ANCIENT CHRISTIAN WRITERS

THE WORKS OF THE FATHERS IN TRANSLATION

EDITED BY

WALTER J. BURGHARDT

and

THOMAS COMERFORD LAWLER

No. 53

CASSIODORUS: EXPLANATION OF THE PSALMS

CASSIODORUS: EXPLANATION OF THE PSALMS

TRANSLATED AND ANNOTATED

BY

P. G. WALSH

Professor of Humanity
University of Glasgow

VOLUME III
PSALMS 101–150
[Psalms 102(101)–150]

PAULIST PRESS
New York, N.Y./Mahwah, N.J.

Library of Congress Cataloging-in-Publication Data

(Revised for vol. 3)
Cassiodorus, Senator, ca. 487–ca. 580.
Explanation of the Psalms.

(Ancient Christian writers; no. 51–
Translation of: Expositio Psalmorum.
Includes bibliographical references and indexes.
Contents: v. 1. Psalms 1–50—v. 2. Psalms 51–100—v. 3. Psalms 101–150.
1. Bible. O.T. Psalms—Commentaries—Early works to 1800. I. Walsh. P. G. (Patrick Gerard) II. Title. III. Series.
BR60.A35 no. 51, etc. [B S1429] 270 s 90-41938
ISBN 0-8091-0441-5 (v. 1) [223'.206]
ISBN 0-8091-0444-X (v. 2)

ISBN 0-8091-0445-8 (v. 3)

Published by Paulist Press
997 Macarthur Boulevard
Mahwah, New Jersey 07430

PRINTED AND BOUND IN THE UNITED STATES OF AMERICA

CONTENTS

TEXT

CASSIODORUS:
EXPLANATION OF THE PSALMS

Commentary on Psalm 101

1. *The prayer of the poor man, when he was anxious, and in the presence of the Lord poured out his supplication.* Though some have believed that this psalm should be attributed to the Lord Saviour, it seems appropriate to introduce in this account the character of the afflicted and grieving pauper, as the title states, for there are many features which cannot be apt for the spotless and holy Word made flesh. First, nowhere do we read that the Lord Christ was anxious, for the anxious person is one who in a situation of serious danger can choose no plan to follow. Second, the text of the psalm includes: *I forgot to eat my bread,* and: *For I did eat ashes like bread, and mingled my drink with weeping. In the face of thy anger and indignation: for having lifted me up thou hast dashed me down.*[1] There are other points too which are reconciled only with the greatest effort if we consent to attach them to the Lord himself. But since it was appropriate that a man grievously wounded and beset with harsh calamities should pour out continual prayer, the character of the anxious pauper is suitably apt, for no sense of shame would repress his voice, and the need inspired by poverty would not deter it. When the psalmist says: *In the presence of the Lord,* he wishes us to understand a prayer poured out before the King's feet like a gleaming mass of gold from the sacks of the soul. As someone has said, you will scarcely ever find that when a person prays, some empty and external reflection does not impede him, causing the attention which the mind directs on God to be sidetracked and interrupted. So it is a great and most wholesome struggle to concentrate continually on prayer once begun, and with God's help to show lively resistance to the temptations of the enemy, so that our minds may with unflagging attention strain to be ever fastened on God. Then we can deservedly recite Paul's words: *I have fought a good fight, I have finished my course, I have kept the faith.*[2] Such are Christ's poor, who are known to intercede not only for their own evils but also for the disasters of the whole world. They are needy in this world, but rich in God. They are empty of vices but full of virtues. They are despised by men but acceptable to Christ. This man who first tortures himself with tearful

affliction shines in the following verses with such splendour of prophecy that one can clearly visualise the gift with which he is crowned in heaven, since he is already renewed with such hope on earth.

Observe that whereas elsewhere names are inserted in psalm-headings, here the poor man introduced as spokesman is anonymous. This is so that Christ's poor may realise that the words allotted to one are attributable to them all. We must further store in our minds that this is the fourth psalm designated as a prayer,[3] but the fifth of the penitential psalms.[4] We must clearly realise that there are two kinds of prayers. The first is when the Lord Christ prays to the Father not for His own sins, for He never had any, but to request that the human nature which He deigned to assume be delivered from the adversities of this world; this is clearly the case with Psalms 16 and 85. The second kind is in Psalm 89, when the venerable character of the poor man is introduced, anxiously crying to God with the humility of penitence. So all penitence is prayer, but all prayer is not penitence, for Christ too prayed, though He committed no act which could have been ascribed to guilt. So these psalms prefaced by the heading of prayer are clearly expounded with their particular qualities.

Division of the Psalm

This poor man, lacking worldly riches but abundantly rich in heavenly virtues, begs the Lord repeatedly at the outset of the psalm that his cry may deserve to reach Him, for worn by continual affliction he says that his bones are fried as if in a pan. There follows an exceedingly tearful, grief-provoking narration which both exposes his needs and recounts his worthy pleas. Then, so as not to appear ungrateful for his correction after all these harsh calamities, in the third section he pursues the Lord's praises with the sweetest vehemence, and says that the Church will be built up at His coming. He prays that though all things will be changed, he himself may abide for ever. A conclusion is added in joyous terms, expressing the fervent prayer that the seed of saints will be escorted to where the Lord dwells in eternal glory. In this way the regular rule for penitents is seen to have been most fully observed, for he began with tears and ended with joy.

Explanation of the Psalm

2. *Hear, O Lord, my prayer, and let my cry come unto thee.* The prophet observed that before the Lord's coming the sins of men were growing unceasingly. So he assumed the apt role of a poor man weeping for the world's disasters with the humility of repentance, asking that the Lord should speedily help him, since so many ills assembled in one were oppressing him. He says: *O Lord, hear my prayer,* the prayer which the devoted spokesman poured out for the deliverance of the whole world. It is the habit of saints to lament the disasters of others as if they were their own. As Paul says: *Who is weak, and I am not weak? Who is scandalised, and I am not on fire?*[5] Next follows: *And let my cry reach unto thee.* This poor man, learned in the divine law, knew that a kind of cloud often confronts the prayers of sinners. Jeremiah says of it: *Thou hast set a cloud before, that our prayer may not pass through it.*[6] The prophet Habacuc says the same thing: *How long, O Lord, shall I cry and thou wilt not hear, shall I cry out to thee suffering violence, and thou wilt not heed?*[7] So mindful of these facts, he made anxious haste that his cry should reach the Lord, so that he should not be late in obtaining a remedy from Him through the obstacle of his evil deeds, for it was clear that he lay prostrate under many calamities. First he spoke of his prayer, and now he has added a cry to enable you to realise that the zeal of his entreaty has increased, observing as you do that his prayer has burst out into the loudest cry. The most devoted Christian must realise that he should preserve the mode of holy prayer which enables him to think of what he prays, to picture in mind Him whom he entreats, to banish all superfluous thoughts, to refuse to admit any other extraneous matter, lest he appear to let thoughtless boars wallow in clear streams, as someone puts it.[8] The roseate hymn of Saint Ambrose, written for Sext and following Paul,[9] had a scent of the same notion: "I shall pray to the Lord in mind and in spirit too, that my voice may not alone sing to God, and my wavering thoughts may not be led a-wandering elsewhere, preoccupied by empty chances."[10] The prayer of those who sing is acceptable to God only if a pure heart carries the same message which the words of the hymn unfold.

3. *Turn not away thy face from me in whatever day I am in trouble.* This most blessed pauper recalled that the Lord through the prophet

Isaiah had rejected the gifts of persistent sinners with the words: *I desire not the blood of steers and lambs and goats. When you came before my sight, who required these things at your hands?*[11] So this man, fearing and pondering repeatedly such words, asks that the Lord should not despise the victim which he was sacrificing, namely his repentance, in the same way as he recalled that the Lord had rejected the sacrificial slaughter by those most wicked men. In the same spirit Psalm 50 says: *A contrite and humble heart God does not despise.*[12] So he begs not to be made a stranger in the Lord's sight. This is the norm of the righteous entreaty, to ask that He in looking on us should ignore our sins, for he forgives us with pity if He does not see them. As has already been said in Psalm 50: *Turn away thy face from my sins.*[13] So quite appropriately we borrow examples of the penitent from a penitential psalm, since it is shown to be an identical idea and a similar plea. He added: *In whatever day I am in trouble. Whatever day* does not denote continuity, but states that there were periods when he was oppressed by the greatest wounds of sins, when the hateful enemy oppressed him. He asked the most devoted Liberator to deliver him, as though he were pinned beneath a cruel beast.

Incline thine ear to me: in what day soever I shall call upon thee, hear me speedily. The entreaty is made in many forms, but it is the one request, that the Lord deign to hear the prayer of the poor man. This figure is called *epimone* in Greek and *repetitio* in Latin,[14] when the same statement is repeatedly made in different words. *Incline thine ear,* that is, 'lend a hearing'; the ear itself (*auris*) gets its name from hearing (*auditus*).[15] The words had not merited the power to mount to Him. The ear of the Lord stands for His clemency with which He genially listens to the prayers of suppliants. Though He hears and sees us all, He is said to hear only those to whom He deigns to attend. Next comes: *In what day soever I shall call upon thee, hear me speedily.* The penitent's supplication swelled commensurately with the humility with which he bent low with prostrate heart. Whereas earlier he had said: *Incline thine ear to me,* he now more confidently asks that he may deserve to be heard more speedily. The person who asks for speedy attention is confident of obtaining his request.

4. *For my days are vanished like smoke, and my bones are fried as in a pan.* He appended the reason for his entreaty, that the intense longing expressed by his prayers might be seen to have sprung from many

miseries, and that the need which he adduces as the result of great calamities might more easily win the goodwill of the fatherly Judge. We see *smoke* coming from a flame but spreading thinly into the clear air; its substance does not remain, though it is seen to be sprung from material fire. So the days of sinners are rightly equated with balls of smoke, for they have been lost by men deceived by activities which are cloaked and foul. The parallel is especially appropriate to the pride of the world, for the more it is raised up, the more it vanishes. This poor man zealously concentrated on the humility of Christ which brings salvation, for he condemned the arrogance and pride of the devil. Next comes: *And my bones are fried as if in a pan.* Just as the bones, in other words strength of mind, of deserving people flourish on good repute when their minds rejoice in happy recollection—in Solomon's words: *Good repute makes the bones fat*[16]—so at the opposing recollection of sins their moral strength is fried, so to say, and shrivels, fearing intensely men's rebukes and the judgments of their own consciences. Or the sinner is fried in this world, since he fears the flames and fires to come, for the person who is apprehensive at the thought of future burning is already fried by terror of the flames. People often ask what is the significance of penitents saying that they endure pains which human nature cannot endure. First, by this exaggeration the magnitude of the offence for which such taxing satisfaction is seen to be offered can be well understood; and secondly, those aware of their huge debts for past sins are not impelled to fresh vices.

5. *I am crushed as grass, and my heart is withered, because I forgot to eat my bread.* Now that he had obtained the goodwill of the Judge through the humblest prayers, he passed to a tearful account of his miseries, so that he could swiftly obtain a remedy by not hiding his suffering from the devoted Physician. The human race is well compared with short-lived grass, for it both possesses the transient joy of greenness and is susceptible to damage when crushed; similarly, as long as we abide by the law and commandments of the Lord we have the vigour of green grass, but then when we are cut off from His precepts by the devil's blade, we at once wither and our hearts are dried up by the barrenness of sin, for the soul cannot obtain the nourishment of His kindness if it is seen to be separated from Him by the action of sins. But those who do not forsake the Lord's commands are always joyful and sunny. Next comes: *Because I forgot to eat my*

bread. He is explaining why his heart is crushed and withered: it is because he had forgotten to eat his bread, by which he knew he could be replenished spiritually. Of this bread the Lord says: *I am the bread of life which came down from heaven;*[17] he could not possibly be complaining of the loss of material bread, since he rejoiced that he was punishing himself by fasting. The nature of sinners is being explained here: when we seek to do wrong, we do not maintain contemplation of the Lord.

6. *Through the voice of my groaning my bones have cleaved to my flesh.* We must investigate the intended sense of *through the voice of my groaning.* The voice of groaning belongs to the person who loses a son, or whose possessions are attacked, or from whom the welcome delight in this world is withdrawn. But the voice in this verse is not that of the groaning of the rich; they groan for the things which the world holds dear, for they desire things doomed to perish, and make no effort to hasten to the Lord's promises. But the most holy man here was afflicted with the groaning at which lovers of the world preferred to jeer. So he added *My* to groaning, to show that he had withdrawn from worldly desires. Next comes: *My bones have cleaved to my flesh.* If you seek to interpret this literally, it cannot befall those grievously afflicted, for only sleek and luxurious people are known to have their bones cleaving to their flesh. But here we seem justified in interpreting flesh as skin, for skin too is flesh. He aims to portray truly extreme emaciation, since the skin is said to have cleaved to his bones. So too the prophet Jeremiah says: *Their skin is fastened to their backs: they have shrivelled, they are become as wood.*[18] But to attain the spiritual meaning instead, his bones means the force of faith by which we stand fast and wax strong; he says that this has cleaved to his flesh because of his brothers' inferior strength, which as yet did not attain constancy in belief in the Lord Christ. So he cleaved to them since he was troubled on their behalf, and was continually worried that they might become estranged from the Lord's kingdom.

7. *I am become like a pelican in the wilderness: I am become like a night-raven in the house.* As I see it, by the names of these birds different kinds of patience are being announced to us. The pelican is an Egyptian bird, similar in size of body to storks, but always naturally emaciated because, so the physiologists tell us, all the food which it swallows it passes out through the bowels by straining, without di-

gesting any of it. Because of this it does not swell with its own fat, because it obtains refreshment from only a little of the juices formed from its food. Pelicans do not fly in large numbers like other birds, but seek consolation in the pleasure of solitude. There is said to be one species of them dwelling in marshes, and another (so the story goes) living in isolated desert places. So this kind of bird most beautifully denotes the hermits who abandon the company of men, and through fear of the Lord discipline themselves by isolated privations.[19] Next comes: *I am become like a night-raven in the house.* Another type of penitent is introduced here. *Nycticorax* is the Greek word for the night-raven, which some have said is a horned owl and others a night owl; others still maintain that it is more like a raven in size and colour, attesting that it can be found especially in districts of Asia. Just as the brightness of the day drives it into hiding, so the onset of night draws it forth; in contrast to the habits of other birds, it begins to be more wakeful and to seek its food when all other living creatures are settling to sleep.[20] Likewise our penitent seeks food for the soul with anxious care in the nighttime; now attending to psalm-singing, now giving alms, now quietly visiting prisons, he wishes to have only God as witness, for His sight is not impaired by the night's darkness. Observe that just as the pelican denotes the hermit and the solitary, so the night-raven indicates the person who stays within his abode and removes himself from the public gaze.

8. *I have watched, and am become as a sparrow unaccompanied on the house.* He passes to a third type of penitent, denoted by the simile of the sparrow, so that in grieving for his worldly sins he might seem to fulfill speedily all the modes of satisfaction. The sparrow is a small bird, but most prudently watchful; it is not easily caught in snares, nor beguiled by the belly's gluttony in its desire for food. Because of its frail physique, it protects itself by a watchfulness unique among birds, so that it may not be trapped by a predator or have its offspring devoured by a snake's ambush. So it flies to the high rooftops of houses to evade suspected disasters, for it is undoubtedly exposed to many dangers.[21] With this sparrow is rightly compared the person in fear of the devil's deceits, who betakes himself especially to the enclosure of the Church, and continues watchful in perfect safety on its summit. The psalmist called it *unaccompanied* because of the charity which makes the penitent a sole figure out of many. He is *on the house*

because of the height of his faith and his bravery of mind. We must also note how this suppliant was initially a greater bird, a pelican or night-raven, and then advanced to the tiny stature of a sparrow; for the penitent goes down step by step, being large at the first stage, modest at the second, and habituated to be wholly acceptable at the third. These birds are compared with men by the figure of *parabole;*[22] they differ in species but are similar in the nature of their habits. This thesis of comparison is called "from the greater to the lesser,"[23] for man is much greater than a sparrow.

9. *All the day my enemies have reproached me: and they that praised me did swear against me.* It is known to be characteristic of the devil's malice to beguile with crafty deceit those of God's servants whom he cannot repress with autocratic assurance, with the result that those who do not yield to open terrorisation are subdued instead by jeering rebukes. This figure is called *irony*[24] or mockery, the surface meaning being other than its implication. So sinners grievously sneered at our penitent as he disciplined himself and seemed to toil to no effect. So that the enormity of their reprobation might be increased, he says that they swore an oath in their execration. It is the manner of the perverted to speak in this fashion: "May I not have the life which this man endures, for he seems to resemble corpses rather than living men." They praised him earlier, when he enjoyed the life of the world, but later they execrated him with an oath when they accounted him as one like to the dead.

10. *For I did eat ashes like bread, and mingled my drink with weeping. . . .* He gives the reason why he was reviled by enemies or acquaintances to his face, as Job clearly endured when his life was disfigured with the most grievous squalor before relatives or friends. This verse is to be handled rather carefully; we must not imagine that, contrary to human custom, wood-ash is the food of penitents. We know that ashes are the remains of charred coals, and we maintain that they are aptly compared to sins, for even minute traces of faults can be removed by the pains of afflictions. Though the surviving traces of sin may be slight, they do not lead us to life. So the prophet in Psalm 50 cries out: *Wash me everywhere clean of my injustice, and cleanse me from my sin.*[25] So this most holy penitent was right to make haste to eat the ashes of his sins so that nothing should be left over to prevent his deserving the kingdom of heaven. Next comes: *And mingled my drink*

with weeping. Though it seems possible for this to happen on occasion, I think that we must seek the spiritual sense for this as well. The drink of souls is the fullness like that mentioned in Psalm 74: *In the hand of the Lord there is a chalice of pure wine full of mixture: and he hath poured it out from this to that.*[26] So it is this drink which we do well to mingle with weeping; it is this chalice which our tears make sweeter, for the heavenly drink enters the recesses of the soul when it is watered with devoted tears. This was the cup which seemed unworthy to those who jeered, this is the food adjudged ghastly by those addicted to luxury. But the Christian should prefer to love the fare by which he can attain the board of the heavenly king. Observe that the whole of this verse is expressed by the figure called *tapeinōsis*,[27] which is known to have the power of reducing some great matter to the most trivial insignificance through the disposition of humility. This figure is found very often in the sacred Scriptures; as Paul has it: *The weak things of this world hath God chosen to confound the strong.*[28]

11. . . . *From the face of thy anger and indignation, for having lifted me up thou hast squeezed me out.* This section is joined to the preceding words, so that the majestic force of that repentance was born of the Lord's anger and indignation, for the verse says: *From the face of thy anger and indignation.* Anger and indignation do not have a bodily face, for they are always present in our imagination when we are afraid. So here a lively description of a fearful person is given, for the psalmist knew that the Lord threatens sinners; in Jeremiah's words: *A lion out of the wood hath devoured them, and a wolf in the evening hath despoiled them.*[29] And the apostle Peter warns us: *Watch and pray, for your enemy the devil as a roaring lion goeth about seeking whom he may devour.*[30] So he was right to fear the face of the angry Lord, for he knew that the Lord had foretold this fate for sinners through His prophets. *Anger* is related to vengeance, *indignation* to moderate emotion, for we show indignation even to our children, but anger with greater vehemence to those rightly deserving punishment. He added: *For having lifted me up thou hast squeezed me out.* Though the character of the poor man alone appears to have been brought before us, our most sagacious narrator inserts the blessings and ills of the whole human race; we have often remarked on this. The Lord very frequently lifts up sinners with His blessings; He bestows riches on them, grants them life, presents them with splendid worldly things,

and causes them to be hymned by all. But once the swollen hearts of mortals have mounted to pride, they are like some outstanding administrator[31] separated from the largesse bestowed upon them, so that they may wisely realise that the goods suddenly snatched from them were not their own. But undoubtedly this wringing process is a blessing. As is stated elsewhere: *It is good for me that thou hast humbled me, that I might learn thy justifications.*[32] From this experience compunction is born, and healing is obtained for souls. This penitent of ours recounts this not without gratitude and reformation.

12. *My days have declined like a shadow: and I am withered like grass.* Our penitent most splendidly remarked that after Adam's transgression his days have declined like a shadow, because the Lord Christ, the true Sun, had forsaken them and without Him all life is in shadow; and just as a shadow has no substance, so our days waste away in useless living. So his days declined because he declined from the Lord. The individual's decline is commensurate with his separation from God's fullness. Next comes: *I am withered like grass;* the person whose days had declined must inevitably have withered like grass. With the withdrawal of that blessing of life which invigorates us and makes us green and blossoming, we are wholly consigned to the barrenness of sin unless we sprout again through the dew of divine mercy into new grace. The sorrowful narrative of great afflictions is complete; let us now see what the third section seems to reveal to us.

13. *But thou, O Lord, endurest for ever, and thy memorial to the end of the world.* After rendering most worthy satisfaction and fittingly lamenting his ills in general, the penitent now raises his head, so to say, and breathes with a certain freedom. He embarks on the third part with spirit lightened and refreshed, matching his earlier self-condemnation and self-humiliation with trusting joy in the Lord's praises. So he embarked upon his praise in the best possible way with mention of the coming of the Lord, through whom he knew the world would be saved. Next comes: *And thy memorial to the end of the world.* By memorial is meant the saving promise of the Lord's incarnation soon to come; that promise is such that no era, no forgetfulness can alter it, but it continues ever unmoved through boundless ages, stored in the bosom of the memory.

14. *Thou shalt arise and have mercy on Sion, for the time of having mercy on it is come.* This most holy pauper instructs us on the power

which the prayer of a simple and faithful man can exercise. Earlier he accounted himself unworthy even of men's gaze, forgoing the pleasure of free movement even in daylight; he ate ashes like bread and mingled his drink with weeping. But now, if it is not impious to say so, he forces the Lord Himself to make good His promises, urging Him to look out on the toiling world with the devoted love of His coming. *Thou shalt arise* is addressed as if to one sleeping, one who had postponed his aid for too long. So that the Lord could be seen to perform all things in the order disposed by His will, he says: *The time of having mercy on it is come;* not that the time reminds Him, but rather that He orders the most appropriate times by deliberation. This was the time of which Paul says: *But when the fulness of the time was come, God sent his Son made of a woman, made under the law, that he might redeem them that were under the law.*[33] And elsewhere: *Behold, now is the acceptable time, behold, now is the day of salvation.*[34] This is the so-called argument from time,[35] usually regarded amongst orators as most effective, for what can obstruct when the appropriate moment beckons? Sion is the mountain which rises at Jerusalem, and which as we have often said signifies the Church. The Lord truly had mercy on it when He gathered it from the nations and established it with a most sacred foundation.

15. *For thy servants have regarded the stones thereof as pleasing, and they shall have pity on the earth thereof.* This verse is to be interpreted with discernment so that we can acknowledge the intended allegorical identifications of servants, stones and earth. The Lord's *servants* denoted the apostles and prophets who carried out His service with devoted minds. They were pleased with *the stones* (in other words, Christians invigorated by divine strength) when they observed that their preaching was efficacious in them. They also took pity on *the earth,* that is, on sinners gathered from the Gentiles in Sion, who were indeed like the earth, for they smacked of the things of the flesh. Observe how appropriate are the words attached to these. He called the stones pleasing because the Lord's servants were content with their commitment which the Lord had bestowed; and he added: *They shall have pity on the earth,* because through Christ's mercy those befouled by earthly stains were to be cleansed.

16. *And the Gentiles shall fear thy name, O Lord, and all the kings of the earth thy glory.* These sentiments are produced against the wicked

superstitions of that era, for the true Lord was not feared when the world was devotedly in thrall to idols. But when His saving coming brought brightness, the Gentiles were converted through fear. It is to them that the earlier phrase, *they shall have pity on the earth thereof,* refers. Moreover, the kings of the lands believed in His glory, in other words, they subjected their bodies to the divine commands, and through the Lord's gifts were able to become rulers of themselves. These are the persons referred to earlier as *the stones thereof, whom thy servants have regarded as pleasing.* They now in very truth recognize the Lord's glory, for they stand firm in strength of faith.

17. *For the Lord hath built up Sion, and he shall be seen in his majesty.* This verse is appended to the previous words: all the Gentiles shall fear the Lord, and the kings shall be in awe of His glory, because Sion which is mother Church has been built up and fashioned from living stones, and in her the Lord's worship will prevail without interruption till the end of the world. This Lord who built up Sion *shall be seen in his majesty* in the truth of the body which He assumed, when He separates the goats from the lambs, dispatching the wicked to hell and bestowing eternal blessedness on the just.

18. *He hath had regard to the prayer of the poor, and hath not despised their petitions.* He calls Christ's faithful the poor, for as has often been said, they are needy in the things of the world and rich in Him alone. So they were filled with the holy Spirit, as this spokesman is, and poured out entreaty to the Lord that He should now bring forward His coming, and no longer delay the prayers of His holy ones. He says that the prayer of the poor has been heard, for He from whose eyes undoubtedly nothing is hidden beholds all motions of the mind. In God to have regard means not to despise.

19. *Let these things be written unto another generation: and the people that shall be created shall praise the Lord.* The poor man, who has sorrow at the recollection of his sins and is weary from vigils and remorse, is now adorned with what one might call a prophet's distinction, and he urges that the age to come may learn through the testimony of Scripture what he knew he had proclaimed in his own day. Thus the truth would not be uncertain to observers once they knew that it had been foretold so many generations before. By *another generation* is meant in particular the Christian people, who follow after that

earlier one. Note the words that follow: *And the people that shall be created shall praise the Lord. Shall be created* refers to the future, and means "shall be reborn through the grace of baptism." Undoubtedly the Lord will be praised by this people for whose salvation He came, for whom He endured execution, and for whose hope He rose from the dead on the third day. This people will praise the Lord with a new canticle; as was said in another psalm: *Sing to the Lord a new canticle.*[36]

20. *Because he hath looked forth from his high sanctuary: from heaven the Lord hath looked forth upon the earth.* These were the words which he earlier said were to be written down. So that you might acknowledge the power of the truth itself, he spoke as if what was to be repeatedly enacted in future ages was already performed; *He hath looked forth* denotes time already past. But let us enquire from where He looked forth; it was from His high sanctuary, namely heaven. He looked forth on us when He took on the frailty of our humanity, for it was through Him that we became free, immortal, and endowed with the highest hope if we deserve to be converted to Him with humble hearts. So that the sense may appear clearer to us, there follows: *From heaven the Lord hath looked forth upon the earth;* as we read elsewhere: *The Lord whose seat is in heaven.*[37] So from there He looked out upon the earth, that is, on the frailty of our bodies which were held in subjection to the vices of the world. Observe that the psalmist wrote: *He looked forth* in both clauses, to make it clear by the verbal similarity that the meaning was identical.

21. *That he might hear the groans of the enchained, that he may loose the children of the slain.* He has given the reason why, *from heaven the Lord hath looked down upon the earth,* namely, to hear the groans of the enchained. *The enchained* means here not persons bound with mortal bonds but holy men held tight by the constraints of law, and seen to abandon the errors of harmful liberty. Of them Solomon says: *Give ear, my son, and take counsel, and cast not away my advice. Put thy foot into the fetters of wisdom and thrust thy neck into her halter.*[38] And a little later: *And her fetters shall be a strong protection for thee, and her halter a robe of glory.*[39] So the enchained are those whom the Lord has deigned to hear groaning and crying to Him, begging Him to free a world enmeshed in its sins by the kindness of His pity, and by His divine power to loose the children of the slain, who were slaughtered

by the devil's deceit, from the errors of their fathers. This is declared to happen every day in the Church through the solemn charisms bestowed.[40]

22. *That the name of the Lord may be declared in Sion, and his praise in Jerusalem.* He has described what was to come with astonishing brevity. The name of the Lord Christ was declared in Sion when the apostles, as we know, first spoke there in diverse tongues of the great things of God.[41] The outcome of this was that the Lord's holy precepts gushed down from the neighbourhood of Jerusalem as though from the clearest fountain through the Church at large. So it is clear that the groans of the enchained were heard so that the saving Lord might come and strengthen His Church in the most sacred religion.

23. *In assembling the people together, and kingdoms to serve the Lord.* He is still recounting the reasons why the groaning of the enchained was heard: it was so that the people should assemble together and make the Lord's praises resound. By saying *together*, he shows the strength of Catholic unity, for though this people is assembled from different regions of the world, they come together since they are gathered in the one regimen of faith. This is the witness of the prophet Ezechiel: *Thus saith the Lord God: Behold, I take the whole house of Israel from the midst of the nations into which they have entered there, and I will gather them from all who encompass them, and I will bring them to their own land, and I will make them one nation.*[42] And Paul says: *One Lord, one faith, one baptism: one God and Father of all, who is above all men, and through all and in us all.*[43] So they are truly said to assemble together who hasten with devoted mind to believe in the inseparable Trinity which is the one God. There follows too the happy change, so that the kingdoms of earth and heaven serve the Lord, and they are then all the more free since they are bound to their Maker in faithful service.

24. *And answered him in the way of his virtue.* How well is the nature of the Christian religion expressed in the two words *via virtutis* (the way of virtue), which we tread in sorrows and traverse in afflictions! But all this we endure in Christ's name with the greatest hope. So the devoted congregation of saints replies to this virtue which the Lord Christ proclaimed. For since He is summoning us to a good life, it is the person known to be obedient to His commands who is seen to answer Him. So it is not with tongue but with life, not with

voice but with faith, not with shouting but with the heart that we make reply. It is clear that all this is attributable to the Catholic Church.

Declare unto me the fewness of my days. In the midst of the Lord's praises, which he has recounted with manifold variety, the poor man now longs to acknowledge the end of life, so that he may deserve to pass quickly to the happiness which the Lord has promised to His saints. It is not through love of life that he longs to know the end of his days, but that continuing with these praises he may swiftly pass to that rest in the heavenly kingdom. So he spoke of the fewness of days because he knew that they must at some time come to an end; when compared with eternity, the duration even of the whole world seems exceedingly short, for we must not describe as long what must come to an end.

25. *Call me not back in the midst of my days: thy years are unto the end of time.* The aspiration of the first request is clear. He was not begging for length of life when he asked that he should not be called back halfway through his days, in other words, in the course of his life; it would be the person who returns to his old sins who would be called back in the midst of his days. He is in fact pointing to the period of youth, when often we seek hazardous desires, and the heat of that age leads us to love sins more. But the person who makes this prayer realises that he has now been freed by great kindness, and does not wish to lose what we know he has gained by God's gift. Next comes: *Thy years are unto the end of time.* He had reasonably asked that he should by no means be called back halfway through his days, for he was hastening with great longing to reach the Lord's eternity, where the saints will rejoice with the Lord in unending gladness, when in Paul's words: *God will be all in all.*[44] The phrase, *thy years,* is addressed to the Lord in metaphor, for years are properly confined to those who experience changes of time. But the psalmist expounds the eternity of the Lord in the three ensuing verses, which we cite together so that both His eternity and His activity in the world may be manifest in the one declaration.

26. *In the beginning thou didst found the earth, O Lord: and the heavens are the works of thy hands.* 27. *They shall perish, but thou remainest: and all of them shall grow old like a garment.* 28. *And as a vesture thou shalt change them, and they shall be changed. But thou art the self-same, and thy years shall not fail.* When he says: *In the begin-*

ning thou didst found the earth, O Lord, he reveals what sound minds cannot deny, that the Creator is known to have existed before His creatures, without any beginning. Observe here that with marvellous brevity he has obliterated the opinions of philosophers, the first of which is that the world was created by no-one, and the second that it will remain without end.[45] But with the words, *in the beginning thou didst found the earth, O Lord, and the heavens are the works of thy hands,* that first heinous belief is refuted; and the declaration, *they shall perish,* made it clear that the heavens will have an end, so that no person through error propagated by the Gentiles should place his trust in the stars, once he realised that they were not immutable. I consider, however, as more worthy of examination the question why he said that the heavens were works of hands, when all things were made by the Word. The answer is that we must interpret *hand* here as the power of His command. As he says elsewhere: *For he spoke, and they were made: he commanded, and they were created.*[46] The outcome is that Scripture is seen not to contradict itself, since the words are expounded most aptly according to their context. He added: *But thou remainest.* Just as he reveals the Lord's eternity at His creation of all things, so he stated that He remains in the glory of His majesty after the transformation of the heavens. His use of the phrase, *all of them,* does not in my view refer to the angels and spiritual creatures, who will abide in their high rank, but to the things known to be subject to change; this figure is called *synecdoche,*[47] the part for the whole, a figure most frequently used in the divine Scriptures. His expression, *shall grow old like a garment,* seems to be explicable by the frailty of the flesh, a comparison found also in the gospel-words: *Is not the life more than the meat, and the body more than the raiment?*[48] We use the expression "growing old" of a thing which like a garment is obliterated in death. He added: *And as a vesture thou shalt change them, and they shall be changed.* We must perhaps interpret vesture as the heavens, for they cover the earth like a veil, and like other things suffer change. To demonstrate that the Lord's works will now abide for ever, he says: *Thou shalt change them, and they will be changed,* for they will never return to this corruptible state; if they were subject to corruption any further, they would not be described as changed. As the prophet Daniel attests: *For wisdom, fortitude and understanding are his, and he changeth times and ages.*[49] The psalmist added: *But thou art the self-*

same, and thy years shall not fail. Same is set against what precedes, for while those things are changeable, the Lord continues ever unchangeable; *self* denotes His omnipotence, for He is truly His unsupported self when He ever performs deeds worthy of himself. *Thou art* briefly announces His nature; for the one who needs no helper to exist knows that He exists of Himself. Thus by these three verses both the changeability of creatures and the eternity of the Lord are described with remarkable brevity.

29. *The children of thy servants shall dwell there, and their seed shall be guided rightly for ever.* Now that his prayer has been most wisely and usefully completed, this most holy pauper reaches the end of the psalm, rejoicing in the forgiveness of his sins and the hope of future resurrection. Here he briefly rounds off the whole message. He rejoices that he will dwell with the Lord's holy ones, where the glorious hope of the faithful and the eternal rest of the just reside. By *the children of thy servants* he means disciples of prophets and apostles, whom they brought to birth by holy preaching through the womb of faith. Paul says to them: *My little children, with whom I am again in labour;*[50] and again when writing to Timothy he put at the head of the letter: *To my dearly beloved son,*[51] for he had begotten him, but in faith not in body. *They shall dwell there* points to the abode of blessedness which the Lord possesses and of which He says: *Father, I will that where I am they also be with me,*[52] that is, in the eternal kingdom where lies eternal joy and unending tranquillity. Your awareness that the children of the servants are with God must be joined to the certainty that the servants themselves, in other words, His apostles and preachers, are also there; if a place of blessedness is granted to the disciples, can it possibly be refused to the teachers themselves? It is scripture's way sometimes to speak of lesser things in such a way as to appear to embrace also the greater. For example, in the words of another psalm: *If thou didst see a thief, thou didst run with him, and with adulterers thou didst set thy portion.*[53] Lesser sins are mentioned there in such a way as to make us think of greater ones. Next comes: *And their seed shall be guided rightly for ever. Their seed* means the works of the faithful, which are sown in this world so that their praiseworthy fruit may appear in the eternity to come. Observe why the expression, *shall be guided rightly,* is used; it is because what is obtained there is set in the straight course of eternity, where there can be nothing crooked

or bent. There the saints will rejoice with the Lord Saviour in wishes that are righteous and steady.

Conclusion Drawn From the Psalm

How happily has this troubled person lamented, until by afflicting himself he attained joys! Earlier he was like the pelican, and in later verses is to be compared with the phoenix; earlier a night raven, later an eagle; earlier a sparrow, but subsequently he became a famed dove. These are the transformations experienced by those who subject themselves to the Lord with pure minds. Men may gain royal titles, but they are trivial; their purple garments may win praise, but they often become grimy on those who wear them. Observe how the world is conquered by rags, and the devil overcome by lamentation. He whom no cohorts are enough to resist is prevailed upon by the prayer of a single pauper. Those deserving of the title of sages, men of eloquence, truly splendid orators are they who as victors gain the possession which is by no means withheld from them by the opposition of an enemy. In short, they obtain an inheritance which they invariably win without toil, and which they never at any time forgo through death. What a blessed condition is that of penitents! It converts the guilty into the just, the sad into the unfailingly joyful, the mortal into the wholly immortal. In this world they associate with the wicked for the moment, but in the next they will gain partnership with the angels in eternal blessedness. So let us realise that this man is the fifth in the role of penitent,[54] who defended himself by not defending himself, who washed himself clean by not washing himself, who cleansed himself by not cleansing himself. If we deserve to attain his poverty, we undoubtedly overcome all the kingdoms of the world.

Commentary on Psalm 102

1. *A psalm for David himself.* After the unfolding of those most humble prayers of the blessed pauper, and of the groans of such great repentance, the whole of this psalm is filled with praise of the Lord, so that the joys of proclamation may through devoted arrangement follow upon the preceding tears. So, as we have often stated, the phrase,

for David himself, is set down so that we may not attach anything to the earthly king of that name, for the heavenly praise unfolds with obvious meaning. The psalm is lucid, matching the clarity of its heading, so that we can apprehend without difficulty the content of its words.

Division of the Psalm

The prophet speaks throughout the whole psalm. In the first section he addresses his soul, bidding it to bless the Lord and in no way to forget His kindnesses. In the second narration he tells of the gifts which the Lord bestowed on Moses and the rest of His faithful, so that we may realise that He was always generous from time immemorial. In the third section he directs his words to the angels. He addresses the heavenly Virtues, and invites the other creatures endowed with reason to busy themselves continually with the Lord's praises.

Explanation of the Psalm

Bless the Lord, O my soul, and let all my inner parts bless his holy name. The prophet, aware that men's minds are engulfed in different delusions and do not remain ever constant in true contemplation, in his sanctity addresses his soul. He urges her now that she is delivered from various disasters to remember the Author of all kindnesses, so that she may not think that what has been clearly granted by the Lord alone is to be ascribed to herself or to any other. Converse with one's soul is an acceptable and most honourable form of discourse. His purpose is to make all men realise that they should in every way seek that most salutary counsel which the prophet is seen to have offered to himself. Next comes: *And let all my inner parts bless his holy name.* The inner parts of the soul are manifold thought and the power of reason. He wished them to accord with his soul, so that the Lord's praise might sound forth with united strength and faithful harmony. The soul often wishes to achieve something, but is seduced by imaginary fancies. But the holy man intent on the Lord's praise desired no part of him to deviate, but that all should sing together in a single harmony, for their possible discord would be blameworthy.

2. *Bless the Lord, O my soul, and do not forget all his repayments to*

thee. He echoes the first verse with a beautiful repetition of words to arouse the greatest enthusiasm by this duplicated statement, so that his soul should not appear too sluggish for such a task through guilty negligence. He warns her above all to remember that she has received all that she has through Him; the person who cannot forget kindnesses bestowed never ceases to give praise. Observe too the word *repayments,* for one kind of repayment was owed to men's sins, but another is seen to be paid, for they were forgiven. It is this which it is right that no-one should forget, for the person liable to punishment then became worthy of honour. What these repayments of the Lord are he next relates, and if a man ponders them he praises the Lord's kindnesses with his whole mind.

3. *Who shows mercy to all thy iniquities, who heals all thy illnesses.*
4. *Who redeems thy life from destruction, who satisfies thy desire with good things.* 5. *Who crowns thee with compassion and pity. Thy youth shall be renewed like the eagle's.* In these three verses the repayments of the life to come, which the Lord bestows on His saints with devoted pity, are recounted in a fivefold division. This figure is called *synathroismos* or gathering,[1] when harsh charges or most sweet benefits are gathered together in one heap. First He shows mercy to their sins, when He forgives their faults and deigns to welcome sinners in peace. Second, He heals all the sicknesses of the faithful, when untroubled life and immortality without end is granted them at the resurrection, that is: *When this corruptible puts on incorruption, and this mortal puts on immortality.*[2] Third, He will redeem our life from destruction when He dislodges us from the disaster of eternal death, so that we may not hear the words: *Go into everlasting fire, which was prepared for the devil and his angels.*[3] Fourth, He satisfies the desire of the blessed with good things when they are told: *Come ye, blessed of my Father.*[4] Fifth, He crowns with compassion and pity when He now restores worthy rewards to the blessed; in Paul's words: *As for the rest, there is laid up for me a crown of justice which the Lord the just judge will render to me in that day.*[5] This is perhaps the meaning of the five loaves with which He satisfied the people's long fasting,[6] for this and similar incidents are seen to have happened earlier as a great foreshadowing. But we must analyse why the example of the eagle is brought in. When this bird is advanced in age, its hooked, hornbilled lip is said to swell to such a size that it cannot gather its food with the usual freedom; and

realising this possible source of mortal danger, it is said to smooth out its mouth on a rock until it removes all that blocks it. After this it regains its former bodily health by its usual intake of food. In the same way the soul regains its earlier health, provided that it does not cease to rub off its sins on the Rock which is Christ the Lord, for it returns to the food of salvation when through the Lord's gift it spurns the sins which are hindrances to eternal life.

6. *The Lord doth mercies and judgment for all that suffer wrong.* After his mention of the Lord's repayments, which He is properly believed to be able to proffer to those converted in the world, he now briefly states that the Lord performs mercies for them that hope in Him, and takes vengeance for all those who suffer wrong. Accordingly none of them can be in doubt about what is said, once they realised that the Lord Himself is identified by this definition. This verse is uttered as a mode of definition, when a person is being denoted by what he uniquely does. When you ask, "What is the Lord?" the answer you give is: *He who doth mercies and judgment for all that suffer wrong.* So the Lord God is adequately identified, since the words could not be apt for any other. He does mercies to those who have shown mercy; as Christ says in the gospel: *Blessed are the merciful, for they shall obtain mercy.*[7] Next comes: *And judgment for all that suffer wrong.* This is promised to those adorned with the gift of patience, of whom He says: *Revenge is mine, I will repay.*[8] Those who long to avenge themselves by force, and hasten to satisfy their rage by attacking an enemy, do not leave vengeance to the Lord because they believe that they themselves can exact the punishment which they ought to demand from the Judge. Most holy prophet, you have offered wholesome counsel to your soul, by which the world too can experience consolation. You have addressed yourself so as to speak to us; you have profited yourself in such a manner as to save us as well beyond all doubt.

7. *He hath made his ways known to Moses: his wills to the children of Israel.* He had earlier stated what repayments the blessed people deserved in the life to come; now he passes to the second section, and demonstrates by the illustration of one man the great benefits which the Lord has granted even here on earth to His servants; thus no-one could have doubts about the repayment to come. But observe how Moses and Israel have been denoted in different formulations. *He made his ways known to Moses,* when He revealed to him the justice of

His power, so that Moses should commit the Law to writing, teach good morals, and walk with steps of perfect faith on the paths of the Lord. Next comes: *His wills to the children of Israel.* He wrote *wills* rather than *ways* here because the whole of Israel after receiving the Lord's word did not walk in His commands. We know of the revolts which that people raised, so that they deserved to hear the words of the Judge: *This people is stiff-necked.*[9] So he says that the wills rather than the ways of the Lord became known to them, for a large section of them had the temerity to diverge from the Lord's way. But you are to realise that the pattern prescribed for Moses is set down here so that you may be aware that the Lord performs this same service every day, and can go on doing so until the end of the world.

8. *The Lord is merciful and compassionate, patient and plenteous in mercy. Merciful* describes the person known to be most clement by nature. He is *compassionate* when he bestows the gifts of his mercy. A person can be merciful and compassionate in isolated cases, but none except the Lord can be found to be merciful and compassionate by nature. Here *merciful* is put first, so that you can applaud the compassionate Lord not momentarily but continually. This figure is called *paronomasia* or *denominatio;*[10] it arouses the emotions of the listener through similarity of words. He added *patient,* an attitude which the merciful person must necessarily embrace, for no-one is merciful who is not patient. So Paul remarks: *Or despisest thou the riches of his goodness and long-suffering? Knowest thou not that the benignity of God leadeth thee to penance?*[11] Christ says of Himself: *These things hast thou done, and I was silent. Thou thoughtest unjustly that I should be like to thee.*[12] Next comes: *And plenteous in mercy.* He is truly plenteous in mercy who though He hears utterly blasphemous words *maketh his sun to rise upon the good and bad, and raineth upon the just and the wicked,*[13] who bestows the spirit of life with great devotion, who waits for those who stray so that they may condemn their wrongdoings.

9. *He will not always be angry, nor will he be wroth for ever*—understand "to those who acknowledge Him with devoted satisfaction, who love to return to Him, who in company with their Maker despise the enticements of the world." On the other hand He will be angry with those to whom He shall say: *Go into eternal fire.*[14] What great unhappiness, to perish beneath the gaze of the devoted Lord, so that you are slow to satisfy Him whom you know you have wronged, especially

when you realise that your entreaty is not vain if you are aware that you offered it with sincerity of spirit! This verse can be applied also to the Jewish people, who we know are to be converted at the world's end. On this Paul says: *Blindness in part has happened in Israel, that the fullness of the Gentiles should come in, and so all Israel should be saved.*[15]

10. *He hath not dealt with us according to our sins, nor rewarded us according to our iniquities.* This is a judgment relevant to all, for there is no person who does not possess His grace without payment, for the Law confines all things under sin. As Paul attests: *For God hath enclosed everything in unbelief, that he may have mercy on all.*[16] But He bestows the Spirit on good and evil persons in common; He grants them salvation, removes their needs, and is good to all alike. The psalmist added: *Nor rewarded us according to our iniquities;* for He shows such devotion to those who entreat Him that He deigns to forgive them all the more when each individual is eager to condemn himself by making satisfaction.

11. *For according to the height of heaven above the earth, the Lord hath strengthened his mercy towards them that fear him.* Let us more carefully examine the meaning of this comparison. He says that the mercy with which the Lord rewards the faithful rises above their merits as much as the top of heaven can be distanced from the earth. The comparison has this further point: just as the sky covers the earth and assigns to man the benefits appropriate to their seasons—now by pouring down rain, now by providing sunny weather, now by cooling the air with most health-giving breezes—so too the Lord's mercy is seen to afford varying aids to our frailty. It supports to correct, lashes to instruct, tests to offer help, and by these differing provisions of blessings His one desire is to lend aid to sinners. To make the force of the whole statement intelligible, we can summarise thus: the possibility that the Lord does not protect those who serve him with the greatest integrity is as remote as a divine prescription that the sky should not cover the earth.

12. *As far as the east is from the west, so far hath he removed our iniquities from us.* He has offered another most beautiful comparison with God's kindness. *The east* is the beginning of our goodly life, *the west* the attitude moulding evil behaviour. We were in the west when we were held tight by the bonds of sin, but we are in the east when the true Sun visits us through the water of rebirth, and dispels the dark-

ness of our sins. So when our sins are forgiven us, our iniquities are removed as far from us as the bright day can be from the shadowy night. Alternatively, the east denotes God's kingdom and the west hell, which is as far removed from the abode of the blessed as the poor man set in Abraham's bosom states: *Between us and you there is fixed a great chasm.*[17]

13. *As a father hath compassion on his children, so hath the Lord compassion on them that fear him.* Notice that now the psalm is concerned with no foreign or remote comparisons; the words are associated with the very heart of fatherly love. He shows compassion like a father to those whose Father He is; He disciplines them like children, for they have deserved to be heirs of His kingdom. Next comes: *So hath the Lord compassion on them that fear him.* The word *so* denotes to us His attitude of fatherly correction. A natural father who wishes to school his son in right actions often disciplines him and often whips him; as Solomon says: *If you love your son, frequently chastise him while he is still young,*[18] and the rest. Those parents truly love their children when they are devotedly severe with them, and in the same way our Lord whips every child whom He accepts,[19] and draws those who fear Him towards a zeal for righteous aspirations.

14. *For he knoweth our fashioning. Remember, Lord, that we are dust.* This section is to be joined to the previous words. The reason is being given why He pities us as a father does, namely because we have dislodged ourselves from our natural worth. Driven from the condition in which the Creator formed us, we are seen to be a mere fashioning. So the psalmist rightly asks that we be helped, for he had no hope in his own powers. Next follows: *Remember, Lord, that we are dust.* He is actually saying: "Remember, Lord, not that You created us from mud, not that in Your generosity You made us immortal, not that You deigned to fashion us to Your own image and likeness"—for all these facts could rouse odium instead against the sinner—"but that through the barrenness of sin we are now reduced to dust. Have pity on those who have unhappily ruined themselves; help those who have shown no inclination to abide in Your gifts. You alone are devoted to sinners because they have grievously harmed themselves by their evil actions."

15. *Man's days are as grass, and as the flower of the field so shall he flourish.* There are types of definition which are expounded by certain

comparisons to things, for example: *I am the way, the truth and the life.*[20] Clearly in this and the following verse a similar definition is fashioned. As if you were asking: "What is man?" the reply is given: *His days are as grass*, the grass which sprouts most luxuriantly but withers most speedily. Grass quickly raises its head to the air after rain, but its neck droops in the heat. Then, to prevent your thinking that this comparison contains any suggestion of stability, he added: *And as the flower of the field so shall he flourish.* A flower of the field fades much more quickly than the observed life of green grass; though it seems most beautiful in bloom, we find that it soon disintegrates and disappears. Likewise our weak humanity has its beauty, and the distinctions and riches of the world are most acceptable, but they do not last very long. So the human condition is justifiably compared with these transient things, because when abandoned by its vigorous strength it invariably hastens with headlong speed to the fate of death.

16. *For the spirit shall pass in him, and he shall not be: and he shall know his place no more.* The comparison in the previous verse was made to establish this parallel. It describes what man is, namely a spirit passing through the present world in which it cannot remain for very long. So those who wax arrogant, rejoicing that they are uplifted by worldly happiness, should hear that the spirits pass from our poor bodies as rivers pass through flooded regions; how empty are the areas which seem to teem with torrents, once the waters retire! We must not, then, be presumptuous about our fleeting breath, but rather concentrate here on what we know profits us in the time to come. But to forestall possible belief by any individual that souls will return to this world by metempsychosis, as certain crazed persons have believed,[21] he added: *And he shall know his place no more*, in other words, he cannot return to this world to live through his life again. Human weakness is convicted by its own frailty. Man, you have heard what you are; now listen to what you will be if you reject the slightest fear of the Lord. This figure is known as *parison* or balancing statement,[22] when we join together good or evil things in clauses of differing kinds.

17. *But the mercy of the Lord is from the world's beginning for all time upon them that fear him, and his justice unto children's children.* The human condition was first truthfully recounted because of the unlawful liberties of the arrogant; now he inserts the hope which must console the faithful, for though in ourselves we are frail and transi-

tory, through the Lord's mercy we are made wholly enduring. Thus we must observe how frail we are, but we can simultaneously hear what we achieve through the Lord's grace. Notice that he said: *From the world's beginning,* that is, from when the world first began to be ordered, and different creatures through the Creator's bounty burst forth. So it seems to me a fitting interpretation here that, as many of the Fathers have said, Adam was recalled to the Lord's grace, for he was the first person in the world; Abel, Noe, Abraham and the other fathers were also in the world, but not at its beginning. As for the phrase that follows, *for all time,* it denotes the Lord's eternity in absolute terms, for He is seen to be merciful before the world, in the world, and after this world. Consider also the addition: *Upon them that fear him,* which is to prevent those persons who in their wicked projects scorn to obey Him from believing that His mercy is to be granted to them. Next comes: *And his justice unto children's children.* We must interpret *children,* as has often been said already, as the actions of each one of us, and *children's children* as the most just repayment for our deeds; for just as in a sense we are fathers of our behaviour, so our actions spawn the repayment for them. This repayment every just man will receive when set in eternal blessedness. This explanation is apt because many of the faithful have not had children, either as the result of barrenness or out of zeal for virginity. But if you wish to interpret the verse literally—I pray you do not—very many of the saints are cheated of this promise. Then too in what follows the spiritual interpretation is maintained.

18. *For those who guard his covenant, and keep in memory his commandments, to perform them.* These are the children whom he mentioned earlier, who keep the Lord's precepts, who are mindful of His commandments in their deeds rather than in their zeal for song. Even if a person mouths the psalter, he is not mindful of it unless he carries out its precepts; the Lord's precepts were uttered to be executed, not merely to be bawled in song. So the most learned father Augustine in his discussion of this psalm maintained that he did not memorise the psalter, or recall the words of the entire Law;[23] he was doubtless rousing the eagerness of all not merely to listen, but above all to act. The memory is the faculty by which the mind recovers what it knows has been heard, seen and done.

19. *The Lord hath prepared his throne in heaven, and his kingdom shall*

rule over all. He passes to the fear-inspiring proclamation of the Judgment to come, so that sinners' minds may not wax arrogant through not fearing future vengeance for their evil deeds. He says He has prepared His throne, referring to the time when the Lord Jesus mounts to heaven, sits at the right hand of the Father, and will come from there to judge the living and the dead. So that you may not be gnawed by any notion that the Lord is powerless, he says that He Himself who is to judge the world has prepared His throne. He added: *And his kingdom shall rule over all.* He did not wish pagans to believe that their demons would have any dominion, so he said that He who prepared His throne, the Lord Christ, would rule.

20. *Bless the Lord, all ye his angels, you that are mighty in virtue, who do his word, hearkening to the voice of his orders.* Whereas earlier the prophet spoke about men, he now comes to the third narration in which he addresses heavenly creatures, saying that they must celebrate the Lord's praises. Since among the angels there is a great separation, he says that only they who are known to obey His commands are worthy to proclaim the Lord, thus showing that only those men and spiritual creatures who obey His wishes are admitted to the service of so great a Majesty. The words of his injunction are, *all ye his angels,* and *his* refers to those who have had no thought of abandoning His dominion. There follows a more specific phrase, *you that are mighty in virtue, who do his word.* It is those who obey His commands who are mighty in virtue. The devil too is powerful, but in wickedness not virtue, in arrogance not distinction. The true sense of *mighty* has reference to those who strive to obey the Lord's word. So that no ambiguity should remain, he inserts with greater emphasis, *hearkening to the voice of his orders;* the implication is that they should be humble not proud, for it is they who both know and revere their Maker who are worthy to bless Him.

21. *Bless the Lord, all ye his hosts, you ministers of his that do his will.* He considered that this great, utterly sublime topic should be reinforced by repetition of the invitation, so that men's weakness should realise how very salutary it is to obey the Lord when the power of the heavens campaigns to do His will. Observe too the aptness of the diction. Earlier he said: *Who do his word;* so that you would not understand *word* as man's usual utterance which strikes the air, he added here: *That do his will.* For the angels, the Lord's word is His will, for

the sublime and spiritual substance of the blessed angels recognises the truth of the Lord's will on beholding Him. There is no need of speech, for the Godhead favours and reveals Himself to them; God does not beat the air by addressing them, but directs their wishes to His own will by inspiring them. This will be the case also, we believe, with blessed men, once they have attained the rewards of the eternal kingdom.

22. *Bless the Lord, all his works, in every place of his dominion: O my soul, bless thou the Lord.* The word *bless* is now repeated a third time. This figure is called *epembasis,*[24] the splendid figure of quite frequent repetition of what has been said, aimed at rousing the spirits in utterances of praise or blame. Initially he stated that those who carry out the Lord's commands must bless Him; now he advises the very creation of the Lord that it should praise its Maker, so as to embrace things on earth and in heaven; for since all is His work, all things must bless their Creator. Next comes: *In every place of his dominion.* Just as no creature by his command is exempted from praising the Lord, likewise no place is detached from such a duty. The phrase, *in every place of his dominion,* allows no exemption, for He is Lord everywhere. Perhaps he is denoting the Catholic Church, which through the Lord's gift was to show belief throughout the whole world; for she blesses the Lord everywhere, praises Him everywhere, and celebrates her boundless gratitude in songs of exultation. He added: *O my soul, bless thou the Lord;* the same phrase which formed the most handsome beginning has brought the psalm to an end. Now since in the divine Scriptures the entire content is rich with the abundance of mysteries, this similarity, as has already been said at Psalm 8,[25] in my opinion denotes those who have entered the hall of the faith with pure hearts, and through the Lord's gifts are bringing their lives to a glorious end. It is a worthy admonition, by which the faithful soul can console itself, and which can be taken up like an invincible shield against all eventualities; for if we ever bless Him, we are continually guarded by Him.

Conclusion Drawn From the Psalm

We acknowledge the abundant generosity by which this blessing of the Lord is granted to those who fear Him. Let us hasten to fulfil these commands, so that we may deserve to obtain the rewards. We have a Lord who is both devoted by nature and most generous in the gifts of His mercies. Who would hesitate to make requests of Him who is offended if He is not entreated? So let us all as one bless the Lord, and let us hymn His works with the exultation of song. What a sacrilege it would be, since every creature is bidden to bless the Lord, if man who is known to have been created in His image and likeness ceased to praise Him! We have heard with what virtues the blessing of the Lord is associated; it is especially apt for the chaste, the most humble, and those who perform the Lord's other commands. So all that is debased is excluded from our midst. The entire malice of the world is expelled. Our tendencies are better governed. The devil is shut out with his followers. So once we have heard of this great gift, let us be filled with abundant hope, bless the Lord with pious works, and sing to our Maker with righteous deeds. When the Judge makes His selection, he will not reject us if He knows that we have performed His commands here on earth.

Commentary on Psalm 103

1. *A psalm of David.* We have often said that *psalm* denotes those actions of men which in their worth are directed towards an understanding of things divine. The instrument which has the specific name of psalm[1] is fashioned to represent this; it has a drum on top in which the sweetest melody is controlled with tuneful sound. *David* is added merely as spokesman. But clearly the whole narrative is to be told of the Lord Christ, who in the beginning made heaven and earth. The psalm has been designed with an arrangement allowing you to grasp that certain things are said here which you realise were left unsaid in the book of Genesis. So we shall offer a literal explanation of appropriate acts, and offer a spiritual understanding, derived from our predecessors, of matters which can offer knowledge of our faith. We should therefore be eager and ready to listen, for that most eloquent person father Augustine declares[2] that we should carefully study and most scrupulously discuss this psalm.

Division of the Psalm

The prophet wishes to demonstrate that the state of the world shows forth the divine mysteries. He is seen to reveal certain teachings to us in the first place by the fashioning of heaven and earth, so that we may acknowledge that all things are truly in harmony with each other, created as they were by a single Maker, since they demonstrably reveal certain similarities to each other. Secondly, he recounts works of the Lord cloaked under various figures. Thirdly, he proclaims that he will continually in the eternal life to come recite those praises of the Lord which he had sung also in the brief span of his life on earth.

Explanation of the Psalm

Bless the Lord, O my soul: O Lord my God, thou art made exceedingly great. Thou hast put on praise and beauty. The prophet invites himself to bless the Lord, and since he knew that the grace of unity is preeminent in the Catholic faith, he addresses to himself alone the advice which he should offer to all. Blessing the Lord means confessing His great works, so when He is the subject of some exalted utterance, each of us should give service to the truth. This initial sentiment has reference to the entire content up to the end of this lengthy psalm. After addressing his soul, as we have mentioned, he suddenly changes direction and says: *O Lord my God.* This figure is called *proanaphonesis*,[3] when in discourse on other things we suddenly address words to God. He confidently maintains that his God is the Lord shared by all; this is to demonstrate that when he proclaims himself God's servant, he has no truck with the devil. He did not wish that traitor to seek any support from him, but to acknowledge him as belonging to another. Next comes: *Thou art made exceedingly great.* We must carefully investigate the force of these words. When is He not great, that He should be made great by men's praises? What can be added to Him when He is the wondrous and incomprehensible Fullness of virtues? But the Lord is made great among men when His great and lofty nature becomes clear to them, so that they realise that He is the Creator, the One who bestows all good things, the Redeemer and lastly the Judge. As the result of this, the Lord of the redeemed is rightly said to be made great, for every day He becomes a source of wonder through the devotion of believers. It is in this way that He is said to be sanctified, glorified, blessed, and the like. He added: *Exceedingly,* and rightly, for the Lord is praised by the mouths of the converted, and those who have for long polluted themselves with wicked crimes are joining the band of the saints; the word, *exceedingly,* is most appropriately applied to what is performed with the entire thrust of the heart. Next is explained the reason for His being made exceedingly great: *Thou hast put on praise and beauty.* Putting on means acquiring what one did not have. When did God not have beauty, He who ever bestows all lovely things on His creatures? Here, however, the incarnation of the Lord Christ is clearly being expounded, and this human body He assumed within time; through it in bestowing His devotion He experienced the praise of mortals; for men had abandoned the worship of the true Godhead, becoming slaves to zeal for images and to false religions. But at His coming, though He had never been absent in His divinity, both the praise and the beauty of that heavenly Majesty became celebrated. The psalmist says that the Lord is clothed in the things in which the Catholic Church is known to be adorned.

2. *Clothed with light as with a garment, stretching out heaven like a skin.* These twenty-two verses up to the next division unfold through the figure of *parabole*[4] with the most beautiful allusions; this figure occurs when things dissimilar in kind are compared. *Light* denotes the Church, of which Scripture says: *Who is this that ascends, clad in white?*[5] Clad in white means in brightness; it is rightly understood of the garment, so to say, of the Lord Saviour, which has no spot or wrinkle.[6] The Church is shining white; of her members Paul says: *You were heretofore darkness, but now light in the Lord.*[7] The tunic which could not be split at the time of the passion[8] also signified the Church. It is she of whom it is said: *Clothed with light as with a garment.* Next comes: *Stretching out heaven like a skin.* The statement that the Lord stretched out heaven is a good one, since we know that He admits harlots and tax-collectors; for though in justice heaven belongs to the just, through the bestowal of grace it has become also the abode of sinners. The comparison of heaven with a skin is not idle; just as a skin covers all our limbs, so the encompassing vault of heaven encloses all creatures. Some people have thought that heaven also denotes the just

man whom the Lord is known to stretch out by grace, just as a taut skin can swell in size.

3. *Who covers his higher places with waters, who makes the cloud his chariot, who walks on the wings of the winds.* Though the psalmist is found to be expounding the physical order (for waters are set above the heavens, as we both read in Genesis and as he himself states: *And let all the waters that are above the heavens praise the name of the Lord*),[9] none the less an indication of sacred baptism is being revealed to us here. So we must interpret heaven, as has often been stated, as every just man, whose upper places, in other words, the improvement of his faithful soul, are irrigated by the waters of salvation. All these topics are so ordered by the writer that the heavenly words both seem to denote the activities of the Church and also to attest the state of the world in a most truthful narration. Next comes: *Who makes the cloud his chariot.* The phrase is appropriately interpreted in the literal sense, for after the resurrection the Lord ascended to heaven before the eyes of the apostles. As we read in the Acts of the Apostles: *When he had said these things, a cloud received him out of their sight.*[10] But we are also seen to interpret this most appropriately by regarding the cloud as the preacher of the Lord's word, through whom Christ ascended in His members when He had cleansed the minds of sinners from the wickedness of this world. He added: *Who walks on the wings of the winds.* We know that winds fly, as it were, on wings in the waving motions of the atmosphere, but the Lord walks on their wings when He performs His wishes much more swiftly than the courses of the winds. Or preferably we must interpret the winds as the souls of the just, for they are schooled by the two Testaments and thus transported on twin wings to heavenly joys. The Lord is rightly said to walk on them, for He reveals the mercy of His activity in their persons. Observe too in this verse and others that follow that he prefers to reveal the Lord through His actions; this is the second type of definition, which among the Greeks is called *ennoematike* and in Latin *notio;*[11] for though the Lord defies definition in His nature, He is splendidly known through what He uniquely performs.

4. *Who makes his spirits angels, and his ministers a burning fire.* We must bear in mind that there is special mention here of the angels, a topic not more prominent in the book of Genesis. The actual words here are to be analysed more closely. *Spirit* is the general term for a

bodyless, powerful substance performing visibly or invisibly a function invested in it by the Godhead. Now the term *angel* denotes not nature but obedience; it is a Greek word which in Latin means *nuntius* (messenger), for when dispatched they become angels, though by nature known to be spirits. He added *His* to indicate those who obey the Lord's wishes with upright intentions. The order of words is: *Who makes his spirits angels.*[12] Next comes: *And his ministers a burning fire.* Every person who performs the divine wishes and is always fired by the warmth of charity is a minister of God; such a man becomes a heavenly fire when by the word of preaching he is shown to have the power to burn and consume wicked deeds of sinners. The Lord Himself similarly says: *I am come to cast fire on the earth;*[13] this is, life-giving fire, the fire of salvation which nurtures souls as it consumes sins.

5. *Who has founded the earth on its own stability: it shall not be moved for ever and ever.* It does not seem possible to take this verse in its literal sense; since we have read that this earth is to be changed, how can it possibly not be moved for ever and ever? But let us prefer to interpret this stabilised earth as the rock-solid Church, which is called the earth because it is seen to be assembled from earthly men. As the psalmist says elsewhere: *The earth is the Lord's and the fullness thereof.*[14] Christ is rightly called its stability, for He is its unshakeable foundation and invincible rock, of which Paul says: *For other foundation no man can lay, but that which is laid, which is Christ Jesus.*[15] If we continually remain based on Him, we are in no way moved; the superstructure cannot be shaken as long as that which contains it stands firm. Thus the total truth of this statement will be established for us by reason. From time to time the holy Spirit makes statements which are most perplexing when taken literally, in order that we may seek the spiritual sense by closer scrutiny. The expression, *it shall not be moved for ever and ever,* must clearly be applied to all the statements of the three verses. This figure is called *hyperbaton,* for the order of words is unfolded at greater length.[16]

6. *The deep like the mantle of its clothing: above the mountains shall the waters stand.* This verse cannot be given the historical sense either, though it seems to speak of the flood which submerged the world; for the time of the deluge was now past, and the prophet is pronouncing what is to happen in the future. So it is necessary to seek instead the spiritual sense, since the chronology cannot accommodate the literal

meaning. *The deep* is the term for a most abundant mass of water, and is frequently used in both the bad and the good sense. Here it is appropriately used to denote superstitious persons and persecutors, for just as a mantle covers the parts lying beneath, so they have cloaked the universe in the foulest superstition, with the result that they have seemed to overwhelm not only ordinary folk, but also holy and most outstanding persons with bodily tortures, but for their own destruction. Here *deep* is used in this bad sense, but we meet it also in the good sense, as in the statement: *The judgments of the Lord are a great deep.*[17] This manner of speaking is clearly to be set among the peculiar usages of divine Scripture. Finally follow the words: *Above the mountains shall the waters stand.* They stood above those who are called mountains because of the immovability of their faith when assailed with various punishments and deaths. We are to interpret *the waters* and *the deep* here as wicked men who hasten to submerge holiness as a mountain of waters can cover what lies beneath. The next verse shows that it is preferable to interpret it as referring to the arrogant and the wicked. Some wish to attach the literal meaning to this passage, stating that the deep surrounds the edge of the earth, for just as the outer parts of our bodies are covered by a mantle, so the world is said to be enclosed by the surrounding flow of the ocean.

7. *At thy rebuke they shall flee: at the voice of thy thunder they shall fear.* Who will flee except the deep, the waters which seemed to overhang Christ's mountains? Though they had inflicted various types of slaughter on His saints, they themselves were routed by the words of the apostles, abandoned their superstition, and—the greatest form of victory of all—their feelings opposed their purposes. Next comes: *At the voice of thy thunder they shall fear.* The preaching of the saints is described most beautifully by this comparison with the words, *at the voice of thy thunder,* to make you feel that it was no human utterance but the sound of heavenly power. Men in numerous places feared the thunder of their proclamations when the awful judgment was pronounced, when they heard that the devil would perish with his followers; and though they had behaved wantonly in this world, they themselves with minds transformed condemned their crimes.

8. *The mountains ascend, and the plains descend into the place which thou hast founded for them.* He still continues with metaphorical allu-

sions. The Lord allowed the arrogant and wicked to swell to the size of mountains for as long as He willed, and again at His decree He made them shrink to the lowliness of valleys. In the same way a respite was granted to persecutors to rise to the heights, and then they declined and became subject to the Christian people, thus teaching us that all things occur through the ordering of Him whose will cannot be opposed. As the Lord Himself said to Pontius Pilate in the gospel: *You would have no power against me, unless it were given you from above.*[18] Notice that here *mountains* is used in the bad sense, whereas earlier it denotes most faithful persons; we have said that this variation is often found in the divine Scriptures. Next comes: *Into the place which thou hast founded for them;* those who have now become the plains descend to the place where the firmly founded Church is, and will remain deep within her abode, for even the very sinners have limits set upon them, and are not permitted to go beyond the loosening of the reins which is permitted them. Scripture puts it succinctly: *The iniquities of the Amorrhites are fulfilled.*[19] This is to make you realise that all things are appointed under the Lord's will. The words that follow also clearly explain this.

9. *Thou hast set a bound which they shall not pass over, neither shall they return to cover the earth.* If you seek to interpret this literally, he is speaking of the copious waters, which as the flood recedes cannot possess the lands any longer. As Genesis has it: *I will establish my covenant with you, and all flesh shall be no more destroyed with the waters of a flood, neither shall there be from henceforth a flood wasting the earth.*[20] But if you look for the spiritual sense, this can be appropriately interpreted as referring also to the ritual of the pagans. Having abandoned their wickedness, they will never return to that wanton behaviour to submerge the human race with the deluge of their superstitions, for God blocks their way. The limit imposed on them was the coming of the Lord Christ; as His religion increased, all forms of idolatry fell away with their creators. Let us observe too the rebuke with which these words are uttered; human beings with reason are to reflect that they must not despise the Lord's precepts when the very elements are known to obey His commands.

10. *He who sends forth springs in the valleys: between the midst of the hills the waters shall pass.* When the nature of the earth is described, the more hidden cause is revealed to us by most beautiful allusions. It

is certain that the valleys overflow with abundant waters, and that in them are numerous springs where the fields are flat. But preferably we should interpret this as the divine waters ever bubbling out of the humility of men, here represented as the valleys. We can interpret the spiritual sense of mountains here as the heretics and the arrogant, amongst whom the divine Scriptures run with enduring richness, for in this world it is the common experience for good and evil persons alike to hear them. The expression *shall pass* is well turned, for they are seen to have fertilised such men to no profit; for if, as some say, the psalmist had wished us to interpret the hills as righteous preachers, he would have said that the waters were flowing from the very hills, not that they could pass by the hills set in their midst.

11. *All the beasts of the woods shall drink of them: the wild asses shall await their thirst.* We must interpret the beasts of the woods here as the Gentiles, who have abandoned their most aggressive manners and emerged from the worship of idols as though from the shadowy woods, to drink the waters which in the gospel the Lord promised to the Samaritan woman with the words: *He that believeth in me, out of his belly shall flow rivers of living water.*[21] Next comes: *The wild asses shall await their thirst.* Whereas he said that the beasts of the woods were drunk with the rushing waters, of the wild asses he merely stated that they await their thirst, for they are the Jews who neglected to drink the streams of divine love. The wild ass is the woodland donkey, said to have the grossest heart of all animals; it is a species of animal which is as enduring when tamed as it becomes most savage when reared in rough living by confining forests. The obdurate Jews are justly compared to such animals, for hardened by savagery of mind and thick-skinned asininity, they are not content to seek their fill quietly from the cups of life. As for the expression, *shall await*, it points to our frequent observation that when Elias and Enoch come at the end of the world, the great crowd of Jews will come to believe. Wretched are they who thirst for so long, who show no desire at all to be filled. Life is a punishment for them, for they are tortured by so great an expectation.

12. *Over them the birds of heaven shall dwell: from the midst of the rocks they shall give forth their voice.* The meaning is: Over the things mentioned earlier in *He who sends forth springs in the valleys*, the birds of heaven shall dwell. Birds are known to love valleys and the streams

that water them. The additional words *of heaven* are not idle. If he had wished us to interpret the sense merely as "birds," it would have been enough to say this; but instead he wishes us to understand by the birds of heaven the souls of bishops comporting themselves in a saintly way, for by their holy preaching they dwell over the Lord's people. He added: *From the midst of the rocks they shall give forth their voice.* These birds described as heavenly will sound forth not from the earth, not from the trees, but *from the midst of the rocks* when they are seen to be preaching in following the example of apostles and prophets. All the faithful are aptly called rocks because Christ too is called a rock. The Lord Himself said to the apostle Peter: *Thou art Peter, and upon this rock I will build my Church.*[22] So all who strengthen their words with the sayings of apostles and martyrs are preaching from the stability of rocks.

13. *Watering the hills from his higher regions: the earth shall be filled with the fruit of thy works.* Earlier he said that the high mountains were passed and the lowest valleys irrigated with springs; now he proclaims that the mountains themselves are sprinkled with the heavenly waters, so that no area might seem excluded from the Lord's bounty. Paul, who was earlier a prominent and vehement persecutor of the Church, was imbued with the water of the Spirit, and what fertile fruits he was known to bring forth for Christians! The Lord every day works to make teachers of pagans after their conversion into masters of the faithful. Such men are watered from the higher regions when they are converted and they realise that they have erred. Next comes: *The earth shall be filled with the fruit of thy works.* True, the earth bears its fruit, but how will this earth which can be trodden underfoot achieve abundance of fruits? The earth is filled with fruits when sinners change for the better, and through the Lord's bounty obtain things most useful and wholesome. The earth is filled when a person is freed from obduracy and is seen to accept the Lord's proclamations.

14. *Bringing forth grass for cattle, and herbs for the service of men that he may bring bread out of the earth.* He refines on his earlier words, making the earth which is soaked with heavenly rain bring forth grass for cattle, in other words, provide alms for those who seek them in sundry places. Of them it is said: *Give to everyone that asks you.*[23] They are called cattle because their belly's gluttony makes them shameless, and like cattle they wantonly voice their need; as long as they are

hungry they are wholly unable to restrain their cries. *Herbs for the service of men* means that necessities should be given to the person of whom it is written; *Let alms sweat in your hand until you find the just man on whom to bestow them.*[24] The persons called *men* here are those who abound in reason and who cloak their need by strength of endurance; so two types of needy person are described by such allusions. Next comes: *That he may bring bread out of the earth.* Bread is brought out of the earth when the Lord's commands are fulfilled, so that out of the visible things of the flesh may come food on which the soul may feast with heavenly refreshment. Christ is in truth our bread; He is brought out of the earth when something is bestowed on the needy out of consideration for Him. Alternatively this can be applied to preachers who have mercifully satisfied the needs of the ignorant with the riches of heaven.

15. *And wine cheers the heart of man, that he may make his face cheerful with oil, and bread strengthens man's heart.* He had said earlier: *That he may bring bread out of the earth,* but so that you would not interpret this as the common bread by which our flesh is nourished, he appended these three statements which are to be understood in the spiritual sense. Scripture often attests that the heart stands for the rational intellect, so wine cheers the heart of man when it is consecrated and becomes the blood of Christ the Lord. We are permitted to become intoxicated with this; as Scripture has it: *And thy chalice that inebriateth, how goodly is it!*[25] This is truly the wine that cheers the mind, not that which leads to guilt and vices. This is a sober intoxication, a blessed fullness which is rightly said to cheer because nothing blameworthy is found in it. His face is made cheerful with oil when the royal chrism is applied, but the face is that of which Scripture says: *Come ye to him and be enlightened, and your faces shall not be confounded.*[26] Next comes: *And bread strengthens man's heart.* Once again *heart* is to be understood as wisdom; if you were to interpret it physically, bread surely strengthens the other parts of the body besides the heart. Observe the peculiar sense of the words, and you may realise that the expression is intended to describe the understanding of heavenly things. He says that wine cheers the heart of man; should you interpret this as the wine of the world, it is known to cheer for a time not only the heart but the whole body, though often it fires men to brawls, and incites them to excessive boldness. But *heart* stands for the

mind by which we are said to have understanding, and are thought to distinguish things good and bad. Again, if we were to consider *oil* here as that in common use, how could it make the face cheerful, when it is the spirit's joy which shows on men's faces? And how can bread strengthen the heart alone, when we take it to refresh the whole body? These statements are to be related to those parts of the soul which make perfect Christians.

16. *The trees of the forests shall be filled, and the cedars of Libanus which thou hast planted. The trees of the forests* denotes the common folk of mighty communities who joined the Catholic Church from thorny and uncultivated nations. They denote especially the lower orders, whereas *the cedars of Libanus* indicate the noble and the powerful, who are seen to stand out among the human race like cedars. But to distinguish them also from heretics and pagans who are supported by the greatest power in this world, he added: *Which thou hast planted,* in other words, "which by Your predestination have been set in the most beauteous paradise of religion." As He says in the gospel: *Every plant which my heavenly Father hath not planted shall be rooted up.*[27] The meaning of the proper name should not be ignored either, for it is said to denote some message to us; Libanus means whiteness.[28] Now power in this world seems to be a kind of gaiety in which rich and powerful individuals, lofty and tall, are born so to say on mount Libanus, but by the Lord's gift have attained the true religion.

17. *There the sparrows shall make their nest: the house of the coot is their guide. There,* that is, *in the cedars which thou hast planted, the sparrows shall make their nests.* The sparrow is a tiny, exceedingly watchful bird which denotes the lowliness of monks, who in the cedars of Libanus, that is, on land bequeathed by Christian potentates, are known to build monasteries for themselves like nests, so to say, in the branches; and sustained by their resources they twitter away like sparrows with unceasing voices, hymning the Lord's praises. This is the life of heaven on earth, the imitation of the faithful angels, living the life of the spirit in the flesh and declining to love the vices of the world. They despise the present world, and always seek the joys of future blessedness; and in the end become the temple of Him whose image the human condition assumed. This is truly a beautiful paradise, in which so many fruits of the virtues blossom. Their chosen path is to prevail over their foes by avoiding grappling with them, and to prevail

by endurance. Their entire triumph lies in the suffering of their own bodies, and they effectively overcome their opponents when they yield with praiseworthy humility. They are truly Christ's soldiers who put no presumption in human powers, but are sure that they can overcome all obstacles by the Lord's strength. They do not have disputes with others, but always arraign themselves. They take pity on all, refusing to spare only themselves. They are inflamed with heavenly charity, and hasten to share with others the blessings which they desire for themselves. (But there is great glory for the tree in which this nest is contained, for if it is known to embrace such a way of life, it is to be assured that it has been planted by the Lord.)[29] Next comes: *The house of the coot is their guide.* The coot is a gentle, black bird, smaller than the duck but similar in physical shape; it settles happily on marshes. It will symbolise those to be baptised who persevere in the grace from the most holy font. So their lodging, that is, their perseverance after baptism, is the guide to the sparrows who nest in the cedars, for the sacred font is the guide of all Christians in leading them to the kingdom of heaven.

18. *The high hills are a refuge for the harts: the rocks for the urchins.* The hart is, as we have said, the devourer of poisonous snakes which leaps over thorn-bushes and is endowed with the utmost agility; it loves to dwell in the highest mountains. Rightly compared with it are the faithful who devour the devil when they transform his wicked deeds into the Lord's praise and glory, and by their goodly way of life leap over the vices of this world as though they were thorns. They dwell among the mountains, that is, among apostles and prophets who have deserved by their holy preachings to be immovable peaks in the world. The urchin is what we call the hedgehog, a most timid creature which is always armed by nature's provision, for the sharpest and most sharply packed bristles like thick hair protect its skin. But this natural defence does not suffice for it, but it always takes refuge in rocks in case it can be intercepted by some ambush. Aptly compared with this is the person shaggy with his sins, who in fear of future judgment is known to seek refuge in the most steadfast rock which is Christ. So these creatures appropriately denote for us persons who never dissociate themselves from the firm stance of the Lord. Observe that sparrows seek the heights of cedars, coots defend themselves by dwelling on waters, harts make for mountains, and urchins fortify them-

selves with the protection of rocks. In this way, by citation of diverse birds and animals, the varying lives of Christians are signified to us.

19. *He made the moon at the right time: the sun knows its going down.* He makes the transition from earthly to heavenly things, but these too are denoted by certain parallels. The moon, as we have often stated, signifies the Church, which was created in days when it experienced decrease and growth, but its decline is such that it is always renewed at the return of its fullness. We rightly interpret the sun here as the Lord Saviour, of whom the wicked will say at the end of the world: *We have erred from the way of truth, and the light of justice hath not shined on us, and the sun has not risen on us.*[30] This could certainly not be said of the sun which we all share, for Scripture speaks of Him: *Who maketh his sun to rise upon the good and bad.*[31] So He knows His going down, that is, He acknowledges the glory of His passion in the words to His disciples: *The hour is come, and the Son of man shall be betrayed into the hands of sinners.*[32] So after those kinds of Christians seen to be denoted earlier with their different senses, clearly the additions relating to the Church and the Lord Himself have been made to enhance the things created.

20. *Thou didst appoint darkness, and night was made: in it shall all the beasts of the woods go about.* 21. *The whelps of lions roaring to snatch and seek their meat from God.* We have combined the two verses here because of the necessary interconnection of the words. He appointed darkness when during the time of the passion the world grew dark at the sixth hour.[33] Then indeed night was made for the disciples and believers, when Peter was disturbed by error induced by anxiety, and by his third denial had lost the clear light of faith.[34] Night too came upon them who gazed and believed in unison that Christ was dying in the flesh on the cross. So on that night the beasts of the woods, in other words, the demons, and the whelps of lions, whom devils brought to birth by corrupting their wills, went forth seeking people to devour so that they could find meat for their malice. But this happened with the forbearance of the Lord, for nothing can be performed by anyone which the Lord does not allow by secret decree, for purposes of trial or vengeance. Whelps (*catuli*) are so called because they are skilled (*calleant*) in following the scent of their nostrils.[35] It should not trouble you that earlier we said that the beasts of the woods must be interpreted as the crowds of Gentiles,[36] whereas here they seem to

denote the devil and his agents, for this is a very frequent phenomenon in the divine Scriptures. A single object can be applied to quite differing persons, as we have remarked with reference to the mountain and to the lion.

22. *The sun arose, and they were gathered together: and they shall lie down in their dens.* When the darkness fell at the Lord's passion, demons were permitted by the Lord to burst forth seeking food for themselves, because they could search out the hearts of waverers. But when the sun rose, in other words, when the holy resurrection was manifest, they were quite unable to endure His majesty, and they tremblingly hid in their dens, that is, they took refuge in the hearts of the obstinate, intending, because they could not persuade all men, to possess at any rate those whom they had deceived. The sun (*sol*) got its name because it alone (*solus*) shines in such a way as to create daylight.[37]

23. *Man shall go forth to his work, and to his labour until the evening.* As he had earlier said that the sun had risen, he appropriately added that in this life every individual goes out to perform his tasks. This is the practice of mortals; as long as we are in this world, at the approach of day we busy ourselves with different sorts of activity. One man cultivates a field, another engages himself in wars; one learns, another teaches. A few reign, and the many serve. Whatever actions frail mortals undertake are seen to be ended with *the evening,* that is, with the end of life.

24. *How great are thy works, O Lord! Thou hast made all things in wisdom: the earth is filled with thy creation.* After recounting the works of creation in figure and discoursing on the mysteries of our faith, the prophet comes to his second mode of utterance, in which he appropriately proclaims the Father's praises, following upon such great marvels. By beginning with *how,* he stated his ability to marvel rather than to explain. It was right to embark in this way on the praises of Him whose eulogies no creature can sufficiently fulfil; this task is found not only difficult for men but also immense even for angels. The lower creatures declare the greatness of His works. Next comes: *Thou hast made all things in wisdom.* This wisdom, then, is the Son; in Paul's words: *Christ the power of God and the wisdom of God;*[38] *through him all things were made, and without him nothing was made.*[39] And to reveal the cooperative nature of this power, the psalmist says to the Father:

"Thou hast made all things through the work of the Son." Paul says the same thing too of the holy Spirit: *All these things one and the same Spirit worketh, dividing to every one according as he will.*[40] We can infer from this that the cooperation of the holy Trinity can be clearly acknowledged from these examples. He added: *The earth is filled with thy creation;* not that the earth is everywhere filled with similar things, but though deserts seem to be bereft of living creatures through the sun's heat or excessive cold, none the less the earth is filled with the things which are the Lord's creation. Or preferably we must interpret this as: "The whole earth is filled with the creation of the Catholic religion which the Lord Saviour established, for the universal Church has deserted to the Lord." Of this creation Paul says: *If then any be in Christ a new creature, the old things are passed away. Behold, all things are made new.*[41] And elsewhere: *Putting off the old man with his deeds, put on the new man, who according to God is created in justice.*[42] So the whole world is filled with this creation, which is why another psalm says: *And he shall rule from sea to sea, and from the river unto the ends of the earth.*[43]

25. *This is the great wide sea: there are creeping things without number, creatures little and great.* In this section too up to the psalm-division the figure of *parabole*[44] unfolds with diverse and beautiful comparisons. Though at the beginning of this verse he seems to speak of the sea on which ships sail, we can aptly interpret it as referring to this world, in which as we know innumerable traps of the devil lie concealed, and our shifting will is moved by the malice of demons as though by waves. They make the world a sea when they induce shipwreck, for there is no doubt that the person submerged by the whirlpool of sins is exposed to most monstrous waves. *Mare* (sea) gets its name from *meare* (to journey),[45] because the sea is always advancing and retreating. These spirits, which for us are beyond counting, are comprehended by God who numbers the grains of sand in the sea and the drops of rain; and so that they should not remain beyond understanding, the psalmist has limited them in extent rather than in nature. In short, they are said to be *creatures small and great,* for amongst them, as we know, some are greater and others lesser in wickedness.

26. *There the ships shall go: this sea-dragon which thou hast formed to mock him. There* means in the world, which was earlier described as

the sea. The ships aptly symbolise the churches which survive the hazardous waves of the world through the timber of the glorious cross, and they transport the people who have believed in the sign of faith. Christ dwells in these ships, and if awakened by believers He bids the most monstrous storm to abate, and it abates.[46] Next comes: *This sea-dragon which thou hast formed to mock him.* Here he openly refers to the devil, rightly called a dragon because of the poison which he breathed into the first woman Eve by his baneful promptings. He was created good; as we read in Genesis: *God made all things very good.*[47] But once he sinned through his own will, he was so shaped by God that the angels mocked him, for he was deprived of his innate worth through his accursed perversity. The Lord says in the book of Job: "*Nothing has been made like him upon the earth,*[48] to mock him with My angels." He is mocked by God's angels, whether in most just rebukes because having been created to serve the Lord he is found to be enmeshed in foul subversions, or rather because the souls of those who confess to him are removed from his wicked power by heavenly command. He is mocked also by the faithful when they shun his exhortations to vices with loathsome horror. You hear of the dragon, but you must not fear at all his harsh person, for by the Lord's kindness he has been moulded to be the object of possible derision even to men. Call on Him who grinds him underfoot, and you begin to cease fearing the devourer; as Scripture has it: *Thou shalt walk on the asp and the basilisk, and thou shalt trample underfoot the lion and the dragon.*[49]

27. *All things expect of thee that thou give them food in due season.* This verse expresses what has been said also elsewhere: *All things are in thy will, and there is none that can resist thy will.*[50] When he says *all things,* he shows that everything lives by God's will, for He was their Creator. That spiritual dragon whose food lies in deceiving men succeeds by his own power in achieving anything only if the Lord allows it. The person abandoned by God because of his wicked acts becomes the food of the devil. So if we are unwilling to be consigned to the enemy as his food, we must not be earthly, for in the beginning he was condemned by a curse to eat the earth; as Scripture has it: *Upon thy breast and belly thou shalt go, and earth shalt thou eat all the days of thy life.*[51] But if through the Lord's mercy we become heavenly, we are made wholly strangers to the devil's food. He further added: *In due season,* so that the Lord may not merely provide food for His crea-

tures, but also bestow it at the appropriate time. The devil sought to tempt Job, but he could achieve this only when the Lord's power allowed it. That most holy man knew that he was being tried by God's permission, and he would reply to every point: *The Lord gave, and the Lord hath taken away. As it hath pleased the Lord, so it is done. Blessed be the name of the Lord.*[52] This is a true and strong affirmation that all things, as has been said, lie in the will of the Lord.

28. *What thou givest to them they shall gather up: when thou openest thy hand, all things will be filled with fruitfulness.* He still continues expounding his previous statement: when troubled by the devil's wickedness, we are not to believe that he presumes to act by his own power; rather we must have recourse to Him without whose permission he can do nothing whatever, and then he departs conquered with all speed. The psalmist says: *What thou gavest to them, they shall gather up,* so that you may realise that they will be able to gather only what is given to them. There follows what you can assume refers to happy fortunes: *When thou openest thy hand, all things will be filled with fruitfulness.* Clearly the causes of all things lie in the source from which fruitfulness is granted and abundance bestowed without limit. *Hand* denotes the power by which He fills all things abundantly, and orders everything wonderfully.

29. *But if thou turnest away thy face, they shall be troubled: thou shalt take away their spirit, and they shall fail and return to their dust.* He now speaks of those who utterly deny that God's gifts have been granted them, attributing such gifts as far as they could to their own powers. Paul opposes them with the words: *For what hast thou which thou hast not received? And if thou hast received, why dost thou glory as if thou hast not received it?*[53] In another psalm we read of such a person: *In my abundance I said I shall never be moved.*[54] When the Lord turns away His face from such people, they are stripped of their great protection and are undoubtedly confounded; and as soon as that spirit of pride which they had assumed from abundance of possessions is taken away, they are utterly resourceless and they return to most salutary conversion from wandering induced by overtrust in themselves. So these persons should seek remedies, and expose their wounds so that they can be cured, and say: *Hear me, O Lord, since my spirit hath fainted away. Turn not away thy face from me.*[55] To them the Lord extends effective healing. Once the spirit of pride, by which they were fired in

their wandering, is removed, they must *return to their dust*, that is, to humble confession in which they acknowledge the poverty of their frailty; and they begin to be happier when they abandon their presumption. At this point we must analyse the Lord's dispensation by which the world is ruled, the economy and peculiarity of its divisions; when He gazes on us, all that will be profitable ensues, but when He turns away, our human need surrenders when stripped of its salutary protection.

30. *Send forth thy spirit, and they shall be created: and thou shalt renew the face of the earth.* Observe that the medicine which was awaited has come forth. Those who humbly acknowledged that they were dust were the ones who were renewed, for this is the fortune of those who are restored by divine grace, and are seen to have escaped the hazards of death. The Lord creates us as often as He deigns to restore us from the old age of sin into the status of new man. As we read in Psalm 50: *Create a clean heart in me, O God.*[56] Observe too that when we faltered he spoke of our dust, but when we are restored he proclaims it as the work of the Lord's spirit, so that none can attribute to his own merits what he has received through the gift of the Creator. Sacrilegious persons must hear that the holy Spirit is Creator, for he says: *Send forth thy spirit and they shall be created.* Hear a passage from elsewhere in which the holy Spirit is announced as Creator: Job speaks of *the divine spirit which created me.*[57] He both calls the Spirit divine, and clearly shows that the Spirit is both God and Creator.

31. *May the glory of the Lord endure for ever: the Lord shall rejoice in his works.* The goodly teacher still teaches the same lesson in case we are puffed up and go astray; he prays that what can at no time fail should continue to exist. He says: *May the glory of the Lord*—and of no other—*endure for ever*, that is, always, because there is no end to His praise; for in this world the Lord's praise continues unceasingly among the faithful, and after this world it will be discharged eternally by the blessed. The expression, *shall rejoice*, is a promise of the future, not of the present. Observe that everywhere the psalmist speaks of *His* works, not yours; the frequent admonition is to ensure that we do not follow the lunatic error of Pelagius, whose wicked poison we clearly sense from this passage, and against which the heavenly antidote is proffered on so many occasions so that future hazards may not oppress us.

32. *He looketh on the earth, and maketh it tremble: he toucheth the mountains, and they will smoke.* He now speaks of those who are enlightened by the Lord's grace, and who tremble at their past sins when they realise that they have gone grievously astray. Such trembling of the humble is safer than the mad presumption of the arrogant. Peter deserved to be received with pardon once he had shuddered at the great sin which he had committed. Another prophet likewise says: *On whom does my spirit rest but on him that is poor and quiet, and trembles at my words?*[58] Paul offers the same advice: *With fear and trembling work out your salvation.*[59] You see, then, how desirable and how steady this trembling is, for it brings both pardon and salvation. But observe to what persons these experiences befall, namely those whom He has deigned to look upon. Next comes: *He toucheth the mountains, and they will smoke.* We must interpret the mountains here as sinners swollen with excessive pride, who on being assailed by the Lord's anger and deprived of their worldly possessions have hasty recourse to wholesome tears. They emit, so to say, smoking clouds of regret like sweet incense, and on mounting to the heavens this is seen to obtain the mercy of the Lord Christ. *Smoke* here is used in the good sense, for it makes us attain the grace of forgiveness.

33. *I will sing to the Lord as long as I live: I will sing praise to my God while I have my being.* Having completed two sections with varying verbal allusions, he passes to the third mode of utterance, in which he says that he will sing the Lord's praises for ever. *When he says I will sing to the Lord as long as I live,* he is denoting the period of his likely life in this world. This life becomes truly life-giving if the Lord's praises are sung with uninterrupted exultation. So that you would not believe that these praises could be finished at death, he added: *I will sing praise to my God while I have my being,* that is, in the future life in which our being is eternal, and psalmody knows no end. The phrase, *while I have my being,* is splendid; for since on becoming immortal he is eager to sing praise while he has his being, he is seen to be desirous of uttering the Lord's praises perpetually. This indication makes it clear what will be the activity of those who deserve to be blessedly admitted into that native home. They will praise the Lord continually because they will always behold Him, for the beauty of that sight beyond description arouses the unending praise of every committed person.

34. *Let my praise be sweet to him: I will indeed take delight in the Lord.* There are two points here, but they harmonise with each other in balanced association. Our praise becomes sweet to the Lord provided that we take delight in the Lord; and the more He grows sweet in our eyes, the dearer we become to Him. Each one finds in himself the person he can become in the presence of the Majesty. The loving person meets affection, the indifferent one is rejected, the one who shows longing is sustained. So the Godhead must be most sweet to us so that our life too may be made acceptable to Him. It is on our own behalf that we are commanded to love the Lord with our whole heart, our whole soul, our whole strength, so that we may deserve to receive affection in return in that measure by His gift.

35. *Let sinners find failure from the earth, and the unjust so that they be not more. O my soul, bless thou the Lord.* Sinners find failure from the earth when deprived of earthly greed and are through God's grace roused to enthusiasm for better things; and similarly wicked men fail when they now cease to be evil. This verse is a prayer rather than a curse, for when every just man longs that God's Church may gain increase, he prays that sinners may be surely converted, especially as he knows that the Lord's coming for which we long can be held back until the number of the predestined is achieved. Next follows: *O my soul, bless the Lord.* The beginning of the psalm is worthy, and worthy too is its end, the command to bless Him who never at any time ceases to bestow gifts on the faithful. This identity of sentiment at the beginning and the end is as in the previous psalm to be interpreted in my opinion as referring to those who through the Lord's gift have joined a religious beginning of their lives to a glorious end.

Conclusion Drawn From the Psalm

We have heard, goodly king, the great mysteries which you have poured out for us from the hidden store of truth. You have taught us how the heavens extend, how waters lie above the heavens, that the moon was made for seasons, that the sun knows its setting, a mighty mystery.[60] Let those whose studies are superfluous, who delude themselves with empty calculations about the course of the stars, learn instead that this is the true condition of the universe. Let them listen to the heavenly Master, the truthful Teacher, the Author who tells of the creation. Why do they hasten to foolish researches, and in their desire to be students of false notions, squander occasions for ascertaining the truth?

Commentary on Psalm 104

Alleluia. This beautiful word has made its first appearance here. You do not find it used by anyone earlier,[1] though there were many Hebrew writers of early date. We must realise that *alleluia* is designated as neuter gender; saint Jerome in his commentary on this psalm[2] clearly states this, and we believe that he found it in Hebrew sources. So whenever a citation occurs we shall follow the rule established by that most learned man, that the word must remain unchanged and entire, for it has not been transmuted by the supposition of any tongue. *Alleluia* among Jews means, "Praise God"; *allelu* connotes praise, and *ia* denotes the invisible God. It is one of the ten terms for God expounded by Jerome in his letter to Marcella. He said: "The first name of God is El, that is, strong. Next come Eloim and Eloe, both meaning God." (This is why the word is often found repeated, as in: *O God, my God, look upon me,*[3] and: *My God, my God, why hast thou forsaken me?*[4] and: *O God, my God, to thee do I watch at break of day,*[5] and the like.) "The fourth is Sabaoth, meaning 'of armies'; the fifth, Helion, which we render as 'exalted.' The sixth is Esereheie, which in Exodus means 'He who sent me.'[6] The seventh is Adonai, which we usually render as Lord. The eighth is Ia, which is applied only to God, and is the final syllable pronounced in Alleluia. The ninth is Tetragrammun, meaning 'the inexpressible.' The tenth is Saddai, meaning 'strong and capable of performing all things,' "[7] and so on.

Alleluia is clearly a new address, notable for its brevity. The churches use it as a votive prayer, and it is fittingly suited to sacred festivities. The tongues of cantors are adorned with it, and the Lord's basilica joyfully responds with it. Innovations are always being introduced to it with varying tropes,[8] as though it is an insatiable blessing. So we must expect the words of psalms to be sweet, when so sweet a proclamation precedes them. We are able to grasp what can follow, for the heading itself is praise. We must further observe that through all these twenty psalms which bear the preliminary heading Alleluia (they are Psalm 104 here, and Psalms 105–6, 110–18, 134–5, 145–50) the great works of the Lord are described, and in them there is rejoicing with copious exultation. Perhaps their number denotes the glory of the New and the Old Testament in balanced alliance, so that the Creator's power must always and everywhere be praised; we can find no more obvious reason why Alleluia is inserted only in these psalms.

Division of the Psalm

The prophet is aware that the Jewish people has often offended the Lord, for they placed their hope in temporal matters and benefits. So in the first section he warns the faithful always to seek Him in spirit. In the second, he strengthens their hearts by citing the examples of patriarchs, showing that they were not abandoned by the Lord because they submitted to His dominion. In the third part he enumerates the number and the nature of the gifts which the divine power bestowed on their fathers. He describes the dangers and the distinctions of Joseph, and recounts the Jews' entry into Egypt. In the fourth section he recounts how the people of Israel were delivered from their enemies at the Lord's command through Moses and Aaron amidst the various pestilences of the Egyptians. In the fifth, he describes the great gifts which the Lord bestowed on the Jews in the desert, their purpose being not to cause them joy in temporal blessings, but to soften them with great kindnesses, so that they would preserve His justifications and maintain the Law with devoted hearts. In this way the lengthy psalm is completed in sections by abridgment of the divisions, and becomes sweet.

Explanation of the Psalm

1. *Confess to the Lord and call on his name: declare his deeds among the Gentiles.* In this verse the order of words consists of three parts. First he says: *Confess to the Lord,* in other words, praise Him and gain the grace of the Godhead for yourselves by good deeds, for praise of the Lord comprises both bestowing honour on Him with the tongue, and

performing His commands by deeds. We must understand confession here as that which unceasingly celebrates the Lord's praises, for the words that follow also indicate such prayer and action. Secondly he urges us to invoke the Lord, so that after our service of most sacred praise we can gain His receptive ear; our introductory words must be pleasing so that the Judge may be appeased and listen to us. Thirdly he says: *Declare his deeds among the Gentiles.* This can be aptly referred to the glorious evangelists, the most holy apostles, and nowadays the priests, who as we know announce His great deeds through all peoples.

2. *Sing to him, hymn him: relate all his wondrous works.* He explains his earlier words: *Confess to the Lord. Sing* refers to the hymns which we are to offer, *hymn* to the performance of pious deeds. Then he spoke of *wondrous works,* once they had been prefaced by the two preliminaries. *All* denotes those which he is to mention. It does not lie within human powers to recount all the works which the Godhead's power performs; as he is to say in Psalm 105: *Who shall declare the powers of the Lord? Who shall set forth all his praises?*[9] This figure is called the whole from the part,[10] which you will often find in the heavenly Scriptures; the celebrated passage of the gospel, *the Word was made flesh and dwelt amongst us,*[11] cannot otherwise be rightly understood, for it sounds as if He did not simultaneously receive a soul, though He deigned to set it free especially.

3. *Be praised in his holy name: let the heart of them rejoice that seek the Lord.* To ensure that no-one when performing a good deed perhaps attributes it to his own powers, the circumspect teacher warns men that in their frailty they must glory in the Lord and not in their own opinion, and that they must avoid false boasting, since they know that these acts are granted them by the Godhead. As we read in another psalm: *In the Lord shall my soul be praised.*[12] So he does not forbid us to be praised, for praise cannot be denied to good actions, but he bids us be praised in the Lord, for He grants us the deeds which we do well. So that they would gain consolation from such action, he added: *Let the heart of them rejoice that seek the Lord.* This means that a person rejoices if he is proclaimed in the Lord, but not if he is praised for some personal ability. It ought to be an important and splendid thing for us when there is praise of the name of Him who bestows on us benefits which will be profitable. So it was an act of extraordinary

shamelessness for some people to say anything against this admonition, for it is not so much these numerous testimonies as virtually the whole Law which has been issued against them.

4. *Seek ye the Lord, and be strengthened: seek his face always.* He urges those who have chosen to seek Him to gird themselves for the rewards to come. But this longing, this search is not to be limited in this world by any time, for he added: *Always,* and especially as we read: *He that seeketh, receiveth, and he that seeketh findeth, and to him that knocketh it shall be opened.*[13] As for his phrase, *seek his face,* it means His presence, which only the humble and devoted person seeks. Only a person sure of his devotion can long for the Judge; when he desires the Lord's presence, he isolates himself from debased activity. Paul sought the face of the Judge when he said: *I have fought a good fight, I have finished my course, I have kept the faith. As to the rest, there is laid up for me a crown of justice, which the Lord the just Judge will render to me in that day.*[14] Such was the prophet, then, who justly sought the face of the Judge, for through the Lord's pity he sensed beforehand that he was to gain the crown.

5. *Remember his marvellous works which he has done, his wonders and the judgments of his mouth.* He passes to the second section, in which he recounts the names and blessings of patriarchs, so that the devoted people could observe that none of them served the Lord with a devotion that proved fruitless. *The marvellous works,* then, refer to the dividing of the Red Sea, *the wonders* to the plagues with which He visited Egypt, and *the judgments of his mouth* to the fulfilment of all that He is known to have promised His servant Moses. So in one short verse he has with brief preliminary stated as a generalisation what he was next to describe in more detail. He wishes the whole of this to be understood as referring to the Lord Christ. This is the argument called *a persona,* relating to the person.[15]

6. *The seed of Abraham, his servants: ye sons of Jacob his chosen.* We must supply here *remember* from the previous verse. We must however observe the marked difference by which the prophet calls the seed of Abraham servants, but labels the sons of Jacob the Lord's chosen. The froward Jews whom he wishes us to understand here were the seed of Abraham's flesh, and he rightly calls them servants because under pressure of their infidelity they refused to be sons. The Lord said to them: *If you were the sons of Abraham you would have done*

the works of Abraham.[16] *Sons of Jacob* denotes the most faithful Christians known to be the Lord's heirs.

7. *He himself is the Lord our God: his judgments are in all the earth.* The seed of Abraham and of Jacob are warned to believe that our Saviour is not the God of one race but the Lord of the earth. Just as the Church extends everywhere, so His judgments are undoubtedly diffused throughout the world. By speaking of the Lord Himself, he warns us that we must understand Him as the One whom the Jewish people decreed should be crucified. Those who do not accept this statement proclaim that they are in a special sense foreign to the patriarchs.

8. *He hath remembered his covenant for ever, the word which he enjoined to a thousand generations.* He *remembered* when He fulfilled His promises. *For ever* means to eternity, for whatever the Lord has promised will remain with enduring stability. *His covenant* points to the preachings of the prophets which they foretold about the incarnation of the Word. Next comes: *Which he enjoined.* Enjoining means saying something through another, which is precisely what happened when the prophets were charged with foretelling the events to come. *To a thousand generations.* The round figure is used for an indefinite number, which is however brought to a close at the end of the world, in the course of which one generation of men is succeeded by the next.

9. *Which he made to Abraham, and his oath to Isaac.* 10. *And he appointed the same to Jacob for a law, and to Israel for an everlasting testament.* This refers to his earlier statement about the Lord's covenant. The promises or oaths which He made in the Old Testament to the patriarchs Abraham and Isaac He *appointed,* in other words, established, for Jacob and Israel in the New, which is the eternal Testament; for Jacob and Israel, as we have often said, usually denote the Christian era. The New Testament is aptly called eternal because none at any time succeeds it, for in it lies the complete perfection of all promises.

11. *Saying: To thee will I give the land of Chanaan, the lot of your inheritance.* Chanaan means humble,[17] so he means that Christians will fittingly obtain the land of the humble. This is the eternal Testament mentioned before, for this land of humility and prostration is accepted by the faithful to be preserved as an eternal gift. The lot of our inheritance denotes the painful privations of the world, which the Lord by

His passion dispersed for the salvation of all. His taking on human flesh is seen to be our inheritance, by which we receive the eternal patrimony of heavenly life if we are found worthy doggedly and most virtuously to lend belief to it. The image of *funiculus* (the lot) is adopted from the thin ropes by which fields and property were marked off by a stretched cord.

12. *When they were but a small number, very few and sojourners therein.* 13. *And they passed from nation to nation, and from one kingdom to another people.* He proceeds to the third section, in which he next recounts all that the divine power bestowed on the patriarchs. Observe what next ensues.

14. *He suffered no man to hurt them, and he reproved kings for their sakes.* 15. *Touch ye not my anointed, and do no evil to my prophets.* Here he denotes the time when the king of the Egyptians received a heavenly warning not to presume to harm Abraham, and as we know Isaac was similarly rescued.[18] This clearly demonstrates divine protection; their salvation was afforded not by human powers but by the gift of heaven. We must also observe that he chose to call the patriarchs mentioned earlier Christs or anointed ones, though anointing had not at that time been performed, for the practice began with Saul. But they were Christians in spirit, and known to be men of devoted faith in Christ—for example, the Lord says of Abraham, *He desired to see my day: he saw it, and was glad*[19]—so they were rightly called by that sacred name, since they were known to embrace faith[20] in Christ, The words set down are the Lord's own: *Touch ye not my anointed, and do no evil to my prophets.*

16. *And he called a famine upon the land, and he broke in pieces all the support of bread.* He points to the era of the Pharaoh, when in Egypt harsh famine stalked abroad for seven years. Though famine has no substantial being—for just as the absence of the sun is called night, so famine is the disappearance of supplies—it is said to be called down as though it were an existing person with the power of hearing. But such expressions are common in the divine Scriptures; as Paul has it: *He calleth those things that are not as those that are.*[21] Next comes: *And he broke in pieces all the support of bread,* in other words, He reduced to nothing the wheat-harvest, and this is truly known to be men's support. As he said in the previous psalm: *And bread strengthens man's heart.*[22]

17. *He sent a man before them: Joseph was sold as a slave.* Before the patriarchs, whom he mentioned earlier, the Lord sent Joseph, rightly called a man because in his many sufferings he bore everything with manly spirit. We must also note that he says that the Lord sent the one who was perplexed by the wicked conduct of his brothers. God knows how to turn to good account the evil deeds of others, and just as sinners misuse His commands detestably, so the actions of most wicked men are transformed by His dispensation to a successful outcome. Joseph when sold into slavery attained glory, and he subsequently took pity on the brothers who had planned to destroy him cruelly. In this way all his reverses turned out happily for him, so that the crafty sale of Joseph became the Lord's errand. As he said to his brothers: *For God sent me into Egypt for your preservation;* and again he says: *You planned evil against me, but God turned it into good.*[23] He next explains what he endured: the order of words is: *He sent before them the man Joseph, who was sold as a slave.* We must supply the word *who* so that the whole expression can make sense.

18. *They humbled his feet in fetters: the iron pierced his soul.* Joseph was put in prison by Potiphar, the Pharaoh's commander, though we find no mention of fetters. But it was possible that a person consigned to an underground prison was also fettered with iron bonds, especially when accused of so great a crime. There is no inconsistency in the statement there[24] that he was put in charge of the prison because of the mercy shown by the guard, for the fetters could have been applied first, and the responsibility could have come later. What this amounts to is that a right understanding of the divine Scriptures entails belief in each individual passage. So Psalm 103 says: *Who makest thy spirits angels,*[25] though we do not read this in Genesis; but the holy Spirit omits certain things in the earlier account so that the later one may gain favour by recounting something new whilst preserving the truth of the matter. So the psalmist tells of Joseph's feet humbled in fetters to denote physical affliction. He added: *The iron pierced his soul,* to show that even his soul was not exempted from punishment, for though it is subject to suffering in condoling with the body, it has also its peculiar punishment when tortured by grievous reflections. The iron pierced his soul when he was reduced to such extremities that in the course of evils unjustly suffered he feared that charges of falsehood should also be laid against him. *Iron* here denotes the affliction

of grim necessity rampant in a troubled soul when it is anxious about the future and already endures the evils which it does not cease to fear. This is the meaning of the utterance in the gospel when Simeon says to Mary: *And thine own soul a sword shall pierce*,[26] showing that the mother would bear the glorious sadness of the Lord's passion. We believe that this type of expression is to be counted among the peculiarities of divine Scripture.

19. *Until his word came. The utterance of the Lord inflamed him.* This verse is appended to the previous statement. He is saying that Joseph's reflections were most bitter until the time came when his word was sought by king Pharaoh to interpret the dream;[27] then he both gained glory and joyfully emerged from the confinement of prison. The phrase, *his word*, denotes the speaker's own utterance, but it was not his own, for it had been imparted to him by divine inspiration. The following words then follow: *The utterance of the Lord inflamed him. Inflamed* means vigorously stirred him to speak, so that he declared the future in the prince's presence with the confidence of the truth. He received within him the light of the heavenly flame, so that he foresaw events which were beyond the grasp of philosophers and teachers of that kingdom.

20. *The king sent, and he released him: the ruler of the people, and set him at liberty. Sent* means sent his ministers who obey royal commands. *The king* refers to Pharaoh, in whose kingdom he had been consigned to prison. *Released*, that is, from the charge on which he had been held. Next comes: *The ruler of the people, and set him at liberty.* The ruler is Pharaoh whom he earlier called the king; he has varied the vocabulary to lend grace to his words. *Set him at liberty*, that is, allowed him to emerge from the confines of prison; Joseph had freed the lord of the earth from the anguish of his reflections, so he now ceased to suffer imprisonment. But so that release alone should not be seen to be the limit of the concession to him, the psalmist mentions also the honour with which he was enriched.

21. *And he made him master of his house and ruler of all his possession.* 22. *That he might instruct his princes as himself, and teach his elders wisdom.* In these two verses he clearly describes the power which Pharaoh gave to Joseph. He made him master of his house and ruler of all his possession when he ordered that he mount a chariot, and that proclamation be made in the ringing voice of the crier that Joseph was

the second lord of the kingdom after Pharaoh.[28] This power is retained even today by prefects, who pass judgment by power solemnly deputed and are known to have the greatest sway over all provinces. In these matters Pharaoh gave Joseph the dominion which he himself wielded, but in the following verse the role accorded him is seen to be greater than Pharaoh's own, for the words are: *That he might instruct his princes as himself.* We must interpret this according to Pharaoh's pagan understanding. He thought that the leaders of his people could attain the wisdom to be able to interpret their own dreams, and also that their knowledge could be advanced to such a pitch of learning that they could speak inerrantly when consulted on doubtful matters. If he had consigned them to the holy man to be schooled in the faith—and clearly he would have pleased the Lord by doing this—the administration of the synagogue would have been established afresh for the Egyptians. But Scripture does not say this, and we must believe that Pharaoh did not at all desire Joseph's religion, but sought merely the splendour of his prophecy after the manner of pagans who wish to know the future, but do not seek to investigate the source of this revelation.

23. *And Israel went into Egypt, and Jacob dwelt in the land of Chanaan.* He aptly runs through the order of events after those which we have described. On Pharaoh's orders, Joseph's relatives were brought to the regions of Egypt where Joseph held sway, as the sweet words of Genesis recount. The person cited as Israel is also Jacob; so as not to repeat the same expression, the psalmist varied the diction of his revelation by using the different names. Israel in fact on leaving Egypt dwelt in the land of Chanaan; Chanaan was the son of Ham, the grandson of Noah, from whom we read that the Egyptians derive their origin.[29]

24. *And he increased his people exceedingly, and strengthened them over their enemies.* He increased his people by abundance of births, for there was hardly a woman there who did not have a child. He strengthened them over their enemies when the Egyptian masses were sorely afflicted by the notorious plagues, while the Israelites grew stronger. Here a general statement is made in brief of the events; he next explains in detail how they occurred.

25. *He turned their heart to hate his people, and to deal deceitfully with his servants.* He comes to the fourth section, in which he relates that

the Egyptians entertained the most savage malice for the Jews, and subjected them to the harshest tasks. By granting a happy lot to the Israelites, the Lord turned the Egyptians' hearts to hatred and deceits; not that He is the Author of evil, but by granting kindnesses to others He stirred their minds to envy. It is inevitable that wicked men wax indignant at the happy fortunes of others, for they know that they cannot merit like treatment. So at the sacrifices conducted by Cain and Abel, He rejected the offering of one, and gladly accepted that of the other. Next comes: *And to deal deceitfully with his servants.* The outcome of the hatred which they conceived was that the Egyptians turned savage and had recourse to deceitful ways. An indication of this is when they bade the Israelites to make bricks, and to redouble their labour denied them straw, and the other impositions which the Jewish people in their devotion to the Lord endured in the course of that most harsh slavery.

26. *He sent Moses his servant, and Aaron, that man whom he chose.* It is clear that these were chosen by the Lord to be witnesses before Pharaoh, with the result that he allowed the people pleasing to the Lord to depart unharmed. What devotion beyond reckoning the Almighty showed! He whose dominion no creature could oppose, sought this outcome from a frail man to teach us the emphatic lesson in our weakness with what self-control we ought to live, since the holy Creator is known to have achieved His wishes with such great clemency. Let us note that this type of utterance too is peculiar to divine Scripture: the expression "whom he chose" would have been sufficient, but he added: "That man" to make the choice clearer. We find this kind of expression very frequently in the divine Scriptures, for example: *In the very place where he dwelt.*[30]

27. *He set among them words of his signs, and wonders in the land of Chanaan. He set* means He implanted in Moses and Aaron the words of His signs and wonders which they proclaimed that the Lord would perform. *Signs* are definite outlines of future or past events; *wonders* refers to marvellous happenings which have not previously occurred in the order of nature. A prodigy (*prodigium*) is so called because it tells the future (*porro dicat*).[31] These signs and wonders occurred in Egypt to foretell something to the Christian people yet to come, as the authority of many Fathers states. We advert to this most appropriately in the relevant passages.

28. *He sent darkness, and blotted them out because they grieved at his words.* We read that the Egyptians endured among the other plagues a darkening of the daylight, but we would interpret this better as the darkening of their hearts for despising the Lord's precepts. *They grieved* means that they received with asperity, or rather they rejected with wounding curses. In recounting the plagues he has made an apt beginning; they could not have experienced the rest if they had not suffered a darkening of their intelligence and a most profound blindness. The experience of sinners shows that the same thing happens also today.

29. *He turned their waters into blood, and destroyed their fish.* He speaks of the second plague of which we read in the first narrative of Exodus,[32] but the plagues themselves were signs of future disaster. *He turned their waters into blood,* because they were doomed to perish in the waters of the Red Sea. Their fish too were destroyed so that no hope of life should appear to be left to them, for what we know was nourished by the basic provision of nature died amongst the waters.

30. *He sent frogs against their land, in the inner chambers of their kings.* This is the third plague. He granted them companionship with frogs, because as we know they too were to obtain a watery home. Not even their kings, in other words, their leaders, were excepted from this sign, for they were doomed to die by drowning in the bottomless depths. But in the general chaos the more remarkable thing seems to have been that not even the king's dwellings were seen to be free of this plague, though they had the service of many to remove such monstrosities; this gives us clearly to understand that divine commands cannot be obstructed by any resources or consolations.

31. *He spoke, and there came the cynomyia*[33] *and scaniphs in all their territories.* The fourth plague follows; He spoke, and it came. The two statements are very meaningful in combination, for no delaying obstacle can impede the divine command. If you clearly observe even the verbs which we find associated here, some delay is involved in pronouncing the syllables; but the Lord's command wastes no time, for His wish is already performed. *Cynomyia* means dog-fly, which bites much more savagely than other flies and is more violent in its assault, which is why it has obtained its name, derived from a hostile and most fierce beast. The *sciniph* is a species of gnat which is troublesome through its implanted sting, and which is commonly called zinzalas.

Persons swollen with foolish self-satisfaction should note that the Pharaoh, so fierce and grim, could not cope even with flies, though he boasted in the great pride of his kingdom. The psalmist speaks of *all their territories*, so that as far as the Egyptians were concerned there was no place which they found excepted from this destructive calamity.

32. *He set their rain into hail: a burning fire in the land.* 33. *And he destroyed their vineyards and their fig-trees: and he broke in pieces all the trees of their lands.* The fifth form of vengeance is recounted. This statement is like the earlier one where he said: *He set among them words of his signs;*[34] *He set* means He established and decreed. The delineation of the plagues of the Egyptians still continues, describing how the rain bestowed to fertilise the earth was transformed into the damaging waste caused by hail, the impact of which is no less destructive than the fall of a dense shower of stones. As we know, this is a sort of fire of liquid in the fields, for with its harmful touch it scorches such fruit as are struck by its stony onslaught. *A burning fire* denotes lightning, the ravages of which occur at the outset of a storm. Next comes: *And he destroyed their vineyards and their fig-trees, and he broke in pieces all the trees of their lands.* His phrase, *broke in pieces*, has reference to the earlier mention of hail or lightning, the violence of heaven which assails the fields like enemy missiles. So that you would not think that only vineyards and fig-trees were destroyed, he added: *All the trees of their lands.* He wanted you to be quite certain that the harvest too was ruined, since you realised that the trunks of trees had been shattered; for the greater implies understanding of the lesser.

34. *He spoke, and the locust came, and the bruchus, of which there was no number.* 35. *And devoured all the grass of their land, and all the fruit of their earth.* This is the start of the sixth plague; we see that the narration is similar to the earlier statement: *He spoke, and there came the cynoyia and sciniphs.* The locust is the mother of the bruchus, which it breeds with oppressive abundance; it descends on its prey like a gathered army with its offspring. To prevent your believing that its arrival had no effect, he says that all the fruit of that land was devoured by them.

36. *And he slew all the first-born in the land of Egypt, the first-fruits of all their labour.* He passes to the seventh and, so far as this psalm goes, last plague, at which the Egyptian people were now subdued and

yielded before the great number of these evils. How could they bear any more, since they had lost all life's pleasures, and realised that they were stripped of their very victuals? This is how the person who thinks that he must war on the divine commands is brought to nothing step by step. A question seems to arise here: why does this psalm recount seven plagues suffered by the Egyptians, when there are ten described in the version in Exodus? We have often stated that in the divine Scriptures the whole is to be understood from the part. For example, we read in the gospel: *The word was made flesh, and dwelt amongst us,*[35] as though He did not at the same time take a soul, though it was this which He deigned especially to deliver. We realise that in this case the mention of the flesh must include also the acceptance of a soul; you find this proclaimed in many places. There is the additional point that the number seven is known to have been perfected by the power of the holy Spirit. So he aptly embraced ten plagues within the narration of seven, so that you might grasp the entirety of the whole from hearing mention of the part. Moreover, it was fitting that he should describe a well-known incident with variation of narrative, for he was proclaiming the punishments of the Egyptians and the like number of blessings of the Jews. In this sense the account here does not differ, but is most splendid because of its variety. Alternatively, and this is father Augustine's view,[36] encomium is not shackled with the law of historical narrative. The writer who compiles a history counts it necessary to record everything most fully, but the eulogist will find it enough to touch on a few themes out of many. So he mentions the earlier ones briefly because he is not here instructing the ignorant, but recounting to an audience which can recall. And since in the section which follows he is to state that the Lord conferred seven kindnesses on the Jewish people, he prefaced this with the account of how their enemies the Egyptians sustained seven plagues, so that (as I see it) the number of good and evil experiences in the psalm might win approval.[37]

37. *And he brought them out with silver and gold: and there was not among their tribes one that was feeble.* Now that he has recounted the plagues which the Lord inflicted on the Egyptians, he passes to the fifth section, in which he says that as many kindnesses were bestowed on the Jews. He says: *He brought them out with silver and gold.* The first kindness, then, was that the people who were oppressed with

long slavery did not leave needy and empty-handed. We read that the Israelites on departing received at the Lord's command gold and silver from the Egyptians,[38] not apparently through hasty theft but as the reward of long activity. Because there can be no doubt that all the Lord's orders are just, this action which was known to be done by His command was clearly guiltless. So a second kindness follows: in that imposed migration no-one can have been troubled by bodily sickness. This was so that they could energetically fulfil all that the Lord commanded them to do.

38. *Egypt was glad when they departed, for the fear of them fell upon them.* We must carefully ponder this verse. It is clear that Egypt was not glad at the departure of the Jewish people, for they decided that they should pursue them. But once those who had decided to attack the Jews had drowned, the ones who had remained in Egypt were extremely glad because they had not suffered a similar fate. He is explaining this reason with his words: *For the fear of them fell upon them.* This fear lay in the fact that the very elements seemed to have warred in support of the Jewish nation. Notice too that by the figure of metonymy, which in Latin is called *transnominatio*,[39] he says that Egypt and not the Egyptians was glad; the content is indicated by the container.

39. *He spread a cloud for their protection, and fire to give them light in the night.* Both boons are known to have been granted to offset the harsh weather. A cloud was sent to temper the sun's heat, and fire was vouchsafed to remove the darkness of the night. This is the third gift known to have been granted to the people of Israel.

40. *They asked for flesh, and the quail came: and he filled them with the bread of heaven.* Observe how their aspirations were met. The Jews asked for flesh, and they obtained quails; we know that meat on poultry is undoubtedly as sweet as that on quadrupeds. Secondly, they asked for one thing and two came, for the next words are: *And he filled them with the bread of heaven.* These incidents are quite well known from our reading of Exodus, for quails rained down like the heaviest shower, and the Jews received manna to get their fill.[40] But to demonstrate that this was a prefiguration, he spoke not of manna but of the bread of heaven, so that the Lord Saviour's coming could be visualised in this blessing, for he is *the living bread which came down from*

heaven.[41] The meaning of manna, as was stated at Psalm 77, is "What is this?"[42] He disposed of the problem surrounding the name, and with the statement: *He filled them with the bread of heaven,* he explained the answer to the question about manna, for the Lord of heaven is indicated by the phrase, and the nature of manna is clearly acknowledged.

41. *He cleft the rock, and waters flowed: rivers ran down in the dry land.* This event too, the rock spouting forth watering streams, was a prefiguration of the Lord Christ. Christ the Lord is the spiritual Rock who wells forth with the waters of life from which the soul's longing takes its fill, and cannot experience further thirst. *Rivers ran down in the dry land* is directed towards sinners among the Gentiles. They are rightly called dry because they will be drained of their scorching sins. Once invigorated by the Lord's rain, they will sprout into new creatures. The Lord says of them: *For the Son of man is come to seek and to save that which was lost.*[43]

42. *Because he remembered his holy word which he spoke to his servant Abraham.* 43. *And he brought forth his people with joy, and his chosen with gladness.* In these two verses the reason for the miracles which he mentioned earlier is given. They are said to have been performed because they were known to have been promised to Abraham. Notice his statement, *he brought forth his chosen with gladness,* for those who grumbled were smitten with the Lord's anger.

44. *And he gave them the lands of the Gentiles, and they possessed the labours of the people.* 45. *That they might observe his justifications and seek after his law.* He passes to the seventh blessing. First he spoke of their being brought out with silver and gold: second, the absence of any enfeebled person among them: third, the cloud spread over them, which both provided light in darkness and removed the sun's heat during the day: fourth, the gift of quails: fifth, the mention of their being filled with heavenly bread: sixth, the welling forth of watering streams in the most barren region: and finally he describes how the truth of the promises to them was fulfilled, for the Lord gave them the lands of the Gentiles, and with the most abundant devotion bestowed on them the labours of their enemies. His expression, *the lands of the Gentiles,* seems to refer to possession of territories, *the labours of the people* to the riches gathered over a long period. So that the hearts of mortal men would not cling to the things of the present, He bestowed

spiritual blessings, constraining them both to seek and to maintain His commandments, so that they should not pin their hope only on temporal things; for even if these things captivate them for the moment, they do not lead them to the kingdom of heaven. As Paul puts it: *If in this life only we have hope in Christ, we are of all men most miserable.*[44] *His justifications* are that we love God with our whole heart, and our neighbours as ourselves, that we honour our father, hold our sons dear, and perform the other just deeds laid down in the various spheres of life. The psalmist warns us to maintain these, because the instruction in such matters is clear and absolute. The Law laid down that men should rest on the sabbath, that a yearling lamb should be sacrificed at the Pasch, that the priests should approach the altar in sacramental garb, and the other commands of this kind known to have been imposed by the Lord. But these and the likes of them are to be sought not in the physical but in the spiritual dimension. This was why he added: *That they might seek*, for he was aware that the commands of the Law are the shadow and mirror of things to come.

Alleluia. You must realise that it is not insignificant that *alleluia* is in some psalms placed at the beginning and end, but in others set only as preface in the heading. Those which harmonise at the beginning and end in this way are in my opinion to be interpreted like the psalms which have the same beginning and end, like Psalms 102 and 103 earlier. Alternatively, a statement renewed in repetition always penetrates with greater emphasis; for example: *Not so the wicked, not so*,[45] and: *So be it, so be it*,[46] or: *Amen, amen I say to you*,[47] and: *Abba, Father* (for Abba means father).[48] Perhaps there is another reason for the repetition which lies hidden, but we have not succeeded in obtaining another explanation from our mentors, nor has any further notion been granted to ourselves.

Conclusion Drawn From the Psalm

Observe that the double alleluia has been sung. A psalm abounding in praise of heaven has been completed, which both truthfully recounted past events and gave us wholesome advice about the future. The Egyptians suffered the vengeance which they utterly deserved, the Jews received heavenly gifts. Each of us must now anticipate the repayment of that people whose example we follow. We must survey with the heart's eye the statement at the end of the psalm, that we must direct ourselves with total concentration of mind towards the Lord's justifications, living within His law. If we have obtained temporal blessings, as Abraham, Isaac, Jacob and the rest of the faithful who flourished with copious resources did, we must none the less concentrate on the means by which we can be guided to the kingdom of heaven. The things which make the world seem attractive have no place in eternity. We must remember that this is the second of the psalms[49] which in relating the miracles conferred on the Jews announce the future sacraments of the Christian people by the figure of allegory, which says one thing but means another.[50]

Commentary on Psalm 105

1. *Alleluia.* Observe once more the return to us of alleluia-joys. This is a brief instruction that we must sing to the Lord with rejoicing throughout the psalm. But let us observe that we find no change in the heading, or in the reason for it, from the previous one. The heading is *Alleluia,* the reason is confession, which is wondrously and exceedingly fruitful for praising the Lord. How many mouths has this theme opened? With it Moses and the men, and his sister Mary with the women, celebrated the crossing of the Red Sea in God's praise.[1] With it Deborah sang out in happy exultation;[2] many of the prophets too poured forth various songs in proclaiming so great a miracle, and rightly, for these miracles attest the mysteries of the entire redemption of men. We are delivered from the Egyptians when by God's gift we are freed from the works of the devil. We cross the Red Sea when we receive the sacrament of baptism. We are fed in the desert when through the dispensation of divine grace we get our fill from the bestowal of the good things of this world. We are led to the land of promise when through the gift of heavenly devotion we enter the blessed native land. It is right, then, that this theme should be often repeated and proclaimed, for it is adorned with the foreshadowing of such great marvels.

Division of the Psalm

The Jewish people is ushered in, uttering their confession. They have abandoned the infidelity of their fathers, and through the Lord's pity are led to His devoted love. This is to enable us to understand that they too when converted aptly sing alleluia because they are redeemed. So in the first narration, the prophet begs to be associated with the people who have found favour and who were to be gathered from the nations at the Lord Saviour's coming. In the second section he recounts the sins which their fathers committed in Egypt, when they failed to acknowledge with virtuous hearts the wondrous deeds of the Lord. But he maintains that the Lord in His devotion freed them from their enemies. In the third part he relates that they relapsed into eagerness to sin, but says that the Lord was appeased by the prayers of His chosen one Moses. In the fourth, he maintains that the Jews renewed their wicked ways, and that the Lord had decided to destroy them but was placated by the entreaties of His servant Phineas. In the fifth section he relates that Moses was irritated by them at the water of contradiction, and that later they cruelly killed their children during their worship of idols. By reason of this the Lord was more fiercely angered and consigned them to slavery under the Gentiles, but then took pity on them and made them glorious in the sight of their enemies. In the sixth, he prays for what he knew would come, that the Catholic Church should be assembled from all the nations, and sound praises together to the Lord with unending exultation. Now let us traverse the sections of the psalm along the revealed paths of the divisions.

Explanation of the Psalm

Confess to the Lord, for he is good, for his mercy endures for ever. Just as the previous psalm stated that the confession there should be directed towards the praises of the Lord, so here he earmarks this confession for the application of the healing of repentance. But undoubtedly this too is relevant to the Lord's praises, for the gesture of sparing the person who confesses manifests greater glory of devotion than does extending pardon to one who lives without giving offence. What happens here is that the gathering of Jews who are penitent and have been corrected by divine inspiration speaks to the rest of the people, urging them to condemn the evil of their former error and to return to the divine clemency. So that no individual would be deterred by the great number of his faults, the psalmist added: *For he is good.* Who would hesitate to return to Him upon hearing that He can come most swiftly to our aid? The Lord is rightly called good, for He feeds the deviant, awaits the wanderer, and *makes his sun to rise upon the good and bad, and rains upon the just and the unjust.*[3] This too is uttered by the voice of Truth itself: *None is good but God alone.*[4] He added: *For his mercy endures for ever.* Once they have heard that the Lord is good, he does not wish human indifference to cease making eager and diligent entreaty, so he explains the reason for the remedy so that through the Lord's gift they may hasten to speedy confession. *For ever* denotes the course of this life in which all sinners are wretched, and it is right that our hearts should be converted and ask for mercy; for at the Judgment which we know is certain, confession of sin brings condemnation.

2. *Who shall declare the powers of the Lord, shall make all his praises heard?* The people mentioned are wholly impressed by the divine works, and say that the human mind cannot take in the full account which they should give of the Lord's majesty. *Who* denotes no-one, for whose mind suffices to ponder, or whose tongue to make utterance, so that His immeasurable greatness can be told on one person's lips? This is why we must rightly say: "Not if I had a hundred tongues, and a hundred mouths, and a voice of iron."[5] He further added: *Shall make all his praises heard?* We must supply *who* here as well to attain the full meaning. The phrase, *who shall make all his praises heard,* offers a pleasing variation of diction. The things known to be spoken can be heard. We must consider this manner of speaking too as one of the peculiarities of Scripture.

3. *Blessed are they that keep judgment and do justice at all times.* Now that he has denied that the Lord's praises can be grasped, he makes a statement with which the human race can console itself. They cannot fulfil His praises, but they can at any rate keep His judgment and justice. Keeping judgment means passing right judgment among others, whereas doing justice means acting fairly. Alternatively he is calling those blessed who keep judgment in the faith and manifest justice in action. But note that he added: *At all times;* as Christ says in

the gospel: *He that shall persevere to the end shall be saved.*[6] So such men are rightly called blessed, for they maintain the Lord's commands with pure hearts. This is the third type of definition, called in Greek *poiōdēs* and in Latin *qualitativa*,[7] which shows what a thing is by explaining what it is like.

4. *Remember us, O Lord, in the favour of thy people: visit us with thy salvation.* The devout Jews pray that they may be numbered among those who have pleased the Lord with faithful deeds; we know that the people of Israel was divided between those who were defiant and those who abided by the Lord's commands. So the people here humbly entreat that they may be counted in the company of those to whom eternal blessedness can be granted through the grace of the Godhead. So that the absolute perfection of their faith may be acknowledged, they pray that they may be visited by the Lord Saviour, at whose coming they knew that they would be saved, for He is the salvation of whom blessed Simeon says: *Now thou dost dismiss thy servant, O Lord, according to thy word in peace. Because my eyes have seen thy salvation which thou hast prepared before the face of all peoples; a light to the revelation of the Gentiles, and the glory of thy people Israel.*[8]

5. *That we may see the good of thy chosen, that we may rejoice in the joy of thy nation: thou mayst be praised with thy inheritance.* This is the purpose of their request to be visited by the saving Lord, that they might behold His goodness which He was to bestow on the chosen by the gift of His coming. Thus they could rejoice with the Christian people who were to be exultant at His incarnation. This is the Lord's nation, gathered from the diversity of peoples to be one flock and one shepherd. Next follows the sweetest reward of these actions, that the Lord *be praised with his inheritance.* The two are combined, for when the Lord is proclaimed, His faithful servant is undoubtedly praised. As the previous psalm stated: *Be praised in his holy name.*[9] So this faithful people hastened with such great longing to the sight of the Lord, and mingled with the Christian throng with such great love that it is sacrilegious to imagine that He was not seen in spirit when we know that He was sought with such great favour. As Christ says in the gospel: *Abraham rejoiced that he might see my day: he saw it, and was glad.*[10]

6. *We have sinned with our fathers: we have acted unjustly, we have wrought iniquity.* He passes to the second narration, where the people

described prostrate themselves in humble satisfaction to manifest the confession mentioned at the beginning of the psalm. They say that they have sinned with their fathers because they are sprung from their loins. True, the intervening period is long since their fathers in Egypt were granted those miracles in the flesh and gave the Lord no answering satisfaction, and the generation being described in song by the sequence of this psalm was much later in time. But there is no doubt that they reenact the sins which they were known to shoulder because of the wickedness of their parents. The Pelagian heresy does not admit this, believing that original sin could in no sense have passed to Adam's descendants. But those who do not through the Lord's grace detach themselves from their forbears' sin err together with them. Father Augustine has proved this in the very careful argument in his books.[11] But now with the Lord's inspiration the mind of the people was pricked and regained its sanity, so they rightly desired to be cleansed of their parents' sins, having begun to isolate themselves from their obligations. So that the resolution in this purest of confessions should be made clear, they confirm it with triple repetition. *We have acted unjustly* is the same as *we have sinned; we have wrought iniquity* is the same as *we have acted unjustly*. Each one of us is forgiven more quickly according to the emphasis with which he condemns himself. This figure is called *schesis onomatōn*,[12] in other words, a crowd of combined expressions denoting the one thing in different words. There is another explanation at this point which has come down to us: a person sins with his ancestors if he does not renounce similar vices, but commits the same faults as, to his knowledge, his forbears did. But none the less the guilt of original sin cannot be removed from descendants except by the Lord's grace.

7. *Our fathers understood not thy wonders in Egypt, and they remembered not the multitude of thy mercies. And they provoked thee to wrath going up to the Red Sea.* Two faculties, the understanding and the memory, approve kindnesses bestowed, but the people claim that their faithless fathers revealed neither. *They understood not* makes the point well. They saw that the marvels were being afforded them, but they were not seen to acknowledge why this was happening. The Egyptians were assailed by ten plagues so that the Jewish race should devoutly observe the ten commandments still to come. They were released by the Pharaoh so that they in turn might abandon the devil and

his agents. But they viewed these events with the eyes of the flesh, and made no attempt to seek the rewards of spiritual grace. They were unmindful of the Lord's mercy when they beheld the Pharaoh's army before the Red Sea was sundered, and they believed that they had lost all means of escape; and they spoke against Moses, saying that it would have been better to submit to harsh slavery rather than that the entire race should perish in the desert. It was consequently inevitable that they should provoke the Lord when going up to the Red Sea, for they did not believe that what they heard promised by His omnipotence could come to pass. The result was that they neither understood the Lord's power nor remembered His kindnesses with devoted heart. The expression, *provoked to wrath*, is good, implying that in Himself He was calm and kindly, but that they made Him hostile and angry towards them. Clearly the phrase, *going up to the Red Sea*, was dictated by the topography; Egypt is said to be lower than the surrounding regions, and as they departed they seemed to be making for higher ground.

8. *And he freed them for his own name's sake, that he might make his power known.* The phrase, *for his own name's sake*, seems to me to point to the Lord Saviour, whose name is appropriate for the rescue of those in danger. When God delivers sinners, He does not help them because of their merits, but to demonstrate the power of His name, so that He is clearly seen as devoted if He grants abundant kindnesses to the undeserving. As for the claim that He made His power known, the psalmist means not to physical eyes but to those with spiritual insight; if He had made His power known to all, the stubborn people would certainly not have sinned through disbelief.

9. *And he rebuked the Red Sea, and it was dried up: and he led them through many waters as through the desert.* He has called the hidden command of the Godhead a rebuke; nowhere in Exodus do we read that the sea was rebuked by the Lord's voice. All that He commands He performs with unseen movements. He addresses the elements which have no faculties of sense as though they listened; such is the power of His command that objects without hearing can obey. We must not assume that the entire sea was dried up, but only as much as afforded them a path; it was in fact a greater miracle that the sea-waves stood still with their sides sheared. The flowing waters ceased to flow, and halted with a stability suited to mountains. Next comes: *And he led*

them through many waters as through the desert. A desert becomes such above all because it is deserted by any inflow of waters, so that no living creature can survive there because of the natural hazard of its barrenness. So the Jews were led out through the depths as if through a desert-tract, arid and extremely barren, thus showing that the path through the waters became so dry that it was virtually a dusty track.

10. *And he freed them from the hand of them that hated them: and redeemed them from the hand of enemies.* Though it was itself a blessing that He freed them from the control of a foreigner, the psalmist extended the range of the gift by saying: *From the hand of them that hated them.* It was not possible that they would spare the Jews when they were attacking them so savagely. We interpret this also as referring to the confederate band of demons, which both hates and smites the human race by goading them to sin. Next comes: *And redeemed them from the hand of enemies.* If you were to interpret this in the literal sense, it does not seem to square with the facts, for He made no payment to the Egyptians to free the Jews; in fact He redoubled the hardships caused by the plagues owing to their arrogance. We must believe that this is said in the spirit of prophecy with reference to Christian times, when the Lord Saviour redeemed enslaved sinners from the devil's dominion with His precious blood.

11. *And the waters covered them that afflicted them: not one of them was left.* This can apparently be interpreted literally, for there is the well-known account in Exodus. But *none of them was left* refers not to the whole Egyptian nation but merely to the crowd of pursuers who were known to have been destroyed there, down to the most insignificant. Those Egyptians who rejoiced at the Jews' departure—in the words of the previous psalm: *She was glad when they departed*[13]—had survived, but they were not in like case.

12. *And they believed in his words, and they sang his praises.* By saying *they believed* after such a miracle, he is pointing to their hardness of heart, because they chose to believe not before the outcome of the event but as the result of miracles. Though it is good to lend assent to things seen, it is much better to have believed in what was promised. As Christ says to Thomas in the gospel: *Thou hast believed because thou hast seen. Blessed are those who have not seen, yet believed.*[14] The addition: *And they sang his praises* denotes the hymn in Exodus which says: *Let us sing to the Lord, for he is gloriously magnified,*[15] and the rest which

the Jewish people sang with great exultation after the miracle was enacted, as was stated in our explanation of the psalm-heading.

13. *They were quickly done, and they forgot his works: they did not abide his counsel.* He passes to the third narration. *They were quickly done;* it is as if he were saying: "They changed course with the greatest speed, for after singing praises to the Lord for the wonders He had bestowed, a little later they raised sacrilegious murmurs against Him." *They did not abide his counsel* when they nursed lack of hope before the emergence of the blessings which He had prepared. The Lord, who had freed them with such great miracles, had not allowed them to endure any shortage of foodstuffs. But they refused to await His dispensation, and anticipated the heavenly counsel as human frailty tends to do, for with the intention of making provision for itself with excessive haste, it unguardedly anticipates the plan of the Godhead.

14. *And they desired their desires in the desert, and they tempted God in the place of drought.* This was their total failure to abide his counsel. They sought food in the desert without trust, and grumblingly demanded that water be given them. This figure is called *cacozēlon*[16] or evil striving, when the intellect lacks judgment, and headlong speed of action is deluded by hope of some good. *They desired their desires;* this type of utterance is extremely frequent in the Scriptures. For example: *With desire I have desired to eat the pasch with you,*[17] or again: *He that curseth his father or mother shall die the death,*[18] or: *The Lord chastising hath chastised me,*[19] and the like. The duplication of words shows the excessive degree of longing.

15. *And he gave them their requests, and sent fullness into their souls.* Since they sought temporal gifts, they rightly obtained blessings of the flesh. We say that the soul finds fullness in two ways, when it is refreshed in its physical weakness by bodily food, and when it is filled with spiritual joy. Here he is saying that their souls were fattened on flesh and drink, so that their very wishes which had sinned through despair were overcome by the material things which became available.

16. *And they provoked Moses in the camp, and Aaron the holy one of the Lord.* Their bellies' fullness was followed by rebellion, which often rouses occasions of destructive danger. We say that a person is provoked when roused to anger by wicked deeds or very harsh words of others. The verse points to the incident when Dathan and Abiron roused strife and sought distinction for themselves.[20] So their punish-

ment ensued; for they provoked the holy men, which led to their own destruction, for they spoke through jealousy, and this is acknowledged to have displeased the Lord. This is aptly mentioned among the Lord's praises because He is seen to have avenged His servants.

17. *The earth opened and swallowed up Dathan, and covered the congregation of Abiron.* As Numbers attests,[21] it is clear that this befell the men who with the poisonous teeth of envy sought the heavenly favour bestowed on Aaron and Moses. Thus Dathan and Abiron wantonly seized for themselves the distinction which had been bestowed by the Lord's kindness on Aaron and Moses. A similar end came on both of them because their motive in causing division was the same. They were swallowed up by the earth because they were redolent of earthly things, so that the nature of their punishment itself witnesses to their criminal deeds.

18. *And a fire was kindled in their gathering, and the flame burned the sinners.* This happened to the two hundred and fifty associates of Dathan and Abiron who unhappily supported their requests to the point of presuming to hold the censers, as the text of Numbers recounts.[22] *Synagoga* denotes here not the temple but the congregation which we know was charred by the divine fire, so that those who had sinned in presuming to offer incense were consumed by the heavenly flame. He added *their* to *gathering* to make you realise that it was detached from the people of the Lord. *Flamma* (flame) gets its name from *flagellum,*[23] the tuft in its tail.

19. *And they made a calf in Horeb, and they adored the graven thing.* This too is made clear in the account of that well-known story, when the Jews were quite unwilling to brook Moses' absence, and with unnatural inclination made for themselves a god of metal on Mount Horeb in the desert.[24] Why, they were much worse than the very mules, for it was not even a living beast which they regarded as worthy of adoration in their ludicrous devotions! The meaning of *Horeb* is Calvary; those traitorous men with sacrilegious presumption dishonoured the Lord's worship, just as their descendants were to crucify the Lord Christ in the place called Calvary. I think that we should also bear in mind the words here: *They adored the graven thing,* for we read in Exodus that it was a molten calf fashioned from various ornaments and of monstrous appearance. We must interpret these as a description of two different things. First they adored the calf in the desert,

and later they worshipped graven images in the land of promise, as the psalmist is to say later.

20. *And they changed their glory into the likeness of a calf that eateth grass. Their glory* was the Godhead which they adored, and which they lost by a wretched interchange. Their fate up to the present day has been the abandonment of the Creator of heaven and earth, and the construction for themselves of a deity in *the likeness of a calf that eateth grass.* What a wicked sin to have allowed themselves to be deceived when they had been enlarged by that splendid vision of wonders! What kind of crime was it to believe that a dumb animal was like to God, when it would have been sacrilege to compare it even with men? It was the lack of endurance of the ficklest men which caused all this, a trait which always leads to sins, and casts us into destruction. If you analyse truthfully the root of the matter, there is no wickedness which is not the offspring of want of endurance. Opposed to it the true remedy, the firm, unwavering protection is this: *With expectation I have waited for the Lord, and he was attentive to me.*[25]

21. *They forgot God, who saved them, who did great things in Egypt.* 22. *Wondrous works in the land of Chanaan, terrible things in the Red Sea.* Great odium is heaped on the Jews for their forgetfulness. What kindness could they have recalled, when their liberation did not succeed in remaining in their memory? He speaks of *great things* to ensure that what was seen to be detached from their thoughts was not considered of small import. Even if they could not be kept in unfaithful minds as benefits conferred, they ought at any rate to have been remembered for the importance of the events themselves. He further spoke of *wondrous works* which they ought not inexcusably to have thrust from their minds, however fickle they were, Finally he added: *Terrible things,* which usually make a more lively impression on human spirits, for when the fear of them returns they are not expunged from the memory. What stupidity, what lunacy is upbraided here! To think that they could have turned from such great works performed by so great an Activator! Note how many events He has concentrated by the addition of single words; this figure is called *auxesis*[26] or increase gradually mounting to higher levels, a technique extremely powerful in speeches of both praise and abuse.

23. *And he said that he would destroy them, had not Moses his chosen stood before him in the breach, to turn away his wrath, lest he should*

destroy them. The text of Exodus recounts all this. The Lord told Moses that in His anger He had consented to destroy the people who sinned so offensively. But Moses *in the breach*—in other words, the destruction which the people deserved to experience—confronted the Lord with the words: *If you forgive them the sin, forgive them: if not, strike me out of thy book.*[27] What a holy man, most worthy of all praise! When he came down from mount Sinai to the camp and saw the people exultantly and sacrilegiously posturing before the idol, he was roused to anger, broke the tablets in front of them, and ordered one or other of them to be slain by the sword. But when comprehensive disaster loomed, he prayed that he himself should be destroyed rather than that the entire nation should perish. Both attitudes were devoted and splendid. Moses was right to converse with the divine clemency, for he loved to carry out its decrees; at the same time that power is revealed by which we often escape the punishment of deserved death through the prayers of the saints. Not that anyone can change the Lord's dispositions, but must realise that the outcome is foreknown by Him.

24. *And they set at nought the desirable land. They believed not in his word.* He passes to the fourth narration, in which he says that the Jews kept in mind neither the promises for the future nor the wonders which had been performed; so these seemed of no account, for they always regarded what they saw and heard from the material aspect, and once we have obtained some bodily need we quickly scorn it. But notice how important that land was to those with understanding, for it was said to be desirable, but to the Jews it seemed of no account because they did not grasp any spiritual dimension. Next comes: *They believed not in his word. Word* denotes the Son, in whom that most sacrilegious people did not believe. Alternatively the literal sense is apt here, for they murmured because they preferred to attach no credence to His promises. Their infidelity helps us to understand a lot about them, but on all counts there is guilt.

25. *And they murmured in their tents: they hearkened not to the voice of the Lord.* While they grumbled they heard nothing of the Lord's voice. This frequently happens to people preoccupied with their own utterances, for they cannot hearken to other things. Notice that the word *hearkening* is applied in common use only to suppliants and not to those in higher positions. So because here the psalmist says that the

Lord was not hearkened to, it is clear that we must reasonably regard this as one of the peculiar usages of divine Scripture. He added: *In their tents*, so that this would be seen to have happened not when they were toiling but when they were at leisure. Greater odium at their sin accrues to them since they were at leisure when they grumbled.

26. *And he lifted up his hand over them to overthrow them in the desert.* 27. *And to cast down their seed among the nations, and to scatter them in the regions.* Here the Lord's justice is first stated so that His ensuing devotion may be appreciated with greater glory to Him. The psalmist says that the Lord's power rose against them to exact vengeance on their transgressions and to overthrow them in the desert, because they refused to listen to the Lord's commands; and subsequently to humiliate their seed, that is, the rest of them, among the nations, whereas for a long time they had been famed and preeminent amongst all races. Finally he intended to scatter them through the regions when they were laid low and despised, so that they should have no presumptuous expectation for the future that they would gather together.

28. *And they were consecrated to Belphegor, and they consumed the sacrifices to the dead.* 29. *And they provoked him with their enthusiasms, and destruction was multiplied among them.* In these verses the Jews' greater excesses and the Lord's fiercer anger are subjoined. They were seen not only to have sacrificed on the spur of the moment, but even to have consecrated themselves to Belphegor the idol of the Gentiles.[28] They had so far seceded to the worship and ritual of demons that they were clearly servants of devils and no longer of the Lord. *The sacrifices of the dead* is a very apt phrase, because it was attested that worship was paid to dead persons whom the Gentiles reckoned to be immortal gods. Note carefully that he says that destruction was multiplied among them whom the Lord was to spare through the prayers of His holy one. He said that the retribution due was multiplied because of the mass of their sin, so that the clemency extended to them might be greater because more numerous offences were being forgiven.

30. *Phinees stood and made a prayer, and the slaughter ceased.* 31. *And it was accounted to him as justice, to generation and generation for ever more.* The verb *stood* itself shows firmness of mind; in that general anxiety he alone dared to assume the trusting role of one begging for

mercy. Though we read that he ran through with a weapon the Jew who contrary to the Lord's command was having intercourse with the woman of Midian[29] (for he is known to have done this with heavenly zeal), it deserved to be called a prayer rather than an action, for whoever concerns himself with good acts is making a prayer. He did not blanch from the murder of that man since he was punishing the stain of adultery. After shedding that blood he was so guiltless that he deserved praise from the mouth of the Judge Himself.

32. *They provoked him also at the water of contradiction, and Moses was afflicted for their sakes.* 33. *Because they exasperated his spirit: and he distinguished with his lips.* He passes to the fifth narration, in which is recounted the offence when water was demanded with sacrilegious grumblings after the manifestation of all the miracles. As we know, it was sought in such a manner that it appeared to be a contradiction rather than a request. As we read in Numbers, Moses on that occasion was indignant at the excessive impudence of the Jewish people, and distrustingly rebuked them with the words: *Hear me, rebellious and incredulous ones; can we bring you water out of this rock?*[30] Moses himself also sinned with these words, for though such great miracles had been earlier received, he did not believe that the Lord would do what He did. Moses *distinguished with his lips* these words from his earlier constancy; he separated the two when he spoke these words doubtingly, whereas he had made those promises earlier with wholly undoubting faith. We claim that this type of utterance is peculiar to divine Scripture, for neither secular literature nor common usage practises it. Moses preserved his holiness, and the only punishment with which he deserved to be afflicted was that he did not enter the promised land; he did not presume to make great promises about the Lord. After his death the Lord when speaking to Josue said: *Take courage, therefore, and be very valiant, that thou mayst observe and do all the law which Moses my servant hath commanded thee.*[31] By calling him *My servant,* He showed that the grace of His devotion had remained in Moses.

34. *They did not destroy the nations of which the Lord spoke unto them.* 35. *And they were mingled among the heathens, and learned their works.* 36. *And served their idols, and it became a stumbling-block to them.* The Hebrew people, as though it had not been enough that they had sinned in the desert, became forgetful of the Lord's commands after entering

the land of promise, and joined in forbidden alliance with the nations which they had been bidden to destroy because of their worship of idols. To their crimes they added the wickedness of additionally polluting themselves with the superstition of heathens, so that the land of promise granted them by the Lord's generosity as a great reward became a stumbling-block to them. They were the most wretched of men, for they translated God's gift into sins; what He had given them for their favour turned by their transgression into ruin. This is a way of warning us to use rightly the blessings bestowed by divine generosity, so that we do not perish as a result of the gift by which we are known to have been aided. *Scandalum* (stumbling-block) is a Greek word meaning "the left side,"[32] because it led their minds leftwards through debased imitation.

37. *And they sacrificed their sons and their daughters to devils.* 38. *And they shed innocent blood, the blood of their sons and daughters.* Though we do not read in the divine Scriptures that human blood was shed in sacrifice to devils by the Jews who entered the promised land, there is no doubt from the evidence of the ensuing age that this could have happened, for the Scripture of the psalms is also established as an indication of the truth. Observe how the wickedness of sinners is built up in this true account. First he said: *They shed innocent blood,* and so that we should not think of this as strangers' blood, he added: *Of their sons and daughters,* the safety of whom is very dear in our human relations. So they did not spare the ones for whom devoted parents do not hesitate even to die.

Whom they sacrificed to the idols of Chanaan. 39. *And the earth was murdered with blood and was defiled with their works, and they practised fornication in their observances.* In these two verses he still continues with amplification, the figure called *climax* in Greek and *gradatio* in Latin,[33] for our thought rises by stages, so to say, in praise or in blame. We have mentioned this shortly before, but we are not reluctant to state repeatedly what the authority of Scripture is seen to repeat. Because he had said that the blood of sons and daughters was shed, the odium swells further and the crime is magnified when it is stated that these pledges of love were sacrificed to grisly idols. We must accordingly interpret *the murdered earth* as cruel persons who by their wicked sacrifice slaughtered themselves instead, for by murdering their sons the parents themselves seemed to be obliterated by so sacrilegious a crime. The phrase, *the murdered earth,* is a metaphorical usage, since earthly men are said to have been killed by evil deeds. He explained what he meant by murdered earth; foolish men dominated by the flesh were brought low by most evil activity, for they clearly practised fornication when they polluted themselves by adulterous superstitions.

40. *And the Lord was angry at heart with his people: and he abhorred his inheritance.* 41. *And he delivered them into the hands of the nations, and they that hated them had dominion over them.* 42. *And their enemies afflicted them, and they were humbled under their hands.* This too is expressed in metaphorical language, for disturbance of spirit can certainly not overtake the Lord; but it is our human tendency to label as anger the power of His vengeance when it is roused. But what did He do in His anger? He turned away from them, demonstrably the worst of all evils; when the sustaining element is withdrawn, inevitably destruction at once follows of the things which are sustained. Those who clearly gloried in idols were consigned to the shame of slavery. Next comes: *And they that hated them had dominion over them.* Though any dominion by Gentiles seems most oppressive, he added: *They that hated them,* so that their enslavement to a hostile power should be more grievous, for perpetual hatred spells perpetual anger. Finally, note what follows: *And their enemies afflicted them, and they were humbled under their hands.* They experienced such a change of fortune that after refusing to serve the loving Lord they were found to be subjected by just judgment to enemies who hated them.

43. *Many times did he deliver them, but they provoked him with their counsel, and they were brought low by their iniquities.* 44. *And he regarded them when they were in tribulation, when he heard their prayer.* The mercy of the Godhead is explained here in a twofold way. He sent them prior benefits, but their human wickedness did not cease; He inflicted vengeance, and again deigned to bestow mercy on them in their trouble. This was to make us understand that He both bestows prior blessings and offers fresh help to us when we are scourged. You find this in these verses, if you concentrate carefully.

45. *And he was mindful of his testament, and repented according to the multitude of his mercy.* He explains the reason why the people of Israel were heard though they quite frequently sinned, and did not meet the destruction they deserved because the Lord pitied them. It was be-

cause of his testament, that is the New Testament which is eternal, in which shone forth the Lord's coming, and which will not be changed by any successor. He was promised to Abraham because He was to be born of Abraham's seed, a fact hidden from the prophets but revealed at the time of the gospel. *He repented* is a phrase adapted to human usage, for when the human race repents it tends to change its practices. But with the Lord all things are ordered and proceed in fixed ways, and nothing new contrary to His foreknowledge occurs, since He knows all that is to take place. It was necessary for Him to speak to us in our language, for He took on the nature of mortality to endow us with eternal life. But observe that the repentance of the Lord is said to take place when He perceives that we too are repentant. His attitude towards us is shaped by His testing our attitudes towards Him. He added: *According to the multitude of his mercy.* That Mercy overcomes all sins, and deigned to go as far as taking on our flesh. It is justly called the multitude of His mercy, for we know that the world was freed through it.

46. *And he gave them unto mercies, in the sight of all those that had made them captives.* He says that they were given to mercies because they received different charismatic gifts. Through the Lord's mercy some of the people flourished as apostles, some as martyrs, some as confessors; thus the Gentiles could subsequently revere them through observing their miracles, whereas earlier they possessed them as lowly chattels. Or preferably this can be applied to the devil or his agents, so that they received their freedom before the eyes of those whose wickedness had earlier apparently made them captives. So Paul speaks of: *The prince of the power of this air, who worketh on the children of unbelief;*[34] and elsewhere: *That they may recover themselves from the snares of the devil, by whom they are held captive at his will.*[35]

47. *Save us, O Lord our God, and gather us from among the nations, that we may confess to thy name and may glory in thy praise.* The people to whom we have allotted the words from the beginning of the psalm have now had their abundant fill of the Lord's praise, and in the sixth narration beg the Lord Father to bring His Church to fullness from the gathering of the nations. They further add: *And that we may glory in thy praise,* not in man's boasting but in Thee, whose glory truly resides together with unending joy. Observe that the Father is said here to save; we read also that the Son saves, as in the words: *The Son of*

man is come to save that which was lost.[36] It is proclaimed that the holy Spirit also saves, as in the letter to Titus: *He saved us by the laver of regeneration and renovation of the holy Ghost.*[37] In this way the equality and unity of the indivisible Trinity are denoted by similar words and powers.

48. *Blessed be the Lord God of Israel from everlasting to everlasting: and all the people will say, So be it, so be it.* This is the praise which in the previous verse he desired the gathered people to proclaim. Even today holy Church sings it in consoling herself at the present time with this great blessing. But he says that this is to be done from this generation for ever, so that the unending praise must never experience satiety. But since the devoted Jewish people is singing these cited words of praise, which is that other people which says: *So be it, so be it?* I think it is the uncircumcised who at the time when this psalm was being sung were not in the faith, yet were introduced here by the power of prophecy as future participants. So in their love of the community they said: *So be it, so be it.* Similarly today in churches when the priests recite a prayer, the reply is given *amen*, meaning *so be it.* So already in those days the people who now make the same reply were being denoted. It is more appropriate to interpret these words in this sense than to regard them as the closing words of books, as some prefer.[38]

Conclusion Drawn From the Psalm

The festive alleluia has been sung, and the whole composition has matched its heading. Though different themes have been stated, they are seen to have harmonised like the sounds of a tuneful instrument into an agreeable unity. So let us entreat with the greatest longing that He who ever makes straight what is crooked, makes sweet what is bitter, and makes eternal what is transient, may allow us to be part of the people pleasing to Him. So we too may glory in the Lord Christ, and deserve to say in community: *Blessed be the Lord God of Israel, from everlasting to everlasting.* We must remember that this psalm, though it contains: *We have sinned with our fathers, we have acted unjustly, we have wrought iniquity,*[39] should not be set with the penitential psalms. To begin with, the festive alleluia is set in front of it. Secondly, the Jewish people speaks, whereas individuals are allotted as spokesmen in the penitential psalms. Thirdly, its content is more historical than a lamentation of faults. Moreover, in many psalms you find brief mention of satisfaction for sin, though they are clearly not associated with the theme of repentance.

Commentary on Psalm 106

1. *Alleluia.* Since this psalm is prefaced by the same heading as the previous two, we think it appropriate to describe their interconnection with a single explanation, so that the gift of so great a mystery can be more easily understood. In the first alleluia, the Jewish people are being commended and there is no complaint in their regard. In the second he tells of those of the same race who sinned with most numerous offences, and through the Lord's pity returned to His grace. But here the Christian people is being warned that they must make the Lord's praises resound in return for the kindnesses bestowed on them. Thus one can summarily realise what is to be looked for in each of the three. So, as we have said, the prophet now warns the Christian people saved by the Lord's redemption to sing Alleluia afresh by confessing past events. The tone here is sweet, and the language joyful. So let us reverently listen to these great and astonishing events which are preceded by the glory of this great heading.

Division of the Psalm

After the confession of the Jewish people discussed in the previous psalms, the prophet passes to the Christian people who wandered through the tracts of the entire world in lonely and vagrant paths of superstitions. In the first section he reminds them that they must confess the Lord's praises, for they have been redeemed by His precious blood, and have attained churches, whereas before they were the plunder of foolish error amidst the altars and groves of demons. The second section states that thanks should be rendered to the Lord, for He has filled the fasting souls of the Gentiles with the food of truth, the abundance of His religion, and with His invincible power has prised open the bonds of their sins. In the third part he enjoins that the Father be thanked because the Lord Christ at His coming has broken down the bronze gates and iron bolts[1] of the devil by the majesty of His omnipotence. The fourth section warns us that the sacrifice of praise is to be offered to the Lord Christ by the priests, who as we know control the helm of the churches as though they were ships amidst the massive waves of the world; and it describes how the divine power deigns to assist them in their trials. The fifth section again says that the Lord is to be praised by priests and elders, for by His heavenly gift He has transformed the world, foul with the barren waste of sin, into the most lovely sweetness. On seeing this the upright in heart will rejoice with great exultation. We must further note that the sections mentioned are seen to commence with similar verses. This type of composition is usually called by the masters of secular literature "intercalation."[2] The repetition is frequent, so that the essential advice should become pleasant by being often restated.

Explanation of the Psalm

Confess to the Lord for he is good, for his mercy endures for ever. The prophet foresaw that the Christian people would obtain grace at the Lord's coming. To ensure that no negligence should cause them to procrastinate through their confidence of gaining this great benefit, he urges them both to lay bare their sins and to sound forth the Lord's praises. As we have said, *confess* bears both these senses; it is the person who first appeases the Lord with confession of his sins who embarks with profit on the Lord's praises. Next comes the addition: *For he is good*, so that sinners may have the confidence to entreat the loving Lord after making satisfaction. *For ever* here means till eternity, for there is no time which is ascertained to be removed from His mercy; in this world He habitually spares us, and in the next He will deign to bestow eternal rewards on the faithful. In this way He is shown to be always good, always merciful to His suppliants, for even when He judges He is good, for justice is good.

2. *Let them that have been redeemed by the Lord now say it: he hath redeemed them from the hand of the enemy. Say it* means "say Alleluia" as in the heading, and let them console themselves with happy cries of

exultation, for they have deserved to attain the Lord's grace. He denotes especially the peoples of the Gentiles, for they have been redeemed by the Lord's blood, and through His pity have been removed from the devil's power. So stiff with obstinacy and so foolish was the devil's band that they could at no time have been released except by the shedding of His sacred blood. The following words make clear that the passage refers to the Gentiles.

3. *He gathered them out of the countries, from the rising and from the setting of the sun, from the north and from the sea.* By the figure of *periphrasis*, which in Latin we call *circuitus*,[3] he explains the power of the devil's hand spread through the entire world. In this way the blessing of the holy incarnation can become known to mankind, for by the power of its majesty it chained fast the author of wickedness, and snatched from him when he was bound those vessels of death. He first mentioned: *Out of the countries*, and so that you would not think that they were gathered from only a few, he added: *From the rising and from the setting of the sun, from the north and from the sea.* After designating three cardinal points of the world, he wrote *the sea* instead of the fourth, the south. On that side he wanted us to interpret it as the ocean, which is said to surround the entire edge of the earth. The description in Genesis is similar, where the Lord promises the whole world to the seed of Abraham with the words: *Lift up thy eyes, and look from the place wherein thou now art, to the north and to the south, to the east and to the sea*,[4] which is the west. *Occasus*, the west, is so called because it is *horarum casus*,[5] the falling of the hours. So whereas here he cited the sea for the south, there it clearly stands for the west. The word can be aptly used for any part of the world, since the sea is said to enclose the whole earth within the circle of its wanderings. So obviously this general unification is interpreted as referring not to the Jews but to the Catholic Church, which we know is assembled from the whole world.

4. *They wandered in a wilderness, in a dry region: they found not the way to the city for their habitation.* 5. *They were hungry and thirsty: their soul fainted in them.* Though the different nations rejoiced in the abundance of their populations, they none the less dwelt in a wilderness because they were known to have no truly genuine teachers and no Church, for the superstitious Gentiles had not yet found the way to

the Lord's city, where they were to dwell, since they were sacrificing to idols. The hungry and thirsty denote the men of this world with curiosity who sought the paths of truth with various beliefs, but because they had not believed in the Author of truth, they could not be found dwelling in the true wisdom. Next comes: *Their soul fainted in them. In them* means that their spirit became weary and yielded before their laborious pursuits, because they sought to search for God in a way in which they could not find Him.

6. *And they cried to the Lord in their tribulation, and he freed them from their needs.* 7. *And he led them out into the right way that they might go to the city of habitation.* Just as he described their wanderings in the two previous verses, so now he recounts their return to the Lord's gifts in two further ones. *They cried* means that they sought with great longing. This remorse comes from the Lord, impelling us to seek with longing what we know is profitable. To denote the force of the word *cried,* he added: *In their tribulation.* The heart's cry is summoned with all its strength when there is fear of looming danger and human confidence recedes. Observe now what this cry produced. They were freed from their needs and acknowledged the path of truth, so that having long wandered in trackless error, they took the way of most holy religion and happily attained the hall of the blessed Church.

8. *Let the mercies of the Lord confess to him, and his wonderful works to the children of men.* He passes to the second section, in which he now warns the faithful not to cease thanking the Lord, for they have obtained abundant kindnesses. The statement that His mercies must confess to Him is a true and wholesome one, for all that is praiseworthy in us is assuredly the gift of His clemency, for He looses our sins, bestows hope, and leads us to the gifts of His bounty. His use of the plural *mercies* means that He bestows gifts on many, but of differing kinds. *But everyone has his proper gift from God, one after this manner, and another after that.*[6] So it is always appropriate to confess to the devoted Lord, for He both delivers us from dangers and enlightens us with the brightness of His love. As for the *wonderful works* which He performed at the time of His incarnation, the psalmist says that they are to be proclaimed to posterity through the evangelists and the apostles, as we know was done. Remember that this verse is repeated unchanged throughout the four divisions to the end of the

psalm, so that just as he says that the Church has gathered from the four quarters of the world, so the praises of His mercy were offered with devoted hearts from the four cardinal points of the earth.

9. *For he hath satisfied the empty soul, and hath filled the hungry soul with good things.* A soul is empty when it is possessed by the corruptions of the world, and does not hasten to return to its Creator with any devotion. He says a soul is hungry when it is now visited by divine grace and longs to attain the Lord's healing. This happened among the Gentiles, who were at first intent on empty longings for idols, for at that time they were empty and idle since they were beguiled and deprived of good fruits. But secondly they were hungry and filled when they were admonished by the pitying Lord, and had translated their aspirations into an eagerness for repentance.

10. *Sitting in darkness and in the shadow of death, bound with chains, in want and in iron.* The life of the Gentiles who lived before the Lord's coming is described in this verse. They were sitting in darkness since they were void of the light of faith, and were made blind with the darkness of infidelity. When he says that they were sitting, he shows that they had remained there in extended torpor. *The shadow of death* was the vicious life of this world, which bore the most foul image of future death. They were *bound with chains*, for they were held fast in the nooses of sins through the devil's domination. Their *want* refers to their lack of good, that want known to afflict not the body but what is worse, the soul, and is much more grievous than any poverty. *Iron* denotes the obstinacy of wicked men, for we often say that a thing demonstrably hard is like iron.

11. *Because they exasperated the words of the Lord, and provoked the counsel of the most High.* 12. *And their heart was humbled with labours: they were weakened, and there was none to help them.* We must note the figure of *parison*[7] or balanced statement in these two verses. He explains in the first verse how they sinned, and in the second the punishment they received. You will often find this figure by careful reading of this psalm. He speaks of those *sitting in darkness and the shadow of death*, for by acting in opposition to the Lord's prescriptions, they were rejecting a life according to His laws. It was inevitable that they should suffer the anger of Him who they thought was to be despised. Finally observe the following words: *And provoked the counsel of the most High.* They certainly provoked, for having shown themselves

arrogant in times of prosperity they were brought low in afflictions and hardships. This was just counsel, a most health-giving healing, that the worldly disease should be cured by the opposing gift of a remedy. He added: *They were weakened,* in other words, dislodged from their worldly confidence, so that once they had lost the incentives towards arrogance they might more easily attain the remedies of repentance. The words, *and there was none to help them,* were appended; understand "no other," for no-one lends aid to a person in danger except one whom almighty God has bidden to offer help.

13. *And they cried to the Lord in their affliction, and he delivered them from their needs.* 14. *And he brought them out of darkness and the shadow of death, and broke their bonds asunder.* Observe why they were humbled and weakened, so that they should cry to the Lord, confessing their sins. When they were puffed up, they were silent, and like cattle without sense they uttered no wholesome word. But remorse set in, and then they spoke words of profit. Observe the distinctions with which the Lord's mercies are expounded. First, *he delivered them from their needs,* for they were oppressed by slavery to the devil. Then He brought out of the darkness of their superstitions their souls polluted with the filth of sins. Thirdly, *He broke asunder* (the psalmist did not say "loosed") *their bonds.* In this way the devil's tyrannical power was broken asunder at Christ's coming, so that Satan can never recover that domination which he had.

15. *Let the mercies of the Lord give glory to him, and his wonderful works to the children of men.* He passes to the third section, where he repeats the verse already spoken in the second part. These are intercalated as though set in mid-path (*in medio calle*),[8] in other words, placed on the route of the poem. He is urging them, now that they are freed, to give thanks because the divine power has broken the gates of sins and the bolts of all wickedness.

16. *Because he hath broken gates of bronze, and burst iron bars.* This is the reason why he says we must confess to the Lord, because on behalf of our freedom He has burst open gates of bronze and bars, so that by His direction we can pass through this life safely. The *gates of bronze* are the sinful habits of men, which enclose us in the halls of sinners so that they afford us no freedom to depart. It seems not unreasonable for us to interpret *iron bars* as the impure spirits which we know block those gates of sinners so that those who are imprisoned cannot

emerge. These two metals are apparently cited to indicate the strength of sins; human strength despaired of breaking them, but the power of God shattered them when in pity He gazed on endangered men with the light of His coming.

17. *He took them out of the way of their iniquity, for they were humbled for their injustices.* Though the Lord is seen to fill all things by the presence of His majesty, He distances Himself from sinners so that they do not draw near Him except when through His pity they approach Him with remorseful hearts. The extent of the harm caused by His abandoning them is clearly explained. He says that they were humbled because of their injustices. This was not the humbling which is life-giving. The humility which raises us is not the same as the humiliation which bears us down. The person who has not deserved to obtain the necessary healing is brought low into death.

18. *Their soul abhorred all manner of meat: and they drew near even to the gates of death.* So far as the literal sense is concerned, the condition of sick persons is being described, when they are known to incur the hazard of death through aversion from food. But we should prefer to interpret the meat here as spiritual, in other words, the law and saving precepts of the Lord. It is from them that the faithful soul gets its life and is renewed by the abundance of heaven; but the hearts of the wicked are starved of them in destructive hunger, for their souls are sick, and they are seen to endure want of goodly possessions. It is a grievous sickness and an accursed disaster not to have a longing for the divine law; for from where can they obtain life if they have not begun to love their life? This was the cause of their drawing near to death's prison, but they did not enter it because they were to be delivered by the Lord's pity.

19. *And they cried to the Lord in their affliction, and he delivered them out of their distresses.* This verse is clearly repeated because the same sentiment was appropriate in a similar situation.

20. *He sent his word and healed them, and delivered them from their destructions.* Here we recognise what a sickness it is to despise spiritual delights, so that only the presence of the heavenly Physician could have removed such danger of sickness; for the Lord Saviour came to renew and heal us, so that lack of spiritual food should not destroy the hearts of sinners. His expression, *he sent his word,* describes the Father's love rather than inequality of powers, for the holy Spirit is

likewise sent by the Son, as Christ Himself says in the gospel: *It is expedient to you that I go. For if I go not, the Paraclete will not come to you, but if I go I will send him to you.*[9] Again, the Son is sent by the holy Spirit, as Isaiah says of Christ: *The Spirit of the Lord is upon me, because the Lord hath anointed me. He hath sent me to preach to the meek.*[10] Moreover the higher is sent by the lesser; for example, Tobias sent the angel.[11] But the Son is not lesser when sent by the Father, nor the holy Spirit than the Son, for the sending is by One and the Same. This verse refers to the harmony rather than the separation of power, for it is often asserted in the divine Scriptures that in the Trinity there is equality of power or nature. These passages have been fittingly gathered by our father Augustine among others in his *Book of Testimonies.*[12]

21. *Let the mercies of the Lord give glory to him, and his wonderful works to the children of men.* The fourth section is begun with the repetition of this verse, for which the previous explanation will suffice. He is urging the priests to sacrifice to the Lord, and not to cease proclaiming His wonders to the people.

22. *And let them sacrifice the sacrifice of praise, and proclaim his works with joy.* It is the person who offers the sacrifice of praise with joy who sacrifices to the Lord, for it is far preferable to offer Him joyful song of psalmody with good works than to slay cattle as victims. He next explains what sacrifices are to be made. Preachers are not to remain silent about His kindnesses, so they must on the one hand render what is due, and on the other appropriate instruction is to be shown to the faithful. The nature of this proclamation is explained most suitably, as *with joy.* The priest must not be melancholy or uncertain, but joyful and most eager, so that the confidence of the preacher can be felt by his hearers. We more quickly incline to believe what we see teachers proclaim with steadfast and grateful hearts.

23. *They that descend to the sea in ships, doing business in many waters.* When he says that they descend to the sea, he refers to the priests who go down to the stormy waters of this world. His word *descend* indicates that this is the lower region of the world, to which he attests descents can be made. *Ships,* as we have often said, denotes the Churches which sail over the stormy waters of this world on the wood of the cross. We descend to and traverse the sea if we position ourselves on the safest of ships where Christ is the helmsman and the apostles and the blessed gathering of holy pontiffs are the oarsmen.

Next comes: *Doing business in many waters.* He still continues with the same comparison. The priests are they who do business in many waters, in other words preach to the Christian peoples. Undoubtedly *many waters* denotes peoples, for when John in the Apocalypse asked what the waters were, the reply was: *They are peoples.*[13] What meaning can there be more true than that which the authority of such great truth corroborates?

24. *These have seen the works of the Lord, and his wonders in the deep. These* are the preachers who recognised His works with spiritual insight. They recognised that the Red Sea denoted baptism, that Jonah's three-day residence without harm in the beast's belly signified the Lord's burial, and other events similar to those performed in the prefigurations of the divine scriptures. So those who examine the works with spiritual assessment take note of the wonders of the deep.

25. *He said the word, and the wind of the storm halted, and the waves thereof were lifted up.* 26. *They mount up to the heavens, and they go down to the depths: their soul wasted away with evils.* He did not wish those who he earlier said could behold the work of the Lord in the deep to become puffed up with any pride, so he now follows with an explanation of the storms and waves which they endured. *He said the word, and the wind of the storm halted,* points to when the Lord with devoted pity checks the storms of our tribulations so that we may not be overwhelmed by mounting evils, but may be freed only by His protection. This delay becomes for us the source of greater danger. A wave is lifted up in human minds when we regard as attributable to our own merits the liberation clearly made possible only by divine grace. But these waves are described in a most splendid narration. *They mount up to the heavens* when they are raised up by windy arrogance; *they go down to the depths* when they encounter desperation and fear. Note what follows: *Their soul wasted away with evils,* precisely because they had gone down under the influence of fear to the deepest depths. *Wasted away* is found also in the good sense, as in Psalm 38; *Thou hast made his soul to waste away like a spider.*[14] But here the words, *with evils,* are added so that we can understand without ambivalence the sense in which the verb is used.

27. *They were troubled, and incensed like a drunken man, and all their wisdom was swallowed up.* He is still discussing those of whom he earlier said that *their soul wasted away with evils. Troubled* refers to

mental disturbance, *incensed* to the immediate explosion of anger. So he says that the wisdom of such men was swallowed up, for wisdom can be found only amongst tranquil and untroubled spirits. *Their wisdom* is excellently directed to those who previously considered themselves teachers, but that wisdom was clearly *swallowed up*, for it cannot exist in troubled minds. So by these examples priests are urged to make entreaty to the Lord so that their hearts may firmly rest in humility, and so may not be agitated by the temptations of the devil.

28. *And they cried to the Lord in their affliction, and he delivered them from their distresses.* 29. *And he turned the storm into a breeze, and its waves were still.* They were like the drunken men whose wisdom seemed swallowed up, but with a wholesome cry they returned to life-giving purposes, for they turned to the Lord and now began to be sober. What the cry for help achieved is explained by: *And he delivered them from their distresses.* The removal of their distresses is recounted allegorically, for there follows: *And he turned the storm into a breeze, and its waves were still.* That most savage storm which could not be endured by human frailty disappeared when bidden into the breezes, and immediately the din of those ravaging evils grew silent at the command of their Master.

30. *And they rejoiced because they were still: and he led them to the haven which they wished for, and delivered them from their distresses.* He speaks of the tendency of those who after dangers emerge weary with toil to rejoice at being delivered from great disaster. *Portus* (haven) gets its name from carrying (*portare*)[15] ships. Appended is the repeated but quite welcome conclusion, that the spirit of the person suffering hardship was delivered from all distresses.

31. *Let the mercies of the Lord give glory to him, and his wonderful works to the children of men.* He passes to the fifth section, where he urges holy Church to give thanks to the Lord because in His devoted pity He has bestowed various kindnesses on the human race. Observe that he repeated the same verse a fourth time, so that the fourfold division of the world which he mentioned earlier: *From the rising and from the setting of the sun, from the north and from the sea,*[16] might be made to harmonise with these sections; in this way faithful confession could be sung identically everywhere and in great throngs everywhere. It was fitting that the single sacred proclamation should embrace the one religion, one people, one Church.

32. *And let them exalt him in the Church of the people, and praise him in the chair of the ancients.* He says that the Lord is exalted, for He is raised above all the powers of heaven and earth; not that anything can be added to Him, but we are to gain increase in exalting Him. When we contemplate and praise Him, He appears as the Highest, beyond measure and beyond comprehension. Here we are to interpret *the people* not as any lowly race of men but as the noble folk who are strong in true religion and who always exalt the Lord by religious deeds. When he says that they are to praise Him in the chair of the ancients, he is bidding all known teachers sitting in the chair of the ancients, in other words, those who have deserved to be successors of the ancient pontiffs, to sound forth the Lord's praises. We have explained sufficiently in Psalm 1 that a chair is given to teachers.[17]

33. *For he hath turned rivers into a wilderness, and the outpouring of waters unto thirst.* He gives the reason why the crowd of the faithful must confess to the Lord, because once the Jews' infidelity was rejected, all fullness came to the Christian people, for the *rivers,* in other words, prophets and apostles, passed to the wilderness of the Gentiles when the Jews refused to believe. Since the stubborn people of the Jews proved totally unwilling to give spiritual assent to God's words, that word of God was diverted like an irrigating stream to all nations, and those who had previously been barren with the aridity of sin became most fruitful. What a marvellous turn of phrase is: *The outpouring of waters unto thirst!* It means that it went to the Gentiles who thirstily drank the heavenly waters, and did not spit it out like the Jews with a contempt that proved deadly.

34. *A fruitful land into barrenness, for the wickedness of them that dwell therein.* He had previously spoken of the summoning of the Gentiles, referring to the Christians, so now he mentions the expulsion of the Jews, a fate said to have befallen them through pride. The land was fruitful when it flourished in its heavenly religion, but it became barren when it spurned the Lord's precepts. Salt moisture is known to militate against crops, because wherever it is prominent it blights the grace of fertility. The reason why this happened to the Jews is appended; it was because of the wickedness of those seen to dwell with crafty hearts in that fruitful land which was the Lord's dwelling-place.

35. *He hath turned a wilderness into pools of waters, and a dry land*

into water springs. 36. *And hath placed there the hungry: and they made a city for their habitation.* These verses refer to the Christian people, on whom in their barrenness was conferred the saving water of sacred baptism. I think that *pools* is used to express the running water which churches have, and from which supplies are drawn off and kept undisturbed in a cistern until the glory of rebirth is conferred. *Stagna* (pools) derives from *stando* (standing).[18] *Dry land* denotes the unbelieving hearts of the Gentiles, which when moistened by the water of baptism flowered with holy preaching. In this happy dispensation were placed those who embraced the Lord's gifts with the most vaunting eagerness. *The city for their habitation* is the Catholic Church, in which those who obey the heavenly commands firmly establish themselves.

37. *And they sowed fields, and planted vineyards: and they yielded fruit of birth.* 38. *And he blessed them, and they were multiplied exceedingly: and their cattle suffered no decrease.* It is those who cleanse their bodies of worldly experiences of sins by means of heavenly instruction who sow fields and plant vineyards. As a result they attain the fruits known to be pleasing to the Lord. It is a happy toil and a wonderful harvest if our work enables us to acknowledge the favour of the Redeemer of the Gentiles. *Ager* (field) gets its name from *agere*[19] (working), because different activities are carried out in the fields to obtain a livelihood. He added: *And they yielded fruit of birth, and he blessed them, and they were multiplied exceedingly. Fructus* (fruit) gets its name from *frui* (to enjoy),[20] and so those who yield spiritual fruit enjoy the Lord's blessing, whereas those whose fate is to be infertile are lopped off like the fig-tree in the gospel, which was found to have abundant foliage but to be barren of fruit.[21] *They were multiplied* when the blessed faithful contributed their holy activities, and through God's grace achieved greater glory by the fertility of their merits. Next comes: *And their cattle suffered no decrease.* We must interpret cattle as the ingenuous people who are healthy in proven faith but without fame in eloquence, better at living than at speaking. They are extremely strong at heart but not in speech, like the ingenuous Paul we read of who gave commands to demons.[22] Such men suffered no decrease, but are seen to have won great favour from the Lord. So the psalmist attests that holy Church contains these two kinds of people.

39. *They were made few, and afflicted through the trouble of evils and*

sorrow. 40. *And contention was poured forth upon their princes, and their vanities seduced them, and he caused them to wander in a trackless region and not in the way.* In these two verses he describes those deceived by the depravity of heretics and led to abandon the Lord's Church. The apostle John says of them: *They went out from us, but they were not of us, for if they had been of us they would certainly have remained with us.*[23] Though they regard themselves as many they are in fact few, for when compared with the universal Church their numbers are found to be extremely puny. They were *afflicted through the trouble of evils and sorrow;* they were particularly afflicted since they were smitten by the devil's plots. Inevitably those known to have abandoned the Author of salvation are attended by trouble and sorrow. Next comes: *And contention was poured forth upon their princes.* The priests of heretics are briefly indicated and censured here, for it is rightly said that contention is poured forth by them because they dispute not by the teaching which brings salvation, but merely by the volubility which brings death; for they accept the divine Scriptures in some passages but abandon them for the most part. Since they have been seduced by their own vanity, they slip into trackless errors, for they abandon the road of salvation, and linger on twisting paths. So they should hearken to the account of where they are walking, and be aware of the possible end of their journey.

41. *And he helped the poor man out of poverty, and established households like flocks of sheep.* 42. *The just shall see, and shall rejoice: and all iniquity has stopped its mouth.* He spoke earlier about arrogant heretics, and now he returns to humble Catholics, abandoning the heretics' arid leaders and renewing the poor among the Catholics with heavenly aid. The poor man mentioned here is the one out of all of them who abandons the enticements of the world and hammers unceasingly on the door of heavenly mercy, so that he may deserve to be admitted to the household which like gentle sheep is adorned with the distinction of simplicity. When the saints see this, they will undoubtedly rejoice because they observe a faithful soul gained by their gatherings. As a result the devil's wickedness falls silent, for he will have no means of opposing the Lord's chosen.

43. *Who is wise and will keep these things, and will understand the mercies of the Lord?* This marvellous psalm closes with a beautiful ending. *Who is wise* bears the sense of: "He who is truly wise guards

the things which were said, and prefers to be Christ's poor man rather than a leader of heretics, choosing to beat on the door of the heavenly King rather than to teach harmful doctrines." He who will be able so to choose and to judge will receive then *the mercies of the Lord*, which cannot be ended at any time.

Conclusion Drawn From the Psalm

Though all the verses of this psalm are recounted with sweet proclamation, my spirit is especially touched with delight by the passage which says that God's Church is to be united from all parts of the world in brief compass. It says: *He gathered them out of the countries, from the rising and the setting of the sun, from the north and from the sea.*[24] But it is worthwhile to scrutinise this verse rather more carefully, for it is an excellent pointer to astronomical teaching. By speaking of the four hinges of the universe, he has sketched the world in quadrangular shape. I have found that this psalm is divided up by the most learned father Augustine.[25] He relates that he has explained it to the people, and so he did not think that it was accordingly necessary to interpret it. I have imitated this practice so far as I could, thinking that all the psalms should be split by allotting divisions to them, and reckoning that the indications provided by the authority of this great Father provide no minor consolations to our explanations.

Commentary on Psalm 107

1. *A psalm-canticle of David.* We observe in this psalm a new feature for scrutiny; it is clear that it is composed of parts of Psalms 56 and 59.[1] But though the words themselves are written as in those earlier psalms, they are aimed at a different sense, for the heading which is always designed to indicate the content of a psalm is different, and it persuades us that those sections earlier set down are understood here in another sense. We have often observed that *canticle* is relevant to the contemplation of divine matters, whereas *psalm* refers to activities, as long as they are seen to harmonise with the divine commands.

The psalm itself attests this in the first verse: *I will sing and utter a psalm to the Lord.* David denotes Christ the King, who is to be the spokesman in this psalm; so we must analyse each part with great care, for the psalms in which He deigns to speak in His own person have a depth and an acuteness deserving of great reverence, so that the value of the great mystery within is shrouded by a thicker covering.

Division of the Psalm

As we have said, Christ the Lord speaks through the entire psalm. In the first section, in His capacity as Man He addresses thanks of praise to the Father's glory, for by shouldering the wondrous secret of the passion He has risen into eternal glory. In the second part He abases His humanity throughout, but also reveals the power of His majesty. Thus you are to realise that there are two natures in the one Person of the Lord Christ. It is not that Christ is split into two sons, as some people impiously maintain,[2] but He speaks as one and the same Son of God now in the flesh which He assumed for us and now with the power and glory of the Word. If you distinguish between the natures of God and man, you will traverse the whole question without coming to grief. As the Fathers briefly instruct us: "Allot the sufferings to the flesh, and the miracles to His divinity".[3]

Explanation of the Psalm

2. *My heart is ready, O God, my heart is ready. I will sing and utter a psalm to the Lord.* The Holiness of the glorious incarnation in recounting His purity reveals how praises are to be uttered to the Lord. He was always ready for such things because He did not have the reservation of sinners towards the Father's praises. The very repetition reveals trust in His promise, for as we know, that which is affirmed by repeated declaration is uttered with the greatest sincerity. The promise which He truly makes about himself we can well make if we trust that our sins are forgiven by His gift. Next comes: *I will sing and utter a psalm to the Lord.* He was justified in saying such things about Himself, for both His speech and His action harmonised with the divine rules. The strings on the psaltery sounded no less, and His

voice did not ring out with any hoarse blare of evil deeds, but His actions were combined with that spiritual canticle in joyful exultation. That was truly a sweet-sounding psaltery, for it sounded forth with tunes that were holy.

3. *Arise, my glory, arise, psaltery and harp: I will arise in the morning early.* After the Lord Christ in the flesh has stated that He was singing and uttering a psalm to the Lord, He now says: *Arise, my glory,* the glory denoted by psaltery and harp. *Psaltery* indicates worth of manners, *harp,* bodily affliction and grief; thus by these He denotes both praiseworthy deeds and His most glorious passion. He added: *I will arise in the morning early.* The order of words follows on most beautifully, for after the indication of the passion this is necessarily seen to be interpreted as the Lord's resurrection, because as the gospel attests He rose from the dead at that time. But if you wish to interpret this also of His members, it is fittingly understood of any faithful individual, for he always arises early in the morning when he is present to praise the Lord in Church through devoted works. Though he keeps vigil deep in the night, he cannot brook the darkness, for he is illumined by the great brightness of His proclamation.

4. *I will confess thee, O Lord, among the people: I will sing a psalm to thee among the Gentiles.* The universal Church is denoted by these words, for as has often been stated many of the Jewish people initially believed, and later the full complement of the Gentiles was admitted. Observe how appropriate words mark out the individual cases. He says He is confessing among the Jewish people, where He spoke with His own voice, but that He is singing a psalm among the Gentiles, to whom the apostles were sent, fulfilling His commands with their holy preaching. He says that He truly hymns what He is known to have achieved through His ministers.

5. *For thy mercy is magnified up to the heavens, and thy truth up to the clouds.* This too is addressed to the Father, for His mercy is magnified up to the heavens, since the heavenly powers enjoy His benefits. Though the distinction of the good angels and the various powers is reckoned very high, they are blessed through His gift. His truth is magnified up to the clouds when those who preach the Word rain on the faithless people like rain-bearing clouds.

6. *Be thou exalted, O God, above the heavens, and thy glory over all the earth.* This refines on His previous words, for He earlier said that the

Lord's mercy was *magnified up to the heavens;* and following that: *Be exalted, O God, above the heavens.* So He whose mercy is clearly possessed by the heavens should rightly be exalted above those heavens. Likewise because He said: *Thy truth up to the clouds,* the apt addition was made: *And thy glory above all the earth.* The things made manifest in the earlier declaration clearly explain themselves here.

7. *That thy beloved ones may be delivered, save me with thy right hand, and hear me.* He passes to the second narration, which we stated was the last part of Psalm 59. So the division is appropriately made here, where we see the section of the second psalm appended. So that you may understand clearly that the Lord's passion has been bestowed in the interests of the faithful, He prays that He may be saved so that the crowd of believers may be freed. Undoubtedly this happened at the time of the resurrection, when the apostles or all believers apprehended the divinity of the Lord Saviour by such a manifestation.

8. *God hath spoken in his holy one: I will rejoice, and I will divide Sichem: and I will mete out the vale of tabernacles.* In this and the ensuing three verses a combination of Greek and Latin words form the figure of *sardismos,* which is the intermingling of different tongues, as already explained at Psalm 59.[4] Now let us return to an explanation of the words. When He says that God has spoken in His holy one, He clearly denotes Himself. Realise the force of *in his holy one.* He did not say: "Through his holy one" as denoting prophets, apostles and others who were pleasing to the Lord, but here He says: *In his holy one,* so that the Word made flesh spoke with the Father in single intent. Next comes: *I will rejoice, and I will divide Sichem.* We must carefully seek out the meanings of all these names, for they are known to reveal to us the secrets of hidden truths. *Sichem* means "shoulders,"[5] which denote the activity which we are wont to perform by the efforts and guidance of our hands. So the sense is this: He says that after His resurrection He will rejoice, because He has meted out His activity, in other words, His grace, to the apostles and the faithful who emulated the glory of His passion and His preaching. He added: *And I will mete out the vale of tabernacles. Vale* denotes humility.[6] *Tabernacles* denotes the churches whose virtue is known to be particularly holy; so the Lord meted out this humility when He apportioned

the gifts of charisms to each of the faithful according to His will. As Paul has it: *But to every one of us is given grace, according to the measure of the giving of Christ.*[7]

9. *Galaad is mine, and Manasses is mine: and Ephraim the strength of my head. Juda is my king. Galaad* is the Latin *transmigratio;*[8] this is truly the Lord's transmigration, for the Gentiles were pricked by His summons and happily changed their allegiance to Him. *Manasses* means forgetfulness;[9] the word denotes the Jewish people, who forgot the kindnesses of heaven and with sacrilegious presumption crucified the Lord Christ, but subsequently through His pity returned to His religion and worship. In this way He attests by mention of these names that both peoples are His. Next comes: *And Ephraim the strength of my head. Juda is my king.* Here He spoke of His passion. *Ephraim* means fruitfulness;[10] it points to the crown of thorns which He endured in His passion, when it was placed on His head. It was more fertile than all fruits, for by that humility it enriched the whole world. He aptly claimed king Judah as His, for His physical descent was from him.

10. *Moab the pot of my hope. Over Edom I will stretch out my shoe: other races are subject to me. Moab* according to Jerome means "away from the Father"[11] or "without the Father," so he would interpret it as the devil, who in his evil activities finds in God not a father but a just Judge. So he is compared to a pot which contains and boils meats, making them agreeable to eat through its bubbling heat. In the same way the devil unceasingly compresses and devours those consigned to him, and by his continuing attacks unwillingly induces them to the humility of confession. So the Lord after the fashion of human persons says that He obtains hope from the devil's persecution, because many who are the victims of Satan's swift affliction are converted and strive to return to the Lord's kindnesses. Next comes: *Over Edom I will stretch out my shoe. Edom* means "things earthly and bloody."[12] The Lord indicates that He will possess it through the preaching of the gospel, for we have pointed out at Psalm 59[13] that *shoe* denotes the gospel which the Lord extended to earthly men, and by universal preaching filled the world with His law. He added: *Other races are subject to me; allophyli* (other races) means foreigners, and denotes the

Christian people who through His pity are gathered from different races. His description of them as subject attests that they will be faithful.

11. *Who will bring me into the strong city, or who will lead me into Edom?* This most apt query made in His human role is set down first so that the ensuing reply may follow. He says that He cannot be led by men's consolation to the place which He longs to reach in order to deliver His faithful. It is His nature which humbly says this, and it also says: *O God, my God, look upon me: why hast thou forsaken me?*[14] and: *He who sent me is greater than I,*[15] and finally: *Father, if it be possible let this chalice pass from me.*[16] The whole is represented humbly by the part, so that the Man is seen to be the all-perfect God. *The strong city* perhaps denotes hell, which could be opened by no human force, but only by Him who is known to have battered down its gates. Hence the words in the preceding psalm: *Because he has broken gates of brass, and burst iron bars.*[17] That city which lay open to admit us was closed to debar us; it lost its title to strength when the Redeemer of the Gentiles entered it. Psalm 23 attests that *gates* is used in both the good and the bad sense when it says: *Lift up your gates, ye princes, and be ye lifted up, eternal gates.*[18] We have said that Edom connotes earthly things. The Lord reached it after the resurrection, when His glory beyond reckoning was revealed, and He became known to all nations as the almighty Ruler. He asks that this request be met in the same way as He asked for the earlier one.

12. *Wilt not thou, O God, who put us off, and wilt not thou, O God, go forth with our powers?* There follows the completion of the confession which He had left unfinished in the previous verse; for the deeds performed at the resurrection could be achieved only by the Godhead. Who could break death's bars or open the gates of the fortified city other than the Lord Christ Himself, who in defiance of the law of human nature rose from the dead on the third day, and revealed the glory of His majesty? Notice carefully that He speaks of Himself in the singular in the course of His earlier verses, but here He says that they have been put off, using the plural, so that we may realise that Head and members are saying such words. *Put us off* means "kept us waiting," for we know that He Himself was delayed from attaining His glory whilst He lingered in this life. Likewise today the glory of all the faithful is postponed until we attain the rewards of resurrec-

tion. Next comes: *And wilt not thou, O God, go forth with our powers?* He is pointing to the time when He was held and betrayed by the crowd of Jews, when He was scourged by their governor, and endured being spat upon by mad Jews. If at that time His divinity had sought to fend off this treatment, all the opposition would have crumbled and been broken. But He postponed showing the wonders of His power to fulfil the due order ordained for His beneficial passion. The faithful experience the same benefit when afflicted by sundry disasters to try them out.

13. *O grant us help from trouble: and vain is the salvation from man.* Here the Lord's humanity in company with His members cries in entreaty that the security of resurrection be granted them from the troubles of this world, so that the storm of this life may at last die down. He is not seeking help from luxurious living, but from trouble; He knows that remedies for this are forthcoming to men through divine clemency. So that no hope in worldly powers should remain, he added: *And vain is salvation from man,* for such confidence is truly feeble and transient.

14. *Through God shall we wield power, and he will bring to nothing those that afflict us.* These are the sentiments of the Lord Saviour and all the faithful, for our spiritual and bodily foes are effectively confronted by God's powers. Those who say that the Lord's flesh and divinity belong to the one nature should also listen to this psalm. The heavenly spokesman Ambrose in his book on the Lord's incarnation[19] rebukes them in these words: "What hellish source has vomited up such sacrilege? The Arians now become more bearable, the force of whose infidelity increases through these men, so that they claim more argumentatively that Father, Son and holy Spirit are not of one substance, for these men have sought to state that the Lord's divinity and flesh belong to the one substance"; and the further comments which that wonderful passage is known to contain. These men must realise that they have been explicitly pronounced as more wicked than those whom the universal Church regards as outsiders.[20] This is quite justifiable, for since the Word made flesh has taken the name Christ, and since the Word is one thing and flesh another, if Christ is restricted to a single nature, as they wish it stated, no more wicked infidelity can be found in my opinion in any heresy. Though various heresies afflict surface injury on His majesty, this alone, sadly enough, had the ef-

frontery to attempt utterly to repeal the very name of our faith. We must realise that this is the sixth psalm of those which we earlier said would discuss the two natures.[21]

Conclusion Drawn From the Psalm

How splendidly joined to each other are the sections proceeding from the same source to achieve the salvation of the human race! Who would not be amazed that what is said earlier in different psalms is clearly assembled so harmoniously here? Similarly David himself in the Chronicles is filled with the holy Spirit, and made the Lord's praises resound with great expressions of joy by assembling sections of Psalms 104, 95 and 105,[22] so that incense compounded of different aromas could happily rise to the Lord's presence; for sentiments which are clearly in no sense at odds with each other are united without difficulty. So let us consider that this psalm too has been fashioned from others so that the hungry soul may feast on the different flavours, and thus be renewed. This is why even today, I believe, cantors are allowed to merge together sections of different psalms. My judgment is that there is another apt feature in the present instance: the action of the Lord made one Church out of the two peoples.

Commentary on Psalm 108

1. *Unto the end, a psalm of David.* This psalm-heading is now familiar through our explanation of these words earlier, so we must apply it to the heavenly King, for all its words are directed towards the Lord Christ. He will speak in this psalm of the wickedness of Judas and the Jewish people, foretelling the mysteries of His passion.

Division of the Psalm

As we have said, the Lord Christ speaks throughout. In the first part He rebukes the Jews who preferred to render evils to their Creator in return for blessings. In the second, the wickedness of the traitor Judas and the faithless people, and the fate awaiting them for that heinous exsecration, are foretold. In the third, He prays in His role as man to be freed from the hazard of the passion, and to attain speedily the glory of resurrection.

Explanation of the Psalm

2. *O God, be not silent in my praise, for the mouth of the wicked and the mouth of the deceitful man is opened against me. They have spoken against me with deceitful tongues.* Our Lord and Saviour in the role of servant which He deigned to assume asks that the Father should not cause the praise of His resurrection to remain unspoken, for in the lowliness of the flesh He was to suffer grim insults from the Jews. *Be not silent in my praise* means "Do not cause it to remain unspoken." There is a fine contrast here: since enemies were speaking lies, He asks that witness to the truth be sung throughout the world to counter them. He longs for them to be refuted by the glory of His resurrection in such a way that they acknowledge the guilt of their own corruption and hasten back more quickly to the remedies of confession so that in their defiance they may not perish for ever. This figure is called *syncrisis*[1] or comparison; it occurs when by drawing a parallel we show that our cause is juster than that of our opponent. But this praise was beyond doubt for it flowed out from the Truth, whereas the utterance known to emerge from the mouth of the crafty and faithless person was seen to be quite false; for how can it be called true when we are told that it is opposed to the Truth Himself? So the mouth which is open denotes the insults which He endured from the Jews. Here however He speaks of a single person because, as has often been said, it is appropriate to speak of a people in either singular or plural. Though one is spoken of by name, we appreciate that this is understood as many. Next comes: *They have spoken against me with deceitful tongues.* They spoke with deceitful tongues when they made trial of the Lord's saintly simplicity with these most cunning words: *Is it lawful to give tribute to Caesar?* and: *Master, we know that you speak the truth.*[2] They uttered these words with crafty forethought.

3. *And they have compassed me about with words of hatred, and have*

attacked me gratuitously. When He says: *They have compassed me about with words of hatred,* He denotes the time when in wicked conspiracy they said to Pilate: *Crucify, crucify.*[3] These were indeed words of hatred and not of truth, for they appeared to be seeking the death of Him who was without stain. The expression, *compassed about,* denotes that mad throng which sounded forth most evil words in all directions. They attacked gratuitously when before the governor they sought the blood of the innocent One with false accusations. He says *gratuitously* because their action could bring them no gain, but instead led to accursed destruction. In the same way as just persons love the Lord gratuitously, since they love Him merely for His own sake and do not seek Him for some temporal benefit, so wicked people curse Him gratuitously because they cannot find a motive for justified hatred. As was remarked in Psalm 68: *They are multiplied above the hairs of my head, who hate me without cause.*[4]

4. *Instead of making me a return of love, they detracted me, but I gave myself to prayer.* 5. *They repaid me evil for good, and hatred for my love.* In these two verses we must make a clear separation between the statements so that the hidden meanings may become clearer. Every sin is committed in one of three ways. The first level of sinning is the failure to render good for good, and the second is rendering evil for evil. The third is the worst of sins, rendering evil for good. Contrariwise, praiseworthy deeds are performed in similar categories, rendering good for good, not rendering evil for evil, and thirdly—the most perfect kind of virtue—rendering good for evil. Observe too that just as the Jews decided to commit the most heinous type, eagerly evincing wicked hatred when they ought to have shown love, so the Lord with perfect devotion responded with the highest good, and as He hung on the cross prayed for the people who with wicked will voted to slay Him.

6. *Set thou the sinner over him, and may the devil stand at his right hand.* He passes to the second section, in which He is to speak first at length of Judas, who was capable of all evils. Then by use of the plural He associates with Judas the wicked Jews, who by imitating his crime revealed themselves as his sons. So in His utter certainty of the future He predicts that over the traitor Judas will be set the devil, who is rightly called *The sinner* because the sin of betrayal took its beginning from him. So that you would have no doubt about the identity of the

sinner, the addition was made: *And may the devil stand at his right hand.* What this means is that Judas deserved to be saved by no confession, but in despair at his wickedness he died by strangling himself with the noose. He could not have free use of the right hand, for he was redolent of the entire wickedness of the left.[5] So each individual is depicted as acting according to the nature of the one who holds his right hand. We have, for example, in the bad sense: *Their right hand is the right hand of iniquity,*[6] and in the good sense: *I set the Lord always in my sight, for he is at my right hand.*[7] So the nature of our entire life is denoted by these senses.

7. *When he is judged, may he go out condemned, and may his prayer be turned to sin.* This is said with reference to the future judgment at which sinners are condemned by a most just sentence, as the gospel passage states: *Depart from me, ye cursed, into everlasting fire which was prepared for the devil and his angels.*[8] Note that He said: *May he go out;* understand "from the gathering of the just." All who depart from this join the ranks of the wicked. *His prayer,* which Judas together with the rest of the apostles had undertaken to carry through, is seen to have become for him the most serious sin, for in it are contained the words: *And forgive us our debts, as we too forgive our debtors.*[9] But what could he forgive his debtors for, when he betrayed the Author of all kindnesses? So it was right that His holy prayer should be turned into sin for Judas, because he sinned and set an execrable precedent.

8. *May his days be few, and his bishopric let another take.* He says that the days of Judas are to be few, hinting that his long life appears to have been diminished through his most savage sin; as He said elsewhere: *Bloody and deceitful men will not live out half their days.*[10] This seems reasonable when younger and older persons are compared; whereas some live to the age of a hundred, the age of those who do not reach fifty is seen to be halved. In the same way the days of Judas' tenure of apostleship became few, whereas others after him remained as apostles by observing the Lord's will. And so that the most sacred number of apostles should not be reduced by the death of Judas, already at that time another was foretold as supplanting him, so that the total of twelve should be preserved undiminished. The *bishopric* is the highest order in the Church. *Episcopus* means overseer, because with the help of divine grace he guards the Lord's flock from his high seat like a most careful shepherd. As the prophet Ezechiel says: *I have made*

thee a watchman over the house of Israel.[11] Observe that this is the first passage in the Old Testament in which this title is found. Paul is clearly suggesting the power of this office when he says: *If a man desires the office of bishop, he desires a good work.*[12] So it is a title not so much of honour as of hard work. The man who takes on supervision of others must continually and sleeplessly keep watch on himself so that the formulation of Paul, *Lest perhaps in preaching to others I myself become a castaway,*[13] may not apply to him. It is appropriate for us to remember what is most clearly stated in the Acts of the Apostles, that this verse was written about Judas. Peter says: *Men, brethren, the scriptures must needs be fulfilled, which the holy Ghost spoke before by the mouth of David concerning Judas, who was the leader of them that apprehended Jesus.*[14] And a little later there follows: *For it is written in the Book of Psalms, Let their habitation become desolate, and let there be none to dwell therein; and his bishopric let another take.*[15] Thus no-one can doubt that this passage is to be wholly related to Judas, and we realise that this psalm is a prophecy about the Lord's passion, the words of the gospel, and the witness of the apostle Peter. We must identify in this verse the figure of *hypexaeresis*, which in Latin is called *exceptio;*[16] for Judas was deprived of the honour of the bishopric, in other words the apostleship.

9. *May his children be fatherless, and his wife a widow.* Though we do not read elsewhere that Judas had a wife or children, we are given to understand from this prophecy that he was a husband and father. When he died, undoubtedly the objects of his affection endured this fate: his wife was left a widow, and his children orphans, for they were fatherless. But if you wish to interpret this in a spiritual sense, his children can be understood as those who emulated him in the betrayal, and his wife as his intention, which is always associated with us like a wife, and from which we beget children when we bring forth our deeds from what we may call our womb.

10. *May his children be dislodged and removed, and beg: let them be cast out of their dwellings.* These words can be related to actual children or to our deeds. *Dislodged* means 'violently expelled', an experience which they grievously lament because they suffer it unwillingly. *May they beg* indicates lack of goodly possessions, so that it is clear to all that those emulating such conduct had no resource of reason. They

were cast out of their dwellings when becoming strangers to the Lord's people, among whom they were seen to have dwelt earlier only in body and not in mind.

11. *May the usurer search out all his substance, and strangers plunder all his labours.* This verse is to be clarified by the comparisons made, so that the obscurity of the general confusion may be removed. When a debtor cannot pay a debt, his creditor obtains a warrant from the judge, and enters his debtor's house. There he plunders all that he can lay hands on, and obtains satisfaction for the money which was borrowed. In the same way the devil, after concentrating many sins in men which adhere to them through their unbending will, obtains power to plunder the substance of a person subject to him, and to have his fill of mutilating people according to his will. This is what is now sought for Judas, that he be left in the power of the devil and stripped of all his possessions. The *strangers* too are impure spirits who are so to say under the devil's command to inflict harm. *Strangers* is a good description as they are known to be outside the Lord's kingdom. They *plunder the labours* of those transgressing the Lord's commands. They are allowed free play until they have robbed them of all their possessions.

12. *May there be none to help him, nor any to pity his orphans.* Good men too are afflicted by the temptation of the devil, but they do not cease to have the Lord as helper to enable them to be freed from looming danger. He says that wicked men are to be stripped of such aid so that their hopeless wickedness continues since that most wholesome medicine is withdrawn. *Pupilli* (orphans) are so called because they are *pusilli* (tiny)[17] children known to be amenable to control because of their youthful years. Likewise the pupil of the eye is so called because it appears quite small in our bodies.

13. *May his children perish: in one generation may his name be blotted out.* Those whom He earlier called orphans He here calls children; and since some men normally beget a long line of sinners, He robbed them of even the hope of posterity, so that their most wicked minds could not console themselves with any blessing. Or preferably we must explain *one generation* as the time when we are born in sins. His request is that rejected by predestination they should not attain a second generation, in other words a rebirth, but perish in those initial

dregs of their sins and fail to escape the noose of death through the benefit of a second birth. These and similar sentiments are uttered about those who will be condemned at the Lord's judgment.

14. *May the iniquity of his fathers be remembered in the sight of the Lord: and let not the sin of his mother be blotted out.* That the sins of ancestors recur to the Lord's memory is a figurative statement. He is asking that Judas be punished for the wickedness both of his own wrongs and of the faults of his fathers. As we have often said, a person is indicted for the sins of predecessors when he is found to be a most eager imitator of their crimes. *In the sight of the Lord* means at the decision of the Judgment, for when the Lord reviews men's sins He undoubtedly strikes down those who committed them. So the prophet elsewhere cries: *Turn away thy face from my sins.*[18] *The sin of his mother* is the well-known obstinacy of the synagogue, which led it to kill the prophets and not to refrain even from sacrifices to demons. He is saying that Judas' mother was that section of the synagogue which shed the blood of the innocent, and not that which brought forth holy men.

15. *May they be against the Lord continually, and let the memory of them perish from the earth.* Now He uses the plural, for it is the insolent Jews whom He wishes us to understand. Just as we interpret one saint as many of the blessed, as in: *Thou art Peter, and upon this rock I will build my church,*[19] so in turn many of the accursed are subsumed into the one most wicked man. Peter embodies a type of the Church, while Judas carries the image of Babylon which will be condemned. So after Judas he rightly speaks of the unfaithful, for those wicked men emulated him in evil deeds. So sinners are *against the Lord continually,* since they are exiled from His kingdom, and when justice is done will be dispatched into the opposing region of hell. Since God is eternal blessedness, the person condemned to everlasting vengeance is aptly said to be against Him. He perishes from the land of the living since he is not seen in the blessed home of heaven. They are not remembered either, since they obtain mercy no longer; for we are said to be remembered by those to whom we afford some benefit.

16. *Because he remembered not to show mercy.* He explains the reason for this most just vengeance. It is because the person who has contemptuously refused to show devoted love to others cannot obtain it himself. As Scripture says: *Blessed are the merciful, for God will have*

mercy on them.[20] Though He has returned to use of the singular, we must still interpret it as the Jewish people who showed no mercy to the apostles or to Christ's faithful when after the Lord's passion they harassed them with unjust persecution. This cannot be understood as referring to Judas, for he passed from this life before the Lord's crucifixion, and thus he could not have persecuted the faithful, since He had no opportunity to pursue them.

17. *And he persecuted the poor man and the beggar, and put to death the remorseful.* We must continue to understand this of the Jewish people, who with sacrilegious audacity slaughtered both Christ and His disciples. It is either desire for riches or a loathsome display of arrogance which usually impels men to persecution, but it is sheer savagery to attack the poor man and the beggar, for there is no aim of glory nor prospect of abundant enrichment from such a deed. After His fashion the Lord relates that He Himself in the nature of the humanity which He assumed is poor and beggarly. He is a beggar in our condition, but rich in His own. As Paul puts it: *Being rich, he became poor for your sakes, that through his poverty we might be rich.*[21] I do not think that *remorseful* can be used of our Head himself, for such a description is unprecedented. I regard it as applicable to the sinner who is pricked by recollection of his faults so that he may deserve to return to satisfaction for them, a conversion attested in countless passages of Scripture. So we must of necessity interpret this as referring to His members, for the Lord Christ was sinless. The Jewish people persecuted the remorseful, as clearly occurred in the cases of blessed Stephen and the apostle Paul.

18. *And he loved cursing, and it shall come unto him: and he would not have blessing, and it shall be far from him.* It is still the faithless people of whom He speaks in: *He loved cursing;* this refers to the time when they said: *His blood be upon us and on our children.*[22] Clearly these words sprang from those who hardened themselves against the Lord with wicked will. That people refused a blessing when they were asked by the blind man who gained his sight: *Will you also become his disciples?*[23] But they replied, when challenged, with what seems the sharpest of curses: *Be thou his disciple, but we are disciples of Moses.*[24] At these words blessing was removed far from them, for they were abandoned, and it was bestowed on the faith of the Gentiles. As the apostle comments: *To you it behoved us first to speak the word of God, but because*

you rejected it and counted yourselves unworthy of eternal life, behold, we turn to the Gentiles.[25]

And he put on cursing like a garment: and it went in like water into his entrails, and like oil in his bones. We must carefully examine how the nature of this sin is denoted by certain expressions. First, the people we have mentioned *put on cursing like a garment,* when at the devil's prompting they unanimously agreed to hand over the Word to Pontius Pilate. This garment was donned as a heavy burden when as we know they clothed themselves with this intention. Secondly, the cursing *went in like water into his entrails,* when they decided to carry out the prompting of that most wicked suggestion. When water enters diseased entrails it always causes damage. Thirdly, weakness flowed in *like oil in his bones,* when they achieved their end with unprecedented corruption, so that it appeared to have penetrated not merely the inner flesh but even the very bones. By speaking of oil he denotes delight in the deed, for oil enters our bodies so gently that it soothes us with a kind of pleasure. Clearly this is the experience of wicked minds when they glory with a sort of delight in their crime.

19. *May it be unto him like a garment which will cover him, and like a girdle with which he is girded continuously.* He still continues with these same comparisons, so that the sin with which the Jews decided to envelop themselves is denoted by the simile of another garment. Earlier He spoke of *putting on,* denoting a shirt; now He speaks of being covered, which seems apt for a cloak. Thus the twin garments denote burdens of heavy sins. Next comes: *And like a girdle with which he is girded continuously. Girdle* here is to be taken not as a woman's garment, but as the belt with which we gird our loins; compare the reference to John in the gospel, and that to Elias in the book of Kings: *With a girdle of leather about his loins.*[26] This word is endowed with a twofold significance. By this simile He says that they were held so fast in the bonds of sins that they were never relieved of their burdens, since they were weighed down by their faithless obduracy. What an unhappy people, saddled with such garments! These are the clothes which make sinners not warm but aflame, which dispatch them into the fire rather than protect them from the harsh cold.

20. *This is the work of them who detract me before the Lord, and who speak evils against my soul.* We must interpret this verse as directed against all unfaithful men, but He seems to attack two heresies in

particular. The Arians disparage the Son's presence in God the Father by attesting that the Son is inferior to Him; they shamelessly label as inferior Him whom men in general confess as Creator of all. The Apollinarists likewise *speak evils against the Lord's soul* when they say that His divinity took on only human flesh and not a soul, and their infidelity does not give way though worsted by numerous proofs. So the words here are properly understood as uttered against these in particular, but also against all heretics in general; they will have no portion in the Lord's kingdom.

21. *But thou too, Lord, Lord, grant mercy for thy name's sake, because thy mercy is sweet. Do thou deliver me.* He passes to the third narration, in which He prays in His role as sufferer that the Lord may hasten the glory of resurrection, and that His foes may be clothed in the shame of confusion. His words, *but thou too, Lord,* are attached to what goes before, that is: "Even though Judas betrayed Me, even though the Jews crucified Me, do You grant mercy so that the glorious resurrection may arise to counteract those deeds." Alternatively, the Son says to the Father, *Do thou, too,* to reveal the power of their cooperation, for all that the Father does the Son too performs. As He Himself says: *All that the Father does, this the Son also does in like manner.*[27] Again: *As the Father has life in himself, so he has given to the Son also to have life in himself;*[28] *that all men may honour the Son as they honour the Father.*[29] The repetition in *Lord, Lord* reveals the feeling behind the sweetest of entreaties. This figure is called *epizeuxis,*[30] for He has repeated the same word in the one verse without any intervening addition. *For thy name's sake,* so that the Lord's worship may be spread through the whole world. Here the great mercy of the Godhead is proclaimed, for no human merits could ensure that our mortal nature could be shown to have been exalted by such great miracles. He speaks of *mercy* because He deigned to take on our flesh, so that through it the most devoted Creator could lend aid to the human race. Next follows: *Do thou deliver me,* that is, from the most savage suffering inflicted by the Jews.

22. *For I am needy and poor, and my heart is troubled within me.* He says that He is needy and poor in the lowliness of the flesh, as has been clearly explained earlier. The poor and needy should listen, and realise that the description of Christ is a source of glory for themselves. Secondly, His heart could be troubled within Him because as we

know He was deprived of life in the flesh for our sake. As He Himself proclaimed as His passion drew near: *My soul is sorrowful even unto death.*[31] All this is recounted in a salutary pattern with two purposes: so that for the sake of heretics the perfect nature of man in the Lord Christ can be revealed, and so that we can be instructed how we are to make entreaty.

23. *I am taken away like a shadow when it declineth, and I am shaken off as a locust.* Here He reveals the ease of the persecution, for He was snatched away from the midst of His disciples by the crowd of Jews with as much haste as the speed with which night's shadow usually departs at the approach of the sun's light. He was shaken off like a locust when He was seen to change His abode during frequent persecutions; namely when He came to Capharnaum from Nazareth, to Bethsaida from Capharnaum, to Jerusalem from Bethsaida. He went round these places on the look-out for sinners, so that the persecuting people could not fulfil their wicked design. The locust avoids the pursuer's hands and flies out of certain glades; He compares Himself with it because it is small, and associates Himself with it because of the speed of its departure. This cannot be inapposite to His humility, for He compared Himself even with worms when He said: *But I am a worm, and no man.*[32]

24. *My knees are weakened through fasting: and my flesh is changed through oil.* Though we are informed by gospel witness that the Lord Christ fasted for forty days and forty nights, we do not read that His knees were weakened; it merely states that He was hungry.[33] So if you relate the effect of this hunger to the knees (that is, to bodily balance, for we put our weight on our knees), the connection is not so appropriate. If this difficulty is not removed, it would be better to interpret *knees* as His members, for they were truly weakened when the apostles were scattered at His passion. What greater evidence of weakness could there be than Peter's denial of Him, and the self-concealment of the rest of the crowd of the faithful? Next comes: *And my flesh is changed through oil.* Oil signifies here divine grace. As has already been said of Him in Psalm 44, *Therefore God, thy God, hath anointed thee with the oil of gladness above thy fellows.*[34] It is the grace which transformed the weakness of the flesh into the glory of immortality. This too seems quite appropriate to Christ's members.

25. *And I am become a reproach to them: they saw me, and they shook*

their heads. He touches on the things which the Jewish folk were to say disparagingly. As the gospel has it: *This man casts out devils by Beelzebub the prince of devils.*[35] And elsewhere: *Is not this the son of Joseph?*[36] And again they say: *Vah! he destroys the temple of God, and in three days rebuilds it,*[37] and the other things which seemed to their foolish minds to be insults, but were in fact things known to bestow healing on us. *They shook their heads* refers to the tendency of people prone to extreme anger; when we blaze with rage, we utter threats with disordered movement of the head.

26. *Help me, O Lord my God: save me on account of thy mercy.* The weakness which He has assumed implores aid; He who lends help seeks mercy. He entreats as Man, bestows as God. This can trouble no-one who proclaims the two natures in Lord Christ for his salvation. We find countless statements of this kind which cannot be explained in any other way.

27. *That they may know that this is thy hand: and thou, O Lord, hast done it.* So that the Jewish people would not claim that the Lord Saviour had been attacked by their own powers, He says to the Father in reference to His passion: "Let men know that this dispensation was set in train by You, O Lord, so that foolish people may not attribute to their own powers what You with great devotion decreed should happen for the salvation of the world." When he says: *That they may know,* He means the persecutors, who certainly did not know. But when He rose again, they very clearly did know that it could never have been fulfilled if the Lord had not permitted it to happen. Next comes: *That this is thy hand,* in other words, Thy power; we must understand "at work."

28. *They will curse, and thou wilt bless. Let them that rise up against me be confounded, but thy servant shall rejoice.* By the figure of *syncrisis,*[38] which is set at the beginning of the psalm, *they will curse* denotes those of whom the evangelist Matthew says: *They that passed by blasphemed him, wagging their heads,*[39] and the Father blesses the Son when He says: *I have both glorified him and will glorify.*[40] But observe those who will curse, who are full of falsehood, who raged cruelly, who hastened to render evil for good; whereas the Father, the Fount and Source of truth, Author of all good and Fullness of all virtues, blesses. The proclamation on each side is marvellous; the faithless people cursed, and the Father's glory praised, the Lord Christ. He added: *Let*

them that rise up against me be confounded. The Jews are they who rose up against the Lord Saviour; they consigned to slaughter Him who in His devotion had come to save them. They were confounded when they became aware of the miracles of His resurrection. Next comes: *But thy servant shall rejoice.* Let us recognise which nature is speaking when He calls himself a servant; God can surely not be anyone's servant? But He is a servant in the sense described by Paul, that *He emptied himself, taking the form of a servant.*[41] In the same way Isaiah too speaks of Christ: *Behold my servant: I will uphold him. My elect, my soul delighteth in him,*[42] and the rest. So heretics must stop regarding the Son as lesser in divinity when they hear His humility in the flesh so expressly stated that the very title of servant is attached to Him.

29. *Let them that detract me be clothed with reverence, and let them be covered with confusion as with a double cloak.* At this point a prayer rather than a curse is allotted to Him, since this is in the interest of a people later to believe. The person who is clothed with reverence is by that time virtually giving thanks for the gift of conversion, and fears as God Him who he earlier thought should be despised as man. *Diplois* means a double cloak, so He asks that they be clothed in understanding of both laws, whereas now they are stripped of both through their lack of faith. The Jews' confusion is their failure to understand the Law, which so often foretold the coming of the Lord Saviour. Alternatively, He wishes to express the kind of truth often uttered in proverbs; let them be clothed in the double cloak of confusion, since they blush before the sight of God and man.

30. *I will give great thanks to the Lord with my mouth, and in the midst of many I will praise him.* This is spoken on behalf of the members, for He prays after the resurrection has been made manifest throughout the world, and a suitable confession to the Father is presented from the mouth of the Catholic Church. *In the midst of many* denotes the universal Church which never ceases to confess the Lord's praises, though the unfaithful still surround it. As long as the world exists, Christ's Church is hemmed in by a crowd of revilers.

31. *Because he hath stood at the right hand of the poor, to save my soul from persecutors.* He explains the reason why He must confess to the Father in the person of His members: it is because His persecutors were confounded, and He Himself was saved. Earlier He said that the

devil stood at Judas' right hand, for Judas was befouled with the dregs of sins, but here He says that the Father stood at His own right hand because He had no sin. Likewise the Father stands by the faithful when He forgives their wrongs. Next comes: *To save my soul from persecutors.* His soul was indeed saved from persecutors when He lent no assent to their wickedness by any debased deed. This too is aptly referred to His members, for they refused to yield to persecutors though oppressed by various tortures. The soul is saved not when it is delivered from death within time, but when it is freed from the prison of this world by a most happy release. As Paul has it: *But I am straitened between two, having a desire to be dissolved and to be with Christ, a thing by far the better, but to abide still in the flesh is needful for you.*[43] And elsewhere: *Who shall deliver me from the body of this death? The grace of God, through Jesus Christ.*[44]

Conclusion Drawn From the Psalm

This is the fifth of the psalms which have discoursed at greater length on lines earlier laid down about the Lord's passion; the earlier ones are Psalms 21, 34, 54, 68. First, all begin with the person of the Lord Christ. Second, they are seen to speak in a prayer. Third, they related the events of the Lord's passion. Fourth, they accord with the words of the gospel in harmonious truth. Fifth, they ended by expressing with great exultation the hope of the faithful. Thus the glory of this psalm was allied to that mystical number conferred on the five virgins and the five books.[45] But though these are great wonders, foretelling our salvation, nothing is clearer or more acceptable than their incorporation of the adorable passion of the incarnate Lord. Everything harmonises, everything matches with glowing correspondence. The virgin brought forth, the Messiah came, the spotless Lamb was slain, the Redeemer rose from the dead, the world heard and believed; yet the Jew still pretends that he does not know what the whole world recognises. Grant, O Lord, conversion to the obdurate, light to those in darkness, faith to unbelievers, so that You may deign to aid those in danger for whom You prayed when nailed to the cross. We rightly pray to You, Lord, for those whom we cannot persuade to act justly.

Commentary on Psalm 109

1. *A psalm of David.* These words are very familiar, for they are so to say pinned to the doors as a royal inscription. But the heading does not say: "Read and depart," but: "Read and draw near." So let us reverently enter to the mighty works of the Lord, for this psalm will discuss fully but briefly both the Lord's sacred incarnation and His almighty divinity. In certain passages He is seen to utter words of similar loftiness or beauty, as at the beginning of the celebrated gospel where it says: *In the beginning was the Word, and the Word was with God, and the Word was God.*[1] So the psalm is, so to say, the sun of our faith, the mirror of the heavenly secret, the chest of the holy Scriptures, in which all that is told in the proclamation of both testaments is spoken in summary. So we must hold it fast in love, for its sweetness swells to attain the worth gathered in its succinct brevity. Now let us fearlessly listen to its divisions, for it is marked out with variation of spokesmen.

Division of the Psalm

The most holy prophet is borne upwards into the hidden heights of loftiest contemplation. In the first verse he recounts the words beyond understanding which the almighty Father spoke to the Son, who is almighty and coeternal with Him, revealing at the same time the nature of His divinity and of His humanity. When He proclaims: *The Lord said to my Lord,* he reveals the nature of His divinity. When he adds: *Sit thou at my right hand until I make thy enemies thy footstool,* and: *The Lord sends forth the sceptre of thy power out of Sion, and thou wilt rule in the midst of thy enemies,* the substance of His humanity is being declared which could receive what it did not have. In the second section, the Father begins to reveal the nature of His divinity to a limited extent, in accordance with the feeble limit of our capacity to understand. He says: *With thee is the principality in the day of thy strength, in the brightness of the saints. From the womb before the day-star I have begotten thee.* In the third part the prophet speaks until the end, again revealing the shape of His humanity when he says: *The Lord hath sworn, and he will not repent,* and the rest. Thus in these sections the Word made flesh, the Lord Christ, could be acknowledged by this threefold illumination.

Explanation of the Psalm

The Lord said to my Lord, Sit thou at my right hand, until I make thy enemies a stool for thy feet. It seems appropriate first to identify the figure by which we can plumb the inner meaning of this exordium of the psalm. *Idea* is the figure which is called in Latin *species,*[2] and through which things invisible are exposed to be seen by the senses. He says: *The Lord said to my Lord, Sit thou at my right hand.* There is a single divinity, a single power, a single eternity. The Father says to the Son words which He did not utter from the mouth, and which the Son did not take in with eager ears. The Father wills, and the Son knows; the Son wills, and the Father knows. But that will cannot be grasped by us, nor can the very notion be clear to our human senses. So there was an appropriate descent to our manner of speaking, so that our feeble humanity could obtain instruction, for the thoughts of man could not penetrate that sequestered perfection. *The Lord to the Lord:* by these titles Their equality of substance and force of strength are declared. This duplication of the one word both aptly mentioned the Persons and clearly revealed the one nature of the Godhead. It should not trouble you that sometimes Jesus Christ is called the Son of David and sometimes the Lord of David. If you investigate the reasons, both are found to be perfectly true. He is David's Son in physical origin, as Scripture says at the beginning of Matthew: *The book of the generation of Jesus Christ, son of David.*[3] And elsewhere the blind cry to Him: *Son of David, have mercy on us.*[4] But He is called the Lord of David in keeping with His divinity by which He is his Creator; a similar position holds even today in our own lives, when a son becomes a bishop and is called the father of his father, not according to birth but by distinction. His birth from David's seed gained him such honour and glory that He was at the same time David's Lord and David's Son. Next comes: *Sit thou at my right hand.* After His glorious resurrection the Son as Conqueror, triumphing over the whole world through His holy incarnation, is offered the seat of honour so that the glory of the humanity which He assumed can be emphasised by this position.

What these words mean is that our Head was known to be put at the Father's right hand, where those persons are to be set who by the gift of the Godhead are detached from the unfaithful; this fulfils Christ's words: *Father, I will that where I am, they also may be with me.*[5] For if you ponder the nature of the Godhead, how can He who embraces all things everywhere in the total fullness of majesty occupy any seat on left or right? As for the statement that the right side is granted to the Son, this is said not so that anyone should think Him greater, but so that the Arians should not sinfully and lyingly proclaim as they do that He is the lesser. He added: *Until I make thy enemies a stool for thy feet. Scabellum* (stool) is so called because one mounts (*scandere*)[6] or climbs on it. Note that here *until* makes limited what is unbounded in time, as though Christ will not sit at the Father's right hand once His enemies have been prostrated to make a stool for His feet. It is common in divine Scripture for the word *until* both to express a short time and to denote eternity. The temporary sense is found in Jeremiah: *Shut thy door a little until the anger of the Lord pass away.*[7] But elsewhere *until* expresses eternity as here, for in Psalm 122 the prophet will say: *So our eyes are on the Lord our God until he have mercy on us.*[8] Similarly there is the comment about Joseph in the gospel: *And he knew her not till she brought forth her first-born son,*[9] as though he did know her after the birth, whereas she remained a virgin. We shall return to the problem and discuss it in its due place; we can term it an idiom or peculiarity of divine Scripture. By *feet* is denoted the eternal stability of the Lord, on which He stands in the power of His omnipotence as though with planted footsteps. Clearly those who daily abandon the opposition of vices and return to the Lord are to be subdued by those feet, and bend low before His preaching like a stool for them. What a blessed stool, for it is set there for His holy feet, and raised above all kingdoms where such high subjection is appointed for it! When a stool is set for Him as He sits at the right hand, this is undoubtedly a reference to those enemies who are converted and are placed on the right.

2. *The Lord sends forth the rod of thy strength out of Sion, and thou shalt be lord in the midst of thy enemies.* The prophet speaks this verse too in his own person, offering in it praise to the Lord Christ. *The rod of strength* is the sceptre of royal power by which the faithful are sustained, unbelievers afflicted, and the ungrateful made to fear. To show that the Son has no need of anything, he spoke of *thy* strength,

because that power is peculiar to His divinity and is eternal. So that you can realise this more clearly, he added that the Lord sends forth this rod *out of Sion*, the Lord being the almighty Father. The Lord Son is also said to be out of Sion; as Isaiah says: *For the law shall come forth from Sion, and the word of the Lord from Jerusalem.*[10] The heretic must hearken to the Father speaking of the power and majesty of the Son; in whose words can he be steeped if he does not believe the Creator Himself? The psalmist added: *And thou shalt be lord in the midst of thine enemies.* He has explained the future effect of the unleashing of the rod of strength; it will ensure that *thou shalt be lord in the midst of thine enemies.* Observe that most merciful *word;* here he has said that Christ is Lord, and does not take vengeance on enemies, for He is Lord over them when the crowd of sinners is converted to Him. His being Lord over the faithful is different from His dominion over the ungrateful, for He trains the faithful by kindnesses and correction, but smites the ungrateful by the punishment of vengeance. By *in the midst* he meant in the soul, in the breast, where the Lord takes rest when the foulness of sins has been washed clean. Or he is saying that Christ is Lord in the Church, which is set in this world amidst the madness of heretics and superstitions. So far the prophet has spoken of the nature of the Godhead and of His humanity. Now let us analyse the start of the second section.

3. *With thee is the beginning in the day of thy strength, in the brightness of the saints.* He passes to the second section, in which throughout these two verses the words are to be understood as spoken by the Father, as was right since He was to speak of the holy begetting of the Son. To demonstrate clearly the Son's coeternity, the almighty Father says of His almighty Son: *With thee is the beginning in the day of thy strength.* The Father Himself is also the Beginning, as in the passage: *In the beginning was the Word;*[11] that gospel denotes the Father as the Beginning in which the Word was. The Son too is announced as the Beginning in the gospel when He says: *I am the beginning, which is why I speak to you.*[12] But there are not two beginnings; just as there is one God, so clearly there is also one Beginning. Undoubtedly we must hold the same belief also about the holy Spirit, for when scripture spoke of the beginning, it added: *And the spirit of God was borne over the waters.*[13] But in this matter holy men cannot see how there is a beginning in the beginning. When Philip saw the Son, he said: *Lord,*

show us the Father. To these words the blameless One replied: *He that seeth me seeth the Father also*.[14] So once through the Lord's grace they have begun to be enlightened by the fullest brightness, they observe Christ the Beginning in the Father who is the Beginning, in company with the holy Spirit. Hence the Arian infidelity should cease to mount. Father and Son are called the Beginning so that their coeternity may be made clear; for if there had been a time when the Son was not, only the Father could be called the Beginning.

Next comes: *In the day of thy strength, in the brightness of the saints*. Observe the force and the distinction of the individual words. *In the day* denotes eternity in which there is one day, and in which the divine power and brightness are beheld by the blessed. Scripture says of this: *Blessed are the pure of heart for they shall see God*.[15] And of the wicked we read: *Let the wicked man be removed, lest he see the glory of God*;[16] for all will see the Son of man judging the living and the dead, but only the most blessed observe His divinity. Where are they who even now refuse to confess the two natures in the Lord Christ? The sinner beholds His humanity, the blessed man simultaneously sees also His divinity. If there were only one nature, as these men falsely maintain, sinners could not at the resurrection gaze only at the flesh which they afflicted, and likewise fail to see His divinity. *The brightness of the saints* refers to when they will gleam at the resurrection like the angels of God, and will be so cleansed and radiant that they can gaze on the Majesty with the heart's eyes. They cannot gaze on that Light unless they are changed for the better; in Paul's words: *We shall all rise again, but we shall not all be changed*.[17]

From the womb before the day-star I begot thee. After saying that the Son was brought forth in the brightness of the saints, He is now to speak of His holy begetting; though this is beyond description, there is brief mention of it. To recount it is beyond words, to understand it is beyond our grasp, and to meditate on it is beyond the powers of all creatures, for it transcends the understanding even of the angels, yet it was made available to us in so far as we could grasp it. God, who remains eternal and unchangeable in His nature, deigned to take on our humanity to renew the old man, to make man immortal from being mortal, to make him justified from being a sinner, to bid him share His kingdom after being an outcast. In His devotion He did not wish to allow His image to disappear among those who confessed Him, that image which the cruel enemy sought to obliterate. Now let us turn to an explanation of the words of this verse. The Father says to the Son: *From the womb I begot thee;* He means: "From the secret depth of My substance, from the Godhead Itself, Entirety from Entirety, Light from Light, Highest from Highest," a concept which no study, no thought can grasp. How can that begetting be understood, when Scripture says: *Who shall declare his generation?*[18] The brevity is wonderful and sufficient in measure for our infirmity, for we cannot take in more, and it is more than enough for our belief to grasp. When He says: *Before the day-star,* He is denoting the boundlessness of eternity. The day-star represents all stars, as the part for the whole; it signifies the coming day. And to indicate something beyond understanding, He speaks of His being begotten before the existence of that which is wont to herald the coming daylight to the world. The beginning of Him by whom all things were created cannot be understood. Now let us turn to the beginning of the third section, in which the prophet again resumes the narrative.

4. *The Lord hath sworn, and he will not repent: thou art a priest for ever, according to the order of Melchisedech.* Here the prophet again relates the Father's promise, as has been explained. He has sworn to the Son who is now Christ, born of the virgin Mary; for what could He promise to the Word alone, when He is known to possess all things eternally in company with Himself? To swear means to make a firm promise before witnesses. To whom could this be more appropriate than to Him who with divine power fulfilled the outcome of His word? This is what the apostle says in the letter written to the Hebrews: *God, meaning to show to the heirs of his promise the immutability of his counsel, interposed an oath; that by two immutable things by which it is impossible for God to lie, we may have the strongest comfort, we who have fled for refuge to hold fast the hope set before us; which we have as an anchor for the soul, secure and firm.*[19] As we have already said, this is why men are rightly deterred from swearing, for they rashly promise by calling God to witness what they cannot carry out. But God swears by Himself, as He promised to Abraham: *As I live, says the Lord, because thou hast heard my voice, and hast not spared thine only son for my sake, see if I do not bless thee,*[20] and the rest. *And he will not repent;* exactly so, for all things rejoiced at so great and splendid a dispensation. One also reads: *I repent of having made man,*[21] when before the

coming of the Flood the hearts of mortal men had plunged into a whirlpool of sins. But these words are uttered after the fashion of human beings when confronted with a situation different from their apparent hopes.

Next follows: *Thou art a priest for ever, according to the order of Melchisedech.* The prophet relates that the Father gave this further promise to the Son; for with whom can these words be truly and clearly associated except the Lord Saviour, who in saving fashion consecrated His body and blood in the distribution of bread and wine? As Christ Himself says in the gospel: *Unless you eat the flesh of the Son of man, and drink his blood, you will not have eternal life.*[22] But the human mind must not imagine that there is anything bloody or corruptible in this flesh and blood—as Paul says: *He that eateth the Lord's body unworthily, eateth judgment to himself*[23]—but rather the substance that gives life and salvation and has become peculiar to the Word itself. Through it are granted remission of sins and the gift of eternal life. It was Melchisedech, that most just king, who by a mystical parallel established this dispensation, when he offered fruits of bread and wine to the Lord.[24] It is certain that sacrifices of cattle which were part of Aaron's dispensation died out, and that the order instituted by Melchisedech remained, which is celebrated throughout the whole world in the distribution of the sacraments. But the obdurate Jews still do not understand this, though both their priest and their sacrifices are known to have been removed from their midst. *Priest* is the special title of Christ who offered Himself to be sacrificed for us once and for all. Of Him the apostle says: *For it was fitting that we should have such a high priest, holy, innocent, undefiled, separated from sinners, and made higher than the heavens.*[25] This is the meaning which the prophet marvellously and clearly describes. The phrase *for ever* points to the Lord Christ, who abides in enduring glory.

5. *The Lord at thy right hand hath broken kings in the day of his wrath.* What the Father is said to have done was clearly and beyond doubt performed also by the Son and the holy Spirit. But it can cause surprise that whereas at the beginning of this psalm the Father told the Son: *Sit thou at my right hand,* the prophet now in turn says that the Lord's power has done its work at the right hand of the Son. This was stated so that through the statement of equal interchange there should be no sense of greater or lesser in this psalm. *He hath broken kings* denotes

those of whom Psalm 2 says: *The kings of the earth stood up, and the princes met together against the Lord and against his Christ.*[26] He broke them when He laid low their pride with the power of His omnipotence, for if they had not been broken they would have stuck fast in the harmful rigidity of their malice.

6. *He shall judge among nations, he shall engineer falls, he shall crush many heads in a land of abundance.* Observe the peculiar senses of the words. In the previous verse he said that kings were to be *broken* because of their tyrannical pride; now he relates that nations are *judged* for their common sins. Both happily tumble from their purposes when they abandon their earlier ill-will through their righteous decision to be converted. Ponder too the statement here that He judges to engineer falls. He engineers falls when He makes sins fall headlong from human hearts and causes harmful faults to vanish by most salutary improvement. This can be understood from the exemplary passage in which he says: *Thou shalt destroy them, and shalt not build them up;*[27] for this would surely not have been said if certain persons were not being destroyed for a happier renewal. Next comes: *He shall crush many heads in a land of abundance.* These are none other than the heads of those who do not have Christ as their head, for those who follow the devil in sundry errors undoubtedly find their heads crushed when they endure correction. By *head* (*caput*) we mean the lofty, distinguished crown of the body which gets its name from *capere* (to take), because it takes in all our senses[28]—sight, hearing, taste, smell, touch—and our members have none of these except touch. So we can rightly call our Head Him whom we decide to follow. He calls a *land of abundance* that which nurtures numerous sinners, a harvest and seedbed, so to say, of vices.

7. *He shall drink of the torrent in the way: therefore shall he lift up the head.* This torrent was disordered persecution by the Jews, of which the Lord Christ drank on the way, that is, in this life, when He endured it in the flesh. The phrase, *in the way,* indicates the onset of violence and the great speed of the journey made by travellers as they drive to another lodging. It is He who heard the words: *Sit thou at my right hand;* who is told: *Thou art a priest for ever, according to the order of Melchisedech;* who crushes the heads of sinners; to whom, because of the merit of His glorious passion, was given *a name which is above all names, that in his name every knee should bow, of those that are in*

heaven, on earth, and under the earth.[29] You who are pagan or Jew have heard that He suffered; now read that He will also be our Judge in the future, so that you may tremble before the almighty God who you consider can be ignored as Man.

Conclusion Drawn From the Psalm

This is the seventh psalm which we have stated is concerned with the Lord Christ's two natures. But since Paul writes to Timothy: *Preach the word, be instant in season, out of season; reprove, entreat, rebuke in all patience and doctrine,*[30] I should like to continue to converse with those of you who consider that there was only one nature created in Christ the Lord. You certainly believe in company with us that in the womb of Mary ever virgin *the Word was made flesh, and dwelt amongst us;*[31] that in the humanity which He took on He suffered and was buried, and on the third day rose from the dead; that he was subsequently seen in the flesh by the apostles and by those who believed in Him; moreover, that He ascended into heaven in the flesh in which He rose from the dead. You proclaim all this up to this point. But why are you subsequently redolent of earthly things, when you have attained things heavenly? Where is the nature with which the Lord ascended into heaven? He could not now perish in death, as Paul attests: *Knowing that Christ, risen again from the dead, dieth now no more. Death shall no more have dominion over him. For in that he died to sin, he died once, but in that he liveth, he liveth to God.*[32] Why should he say: *He liveth to God,* and not: "God lives," if only one nature was created which lives? There is in fact another element, the fact that *He liveth to God,* precisely because He died once to sin. In short, when you hear the words: "He sitteth at the right hand of the Father," do you doubt that He preserves that which alone is appropriate to His humanity? Allow, we beg you, that Christ the Lord be ever called the hope of our salvation, for He can be rightly accorded this title, since He remains with His two united and perfect natures in the glory of the Father for ever and ever. If you weigh your words carefully, you will realise that each time you say that Jesus Christ has only one nature, you are denying that He is the Son of the holy virgin. Ask yourselves what source for your salvation now exists, if your reluctance to confess Him cuts the Lord Saviour off from you.

Commentary on Psalm 110

1. *Alleluia.* Though this word of praise appears to be of general application, it is exploited particularly at points of great exultation and joy. The Lord is praised by His people who are freed from worldly calamity and refuse to endure the slavery of vices. This praise is seen to convey the shape of the joy to come, when the Lord is beheld uninterruptedly by the faithful, and praised without end. As we read in another psalm: *Blessed are they that dwell in thy house: they shall praise thee for ever and ever.*[1] This psalm is also adorned with the sequence of the Hebrew alphabet, which is set down with all its letters at the head of the sentences or sections. It points out to us those just persons who by the gift of divine grace shine out with perfect virtues. Just as earlier alphabetic psalms which have certain letters missing indicate people who are not so endowed with every merit but are known to dwell in the holy gathering,[2] so the psalms with the full complement of letters seem to signify the merits of those outstandingly just. There is a further reason, as father Hilary says, for the insertion of this alphabet: "We know that children and the uninstructed are taught by letters to seek precepts of wisdom. In the same way psalms of this type are put before boys and learners so that their first lessons may be imparted by the letters acting so to say as teachers."[3] Though we have read that some people have learnt the divine Scriptures without knowing the letters, it is easier for our frail natures to learn wisdom by God's grace through letters than to achieve such a remarkable feat. So by this sacred sign we are advised to embark with speed and the utmost concentration on the pursuit of learning, for the very order of letters is set down so that we may ponder on and learn the rudiments.

Division of the Psalm

The nation of the blessed have gathered from different parts of the world, and at the beginning of the psalm they say that they are confessing to the Lord in the gathering of the just, where praise is everlasting and celebration is without end. This first section contains six letters of the alphabet just mentioned. In the second section they say that His faithful are filled with His abundant gift, and together they give promise of the Lord's coming, so that with most eager concentration they may seek the promised inheritance. In this section ten letters are apportioned out. In the third section they claim that Christians have been redeemed, and that the New Testament has been hallowed by eternal grace. This part takes in the remaining six letters, thus rounding off the whole alphabet appropriately.

Explanation of the Psalm

ALEPH, BETH.[4] *I will confess to thee, O Lord, with my whole heart, in the council of the just and in the congregation.* As we have often said: *I will confess* is an ambivalent expression, the meaning of which varies according to the context; for those who lament their sins confess, but so do those who render thanks to the Lord. The first confession is tearful, the second joyful; the first is as we know embodied in affliction, the second in pious eagerness of mind. So here the faithful people exults in abundant joy, giving expression to some shape of the age to come, when these proclamations are uninterrupted, and they celebrate the Lord's praises together with devoted minds. To reveal the sincerity of their purpose, they say that they will praise Him with their whole heart's feeling, so that hostile thoughts may not detract anything from it, and the devil's trickery may not appear to cloud their bright and shining minds. Next comes: *In the council of the just, and in the congregation.* Should you wish to identify the council of the just and the congregation nowadays, it would be extremely difficult to ascertain all the elect in this age in which the Church is filled with a mixture of good and evil persons. But those who confess with their whole heart in this passage are already seen to be singing in that congregation of the just which the Lord is clearly gathering from all nations for the future. Let us observe what these words recount to us. *The council of the just* is a reference to when the blessed will pass judgment with the Lord at the time of the resurrection; as was said in Psalm 1: *Therefore the wicked do not rise again in judgment, nor sinners in the council of the just.*[5] The Lord in the gospel gave this promise in particular to the apostles and to His saints when He said: *You shall sit on twelve seats, judging the twelve tribes of Israel.*[6] *Congregation* denotes the blessed gathering of the whole Church, united from various regions of the world.

2. GIMEL, DALETH. *Great are the works of the Lord, sought out according to all his wills.* They now begin to recount their most devoted confession, revealing the boundless nature of His goodness; for what could be more splendid than to convert the wicked man into the just, the enemy into a son, the captive into a free man? This is to fulfil Paul's words: *Where sin abounded, grace did more abound.*[7] *Sought out* means unique, perfect, unmatchable. He allows the devil to rage so that out of his wickedness the Lord may elicit persons most faithful to himself, and in this novel way joy is born from affliction, and eternal tranquillity from persecution. So that you would not regard this as only partial praise, they added: *According to all his wills.* Whatever He does, He performs outstandingly and in a manner beyond understanding. As is written in Genesis, *God made all things very good.*[8] In this way the praise which cannot be plumbed or measured is embraced in brief compass.

3. HE, VAV. *His work is praise and magnificence: and his justice continueth for ever and ever.* They now in turn explain how the Lord's work mentioned earlier is to be understood. *His work* is glory and beauty, as father Jerome has rendered it,[9] because what He does is extremely praiseworthy and beautiful. We have said that the sense of confession to be adopted here is that which unfolds in words of proclamation. Next comes: *And his justice continueth for ever and ever.* Here we must interpret the Lord's justice as the decree of the future Judgment which abides for ever. *His justice continues for ever and ever,* when He shall say to sinners: *Depart into eternal fire, which was prepared for the devil and his angels.*[10] *His justice continueth for ever and ever* when he shall summon the faithful with the words: *Come ye blessed of my Father, possess ye the kingdom prepared for you from the foundation of the world.*[11] Thus in both respects the Lord's justice continues abiding and unchangeable.

4. ZAIN, HETH. *He hath made a remembrance of his wonderful works, being a merciful and pitying Lord.* They come to the beginning of the second section, in which they show that those most faithful ones were nurtured by heavenly food, in other words, by the coming of the Lord Saviour. So *He made a remembrance of his wonderful works* when He manifested numerous things strange and unprecedented; it could then be clearly observed that God governs all things, when the normal courses of nature were seen to be changed by His sacred

commands. Only He who is known both to have created and to administer the courses of created things can actually change them. The words that follow, *being a merciful and pitying Lord*, are there to show who it was who *made a remembrance of his wonderful works. Merciful* reveals the nature of His devotion, *pitying* the time at which He showed mercy by His coming, and brought succour to the human race by generous devotion.

5. TETH, IOD. *He hath given food to them that fear him; he will be mindful for ever of his covenant.* The words: *He hath given food to them that fear him* essentially denote spiritual food, for who could think that the ordinary run of food was bestowed as a reward on the faithful when we know that it was given indiscriminately to sinners as well? In fact the next words: *He will be mindful for ever of his covenant*, are to ensure that you interpret this as the Lord Saviour's coming. *He will be mindful* expresses a human tendency, for a person is thought to have had something in mind when he fulfils a promise. *For ever* denotes eternity, for He maintains the words of His testament in most constant truth. Just as the Lord Saviour was promised in the Old Testament, so He deigned to come in the New, in which food was given *to them that fear him*, in other words, communion of His holy body and blood, the salvation of nations and the forgiveness of sins.

6. CAPH, LAMED. *He has announced to his people the power of his works, that he may give them the inheritance of the Gentiles.* The thought contained in the three verses is here filled out. *The power of his works* is that which he states in the gospel: *The blind see, the deaf hear, the lepers are cleansed, the dead rise again, and blessed is he that shall not be scandalised in me.*[12] He has announced, in other words, made plain, that is to the Christian people whom He redeemed with His precious blood. They express this with the spirit of prophecy, for with holy faith they believed in the Lord before His coming. He gave them *the inheritance of the Gentiles* when He fashioned the Catholic Church from living stones from all nations. This is the inheritance promised to Abraham: *I will multiply thy seed as the stars of heaven, and as the sand that is by the sea-shore.*[13] They revealed the reason why *he announced to his people the power of his works;* it was to give them the inheritance of the Gentiles. It was the purpose of the miracles that they should believe, and by believing obtain the promised rewards.

7. MEM, NUN. *The works of his hands are truth and judgment: all*

his commandments are faithful. The praises of the Lord are described in this and the following verse in most beautiful and varied sentiments. This is the twelfth type of definition which the Greeks call *kat'epainon* and the Latins *per laudem;*[14] for the works of His power emerge when He spares those who confess to Him, and He converts them from wickedness into blessedness, and again when He assigns due punishment to the obdurate. So the statement that His work is *truth and judgment* is apt. It is truth when He renders promises to the faithful, and judgment is the threat to the wicked, for those who neglect to perform His commands in this life will endure undying punishment in the next. The following words are: *All his commandments are faithful.* Scripture says: *Keep the commandments, and they shall preserve thee.*[15] They are faithful because His words show no divergence into falsehood; they preserve us wholly when by the Lord's help we hasten to keep them.

8. SAMECH, AIN. *Confirmed for ever and ever, made in truth and equity.* The words of men are vainly uttered and vanish; but God's word remains confirmed for ever, for what Truth utters cannot waver. Next comes: *Made in truth and equity.* The commands which were mentioned earlier they said were *made* rather than spoken; so that their worth should be made more apparent, they added: *In truth and equity.* The truth lies in the words being fulfilled, the equity in their being uttered with the weight of justice. Clearly His commands contain these virtues.

9. PHE, SADE, COPH. *He hath sent redemption to his people, he hath mandated his eternal covenant. Holy and terrible is his name.* Here an enthymematic syllogism, which we have frequently instanced earlier,[16] arises. The proposition is: *He hath sent redemption to his people, he hath commanded his covenant for ever.* The anticipated conclusion ensues: *Therefore holy and terrible is his name.* Let us listen to the rest that follows. They have reached the beginning of the third section, in which they proclaim that the Lord Saviour will come, and that He is worthy of fear, love, and praise in unremitting exultation. The words: *He hath sent redemption to his people,* are aptly used, for as captives they were seen to be in need of this; but the price was not one which a tyrant could exact, but one which the person who was forgiven could obtain. The captive gained his redemption; he who had been held in subjection obtained the greater price for it. Next comes: *He hath*

mandated his eternal covenant. We speak of mandating when instructions are given to absent people through intermediaries; this clearly happened when He transmitted the New Testament through the apostles and evangelists to the Gentiles. The word *eternal* is rightly used, because it denotes that no other testament will succeed it in the way in which the Old Testament was seen to be supplanted. The New Testament was a universal consummation, for it rendered the fullness which had been previously promised. Hence it is rightly called eternal, because it is seen to require nothing in addition. They added: *Holy and terrible is his name. Holy* has reference to the incarnation; as He Himself says: *Preserve my soul, for I am holy.*[17] *Terrible* indicates the omnipotence of the exalted Godhead; as another psalm has it: *Thou art terrible, and who shall resist thee?*[18] The two epithets have the purpose of making us love our Patron, and making us fear our Judge. The two are fittingly combined to ensure that love alone may not make us indifferent, and fear alone may not make us despair.

10. RES, SIN, TAV. *The fear of the Lord is the beginning of wisdom. A good understanding to all that do it. His praise continueth for ever and ever.* This is a fine definition of fear of the Lord, *the beginning of wisdom.* Through it we gain access to the Lord as though through a kind of gate. If we are untouched by fear of His judgment, we neglect the remedy of conversion. Let us fear His vengeance, that we may deserve to find His redeeming grace. Next comes: *A good understanding to all that do it.* To prevent your thinking of that wisdom as the human sort which wavers and vacillates in uncertain fortunes, they describe this heavenly wisdom as *good understanding,* that is, true and salutary understanding clearly not embraced by the wisdom described by Scripture as *the wisdom of this world is foolishness with God.*[19] So this is the understanding which is seen to concentrate on fear of the Lord, and which is useful and fruitful, for from it springs what is clearly conducive to enduring glory. They added: *His praise continueth for ever and ever.* Note how the whole purpose of the psalm is stated here. The faithful people, freed from the devil's wickedness, gave voice with thanks to the Lord to the sentiment of their devoted hearts; this is what men of piety must do in this life, and what the blessed as we know are to continue to do in the heavenly Jerusalem. His praise has no end, because His blessings can have no end. He is praised here on earth because He frees sinners; He is proclaimed in heaven because

He crowns those devoted to Him. So this psalm is seen rightly to have incorporated Alleluia in its heading, for it began with the Lord's praise and it likewise ends with His praise.

Conclusion Drawn From the Psalm

How splendidly has the most faithful people rejoiced! They brought joy to us as well in our hearing their joy, for our mental eagerness is enhanced when we drink in the sweet taste of another's joyful utterances. We must not think it idle that this delight of the faithful is set immediately after Psalm 109. Reflect on the sweetness and untroubled attitude of the singers, and you will discover here the image of that reward which the Lord promises to the labourers in the gospel, when He invited them to undertake toil in the vineyard through the gift of His summons. He himself is the denarius which is to be given to those who come early and late in the day.[20] He is the denarius because He bears the crown; He is the one denarius, because He shall have no end whatsoever. The beautiful perfection of the alphabet was added to this psalm so that instruction in the letters might be joined to the pleasure of such great joy.

Commentary on Psalm 111

1. *Alleluia. Of the return of Aggaeus and Zacharias.* Since the psalmist has already set down the bare Alleluia, let us examine what meaning is intended by these additional names. Aggaeus and Zacharias were prophets who prophesied after the transmigration from Babylon under king Darius, long after these verses were sung. When they returned to their native region of Jerusalem and saw the temple restored,[1] they poured forth the Lord's praises with great delight. To represent this, the present psalm as well as the previous one is seen to be interlaced with the letters of the entire alphabet as though with golden guiding-lines. The Christian is to sing this song with the most consummate joy after his sins are forgiven. Remember that this is the fourth psalm which instructs the faithful; it points out how great are

the blessings of the faithful after they are freed from sins, and what is the retribution suffered by the unfaithful.

Division of the Psalm

The prophet speaks throughout the psalm. In his initial admonition, he reveals what the blessed man is to do, and the great benefits which he merits through the Lord's grace; this embraces six letters. The second part points to the coming of the Lord Saviour by which mankind were enabled to become blessed for ever after being sinful and wicked. This section is seen to contain thirteen Hebrew letters. In the third part he attests that the opposite fate emerges for the wicked; this contains the remaining three letters.

Explanation of the Psalm

ALEPH, BETH. *Blessed is the man that feareth the Lord: he shall long exceedingly for his commandments.* The blessed man is brought into prominence in various ways, so that our search for him may not be abandoned through disregarding him; for we must regularly ponder in our minds the means by which we are sure to find eternal joy. Though there can be no blessedness dominated by fear in this world (for this makes people wretched instead) it is clear that no eternal joys are obtained unless they are preceded by fear of the Lord; this fear impels us to long for what can make us blessed. So what follows is: *He shall long exceedingly for his commandments.* Through fear of the Lord we can certainly ensure that He does not exclude us from His kingdom, for we exercise our fear by love of the Lord. *Blessed is the man that feareth the Lord* and what follows is an example of the twelfth type of definition which in Greek is called *kat'epainon* and in Latin *per laudem.*[2]

2. GIMEL, DALETH. *His seed shall be mighty on earth: the generation of the righteous shall be blessed.* The rewards of the blessed man earlier mentioned are now described. But since the Lord proclaims that the humble find the greatest favour with Him to the extent that the poor are called His just ones, we are to enquire in what land they are said to be made mighty, since they are known to be objects of

scorn here. The answer is in that land where the saints will share kingship with the Lord, where human riches or temporal distinctions will not make men mighty, but contemplation of the Lord and His unending praise. This is true might, for no weakness follows in its train. It maintains in eternal blessedness the status it has deserved. *Seed* denotes good works which are sown in this world like seeds so that the fruits of the harvest to come may spring up. *The generation of the righteous* is a splendid phrase; it refers not to physical descendants in this life, but to what we know is begotten by imitation of the just in performance of similar works. The devil too is said to have sinners as sons in the same way; they are told: *You are sons of the devil your father.*[3]

3. HE, VAV. *Glory and wealth shall be in his house; and his justice remaineth for ever and ever.* The earlier description of the benefits of the blessed man is continued. The house of the blessed man is the inner sanctum of the mind, in which all who fulfil the Lord's precepts store their sacred riches and enduring glory. That glory has no end; those riches do not vanish by malevolent theft, but emanate from the Lord's commands, and whatever is gained from them is preserved undamaged for ever. Finally comes: *And his justice remaineth for ever and ever.* Justice is said to be a person's attribute, but is granted by the Lord's gift. Though it is a universal term, it is noted as a personal possession when by divine ordinance it is granted to an individual and resides in him. So that none of us should think that he becomes blessed only for a time, the psalmist added: *Remaineth for ever and ever.* Up to this point the goodly possessions of the blessed man have been recounted; now the means of his becoming blessed are announced, so that he may not merely appear to have expressed an aspiration without also explaining the cause.

4. ZAIN, HETH. *To the righteous at heart, a light is risen up in darkness: the Lord is merciful, compassionate and just.* He comes to the second part of his admonition, in which the Lord's first coming is announced. This made those who confessed Him blessed, and condemned the proud for their wickedness. This coming of the Lord is described with wonderful aptness. A light comes which transcends all light; and he added: *In darkness*, so that it should be more welcome. This is not darkness caused by the sun's absence, but that which overshadows us with the presence of sins. This darkness is within the heart, where the sun of the universe cannot reach. It is dispelled by

that Light which conquered death and ground sins underfoot. The phrase, *to the righteous at heart*, implies that the unrighteous are withdrawn from this Light. Next comes: *The Lord is merciful, compassionate and just.* These words are few, but they take in the actions of all rational creatures. Those who confess find Him merciful, but those who despise the just man will undoubtedly find Him just.

5. TETH, IOD. *Sweet is the man that sheweth mercy and lendeth: he orders his words with judgment. Sweet* means not so much acceptable to men, as welcome to God. *That sheweth mercy,* that is, who gives to those in want. *Lendeth* means that one who is to obtain something in this world lends to those who look hopefully to him in their need. As the gospel has it: *Give to each that asketh of thee, and him that would borrow of thee reject not.*[4] Not the least financial help accorded to one in immediate difficulty is to take back only the amount of money which was advanced.[5] A possible interpretation, however, is that the mercy he shows—that is, his gift to the poor—he is seen to *lend,* for man bestows temporal gifts to recoup eternal ones. But though both expressions seem to refer to practical works of mercy, he is saying that we must not only take pity on the poor man by offering money, or lend it to those who hope for it; we must also offer every kindness of which the destitute person is seen to be in need. So we must energetically do everything which can help our neighbour. Next comes: *He orders his words with judgment.* Ordering of words signifies an untroubled and calm exposition recounted in a way that wins approval; for when the Father of the household comes, we must say to Him: *Lord, thou didst deliver to me five talents: behold I have gained another five over and above.*[6] So the person who *orders his words with judgment* is the person who proves that he has doubled the Lord's gifts, not he who has kept his talent buried with barren care and harmful thrift. This can also be a reference to him who through the Lord's gift has studied the divine scriptures, and either keeps them to himself in fruitless silence or diffuses them with saintly purpose.

6. CAPH, LAMED. *Because he shall not be moved for ever. The just shall be in everlasting remembrance.* He offers the reason why the just man orders his words with judgment: it is because *he shall not be moved for ever,* in other words, he will not be in any way separated from the Lord's glory. Next comes: *The just shall be in everlasting remembrance.* This will be precisely because he is summoned to his reward, whereas

the wicked are told: *I know you not.*[7] So just as those consigned to punishment are said to be forgotten, so the just because of the blessedness which they will attain are said to remain in the Lord's remembrance.

7. MEM, NUN. *He shall not fear the evil tidings: his heart is ready to hope in the Lord.* He means the evil tidings which the wicked shall hear: *Depart into everlasting fire,*[8] and the rest. The tidings seem evil to those who will be afflicted with just severity, for it is impious to claim that the judgment of the Lord is ever anything but just. So that you would not believe that only the blessed have no fear of harmful punishment, there follows: *His heart is ready to hope in the Lord,* so that those who by His aid have trodden underfoot the world's enticements may grasp what He has promised. To them he will say: *Come, blessed of my Father, possess the kingdom prepared for you from the beginning of the world.*[9] *Heart* is used to denote the feeling of the righteous mind, which can seek what was promised without hesitation.

8. SAMECH, AIN. *His heart is strengthened: he shall not be moved until he gazes at his enemies.* Because the heart of the blessed man had been ready to hope in the Lord, the addition follows: *His heart is strengthened.* He despises all transient things, for he is filled with that other delight. The heart of the just man is strengthened, then, when he is not made soft by any success in this world. When he gazes on the power of enemies here, he awaits instead their downfall. He endures the sight of his enemies wielding power in this world so that he can see them humbled in the next. But though here we observe physical enemies battling with us in opposition, he wishes us to understand those enemies as acts of spiritual wickedness which we do not observe here but which we shall certainly identify at the Judgment. When he says: *Until he gazes at his enemies,* we must understand "humiliated and repentant." What a blessed dispensation of the Creator! He makes them appear broken, when they can be scorned rather than feared by us.

9. PHE, SADE, COPH. *He hath distributed, he hath given to the poor: his justice remaineth for ever and ever: his horn shall be exalted in glory.* This statement is relevant to the Lord's precept: *If thou wilt be perfect, sell all that thou hast, and give to the poor; and come, follow me.*[10] This is the distribution which blessedly accumulates, this is the payment which purchases the kingdom of heaven. The person who does

this performs justice because he has fulfilled the injunctions of the Lord, and the Lord ever remains in him, for he received eternal gifts from the Creator who founded the world. Next comes: *His horn shall be exalted in glory.* We have already often said that *horn* stands for power, as the prophet Daniel attests with the words: *The four horns are four kingdoms.*[11] How vital it is to give in the next world to those seen to be prostrate in devoted humility in this life! So far he has spoken of the advantages of the blessed; now he ends the psalm with the affliction of the wicked.

10. RES, SIN, TAV. *The sinner shall see, and is angry: he gnashes his teeth, and pines away: the desire of sinners shall perish.* After he has described the blessed man and his rewards, in the third section he drew attention to the envy of sinners. This figure is called a *paradigm,*[12] when we are encouraged by the happy lot of the blessed, and deterred by examples of the wicked. This figure is found in all these psalms which tell of the disposition of the blessed, though we find it aptly used elsewhere too from time to time; for example, it is clearly exploited in Psalm 1. *Is angry* bears the additional sense of "with himself," for such sinners refused to be raised clear of their wickedness. They realised that they had earlier been too complacent about their transient glory and fleeting power. They saw that others were gaining the blessedness which can never at any time end. Their anger was justified, their indignation genuine, but it was unprofitable in the hour of vengeance. They could only have avoided indignation then if they had become hostile to their vices here. Next comes: *He gnashes his teeth, and pines away.* It is the envious sinner wave-tossed on his malevolence who is described here, for he holds fast to the evil of his anger but can do no-one any further harm. Here he was wickedly roused to harm his neighbour, but at the Judgment he is justly angry with himself, for he is punished for his own ill-will. So Isaiah remarks: *There is no peace for the wicked, says the Lord.*[13] The grinding of his teeth causes him to pine away, his vehemence causes him to grow faint. He bites himself with his own teeth, punishes himself with self-inflicted pain, exacting from himself the tortures which in this life he compelled the innocent to endure. The psalmist added: *The desire of sinners shall perish,* because just as the longings of the blessed will come to fruition when planted in the Lord's kingdom, so the desires of sinners are lopped away and wither.

Conclusion Drawn From the Psalm

How beautifully was this blessed man described through the progression of the alphabet, so that his deeds and his rewards were simultaneously recounted! Who would not believe that he beholds the promises bestowed by the sacred Truth? May He lead us to accept what He has already allowed us to hear. This alphabet, by which this poem was completed, undoubtedly points the way to the perfection of wisdom. Through it an understanding of divine affairs is acknowledged, and the fault of ignorance avoided. It is thus clear that the psalms show a variety of differing sweetness, so that our human weakness as we advance in learning cannot be overcome with distaste.

COMMENTARY ON PSALM 112

Alleluia. Observe how the psalm as it proceeds explains the heading. Since Alleluia means "Praise the Lord," this is how our true teacher and outstanding doctor began. His words cannot mislead because they are known to flow from the fount of truth. How can any statement be more certain than when he who guides our actions is seen to be his own spokesman?

Division of the Psalm

The prophet David runs briefly through the words of the psalm. In the first section he urges the devoted to discharge praises continually to the Lord, and not to cease proclaiming Him throughout the whole world. In the second part he himself carries out what he urges others to do, so that he is seen to be a true master, teaching not by word but by example.

Explanation of the Psalm

1. *Praise the Lord, ye children: praise ye the name of the Lord.* The label *children* is known to be applied to the simplest and purest, for the

Lord himself is called a Child, as in the passage: *Unto us a child is born.*[1] Clearly this period of life was chosen by the Lord for its innocence, for He says to His disciples: *Suffer little children to come unto me, for of such is the kingdom of heaven.*[2] So the prophet does well to urge those persons to sing praises to the Lord who are seen to embark on them with pure hearts; it is not their age but their piety which is singled out. Note too that there is a certain difference in the repetition here. That person praises the Lord who commends himself by praiseworthy action; he praises the Lord's name too when he joins in celebrating the Lord's virtues in pious proclamation.

2. *Blessed be the name of the Lord from henceforth, now and for ever.* In case the children chance to think that merely momentary praise is enjoined on them, he states that He is to be proclaimed now in this world, and praised also in the eternity to come. So that this cannot be understood in a purely local sense either, he states in what follows how He is to be praised everywhere.

3. *From the rising of the sun unto the going down, praise the name of the Lord.* Here he points to the whole Church, so that Christ's praises may not be unheard throughout the whole world which He fashioned. The Lord's warning is just, his imposition is salutary. The creation must acknowledge its Creator, and magnify Him so that He ever swells in its praises. This figure is called *periphrasis,* in Latin *per circuitum;*[3] the world is described in some places by a circle, in others by the four cardinal points, and here by the course of the sun, as though it were a straight line.

4. *The Lord is high above all nations, and his glory above the heavens.* He wishes us to understand all creatures by these two divisions. Let us take *nations* as all earthly things, and by *heavens* understand all heavenly things. He is known to be high above all things, for the heavens themselves are subject to Him. As we read in another psalm: *Be thou exalted, O God, above the heavens, and thy glory over all the earth.*[4] Alternatively, we are to take *nations* as fleshly creatures and *heavens* as spiritual beings, so that He who is known to be the Founder of all things may be perceived to be the Highest, above all creatures.

5. *Who is as the Lord our God, who dwelleth on high?* He passes to the second section, in which he now joyfully discharges the Lord's praises through His deeds. The use of *who* denotes that there is no other who

glories so much in the personal majesty of His power. *Who dwelleth on high* means among His lofty creatures, whom He makes great by deigning to dwell among them. They are the good angels, His saints and the other powers which attain grandeur by the dignity of His presence. Now observe what follows, to prevent your thinking that this Majesty seeks to despise lowly things.

6. *And looketh down on the low things, in heaven and in earth.* The earlier words, *who dwelleth on high,* are explained. He looks down on lowly things so that by His gift they may always become most high. His seat is above devoted lowliness; He visits the humility which puts no hope in itself, but presumes on the Lord's generosity alone. You must interpret this lowliness as a mental attitude rather than as a physical position on the earth, for the next words are *in heaven and in earth,* and what is lowliness in heaven other than the humility by which the holy angels won approval? All heaven's virtues are raised high by that praise. Whatever is faithfully humble is known to be the seat of God's abode and eternal power. *In earth* denotes the holy men of whom Scripture says: *Upon whom does my spirit rest, but on him that is humble and unheard, and who trembles at my words?*[5] Thus lowliness pleasing to God is found in heaven and on earth, just as that pride is found hateful by which the devil fell, and by which men are plunged into the depths of hell. Let those who are puffed up blush with shame, and having listened to the reason, rebuke themselves. Where are they to believe that pride has a place, once they see heaven and earth occupied by humility?

7. *Raising up the needy from the earth, and lifting up the poor out of the dunghill.* Those in need and want should not claim this benefit solely for themselves, for anyone who through God's grace is raised from this blemished body, is exalted from the dunghill and from poverty. In fact, even a king in this world is empty of God's gifts and rolls in the dung, for vices of the flesh are his master. So the Lord raises up those of any rank or age when He bestows the gifts of His mercy.

8. *That he may place him with princes, with the princes of his people.* He makes clear the goal which can be attained by this raising of the poor and needy; they are to be placed *with the princes of his people.* These princes of the people are the patriarchs, prophets, apostles, and all who have been pleasing to God by their praiseworthy life. But you

are not to believe that the preeminence mentioned here is the distinction sought by human aspirations; rather, it is the preeminence granted by the Lord's generosity which is lofty in humility, certain in faith, unflinching in mental strength. As for the addition: *Of his people*, it points to the Catholic Church spread through the whole world.

9. *Who maketh a barren woman to dwell in a house: the joyful mother of children.* Here the earlier ideas are brought to an end, and there is beauty in the closing words. He explains where *raising up the needy from the earth, and lifting up the poor out of the dunghill to place him with princes, the princes of his people*, can take place. It is in the Church, which before the coming of her Bridegroom had been barren, but she became *the joyful mother of children* when at the apostles' preaching she brought forth abundant offspring throughout the whole world, by water and the holy Spirit. Earlier she was dusky, but now she is beautiful. Through that most fecund water she bears children whilst still maintaining her virginity gloriously unimpaired. So she was the barren woman whom the Lord made to dwell rejoicing in His house; her joy was caused by her childbearing and by the number of saints.

Conclusion Drawn From the Psalm

It causes me great wonder whenever I come upon this number, so full of the glory of great mysteries. The aggregate[6] embraces the number of apostles; it separated the people of Israel into tribes, denoting as father Jerome says[7] that the number twelve is the sign of future blessedness. For example, the apostles take first place, the prophets second, the martyrs third, infants carried off after baptism fourth, virgins fifth, the truly penitent sixth, and so on with different degrees of merit down to twelfth place. Paul seems to be referring to this when he says: *One is the glory of the sun, another the glory of the moon, another the glory of the stars.*[8] And elsewhere: *Star differeth from star in brightness; so also will be the resurrection of the dead.*[9] So this psalm, established as twelfth after the hundredth, promises us the shape of our future blessedness; for it commands that the Lord be continually praised by children, in order to depict a parallel to that eternal joy.

Commentary on Psalm 113

Alleluia. Many of the preceding psalms and others which are to follow are prefaced by *Alleluia,* and the adornment of so many psalms with this heading seems hardly otiose. Just as in a melody this one general term embraces various tones, so the one word Alleluia incorporates manifold motives for expressing the force of its proclamation. There is more than one way of saying, "Bless the Lord," and just as this praise is assembled from different actions, so *Alleluia* is applied to various forms of activity and to appropriate discourses. The purpose of this psalm is to proclaim the perfection of the Law, in other words the Lord Christ, manifested to the world by mighty miracles from the beginnings of the Jewish nation; and the parallels between their situation and ours show that every Christian today is likewise set free.

Division of the Psalm

The prophet speaks throughout the psalm. In the first section he recounts the miracles which the Lord bestowed on the Jews and on the Christian people. In the second he asks in the form of a question why the sea fled, and why the Jordan held back its course; to this he attaches the most pleasing reply that the earth was moved by the presence of the Lord. In the third section he shows that the idols of the Gentiles were unprofitable to their worshippers, and he then explains how useful and most wholesome is the Lord's religion to those who espouse it.

Explanation of the Psalm

1. *At the departure of Israel from Egypt, the house of Jacob from a barbarous people.* We must here interpret *departure* as the time when we emerge from the chains of sins. We are freed from the mob of the Egyptians—in other words, of the demons—when we no longer endure the sovereignty of their barbaric harshness, when the ostentation

of this world has begun to be banished from our minds. *Barbarus* (barbarous) derives from *barba* (beard) and *rus* (country),[1] because the barbarous person has never lived in the city, but is known to have dwelt always like a wild beast in the country. We are truly transformed into *the house of Jacob* when we preserve the precepts of Christian belief.

2. *Judaea was made his sanctuary, Israel his power: Israel reigned in it.* We are to realise that the three phrases in this verse have separate explanations. We have said that Judaea refers not merely to the Jewish nation, but can embrace all the faithful; the Lord Saviour is the true Judah, for in Him the kingdom and enduring power of the Israelites —which means those who behold God—is known to lie. So those who follow Him and are circumcised inwardly are rightly called *Judaei*. Israel is called His power because He showed in her the great marvels of His strength; for where does He not have power, since he does all that He wishes in heaven and on earth? Next comes: *Israel reigned in it*, that is to say, "he who beheld God" reigned in that blessed gathering where all the saints are to gather in their entirety.

3. *The sea saw, and fled: Jordan was turned back.* The prophet realised that he was overwhelmed by the great weight of mighty miracles, and so by these two allusions he embraced with the most comprehensive brevity the sources of all vices. We have often said that the sea must be interpreted as the sinners of this world, who like waves swell with bombastic thoughts. *Jordan* we must regard as each and every river which sweeps men away on various desires, and sacrilegiously bears them headlong into the mighty sea. These two, sea and river, which had borne the human race away on diverse pleasures, then witnessed the Lord's coming, and abandoning their practices they made their way back with frantic haste. Though this is recounted in the Old Testament, it is alluded to here in different words and similes, so we can clearly realise that those events of old announced with spiritual understanding the signs of our salvation.

4. *The mountains skipped like rams, and the hills like the lambs of the flock.* Gradually and more clearly he passes to Christian times. Clearly *mountains* can be interpreted as the apostles and evangelists, or all preachers of the word, for they received the heavenly light earlier than the remainder of the lands. They are rightly called mountains because of the towering peak of their holiness and the most solidly based

strength of their faith. They *skipped like rams* as they performed their works, for they were leading the most faithful flock to the Lord's pens with divine help. *Hills* denotes the modest height of widespread believers, whose hearts effectively received the seeds of faith; the word *colles* (hills) gets its name from *colere*, to worship.[2] Reason itself forces us to interpret these words in the spiritual sense, for if taken literally they are seen to be wholly absurd. So observe how pleasantly the earlier parallels are apparently guided towards this sense, so that all are consistent with each other in these most beautiful comparisons.

5. *Why was it, O sea, that thou didst flee? And thou, O Jordan, why wast thou turned backward?* He embarks on the second narrative, which is introduced by a fine question so that the sweetest of replies may follow. This figure is called *peusis kai apokrisis*, or in Latin *percunctatio atque responsio*.[3] The sea is asked, and the river questioned, why they abandoned their usual behaviour to the extent of halting their courses, whereas previously they enveloped and bore off everything. *Backward* is a laudable addition, for we experience comprehensive correction when through the Lord's kindness our practices change direction. This verse: *Why was it, O sea, that thou didst flee? And thou, O Jordan, why wast thou turned backward?* is virtually a repetition of the earlier one.[4] This is another figure, called *epanodos*,[5] or repetition of topics joined to each other.

6. *Ye mountains, why did ye step like rams, and ye hills, like lambs of the flock?* He has maintained the order of the earlier verses. They are set down here as we see them recounted in the first section, but in a different form. First he asks the world through the sea and river why its bonds were loosed, and since the one reply is to follow, he addresses the same question to hills and mountains, which were notably seen to have been skipping. It was the one Creator who made sea and river halt in amazement, and mountains and hills rejoice in their implanted joy.

7. *Before the face of the Lord the earth was moved, at the presence of the God of Jacob.* Here followed the appropriate reply adduced to both questions. Listen, you who are converted; listen, most faithful Christians, to this movement or transformation which happily befell this earth which is the human race. It was caused not by the tremor of mountains but by the profitable conversion of peoples. If you ask the identity of the Lord, he is *the God of Jacob.* When He appeared in

mercy, before His face, in other words, in His presence, the earth which had previously stiffened in the sluggish stupor of death experienced salutary movement. It was dislodged from its superstition to remain implanted with eternal strength in the Lord's worship.

8. *Who turned the rock into pools of water, and the cliffs into fountains of waters.* We must, I think, interpret *rock* as the Jews' obstinacy, which He turned into the pools of sacred baptism when He caused them to pass to untroubled religion. The Lord cites this parallel in the gospel: *The Lord is able from these stones to raise up children to Abraham.*[6] He also made *cliffs*, in other words, the barren and hard hearts of the Gentiles, into watered fountains of divine eloquence, for whereas previously they were arid in barren superstitions, they were later heard pouring forth abundant proclamations of the heavenly word. Up to this point the verses, as we recognise, have been cited by means of the figure of *parabole*.[7]

9. *Not to us, O Lord, not to us, but to thy name give glory, for thy mercy and thy truth's sake.* After his recounting the many kindnesses which the Lord Christ had granted for our benefit, a most genuine and loving request follows, that for His name's sake He should bestow things of profit on the human race, since He certainly could not find laudable merits in the persons of sinners. Though He heaps blessings on the undeserving, we know that what He grants redounds to His own praise. Next comes: *For thy mercy and thy truth's sake.* He asks that the Lord's glory be assigned to these two attributes. His mercy appears when He forgives the sins of the wretched and errant, His truth when He fulfils the promises of future blessedness, or alternatively, as others have it, when He judges the wicked. Clearly both His sparing and His judging enhance the Lord's glory.

10. *Lest the Gentiles should say: Where is their God?* There follows here the reason why the Lord deigns to bestow the gifts of His mercy on those devoted to Him. This figure is called *aetiologia*[8] or the rendering of the reason. He is asking that the wicked allegation very often endured by Christians in this world should be removed; for whenever the bodies of martyrs are tortured by various punishments, this is what tyrants and pagans say: *Where is their God?* as though He cannot rescue those whom He allows to endure tortures so that He can crown them.

11. *But our God is aloft in heaven: he hath done all things in heaven*

and on earth, whatsoever he would. Against the words of mad pagans who ask: *Where is your God?* this most true and complete statement is uttered, that our God does all things that He wills in heaven and on earth. The phrase, *aloft in heaven,* shows Him as powerful over all creatures. Next comes the statement that He does all that He has purposed to do towards His creatures greatest and smallest, so that you may realise that He is almighty, since He everywhere manifests the outcome of His will.

12. *The idols of the Gentiles are silver and gold, the works of the hands of men.* We come to the third narration, in which the prophet mocks the idols of the Gentiles, and hymns the Lord of Israel with apt praise. This kind of pleading is called "demonstrative," and is known to embrace both praise and blame.[9] He jeers at the pagans' gods in five verses, but praises God on high in ten, so that by the very number of words he may demonstrate the difference between the two. But since he had earlier said that God is invisible, performing all that He wishes, here he rightly says that idols are worthy of mockery, for they are fashioned to human shape but known to be strangers to bodily feelings. Though idols of bronze and wood are found, he chose metal of higher value such as pagans regarded as worthy of more reverent adoration. This was so that they would feel shame at worshipping the more tawdry kind, when those formed of precious metal are seen to be despicable. So that you would not think that these statues possess a live existence of any kind, it is stated that those gods were fashioned by pagans' hands, to denote their tawdriness. It is shameful to state that a statue is worshipped by one whose Creator could be identified. How could an idol benefit a man when it could not have existed had he not so desired? Jeremiah too incorporated such lunacy in a fine definition when he said: *It will be nothing save what the goldsmiths wish it to be.*[10] We must repeat to these worshippers those verses of Sedulius, who is the poet so to say of truth: "Wooden one, you make entreaty to logs of wood; you are seen to cry out to the deaf; you seek replies from the dumb."[11] If you seek to discover the true nature of God, listen to Isaiah as he speaks: *I the Lord, this is my name for ever. I will not give my glory to another, nor my powers to graven things. The things that are from the beginning, behold they come to pass as new things, which I shall declare: and before I revealed them I have made you hear them. For I am. Before me there was no other God, and none will be after me.*[12]

13. *They have mouths, and will speak not: they have eyes, and will see not.* 14. *They have ears, and will hear not: they have noses, and will smell not.* 15. *They have hands, and will feel not: they have feet, and will walk not. They shall not cry out in their throats: there is no breath in their mouths.* The most truthful account in these three verses censured those who sought foolishly to allot human limbs to their false gods. What need of a mouth, I ask, had the idol which could not speak? What need of eyes, when it could not see? What need of ears, when it was not to hear? What need of nostrils, when it got no whiff of fragrance? (*Nares,* nostrils, get their name from *gnaritas,*[13] awareness, because they make us recognise smells.) What need of hands, when it knew nothing of things which can be felt? Or feet, when it could not bestir itself? To increase the mockery in all this, he added that they should not be compared even with animals that lack reason, for they have not even a confused cry in their throats, such as cattle are wont to make with their peculiar utterances. There follows the statement which rounds off the whole description, saying that the idols are found unworthy of comparison with men or beasts, because *there is no breath in their mouths.* Undoubtedly utterance, articulated or indistinguishable, is the mark of living creatures; this long catalogue has been most aptly devoted to these matters so that the taunts against pagans should not be brought quickly to a close.

16. *Let them that make them become like unto them; and all such as trust in them.* Perhaps the pagan hears this and rejoices that he is compared to his deities. But he must realise what profit he could gain from such patronage, for he has deserved to pass from the status of rational man to that of metals without sensation. He must realise that his worship has changed into his own damnation, and he must shrink from adoring the idol from which he is seen to have incurred a judgment which brings punishment. Those who have decided to follow such a course are to become like those idols. We must not omit the fact that those who fashion and worship idols are known to be broken with them by the one decree; for it is a parallel wickedness to deceive others by one's works and to bind oneself by nefarious worship. Paul says of these men: *Who changed the truth of God into a lie, and worshipped and served the creature rather than the Creator, who is blessed for ever.*[14] Here too the figure called *sarcasmos,*[15] forceful derision of an

opponent, which we identify as hitting the target of the faults themselves, is seen to be apt.

17. *The house of Israel hath hoped in the Lord: he is their helper and their protector.* Now that he has condemned the wicked deeds of the unfaithful, he joyfully proceeds to praises of the Lord. We know that *the house of Israel* denotes the Church of the faithful people. She hopes in the Lord, for she ever rejects worldly desires and enjoys delight in Him alone. He next explains the benefit accruing to her: He becomes her Helper and Protector whom all creation is known to serve. He is her Helper because He helps those toiling in the flesh in this world in so far as He knows it is useful, and her Protector since He does not allow holy souls to be brought down by any of the devil's guile.

18. *The house of Aaron hath hoped in the Lord: he is their helper and their protector.* He has now revised the general statement in the previous verse, and with splendid repetition has applied it to the priests, so that their exalted rank could be praised not by general mention but by specific proclamation; for Aaron was the first to be chosen as priest among the Jewish people, and by mention of him the order of priests is aptly denoted.

19. *They that fear the Lord must hope in the Lord: he is their helper and their protector.* He has explained the previous phrases, *house of Israel* and *house of Aaron,* for they are the ones who fear and hope in the Lord. These are the two attitudes which make men blessed and happy, and the earlier statement that the Lord is their Helper and Protector is the benefit which they receive.

20. *The Lord hath been mindful of us, and hath blessed us. He hath blessed the house of Israel; he hath blessed the house of Aaron.* He reiterates the same words with fine variation, so that we should believe that the Lord's blessing is granted to such persons by emphasising the reason; for when he says that the Lord was mindful of us, he reveals the grace bestowed by divine devotion. To what possible merits was the Lord Christ's coming owed, that He should both teach erring people and by His blessing save those who turned to Him? *He blessed the house of Israel* by being born of the virginity of saint Mary. He also *blessed the house of Aaron* when He invested himself with the distinction of the priesthood. As another psalm says of Him: *Thou art a priest for ever, according to the order of Melchisedech.*[16]

21. *He has blessed all that fear the Lord, both little and great.* After these specific references, he mounts to the level of the general blessing, where all who have chosen to serve the Lord with pure hearts are blessed in common. He did this in the case of fishermen and of kings, and no class of men who believe in Him is known to be excluded as strangers to His gifts. This figure is known as *anacephaleosis* or recapitulation,[17] when what has been earlier stated more broadly is later recalled to mind briefly.

22. *May the Lord add blessings upon you: upon you and upon your children. Add* seems to have a double sense, referring to the blessing which God for His part bestows on holy ones in this world, or to the additional faithful accruing to your numbers. He achieves this unceasingly in our day and until the world's end, so that the Church as predestined may rejoice when gathered from the nations into one flock, and may enjoy the splendid rule of the one Shepherd.

23. *Blessed be you by the Lord, who made heaven and earth.* Though earlier the prophet has prayed that the faithful might be blessed, he now trusts in that predestination, and says that those who are most just are blessed. Observe the nature of the blessing. He wrote *by the Lord* because the perfection of blessedness is not that a person should be so equipped by his own efforts, but by the Lord. The hearts of the faithful are strengthened by the Word, and the possible source of future blessedness is revealed by it. *Who made heaven and earth* denotes the Word by whose action every creature is perfected; or *the little and the great* mentioned earlier, who by His mercy have attained the joys of the Catholic religion.

24. *The heaven of heavens is the Lord's, but the earth he has given to the children of men.* Since heaven is the term for just men, the Lord Christ is aptly called the heaven of heavens, as He is called the Holy of the holy, the God of gods, and other grandiloquent expressions of this kind. *Caelum* (heaven) gets its name from concealing (*celare*)[18] all things within itself. Whereas the heaven of heavens is attributed to the Lord—as we read in Psalm 67: *Who mounteth above the heaven of heavens from the east*[19]—the earth is allotted to the children of men, so that by the Lord's grace they may there purify themselves by manifold struggles and from the contest of the world attain eternal life. *He has given* has reference to Christ's humanity in the incarnation; for what

could be given to the Word, who with the Father and the holy Spirit has always possessed and possesses all things?

25. *The dead shall not praise thee, O Lord, nor all that go down to hell.* He speaks here of those dead who will be afflicted by enduring tortures. The Lord does not heed their voices, for only those who will sound forth His praises are blessed. As Solomon says: *Confession perisheth from the dead as though from one who does not exist,* and a little later: *But we who are alive and in health praise thy name.*[20] By saying: *Nor all that go down to hell,* he shows that even the saints descend to hell, but that they rejoice in the Lord's praise. Death is known to be the common lot of the just and of sinners, but they are segregated by an extremely long distance. As was said in Psalm 85: *Thou hast delivered my soul out of the lowest hell.*[21]

26. *But we that live bless the Lord, from this time now and for ever.* Now that he has explained the lot of the damned, it was appropriate that the good fortune of the blessed should end this beautiful psalm, for He is Lord of the living and not of the dead. As we read in the gospel: *He is not the God of the dead, but of the living.*[22] But we must understand by the living not the life that we live on earth, which the saints obviously share with the ungodly, but the life of which we read in another psalm: *I will please the Lord in the land of the living.*[23] His human mind avoids descending to earthly goods by rising fittingly to the things of heaven. They can have no end of praises, nor bear any diminution of rewards.

Conclusion Drawn From the Psalm

Like the most beautiful seeds of the pomegranate, these events when stripped of the peel of history have exuded the sweetest honey. There are as many pleasures as there are verses, as many fruits for the soul as there are words. By the comparisons with the people of old, we are warned to abandon the tyranny of this world like the tyranny of Egypt, so that we can attain the land of promise by the route of baptism. Let us fearlessly hasten on; the obstacles confronting us have been dissolved by the Lord's coming. The sea has fled, the Jordan has turned back in fear, the idols of the Gentiles are despised as metal without feeling. The glory of our Lord is worshipped and proclaimed everywhere. So with God's help let us most eagerly seek out the virtues of the psalms, since they both reveal themselves to the faithful and always conceal themselves from unbelievers.

Commentary on Psalm 114

Alleluia. This solemn and genuine admonition rouses us from our sleep in this world, and like some spiritual cock compels us to attend to the works of the faithful. Let us hear this holy utterance, follow the devoted command, and abandon what is ungodly; for praise of the Lord is worthy activity and a reward for toils, since nothing sweeter can be uttered and nothing more wholesome regularly performed.

Division of the Psalm

The prophet has been rescued from the deep pit of sins. While he still stands on the rock of mercy, he gives thanks in the first section because he knows that he has been heard, and he attests that he has successfully invoked the Lord in the face of all death's dangers. In the second section he again cries to the Lord, so that now freed he may attain the eternal rest which he guarantees is to be granted to the faithful by the Lord's gift.

Explanation of the Psalm

1. *I have loved, because the Lord has heard the voice of my prayer.* We know that the Lord's love comes to men under two heads. The first is when He is loved and praised even by the unfaithful for the benefits He has bestowed; as we read of the sinner in another psalm: *He will praise thee when thou shalt do well to him.*[1] The other is the most certain and perfect, when the mind of one devoted to Him is cast down by no adversity caused by the ills befalling him, but in his love of the Lord is

ever fired in the course of his miseries by hope of what is to come. As Paul says: *Who shall separate us from the love of Christ? Shall tribulation? Or distress? Or persecution? Or famine? Or nakedness?*[2] and the rest. So the prophet later explains the attitude of showing love in the midst of afflictions and hardships, because the tribulations and pains bestowed on him the merit of calling on the Lord. So David joyfully exults not in the breadth of his kingdom, and not in worldly happiness, which he knew would fade; but he rejoices that his prayer uttered in hardship has been heard by the most merciful Lord, and he realised that this was of enduring benefit to him. Observe the economy with which he both stated his case and appended the reason for it with the speed of a moment. This figure is called *epitrochasmos*[3] or round statement, which draws together what has to be said, briefly and succinctly.

2. *Because he hath inclined his ear unto me, and in my days I will call upon him. Auris* (ear) gets its name, as we have already said, from *auditus* (hearing).[4] The Lord is aptly said to incline His ear to us, for clearly no human merits cause Him to deign to listen to us. The authority of Truth Itself relates that this occurred at the Lord's coming, when He took pity on the sins of the world and bestowed the healing of the blessed incarnation. Since the prophet had begun to sense the Lord's most abundant devotion around him when he was racked by many tribulations in his days, as he says later in the verse, he proclaims that he called upon the Lord. We label as ours those days when we sin through our own wickedness, and through evil thoughts endure troubled griefs. It is a marvellous statement and a blessed interchange that the faithful man should ever seek blessings, and that the merciful Lord should bestow them with unceasing kindness.

3. *The sorrows of death have compassed me: and the perils of hell have found me.* He is still giving the most fitting reasons why the holy man loved the Lord. These are not the reasons on account of which human persons think they are loved when riding high with haughty distractions or waxing proud with heaps of riches. Rather, he says that he has been attended by God's grace because he was seen to be troubled by griefs and dangers; and rightly so, for these experiences lead to glory, while those earlier ones send us headlong to destruction. Observe how the words though simple are filled with pregnant meanings. He

says he is compassed with *sorrows,* adding *of death* to prevent your thinking that they are modest ones. He further added: *The perils of hell,* known to be more grievous than all tortures. Also following are the words: *Have found me,* implying that I was unprepared, untroubled, and lying outside the Lord's protection; and since he happened to be isolated from such great protection, he was easily exposed to capture.

4. *I found trouble and sorrow: and I called upon the name of the Lord.* You hear the words *trouble and sorrow,* and perhaps you are alienated, but realise what riches this treasure-house bears. These are the troubles which caused him to exclaim to the Lord, these are the sorrows which remedially pierced men's hearts, with the result that the sick man cried out to the true Physician from whom it is certain that reliable aid comes. Notice what outcome the reversal of words brings. Earlier when he was captured, he says that he *was found* by griefs; here when he obtains the remedy, he maintains that he *found* troubles. He becomes aware of the causes of his calamity, for he realises that he has been afflicted so that he may be converted. It is when some disease is felt to be oppressing our inward organs that the doctor is summoned. Next comes: *And I called upon the name of the Lord,* that by His help the sorrow and grief could be quickly overcome.

5. *O Lord, deliver my soul! The Lord is merciful and just, and our God will show mercy.* Having recounted his sufferings, the prophet passes to the second section, in which he cries out to the Lord, asking that his soul be freed from the depth of sins. As Paul says: *Who will free me from the body of this death? The grace of God through our Lord Jesus Christ.*[5] This figure is called *proanaphonesis,*[6] in Latin *exclamatio,* whenever in the course of our speech we suddenly address our words to God. So let us through God's gift examine our afflictions and griefs most carefully, for they lurk quite deep below the surface, often being cloaked by delight in the world and lying asleep. Unless we search them out with divine help, we cannot utter this saving cry within us. When he says: *Deliver my soul,* he admits that without the Lord it is always a prisoner. Next comes: *The Lord is merciful and just, and our God will show mercy.* In the first sentence of the verse he sought the deliverance of his soul, but here he promises that the Lord is merciful and just. He wished to avoid the impression of uncertainty in that

request, and did not want others to be on tenterhooks in the anxiety of their desire. The Lord is *merciful* because He inclined His ear to him, and *just* because He coerced the sinner to seek pardon. He *will show mercy,* for He accepts the son whom He scourges.[7] So realise that these three statements are made to instruct the frailty of the human race, which gapes admiringly at worldly delights, and thinks that pains bestowed for the soul's salvation are harsh.

6. *The Lord guards the little ones. I was humbled, and he delivered me.* He has reversed the order of the previous statement to point to something of great importance. First he asked that his soul be delivered, and then proclaimed the merciful Lord in general terms. Now he states by way of generalisation that He is the guardian of little ones, and then proclaims that he has been humbled and freed. This order of topics was intended to show what we read in the gospel, that though the Lord's flock is gathered from many nations, it is one flock and it has one Shepherd.[8] *The little ones* are they who seem indubitably insignificant in their own eyes, and swell only through the Lord's generosity. Observe the nature of the word *guards,* suggesting an outstanding shepherd defending his flock from the plundering attack of the wolf. But note that he preserves the appropriate order, saying that he was first humbled and later delivered; thus men cannot be resentful at their wounds, for by the heavenly Physician's gift they have been healed.

7. *Turn, my soul, into thy rest, for the Lord has been bountiful to me.* The soul which is alienated from the Lord should sing this in company with the prophet; the sheep which had wandered and had merited a return to the pens, borne on the shoulders of the Protector,[9] should also sing it. So should the son who was dead and has come to life again, who had been lost and was found.[10] So should the devoted people who have been redeemed by His precious blood, and have through the Lord's generosity gained the attainment of the rest for which they longed. So the prophet urges his soul to turn to the Lord, from whom come to him both peaceful rest and the removal of sins. So the rest of which he speaks is given to him by grace, and not possessed in token of his merits. So the following words are: *For the Lord has been bountiful to me.*

8. *For he hath delivered my soul from death, my eyes from tears, my*

feet from falling. The reasons are stated why he said earlier: *For the Lord has been bountiful to me.* But we must understand that the prophet says this with reference to the future by virtue of his foreknowledge, for the words cannot be appropriate to those living in this world; for he says: *He has delivered my soul from death.* When the souls of the just pass from this world, they are freed from that death of which the gospel says: *Let the dead bury their dead.*[11] When he says: *He hath delivered,* he reveals the blessing conferred by God's strength, for he could have been delivered from enduring death only by His power. Next comes: *My eyes from tears.* The tears of the saints dry up precisely when the soul's death is found to be no longer anticipated. Lamentation occurs not in untroubled tranquillity, but in the struggle here where we fear ensuing disaster. He added: *My feet from falling.* When he speaks of *falling,* he shows that sin involves slipping and declining; but such tumbling is rightly not feared in the region of eternal happiness. As has been said, it is when stationed in this world that just men fear the soul's death and continually shed tears, and do not consider their feet in any sense secure from falling. In this world life is a struggle, and so all things are subject to fear; we accordingly realise that the human race is here exposed to three dangers, because it is still involved in this life's struggle; for note what follows.

9. *I will please the Lord in the land of the living.* We must study the reason why he said: *I will please the Lord in the land of the living* with reference to the future, with the implication that the holy men praised by the Judge's words are not pleasing here in the land of the dead, though we read in Genesis: *Enoch was pleasing in God's sight, and God took him.*[12] Job too was praised by the Lord's words.[13] And in the gospel the Lord Himself says of Nathaniel: *Behold an Israelite indeed in whom there is no guile.*[14] But here the prophet said: "I will please; I am already sure, I am already unable to displease Him, and I will harbour no doubt." As Paul says: *Death shall be swallowed up in victory, and this corruptible will put on incorruption, and this mortal shall put on immortality.*[15] Then the just will so please the Lord that they will have no further fear of the opposition of sinners. *In the land of the living* means in the congregation of saints, where all who truly live are gathered, and are segregated from the fate of those who die. As the Lord says in the gospel: *He who believes in me will pass from death to life.*[16]

Conclusion Drawn From the Psalm

Now that we have discussed the purpose of this saving psalm, we must confront worldly pains with strength of mind. Let us say, in the initial words of the psalm: *I have loved, because the Lord has heard the voice of my prayer;* for it is no punishment which impels us to our rest, no grief which guides us there. We must not regard the weeping which provides us with eternal joys as a hardship. Our thoughts must be not on our suffering but on our hope; our transitory ills undoubtedly become less harsh when their most happy outcome is kept in view. So let us ask the omnipotent Christ, who alone can overcome these trials by strength beyond reckoning, to blunt the sharp edge of their oppressiveness, so that what now seems heavy may not be utterly troublesome to us. We shall please the Lord in the land of the living if in this world we make haste to mortify our bodies in the name of His glory.

COMMENTARY ON PSALM 115

Alleluia.[1] The praise of the Lord must at some time so swell in our hearts that we cannot regard with contempt the joys which provoke the cry Alleluia. This is the exclamation of the faithful, the words of the blessed, the holy harmony of the singers, and from it our physical ears are sweetly soothed, and our weary souls renewed with heavenly delight. For the words of the martyrs are to be ushered in; they have waxed strong with glorious proclamation, and through their wondrous suffering have attained the Lord's gifts.

Division of the Psalm

Through the whole of this psalm the words of the unconquered martyrs are related. Initially they recount the Lord's kindnesses. In their uncertainty of what could be offered worthy of them, the glorious chalice of martyrdom proffered by the Lord's generosity occurred to them. In the second part the chorus proclaims itself servant of the Lord and child of the Catholic Church, so that none would regard as pleasing to God the martyrdom of heretics in addition to that of the most faithful.

Explanation of the Psalm

10. *I have believed, therefore have I spoken: but I have been humbled exceedingly.* That venerable assembly of martyrs preserves the order of true teaching, and says that they believed first and spoke afterwards. This is because of those who are to suffer annihilation, for they do not truly believe, but pretend to make definite proclamations about the Lord's great deeds; for after true faith must come holy confession, so that the churlish individual may not hear these words: *But to the sinner God hath said, Why dost thou declare my justices?*[2] Next comes: *But I have been humbled exceedingly.* You should not interpret this as saying that their most true proclamations have been humbled, for in fact they shine forth all the more as they are repressed by the zeal of their persecutors. They say that they have been humbled because while their holy religion grew stronger they themselves were seen to be subject to transient punishments.

11. *I said in the ecstasy of my mind: Every man is a liar.* They do not wish anyone to think that their most truthful confession obtained through the Lord's gift should be attributed to the powers of mortal men, and so they themselves proclaim what humankind possesses as its own, namely that *every man is a liar.* But note that they could not easily come to this realisation if they were not raised to heavenly contemplation in mental ecstasy, when the soul is cleansed of bodily grime and gazes with clear sight on the causes of things. It is evidence of great wisdom that a man should seem to himself unwise. Just as unreflective and foolish people lyingly say that they are most truthful, so enlightened persons know that they are liars. So this undeviating rule should bind us: when we lie through the frailty of the flesh, we should confess the fault as ours, but when we are truthful we should attribute it to God's gift. This aphorism[3] belongs to the figure *paroemia,*[4] for the proverb is widespread through its frequent appearance

in human speech. The words spoken to Saul in the Acts of the Apostles are of this kind: *It is hard for thee to kick against the goad.*[5] It is indeed hard, for he who is seen to have kicked against the prick is pierced through his own efforts. But we must note that the phrase *Ecstasy of mind* can have also a bad sense, as in Paralipomenon: *And thou hast delivered them to ecstasy*—that is, to mental excess—*and to trouble and destruction.*[6]

12. *What shall I repay to the Lord for all the things that he hath repaid to me?* They did well to have doubts of what humankind can repay, for they have nothing good of their own. The word *what* reveals great hesitation, for what can be *proffered* by man to Him, when clearly we are ever kept in being by His gift? So they did well to doubt, for nothing worthy had come to them by their own efforts. But so that they should not be made wholly barren they trusted in the Lord's mercy, and they later expound what they are to repay. But we must carefully scrutinise the words that God has repaid to us what He has bestowed, as if we have first given Him something good and then obtained it as bestowed by Him, whereas Paul cries out: *What hast thou that thou hast not received? And if thou hast received why dost thou glory as if thou hadst not received it?*[7] But we use the word *repay* when we both render good for good and return good for evil. The Lord repays us with good for evil, so as to demonstrate by example what He preached by word. He was beaten with blows, betrayed to the judge, whipped with undeserved scourging, but He bestowed on us the hope of resurrection, and promised us the kingdom of heaven.

13. *I will take the chalice of salvation, and I will call upon the name of the Lord.* This is indeed a worthy promise, but it would be hazardous presumption if it rested on human powers. Who can endow confessors with endurance of tortures except Him who deigned to accept the chalice of suffering on our behalf? To show with certainty that this is impossible for human powers, they next said: *And I will call upon the name of the Lord.* By relying on His help they believed that they were achieving what they thought their bodily frailty inadequate to perform. The death of martyrs is defined most beautifully and briefly as: *The chalice of salvation. Chalice*, because it is drunk in due measure; *of salvation*, because through the Lord's generosity it is served for eter-

nal salvation. Of this chalice the Lord also said in the gospel: *Can you drink the chalice that I shall drink?*[8]

15.[9] *Precious in the sight of the Lord is the death of his saints. Precious* is appropriate, for we know that the death was gained by the Lord's blood, since it was glorified by His passion so that it was outstanding in His sight. We know that the Lord bestows on His servants by great abundance of grace what He himself deigned to endure. What a life-giving death, desirable end, glorious passing, which makes Christ's members imitators of their Head, and ensures that it is precious not by the offering of riches but by the shedding of blood!

16. *O Lord, for I am thy servant, and the son of thy handmaid. Thou hast broken my bonds.* The spokesman passes to the second stage, at which having received the unique gift he cries out: *O Lord, I am thy servant.* He expresses wonder that he has received blessings such as the Lord deigned to take up for the redemption of the world. How could a servant escape wondering, entangled as he was in the condition of the first man, that he was meeting the fate that such great Majesty deigned to have chosen? To state the blessings which he receives engender fear, for by his deeds he deserves displeasure. To emphasise the growth of this admiration he repeated: *I am thy servant,* and he added: *And the son of thy handmaid* to show his humility by this triple confession. *Son of thy handmaid* seems to have been appended to denote the Catholic Church in all its forms, for she is a handmaid in her service and a bride in her marriage. So we fittingly observe that there is no martyrdom except that gained by a servant of the Lord and a son of the Catholic Church. Next follows: *Thou hast broken my bonds.* Here we appreciate that the power of martyrdom is explained, for by its triumphal onset all the bonds of sin are broken. No stain can remain in a person when devoted blood has washed it away. We must observe that this verse was believed to have such power that some claimed that sins could be forgiven by it if a person repeated it at the end of his life by a third confession.[10]

17. *I will sacrifice to thee the offering of praise.* Because the bonds of sin had been broken, he says that he is offering the sacrifice of praise, a sacrifice seen to be most acceptable to the Lord, for he says in the gospel: *Ten were saved, and there is no-one found to give glory to God but this Samaritan.*[11] This man was not of the number who diminished the

Lord's kindness by ungrateful silence, but he promises to repay to God thanksgiving for the blessing received.

18. *I will pay my vows to the Lord in the courts of the house of the Lord.* After he had said that he would offer the sacrifice of praise, he adds: *In the courts of the house of the Lord,* so that you would not believe that it could be discharged anywhere whatsoever. Those courts are the Catholic Church spread throughout the world, in which are contained all most genuine Christians, but not the heretics who are segregated through their empty wickedness. His words: *I will pay my vows to the Lord,* is a promise to offer himself. The vow of all the faithful is self-offering to Christ and abiding in the right belief of the Church. Observe what follows, so that you may recognise the nature of this house of the Lord.

19. *In the sight of all his people, in the midst of thee, Jerusalem.* Notice his information here about the house of the Lord which he mentioned in the previous short verse: it is *in the sight of all his people,* for it is right that He who deigned to suffer for the salvation of all should receive public praise. The Lord is most perfectly aware of it even if it is performed in the recess of the heart. This contributes to the edification of the people, if a good confession is absorbed by the ears of the community at large. As Christ says in the gospel: *He who confesses before men, I will also confess him before my Father who is in heaven.*[12] He added: *In the midst of thee, Jerusalem,* where the Lord's peace resides, and where the unity of the holy people rejoices in contemplation of the Lord.

Conclusion Drawn From the Psalm

This psalm has been hallowed with the splendid honour paid to martyrs; it has been both given to us as an example and bestowed on us for our protection. Let us revere the griefs of such persons, and aspire to pains of this kind for ourselves in the eagerness of our affection. Even if we do not deserve to be crowned with such a consummation, we can at any rate be found engaged in similar pursuits; for why should a Christian wish to avoid such griefs, when he knows that through them he can attain the joys of heaven?

Commentary on Psalm 116

Alleluia. Though there are only two verses, the full glory of a heading is assigned to them, so that we may realise that however few the words uttered in the Lord's praises, they are always as full as can be. None can doubt that the source of praise of heavenly splendour must not be labelled insignificant. Appropriately joined to it is the figure called in Greek *hormos*,[1] for it preserves the continuity of the speech to the end with no change of spokesman or theme, continuing with the one meaning from beginning to end.

Content of the Psalm

Though this psalm does not allow of division because of the small number of verses, it transcends all others in the economy of its utterance. It is the prime particle of the psalms, exhibiting the distinction of the point from which the line grows and from which different types of figures are shaped in most learned diversity.

Explanation of the Psalm

1. *Praise the Lord, all ye nations, and praise him together, all ye people.* We must associate this psalm too with the character of martyrs, for the holy men speak as though they have already completed their glorious suffering, saying that all nations must be roused to praise the Lord, for He bestowed on His servants such things as caused them to be inspired by His exemplary deeds. Where are the Donatists, who lyingly boast that the faith has been bestowed on their gathering alone?[2] That chorus of the saints cries out that all nations must praise the Lord; if only the Donatists even in our company would do what they lyingly claim to perform uniquely. Next comes: *And praise him together, all ye people.* Collective praise is that uttered in unison by all the faithful, and is seen to befit the Catholic Church assembled from different parts of the world. All nations in common are exhorted among the people so that none at the Lord's judgment may claim that they were not included.

2. *For his mercy is confirmed upon us, and the truth of the Lord remaineth for ever.* The reason is given why the Lord must be praised throughout the world: it is because He has fulfilled His promises made through the holy prophets by His coming to us. His mercy towards the Christian people is confirmed and will not be moved for ever, for He who granted it, as we justly believe, protects us with His pity. He added: *And the truth of the Lord remaineth for ever.* The truth of the Lord here means the Son; as He Himself says: *I am the way, the truth and the life.*[3] In the view of the utterly mad Arian, there was a time—this is a sacrilege to utter—when the Son was not. That means that there would have been a time when the Father was without the Truth, the Way and the Life. But since we must believe that the Father was never without them, it befits our salvation and truth itself to confess the Son as coeternal and consubstantial with the Father through all things. In addition Scripture says: *All things were made through him, and without him nothing was made.*[4] If time was created through the Son, how could time exist when its Creator was not? Absurdity always thus attends on base errors. They append a third falsehood: The Father is always predicated as anterior to the Son. Where is the relevant passage? *In the beginning was the Word, and the Word was with God.*[5] You observe that there is no anterior order there. Indeed, in many places the Son is named first, as in the passage of Paul to the Ephesians: *Do you not know that no fornicator and unclean person has inheritance in the kingdom of Christ and of God?*[6] And to the Galatians: *Paul an apostle, not by man nor through man, but through Jesus Christ and God the Father.*[7] And to the Thessalonians: *Our Lord Jesus Christ himself, and God our Father who has loved us.*[8] And the second letter to the Corinthians: *The grace of our Lord Jesus Christ, and the love of God.*[9] So that you would understand the equality of the whole Trinity, he added: *And the communication of the holy Spirit be with you all.*[9] We read also of the holy Spirit as Lord, and placed first. Paul says to the Thessalonians: *The Lord direct your hearts in the charity of God and the patience of Christ.*[10] The holy Spirit is being implored to guide the hearts of believers in both the love of God and the patience of Christ. So citation of one of the Trinity earlier or later will indicate no preference to the listener; human speech cannot express itself otherwise. In God we must reckon there is no disparity or diversity. We rightly believe that where there is one God, no lesser or greater can be found.

Unity knows no number, equality allows no scale. As Scripture says: *Thou shalt not go up by steps to my altar.*[11]

Conclusion Drawn From the Psalm

The tiny psalm is enclosed in the most capacious brevity. What more expansive sentiment can be spoken than that the Creator must be praised all over the world? This is a fertile brevity, a restricted abundance, the broadest of confines, narrows which have no boundary. What sweet and remarkable variation, now expressing saving thoughts in a few aphorisms, now relating great tidings in extended speech, so that weary mortals should not experience distaste in their very diligence; for the pleasant diversity gives them appetite. Perhaps the enquiry may be raised why this psalm contains only two verses whereas by contrast Psalm 118 is seen to be prolonged to 176 verses, and several others are shaped differently according to the nature of the themes. Perhaps this consideration is found to explain it: just as a harmony or beautiful melody of musical power makes a perfect song from different sounds and tones, so these psalms, now short, now of medium length, now very long form a single harmony with the most delightful sweetness. An alternative credible explanation is that they denote the Lord's future kingdom in which the saints' diverse merits shine according to the nature of their deeds, though the one blessedness and eternal sweetness is bestowed on all of them.

Commentary on Psalm 117

Alleluia. We read in the Apocalypse of the apostle John that a huge crowd sings *Alleluia* in heaven, and also that the four beasts and twenty-four elders speak in adoration of the Lord; that the whole army of heaven celebrates together to the sound of the braying trumpet with exultant singing of hymns.[1] So we too must eagerly join in this duty of praise. If we sing with pure hearts, we mingle in devoted adoration with the holy Virtues; what we know to be the blessedness of heavenly creatures becomes the glory and favour accorded to us on earth. So let us examine this psalm, which gleams out with its beautiful facade, for in the initial section it ends the four verses identically, so that by the number of the gospels it can urge the whole world in fourfold exhortation to render praises to the Lord. We cannot call these "intercalary,"[2] for other verses are not mingled with them, but we can perhaps accord them the apt label of "identical-ending," for they close with a similar harmony of words. The psalmist is to achieve this totally in all verses in Psalm 135; we advert to this arrangement more specifically in its due place.

Division of the Psalm

The faithful people are freed from the bonds of sins, and in the first section they offer a general exhortation that each of us should confess to the Lord, for they have gained a hearing in afflictions, and have proclaimed that no man whatsoever is to be held in fear. In the second part they say that we must have confidence in the Lord alone, through whom they know that they have escaped the enmity of the Gentiles, and have attained the remedies of a truly genuine life. In the third section they say that the gates of justice are to be opened; they speak there also of the Cornerstone which is Christ the Saviour. In the fourth, they persuade the other Christians that they must crowd the Lord's halls in shared joy and sweet delight at the coming of the holy incarnation.

Explanation of the Psalm

1. *Confess to the Lord for he is good, for his mercy endureth for ever.* The people of the blessed, freed from their calamity, urge the rest of the faithful to remain constant and wakeful in the Lord's praises. Confession here implies praise and nothing else, either because *Alleluia* prefaces it or because they rejoice that they have been rescued from various hardships by the Lord's pity. The reason for the praise is also appended: *For he is good.* The adjective is certainly apt for God, for when Christ in His physical appearance was called *Good master* by unbelieving Jews, He answered: "Why do you ask me concerning good, when you do not believe that I am the Lord of heaven?" and He

added: *None is good save God alone.*[3] But the text: *A good man out of his good treasure brings forth good things,*[4] seems to say the opposite. But we say that a man is made good through the Lord's grace, for He alone is properly called good in Himself, since He makes men attain their goodness. Next follows: *For his mercy endureth for ever.* The explanation of God as good is clarified, for He confers the gifts of His mercy not only on the undeserving, but also eternally. *For ever* denotes the eternity to come when there is one age and one day without the succession of change.

2. *Let Israel now say that he is good, that his mercy endureth for ever.*
3. *Let the house of Aaron now say that he is good, that his mercy endureth for ever.* 4. *Let all that fear the Lord now say that he is good, that his mercy endureth for ever.* The previous explanation aptly embraces the similar endings for these verses. But we must examine in greater depth why only the names at the beginnings of the verses are varied. The people state: *Let Israel now say* because this embraces the whole population of the blessed. In the second verse, *Let the house of Aaron now say,* denotes the priests, who were accounted worthy of particular mention because of veneration for their office. The third verse adds: *Let all that fear the Lord now say* to signify those mentioned in Psalm 113: *Both little and great,*[5] who with pure hearts show devotion to Christ the Lord in a single fellowship. So this range of names embraces in entirety the generality of the faithful.

5. *In my trouble I called upon the Lord, and he heard me and gave me room.* A personal example is offered to arouse the enthusiasm of listeners, for it is a great incentive to belief to hear thanks given by one who has suffered. But ponder the addition: *Give me room,* for He frees us from the constriction of this world and pityingly receives us into the great expanse of His rewards. He delivers us from temporal evils, but has the power to fill us with enduring blessings. So transient dangers can rage as they will, and fleeting adversities can loom large, for the constrictions which faithful people endure in this short-lived world are removed to the fullest extent.

6. *The Lord is my helper: I will not fear what man can do to me.* 7. *The Lord is my helper, and I will behold my enemies.* Though these verses seem virtually identical, they are sharply distinguished by the individual words. When the people say that through God's help they do not fear man, they denote enemies in the flesh who visibly persecute the

way of life of religious persons. But when they say: *I will behold my enemies,* they wish us to understand them as the spiritual sins which they say will be visible at the Judgment, when the devil and the rest of his agents will appear to human eyes dismantled and condemned. Though the greater part of mankind see only their enemies in the flesh, we are to believe that the people prayed more for what they could not see here. Alternatively, they entreat to be able to behold the hidden enemy so that they may take greater precautions and become immune to his traps. Note that at the beginning of both verses they have repeated the same words. This is the figure called *anaphora,*[6] found also in the verses that follow.

8. *It is good to trust in the Lord rather than to trust in man.* The gathering of the blessed, who are freed by God's gift, and who instruct with fidelity and devotion, pass to the second section, saying that we must trust in God alone and not in man, in Him who makes truthful promises and not in him who beguiles himself with deceitful presumption. How many are the fools who say: "I do what I wish, I have no lord over my will," believing that what is profitable for men is to be regulated by their free will. The apostle James rebukes them with the words: *Your desires surely prompt you to say, Tomorrow we will go into such a city, and we will traffic and make our gain, instead of saying, If the Lord will and if we shall live we shall do this or that,*[7] and the rest. The freedom of will in its evil aspect is accursed, for the sinner abandons the Creator and turns to sacrilegious vices. We lost the use of free will in its good aspect with the sin of Adam, and we cannot return to it except by Christ's grace. As Paul says: *For it is God who worketh in you, both to will and to accomplish according to his good will.*[8] So we must entreat by diligent prayer that no debased desire seize us but that divine inspiration possess us, for whatever wisdom we derive from ourselves we summon with deadly recklessness to our own harm. So they rightly forbade us to trust in man, who of himself can bestow a remedy neither on himself nor on another. As Jeremiah says: *Cursed be the man that trusts in man, and puts the hope of the flesh in his arm, and whose heart departs from the Lord.*[9] So reckless men must cease to play the role which can cause God's sentence to condemn them with greater justice. (Father Augustine has also argued on this matter in extended books against the heretics Pelagius, Caelestius and Julian, and has shattered the armour of their poisonous belief.)[10]

9. *It is good to hope in the Lord rather than to hope in princes.* The change of two words has produced a wholly different judgment. Earlier the people say that they trust, but here that they hope; and earlier in man, but here in princes. So it seems that earlier they speak of physical creatures, but here of spiritual ones. The devil is also called a prince, as in the gospel-passage: *Behold the prince of this world comes, and in me he will not find anything.*[11] Likewise a good angel is called a prince, as we read in Daniel: *Michael your prince.*[12] So they are saying that the hope of man must rest in neither wicked nor good angels, but in the Lord alone. Even if we love the good angels for the devotion they bestow on us, we praise the Lord's blessing which they manifest, and not powers wielded at their own discretion.

10. *All nations compassed me, and in the name of the Lord I have been revenged on them.* The people justly said this, for they had placed their hope in the Lord's protection, and were indicating the toils of the Church which they had first endured in the person of their Head, the Lord Christ, and which they subsequently bore by their own sufferings. Initially when the Christian religion became known, all the nations rose to persecute it, and inflicted various atrocities on the most faithful. But they gained revenge on their persecutors with the help of the Lord when they tamed them by a wondrous conversion, so that those persecutors exacted from themselves the punishment of repentance, whereas for long they had inflicted that punishment on innocent victims. The use of *gentes* (nations) followed by the masculine *eos* (them) is explicable either by the sense, for the people in the nations are denoted, or this is the figure of *exallage* or change, for here the gender of the noun is changed.[13]

11. *Surrounding me they have compassed me about, and in the name of the Lord I have been revenged on them.* The minutiae of the words have to be analysed here, for when sifted, as we have often said, they bring home to us mysteries of no little importance. They spoke first of *nations,* with reference to the suffering of the Church caused by the communities to which the martyrs belonged, for in their passionate cult of demons they ravaged the faithful in many places. But now with this repetition of words they refused to speak of nations, to denote subtly instead the suffering of the Lord, which we know was inflicted in a particular way by the Jews alone. But revenge was exacted from

them in the name of the Lord when many of them repented of their evil deeds, and deserved to acquire the title of Christians. These verses too are to be described as "identical-ending," like the ones at the beginning of the psalm. We should observe that just as often the Head speaks of the members, so now the members make a declaration about their Head.

12. *They surrounded me like bees round the comb, and they burned like fire among thorns: and in the name of the Lord I took vengeance on them.* These verses too continue to refer to the Lord. He was surrounded by raging Jews, and poured out the honey of His passion through the whole world. Bees surround the comb when they store their most sweet liquid in their wax houses. Their intention is to lay by victuals for their own use, but they are the means by which men can satisfy their desires. It is clear that the Jews achieved this when by their bitter designs they brought to pass the sweetest of events for the whole world. *Apes* (bees) get their name from *a pedibus*,[14] being born without feet. *Thorns* denote the sins of the world, by which the Jewish people were fiercely stimulated, and like a crackling fire seethed in their wicked deeds. But by the Lord's grace vengeance was exacted from them too, when in their ignorance of that honey which they had stored away, they turned to the Lord and gained the sweetest satiety.

13. *Being pushed, I was inclined to fall, but the Lord supported me.* The body of the faithful with most authentic voice now speaks, giving evidence of itself. The person who is pushed, and from whom the Lord's strength is removed, falls. Observe the force of the words. They say they were pushed and about to fall, but were steadied by the Lord's support. Only those sustained by Christ's powers do not fall when overturned, as is often the case when deserving individuals are consigned to punishment. They seem to be consigned so that they may fall, in other words, abandon their right belief; but strengthened by the Lord's right hand they do not fall, for they stand steady in the sanctity of faith. Without that stance the unfaithful fall, even when they seem to stand in their unyielding obstinacy.

14. *The Lord is my strength and my praise: and he is become my salvation.* He who is pushed cannot fall when the strength of the Lord is seen to afford him help. But so that the person saved by the Lord's gifts may not be thought merely to avoid dangers, the words, *He is*

become my salvation, are added, for they obtain eternal life through Him who is their means of gaining escape from the collapse of this world. He is the strength and eternal praise of the blessed.

15. *The voice of gladness and salvation is in the tabernacles of the just. The right hand of the Lord hath wrought strength.* The chorus of the faithful expresses delight that while their persecutors thought that they were overcome with grief and exhausted by affliction, they were actually rejoicing in contemplation of God, and finding happiness in their punishment because they knew that it would aid them towards eternal delights. Here *the tabernacles of the just* denote the secrets of the human heart, in which the saints always rejoice though they are oppressed externally. So that you would recognise the source of this joy, they added: *The right hand of the Lord hath wrought strength.* The right hand is Christ, through whom the Father has wielded His power in the exaltation of the saints, as the people are to say later.

16. *The right hand of the Lord hath exalted me.* The right hand of the Lord exalts when He grants the kingdom of heaven to earthly men. What mark of greater power is there than that mortals should put on immortality, and the corruptible put on incorruption?[15] Or that He should grant blessedness to sinners, and victory over the strongest foe to the weak?

17. *I shall not die, but live, and shall declare the works of the Lord.* These words are uttered against the claims which the mad wantonness of persecutors is wont to utter against Christ's Church. But when they imagine that they are erasing the Christian name, they are found instead to extend it further. Such men are rightly told by the faithful: *I shall not die* as you think, but *I shall live* a life of which you are unaware, and which those whose minds are inflated cannot attain. He promises further to declare the works of the Lord, so that the Church may ever gain increase through being noised abroad by such proclamation. What point is there in cruel men's persecuting those whom they observe always thriving on persecutions? How much better would they also live if they were converted, and lamented their deeds!

18. *The Lord chastising has chastised me, but he has not delivered me over to death.* They did not wish arrogant persecutors to make any claims for themselves, so they maintain that tortures and the most fierce savagery of those men are actually the Lord's chastisement, so that the whole of their wicked power is seen as permitted to them for

the correction of the faithful. Why do they preen themselves on their power when nothing is granted to them for their profit? Their cruelty is our correction, the flame of their fury puts us to the test. They should not account themselves better for sinning. The faithful person is not spared to enable us to see that he can be schooled. Here the people say that their chastisement is good, for only persons cleansed of sins committed here are not consigned to death. Observe the words, *chastising hath chastised;* this is a type of utterance often found in the divine Scriptures, as in: *Blessing I will bless thee, Multiplying, I will multiply thy seed,*[16] and the like. This, as we have often explained, is the argument from related words.[17]

19. *Open ye to me the gates of justice, and going in to them I will give praise to the Lord.* The company of the faithful passes to the third section. They wish to enter Jerusalem, and ask with spiritual fervour that her gates be opened to them. So to whom is the word *open* addressed but to the prophets and apostles who received the keys of heaven through their mystical powers? Through these gates of teaching we are admitted, and now established within we truly give praise to the Lord; whereas all that is performed outside the Catholic Church is in no way applied to the Lord's praises. The prophets and apostles are by allegory well labelled *gates,* for gates are the means by which foodstuffs are brought into cities,[18] just as food for souls is known to have been brought in by prophets and apostles.

20. *This is the gate of the Lord: the just shall enter through it.* Since they earlier spoke of *gates,* we must investigate why here they sought to use *gate* in the singular. The reason is that they wished to denote prophets and apostles as the gates of heaven, but to suggest that they all lead to one gate, for all regularly admit to the Lord Saviour, who can also be called a Gate. As He Himself says in the gospel: *I am the gate of the sheep,*[19] and the rest. Next comes: *The just shall enter through it.* As it seems to me, this denotes not the divine Scriptures, through which the unjust also pass, but the Jerusalem which has the Lord Saviour as its Gate, through which only just men will enter. Both senses are excellently combined, being seen to denote this world and the world to come.

21. *I will confess to thee, O Lord, because thou hast heard me, and art become my salvation.* We must interpret this as the confession of a rejoicing rather than an afflicted people. They are giving thanks be-

cause the saving Lord has shone on them, and the Redeemer of the Gentiles has appeared to human eyes. So we truly realise that the Lord's coming was continually awaited by the most just people of earlier times as well. As He Himself says in the gospel: *Many prophets and just men have desired to see the things that you see, and to hear the things that you hear,*[20] and the rest.

22. *The stone which the builders rejected is become the head of the corner.* The Jews' vain activity is expressed by the allusion to craftsmen. Alone of mankind those who still worshipped one God in the world were seen to be builders, while the other nations destroyed themselves by their cult of idols. Builders always work towards the corner so that the solidity of the adjoining walls may be ensured. But the Jews were far from completing the building of their faith, for like madmen they thought that He who was the strongest stone, the cornerstone, was to be despised. The Lord Christ, as has certainly been explained on countless occasions, is metaphorically called the cornerstone because He joined to Himself the two peoples of Gentiles and Jews, coming from different directions as though they were twin walls joined in a firm unity of grace. The prophets, apostles and different witnesses had much to say about this Stone. *Angulus* (corner) is derived from Greek *gonu* (knee), which in Latin is *genu.*[21] When the knee is bent, it is shaped like an angle; among the Greeks it wholly maintains the origin of its name in derivations, as for example in tetragon, pentagon, and the like.[22]

23. *This was made from the Lord, and is wonderful in our eyes.* So that you would not think that this Stone was quarried from rocky mountains, it is said to have been made from the Lord. When the people say *made*, the nature of His humanity is being revealed, for it too is shown to have been created. So Paul too says: *Being made in the likeness of men, and in habit found as a man;*[23] and in another place: *Who was made to him of the seed of David, according to the flesh.*[24] For this stone, which is the beautiful adornment of the building, the clamp of the walls, the enduring strength of the foundations, is wonderful in the eyes of the faithful, who not merely behold Him in the flesh but also see Him with enlightened mind. The Jews too saw Him, but did not regard Him as wonderful, for they gazed solely at the flesh which they regarded as shared by all men. But to the perceptions of the faithful, who

proclaimed Him as Son of God, He seemed wonderful and awe-inspiring, as He did to the apostle Peter, who told Him: *You are the Christ, Son of the living God.*[25]

24. *This is the day which the Lord has made: let us be glad, and rejoice therein.* What sweet and holy words does their belief demonstrably utter to us! Though God created each and every day, He is said to have made in an unique way the day consecrated by the birth of the Lord Christ. It is indeed fitting to be glad and to rejoice in it, for on that day the devil lost his rights, and the world received its salvation.

25. *O Lord, save me! O Lord, give good success.* These exclamations reveal the longing of their great request, asking both that here they may be freed from the disaster of this world, and in the next world attain the most happy lot of being set at His right hand. These are the two requests which the faithful Christian makes, that he may be rescued here from the death of sins and there set in eternal rest. The afflictions which they suffer here, the griefs which they bear out of love for the Lord, bring undoubted prosperity in the next world, for they there attain eternal joys. Bringing *success* means that some harsh experience results in untroubled peace, so that past evils become welcome to us, for we believe that they are to change into eternal joys.

26. *Blessed be he that cometh in the name of the Lord. We have blessed you out of the house of the Lord.* The fourth and remaining section is introduced, in which the sweet gift of praise devoted to the Lord's coming is offered, and the wicked audacity of Antichrist is cleverly condemned. This figure is called *emphasis*,[26] which denotes more than the words say. The expression, *blessed is he that cometh in the name of the Lord*, makes clear that he who is thought to come in his own name is accursed. The people say that He has come in the Lord's name to enable you to realise that it is Christ the Lord almighty, and to prevent our human minds entertaining thoughts about Him in terms of the flesh. The gospel-words also show this when they say: *I am come in the name of my Father, and you have received me not: if another shall come in his own name, you will receive him.*[27] Next comes: *We have blessed you out of the house of the Lord.* This is said to the other Christians by the faithful people of whom we spoke at the outset; they are, so to say, raised to the rank of the priesthood, and they address the people, showing that the Lord's blessing is given to the devoted folk

for their welfare through the priest. So that you would feel no hesitation in accepting this, they added: *Out of the house of the Lord*, in other words, the Catholic Church, the source of the baptism of salvation, of holy communion, of cleansing by anointing with consecrated oil, and of the imparting of every true blessing.

27. *The Lord God: and he hath shone upon us. Appoint a solemn day with packed gatherings, even to the horn of the altar.* When the people say: *The Lord God*, they are reacting to the previous words, so that you are to understand it like this: "We have blessed you out of the house of the Lord, or rather not we, but the Lord God." He blesses through the mouths of the saints, and He shines on us when He separates us from the darkness of sins. Next comes: *Appoint a solemn day with packed gatherings, even to the horn of the altar.* This is now addressed to the blessed ones who could solemnly celebrate feast-days. *Appoint*, in other words, by considered decree keep a solemn day consecrated by honour to the Lord and praise by the saints. *With packed gatherings*, that is, in crowded processions packed by flocks of people and celebrated with festive devotion. The addition: *Even to the horn of the altar*, suggests that some are perhaps being forbidden to leave after hearing the gospel-reading, as many habitually do, for those not filled with the grace of communion do not approach *the horn of the altar*. It is fitting for us, I think, to interpret this as the altar we see, which distributes to us the Lord's body and blood in solemn gathering. But there is also the altar which stands before the sight of the Lord, which we are bidden to approach with minds purified by holy contemplation; and in this physical celebration here we must always train our eyes on that altar there, as we explained already at Psalm 42 in the words: *I will go unto the altar of God, to God who gives joy to my youth.*[28] *Horn* denotes the power which the holy altar clearly possesses.

28. *Thou art my God, and I will confess to thee: thou art my God, and I will exalt thee.* How splendidly this truthful proclamation is repeated in our saying that the God whom we do not cease to adore with pure hearts is ours! In the first sentence the people say: *I will confess to thee*, which is a form of thanks; and in the second: *I will exalt thee*, for in the praises of the blessed uttered through all nations they exalt the Lord Christ, who renders good for evil; who waits with patience until He

can quash enemies, and once they are converted bestows on them the rewards such as His mercy has promised to His saints freely.

I will confess to thee, Lord, because thou hast heard me, and art become my salvation. This verse is repetition, and has already as we know been explained in the third section.[29] We merely state in brief that we must understand this most joyful confession as the outcome of His kindnesses experienced, as the heading *Alleluia* also pointed out to us.

29. *Confess to the Lord, for he is good, for his mercy endureth for ever.* This verse too we see has already been uttered, at the beginning of the psalm; just as it began with Christ, so the conclusion is seen to be in harmony with it. As He Himself says in the Apocalypse: *I am alpha and omega.*[30] So a confession was rightly set at the beginning and repeated at the end, for throughout the whole of our lives we must adopt it, and end with its delight.

Conclusion Drawn From the Psalm

Let us remember that this psalm is purposely interwoven with certain embellishments. At the outset four verses are lent the identical ending, and the end with beautiful repetition echoes the first verse. Moreover the penultimate verse repeats verse 21, so that like the high priest's vestment it could shine out with threads of gold, so to say, and beautiful tracework. The vestment had bells on its fringes; these verses at the close jingle with the words uttered at the beginning. When the high priest entered the Holy of holies, he then wore this garment so that none would be unaware of the approach of the venerable priest, for even if he did not speak, his coming was audible. In the same way this psalm was arranged with such beautiful variation that proclamations of the holy incarnation were grasped by most beautiful indications. May this garment of Your eloquence, devoted King, be our vestment, and by Your help may our actions sound forth the message which Your commands, O Lord, have enjoined. Let us remember that this is the fifth of the psalms proclaimed with wondrous narration of the Lord's first coming;[31] they are perhaps to be compared with the five loaves[32] which with heavenly abundance sated the hunger of the attentive folk.

COMMENTARY ON PSALM 118

Alleluia. Before this joyous psalm, which is as full as can be of the power of things divine, is set the Alleluia, which is desirable so that the merits of this heavenly hymn can be recognised by the glory of its heading; for it is most lofty in the depth of its sentiments, and interwoven with the repetition of familiar words, now proclaiming gifts received, now in turn hoping for those same blessings which have been deserved. Like celebrated rivers, it is seen to flow smoothly, though we know that it runs very deep; but we must with God's help course through it according to the measure of our practice, for up to now we have disciplined ourselves, and not spread ourselves with a sudden overflow. The psalm is adorned with Hebrew letters, for the instruction of those who are novices and amenable to teaching in Christ's school, in such a way that the letter allotted to a verse is joined also to the ensuing seven, perhaps denoting the mystery which lies in the heart's circumcision.[1] So this psalm runs on in its Hebrew tongue in groups of eight verses for each letter, interconnected at all points and completed with equal length of sections. We state that this is the arrangement both for purposes of division and so as to be able to denote the perfect number of just persons; for by means of these letters Hebraic wisdom is learnt, and the consecrated number of divine books is contained.[2] We know that each of these letters has its peculiar significance, since blessed Jerome attests this.[3] It seems otiose to repeat this here, since it has been compiled by the toil of another. Josephus states that this psalm, together with Psalm 144 and the Song of Deuteronomy, were composed in the elegiac metre.[4]

Division of the Psalm

We reasonably claim that the Hebrew letters have bestowed on the moral psalm divisions observable according to their number. Each letter, as we stated above, lays claim to eight verses, and invests the whole poem with beautiful balance. The psalm is not confused by any intermingling of sections, but unfolds new topics by change of letters. Throughout the psalm the speaking is done by a whole chorus of saintly men who have lived at the beginning of the world, or who live now, or who are believed to live in the future. Among them are found apostles, prophets, martyrs, confessors, the orders of the Church, and all who serve the Lord with devoted purity, *a chosen race, a royal priesthood, a holy nation, a purchased people*[5] who are to be gathered from the beginnings of the human race up to its end. Though there is a countless crowd of them, an individual is everywhere introduced as spokesman so that the power of unity in a harmonious Church can be acknowledged. Now let us see what spiritual fruits sprout in this heavenly paradise.

Explanation of the Psalm

1. ALEPH. *Blessed are the undefiled in the way, who walk in the law of the Lord.* Since the longings of all are seized by desire for this title, and one can find no-one unwilling to gain the rewards of blessedness, it was appropriate for the holy men to indicate the path in praiseworthy prayers so that men's troubled minds cannot err through ignorance of the way, for those beguiled by worldly ambitions also account themselves blessed. But to ensure that we do not think that any such course should be chosen, they first spoke of the undefiled in the plural, so that we must interpret this as referring to the faithful as well as to Christ. He alone is undefiled by nature, for He had no sin. The saints become undefiled only when they obtain the gifts of pardon. As the prophet says in Psalm 50: *Thou shalt wash me, and I shall be made whiter than snow.*[6] Next comes: *In the way*, that is, in the Lord Saviour Himself, who said: *I am the way, and the truth, and the life.*[7] It is the just who walk on it, not with bodily feet but with steps of praiseworthy activity; for to make you realise that they had not spoken of the way on which one could go astray, they added: *Who walk in the law of the Lord*, that is, those who either do not sin, or who through the grace of heaven consult their interests by making worthy satisfaction. The phrase, *in the law of the Lord*, is not idle, for there is also the law of sin. As Paul says: *I see another law in my members fighting against the law of my mind, and leading me captive in the law of sin.*[8] Hence the addition: *Of the Lord*, to distinguish this law from that of sin.

2. *Blessed are they that search his testimonies: they seek him with their whole heart.* This sentiment continues to express the earlier sense.

Though the undefiled who walk in the way, that is, advance in the Lord Saviour and His law with devoted mind, are blessed, to these virtues are added: *That search his testimonies.* The nature of this search is next revealed: they have chosen to seek the Lord *with their whole heart.* Heretical backsliders also appear to search His testimonies, but they do not seek the Lord with their whole heart, since through human duplicity they aim to devise new calumnies. The person who through error deserving of punishment is diverted to the vanity of falsehood cannot be said to have set his whole heart on the holy Scriptures. (Hence holy Primasius, the eloquent bishop of Justinianopolis, is known to have composed a book with the title, *The Effect of Heresy.*)[9] Again, those who neglect the teaching of His commandments, and desire earthly joys, do not seem to have set their whole heart on the Lord's testimony. Notice the sequence of this true and holy doctrine. He first says: *Blessed are they that walk in the law of the Lord,* and then: *That search the testimonies* of the sacred books. Only the person known to comport himself in praiseworthy action is worthy to search out these testimonies. The third type of definition, called in Greek *poiotēs* and in Latin *qualitativa,*[10] embraces both these statements. The nature of the blessed man is revealed here in the nature of his actions.

3. *For they that work iniquity have not walked in his ways.* Since the words of the apostle John are true, that *if we say that we have no sin, we deceive ourselves, and the truth is not in us,*[11] it seems that not even the saints walk in His ways, for we know that they have sins. But this question is solved by the words of Truth itself. There are unlawful desires which we entertain by the necessity of original sin, but we are not held fast in them by mental consent. The blessed mind does not walk in them, for they are overcome through God's gift by goodness of heart. We can cite as examples the sudden desire for something beautiful, having a keen appetite for food, being roused by pleasant odours, being suddenly disturbed by some wicked prompting, and the like; these are suppressed by holy prayer and the merest sign of the cross. So it happens that even saints entertain sins by the flesh's prompting, but though the effect on them is by no means mitigated, they are rightly regarded as not having committed these sins. These words, *who walked in the ways of the Lord,* are quite clearly approved by the witness of the apostle Paul when he said: *I have fought a good fight:*

I have finished my course: I have kept the faith,[12] and the rest. The sin which he committed was involuntary when he cried out: *For the good which I will I do not, but the evil which I will not, that I do.*[13] There follows his explanation which removes all shadow of doubt: *Now if I do that which I will not, it is no more I that do it, but the sin that dwelleth in me.*[14] You observe that the accusation is levelled only against those who with wicked delight lend assent to the workings of sins. So *they that work unjustly* are rightly said not to walk in the Lord's ways, for the working of iniquity involves that consent of evil men which is clearly through the Lord's indulgence alien to the hearts of saints. Paul himself offers this warning as well: *Let not sin therefore reign in your mortal body so as to obey the lusts thereof, neither yield your members as instruments of iniquity to sin.*[15] And Solomon says: *Go not after the desires of thy heart.*[16] So what is forbidden here is obedience to sin rather than the promptings which the flesh by its own powers cannot avoid. But let us examine why here they spoke of *ways* in the plural, whereas earlier the singular was used in *blessed are the undefiled in the way.* In that passage they denote the Lord Saviour, the certain Way of those who go to the Father. As He Himself said: *No-one goes to the Father except through me.*[17] But the use of the plural *ways* at this point denotes the prophets and apostles, or any persons whom He taught with truthful proclamation.

4. *Thou hast commanded thy commandments to be kept exceedingly.* They had earlier called blessed the person to whom practices such as these recommend themselves: being undefiled, walking in the way of the Lord, searching His testimonies, and as the most perfect type of living, seeking the Lord with one's whole heart. So that these important matters should not appear open to neglect, there follows the injunction of the Lord's command inspiring reverence, that His commandments be pursued not only diligently but also *exceedingly.* An exceeding person is one who shows no hesitation in any matter, who always eagerly supports a project in hand. What then of the aphorism of pagans which is famed throughout the world: "Nothing excessive"?[18] Observe that Truth enjoins the excessive on us; the Controller of all things ordains that deeds be done without imperfection. *Exceeding* here means abundant and boundless; as another psalm has it: *Thy thoughts are exceedingly deep,*[19] and elsewhere: *Thou art exalted exceedingly above all gods.*[20] Alternatively we are instructed to keep the

Lord's commands exceedingly when it is adjudged that we put them before even our bodily safety. So God's service demands that we transcend the powers of our own abilities, for in that service what is wholly excessive is appropriate, since we ask to have bestowed on us what is without limit. We must also investigate the separate identification of the nouns here, so that no-one may think that they are run together. In the first verse was mentioned *the law of the Lord;* the Lord's law, as Paul says, is *a shadow of things to come,*[21] which must be observed not in the letter but in the order of the spirit. We may cite as examples the law of sacrifices, observance of the new moon, the rite of circumcision, and the other items of this kind which undoubtedly were a foreshadowing rather than an appearance of the truth. In the second verse there is mention of *testimonies;* a testimony is a clear and predetermined condition. Once we are apprised of its determination, we cannot forget previous events. So Jacob says in Genesis, *This heap shall be your testimony*, and: *This stone shall be your testimony.*[22] Then too in Joshue is written: *Bring twelve stones from the midst of the Jordan, that they may be a testimony to your children.*[23] In this sense the divine commands are testimonies for us, when they counsel us not to sin. As the apostle Paul says: *I testify before God who gives life to all things, and before Christ Jesus and the elect angels, that you observe these things.*[24] In the present verse is written *commandments,* which are not shadows of future events as is the law, but have immediate application in visible action. The Lord makes this wholly clear in the gospel, when He says that the first commandment is: *Thou shalt love the Lord thy God with thy whole heart and with thy whole soul, and with thy whole strength,*[25] and the rest. These words were addressed to an individual, so as to be observed by all men through all times. So whether the law, or testimonies, or the Lord's commands are observed, they undoubtedly lead us to gifts of blessedness. These terms and the definitions of them which we have given must be stored in the mind, for we find them often cited in subsequent verses.

5. *Would that my ways may be made straight to keep thy justifications!* Since they have earlier described clearly the life of the blessed person, the faithful people now also interpose in prayer a request for the growth of such blessings in themselves. *Would that* always expresses an aspiration that what we cannot attain by our own powers

we may merit through the generosity of divine mercy. When they say: *May my ways be made straight,* they indicate that human weakness twists them. *My ways* denotes the deeds which we perform in this life. Next is added: *To keep thy justifications.* They now reveal what they earlier desired, for none can achieve observance of the Lord's justifications unless his ways are found to be straightened by the Lord. But let us probe the meaning of *justifications.* The Lord's justifications were many and varied among the people of old; for example, a Jewish servant was to remain in service for only six years, a son was to be schooled by the love and control of the father, a father was to be held in reverence in all matters, God was to be worshipped with the utmost awe and love, a priest was to be held in honour, a neighbour was to be loved as though one's own interests were at stake, and there were other injunctions of this kind laid down by holy Scripture. So these cannot be observed unless seen to be bestowed by the Lord's mercy.

6. *Then shall I not be confounded, when I observe all thy commandments.* An explanation is offered of how the Lord's justifications can be continually maintained: it is by observance of all His commandments. When the spokesman says *all,* he warns that we must not sin against any, for it is written: *If anyone does not carry out the least injunction of the law, he is answerable to the whole law.*[26] Observance means ever keeping in mind the commandments enjoined, so that if any transgression is committed, it is at once corrected by wholesome improvement. But the person who does not observe the commandments will be wholly unaware of the nature of his sin. The apostle James makes this comparison: *If a man be a hearer of the word and not a doer, he shall be compared to a man beholding his native countenance in a glass. For he beheld himself, and went his way, and presently forgot what manner of man he was. But he that has looked into the perfect law and has continued therein, not becoming a forgetful hearer but a doer of the work, this man shall be blessed in his deed.*[27] So the persons who win praise are those who do not lose sight of the Lord's commands.

7. *I will confess to thee, Lord, with uprightness of heart, since I have learnt the judgments of thy justice.* Here confession denotes the praise which befits the blessed people. *Uprightness of heart* is the sacred rule of the Catholic faith, for the twisted guile of heretics cannot confess Him. *Since I have learnt* denotes the discipline passed on to them by

their blessed fathers, not that devised in enthusiasm for perversity, as is the case with some. The judgments of the Lord's justice refer to His deigning to deliver His servants when they struggle under the devil's persecution.

8. *I will keep thy justifications: O do not utterly forsake me!* The beautiful model of blessedness proposed is now complete. They ask the Lord to deign to protect the devoted people by His kindness, now that His justifications have been granted. We have already explained at verse 4 the meaning of *justifications*. Since they knew that the devil's temptations surrounded them on every side—as we read in Scripture: *Your adversary as a lion goes round seeking whom he may devour*[28] they ask to be protected on every side, so that the cruel foe may not be able to find an opportunity for harm. Now let us see what the second letter contains.

9. BETH. *By what does a young man correct his way? By observing thy words*. In the section of the first letter, the faithful people pointed to the spheres of blessedness in which they begged to be maintained; they now under the second letter reveal the time of conversion, and by quoting the Lord's words also state what delights they are to enjoy. So by the figure of *erōtēsis*[29] they propose the question: *By what does a young man correct his way?* The age chosen is that of the New, not the Old Testament, for we are renewed from the condition of the older man to the age of vigour. He is called young by comparison with the old, for the comparative degree often bears the force of the positive. The people explain in the reply that follows how this young man has corrected his way: it is *by observing thy words*, that is, at the time when the Christian people accepted the gospel-teaching, for at that time a person obtained correction, when he condemned the wickedness of old, and attained the gifts of right faith. That person observes the Lord's words who not merely keeps them in memory but restores them by worthy deeds.

10. *With my whole heart I have sought after thee: do not drive me from thy commandments*. The assertion that they have sought the Lord wholeheartedly denotes a further kindness of His, for they would not seek Him if they had not been sought out. As we read in Isaiah: *I shall seek what was lost, and summon back that which had wandered*.[30] In every good deed we are anticipated by the Lord's grace. He deigns to inspire

us to make us wish to entreat Him. Next comes: "*Do not drive me from thy commandments* as one unworthy of Your benefits; since You have made me seek You with all my heart, deign to listen to me as well." He drives from His commandments those whose entreaties to Him are deceitful; as we read in another psalm: *The bloody and deceitful man the Lord will abhor.*[31] Solomon too says: *For the holy spirit of discipline will flee from the deceitful, and will withdraw himself from thoughts that are without understanding.*[32] So the spokesman asks that he be not driven from understanding of the divine law as one unworthy, so that we may recognise that only those found to make wholehearted entreaty gain this understanding.

11. *Thy utterances have I hidden in my heart, that I may not sin against thee.* Though we read that the work of the Lord is to be proclaimed—as Peter says in The Acts of the Apostles: *We cannot but speak the things which we have seen and heard*[33]—here they say that the Lord's utterances are hidden in their hearts, so that they may not sin. Both statements, however, are true. Just as it is fitting for the faithful to proclaim His words at the appropriate time, so must they hide them from nonbelievers. As the gospel has it: *Give not that which is holy to dogs, nor cast your pearls before swine.*[34] Another psalm says: *I have set a guard to my mouth when the sinner stood against me. I was dumb and was humbled, and kept silence from good things.*[35] This is to make us aware that it is a species of sin to proclaim the Lord's utterances to the obdurate. So too the apostle Paul says: *A man that is a heretic, after the first and second admonition, avoid,*[36] and the rest.

12. *Blessed art thou, O Lord: teach me thy justifications.* So that no-one may attribute the sacred teachings to his own powers, they preface their statement with: *Blessed art thou, O Lord;* in other words, "You freely bestow them," for there is no choice which man can make. Blessing here denotes praise of the Lord, for when we bless God we praise His deeds, but when He blesses He deigns to sanctify us. Next comes: *Teach me thy justifications.* Whereas earlier they said: *Thy utterances I have hidden in my heart,* they now say: *Teach me thy justifications,* as if they have learnt none of them previously. It is not enough for the holy gathering which hungers and thirsts for justice to have learnt by word the Lord's commands; they sought to be able to demonstrate them in deeds, in which they knew that they would find

fullness of grace. Hence the words: *Teach me thy justifications;* in other words: "Grant that I may perform actions which are the source of Your habitual justification of Your chosen ones."

13. *With my lips I have pronounced all the judgments of thy mouth.* That band of saints says that they have pronounced the judgments of the Lord's mouth, which He spoke through His prophets and apostles, when they enumerated them with their lips, and proclaimed them to their people. *All the judgments* denotes those written or spoken. But they cannot wholly proclaim what cannot be understood by any knowledge; in the words of another psalm: *Thy judgments are a great deep.*[37] Paul too attests: *O, the depth of the riches of the wisdom and knowledge of God! How inscrutable are his judgments, and how unsearchable his ways!*[38] Christ Himself said to the apostles at the approach of the passion: *I have not told all things to you.*[39] So here the whole is used figuratively for the part, a usage clearly found often in the divine Scriptures.[40]

14. *I have been delighted in the way of thy testimonies, as in all riches.* The Lord Christ is *the way of testimonies,* for when they speak of Him they lead to Him. He is the certain Way, the unwearying Path, the gainful Toil; and whoever attains it is charmed with the delight of riches beyond reckoning. We must note what follows: *As in all riches.* We must interpret these as the spiritual riches of which Paul says: *That in all things you are made rich in him, in all utterance and in all knowledge, as the testimony of Christ was confirmed in you.*[41] But the holy band could not compare worldly riches with the Lord's testimonies, for they are known to have renounced them as a form of filth.

15. *I will be exercised by thy commandments, and I will consider thy ways.* The order of ecclesiastical discipline is preserved. First came their being exercised by the divine commandments, in other words, by the performance with diligent toil of the practice of essential works by frequent activity, and by this means access to the innermost region of understanding of Him. Only the person granted access to heavenly benefits through good living deserves to behold this great mystery. Notice that meditation on the divine Scriptures is usually accounted a good.

16. *I will meditate on thy justifications: I will not forget thy words.* Forgetfulness does not come upon us naturally, but is the outcome of the frailty caused by original sin. Meditation is set against it as a

remedy, so that sacrilegious forgetfulness may not destroy the eminence of memory. They say that they meditate on the Lord's justifications so that they cannot forget what they strive to remember. They realised the failing by which the human mind was oppressed, and devised this resource against it, by means of which the power of forgetfulness could be excluded. Note how apt words are attached to the various aspects. In the previous verse, *I will be exercised by thy commandments*, they spoke of the need for an active role. The Lord's commandments are: *Thou shalt not commit adultery, thou shalt not declare false witness*,[42] and the rest. In these cases it was necessary not merely to hear but also to act, so they wrote: *I will be exercised.* But here they say: *I will meditate on thy justifications;* by justifications, as was explained earlier, is meant that a Jewish servant should not serve for more than six years, which denotes that the blessed people serving in this world should be freed of all subjection at the resurrection. So because this was expressed as a riddle, they said: *I will meditate*, so that frequent repetition might reveal more clearly an understanding of what is to come.

17. GIMEL. *Reward afresh thy servant: I shall live, and I shall keep thy words.* They come to the third letter, in which they confess human need, and commend the Lord's grace in all things. They claim that the proud who persecute the Lord's faithful with unjust agitation are rebuked. *Retribue* (reward afresh) means not "grant to deserving merit" but "bestow again; since You who have granted us the longing of our entreaty, impart also the outcome of our request." In fact the words that follow, *thy servant*, announce this sense. Only he who attributes any good which he is known to have achieved to divine grace rather than to his own merits can be called Christ's servant. The observance of the Lord's commandments is the mark of true life, and by contrast he who is known to be disobedient to them is rightly said to be dead. As we read of the unfaithful in the gospel: *Let the dead bury their dead.*[43] Burial of the dead was the task of the living, but because they were seen to be unfaithful, we know that they were rightly described as dead. Notice the holy confession: their judgment was that they would live if they could keep the Lord's words—and rightly, for he who guards them is undoubtedly guarded by them, and the death which stalks and plunders the wicked will not master him.

18. *Unveil my eyes, and I will consider the wondrous things of thy law.*

In this verse the frailty of humanity and the kindness of the heavenly Majesty are explained. *Unveil* means "remove the veil"; our inward sight is blocked by a shroud of ignorance, and if the covering is not removed through His mercy, we cannot gaze on the holy Scriptures with the heart's eye. So they ask that the blindness of ignorance be removed from them, so that enlightened by divine grace they can behold the Lord's wonders. They attest the nature of these wonders with the words, *of thy law*. Earlier we said that the law was a shadow of future events, containing the meaning of the fullness to come. A spotless lamb was sacrificed at the feast of the Pasch, denoting the slaughter of the Lord Christ. The priest was clothed in a most beautiful and gleaming garment, to offer indications of the future Pontiff and the heavenly King. There were also the Lord's promises, that Israel's people would be led into a land flowing with milk and honey, and undoubtedly this refers to the future age in which abundant joys of highest blessedness offer their sweetness. So that holy people asks to ponder these things with hearts unveiled, for they could not behold them whilst a covering was drawn over them.

19. *I am a sojourner before thee on the earth: hide not thy commandments from me.* On this earth the just are the sojourners who have no lodging of their own in the world. They are situated physically on the earth, but in their praiseworthy mode of life they reside in heaven. As Paul puts it: *Our conversation is in heaven.*[44] They are rightly called sojourners here, for they have no feeling for this alien land, merely cultivating temporarily the earth where their bodies are. The rich man who built granaries and devoted a long life to gathering many possessions was no sojourner; the true sojourners are this band who store their treasure in heaven, so that their hearts are always set on that future fatherland. So the faithful people asks to be made aware of the Lord's commandments, for they are seen not to dwell in the region of Babylon. Each of us can identify a person's ambition by what we see him seek to serve. We have said that the commandments are: *Thou shalt love the Lord thy God with thy whole heart and with thy whole soul,*[45] and the rest. The people asks that these be not hidden from them, in other words, removed from and denied to them, for they knew that from them would come salvation for their souls. So they pray that the commandments known to be concealed from sinners but seen to be proclaimed to the world should not be hidden from them.

20. *My soul hath coveted to desire thy justifications at all times.* Coveting is used in the bad and in the good sense. In the bad sense: *Thou shalt not covet thy neighbour's goods.*[46] In the good sense: *My soul hath coveted to long for thy justifications.* It is a forceful emotion, working most strongly in both directions; what is entangled in the roots of covetousness does not easily slip away. To demonstrate the force of the word, the spokesman added: *At all times,* so that no interruption, no time-lag could block this desire. The unfaithful person too can covet something good for a time, but the holy people entrusted to their perfected desires that which they longed for at all times, for coveting is desiring. No-one desires who does not covet, and again no-one covets who does not desire. So the double protestation denotes the fullest of wishes.

21. *Thou hast rebuked the proud: they are cursed who decline from thy commandments.* Although men's sins are countless, they here maintain that it is the proud who are rebuked, for they are known to be always hateful to God. It was through pride that the angel fell, and through pride that Adam was dislodged from the dignity of his nature. Just as humility is known to be the peace of all virtues, so pride is acknowledged to be the mother of vices. Scripture says of them: *God resisteth the proud, and giveth grace to the humble.*[47] We use the word *increpare* (rebuke) for breaking silence with a noise (*crepare*) and bursting out with biting words. God often does this in the course of the holy Scriptures, when He reveals to men His awesome anger. Next follows the simple generalisation that those who seek to decline from His commandments are cursed. It is a lighter evil for human frailty not to fulfil the Lord's precepts, but it is wicked to decline through pride from the source by which we can rescue our souls from the bonds of sins. It is clear that Adam, who declined from the Lord's command, was cursed, and likewise today those disfigured by a similar sin are cursed. We have already stated earlier what the commandments are.

22. *Remove from me reproach and contempt, because I have sought after thy testimonies.* Notice the words which sounded forth from that band of saints and martyrs. Subdued by various punishments, they seemed to be objects of reproach and contempt to the proud and wicked, and now they ask that the derision and low esteem in which they are held be removed by the manifestation of the Lord's mercy. We read this also in the words of another psalm: *For we are greatly*

filled with contempt, and our soul is greatly filled: we are a reproach to the rich, and contempt to the proud.[48] They sought after God's testimonies, and so they endured such treatment, for we know the injunction: *Blessed are they who suffer persecution for justice's sake, for theirs is the kingdom of heaven.*[49] But at this point we must more carefully examine why the martyrs seek to have reproaches removed from them, for they were aware that these were the source of their crown through the Lord's gift. But this prayer is uttered on behalf of the persecutors, so that once they are converted to the Lord, reproach may be removed from the martyrs, since the persecutors too have embraced the religion which they thought was to be attacked in the persons of others. We know that this has often occurred through the Lord's prompting.

23. *For princes sat and spoke against me, but thy servant was exercised in thy justifications.* The band of martyrs explains that they have been heard by princes sitting as judges who presided over the destruction of innocent people. They were both accusers and judges, a possible cause of still greater fear. But they rightly claim that they are the Lord's servants who in the midst of dangers to their lives pondered the reward which they would receive in the future life from His justification, since they endured such grievous suffering for a time in this world. They were *exercised* for their own betterment, not tortured for their punishment. Spirits like these conquered the world, for they softened the experience of their pain with thoughts of their eternal reward.

24. *For thy testimonies are my meditation, and thy justifications are my consolation.* A strategy was devised against the council of the malevolent, so that reflection on the Lord's testimonies would suffice in the face of their wicked fury. Meditation on those testimonies softens pains of any kind; the person continually intent on the Lord's promises leaves no scope for fear. As the apostle says: *Fear is not in charity, but perfect love casts out fear.*[50] They claimed that the Lord's justifications, which He promised to His martyrs, were their consolation. They gain consolation in present affliction from the hope of future rewards.

25. DALETH. *My soul hath cleaved to the pavement: quicken thou me according to thy word.* The council of the faithful passes to the fourth letter, in which they say that they are held bound by physical necessity, and can be saved only by the Lord's devotion. They entreat that

He remove from them the ways of iniquity, since they had chosen the path of truth. The human condition is explained by most splendid comparisons. A *pavement* is a solid structure of earth set where the ground is softest; it is well compared to our persons, for they too are smoothed over with a similar sheen. So they say that they are stuck fast to their flesh, which is undoubtedly prone to faults. If the soul cleaves to the body, it supports sinning, but if its will is sundered from the body, it supports virtues. So they rightly asked to be quickened through the Word, that is, through the Lord Christ, for they realised that they were being smothered by association with the flesh. We must however examine why this council of the blessed, which had earlier said: *Thy servant was exercised in thy justifications*, here confesses that their souls have cleaved to the pavement. This is to make us genuinely understand that though saintly men enjoy the Lord's grace and gleam with abundant variety of virtues, for as long as they are in this mortal flesh there are faults from which they must pray to be absolved. As the best of masters says in the gospel: *When you have done all things, say: We are unprofitable servants; we have done that which we ought to do.*[51] Scripture says elsewhere: *The just man at the beginning of his speech is his own accuser.*[52]

26. *I have declared my ways, and thou hast heard me: teach me thy justifications.* Having stated that they cleave to the pavement, they have next rightly revealed their sins, and so the words, *thou hast heard me*, follow. What a wonderful balance and astonishing exchange, that they should tell the Lord of their wicked deeds, and receive from Him the rewards of salvation! Who would not be roused by such blessings to seek a reward by confessing to Him to whom you cannot deny what you have done? We must also study the words: *Teach me thy justifications.* This is not so as to hear them, but to perform them. It is the one seen to have performed the tasks entrusted to him who is revealed as acquainted with things divine. Alternatively, they ask that they might grasp those justifications known to have been enjoined in figure.

27. *Instruct me on the way of thy justifications, and I shall be exercised in thy wondrous works.* The sacred troop rightly sought to understand the way of justifications, which had exposed their own ways, in other words, their sins; for unless we condemn these ways, we cannot attain that other. *Instruct me* points to their understanding; they wish to ascertain, as has now often been said, the secret meaning in the Jewish

servant's being freed after six years, in the gift of the seventh fruit of the earth to cattle and to the needy, in the fact that after fifty years any possession was ordered to be restored to the former owner,[53] and similar practices which are seen to meet with the Lord's justifications. They rightly wished to acknowledge these, for they are known to contain the secrets of our future hope. Next comes: *And I shall be exercised in thy wondrous works.* They are indeed exercised in thought and unique wisdom, since they apply the Lord's words to their spiritual meaning. They call wondrous works those which they earlier called justifications; when understood these reveal a miracle, because they are manifest in the present so as to be seen to show things in the distant future.

28. *My soul hath nodded through weariness: strengthen me in thy words.* We gather that after that holy entreaty they were made to wait, for they say that their souls have nodded through weariness, as usually happens to people made to wait in lengthy anticipation. This is to help us realise that divine protection comes to us through the virtue of patience. The soul nods when it relaxes its concentration and wearily seeks leisure and rest, and is seen to fail wholly to attain its aim. Note that the word is *nodded,* not slept; the forgetful and lazy person sleeps, whereas the weary person who is expectant nods. Another psalm has this same word: *If I shall give sleep to my eyes, or nod with my eyelids.*[54] And elsewhere: *Behold, he shall neither nod nor sleep, that keepeth Israel.*[55] But so as to be able to dismiss this fault too from their wearied souls, their follows: *Strengthen me in thy words.* Their purpose was that if their expectation was to be postponed further, their souls would remain steadfast and unchangeable in the Lord's words, for we know that any delays, any weariness, any toils can be wholly consoled by such a remedy, if we ponder with frequent repetition on the Lord's law. (Cassian, that best of educators of God's servants, calls this nodding of the soul *accidie;* he counsels monks that it is to be energetically avoided.)[56]

29. *Remove from me the way of iniquity: and in thy law have mercy on me.* Now that they are borne upwards to that contemplation of truth, they ask for what was vital in this world: that the way of iniquity, in other words, the devil, should be dislodged from his attacks on them, and that they might find the mercy which they desire in the Lord's law. No-one will in fact be justified through the law; as Paul says:

Knowing that by the works of the law no-one will be justified, but by faith in Jesus Christ.[57] And again: *By the law is knowledge of sin.*[58] So they justly ask for mercy in the state in which they believed that they were not forgiven by reason of the bonds of the law.

30. *I have chosen the way of truth: thy judgments I have not forgotten.* The way of truth is the Lord Christ; as He Himself says: *I am the way, the truth and the life.*[59] That most holy chorus said that they had chosen worship of the Lord Saviour amidst the various superstitions on the earth to which worldly people were enslaved. Choosing means nothing other than opting for one out of many. But let us see why they say that they chose, when we read in the gospel: *You have not chosen me, but I have chosen you.*[60] The blessed people, then, rightly made that statement because they had already been chosen so as to be able to choose. As the psalmist says elsewhere: *I have chosen to be an abject in the house of the Lord.*[61] So they rightly said that they had not forgotten the Lord's judgments, since they rejoiced in such a choice.

31. *I have stuck to thy testimonies, O Lord: do not confound me.* They earlier said that they had cleaved to the pavement;[62] and now they relate that they have cleaved to the Lord's testimonies. This is to show that through God's gift they have experienced growth. But since this rests wholly on divine protection, they ask that they should not fall from the benefits which have been bestowed, and plumb the confusion of shame. Their holy awareness had not relaxed through careless complacency; rather they were humbly afraid to lose what they had received. They could have been confounded if they had lost what they held.

32. *I have run the way of thy commandments, since thou didst enlarge my heart.* How variously this way is described, how diversely it is treated! They earlier said: *I have declared my ways,* and next: *Instruct me on the way of thy justifications,* and then: *Remove from me the way of iniquity;* they also repeated: *I have chosen the way of truth,* and they finally say: *I have run the way of thy commandments,* so that we are instructed that the way of the good or the evil life is being described in every possible manner. Preserving the order of truth, they say that they have run the way of the commandments, for they assert that their hearts have been enlarged by the Lord. They could not have either walked or run if their hearts had not been extended by breadth of knowledge, for though we read that the way of the commandments is

narrow, we can run it only with heart enlarged. When the soul receives the light of truth, it is opened to recognitions of many kinds; it is broadened by knowledge of virtues after earlier being narrowed by sins. They did well to say: *I have run*, to show that they have swiftly attained upright faith through the Lord's gift, for the just man runs the way until in Paul's words he attains the palm of the heavenly calling.[63]

33. HE. *Set before me as a law the way of thy justifications, O Lord, and I will always seek after it.* The blessed crowd has advanced to the fifth letter, asking in numerous ways to be maintained in God's law by His gift. We must clearly investigate which law this people seeks to have established, since they earlier said: *In thy law have mercy on me.*[64] These words were spoken with reference to the Old Testament; now they ask that the New Law be set before them with the coming of the Lord Christ, so that once the advent of the holy incarnation had been fulfilled, they might be strengthened by the perfect power of Christian faith. As Scripture has it: *The law shall come forth from Sion, and the word of the Lord from Jerusalem.*[65] Finally, they say that they seek that law continually, for what they demand with great prayers should come is always sought with burning desire.

34. *Give me understanding, and I will search thy law, and I will keep it with my whole heart.* We must ponder the meaning of this renewed request for what he said he had earlier received in the words: *I have run the way of thy commandments.* The fact is that we must go on begging for the Lord's gifts. His giving is constant, since He maintains what He gives, and we continue to seek with praiseworthy desire what we ask should remain permanently in us. This law is searched out by one who is lent understanding by the Lord, and to show the constancy of his devoted perfection, he says that he maintains it with his whole heart by the Lord's gift. By means of all these subtle touches he makes clear that every blessing is bestowed by the Lord and maintained by Him, and ever increased by His grace. Notice the beautiful order in which all the statements develop. They first ask that the law be set before them; this must be the law of the New Testament, for they already possessed that of the Old. Then they ask that they may deserve to recognise the purpose of that law, so that they may keep it with integrity of heart.

35. *Lead me into the path of thy commandments, for I have desired it.* Whereas in the fourth letter they say that they have run the way of the

commandments, here they made a second request to be led on that same path. But here we must interpret these commandments as those of the New Testament; they were earnestly praying to be directed to them, since they had run through those of the Old. In this way the desired perfection of the faith is fulfilled, and holy Scripture is seen not to have been self-contradictory. By their words, *I have desired it*, they are seen to seek the spiritual grace of the New Testament, by which they knew that they were attaining the kingdom of heaven.

36. *Bend my heart to thy testimonies, and not to covetousness.* These words are to be carefully analysed. They ask that their hearts be bent to the Lord's testimonies, which through the Lord's gift we attain not by greedy avarice but by praiseworthy humility. When we bend low, we observe better the things revealed before our eyes, for those who stand upright or bend backwards through vanity are wholly unable to observe the things before their eyes. They added: *And not to covetousness.* That troop of saintly persons realised that covetousness is full of vices, and they ask that this be removed from them so that they could whole-heartedly and wholesomely bend over the sacred Scriptures. Covetousness is the burning desire for temporal possessions; it was through this that the first man sinned and bequeathed to his posterity inflammatory vices. It was through this sin that the devil accused Job, saying that he loved the Lord because of the riches that He had given him and not because of the contemplation which was the cause of his goodness. The outcome refuted this charge, since the holy man repeatedly gave thanks to the Lord in all his adversity. So this blessed people asks that He remove covetousness from their minds, and that they be attracted to the Lord's testimonies solely through love of right conduct.

37. *Turn away my eyes that they may not behold vanity: quicken me in thy way.* Many of the wise of this world have governed themselves by the law of self-control, so as to win the approval of men's judgment rather than the Lord's. But these men wasted their efforts in pointless zeal, for Scripture says: *Do not perform your justice before men.*[66] So now the blessed crowd begs the Lord to divert the eyes of their hearts from such designs, so that they may not become enmeshed in worldly delights through debased habits, for we undoubtedly sin through our eyes as well, when we are seduced by desire for things observed. They begged to be estranged from this vanity, since they knew that this is

the source of the greatest sin. It is through this that people become notorious for being obsessed by various spectacles, and likewise for being carried away by foul love for women, and for evilly desiring possession of the property of others. But to this request is added the aspiration for perfection, that God should deign to enliven them in His way, that is, in the Lord Christ, in whom they are truly quickened because death is overcome by His strength.

38. *Establish thy word to thy servant, in thy fear. Establish* means set or implant, solidify and strengthen so that the sacred utterance does not slip away in fleeting forgetfulness, for it must ever remain immovably in our thoughts. To this statement they did well to append fear, to ensure that we always pray that we may not lose the gifts which we have received, and suffer the heavier fate of having learnt a sweetness which is lost. They added *thy* to fear, and this is quite different from human fear. This people fear in order to love, and seek so as never to cease loving Him whom they fear. Because very many people regard the words of the Lord carelessly, and refuse to listen, regarding them as useless tales, they rightly added: *In thy fear,* in which guilt is not sought and in which we do not embrace the hazards of sloth.

39. *Cut out my reproach, which I have apprehended, for thy judgments are delightful.* In this statement man's greatest vice is expounded. Many people descend to reproach through false suspicion, and they seek to have this fault excised. We often give favourable testimony on behalf of many wicked men, and again in our ignorance we speak evil of good men, and inevitably the person who makes some assertion without knowledge incurs disgrace. Suspicion is very often found to be unfounded, and this is not appropriate to a true Christian; so this suspicion leads to reproach springing from sin. So they rightly sought that it be cut out from them, for it could be a source of guilt. First they confessed their weakness, but now they are found praising the Lord's judgments, for His word is true, and His decree unchanging. So as lovers of the truth they aptly said that the Lord's decree was delightful to them, for they knew that through it they gained both rest and a crown. As Paul says: *I have fought a good fight, I have finished my course, I have kept the faith. For the rest, there is laid up for me a crown of justice.*[67]

40. *Behold, I have longed after thy precepts: quicken me in thy justice.* The holy troop has earlier asked that various benefits be bestowed on

them, but in this verse they say that fullness of favours has ensued because they had longed for the Lord's precepts, which bestow true prudence and salvation. They beg to be enlivened in the Lord's justice, though seen to be still living. This was to enable us to understand that the sole really genuine life is that which the Lord Christ has deigned to bestow. The Lord's justice is the Word made flesh, to whom He assigned all judgment, so that the whole world is to attend for judgment when He assesses us. As Paul says: *He was made unto us wisdom and justice and sanctification and redemption.*[68]

41. VAV. *Let thy mercy also come upon me, O Lord: thy salvation according to thy word.* At this sixth letter, the holy gathering reaches the point of asking that the Lord of salvation be granted to them, so that they may confound their enemies as a result of this great gift, and may advance in the Lord's law by diligent meditation. So they pray that the Lord Saviour may come upon them, for He is the mercy of sinners and the life of the faithful. So that you would particularly heed this mercy, the words that follow are: *Thy salvation;* He is truly this, for through Him salvation came to the nations when He bestowed the healing of His devotion on a sick world. *According to thy word:* in other words, "according to Your pledge which you are known to have promised through the prophets."

42. *So shall I answer them that reproach me with the word, that I have trusted in thy words.* They make this point to us by an absolute statement, to be observed when we are confronted by the guile of adversaries. We must not be silent before those able to listen to reason, but we must respond bravely so that the audacity of men of ill-will does not appear victorious in their eyes. They *reproach me with the word* who say that the Son is the lesser, or who wholly refuse to believe that He suffered in the flesh. As Paul has it: *If they had known it, they would never have crucified the Lord of glory.*[69] We must reply with the Lord's presumption to those who do not listen to salvation-teaching in order to venerate it, but rather to expose it to the injury of reproach. Next comes: *That I have trusted in thy words.* So they say that the reply must be that they have hoped in the words of the Lord, who says: *When you come before princes and powers, take no thought how or what to speak, for it shall be given to you in that hour what to speak. For it is not you that speak, but the spirit of your Father that speaks in you.*[70]

43. *And take not thou the word of truth utterly out of my mouth, for in*

thy judgments I have hoped. They ask that no fear of any punishment may remove from their mouths their confession of the truth, but that they may continue with words of constancy and nothing other, whatever the tortures inflicted. When they say: *Utterly,* they signify that the word of truth has been momentarily removed from some people, as happened to the apostle Peter who denied the Lord three times before cockcrow.[71] But the word of truth was not taken utterly out of his mouth, since he washed away his guilt with tears, and cleansed it with the shedding of blood. There follows the reason why the truth of confession must not be utterly removed from their mouths: it is because *I have hoped in thy judgments.* The Lord's judgments lay in the fact that crowds of martyrs were afflicted with various tortures; but they claim that their hope rose in the course of these, for Scripture says: *He scourges every son whom he receives.*[72] When wicked persons encounter trouble, they despair; but saintly men when afflicted experience instead the hope that they are loved. Up to this point the verses in this letter have contained a prayer, but the rest up to the end of the section are ordered in narrative.

44. *And I shall always keep thy law for ever and ever.* This and the other verses to the end of the letter are not a prayer but a narration. Earlier they begged to obtain, and now they here give thanks for the benefits received. They maintain that they always keep the Lord's law because it is sacrilegious to diverge from it. They can keep it if, as was said earlier, He does not take the word of truth utterly from their mouths. We use *always* to denote the period to the end of the world, but the expression here: *For ever and ever,* denotes that eternity which has no end. Earlier we said that the law was the shadow of things to come, the slaughter of the immaculate lamb, the performing of the rite of circumcision on the eighth day, and the like. How then can they say that they keep the law for ever, when not only are such things unnecessary after the resurrection to come, but they are seen to have been abolished on earth as well? The answer is that in the next world the Lord's law which the most holy people promise to maintain will be different. They know that an ascent is being made through this shadow of the law to the mystery of the eternal law. They know too the practice of the angels and powers who praise the Lord unceasingly; they know that it is an observance of the highest blessedness to gaze upon Him constantly. In short, they are aware of the laws of the

faithful in the next world, which they proclaimed they would maintain without end.

45. *And I walked at large, because I have sought after thy commandments. At large* is what they detailed under the fourth letter; *I have run the way of thy commandments, since thou didst enlarge my heart.*[73] This knowledge is manifold and salutary, and they deserved it for seeking understanding of His commandments. That understanding we rightly define as the charity of which Scripture says: *The charity of God is poured forth in our hearts, through the holy Spirit who is given to us.*[74] On the other hand, sinners' hearts are restricted in the matter of goodness, a point made by Paul when he says: *You are not straitened in us, but in your own bowels you are straitened;*[75] for the straitened, that is, the polluted, heart does not receive God. He who fills heaven and earth is taken up by the mind, which is *at large.* The dwelling must be expansive to deserve to receive such great majesty.

46. *And I spoke of thy testimonies before kings: and I was not confounded.* They spoke of the Lord's testimonies because they had sought and accepted them so as to reply to those who reproached them with the word. With the strength of this support, they say that they were not confused in the presence of earthly kings who could inspire terror with their proud power, but with fearless speech uttered the truth which they had conceived in mind. It is the person whose words are refuted by reasoning who is confounded, whereas no-one can be embarrassed who is strengthened by the testimony of truth. Whatever the pressure of circumstances, we must not deny Him who says: *He that shall deny me before men, I will deny him also before my Father who is in heaven.*[76]

47. *I meditated also on thy commandments, which I have loved exceedingly.* Here they reveal the zeal of their assiduous meditation. Only the person who has perused the commandments by diligent reading can meditate on them. They added: *Which I have loved,* to make this assiduity more clear-cut. A person can never neglect what he loves. Then, in case you perhaps regarded even this love as lukewarm, they added: *Exceedingly;* no love can be found greater than this. Love of the Lord's commandments cannot be modest like any other love; it must be enthusiastic, as is the aim here. So they rightly loved the Lord's commandments exceedingly, for they walked trustingly in breadth of heart.

48. *And I lifted up my hands to thy commandments which I have loved*

exceedingly, and I was exercised in thy justifications. In the previous verse they said *I meditated on thy commandments,* which relates to contemplative virtue, but now they say: *I will lift up my hands,* which relates to the active role, for raising the hands denotes being occupied in good works, whereas the person detained in evil actions lowers rather than raises his hands. Observe in both passages the words: *Which I have loved exceedingly* (in the first passage, *vehementer;* in the second, *nimis*); for both activities must be performed with great vigour so that the person who performs them can through the Lord's pity obtain fruit from them. They added: *And I was exercised in thy justifications.* Earlier they meditated when transported by mental concentration; here they were exercised when they sought to progress by regular action. Observe that in the divine Scriptures *exercise* is usually used in the good sense, but that in secular literature or in common speech it is rarely or never found in that sense;[77] we maintain that this is a usage peculiar to divine Scripture. *In thy justifications* relates to both kinds of activity, pleasurable meditation on the Lord's commandments and loving performance of manual work. These two, as we have often said, are precisely the activities which make Christians perfect. The narration begun four verses earlier ends here with this letter.[78]

49. ZAIN. *Be mindful of thy word to thy servant, in which thou hast given me hope.* The chorus of holy men passes to the seventh letter, in which they wholly commend to our minds hope in the Lord's promises. They desire that the pledge made by truth in its glory should remain firm in our minds, and they maintain that through this hope the faithful endure easily and most gladly the adversities of this world; for who would fear transitory death if eternal life were promised him? Who would spare a thought for the loss of dear ones when he knows that he will be joined to the choruses of angels? Who would fear physical toils when he realises that he will be set in eternal rest? Because of the conventions of human speech, God is told to be mindful, though He cannot forget anything whatsoever; not that it was right to attribute the injustice of forgetfulness to the divine majesty, but they pray that He may quickly bestow the fruit of His most merciful promise on His servants. You will often find these metaphors in the Scriptures. For example, in Genesis: *I will remember my covenant;*[79] or in Exodus: *And the Lord remembered the covenant he made*

with Abraham, Isaac and Jacob.[80] *Of thy word* perhaps denotes the promise which He makes in the gospel: *Blessed are they that mourn, for they will be comforted. Blessed are they that suffer persecution for justice's sake, for theirs is the kingdom of heaven.* And elsewhere: *I shall not leave you orphans,*[81] and similar passages. *To thy servant:* we must understand "fulfil Your promise," for if you try to join the expression to what goes before without any addition, the words cannot make sense. This figure is called *ellipsis,*[82] in other words, omission, when a word is left hanging to make us investigate it more eagerly. Next follows: *In what thou hast given me hope,* that is, in the promise of Your word, fulfilment of which the faithful people rightly sought from the Lord of truth.

50. *This hath comforted me in my humility, because thy word hath enlivened me.* The people bear witness that the hope which they say emerged from the Lord's promises comforted them in the exigencies of this world; for in the course of calamities of any kind, the spirit of the faithful is refreshed when such repayment is contemplated. Who is to fear ambush in this world when he turns his mind to the Lord's promises for eternity? When they say: *Hath comforted,* they indicate that amidst their worldly hardships it was their consolation to be afflicted in this life, and to rejoice in the promise of the hope to come. *In my humility* also denotes this, for holy humility is undoubtedly found to endure all things with patience and thanksgiving. This hope He also bestows in the gospel, when He says to the apostles: *In your patience you shall possess your souls.*[83] Next follows: *Because thy word hath enlivened me.* They give the reason why their humility has consoled them: the promise of so great a Judge has strengthened their spirit of endurance, and the hope derived from that comfort has enlivened them in their affliction, so that they do not fear the death that is transient.

51. *The proud did iniquitously together, but I declined not from thy law.* They indicate the period when the lowly Church was exceedingly troubled by arrogant persecutors. But they say that these attempts were all vain, because the savagery of the malevolent could not harm them. Notice too that the faithful people say that their humility was enlivened, whereas they relate that the proud, in other words, malevolent despots, acted cruelly, and their future was to lie in death, not life. These two words denote the nature of the human race. Those

who strive to obey the Lord's commands are to be called humble, and those swollen with the devil's promptings, proud. Next comes: *But I declined not from thy law;* understand "as those who persecuted the innocent imagined." When they say: *I declined not*, they indicate that they constantly abided by the utterance of the truth.

52. *I remembered, O Lord, thy judgments of old, and I was comforted.* Remembering judgments does not imply deeds deserving retribution, for the person fired by the urge to wickedness is haled back by fear of punishment. When they say: *Of old*, they denote the time when the world began to be ordered. The troop could speak of that era for they are known to have lived long lives in successive generations. If the psalmist had intended to indicate eternity he would have used: *For ever and ever*, a phrase which he often inserts.[84] They say that they were comforted by this thought, for God's power does not forsake His servants. As the psalmist says elsewhere: *I have been young and now am old, and I have not seen the just forsaken.*[85]

53. *A fainting of spirit hath taken hold of me because of the wicked that forsake thy law.* Here the devotion of their holy association is expounded: they say that they are faint with grief because sinners were seen to abandon the Lord's law. Inevitably a holy person feels sorrow at a neighbour's guilt, for the devoted spirit longs for the salvation of all, and is heartbroken on seeing punishment looming over the person who he prays will not sin; he knows that evil gratuitously inflicted is more offensive to his Creator. So the holy troop was tortured not so much by their own punishment as by the sins committed by exercise of tyrannical power.

54. *Thy justifications were a fit subject for my song in the place of my lodging.* The phrase, *fit for my song*, suggests psalm-singing to be conducted with great delight. As Paul has it: *Singing and making melody in your hearts to the Lord.*[86] Singing always lightens labours, and does not allow weariness to creep into the mind consoled by the great sweetness of contemplation. As for the addition: *In the place of my lodging*, this, as we have often said, denotes this world in which all devoted to the Lord Christ are foreigners. We have been expelled in the person of Adam from our abode in paradise, and we have our lodging in this land because we do not possess the blessedness of that native land; so

we are seen to be foreigners in this world. As Paul likewise says, *While we are in this body, we are absent from the Lord.*[87]

55. *In the night I have remembered thy name, O Lord, and have kept thy law.* Undoubtedly the *night* can denote this world in which the darkness of sins reigns; if only it closed our bodily eyes, and did not to our greater danger blind the eyes of the heart! The Lord dispels this darkness when at the time of the Judgment He comes and *brings to light the hidden things of darkness, and makes manifest the counsels of the heart*[88] now nurtured by unlawful transgressions. But the people say that in this night they *have remembered the Lord's name,* since they attribute all His benefits not to their own merits but to God's gifts. As we read in another psalm: *Our help is in the name of the Lord, who made heaven and earth.*[89] And Paul states: *He that glorieth, let him glory in the Lord.*[90] By so doing the faithful person is not shrouded in the darkness of this night, for he is enlightened by the light of the heart. A worthy claim follows: they say that they have kept the Lord's law because they remembered His name in the night. It would have been fruitless to keep the Lord's law if they had attributed anything to their own merits.

56. *This happened to me because I sought after thy justifications.* With *This happened to me* supply "as consolation"; it must be understood of the night rather than of the law, so that what is blindness in sinners is seen to be enlightenment in holy men. This is how believers avoid darkness, though dwelling in the blindness of this world. The reason follows why night became a consolation to them; it was *because I sought after thy justifications.* If they had said "my justifications," they would have continued to suffer the densest darkness, but because they said *thy justifications,* they could not be shrouded in the shadows of the world.

57. HETH. *O Lord my portion, I have said I would keep thy law.* The blessed troop advances to the eighth letter, in which they desire to see the Lord's face because they are known to have obeyed His commandments. *Portio* (portion) is derived from *pars* (part);[91] we belong to the part of Him whose wishes we obey. You find this word often used, as in: *The sons of Levi will have no portion nor lot in the midst of their brethren, because the Lord God is their portion.*[92] So God is rightly called

the portion of the devoted, because they will live in the blessedness of His kingdom. Next comes: *I have said I would keep thy law. I have said,* that is, "I have decided, decreed and promised to preserve the Lord's precepts," and so they had been set in the Lord's portion, that is, in blessed Jerusalem and not in the chaotic region of Babylon.

58. *I entreated thy face with all my heart: have mercy on me, according to thy word.* The Lord's face is here found to be understood in two ways. The people longed for the Christ who they believed with undoubting minds would come, and they sought to gaze on His incarnation, which was to appear as salvation to the world. As another psalm had it: *O God of hosts, convert us and show thy face, and we shall be saved.*[93] *With all my heart,* that is, without hesitation, so that they did not seem dubious about the future, but showed utter certainty in demanding Him there and then. They also ask that the mercy of His coming be fulfilled, for this was promised in countless declarations through the prophets. Or preferably, they seem to ask to be able to gaze on His face at His coming resurrection. As we read in Scripture: *Blessed are the pure of heart, for they shall see God.*[94] And Paul says: *We see now through a mirror in a dark manner, but then face to face.*[95] But because they knew that they were sinners, they beg for His mercy, so that when delivered by grace they may witness what they cannot observe on their own merits. *According to thy word:* that is, the word by which He promises to His saints the most blessed and wholly incomparable vision of His divinity.

59. *For I have thought on my ways, and turned my feet unto thy testimonies.* They explain the sequence of human conversion. We must first quite sternly convict ourselves, and thus make our way to the Lord's commands. With the famed Judgment in mind[96] they had first pondered their ways, in other words, their human acts, but since these were wholly displeasing to them, they turned their feet to tread the Lord's testimonies, on which the person who walks can gain a firm footing. They observed that there were sins in human actions, but that justice flourished in God's commandments, and they wisely abandoned the course which they realised was exposed to hazards. By saying: *I turned my feet,* they indicate that initially they had been ill-directed.

60. *I am ready, and am not troubled: that I may keep thy commandments.* When they say that they are ready, they show that they have

decided to endure any dangers whatsoever in favour of the Lord's commandments. It is the person who has no fear of persecutors and who has dismissed the enticements of this world from his thoughts who attests that he is ready to maintain the Lord's precepts. As the apostle Paul says: *I am ready not only to be bound, but to die also for the name of Jesus.*[97] There are similar words in another psalm: *My heart is ready, O God, my heart is ready.*[98] Next follows: *And I am not troubled.* The unforseen is perhaps a source of trouble; a studied decision does not induce fear. So the Lord likewise gives forewarning in the gospel: *Let not your heart be troubled;*[99] for the person troubled with fearful reflections cannot be called ready. They added the purpose for which they said they were ready, namely to keep the Lord's commandments, which are well and wholly kept when no opposition is feared.

61. *The cords of sins have encompassed me, but I have not forgotten thy law.* When they speak of the cords of sins, they show that each sin which we commit is a noose, for cords are intertwined and twisted bonds by which sinners always confine themselves. As Isaiah says: *Woe to you that draw iniquity like a long cord.*[100] Elsewhere we read: *Each is fast bound with the bonds of his own sins.*[101] This must be ascribed to the body's depravity; but since they state: *I have not forgotten thy law,* why should they say that they are encompassed by bonds of sins? The likelihood is that their flesh was encompassed and bound by the cords of transgressions, whereas their holy spirit fought back against the vices that stirred them, and was not forgetful of the Lord's law. As Paul says: *I with the mind serve the law of God, but with the flesh the law of sin.*[102]

62. *I rose at midnight to confess to thee, for the judgments of thy justice.* The words, *I rose at midnight,* are not otiose. They knew that at that hour the first-born of the Egyptians were smitten,[103] that at that time the bonds of Peter, Paul and Silas who lay in prison were loosed,[104] that the Bridegroom would also come at midnight.[105] So at that same time they rise to give praise, so that they may not stand among the foolish virgins, and the door remain closed on them. The expression, *I rose,* is also meaningful, because we always rise when we hasten to the Lord's praises. *To confess* here means to give praise, for the words that follow are: *For the judgments of thy justice.* If the sense to be understood had been confession of repentance, the words would have been "for Thy mercy," not *for the judgments of thy justice.*

63. *I am a partaker with all of them that fear thee and that keep thy commandments.* Here they have expressed more clearly what they said earlier at the beginning of this letter: *O Lord, my portion.*[106] They were the Lord's portion in the sense that they were seen to take their place among His servants. Observe how they show the force of ecclesiastical unity, saying that they are a part of all the faithful, not of a single church but of the Church throughout the whole world's extent. They were right to say that they had sections everywhere, for such were the words of the whole congregation; they were a part of all that could be pleasing to God throughout the whole world. Observe how humbly they say that they are *a partaker with all of them that fear* God, whereas we read in the apostle: *We are made partakers of Christ.*[107] We recall that certain persons are denoted as partakers of God in Psalm 44 in the words: *Therefore God, thy God, hath anointed thee with the oil of gladness above thy fellows;*[108] for whoever walks in newness of life will be a partaker of Christ. So the gathering spoke humbly here, yet extended the mind of the person with good understanding to the true meaning of what a partaker of the Lord is. As for the phrase, *all of them that fear thee*, they did not wish you to interpret this as those who fear the Lord's judgment with servile fear, so they added: *And that keep thy commandments*, these being people of proved devotion, whose fear is most chaste and whose love invites respect.

64. *The earth, O Lord, is full of thy mercy: teach me thy justifications.* When they say: *The earth, O Lord, is full of thy mercy*, they reveal nothing other than the diffusion of the Christian faith. He has mercifully filled the earth with it so that He may be shown to have made void the claims of totally empty superstition on all sides. Observe too how diligently they seek to learn the Lord's justifications, after repeatedly claiming to have kept them. This is to show that the Lord's commands must be sought unwearyingly, so that with the impulse of such longing our growth can ever be enhanced. As the first verse of the fifth letter had it: *Set before me as a law the way of thy justifications, O Lord, and I will always seek after it.*[109]

65. THETH. *Thou hast dealt in goodness with thy servant, O Lord, according to thy word.* The blessed folk embark on the singing of the ninth letter, in which they give thanks that they have been made humble so that they might with total devotion attain the Lord's justifications. They claim that His testimonies rank higher in their eyes than

all riches. In this statement: *Thou hast dealt in goodness with thy servant, O Lord,* they proclaim the gifts bestowed on them, for the good Lord bestows goodness on His servants. What this goodness is they expound below with the words: *It is good for me that thou hast made me humble, that I might learn thy justifications;*[110] they are not offering thanks for worldly happiness, but for the affliction which wins salvation. They remember that the hardship which squeezes them is a mark of devotion, for they realise that *goodness* is the appropriate term for what helps their growth, not what makes for empty joy and exultation. A doctor deals in goodness when he lances wounds, and so does a father when he beats his son. Though they inflict momentary punishment, they bestow healing as a result of tribulation. So they realised that the Lord was to be honoured with devoted supplications, for through His clemency our afflictions are transformed into joy, though they seem oppressive for the moment. Next comes: *According to thy word,* referring to the text: *He that humbleth himself will be exalted, and he that exalteth himself will be humbled.*[111]

66. *Teach me goodness and discipline and knowledge, for I have believed thy commandments.* We must investigate why they still seek instruction on what they already claimed to have received earlier. Presumably this is because we can never have enough of what is good, just as a blazing fire will rage more widely the more it runs through dry timber. So the apostles burning with the heat of belief said: *Increase our faith.*[112] God, then, teaches *goodness* by breathing into us a desire for charity. He teaches *discipline* when He grants patience in tribulations; He teaches *knowledge* when He is recognised as the One who bestows the things that bring salvation. But God teaches in one way, and a human teacher in another. The human teacher utters words, but cannot impart understanding of these matters, but God first enlightens the heart so that the words may sink into the thoughts of the elect. Next comes: *For I have believed thy commandments.* Commandments are proclaimed to be carried out, so we must ask why they said: *I have believed thy commandments.* It is because of the Lord's promise proclaiming: *He who hears my words and does them is like to a man building his house on a rock,*[113] and the rest. So they rightly added: *I have believed,* because the Lord has promised the greatest rewards to those who obey Him.

67. *Before I was humbled, I offended: therefore I have kept thy word.*

Let us observe how in this verse human life is described. They said earlier that they had sinned since they were held in subjection to original sin. Later they claimed that they had been made humble so that they might be free of the guilt incurred at the root. Finally they have kept the Lord's word because they have deserved to be humbled, for as the apostle James says: *To the humble he gives greater grace.*[114] To restrain the licence of those who often transgress, they say that they have kept the Lord's word, in other words, the holy Scriptures, through His gift by the total concentration of their minds.

68. *Thou art good, and in thy goodness teach me thy justifications.* The spokesman asks the good Master to deign in His goodness to teach His disciple. This figure is called *paronomasia* and in Latin *denominatio*,[115] when the similarity of words gains the attention of the listener.

69. *The iniquity of the proud hath been multiplied over me, but I will seek thy commandments with my whole heart.* He fittingly seeks the resource of goodness, since he was about to enter the uncertainty of conflict, so that in his struggle he could declare the Lord's justifications which he had learnt by his reading, for the commandments are perfectly learnt when they are carried out. He says that the iniquity of persecutors has been multiplied over him, and accordingly he requests that his devoted humility should not be stained by the oppressive punishment of the proud. But note the ensuing words in the face of that most cruel faction: *But I will seek thy commandments with my whole heart*, so that the more they strove to seduce him, the more he was seen to cleave to the Lord's commands. This is how those who have tried to prevail over the saints by wielding transient punishment are themselves splendidly vanquished; the greater their exertions to prise the saints from the Lord's law, the more they caused them to ponder His commands.

70. *Their heart is curdled like milk: but I have meditated on thy law. Curdled* is used in a good and a bad sense. In the good sense, as at Psalm 67: *A curdled mountain, a fat mountain.*[116] But here we must interpret it in the bad sense, for he wishes us to understand that the iniquity of the proud, which he earlier witnessed was multiplied over him, has hardened, for through wicked plotting it has become concentrated as milk does into a thicker substance. *Lac* (milk) gets its name from *liquor* (liquidity) because it pours out of an internal substance rather than forming the natural liquid of the body; *a* changes into *i*, as

amicus changes into *inimicus*, and so on.[117] But the more hardened they became in evil, the more the spokesman could not detach himself from the Lord's law, so that their cruel obduracy was overcome by his devoted perseverance.

71. *It was good for me that thou didst humble me, that I might learn thy justifications.* The spokesman said it was good for him that he was subjected to savage punishments, with no thought of the present but a longing for the future; for he had begun to get a taste of the sweetness known to excel all sweetnesses. This lowliness touches the famed roofs of Jerusalem, for just as pride submerges us in hell, so humility raises us to heaven. Next is explained the nature of the conflict waged by this lowliness. His phrase is: *That I might learn thy justifications*, in other words, "That I might carry out Your teaching." Perfection of learning occurs when the Lord's precepts are demonstrated in faithful action.

72. *The law of thy mouth is good to me above thousands of gold and silver.* How often in this letter does the troop of saints speak of goodness! They reverted to it often because the sweetness of that goodness grew more and more on them. Let us reflect on the force of the expression which they use, *of thy mouth;* they attest that the gospel precepts which were uttered by the mouth of the Lord Christ rather than the precepts of prophets or apostles are most precious to them. Next comes: *Above thousands of gold and silver.* Gold and silver seem to be conspicuous among the things desired by men. But because that goodness could not find a parallel comparable to it, they first inserted *above thousands*, a phrase denoting what is without limit and beyond comprehension, so that by such an addition comparison with gold and silver would appear cheap; for whatever the objects mentioned, *above* always goes beyond them. So we have here a comparison without similarity, a prize without limit, love without end. Such great affection deserved to be signified in such a way that nothing could be made equal to it.

73. IOTH. *Thy hands have made me and formed me: give me understanding, that I may learn thy commandments.* The splendid troop advances to the tenth letter, in which they ask that understanding of the commandments be granted them so that they may enjoy the benefit of truly genuine life. They pray that the Lord's mercy may be without stain, so that they may not be confounded at the Judgment. If we

sought to draw together the arguments about this verse, we would disgorge the length of whole books rather than recount anything with the promised brevity. Let it be enough for us to express with God's help some understanding of the subject by abbreviated reflections. We read: *The heavens are the works of thy hands;*[118] we also read: *And his hands formed the dry land.*[119] We have the same thing here: *Thy hands have made me and formed me.* But all these words are metaphorical, for possession of hands is a physical attribute. If you wish to grasp the peculiar nature of the Lord's activity, listen to this: *He spoke, and they were made: he commanded, and they were created.*[120] So the power of His activity is by human tendency labelled His hands, for we are accustomed to work with our hands. Some would relate *have made* to the soul, and *formed* to the body, because it is known to have been formed from the mud of the earth. His creation rightly cries to its Creator: "*Give me understanding,* for I am known to have been formed by You." But you will ask what sort of understanding they sought, since they could not find it by human reason. It is the pure, contemplateable, devoted understanding which Adam's uncorrupted simplicity possessed before his sin, and not the understanding by which men seem to themselves to be wise and to excel the brute beasts in some degree. So they seek understanding to get to know the Lord's commands, so that by devoted obeisance the holy troop may deserve to obtain the understanding which Adam had lost through disobedience.

74. *They that fear thee shall see me and shall be glad, because I have greatly hoped in thy word.* A most splendid reason for bestowing pity is offered to the devoted Lord, that if He grants it to any one of the holy gathering, He will fill the spirits of all with great joy. They knew that His clemency wished to achieve the aim of strengthening the hearts of the faithful, and they entreat that the effect on them may be that the devotion of all can be increased. Our holy awareness progresses by observing the rewards of another, since the examples set before us always further our imitation of praiseworthy actions. They further added the reason why they should certainly obtain their request: it is because they proclaim that they hope in the Word which is Christ the Lord. Hope in Him never deceives; the mind deserving to be implanted in such great truth cannot be beguiled by transient desires.

75. *I know, Lord, that thy judgments are equity: and in thy truth thou hast humbled me.* Since elsewhere we read: *Thy judgments are a great*

deep,[121] and again: *God's judgments are unsearchable,*[122] we must investigate why the psalmist said here: *I know, Lord, that thy judgments are equity.* Whenever we read of what is unmeasured and unsearchable, we must interpret it as that eternal judgment which we cannot wholly understand here on earth. But the point here refers to the situation in the present world which the people attest that they know. It refers to the humbling and correction of the man who sins through mental pride, and the acceptance by God's mercy of the person who makes entreaty to Him. Who could doubt that His judgment is of the greatest equity, so that those who sin through pride are cleansed through devoted humility? Note that the expression here is not "I have believed" but *I know,* in other words, "I have experienced." This was to show that they have come to know this equity of the Lord through their sufferings and blessings.

76. *O let thy mercy now be for my comfort, according to thy word unto thy servant.* They rightly begged for mercy, for they had earlier in their humility confessed that the Lord's judgments were just. Amidst manifold labours and cruel encounters with tortures, they sought that mercy which would console them in these trials, so that they could endure the hardships of the world which they knew had been profitably imposed on them to cleanse their sins. They did not ask that such pains be removed from them, but rather sought consolation in them. Consolation comes when He grants patience in miseries, mitigates harsh tortures, and relieves the griefs of an afflicted mind with the promise of blessedness. Next follows: *According to thy word unto thy servant.* Supply "Let it be," shared with the previous phrase. The sense is: "According to the promise by which in the gospel He pledged that He certainly would not forsake the afflicted in their sufferings."

77. *Let thy tender mercies come unto me, and I shall live: for thy law is my meditation.* This is a sufficient explanation of what we obtain through the Lord's mercy, namely eternal life. When they asked that this be granted them, they begged to deserve true life, for the sole life which can be properly so called is the life troubled by no anxiety and saddened by no apprehension of death. The gospel says of it: *If thou wilt enter into life, keep my commandments.*[123] It should not trouble you that "eternal" is not added, for such is the force of the word "life" that when cited alone it is understood rather as eternal. So they say that

they should deserve this kind of life because their meditation was seen to be dominated by holy works. *Meditation* here is to be interpreted not merely as reading but rather as the works laid down by the law, for we are not made blessed merely by the meditation of repeated reading. That meditation makes us blessed which seeks the kingdom of heaven by holy works. As Paul puts it: *For not the hearers of the law are just before God, but the doers of the law shall be justified.*[124]

78. *Let the proud be ashamed because they have done unjustly towards me: but I will be employed in thy commandments.* It does not befit the holy people to attack their adversaries with a curse, since Christ Himself says: *Love your enemies, and pray for them that calumniate you;*[125] they themselves added: *But I will be employed in thy commandments,* so that you would realise that they had done nothing contrary to rule. But *let them be ashamed* is addressed to their improvement, not to eternal punishment. The conscience of the sinner is rightly shamed when his earlier evils are condemned by his own wish, and he begins to hate what earlier he seemed to love. What they pray for is that the outcome for the proud should be that they are no longer seen to revel in unlawful adventures. Next follows the likely reason why the proud are to be ashamed; it is *because they have done unjustly towards me.* What can be called more unjust than the desire to persecute those seen to be concerned with the most sacred commandments? Next comes: *But I will be employed in thy commandments.* In the face of the traps of enemies and of the pride which vaunts itself in swollen wrongdoing, they set the wholesome remedy which is nothing other than practice of the commandments. They did not war or struggle against faithless or cruel men at all, nor involve themselves in disputatious verbal arguments, but assaulted by empty words as though by blasts of wind they carried through their purpose with untroubled mind; thus their opponents might fall all the more quickly, since they were opposed by no mere human powers. Undoubtedly this kind of patience is the adornment of Christians.

79. *Let them that fear thee be converted to me, and they that know thy testimonies.* Appropriate phrases are designated to distinguish individuals; earlier it was said of the proud: *Let them be ashamed,* whereas it is said here of initiates: *Let them be converted to me,* which means "to Thee." It is right to interpret those who turn to the Lord as those who have begun to take their place in the gathering of the Church; at this

stage they had begun to fear but had not yet been converted with full commitment of mind. The additional phrase, *And they that know thy testimonies*, refers to those already steeped in the divine reading but not yet instructed in the work of salvation. *Let them be converted* could not refer to those made perfect who were radiant with both sacred reading and devoted activity.

80. *Let my heart become undefiled in thy justifications, that I may not be confounded.* They entreat that their hearts may become undefiled by forgiveness of sins rather than through the nature of their merit. As the beginning of the psalm stated, the person whose sin is forgiven is undoubtedly cleansed, and only the one who through divine grace has deserved to obtain the purity of forgiveness can don the marriage-stole. When that time comes, only he whose sins are forgiven is not put to shame. Observe too that after mention of their outstanding virtues the band of saints prays that their hearts may become undefiled. This is so that no human being may presume that he has what undoubtedly only the holiness of the Lord Christ possessed. Having confessed that they were made and fashioned by the Lord's hands, having stated that they were justly humbled to bear numerous sufferings, and being employed in the Lord's commandments and pondering also on His law, they do not dare to say that their hearts are undefiled, but they pray for the outcome not yet attained at the resurrection, when they will hear the words: *Come ye blessed of my Father, possess ye the kingdom which was prepared for you from the beginning of the world,*[126] and the rest. Note how the same word is used for different purposes. They asked that the wicked should be shamed, so that they would seek correction; and they ask that they themselves be not shamed so that they may escape the death of condemnation.[127]

81. CAPH. *My soul hath fainted after thy salvation, and I have hoped in thy word.* The pilgrim people on this earth sing the eleventh letter, in which they happily confess their extreme longing for the Lord's coming. They further relate their great sufferings from the persecution of the proud. Finally they ask that by the Lord's gift they may persevere in His commandments. The word *defectus* (fainting) is used also for the termination of something, as in: *The swords of the enemy have failed (defecerunt) unto the end.*[128] It is also on occasion used to express intense longing, as in: *My soul hath longed and fainteth for the courts of the Lord.*[129] Likewise here the holy congregation says that its

soul has fainted for the most burning love of the Lord Saviour. This is the tendency of human beings; if we utterly long for something, we seem to show weariness and fainting in the matter when we are on tenterhooks and cannot attain what we long for. So if a most kindly father is impatient at heart for the arrival of a most dear son who is long awaited and delayed, or if the chastest of wives likewise impatiently awaits a most sweet husband, do they not *faint* with the exhaustion of love in their longing demand to see their dear ones? So *my soul faints* means it is weary and exhausted, a feeling resulting from extreme longing. So let us ponder the extent of this most holy longing; they wearied themselves with such intensity of mind that they reached the point of most blessed fainting. But so that this fainting should not appear as loss of faith, they say that they have *fainted after* His *salvation,* which is what Jesus means in Hebrew. Then, so that none should perhaps question the need for such feeling, they added: *And I have hoped in thy word,* in other words, in the only-begotten Son who is: *The power of God and the wisdom of God,*[130] of whom we read elsewhere: *The word was made flesh and dwelt amongst us.*[131]

82. *My eyes have fainted in thy word, saying: When wilt thou comfort me?* This saving and strengthening fainting is repeated; it does not spring from weakness of mind, but is rather the outcome of glorious strength of spirit. Earlier they said that their soul had fainted in extreme longing for the Lord Saviour; now they relate that the eyes of their heart have fainted with such a desire. These are the eyes which can speak inwardly; as Scripture has it: *I cried with my whole heart, Hear me, O Lord.*[132] Though it is the tongue which usually speaks, here we read that the eyes said: *When wilt thou comfort me?* Clearly, then, these are the eyes of the understanding, the inner sight of the heart, which effectively entreat the Lord, and cry out, as it were, with silent words. It is no common or usual expression to say that the eyes speak; we must inevitably say that this manner of composition is peculiar to divine Scripture. Observe too the force of *in;* they said: *In thy word,* not "from thy word." To faint from the Lord's utterance is actually privation of all that is good, whereas fainting in His word spells perpetual increase. They say that they have borne this most powerful fainting for so long until the anticipated incarnation of the Lord should appear to the eyes of their heart. So we clearly acknowledge that even if the just have not beheld the Lord's coming with their

bodily eyes, they have ever gazed on it with the eyes of faith. As the Lord says in the gospel to His disciples: *Abraham desired to see my day; he saw it, and was glad.*[133]

83. *For I am become like a wineskin in the frost: I have not forgotten thy justifications.* Earlier they had sought comfort; now they give the reason why the Lord should help them. A skin in frost is deprived of its natural heat, and contracts with the stiffness of the frost. In the same way the bodies of the saints, when emptied of the heat inciting them to vices, are drawn to the blessing of conversion, and once they are wasted by a happy fate, the outcome is as the next words describe; they can by no means forget the Lord's justifications. The wineskin denotes the human body, and the frost indicates the blessing of conversion through which our wanton flesh is contracted by the tribulation of repentance. The heat of faith grows to the degree that it is withdrawn from the body's flame. But this wineskin belongs to the blessed; it causes the soul which confesses to profit from its own contrition. You should not regard it as improper that men are compared to wineskins, for when the Lord is to speak of the proclamation of the faith in the gospel, He says: *No-one puts new wine into old skins; otherwise the skins break, and the wine runs out, and the skins will perish. But new wine they put into new skins, and both will be preserved.*[134]

84. *How many are the days of thy servant? When wilt thou execute judgment on them that persecute me?* The band of saints knows that the Lord's members are subject to the devil's temptations till the end of time, and they ask when this world will come to an end, so that vengeance in store may be exacted from the persecutors, that is from the devil and his agents. It was not that they wished to know the period of their lives, but they were demanding the swift arrival of the future judgment, at which there will be rest and eternally abiding joy for those who are then blessed. You may possibly wonder why they wished to know of the world's end, whereas we read in the Acts of the Apostles: *It is not for you to know the times or moments which the Father hath put in his own power.*[135] First of all the disciples asked the Lord Christ this very question, and it was appropriate that the holy band as forerunners of the apostles should say what the apostles were to utter. Secondly, we must realise that the blessed folk sought an end to their evils, and they could not witness this until after the end of this world.

85. *The wicked have told me fables, but not as thy law, O Lord.* The

wicked here are clearly the heretics or the Jews, whose perverted prattling is seen to recount some foolish nonsense to them, for abandoning the order of truth they are known to be zealous for the most untrue fictions. Such teachings are wholly at odds with the Lord's law, for whereas it teaches the truth, those men strive to persuade us with deceits. Realise, you madmen who depart from Catholic truth, that your beliefs are compared to groundless fables. To whom do you believe yourselves acceptable, when you realise that you are branded with such an accusation by the holy Spirit?

86. *All thy statutes are truth. Unjust men have persecuted me: do thou help me.* In contrast to those words of theirs about heretics: *The wicked have told me fables,* they here proclaim that all the Lord's statutes are truth. Truth speaks the truth, but faithless men seek to obscure it with what we might call clouds. As the next words put it: *Unjust men have persecuted me,* denoting injunctions to wickedness, persuasion to falsehood, and any other means of aggression usually adopted by evil persecutors. They added: *Do thou help me,* as though they were confronting a monstrous beast, a most cruel foe, a savage lion, and the other opponents which fearful suspicion urges us to avoid.

87. *They had almost made an end of me upon earth, but I have not forsaken thy commandments.* When they say: *They had almost made an end of me,* they reveal the excessive extent of the persecution, but also they assert that by the Lord's gift they have not given way. The expression, *made an end of,* denotes both accomplishment and failure; if you carefully examine the force of the passage here, you will realise that they had accomplished rather than failed. So the gospel says: *It is accomplished,* meaning completed, *and saying this, he gave up the ghost.*[136] But if you have a mental picture of the butchery of dying men, you will think of them without pity as virtually *made an end of. Upon earth* means in this world, where the martyrs have endured. They added: *But I have not forsaken thy commandments,* so that their constancy could hold out to the end. As we read in Scripture: *He who perseveres to the end shall be saved.*[137]

88. *Give me life according to thy mercy, and I shall keep the testimonies of thy mouth.* Following that unique longing for the Lord Saviour, and the bodily tribulation described by the parallel of the wineskin, and the noble punishments which they endured, they appear to be asking to be lent life, as though they had not been living up to now;

and they promise that they will keep the testimonies of the Lord's mouth as though they had not been keeping them previously. But *Give me life* means: "Set me in eternal life, where there is life for the saints who are afflicted by no opposition." The statement: *I shall keep the testimonies of thy mouth,* does not imply that they did not keep them at that time, but gave promise that with the Lord's help they would keep them until the close of their lives. Or as some have it, these are the words of saints who longed for martyrdom, who a little earlier said: *Unjust men have persecuted me: do thou help me,* and later: *They had almost made an end of me on earth;* so these authorities reckon that the words must have reference to a longing for martyrdom. They asked to be given life through a glorious death, so that by losing this life for the faith they might purchase eternal rest, and then win eternal distinctions when the unfaithful believed that they were annihilated. But the chorus of the faithful takes note of human weakness, and says that this will be granted according to the Lord's mercy, for He gives life to what is dead and strengthens what is weak.

89. LAMED. *For ever, O Lord, thy word standeth firm in heaven.* The heavenly folk reach the twelfth letter, in which they detail the power and works of the Lord, and state that all transient things can have an end, but that His commands by no means come to a close. But since earlier they had said: *They had almost made an end of me on earth,* they expressed wonder at the power of the Lord, who does not permit the existence of the Church to be destroyed, no matter how harsh the persecution; and they leapt up with devoted cries, saying that the Lord's word *stands firm in heaven,* in other words, in each and every holy man on whom He has bestowed life instead of death, and joy instead of affliction, so long as they follow His commandments with devoted humility. Heaven lies within them, for they clearly live a heavenly mode of life. Alternatively, *in heaven* means in the angels, archangels and powers of heaven, in whom the holy Majesty dwells by reason of the purity of their allegiance. The Word always remains in them, for they too continually stand firm with the most constant will in the Lord's service. But on this passage some ask how the Word stands firm in heaven, whereas Christ Himself says: *Heaven and earth will pass away, but my words will not pass away.*[138] The answer is that these undergo change, but the Word stands firm in heaven, for He dwells in all the things of heaven with the glory of His majesty.

90. *Thy truth endures till the end of time: thou hast founded the earth, and it continueth. Till the end of time* denotes the periods in which the two peoples lent belief through the Lord's gift. The one people is that of the law and the prophets, the other that of the gospels and apostles, in which lies *Truth,* in other words the Lord Christ Himself, who granted them both belief and adhesion to the foundation of the faith. Why this Truth did not fail in these times is next explained with the words: *Thou hast founded the earth, and it continueth.* The phrase is better understood of holy men, who were *founded* so as to continue to believe in the Lord Christ; for if He had not founded them, neither the first age of the patriarchs nor the second of the apostles could have believed or endured. Whereas if you interpret *earth* as the whole world, which we read is suspended in its mighty mass, how are we to say that it continues, when the divine reading affirms that like heaven it must be changed?

91. *By thy ordinance the day goeth on, for all things serve thee.* Whenever *day* is used in the singular, it denotes the day to come which is one and eternal, and has no night. Scripture says of it: *And the Lord shall be for thee an everlasting light.*[139] So that none would think that this great wonder brooks any argument, they added that all things serve the Creator, who orders everything both temporal and eternal according to His will. But an objection may be raised about the unfaithful, who are seen not to serve the Lord, for they distance themselves from dedication to Him. But they too serve when they are judged, for the person found worthy of punishment does not get away scot-free. Alternatively, we must understand the mention of *all things* as referring to those for whom the day will be unending, for they endure the darkness of infidelity at no time.

92. *Unless thy law had been my meditation, I would then perhaps have perished in my lowliness.* They claim that they might have perished amidst the disasters which they endured, if they had not had the benefits of meditation on the law. This allows us to realise the value to us of meditation on the law, for it could deliver them from such great dangers. Such meditation on the law enjoined reflection or action, so that moulded so to say by their inner counsellor, they could fearlessly overcome rabid tortures. *In their lowliness* means in the affliction which they endured with devoted concentration, and from which they rejoice that they are freed, once they have deserved to attain holy

martyrdom; for *lowliness* is both endured by necessity and undertaken willingly. Those charged with crimes endure it, and those most holy in purity practise it.

93. *Thy justifications I will never forget, for by them thou hast given me life.* They promise devotion without qualification after the gifts which they have deserved to attain through the Lord's clemency. Other things can perhaps fade from the memory, but none of the faithful forgets the kindness by which life is proffered to them. So it had always been essential to be mindful of the justifications from which they are seen to have gained the gift of life. As we have already said, *justifications* are the understanding of the signs to come through events in time; the slaying of the spotless lamb at the Pasch, the journey to salvation afforded by the Red Sea, the gaining of the promised land by the people led in by Joshua. It is clear that all these events offered indications of the perfection to come. So we must not in any way forget these justifications, which afforded us the initial bases of our faith; for no-one can acknowledge the favour of a gift unless he recalls how events were seen to have their beginning.

94. *I am thine: save thou me: for I have sought thy justifications.* We read elsewhere: *The earth is the Lord's, and the fullness thereof: the world and all they that dwell therein.*[140] But this band here trusts in the reward of a special grace of the Lord, and says: *I am thine.* The person seen to involve himself in any impurity cannot truly say: *I am thine*, for one who is a slave to vices does not deserve to serve the Lord of the saints. The apostle Paul could employ such an expression without shamelessness when he cried: *To me Christ is life, and death is gain;*[141] and again; *I live now not I, but Christ lives in me,*[142] and the like. We must also ponder the fact that though they claim to be the Lord's, they still ask to be saved; they mean at the future judgment, when the blessed are admitted to eternal rest. They subsequently added the reason why they sedulously sought this salvation: *For I have sought thy justifications.* Other people seek honours, look for marriages, desire worldly joys; but this band considered that their riches were beyond reckoning if they were seen to seek the Lord's justifications with unremitting eagerness. We must ask further why they seek these justifications so often: it is to ensure that no-one thinks that the indications in the Old Testament can be ignored.

95. *The wicked have waited for me to destroy me: but I have understood*

thy testimonies. They *waited to destroy me* refers to the fact that evil counsellors coaxingly sought to pierce their souls with the wound of wickedness; for if the punishment had been immediate, the verb "hastened" rather than *waited for me* would have been used. That persecution is more oppressive which defers the crown of martyrdom, and unceasingly urges death for the soul. However, they reveal the remedy by which they were able to avoid this fate, for by understanding the Lord's testimonies they could not be induced to commit sacrilegious sins. So it is clear that only those delivered from such danger by the Lord's enlightenment make their escape. We must interpret *I have understood* as "I have performed"; as another psalm has it: *Blessed is he that understandeth concerning the needy and the poor.*[143] How could it profit the poor man if they merely understood that he was needy, and helped him with no gift? So understanding of the commandments means holy action.

96. *I have seen the end to all perfection: thy commandment is exceeding broad.* They had entered into the riches of God's depths, and had seen what could not be explained in detail, so they finally embraced what they had to say in a pithy statement, claiming to have seen the end to all perfection. Perfection is the full attainment of all virtues, and Christ is the end to this perfection. They rightly state that they have seen Him, for at that moment with enlightened minds they believed that He would come. But if you wish to interpret this literally, it can be taken in the sense that an end is always seen to be set on secular affairs, whereas the Lord's commandments have no end, because they extend with the broadest power. This is stated in this way to ensure that none of us may longingly aspire to worldly ambitions, realising that an end is set to them, but should with outstanding haste seek the Lord's commandments, which we recognise as ranging most widely. Their statement: *Thy commandment is exceeding broad,* is not idle; it denotes the love which we are bidden to direct to God and our neighbour. What can be said to be wider than that which embraces the entire law and the words of all the prophets? Of this love Paul says: *The charity of God is poured forth in our hearts by the holy Ghost who is given to us.*[144]

97. MEM. *O how I have loved thy law, O Lord! It is my meditation all the day.* The blessed people, who had made progress by the deepest meditation on the prophets and the gospel, is under this letter ushered

in to maintain that they have understood the divine commands more than did their teachers and elders, and so they claim that the sweetness of the divine Scriptures, sweeter than honey and the comb, has sprung forth on their lips. The word *how* promises that they will tell how they have loved the Lord's law with outstanding zeal. So they loved, not feared, the law, for it is fitting for holy men to perform the Lord's command through love not worldly fear. It is more acceptable that a person performs an action in love than merely in faithless fear. They next explain how they have loved with the words: *It is my meditation all the day.* We must interpret *all the day* as unbroken time, as we likewise read elsewhere: *I will bless the Lord at all times: his praise shall be ever in my mouth.*[145] Their holy awareness always had the light of day, for in the enlightenment of their hearts they knew nothing of the darkness of unbelief. What unfailing meditation, for which this world's daylight is insufficient! Our belief in the ability of human weakness to attain such constant meditation can be established on these grounds: a person who orders and controls any matters whatsoever with his eye on the Lord, taking food in moderation and sleep to the appropriate degree, is meditating on the Lord's law in all things, for he is recommending himself by honourable and praiseworthy action. As Paul puts it: *Whether you eat or drink or whatsoever else you do, do all to the glory of God.*[146]

98. *Through thy command thou hast made me wiser than my enemies, for it is ever with me.* These enemies are to be understood as the obdurate Jews, the heretics or the pagans, who have either failed totally to understand the Lord's commands, or are known to refuse to carry them out through misguided zeal. The people say that they have been made wiser than these enemies because they both devotedly accepted the Lord's command and abided by it with genuine integrity. They added the cause of their becoming wiser than their enemies: *Through thy command,* for by obeying faithfully they undoubtedly rose above all who sinned. This is the truly blessed glory and kingship of the good, to rise above the proud, to excel worldly powers, and to abide with constant minds in holy humility. They appended the phrase: *For it is ever with me,* meaning: *Thy command.* But let us examine what this command is which abides in this failing world: it is love of God and one's neighbour, for by that command we both love the Lord above all things and have the most perfect affection for our

neighbour as for ourselves. So they rightly said that they must keep this command for ever, for through it the blessed continually enjoy holy awareness of what is right.

99. *I have understood more than all my teachers, because thy testimonies are my meditation.* They appear to part company with that most holy humility of the blessed if we seek to interpret this as a claim to be superior to Moses, the prophets and the apostles who have instructed the Church with the purest faith. But let us advert to the previous verse, and here this entire false objection vanishes. There they said not "more than our fathers," but *Wiser than my enemies,* who are precisely those who taught the Lord's law with debased purpose. Here they refute rather than rebuke the teachers, denoting the Pharisees who restricted themselves to the letter, and disregarded spiritual understanding. The Lord often refutes them in the gospel, but their stony hearts did not deserve to experience the way of truth. So the evangelical band rightly claims that their understanding is better than that of all such teachers, because they rejected their teachers' base errors, and received the true teaching of the Lord Saviour. But they explain the reason why they understood better: *Because thy testimonies are my meditation.* The Lord's testimonies were not the meditation of those who through their most false opinion had far different sentiments than what had been enjoined.

100. *I have had understanding above the elders, because I have sought thy commandments.* This is not proud boasting, but the truth. *Elders* is the term which we use for those who excel in ripe wisdom and are considerably older than ourselves. Scripture says of them: *Ask thy father, and he will declare to thee: thy elders, and they will tell thee.*[147] We also use *elders* for persons of mature age who are most inconstant in their tendency to vices; the gospel writes of them: *The priests held counsel with the elders to put him to death.*[148] In this passage the people term as elders those hoary in body rather than in mind. They rightly say that they have understood more than these, for they venerated as their Creator one whom those others despised with sacrilegious minds. Often younger persons understand the divine Scriptures better than their elders; for example, Jacob, who submitted himself to the blessing and received the reward of the first benediction promised to his brother;[149] or Samuel, who understood better than the priest;[150] or Daniel, who knew better than the false elders whom he condemned to

death when filled with the spirit of God.[151] Certainly the new people had better understanding than the older Jewish people, for they happily accepted the Lord Christ who the Jews with mortal damage to themselves believed was to be despised. To enable the people to prove this with the testimony of truth, there follows the reason why they had understanding above the elders; it was *because I have sought thy commandments.* If the elders had sought the Lord's commandments, the younger ones could by no means have regarded themselves as wiser. Observe how the passage preserves the order of truth. They speak of *thy commandments,* not the commandments of debased men, of whom it is said: *Not knowing the justice of God and seeking to establish their own, they have not submitted themselves to the justice of God.*[152]

101. *I have restrained my feet from every evil way, that I may keep thy word.* It clearly emerges from this verse that both the enemies mentioned earlier who did not know the Lord's law, and the teachers who were gripped by the blindness of ignorance, and the elders, did not have a truly serious grasp of faith; for the people say that they have restrained their feet from every evil way trodden by those men, so that they could not be brought down by their wickedness. This is the surer explanation, for authority flashes like lightning to make itself clear. But let us examine what the words of the verse bring forth for us. *From every evil way* denotes the debased and most wicked promptings of heretics, with which they seek to charm us with a sweetness presaging destruction. The people added: *I have restrained my feet,* as though they sought to go to where they could have fallen into the black pit. For the guilt of original sin drags us ever headlong towards vices, and if we are not protected by the Lord's grace we are most easily beguiled by foul persuasion. That restraint achieved by the Lord's help is salutary, for we do not allow the development which is known to be full of dangers. *My feet* denotes the mental assent which by its footsteps, so to say, leads to sin and forces us on to evil ways, if the Godhead's devotion does not drag us away. Next comes: *That I may keep thy word.* The Lord's word could not be kept unless that baneful prompting is seen to have been banished. As Paul has it: *You cannot drink the chalice of the Lord and the chalice of devils: you cannot be partakers of the table of the Lord and of the table of devils.*[153]

102. *I have not declined from thy judgments, because thou hast set me a law.* The people clarified their earlier statement: *I have restrained my*

feet from every evil way, so that they might not decline from His judgments to the slightest degree. The purity of perfect blessedness is maintained when the debased wickedness of heretics is spurned. *From thy judgments*, then, means: "What Your holy will has appointed and given to us as our rule of life." Not to decline from them means precisely to stick fast to the right way, in other words, to attain the joys of heaven. There follows the reason which they approve: *Because thou hast set me a law.* Though the Lord bestowed the law through Moses, and commanded that it be observed unbroken, it is appropriate that we interpret *thou hast set me a law* as referring here to the gospel. The law which He bestowed through Moses put before us the task of the schoolmaster, but this law has bestowed on us the fruit of total fullness. So the holy people rightly rejoiced in the law which they had already accepted by believing in it. Now see what follows.

103. *How sweet are thy words to my throat, above honey and the comb to my mouth!* Though these comparisons are seen to denote something outstanding, they cannot be equated with things spiritual unless the word *above* is invariably used. So under the ninth letter it was stated: *The law of thy mouth is good to me, above thousands of gold and silver*, so that you may realise that such things are outstanding among men, but inferior to God's sweetness. So the blessed people in their great abundance are bloated by spiritual delights, and cry out: *How sweet are thy words to my throat!* By saying *how*, they claimed that they experienced great sweetness, but that their tongues could not express it. But since all taste is savoured by the palate, we must ponder why they spoke of their *throat*. The throat is the passage to our gullet, in which no sweetness is experienced, since the food has already been swallowed. But the people wished to speak simply of the Lord's utterances, so they specified the throat so that the nourishment could pass quickly to the inner reaches of our hearts. The Lord's utterances have no savour on the palate, but become sweet instead when gulped down. Next comes: *Above honey and the comb to my mouth. Honey* has particular reference to the Old Testament, *the comb* to the New; for though both are sweet, the taste of the comb is sweeter because it is enhanced by the greater attraction of its newness. Additionally, *honey* can be understood as the explicit teaching of wisdom, whereas *the comb* can represent that known to be stored in the depth, so to say, of the cells. Undoubtedly both are found in the divine Scriptures. They added: *To*

my mouth, for they were indeed proclaiming with their mouths the wisdom which they had swallowed with their throats. The prophet Ezechiel likewise says of the Lord: *Son of man, eat all that thou hast found: devour this book, and go and speak to the children of Israel. And I ate that book, and it became as sweet honey in my mouth.*[154]

104. *By thy commandments I have had understanding: therefore have I hated every way of iniquity.* The people were schooled in the Lord's law, and had heard the message: *My son, walk not with the wicked: divert thy foot from their paths. For their feet run to evil, and make haste to shed blood.*[155] They had also heard: *Thou hast destroyed all them that are disloyal to thee.*[156] And elsewhere: *You that love the Lord, hate evil,*[157] and the other passages proclaimed to the same effect in the divine reading. When they heard such instruction in the Lord's commands, they realised that the way of iniquity was to be wholly accursed, for it could not be pleasing to the just Lord. Worldly affairs must be loathed so that all our devotion may be bestowed on the things of heaven. It is fitting that we curse the things that are evil, because from time to time only necessity deters us from debased deeds, for the mind which has conspired with some delight in them seems to remain conscious of them. But the will of the faithful people distances itself from those things, once it has condemned them with the intervention of loathing. Thus they pollute themselves neither in aspiration nor in action, since they purify their minds by such cursing.

105. NUN. *Thy word is a lamp to my feet, O Lord, and a light to my paths.* The blessed troop passes from the thirteenth to the fourteenth letter, in which they rejoice that the lamp of the Lord's word shines out for their feet, and they commend their souls to Him with the most humble satisfaction. They seek their recompense from the Lord not in terror of punishment but with desire for reward. Thus in their knowledge that the night of this world is enmeshed with varied hazards so that it contains snares in one place and rocks in another and the deepest abysses in a third, they give witness that the Lord's word shines before their feet. They fear that if the true light were absent, they would fall into the destruction which they could not avoid by their own foresight. *Word* here must be interpreted as that sown by the mouth of the prophets through the holy Scriptures. They did well to call this *a lamp*, for the lamp is employed by men to dispel the deepest darkness of night. As the apostle Peter says: *We have the more firm*

prophetical word, whereunto you do well to attend, as to a lamp that shines in a dark place.[158] Similarly the Lord says to His apostles: *Let your loins be girt, and lamps burning in your hands.*[159] Luke did well to add *burning,* because of the foolish virgins, for when their oil ran out they could not attend on the Bridegroom's coming. But the Word which is consubstantial with the Father in the nature of His divinity, *who enlightens every man that comes into this world,*[160] and who says of Himself: *I am the light of the world,*[161] cannot be called a lamp. This distinction is made also in the gospel. John is called: *A burning and shining lamp,*[162] and again: *He was not the light, but he was sent to give witness of the light.*[163] Next follows: *And a light for my paths.* They continued with the same metaphor, saying that the Lord's word, that is, the utterances of prophets, provided a light for their paths; for it is through them, in the course of our being instructed towards the path of a good life, that we are enlightened in heart, and walk with straight steps.

106. *I have sworn, and am determined to keep the judgments of thy justice.* Following the enlightenment of the word, which they claimed shone before their feet, let us see if the blessed people could swear contrary to the commandments, for in the gospel it is written: *Thou shalt not swear, neither by heaven, nor by the earth, nor by Jerusalem, nor by thy head,*[164] and the rest. But swearing does not always denote taking oaths by which we invoke the Godhead in promising not to transgress our pledges in a fickle manner. Their sacred devotion had enjoined upon themselves the decision to keep the Lord's judgments in each and every danger. The very word denotes its purpose, for *iurare* (swear) is *iure orare,*[165] in other words, to plead what is right, so that one may not go astray and seek to renegue on one's promise. This is how the saints swear, in other words, make firm decisions, for they have already been strengthened by the Lord's gift. Indeed, in the gospel the Lord, who had come to save the poor and the wounded, restrains the weak from seeking to make rash promises which they certainly could not fulfil by their own efforts. *The judgments of his justice* lie in His exalting the humble, bringing low the proud, and relieving by the gift of His mercy those prostrated in humble satisfaction. This is what the next verse reveals.

107. *I have been humbled, O Lord, exceedingly: enliven thou me, according to thy word.* When Christ's members state that they have been

greatly humbled, they reveal that they have undergone the dangers of many persecutions, and thus in accordance with the Lord's promises they seek to be enlivened, for through the condition of the flesh they were seen to be fixed in death. *According to thy word,* that is, the promise which He gives: *Come unto me, all ye who labour and are burdened, and I will give you rest,*[166] and the passages of a like kind. They also know that through this humility the Lord Christ overcame the devil's pride. They know that the Lord suffered all the things which He commanded His saints to bear, and they rightly in their humility seek the remedies by which they knew they would be saved. So through this humility the faithful advance above kingdoms; through it the arrogance of tyrants is overcome; through it martyrs live for ever. The person who is deprived of this virtue cannot be called perfect.

108. *The free offerings of my mouth make acceptable, O Lord, and teach me thy judgments.* Earlier they said that they were humbled exceedingly, but so that you would not regard their prostration as an act of necessity, they added that the free offerings of their mouth could become most welcome to the Lord, offered as they were by a devoted spirit amidst fierce hardships. The offering of praises to the Lord is most acceptable even in time of leisure, but is clearly more outstanding in affliction, when physical weakness is not overcome though oppressed by pain, but the soul is content, and aroused the more to praise the Lord. *Free offering of the mouth* denotes the sacrifice of pious praise, offered not with an eye to any worldly advantage but with the aim of personal devotion, so that we love the Lord for His own sake and revere the Creator, who *rains on the just and unjust,*[167] who is good beyond all reckoning. So they ask that their devotion be made acceptable to the Lord, that appeased by this offering He may teach them His judgments which He deigns to reveal to faithful hearts. But let us ponder the splendid warmth of their hearts, which leads them to seek eagerly what they state they have quite often obtained. As they say under the ninth letter: *Thou hast dwelt in goodness with thy servant,*[168] and again: *Teach me goodness and discipline and knowledge;*[169] in this sense both statements are clearly intelligible. We must continually hope for what we always gain by asking for it.

109. *My soul is in thy hands always: and I have not forgotten thy law.* When wicked brigands were afflicting the just man's soul, and were

seeking to ensnare it with various traps, they declare with the greatest wisdom that it reposes in the Lord's hands, where no violence of aggressors can approach it. So we read in Scripture: *The souls of the just are in the hands of God, and torment shall not touch them.*[170] And in the gospel: *My sheep hear my voice*, and a little later: *And no man snatches them from my hand.*[171] They added: *Always* so as to appear to leave no scope for crafty infiltrations. The phrase, *in thy hands*, means in His power, for He can govern for their good the persons known to have entrusted themselves to His judgment. Next follows the reason why their soul is believed to have been placed in the Lord's hands: it was because they were seen not to be forgetful of His law. By not deviating at all from His saving precepts we pass under His protection. This precept is everywhere laid down, and we are specially warned of it, that we should turn back to the law in such a way as not to depart from it.

110. *Sinners have laid snares for me, but I have not erred from thy precepts. They have laid* means they have stretched out and sprung; they could not have been merely laid idly. A snare without bait does not catch a bird; the more effective deceit is that which beguiles with something pleasant. The devil's snare was armed with thirty pieces of silver when it trapped Judas and choked him to death.[172] It caught Saul by proud jealousy;[173] it drew the noose tight on Cain through envy of his brother;[174] and there are other examples of the devil's rage continually attacking the continuing life of this world, for in the forest of the world you find as many snares as you observe vices. But no earthly power could prevail against this saintly fellowship, for the life which they led accorded with heaven. As another psalm has it: *Our soul hath been delivered as a sparrow out of the snare of the fowlers. The snare is broken, and we are delivered.*[175] Next follows the heavenly antidote which is known to war on the poisons of this world; it lies in not having diverged at all from the Lord's precepts. He who does not diverge from them is not trapped by any deceit; for the ambush does not lie in those precepts, but adjoins them.

111. *I have acquired thy testimonies as an inheritance for ever, because they are the joy of my heart.* Profitable ownership is said to be attained in many ways, but the son who boasts succession to his father is held in great honour, for the legitimacy of a name and the mark of greatest affection lies in winning the approval of one's elders and rejoicing in

unshakeable ownership. The *testimonies* of the Lord are the most sacred precepts to which Moses witnesses before the people in the book of Deuteronomy, saying: *I call heaven and earth to witness to you this day.*[176] And elsewhere: *Be my witnesses, and I will be your witnesses, says the Lord.*[177] Paul too says: *I bear witness before God and Christ Jesus and the elect angels.*[178] So these are the testimonies which the blessed people rejoiced at having gained as an inheritance for ever, for we enter on such an inheritance not for a brief period, but for ever. Next follows: *Because they are the joy of my heart.* They rightly said that inheriting the heavenly kingdom for all time was their heart's joy, for the person seen to rejoice in such an acquisition deserves to attain it.

112. *I have inclined my heart to do thy justifications for ever, for the reward.* The most holy band has hearkened to the instruction continually prompted by regular reflection: *Learn of me, because I am meek and humble of heart.*[179] It was essential that their hearts should incline in every way to perform the Lord's justifications, for following the instruction of such teaching they energetically spurned the haughty respectability of the world. Doing justifications means performing the Lord's commands with feelings of humility; breaking bread for the hungry, clothing the naked, sympathising with others' calamities, and the other activities which the Creator's devotion has deigned to recommend to the human race. But we must ponder the words, *for ever,* because all that we have mentioned earlier can be performed only so long as we are troubled by the disasters and need of this world. Who can show pity to a person in tribulation in that future age, when we know that there is no wretchedness in the heavenly kingdom? The solution is that the person who performs these works in this world with the zeal of love is known to do them for ever, for he will receive the reward for these actions throughout eternity. They added: *For the reward.* This is the reward which the saints will hear: *Come, blessed of my Father, possess ye the kingdom prepared for you from the beginning of the world,*[180] and the rest. It is a great reward, the outcome of the Lord's generosity, to become a dweller in the eternal kingdom, a companion of the good angels, to attain the fatherland which is the source of undying delight and which is never quitted in any journeying. They will remain there, implanted in that contemplation, continually looking to Him in whom they ever rejoice.

113. SAMECH. *I have hated the unjust, and have loved thy law.* The

swarm of Catholics passes to the fifteenth letter, under which they say that the unjust, in other words, the opponents of the law, have been an object of hatred to them. They state that they have loved the Lord's law, and ask that they should be taken up by His devotion and thus be enabled to escape the evils of the world. They further ask that their flesh be subjected by fear of the Lord, so that it cannot be condemned at the divine judgment for transgression of the law. At this point the question raises its head as to why the faithful people appear to have made a statement opposed to the gospel commands. They say: *I have hated the unjust*, though the commandment says: *Pray for your enemies, do good to them that hate you.*[181] But if you ponder the relevant occasions, you will see that there is total consistency. When Christ instructs us to love our enemies, the fire of opposition and the heat of injustice are tempered, so that we are far from appearing to render evil for evil. We are patient in the face of all insults, like Christ when He endured being spat upon and being scourged. But when the time for martyrdom confronts us, we are bidden to hate those who wickedly suborn us, for we must spurn our very sons and parents if they oppose us, by making our intentions foreign to theirs. It often happens that persons who are not frightened by fire or subdued by the sword are seduced by the coaxing of relatives. This is why Scripture says: *If any man come to me, and hate not his father and his mother and wife and children and brethren and sisters, yea, and even his own life also, he cannot be my disciple.*[182] The fact is that no person should be preferred to God; but if His love is put first, it is right that we love our relatives when no opposition to the faith militates against them. So once we take account of the occasion, both injunctions can be squared with each other with absolute truth. As Scripture says: *There is a time to embrace and a time to be far from embraces;*[183] then, after protracted discussion, comes: *There is a time for everything.*[184] We must realise that we have in this verse the argument called the *ex contrario* in the *Topics,*[185] when we enclose our judgment in a single proposition from different examples.

114. *Thou art my helper and my upholder, and in thy word I have hoped. Helper* has reference to the fulfilment of the commandments, for without His help we cannot inaugurate or succeed in completing any good action. He became our *Upholder* by the mystery of the holy incarnation, through the agency of which He upheld man to prevent

his utter destruction by the law of sin. Note too what follows this upholding: *And in thy word I have hoped,* in other words, "I have placed my highest longing in the protection of Your divinity, where hope is possible and where hope most solidly based does not deceive." As Scripture has it: *Who has hoped in the Lord and been confounded?*[186] And again: *Mercy shall encompass him that hopeth in the Lord.*[187] So they hope for the coming of the Redeemer of the nations, so that He can wipe away the blemishes of the world, bring to life the dead, heal the sick, and through the death of death itself release what had been bound by the law of sin. Thus in one short verse is enclosed the perfection of our whole religion.

115. *Depart from me, ye malignant, and I will search the commandments of my God.* Those heretics who desire to ascertain the truth often profitably stimulate us in fulfilling the Lord's commands, but they are also wilful in their study of the sacred readings, and are seen to rail at us and to block our progress. The Lord proclaims that they are to be segregated from us, for they seek to rend apart the Lord's Scriptures with their mad assertions. What can human language achieve, when the aspiration of heretics is that their belief be withheld? Another passage bids them: *Depart from me, all ye workers of iniquity.*[188] When you see that a person is unwilling to be converted, the proper course is to succeed in avoiding him, for if such men are present and continually join battle with contentious malice, devising lies with sophisticated foolishness, we cannot be found adequate to search out the Lord's commandments, since we are preoccupied to the full extent of our souls' power.

116. *Uphold me according to thy word, and I shall live: and do not confound me in my expectation.* Now that they have routed the faithless and are cleansed of intimacy with wicked men, they ask to be supported by the Lord so that they can be saved by the promise of His word. It would perhaps be presumptuous to say to the Lord: *Uphold me,* without adding the promise which can never mislead. But when they say: *I shall live,* they speak of the time to come, for we do not truly live in this world where we sin in the frailty of the flesh. Their *expectation* was that in their great devotion they would encounter Christ's mercy. They ask that they realise this hope at the Judgment to come, so that they cannot be robbed of their expectation through misleading themselves and being confounded. This doubt is always

present in holy hearts until the heavenly promise is realised. There is a similar expression elsewhere: *With expectation I have waited for the Lord, and he was attentive to me.*[189] So the expectation is blessed when the promise is certain; for why should faithful hope meet disappointment when He who gives the promise cannot experience change? So the expectation of the saints is to deserve the kingdom of heaven and companionship with the angels, and above all the continual vision of Him who ever grows sweet in the hearts of the blessed.

117. *Help me, and I shall be saved: and I will meditate on thy justifications always.* Though these words are found often repeated, there are great mysteries being announced to us in such frequent occurrence. We must apply them to our minds' longing, and they cannot be divorced from them for any period, for though we receive blessings from the Lord, we must always beg Him to impart them constantly, so that the kindnesses bestowed may not forsake us through a crisis of faith. We should not regard the repetition as without point, so that we may not appear to have negligently disregarded what it is important for us to know. They added: *And I will meditate on thy justifications always.* They give the reason for their obeisance, so that after receiving salvation they may not appear ungrateful for the gift which has been bestowed. But when they promise to meditate always on His justifications, they are continually longing for their salvation to be maintained, for by such a course the devil wholly loses his opportunity. We can interpret *justifications* in two ways, either as those which we perform here and now in confessing our sins, like the gospel-example when the tax-collector confessed his sins and emerged justified from the temple;[190] it is appropriate, as long as we are in this world and cannot be free of sins, always to prostrate ourselves in this justification. But because *always* follows, a word which we know transcends all time, the passage may not seem to you to befit this world, but may encourage you to give some thought to the eternity to come. The saints meditate on the Lord's justifications always when they shall combine their longings with those of the bands of angels, when they shall sing the Lord's praises with lasting exultation, when in Paul's words: *This corruptible has put on incorruption, and this mortal has put on immortality.*[191]

118. *Thou hast despised all them that fall off from thy justifications, for their thought is unjust.* This explains why there was regular and dili-

gent meditation on His justifications. Such a judgment to follow rightly roused fear, for those who abandon His justification are despised by the Lord. Since justification of sins lies in pure confession of the mind, the proud are rightly spurned by the Lord, for they are unwilling to heal themselves by such a remedy. Their unjust thought lies in their willingness to sin and in their unwillingness to pay satisfaction to the most just Judge. So such persons are justly deprived of the grace of absolution, for in spite of such frequent warnings they have not deigned in this life to make entreaty to the devoted Lord.

119. *I have accounted all the sinners of the earth prevaricators: therefore have I loved thy testimonies.* Unless this statement is quite carefully analysed, it seems to contradict Paul, who says: *Those who have sinned without the law shall perish without the law,*[192] whereas here they attest that all the sinners of the earth are prevaricators.[193] How can anyone be outside the law if all are to be accounted prevaricators? Prevarication is nothing other than contravention of the established law. But both statements are true, since they issue from the one fount of truth. When Paul says: *They shall perish without the law,* he speaks only of the rules known to have been written on tablets of stone by the Lord's finger on mount Sinai. But there are other laws by reason of which people will fall under divine sentence; for example, the transgression of Adam, for which the human race would have to be judged if it were not delivered by Christ's kindness. Gentiles are also bound by natural law not to do to another what they are unwilling to suffer themselves; so Paul also says: *The Gentiles who have not the law do by nature those things that are of the law.*[194] So you see that it is rightly claimed here that all persons capable of sinning through some fault are prevaricators. All are accounted prevaricators either of the law which was first transgressed or of that bestowed through Moses, for no person born on earth is found to be exempt from these. So it was inevitable that they should love the Lord's testimonies more earnestly, since they were seen to consign all sinners to the ranks of prevaricators. They believed that through those testimonies a remedy could accrue to them, for it was through them that with urgent longing they made their way to Christ's grace. Once the law sentences us, there is only one grace which wholly acquits us, the grace which frees the shackled, which makes sons out of slaves.

120. *Pierce thou my flesh with thy fear, for I am afraid of thy judg-*

ments. The gathering of spiritual men is aware of the cause of this transgression of the law incurred by the human race, and prays that by a new and unprecedented punishment their flesh, which they regard as a most fierce aggressor or an untameable wild beast, be not merely bound but also pierced. The vices of the flesh are the earthly sins which cause us to transgress the law of the commandments when they entice us away from the path of truth. How rightly they beg to be pierced with the Lord's fear, so that they may not be detached from Him through a freedom that brings harm! Thus by a single word they showed how the Christian should regard the flesh, and they detailed the devotion with which he should plead with extreme vehemence against his own body. The fear is fear of the future judgment, so that by mortifying the body here they may make it eternal in heaven, and by saddening it for a time here they may make it perennially joyful in the next world. Observe the phrase, *with thy fear:* this is the chaste and perfect fear which not only keeps fear of punishment in view but also feels strong apprehension of loss of grace by which the faithful person lives, and through which every Christian is renewed. But let us scrutinise the nails which pin us to the Lord's crucifixion. They are the charity which causes us both to ignore our tortures and to love more the dangers of death itself. How happy is he who is pierced by this nail, and afflicted by such a wound! Paul was transfixed by this nail when he said: *To me to live is Christ, and death is gain.*[195] The one who prayed *now dismiss thy servant in peace, because my eyes have seen thy salvation*[196] was pierced by the prick of awareness. Lastly, the Church proclaims in the Song of Songs: *I am wounded by love.*[197] So the holy people prays to be pierced by fear of the Lord, so that by dying they may live, whereas earlier by living they were dying.

121. AIN. *I have done judgment and justice: do not give me up to them that persecute me.* The Lord's members that live for ever have reached the sixteenth letter. Here with one voice they entreat the coming of the sacred incarnation, saying that it is the moment for the divine power to be revealed for the destruction of the proud. So let us concentrate on the words spoken, so that no waywardness may contemplate the arrogance hateful to holy men. Whoever judges himself and condemns with just malediction his wicked ways before the Lord's scrutiny, *does judgment.* But to ensure that you do not think that this is a flattering rather than a truthful exercise, they added: *And justice,* for

we judge ourselves justly when we punish our own transgressions. So it is equity itself which delivers us from punishment, equity which frees us from guilt, as long as we acknowledge that we are enmeshed in evil deeds. Since they had now wholly discharged devoted satisfaction, and have condemned their sins, they now ask not to be consigned to sinners. This was their earlier request: *Pierce my flesh with thy fear,* so that the guilty body may be subjected to the judgment of the soul, and may be a better servant when pinned down, since it would play the wanton if uncontrolled. *Them that persecute* are the devil and his agents, who pursue us with unceasing malevolence, and tear us apart with savage rending when we are consigned to them. We recall the sufferings of the most holy Job, the huge calamities which he endured, for he realised that he had been given over to them. We know also the extent of Joseph's and again Susanna's sufferings when they were consigned to the hands of wicked men. It is through being reminded of this that we ask every day: *Put us not to the test.*[198] Sinners too are handed over to suffer scourgings appropriate to their crimes. As Paul says of the wicked: *God delivered them up to a reprobate sense, to do those things which are not convenient.* Elsewhere he says of sinners: *I have delivered them up to Satan, that they may learn not to blaspheme.*[199] So the holy people beg that they may not be surrendered to their persecutors, whose impure spirits were angry because they saw that their attacks and incitements were condemned by them. This is the hatred which gains Christ's affection, for one can be loved by Him only if regarded with loathing by His bitterest foes.

122. *Uphold thy servant unto good: let not the proud calumniate me.* They seem to have asked: *Uphold,* when tugged by the devil's arm, to avoid falling, for we are upheld by the Lord's mercy when beaten down by the power of our sins. It was fitting to say to the Lord: *Uphold me unto good,* because they knew that the opposing force had driven them into evil. The use of *servant* is the mark of freedom, for *servus* (servant) is derived from *servare* (preserve),[200] for the pitying hand of their Lord saved them from looming death. So they rightly call themselves servants, for they have been preserved from their souls' deceit. Hence *servant* here is seen to be a title of liberation and honour; only the person who has joined the ranks of saints is Christ's servant. *The proud calumniate* when they confront us with heretical arguments expressed with the forceful weight of falsehood, so that the holy men

rightly begged to be upheld by the Lord so that they could not be brought low by their disputation. Alternatively, these words better refer to impure spirits who wickedly calumniate us. Since they are chiefly guilty of the sins which we commit, they do not wish us to be freed by being forgiven, for though they deceive us they also ever accuse us. It is not surprising that the devil should calumniate sinners, for he sought to tell the Lord Christ: *All this will I give thee, if falling down thou shalt adore me.*[201] And again: *I shall set my seat to the north, and I will be like the most High.*[202] So he is rightly termed a calumniator, for while performing cruel deeds he always lays accusations against the devoted. Scripture elsewhere says of him: *He shall humble the oppressor, and he shall continue with the sun.* So they most justly ask that the humble be not betrayed to the proud, the ingenuous to the liar, the pious to the ungrateful, for the persons whom those persecutors cannot seduce they treat with more savage violence.

123. *My eyes have fainted after thy salvation, and for the utterance of thy justice.* This usage of the plural *eyes* often troubles people, for the heart has a single gaze, and this cannot connote the eyes of the body for they could not observe any such vision over such a length of time. But it is the holy band, clearly identical with the Church, which speaks, and so they rightly used the plural, *my eyes.* So elsewhere we read of her: *Your eyes are as doves on the abundance of waters,* and again: *Your eyes are like doves, masking your silence within.*[203] So they say that these eyes have fainted after the Lord's salvation, because of the holy coming of the incarnation, which they bore with such longing that it could allow them no rest. So they were right to faint, because they had no period of leisure. *Salvation* denotes the Lord Saviour, of whom it was said: *Save, O Lord, thy people, and bless thy inheritance.*[204] Next follows: *And for the utterance of thy justice,* that is, of the words of the gospel which He was to utter to the people soon to believe.

124. *Deal with thy servant according to thy mercy, and teach me thy justifications.* They continue with their diligent entreaties, for there must be no weariness in petitioning, since the generosity of the Donor cannot be exhausted. They made unlimited requests, for they asked that blessings be granted them according to God's mercy, and just as that mercy is unending, so His gifts are known to be never-failing. They did well to add: *With thy servant,* for one who desires another as master at once gives way. According to their custom, they invariably

beg for the justifications which in their piety they have already obtained. This incessant demand is likewise indicated by the Lord's prayer, where it says: *Give us this day our daily bread.*[205] It is right to make continual entreaty of Him, for He is offended if He is not petitioned. Notice too the aptness of the words with which these matters are distinguished. Earlier they asked that mercy be dealt to them, whereas they begged entreatingly that His justifications be taught them.

125. *I am thy servant: give me understanding that I may know thy testimonies.* Though we must beg the Lord with continual prayers for everything helpful to us, we must regularly beseech Him most of all for an understanding of the divine Scriptures, for the more they are apprehended, the sweeter they are found by holy minds. In their knowledge that the almighty Lord is most generous to His subjects, they say: "*I am thy servant, give me understanding,* for it is Your habit to bestow what is requested justly and trustingly." Though all things acknowledge that they are subject to Him, it is a mark of great merit to be called His servant. Only the person who serves His will can truly be called His servant. Note the meaning of: *That I may know,* "that I may keep what has been given to me"; for knowledge is what clearly comes to our attention and is not dissipated by any forgetfulness.

126. *It is time, O Lord, to do: the wicked have dissipated thy law.* The devoted people foresaw that in the days of Antiochus[206] the Lord's law would be polluted with cults of demons by the Jewish people, and in their sickness they cry out as though to a physician that it is time to lend help, so that the people's health may not be ruined by mounting illnesses. They say: *It is time to do,* not to put off, what is expedient. He had commanded through the law and the prophets that the true Lord be worshipped with the most devoted piety, but since the Jews' obstinacy spurned this injunction for their own destruction, the faithful people cries: *It is time to do,* in other words, time to appear as Saviour to the world, to loosen sins, to conquer death, and to lay low the devil with his troop. This is what the Lord's doing is, to come at the prophesied time. In the words of the prophet: *In an acceptable time I have heard thee, and in the day of salvation I have helped thee;*[207] and as Paul says: *Behold, now is the acceptable time; behold, now is the day of salvation.*[208] All that the Lord does is fulfilled in the most suitable sequence; nothing must come to pass until in His mercy He allows it.

This is why it is always profitable for us to have patience, to await orders, to ask for what avails us. The Ruler knows the time for action. They added the reason why He should fulfil the request, because the Jews have dissipated the law which He had ordered them to maintain undamaged. Dissipating the law means living in a way other than its precepts advised, and to do this all the more because the law is known to have condemned such action with every malediction. The rhetoricians have set this argument among the more forceful precepts, for when entreaties are being entertained, the most suitable moment aids them.

127. *Therefore have I loved thy commandments above gold and the topaz.* Commensurate with the dissipation of the law by sacrilegious boldness was the haste with which the devoted mind sought to fulfil its commands. Love for noble religion grows whenever the recklessness of the wicked seeks to assault it. Hence the additional word: *Therefore.* So keeping respect for the Lord's commands was for the most holy band worth more than gold and jewels, which mankind regards as most precious. Gold and jewels charm our human eyes for the moment, but the law is the means by which the blessed mind is led to eternal rest. The topaz, as some writers state, is a kind of stone which is rarely found, and is precious for what it brings. It is said to have two colours, one of the purest gold, and the other gleaming with the brightness of the air. It has a rosy richness, a chaste purity, quite like the chrysoprase in size and colour, shining brightest when struck with the sun's rays. It excels the most precious lucidity of all other gems, and uniquely attracts the most eager pleasure of the eyes to gaze on it. If you seek to polish it, you darken it; if you leave it in its natural state, it shines. It is said to be admired even by kings, to the point that they acknowledge that there is nothing among their riches comparable with it. They say that it originates in the island of Topazion in the district of the Thebaid, from which it got its name.[209] We must not speak of it at length to avoid depicting by studied praise as admirable what Scripture says is worthless.

128. *Therefore was I directed to all thy commandments: I have hated all wicked ways.* Inevitably, in their love of the Lord's law above that of gold and jewels, they had to appear wholly responsive to all the commandments; a person set right by divine inspiration cannot neglect such instruction, and regards gold as earthly filth, and jewels as cheap

pebbles. It is the act of a madman to love things which will not profit him. The holiest men must yearn for what can bestow rewards which will never fade. So it was appropriate that in deserving to love the most upright way they should hate the path of wickedness. The wicked way is that which leads us to vices; the upright path of virtues bestows pardon and salvation on us. How zealously and repeatedly this message washes over us, to make us realise the nature of the aspirations on which they feast with delight. They regard as sweet beyond all else what they think must be repeated again and again.

129. PHE. *Thy testimonies are wonderful, O Lord: therefore my soul hath sought them.* The prayer of the saintly people enters the seventeenth letter. They state that they have opened their mouths and drawn breath so that their prayer may be heard, and that their devoted tears have outpoured the discharge of waters because the Lord's law has not been observed by the Jews. Notice how they have embraced the definition of testimonies in a single word: *Thy testimonies are wonderful, O Lord.* They are indeed wonderful, for through them heaven's power became known to earthly men, and they gave to the insignificant that knowledge by which the lofty nature of the angels is filled with blessed delight. We can continually seek out and investigate these testimonies with diligent reflection. It is not appropriate at this point to be fearful about the words: *Seek not the things that are too high for thee, and search not into things too difficult for thee,*[210] for the testimonies have been proclaimed to us so that our minds may ever search them out with devotion and care. The tidings which were proclaimed for investigation cannot be called too high and too difficult. This is the fifth type of definition, called in Greek *kata tēn lexin* and in Latin *ad verbum,*[211] for the nature of the Lord's testimonies is explained as wonderful.

130. *The declaration of thy words giveth light to me, and giveth understanding to little ones.* The Lord's words are those predicted by the authority of just men. Scripture says: *Behold, a virgin will conceive and bring forth a son, and his name shall be called Emmanuel.*[212] And elsewhere: *All flesh shall see the salvation of God.*[213] But these words, shrouded in the darkness of extended time, were made clear by the brightness of the Lord's coming, for what was kept hidden in the sacred writings was made manifest by Him. It was then that the Word was made flesh, that the Virgin gave birth. Then the dumb spoke, the

deaf heard, the lame walked with upright step, and the other miracles occurred which paid tribute to the Lord of virtues. This *declaration* deigned to enlighten by the force of His power the darkness of our nature which lay in shadow, and gave *understanding to little ones*, who acknowledged their lowliness and the poverty of their powers. These little ones are not to be measured by years but by the simplicity of their thinking. Of them Scripture says: *Suffer little children to come unto me, for of such is the kingdom of heaven.*[214] He grants them here on earth a pure and most innocent understanding, and He will give them in heaven an eternal reward.

131. *I opened my mouth and drew in breath, because I longed for thy commandments.* If you are attracted to a literal interpretation here, it explains the tendency of a speaker. First the mouth is opened, the breath is drawn in, and then the tongue is moved to allow the voice to sound forth. But if you interpret spiritually, as you should, the mouth connotes the entry to the mind which is opened when we hasten to learn something. It draws in breath when by the divine gift it is filled with a spirit of wholesome longing, and begins with constant heart to seek what previously it was known to have sought only through God's grace. So the weak little ones opened their mouths and drew in breath, in other words, strength for action, which they could not attain of their own accord. So that you may better realise that this first part is addressed to the good of the understanding rather than to the function of speaking, there follows: *Because I longed for thy commandments.* They first expressed zeal of will, to explain later their longing for the commandments; the sequence could not be logical if they said that they would first speak and then long for what was to their benefit.

132. *Look thou upon me and have pity on me, according to the judgment of them that love thy name.* The Lord often looks in anger, and more often gazes to destroy, as when He looked on Sodom and Gomorrha, and on the camp of the Egyptians. But He also looks with favour, as He did on the gifts of Abel. He has gazed too on the sons of the poor, and has not spurned their prayers. So that this passage would not be taken in the hostile sense, they at once added: *And have pity on me.* As has often been mentioned, this is rightly called pity, because it is bestowed with abundant love on the pitiable. The utterance of the prayer did not stop there, but added: *According to the judgment of them*

that love thy name. The Lord's judgment is the bestowal of the aid of mercy on them that love His name, so that the expectation of the faithful may not be cheated, for it is always raised by reflection on Him.

133. *Direct my steps according to thy word, and let not any iniquity have dominion over me. My steps* denotes movements of the soul, for just as by our steps we move from place to place, so by those paces of the soul, so to speak, we advance to things better or worse. The blessed troop asked that these steps be directed according to the Lord's word, so that they should not be seduced by evil vices, and slip into deadly errors. *According to thy word* means "according to the commands which You lay down for improving the life of the human race." Next comes: *And let not any iniquity have dominion over me.* It was essential that if the Lord were to deign to direct their steps according to His word, no iniquity should prevail over them, for it could not be so utterly banished that it could not assault them further. But when it does not prevail, we escape it, whereas slavery to it consigns us down to destruction. The phrase, *any iniquity,* is not idle, for they know that if it prevails over them at any point, it carries them off, and it is no use keeping the law in many matters if we are seen to transgress it in any respect. Scripture says: *If anyone keeps the whole law but offends in one point, he becomes guilty in all.*[215]

134. *Redeem me from the calumnies of men, that I may keep thy commandments. Calumnia* (calumny) is derived by citation of opposites from *capitis alumna* (fosterling of the head), though it attacks the head of another and is hostile to it; in the same way *bellum* (war) is something not good, and *lucus* (grove) is something which has no light.[216] Calumny is a lying attack of dangerous falsehood, which through zeal for wickedness is always directed at good men, striving to blacken some activity regularly performed with upright conscience. The just men endured this in a zealous and hostile attempt to divert them from the path of righteousness. I say nothing of earlier individuals, but what great sufferings David endured when he spared Saul, and on that account was guilty in that unjust king's eyes, since he was known to be merciful to him![217] What calumny, I ask, was roused when the young women said: *Saul slew a thousand, and David ten thousand?*[218] So men's calumnies are arguments devised against the dignity of truth, and the

saintly troop rightly prayed that these be shifted from them, so that they could seek out the Lord's commands with all opposition removed.

135. *Make thy face to shine on thy servant, and teach me thy justifications.* We read that the countenance of holy Moses was made so bright by the Lord that the people of Israel could not gaze on him, so he spoke to them with his features veiled because they could not look on his heavenly brilliance. The face of Moses was in fact the brightness of the law which they could not endure because they heard it with hearts veiled. So the holy people beg that they may behold the Lord's face in brightness and not veiled, so that they may deserve to be wafted by the grace of His clear light, and may then encounter no obstacle in their desire for the sight of Truth itself. The holy troop can long the more for the coming of the Lord Saviour, by whose countenance the dark abodes of sin are illumined, and who bestows life on the dead and unfailing remedies on those who have lost hope.

136. *My eyes have exceeded the discharges of waters, because they have not kept thy law. Discharges of water* denotes abundant tears, which they say were so copious that they outpoured the waters of springs. They *exceeded* them, since spring waters run along without consciousness, whereas the tears poured forth with the heart's affliction; they could not be greater in extent than the waters, but they excelled them in the nature of their most blessed remorse. We pour out these tears when we are pained by recollection of our sins, for if we kept the Lord's commands, we would certainly experience joy, and not the heat of lamentation. But since we cannot avoid such sins through the exigencies of the flesh, may the Lord bestow on us the tears by which we may be cleansed from the filth of our sins. I think that we must also realise that they say that satisfaction is paid through the eyes, the medium by which we are known usually to solicit the enticements of this world, so that the guilt is rightly expiated through the organs by which the transgression was committed. This practice finds very frequent mention in the divine Scriptures, for example, in Psalm 6: *Every night I will wash my bed: I will water my couch with my tears.*[219] And elsewhere: *My tears have been my bread day and night.*[220] This figure is called *hyperbole*,[221] when the character of a statement is pronounced with greater and exaggerated weight. The holy band was constrained to weep to wash away all their sins with a copious shower of tears.

137. SADE. *Thou art just, O Lord, and thy judgment is right.* Having triumphed over their flesh, the band of saints passes to the eighteenth letter, in which they proclaim the Lord's justice, and state that they revere His burning utterances with unremitting love. Finally they plead for an understanding of his testimonies so that they can obtain eternal life. After earlier saying that their sins were expiated by gushing tears, they now with faithful hearts praise the Lord's judgments with the words: "*Thou art just, O Lord, and thy judgment is right,* for You enjoin affliction on sinners so that Your medicine can save them"; for at no time of joy did they manifestly endure correction, and in no other way could the divine kindnesses be recognised. If a sinner continually prospered without coming to grief, he would imagine that this was achieved by his own merits. Both statements are just and most appropriate; the transgressor is corrected by making satisfaction, and the Lord's justice is declared by humble confession. It was by this statement that Daniel gained safety among the lions' most savage maws; it was by these words uttered by the three boys that the flame was extinguished; this was the declaration that Jeremiah repeated often in his lamentations. So we too must recite this verse in each and every danger and in all joys, for such a confession both delivers us from hardships and maintains us in prosperity.

138. *Thou hast commanded thy testimonies as justice, and thy truth vigorously. Thou hast commanded* means "You have laid down." As we have already said, *testimonies* are utterances to which we witness. They contain justice and truth, justice because they distinguish all things fairly, and truth because they repay what has been promised. So they rightly loved and sought out these testimonies so eagerly because the unfathomable and awesome power of the Lord was allowed to be recognised by such witness. *Vigorously* can be attached aptly to both *justice* and *truth;* for that the Lord should command justice vigorously imposes a sanction which will be profitable, and to implant truth vigorously in men's minds offers a surety.

139. *The zeal of thy house hath made me waste away, because my enemies forgot thy words.* Wasting is the unavoidable contraction of some illness which causes us gradually to seep away, since it eats away the body's solidity with painful affliction. They attest that this has befallen them through zeal for the Lord's house, which He did not allow to be damaged by the onslaught of wicked men. *Zeal* is used in

both the bad sense and the good sense; in the bad sense, as in: "Zeal and envy have devoured the house of Jacob";[222] and again, we read in the Acts of the Apostles: *When they saw this, the Jews were filled with zeal, and they laid their hands on the apostles.*[223] This kind of zeal always leads to sins, lays ambushes, cuts off the path to salvation. The word is used in the good sense: *The zeal of thy house has consumed me,*[224] and Elias says: *With zeal I have been zealous for the Lord God of hosts, for the children of Israel have forsaken thy covenant.*[225] Then too Phineas the priest, on seeing the Israelite engaged in sexual intercourse with the Moabite woman, in zeal for the Lord's command ran them both through with the sword.[226] His zeal was so effective that it alone diverted the Lord's anger. Indeed, this kind of zeal bestows salvation, keeps faith, maintains chastity and protects God's Church with splendid vigour.

140. *Thy word glows exceedingly, and thy servant hath loved it.* The Lord's word is ablaze, for it cleanses men's hearts when they are befouled with worldly grime. Just as the blazing heat of the furnace melts down metals and burns out their faults by necessary purification, so the Lord's word cleanses the thoughts of the humble by wiping away the stains of sins. The heart of Cleophas burned with this fire when she said: *Was not our heart burning within us when he opened to us the scriptures?*[227] Jeremiah too was aflame with this fire when he proclaimed: *There was a blazing fire in my bones.*[228] All the others who abounded in victorious love were likewise ablaze with this fire. So this fire denotes the words of Christ; as He says in the gospel: *I am come to cast fire on the earth, and I will that it be kindled.*[229] They added: *Exceedingly,* so that you would interpret this as hyperbole directed towards salvation, not death. There also follows: *And thy servant hath loved it.* They loved it precisely because they knew that it bestows life, and they glorified it because they knew that it was bestowed to heal the human race.

141. *I am quite young, and despised: I have not forgotten thy justifications.* This verse seems applicable to many holy persons. We see such a one mirrored in the person of Joseph, who was despised by his elder brothers, and as we know was sold as a cheap serf to slavedealers. But he did not forget that the Lord's justifications were embodied in him when he comported himself in all things with devoted will. We know that he was mindful of his Liberator, for he was seen to lend obedience

to His precepts. David too can recite this verse in his own person, for it was not expected that among his brothers he would attain the heights of kingship because of his feeble years. But he kept the Lord's justifications with such devotion in his memory that the Lord Himself said: *I have found David, the son of Jesse, a man according to my own heart, who does all my wills.*[230] Finally, these words can be spoken by what is clearly the buttress of the whole Church: the adopted people, the people of grace, the new people who are later in time but prior in distinction of faith. So we do well to assume that the blessed troop of saints, known to embrace all the faithful and all the most blessed, are speaking throughout the psalm.

142. *Thy justice is justice for ever, and thy law is the truth.* This verse distinguishes between the justice of the Lord and His law, by applying to them their peculiar meanings. However great human justice is, it is undoubtedly transient, like the justice of philosophers seen to behave with moral propriety; but their justice when isolated from God's worship gains the proper title of vainglory. But the Lord's justice remains for ever, for whoever maintains it will rejoice in eternal blessedness. The Jews too seemed to have justice, but their concern was rather for the letter, and they did not believe that in this justice there were mysteries to come. But the Christian people has grasped and preserves for ever the Lord's justice, for it is of itself eternal. I think that we must hold the same view of the law, for those who have deserved to grasp it are filled with heavenly truth. The truth of the law is the Lord Christ, who says of Himself: *I am the way, the truth and the life.*[231] So the statement: *Thy law is the truth,* is rightly definitive, for that truth is Christ the Lord.

143. *Trouble and anguish have found me, but thy commandments are my meditation. Trouble and anguish* are great gifts for holy men, because they know that when they are squeezed by the burden of such trials, they sweat out their sins and strain towards the joys which have no end. As Paul says: *Who shall separate us from the love of Christ? Shall tribulation, or distress, or persecution, or famine?,*[232] and the rest. These sufferings are a kind of antidote for blessed men, bitter to drink but health-giving and efficacious. Next comes: *Have found me*—understand "waiting, unmoving, ready to grapple with them." They further add that aid which they knew had undoubtedly been the source of healing in diverse sufferings: *But thy commandments are my medita-*

tion. By what troubles or hardships could they be downtrodden, rejoicing as they did in such meditation? Though their feeble bodies were afflicted and their suffering flesh was tortured, they knew that a spirit intent on the divine Scriptures was translated into rest.

144. *Thy testimonies are justice for ever: give me understanding, and I shall live*. Once again they denote the power of the testimonies by the technique of definition, for if you ask what are the Lord's testimonies, the reply is *justice for ever;* and so fired by such hope, each individual despised what they knew to be transient. There was also a definition under the previous letter: *Thy testimonies are wonderful, O Lord.*[233] They added: *Give me understanding, and enliven me*. Earlier they had said that they were young and despised,[234] but now they are more mature than the elders, and in the midst of adversities they seek understanding so that they may recognise that this world's hazards are to be accounted as mere passing winds. They could be enlivened provided that they judged such things to be unworthy of regard. They could thus survive the death of martyrdom, and rejoice in unending exultation. What a life-giving death, blood more precious than all princely purple, for you deserve to see an end to afflictions and hardships, and in addition you await the attainment of the kingdom of heaven!

145. COPH. *I cried with my whole heart, Hear me, O Lord: I will seek thy justifications*. The most venerable chorus embarks upon the nineteenth letter, in which they promise to seek the Lord's justifications, and to take joy in His word with a confession preceding that promise. They add that they have realised that the Lord's testimonies have been founded for ever. Now let us turn back to this verse. The cry of the faithful, then, is the feeling of devoted minds not merely uttered in words but declared with fierce emphasis of heart. The people of the Jews grumbled and cried out, and were not heard by the Lord; but Moses was silent, and the Lord said to him: *Why criest thou to me?*[235] the sense being that the highest One hears the thoughts developed with devoted concentration. *With my whole heart* was added to prevent your thinking that we should have other thoughts when we cry to the Lord. The whole spirit should be intent on religious reflection alone, so that the mind may not be divided and be unable to obtain the outcome which it demands. Observe too what they sought with their whole heart and strength; not worldly riches, not marriage with noble

women, not momentary distinctions, but the Lord's justifications which the holy mind always desires and seeks *above gold and the topaz.* The words, *I will seek,* refer to the justifications which they ought to carry out, not merely to acknowledge in their reading. Only the person who fulfils those justifications with devoted heart truly seeks them.

146. *I cried unto thee, Save me, and I shall keep thy commandments.* They detail the cry mentioned earlier. *I cried with my whole heart* is identical with *I cried unto thee.* Only the person who directs his entreaty with full feeling of the heart cries out to the Lord. When they say: *Save me,* they wish this to be interpreted as not in the body but in the soul, where they could truly preserve the Lord's commands. The person willingly subject to bodily sufferings could not seek the safety of the flesh.

147. *I came early to maturity, and cried out: and I hoped in thy word.* All who attain the moderation of old age in the days of their boyhood, and develop the utmost seriousness of mind before the count of years can turn their hair gray, *come early to maturity.* What praise is it for the old if their frailty is cocooned in extended comfort and they attain tranquillity induced by weariness? By contrast, what glory it is for the young if in the very heat of youth they restrain themselves with the discipline of good manners! As Jeremiah says: *It is good for a man who has borne a heavy yoke from his youth. He shall sit solitary and hold his peace, because he has shouldered a heavy yoke.*[236] Next comes: *And I hoped in thy word.* This is precisely the point of their coming early to maturity and crying out; with minds intent they did not cease to hope in His Word, that is, in the coming of the Lord Saviour. Though holy men are fired by great longing, they always add further heat to their anticipation, since the more their expectation is protracted, the more their coming blessedness is desired.

148. *My eyes have turned early to thee at daybreak, that I might meditate on thy words.* In the previous verse they say that they have come early to maturity, and this denotes the period of youth. Now they mention the hour of the day. *My eyes have turned early to thee at daybreak* means simply that the eyes of their hearts believed in the coming of the Lord Saviour before His arrival shone forth. *Daybreak* denotes the beginning of light, the pointer to the arrival of day, for after the darkness of sins in which this world was held subject, the

life-giving presence of the Lord gleamed forth. Alternatively, it denotes the Lord's resurrection which occurred at daybreak. The gospel says: *Just when day was breaking, Mary came to the tomb,*[237] and the rest. Next comes: *That I might meditate on thy words.* The reason is given why their devoted minds rose before daybreak, not to till the fields, not to anticipate the greetings of the powerful, but to meditate on the Lord's words, which can never elude devoted prayers since their sweetness seems to grow perpetually. As was said in the thirteenth letter: *How sweet are thy words to my throat!*[238]

149. *Hear thou my voice, O Lord, according to thy mercy, and quicken me according to thy judgment.* Let us observe with what wonderful humility the Lord's true servants entreat Him, and let us realise that we must take nothing for granted if some prosperity smiles on us through God's grace. Their spokesman who transcended his youth and cried to the Lord in his youthful years, who rose at daybreak, always seeks mercy in his praises and prays to be enlivened, for we must not show presumption in any actions, but rely solely on the Lord's devoted love. When they say: *Hear my voice, Lord, according to thy mercy,* they have nothing to offer with confidence to counteract their sins, but they seek nothing other than the mercy which makes the wretched happy, captives free, the dead alive, the mortal eternal. Next follows: *Quicken me according to thy judgment,* the judgment by which You spare those who entreat You, by which You mercifully forgive those who condemn themselves. When they added: *Quicken me,* they were confessing that they were dead by the law of sin, for only the person who has no proper life in him can be quickened.

150. *They that persecute me unjustly have drawn nigh, but they are gone far off from thy law.* The prophetic spirit of the blessed knew what dangers overhung them oppressively, and they sought mercy beforehand so that they could not be overcome by any cruelty in the course of them. Persecutors draw nigh when on top of all else they go as far as lacerating the flesh. So the Lord's passion was described in Psalm 21: *Depart not from me, for tribulation is very near;*[239] and in the gospel; *Rise, let us go. Behold, he is at hand who will betray me.*[240] They made the splendid addition: *Unjustly,* to make a necessary distinction, for guilty people can also suffer persecution when the brigandage which they have committed is punished; so the gospel adds to the words: *Blessed are they that suffer persecution,* the phrase: *For justice's*

sake.[241] *Unjustly* is apt here because they suffered evil things instead of good. The persons to whom they proclaimed salvation thought that they should be subjected to death. Next comes: *But they have gone far off from thy law;* that is, the nearer the persecutors drew nigh to punish the saints, the further they withdrew from the Lord's law. Inevitably those who hasten to evildoing in wicked ways abandon justice, because only those who obey the Lord's rules can draw near to Him. This figure is called *syncrisis,*[242] used when we show that our cause is superior to that of our opponents; for they say that they have borne persecution unjustly, whereas their enemies are far removed from the Lord's law.

151. *Thou art near, O Lord, and all thy commands are truth.* They say that in the face of that overhanging and most violent persecution, the Lord's proximity is their remedy, for they knew that aid to salvation would come from Him. They say: "*Thou art near, O Lord,* for You are fully and wholly everywhere, not bounded by space but Yourself filling and embracing all space." When the prophet wished to show this ubiquitous presence, he said elsewhere: *If I ascend into heaven, thou art there: if I descend into hell, thou are present. If I take my wings before daylight, and dwell in the uttermost parts of the sea, even there also shall thy hands lead me.*[243] But when they say to Him: *Thou art near, Lord,* they confess that He is not unaware if we behave wickedly, and that He does not turn away when we shun Him. So the one salvation is to hasten to Him, for you cannot escape from Him. They further added: *And all thy commands are truth.* This can be said by the one who has lent credence to the Truth which is the Lord Christ, and who has undertaken His commands with salutary perfection; but the Jew who refused to believe the truth cannot say such things.

152. *From the beginning I have known of thy testimonies, that thou hast founded them for ever. From the beginning* denotes the first stages of the world, when the term "holy men" began with the just Abel, who though innocent was slain by his wicked brother as an exemplar of the Lord Saviour. They knew *from the beginning* too, when the offered gifts of the priest Melchisedech were taken up as a prefiguration of the Lord's body. They also knew *from the beginning* when Abraham offered his son for sacrifice as a symbol of the Lord Saviour;[244] so too other passages of a similar kind contained in readings of the sacred books. These were undoubtedly *founded for ever* since they are seen to

be attested by truth itself. They did well to say that they were founded, for this referred to the foundation which is Christ the Lord. He is the unique and solid Foundation; as Paul says: *For other foundation no man can lay but that which is laid, which is Christ Jesus.*[245] So it is clear, as has often been said, that the faithful behold the Lord Christ in mind, and acknowledged His sacred coming in the prefigurations present in the Old Testament.

153. RES. *See my humility, and deliver me, for I have not forgotten thy law.* As you see, the people victorious over vices enter upon the twentieth letter, in which they seek to be enlivened because they have sought the Lord's commands with the greatest eagerness. They state that salvation is remote from sinners because they have not acted similarly. They also attest that the beginning of the Lord's words is truth. But to return to the starting-point of this letter, they say: *See my humility.* Here this seems to apply to martyrs, whose bodies are so afflicted by massive torture that they are accounted not as human beings but as cheap cattle. A later psalm is to say of this humility: *For we are greatly filled with contempt, and our soul is greatly filled: we are a reproach to the rich and contempt to the proud.*[246] Listen also to Paul humbling himself: *But I am the least of all the apostles.*[247] But let us clothe this humility in a purple cloak, so to say, for the Lord likewise says: *But I am a worm and no man: the reproach of men and the outcast of the people.*[248] The devil's pride was conquered by this humility, so that he fell from the opposite status to prevent him from rejoicing in profitable presumption. Next comes: *And deliver me*—surely from nothing other than the necessity of oppressive punishment, danger of death, and all that blessed martyrs can endure in that conflict. The holy people could certainly not have begged to be freed from their humility in retirement, for their proclamation of it was unchangeable and devoted. By *law* here they mean the pronouncement: *Every man that exalts himself will be humbled, and he who humbles himself will be exalted.*[249] So they rightly said that they had not forgotten this law, for they persevered in it until the end of life.

154. *Judge my judgment, and redeem me: quicken thou me for thy word's sake.* This verse is to be scrutinised with careful devotion, so that the troop of saints may not appear arrogantly to have sought to be judged; far be it from them, for Scripture says of them: *The just with his first words is his own accuser.*[250] By their *judgment* they mean their

belief in the Word, their acceptance of the Lord's incarnation with pure hearts. That is indeed a safe judgment, for none could fear the Lord's judgment with regard to it. In these judgments which the saints make through God's grace by sound belief, they always achieve security, and they rightly request the Lord's scrutiny in them, because they know that they will be glorified in them. Observe how beautifully the designation is made; this argument is called the *a coniugatis*,[251] when a word is fashioned by harmonious association from another. Next comes: *Redeem me.* Whom could He redeem, except the believer? For whom above all would He shed the blood of redemption if not for the faithful servant? They added: *Quicken me for thy word's sake;* this is no doubt the promise He made that *he who believes in me will not die, but will have eternal life.*[252]

155. *Salvation is far from sinners, because they have not sought thy justifications.* In the first verse of this letter, they had stated that they should be rescued from persecutions because they had not forgotten God's law; now by the most apposite contrast they say that salvation is distant from proud persecutors since they have made no attempt to seek the Lord's justifications, for the dual purpose of rousing the committed with the prospect of pious behaviour and deterring the wicked with the spectre of damnation. I think this must be understood in particular of the Jews who made their salvation, in other words, the Lord Saviour, far from them by not believing in Him. Though they could have believed, they were wholly unwilling to investigate the justifications of the Old Testament, in which, as has often been remarked, the coming of the Lord Saviour was prefigured. So they were rightly removed far from salvation, for they spurned the Author of salvation; for though Pilate offered them the Lord Christ, they preferred with obstinate hearts to receive the acquittal of the robber Barabbas who was one like themselves.

156. *Many, O Lord, are thy mercies: quicken me according to thy judgment.* The Lord's mercies are those by which He deigns to aid the afflicted and the wounded in various ways. For example, Joseph who was kept enclosed in the bonds of imprisonment, or Jonah swallowed by the whale, or Susanna whom He freed through Daniel's judgment when she was labouring under a false charge, or the thief whom He also saved through his spontaneous confession. Then too there were the other kinds of mercies which no man's knowledge can explain.

Next comes: *Quicken me, according to thy judgment.* In each instance we must most carefully observe what kind of judgment is being sought, for it is not appropriate to our trust as men to demand the treatment epitomised in: *Enter not into judgment with thy servant.*[253] *Judgment* is quite simply what we must seek when we prostrate ourselves in humble satisfaction, when we lay aside excuses and confess our sins; for at that moment the Lord's judgment embodies pity for such suppliants, since an entreaty is meritorious if one in humble and suppliant posture asks to be quickened according to the Lord's judgment. When the Lord judges He pities, and when He pities He judges; for He neither pities without judgment nor judges without pity. To Him the psalmist says: *Judgment and mercy I will sing to thee, O Lord.*[254] Clearly all virtues repose in Him; they do not enter or leave Him, for they are known essentially to dwell in Him.

157. *Many are they that persecute me and afflict me, but I have not declined from thy testimonies.* The injury inflicted by extremely harsh persecution is magnified, for the one individual says that he has suffered the attacks of many abominable persons. The Church receives countless palms, and the blood of martyrs is consecrated throughout the world, since the mad rage of savage persecutors in their onslaught on innocent persons has not succeeded. The number of the elect has grown the more the anger of tyrants has flared up. In the course of all this they witnessed that they have not declined at all from the Lord's testimonies. The devotion maintained when one is surrounded by mortal hazards is hailed with greater warmth.

158. *I beheld men not preserving the pact, and I pined away, because they kept not thy words.* A *pact* is a stated agreement between persons who are at loggerheads, out of an impulse for friendship. It gets its name from *pax* (peace), because it is an act of peace.[255] So the means by which the human race was recalled to the peace and harmony of the Lord when they were detached from divine grace is rightly called a pact established under both old and new laws. So the Lord's pact means that whoever surmounts persecutions wins the crown through glorious election. It was this pact which these men did not preserve, for after being converted in frail forgiveness they succumbed to the whims of their persecutors. When the holy troop observed this, they were troubled at having lost comrades in the faith. To reveal the depth of their grief, they said: *I pined away*, which is what weary bodies

usually suffer in lengthy sickness. They revealed the cause of their pining: it was because the transgressor failed totally to keep the Lord's words. The words of the Lord are these: *He that perseveres to the end will be saved.*[256] Or alternatively they are referring to the pact of the Old Testament, when the Jewish people heard the Lord's words and said: *All that the Lord hath spoken we shall both hear and do.*[257] But when they adored alien gods and polluted themselves with the most foul worship of demons, they abandoned with execrable forgetfulness the pact to which they had initially lent assent. Inevitably the holy men lamented this to the extent of physical wasting, for they saw that their fellow citizens and parents had neglected the Lord's words, and with most devoted grief they bewailed their lapse into false notions.

159. *Behold, I have loved thy commandments, O Lord: quicken me thou in thy mercy.* Observe how similarity of words has adorned both arguments. In the previous verse, they said: *I beheld men not preserving the pact, and I pined away;* now they say: *Behold, I have loved thy commandments.* They sought to deserve His eyes upon them, for He dealt with their enemies with the zeal of devoted love. But once they had recounted the savagery of the persecutors, and the punishments imposed, they pass to the charity which commends all things; for if they had endured such treatment without living the Lord's commandments, they would not have had a blessed crown, but merely have exhibited sinful boasting. As Paul says: *If I should deliver my body to be burned, and have not charity, it profiteth me nothing.*[258] If a person grumbles as he endures the tortures of martyrdom, there is a sense in which he seems ungrateful to the Lord's law; he should love the means by which he believes he attains eternal joys. The Lord pays more favourable attention to attitudes of mind than to the pain of physical suffering, just as He witnesses almsgiving offered with a joyful heart. So they rightly begged the Lord to be enlivened, for they had spurned worldly life in a spirit of true religion.

160. *The beginning of thy words is truth: all the judgments of thy justice are for ever. The beginning of thy words* seems to me to denote the start of the divine Scriptures. This is nothing other than the first words of Genesis: *In the beginning God made heaven and earth.*[259] We know that all things are included and denoted in this phrase, for heavenly things are included under heaven, and we must interpret *earth* to include earthly creatures. So the phrase, *the beginning of thy words*, is

seen to be the perfection of the whole of truth. Truth speaks words of truth from the beginning, and marshals His words of truth until the end. Scripture says of these words: *Heaven and earth will pass away, but my words will not pass away.*[260] Whatever comes down from that fount of truth remains fixed in unchangeable strength. Just as Scripture says: *The beginning of wisdom is the fear of the Lord,*[261] so the same order of words is fashioned here: *The beginning of thy words is truth.* Since they had touched upon what was performed at the beginning, there follows what is certain to take place after the end of this world, when the Lord's judgments will abide for ever. Christ says to the just: *Come, blessed of my father, possess ye the kingdom which was prepared for you from the beginning of the world.*[262] But to the wicked He will say: *Go into everlasting fire, which was prepared for the devil and his angels.*[263] These judgments of justice itself will undoubtedly be everlasting, since no time will alter nor any event undermine its decree. So the single verse has embraced both the beginnings of our faith and the things still to come.

161. SIN. *Princes have persecuted me without cause: and my heart hath been in awe of thy words.* The gathering of saints embarks upon the twenty-first letter, in which they say that through the Lord's affection the persecutions of cruel men are most welcome to them. They also relate that they have uttered praises to the Lord seven times a day, and they further proclaim that their ways are known to Him. We must interpret *princes* here too as persecutors who have launched bloody attacks on Christians with the authority of rulers, as was foretold: *They will deliver you up in their synagogues, and they will scourge you, and you shall stand before kings and governors for my sake, as a testimony to them and to the Gentiles.*[264] It is in this sense that we call the devil too a prince, for he claimed for himself the primacy in wicked deeds. *Without cause,* because the Christian religion troubles no-one; on the contrary, in keeping with the Lord's precept, it prays for all who ineptly strive to afflict it. As scripture says, *Pray for your enemies, do good to them that hate you.*[265] They did indeed suffer attack from princes without cause, for there were no commands that princes be spurned or that tribute be withdrawn from them. Scripture says: *Be subject to all higher powers, for there is no power but from God.*[266] And in the gospel, when the Lord was asked about tribute, He said: *Render unto Caesar the things that are Caesar's, and to God the things that are*

God's.[267] Christ also paid tribute for Peter and for himself from the mouth of the fish,[268] so that it may be undoubtedly clear to all that the most shameless persecution was launched *without cause* against those who chose to conduct themselves in a way of life which caused no harm. They added that by refusing to fear such treatment they stood in awe of the Lord's commands; for whereas the persecutors threatened temporal destruction, the saints were fearful of the death that is eternal, in case they should be acquitted by human judgment but incur everlasting damnation. They feared the words spoken by the Lord in the gospel: *Fear not them that kill the body and are not able to kill the soul: but rather fear him that can destroy both body and soul in hell.*[269]

162. *I will rejoice at thy words, as one that hath found great spoil.* Comparison is made with men at war, who both exult at victory over the enemy and rejoice at having gained many spoils. But let us ponder the way in which these devoted minds seem to have likened themselves to cruel men. Though martyrs died by a lowly end, they *found great spoil* because they both obtained heavenly rewards and rejoiced that even their persecutors had been converted through the Lord's pity. So the very people who had deprived innocent persons of their lives became their spoils instead. This is why they say that they rejoice at the Lord's words—that is, at the counsels He has given—like a victor hastening with eager zeal to seize the booty of the slain. The comparison is being made with the joy of the triumphant victors, not with eagerness for bloodshed. The parallel is often deployed in the sacred writings to express certain meanings. The Jewish people despoiled the Egyptians when through the Lord's kindness they were freed from lengthy slavery. David obtained spoils when he laid low the pride and wickedness of Goliath. The Lord Himself triumphed over the devil when He chained his strength and delivered the vessels of death, which He conveyed to the safety of salvation. Finally the Christian people itself rejoiced *as one that hath found great spoil*, at the Lord's words, which they rescued from the unbelieving Jews for the benefit of their salvation.

163. *I have hated and abhorred iniquity, but I have loved thy law.* We must store in our hearts the fact that through their hatred of evil things, they approved love of the good, for if our minds consent to entertain wickedness, they cannot in any way sincerely attach themselves to the Lord's law. As Christ says in the gospel: *No-one can serve*

two masters.[270] True love is that which maintains regard for the truth with such unbending purpose that it utterly abominates all that can be opposed to it. So they say that they hate not the wicked man but wickedness, as is right, and that they have so loathed it as to render it wholly foreign to them, so that they loved the Lord's law with perfect will. The argument is assembled from the contrasting difference between things.[271] The Lord's law, as has often been said, is that which was performed with secret meanings; for example, that a Hebrew slave should serve for six years, that a yearling lamb should be sacrificed, and similar practices which can relate to the meaning of the New Testament. They rightly state that they have loved these things, so that none should believe that they are to listen to them with any indifference.

164. *Seven times a day have I given praise to thee, for the judgments of thy justice.* Should we wish to interpret this number literally, it denotes the seven offices with which monks in their devoted piety console themselves, namely, matins, terce, sext, none, vespers, compline, nocturn; the hymn of saint Ambrose, sung at the sixth hour, also attests this.[272] But if you seek a spiritual significance, you more wisely interpret this as the expression of continuing activity, like: *I shall bless the Lord at all times: his praise shall be ever in my mouth.*[273] So too the weekly period, always circling through the number seven, stretches before us as an extended line, for all that happens in the duration of this world is enclosed by this number. It is used for example of an indefinite number in the text: *A just man falls seven times, and rises again;*[274] the number of times the just man falls is unlimited, but inevitably occurs whenever he falls to rise again. A similar usage is found in: *Render to our neighbours sevenfold in their bosom,*[275] where sevenfold means many times over; and again in Moses' words: *Whoever shall kill Cain shall be punished sevenfold,*[276] meaning many times over, and in other such passages. To ensure that you would interpret these praises as unbroken, they next added: *For the judgments of thy justice,* doubtless because He spares the suppliant and is so devoted to the humble that He not merely forgives their faults but also bestows eternal rewards on them.

165. *Much peace have they that love thy law, and to them there is no stumbling-block.* Since God resides untroubled in undisturbed purity, it is inevitable that those who love His law should be granted the joys

of peace. *Much peace* is to be understood as purity of mind and abundance of faith, which we aptly set against vices. But the person who proclaims himself the servant of the Lord is subject in this world to hardships and dangers. The Lord says to the apostles who were to be ravaged by various forms of persecution: *My peace I give to you, my peace I leave to you*,[277] so that it may become clear that the Lord's servants always enjoy peace of mind in spite of appearing to be molested by various physical tribulations. Next comes: *And to them there is no stumbling-block*, suggesting precisely that since they love the Lord's law they suffer no stumbling block, nothing unpropitious, in it; whereas the Jews do, for of them it is written: *To the Jews indeed a stumbling-block, and to the Gentiles foolishness.*[278] *Stumbling-block* describes an affronted mind at odds in its thinking with the advice given to it, and we know that this is foreign to those who love the Lord's law. We must love the whole of what it is seen to contain; otherwise the person who objects to any part of it, however small, does not love the law. We must pray that through the Lord's mercy we can gain understanding of what our weakness does not allow us to apprehend. The experience of a stumbling block lies in being separated from the Lord's elect; this happens to all heretics who cut themselves off from the unity of holy Church through debased wickedness.

166. *I looked for salvation, Lord, and I loved thy commandments.* This verse expressed in such a sequence is appropriate to both the faithful of old and to those of today, if we agree to interpret it as referring to the two comings of the Lord. It is relevant to the faithful of old if you relate it to their expectation of the incarnation; and it is appropriate to the saints who began to believe after the gospel-command, for they still await the coming of the future judgment. Those men of old could not have loved the Lord's commandments if they had not longed for them in their fullness, and likewise the saints could not have loved them if they had not awaited the Lord Saviour's coming with the most chaste fear, for the Lord's salvation is that bestowed on the Gentiles, which was foretold to Joseph through an angel, and which Simeon who was to be dismissed in peace acknowledged.[279]

167. *My soul hath kept my testimonies, and hath loved them exceedingly. Kept* refers to the endurance of martyrdom to avoid appearing to lose what their religion contained; *loved* to the charity which is stronger than all tortures, which conquers flames, overcomes swords,

and rises above all things with its heavenly power. But this love is to be practised not casually but exceedingly, for it unfolds through the efforts of the entire spirit, so that it does not withdraw at any time, or become flaccid through weariness of spirit. By its action it attains the result described by Paul: *I have fought a good fight, I have finished the course, I have kept the faith. As to the rest, there is laid up for me a crown of justice which the Lord the just judge will render to me in that day.*[280]

168. *I have kept thy commandments and thy testimonies: because all my ways are in thy sight, O Lord.* In previous verses they discussed commandments and testimonies separately; here, in bringing this letter to a close, they united the two so that you would grasp that both were kept together. So they say that they have kept the commandments and the testimonies, and then they added the reason why they could do so. It was because the Lord deigned to observe all their ways, so that they attributed their success not to their own strength but to divine power. Their ways would have been confused in blind darkness if the true Light had not deigned to gaze on them. This admission, that their ways lay exposed to the perennial Sun and the eternal Light, is indeed the utterance of the blessed, for they say that error could not have overcome them, since they claim that the Author of light was observing them. Adam after his sin hid his path, as did Eve, and Cain hid the murder of his brother; none of them could say: *All my ways are in thy sight, O Lord,* for they knew that they were seen to perish.

169. TAU. *Let my prayer draw near to thy sight, O Lord: give me understanding according to thy word.* With the Lord's help the twenty-second letter has been reached, in which the longing of the band of saints to draw near to Christ is commensurate with their proximity to the close of the psalm. The whole composition is relevant to the Lord Saviour's coming. The devotion of the faithful awaited it with an indescribable longing, so that He might deign to summon back the lost sheep through the kindness of His love; for when they begged that their prayer should draw near to the Lord's sight, they revealed that the presence of sinners is exceedingly far from Him, for only things cleansed by the purest holiness draw near to Him. Next follows: *Give me understanding according to thy word.* So they are asking for sagacity in the Lord's utterances, lest they sink into vanity through mere human wisdom; and they more eagerly cleanse themselves of vices the

more they come to enjoy the proximity of virtue. They do not seek worldly understanding, but understanding in accordance with God's word, which is always profitable for life. Knowledge of it is true knowledge, and its wisdom is eternal. But there is that other knowledge, knowledge of this world, the fruitless toil and empty argumentation in which some indulge; they investigate the courses of the stars, and entrust men's lives to the power of the constellations. If this learning were accepted and taught, there would be no recourse to the power of the Creator, though we know that all thought which takes refuge with Him is perfect.

170. *Let my request come in before thee, O Lord: deliver thou me according to thy word.* The holy entreaty gradually mounts; whereas before they had said: *Let it draw near,* they now ask: *Let it come in.* The first request was to approach, the second to have the chance of entering into God's sight, so that we should attribute nothing to human powers, but realise that everything is fulfilled by His grace. This presence reveals the extent of the power of devoted prayer; we are represented by it, since we know that it can be offered to God's sight. As is said in another passage: *Let my prayer be directed as incense in thy sight.*[281] Whereas earlier they said: *Give me understanding according to thy word,* they here say: *Deliver me according to thy word.* In the first passage they wish to see the things of heaven for which they long, and in the second to be cleansed of the stain of earthly concupiscence. The Lord's word provides both, for it can save us by its manifold power. As Scripture has it: *Who has hoped in the Lord, and been confounded?*[282]

171. *My lips shall belch forth a hymn when thou shalt teach me thy justifications. Ructare* (belch) derives from *rumpere* (break)[283] because the digestive process breaks through the barriers of the stomach and forces its way out into the air above with a loud report from the mouth. How the spokesman had sated himself with the sweetmeats of the prophets, for he belched forth a hymn to the Lord with joyous exultation, for this exhalation comes from the depth of men's minds! When the Lord makes men's resourceless thoughts replete, the outcome is that a hymn to Him is poured forth with the intoxication that brings salvation. Observe that often a prophetic utterance is denoted by this word. For example: *My heart has belched forth a good word,*[284] and again: *I will belch forth things hidden from the foundation of the world,*[285] and elsewhere: *Day to day belches forth a word.*[286] So a hymn is

belched forth when the tongue is filled with the spirit of the Lord, and does not as is usually the case in common speech apply itself to the opinion of the human mind, but its speech is ordered to express the heavenly understanding of divine thought. Next comes: *When thou shalt teach me thy justifications.* The order of words is this: *When thou shalt teach me thy justifications, my lips shall belch forth a hymn.* They promise the favour of their devotion when they have received the Lord's gifts. This type of argumentation is reckoned as outstanding among orators.

172. *My tongue shall pronounce thy words, because all thy commandments are justice.* The holy band knew that an account was to be rendered for any idle word, so they say that they are uttering the Lord's words to them that seek them, for from these words the soul's salvation is obtained, and dangers of tumbling down are avoided. It is most blameworthy, when the divine Scriptures full of such great gifts are available to us, and the might miracles of the Lord shine before us everywhere, to abandon the words of life and transfer our attention to the foolish prattle of the world; it is by this means that we become concerned with things that harm us, as though some benefit appears to accrue to us through them. For this reason Scripture threatens that we will render an account for any idle word.[287] So their holy minds pronounced the Lord's words so that they could gain glory rather than incur the shame of guilt. The reason follows why the Lord's words must always be proclaimed, because all His commandments gleam with the glory of justice. This is most aptly worthy of constant proclamation, for it aids the speaker and builds up the understanding of the listeners.

173. *May thy hand be there to save me, for I have chosen thy precepts.* When they speak of *thy hand* being there, they mean the Lord Saviour, who was born of the seed of David in the flesh, and through whom all things were made and are governed. We must interpret *hand* here as the right hand, for the Lord Himself is denoted by different names. As Isaiah says: *To whom is the arm of the Lord revealed?*[288] Elsewhere we read: *The right hand of the Lord hath exalted me.*[289] So the Lord Christ is signified by the terms hand, arm, right hand. This mode of speech is often found in the psalms, and we reasonably claim that it is peculiar to divine Scripture; for example: *May thy ears be attentive to the voice of my supplication.*[290] This is called the optative mood. So

they ask that the Lord Saviour should come, for they knew that in company with the rest they were to be saved through Him. As for the phrase, *I have chosen thy precepts*, they bear witness that they have disregarded all dangers out of love of the Lord, for no-one chooses anything good unless he is taught to despise all that is opposed to the good.

174. *I have longed for thy salvation, O Lord, and thy law is my meditation.* The prayer of the saints is now more clearly and more simply addressed to the Lord Christ. The blessed men in unity revealed openly what they previously seemed to seek in riddles. They had longed to see Him who even at that time they believed would come to them from the virgin's womb. To demonstrate that the knowledge had reached them from the divine Scriptures, the words, *and thy law is my meditation*, follow. They had longed for the Lord Christ as revealed by the prophets, for they knew that His coming birth had been foretold by them; and inevitably He was sought with great love, for they had learnt that His coming for the salvation of the human race was signified all those centuries before.

175. *My soul shall live, and shall praise thee: and thy judgments shall help me.* They speak to Him whom they had longed to behold, promising that their souls will live for ever, for they knew that they had gained salvation by belief. *Shall praise thee*—with a new song, as they should, since they have been saved and made new. The *judgments* refer to those which the Lord promised to pronounce over His servants with the words: *Come ye, blessed of my Father, possess ye the kingdom prepared for you from the foundation of the world.*[291] They believe that they will be helped perfectly when the ranks of the just are set at His right hand.

176. *I have gone astray like a sheep that was lost: seek thy servant, because I have not forgotten thy commandments.* Though this psalm contains different persons as spokesmen, at one time most faithful figures of the Old Testament and at another those chosen in new rebirth, some enduring martyrdom and others constant in diligent meditation on the Lord's law, it has none the less been made clear that the Catholic Church speaks in Christ's members, for at the close of the psalm a statement is made which is clearly apt for the Lord's bride. The common man who had gone astray in Adam by the law of sin, and who could not return to the Lord's sheepfold by his own efforts

because he had lost the gift of wisdom which he previously possessed, says: *I have gone astray,* meaning "I left your path and blindly entered the trackless wastes of sins"; so he was readily exposed to plundering, for he did not have the protection of his Shepherd. They appended the gospel-image: *Like a sheep that was lost,* for the sake of which their Shepherd abandoned the ninety-nine on the mountains,[292] and in searching for it was attacked by the ambush of the Jews. Then through His cross He greatly increased His flock, and does not abandon the search nor cease to gather them together. The holy gathering of the faithful is a single sheep, for there is one flock and one Shepherd.[293] Observe the frailty of the object with which mankind is compared when abandoned by Christ's grace. They are likened to a wandering sheep exposed to dangers, to the plunderings of wolves. Flight does not deliver it, physical force does not defend it. It endures the pleasure of him who waylays it, for it has no strength of body to defend it. *Which was lost* is a good description, enabling you to realise that it was found by the mercy of the Lord, who gathers back all that wanders, and by the goodness of His devotion regains what was lost. But that nature which had become weak and was demonstrably frailer than anything, at the Lord's incarnation conquered, overcame, and became loftier than all things, though it seemed more lowly. As the apostle says: *But to which of the angels said he at any time: Sit on my right hand until I make thy enemies thy footstool?*[294] Next comes: *Seek thy servant.* Christ is told: "Seek, because human weakness cannot seek You out." The statement is added which has been made often already, but which suitably concludes the whole psalm: that this just man is sought because he is known not to have forgotten the Lord's commandments.

Conclusion Drawn From the Psalm

We must embrace this psalm most fondly, for it has ended with this splendid confession. It is great in length, as deep and wonderful as the ocean; it is a paradise in the beauty of its outstanding content, for it is adorned with blossoms of the virtues, and the unfading garland of all the saints has sung it through the medium of the Hebrew alphabet. We can seek certain parallels from the natural world. Cranes fashion their flight in the shape of Greek letters, and such is the power of this impulse that although the birds do not know the outlines of the letters, they none the less fashion them by the guidance of instinct. So we have seen the affirmations of the psalm set in the highest heaven like the brightest stars; we have seen the boundless sea filled with the fish which the apostles' nets drew in at the Lord's command. Let us also observe that the very order of the psalms announces to us no mean mysteries of the age to come. It was appropriate that songs in stages[295] should attend this Church, which is gathered from the whole world and has lingered on the Lord's praises, so that they indicate a picture of what is to come at the end of the world. When at the Lord's prompting the aggregate of all the blessed has been gathered, the happy throng is to be raised up and mount to the heavenly Jerusalem. So we must remember that this is the third of the alphabetic hymns delineated with the entire alphabet, Psalms 110, 111, and the present one. Since they are stamped with this threefold distinction, they clearly denote to us the Trinity which perfects our faith. This number three is rightly associated with the future Jerusalem, for it is strengthened by the power of total purity. Four alphabetic psalms, 24, 33, 36 and 144, are fashioned with the tally of letters incomplete. They accord with the four cardinal points of the world, and aptly denote the Catholic Church which is still active in the world; for the Church is still imperfect until it suitably obtains the number of the predestined. In this way the collection of these psalms is seen to reveal the mysteries of mighty matters. This is also the fifth psalm, as has already been stated in previous psalms, in which the blessed troop has sung of all that pertains to ecclesiastical discipline. It is deservedly connected with the number 118, for we read that Noah's ark, which represented the type of the Church in a special sense, was fashioned in a hundred years;[296] now the letters *iota* and *eta* as the Greeks form them make the number eighteen; so the number 118 is shown to contain within it both the reward of the crown and the glory of the holy name.[297]

Commentary on Psalm 119

A canticle of steps.[1] A series of new and remarkable headings is now inaugurated, though the words have been encountered in our explanation of the previous psalm.[2] Their purpose is to unfold in fifteen ordered steps the blessedness of the faithful people, celebrated in that previous song in which their wide-ranging merits are assembled, to elucidate the mystery of the New and Old Testaments. The number seven, as has often been said, denotes the week occasioned by the sabbath of the Old Testament; the number eight signifies the Lord's day, on which He clearly rose again, and this is relevant to the New. When joined together, they are seen to make up the number fifteen. The psalmist begins with renunciation of the world, for he shudders at the worldly ways which constitute the burden of his ills. From this base he mounts by the steps, so to say, of merits, and reaches the perfect and eternal love of the Lord, which as we know is set at the very summit of the virtues. We explain this progression more clearly in its due place. But I think that I should advise you that through the bounty of divine grace, fifteen steps are laid in these psalms to denote in various ways the saints' merits, just as there was the same number in the temple at Jerusalem, which we know was completed by Solomon. This was so that the present order of the psalms, prefigured in that building, should be seen to be foretold, for that earthly construction seemed to bear the likeness of the heavenly temple. So when we hear the word *steps* in the psalms, we are not to think of anything material to be mounted by physical movement, but we should interpret it as the mind's ascent. The word *canticle* has been placed first so that we may apply it rather to the progress of the soul. *Step* here is the ascent of humility, confession of sins, as was stated in Psalm 83: *In his heart he has disposed to ascend by steps, in the vale of tears.*[3] We shall deserve to mount these steps only if we prostrate ourselves for our sins. So let us continually entreat the Lord. We must realise that these steps are thought to allow only ascent and not descent. What we call *cantica graduum*, canticles of steps, are known to be entitled in Greek *ōdē tōn anabathmōn*, songs of ascending steps, denoting that these steps lead only to the heavens. So we must consider that these are songs of persons now blessed, who through the Lord's help cannot now be drowned by any deceit. So we are justified in saying that the famous ladder of Jacob can perhaps be compared in some degree with these steps; for that ladder had upon it persons both mounting and descending, whereas on these steps the blessed merely mount. Some commentators think that the fifteen additional years accorded to king Ezechias are related to this parallel, so that the number fifteen is shown to have signified also the course of his perfect life.[4]

Division of the Psalm

The prophet speaks throughout the psalm. In the first part, he cries to the Lord, asking to be delivered from wicked lips and a deceitful tongue. In the second, he is fiercely afflicted because in lingering too long in this life and enduring the vices of others he is weighed down by an assortment of ills.

Explanation of the Psalm

1. *In my trouble I cried to the Lord, and he heard me.* The first step of the virtues is taken, in which the prophet abandons earthly vices, and with tearful confession begs to be freed from the affliction of this world. As a beginning, he proceeded to abandon the sins of the flesh, and thus to make entreaty to the Lord. The person who mounts one step leaves ground-level, but is still admitted to a lowly position when accorded only the first step of the climb. But undoubtedly he who can be encountered even on this step will now possess the merit of one of the blessed. So we read in Scripture: *Blessed are they whose iniquities are forgiven.*[5] So they say that they have been heard, since they had cried out in tribulation. The Lord cannot fob off the person whom He hears entreating Him with remorseful heart. As we read in Isaiah: *Whilst thou art still calling, I will say, Here I am.*[6] Observe too the most beautiful order of the words: first the affliction is mentioned, then comes the exclamation, thirdly the hearkening, so it is clear that the prayers of the faithful reach the Lord in this fixed sequence.

2. *O Lord, deliver my soul from wicked lips and a deceitful tongue.* Set as they are in the vale of lamentation (though we now know that this is one of the steps for faithful souls), they ask to be delivered from harsh allegations and from enticements ordered with crafty persuasion. The person who has begun to abandon the world through loathing of its vices endures *wicked lips* at the first stage of conversion, when his decision is mocked by evil reproaches. Wicked people say to him: "Why do you torture yourself, fleeing from worldly honours and

abandoning human attractions, with the result that you both lose the world and fail ever to attain what you long for?" But these are words placed on lips that deceive, for they are not reinforced by any reflection from the heart. When they are ineffective, their advocates turn to crafty enticements, and say: "Do not circumscribe yourself, do not weary yourself with fasting; there is time to do these things later." They presume to speak on behalf of the body, but are seen to impose problems of all kinds on the soul. So these are the *wicked lips and deceitful tongue* which the person initially suffers who is converted to the Lord's commands. Though he thinks that the words are trivial, they were the reason for the fall of the human race and the imposition of the condition of death, for when the serpent approached Eve, he first said to her with *wicked lips: Why has God commanded you not to eat of this tree of Paradise?*[7] When she replied that she was forbidden by the Lord, he said with *deceitful tongue, Eat and you shall be as gods.*[8] So you see that entreaty was made with all the prophet's strength that he be delivered from these words of persuasion, for he knew that the human race had been beguiled by them.

3. *What shall be given to thee, or what shall be added to thee against a deceitful tongue?* After the previous exclamation, and the fear of overhanging dangers, the prophet returns to his questioning as reflective people are wont to do. He is in doubt, and asks what remedy is to be afforded him in the face of such monstrous wickedness, so that he may safely avoid by some erected defence the weapons launched against him. Whereas earlier he spoke of both wicked lips and a deceitful tongue, here he mentions only the deceitful tongue which embraces both, for a deceitful tongue always presupposes wicked lips. So that the help should not be slow in coming, the medicine which is requested follows. This figure is called *erōtēsis* or asking,[9] when a person proposes to himself for his own exercise a question to which he himself replies.

4. *The sharp arrows of the mighty, with coals that lay waste.* So he has found the remedy which he anxiously sought, the appropriate benefit both to destroy wicked lips and to confound a deceitful tongue by the Lord's power. *The sharp arrows of the mighty* are the words of the divine law, by which the hearts of heretics or of crafty flatterers are pierced as though by darts. As Scripture has it: *The arrows of children are become their wounds.*[10] *Of the mighty,* because no-one can rightfully

impede the person whom the divine power wishes to save; *sharp*, on account of the very speedy effect of the action, for no delay is set in the way when that healing is afforded. Some have sought to interpret *coals that lay waste* as the foulest sinners who are snuffed out by evil deeds, the fear and recollection of whom cause us to forsake our vices, since we fear to commit such sins as we know they perpetrated. But there is another possible interpretation. We can regard *coals that lay waste* as prayers kindled by the fire of love, which so cleanse and purify us of our vices that through heaven's kindness we experience the abandonment and destruction of what the devil had erected in us. Or preferably it is what Isaiah describes: *And one of the seraphims flew to me, and in his hand he held a live coal which he had taken with the tongs of the altar. And he touched my mouth, and said: Behold, this hath touched thy lips. And he said: Behold, I have taken away thy iniquities, and I have cleansed thy sins.*[11] This is now achieved by the benefit of the holy cross, when we seal our lips with remembrance of the Lord. Perhaps it is justifiable to say that the *coals that lay waste* are the sign of the cross, for it routs the sins of believers, though the faithless think it has been exstirpated.

5. *Woe is me that my sojourning is prolonged: I have dwelt with the inhabitants of Cedar.* He passes to the second section, in which he condemns the vices of the age, and regrets the long extent of his life. *Woe is me* are the words of one grieved because wearied by the interminability of life in this world. Undoubtedly different holy people have uttered this complaint. As Ecclesiastes says: *And I praised all the dead more than all who continue living.*[12] The apostle Paul also cries: *I have a desire to be dissolved and to be with Christ.*[13] So it was right for the prophet too to grieve at this point, for he burned with a closely similar love of the Lord. *Sojourning* denotes pilgrimage; we give the name of sojourners to those who dwell temporarily in others' lands, far away from their native soil. It is rightly used of those whose mode of life is ever in heaven, but who are still detained here in body. His expression, *is prolonged,* denoted the feeling of extreme longing, for though our time here is known to be short, it is still long for one who desires to behold the blessed land. Next comes: *I have dwelt with the inhabitants of Cedar. Cedar* is a Hebrew name which in our tongue means darkness,[14] and refers to lovers of this world involved in acts of darkness who prefer to love the things which we know are the source of

death. By way of brief explanation of the origin of the word: Cedar was the son of Ishmael,[15] and gave the name to his tribe, the boundaries of which extended to the Medes and Persians; they are now called Saracens. The prophet fittingly denotes sinners by this name, and grieves that he still dwells amongst them. Inevitably a good person is afflicted when enclosed and mingled with evil men. These words we appropriate for one who stands on the first step and has come to spurn the earth which he has abandoned by a blessed change of life.

6. *My soul hath been long a sojourner with them that hated peace.* He sorrowfully repeated his sojourning which he mentioned earlier, so that it appeared not only long but also oppressive. So that you would not regard this journeying abroad as merely bodily, he added: *My soul,* for the saints' minds endure sojourning here where they are known to dwell without pleasure. There follows the most painful reason why this sojourning was most bitter: he himself was patient and kind, but he was seen to dwell in this world with brawlers and men crippled by heretical wickedness. The man who hates peace is he who does not love Christ, for Christ is known to be our peace. As Paul says: *He is our peace, who has made both one.*[16] How grievous it is to hear Him blasphemed, when we ought to prostrate ourselves perpetually before Him in humble prayer.

7. *I was peaceable: when I spoke to them, they fought against me without cause.* Earlier he had said: *My soul has been a sojourner with them that hated peace.* But he did not wish to be considered angry or troublesome through any disputes, so he added: *I was peaceable*—understand "towards the enemies of peace, his opponents, those who showed hatred to him"; he has fulfilled the words spoken through Paul: *If it is possible, as much as is in you, have peace with all men.*[17] Then too the Lord Himself says in the gospel: *Love your enemies, do good to them that hate you.*[18] This is notably the highest virtue of the Christian, always to be found mild-mannered amidst the disorders of the present world. But to show that this very peace did not seem damaging to sinners, for they were not impeded from evildoing, he added: *When I spoke to them, they fought against me without cause.* The peaceable man merely spoke; he did not persecute them or do them harm, but honoured them with the kindest words, words comparable with the sweetest drink. But their hearts were hardened and unmoving. They fought against him without cause as though he were a foe, an enemy, an evil counsel-

lor. *Impugnare* (to fight against) derives from *pugna* (fight), behaviour befitting wild and proud individuals. He was assailed without cause when he suffered the most untrue allegations, hurled with fiery malice. We use the expression *without cause* for suffering endured without preceding guilt, when we are attacked with wilful wickedness and without motive. These are the men from whom he sought deliverance, and of whom he said: *From wicked lips and a deceitful tongue deliver me.*

Conclusion Drawn From the Psalm

You see the prophet abandoning things of earth and now holding the height of glorious virtue, but still grieving because he knows that he sojourns with the wicked. So let us look at the nature of his advance to the second step, for with the Lord's help the first step has been revealed to us.

Commentary on Psalm 120

A canticle of steps. Though we can say nothing new about these headings, we have still to speak of the gradual ascent of the psalms. Initially the prophet is afflicted, like the tax-collector who beat his breast and did not raise his eyes to heaven.[1] He begs to be delivered from wicked lips and a deceitful tongue. But now he has recovered his breath and advanced to the second step. He has raised his eyes to the mountains, that is, to the holy intercessors by whose support he sought to win heavenly blessings. The prophet speaks these words in his own person, though he himself is such a mountain and a wondrous patriarch. His purpose in saying that he has fittingly mounted these steps is to reveal to us in our ignorance the types of the virtues in distinctive narration.

Division of the Psalm

The prophet, as we have said, mounts to the heavenly Jerusalem through God's generosity. In the first section he says that he has raised his eyes to the deserving saints so that by their prayers he may gain the help which he entreats; thus his mind may not yield before hostile attack. In the second section he promises himself without hesitation what he knew he had entreated with a pure mind, teaching us that whenever we seek blessings with constancy of heart we may believe that they are accorded us without a shadow of doubt.

Explanation of the Psalm

1. *I have lifted up my eyes to the mountains, from whence help shall come to me.* 2. *My help is from the Lord, who made heaven and earth.* From these verses a categorical syllogism[2] is hatched, as a bird hatches an egg by warming it. This is how the syllogism runs: My help is from the Lord, who made heaven and earth. Every person whose help is from the Lord who made heaven and earth gets his help from the true God. So my help is help from the true God. Now let us deal with the words of the psalm. The prophet was now perched on the second step, but was hastening to mount higher, so he says that he has raised his eyes to the mountains, to show that the Lord's rewards are sought with greater longing according to the generosity with which they are seen to be bestowed. As Psalm 118 says amongst other things: *My soul hath coveted to long for thy justifications at all times,*[3] and in Psalm 83 are the words: *My soul longeth and fainteth for the courts of the Lord.*[4] When he says: *I have lifted up,* he shows that he has advanced to a kind of contemplation, for lifting up means raising something to a higher level. *My eyes* means nothing other than the heart's vision, of which Scripture says: *Open thou my eyes, and I will consider the wondrous things of thy law;*[5] and again: *The precept of the Lord is bright, enlightening the eyes.*[6] If you were to interpret these as the eyes of the body, what advantage could they gain by deciding to focus on mountains planted with woodland or dotted with unsightly rocks? But if you investigate the phrase in the spiritual sense, it is markedly helpful; we can believe that he has raised his inward eyes to holy men, or to the divine books, or to the lofty angels who in their greatness and strength are truly mountains, and from whom fitting help was also obtained. But in case we perhaps set our hope in the mountains mentioned, the second verse reveals the true Source of possible help to us, the Source

which orders all things by a saving dispensation; thus our hope in the mountains is such that we realise that it is the Lord who lends help through them. It is from Him that the necessary benefit, the saving protection, the unshakeable blessing comes. As Paul says: *Neither he that planteth is anything, nor he that watereth, but God that giveth the increase.*[7] So that you would not think that this was some other lord—for the term is ambiguous—he says: *Who made heaven and earth,* thus denoting the Word by which all things were made.

3. *May he not suffer thy foot to be moved, neither let him slumber that keepeth thee.* After earlier asking that help come to him from the Lord, he suddenly changes direction and addresses his soul, urging it to continue with unflagging strength in its saving request. The *foot* is the extremity of our body, which at the mind's command transports us to different places. By comparison with this we call our thoughts our feet, for we make our way into good or evil situations through them. So it is these feet, by which the devil fell and the first man was laid low, of which the prophet speaks to his soul. He prays that they may not be subverted by the slippery nature of sins, and that he may not experience destruction within, while his body remains unharmed. Such a slip is in the nature of pride, which often drives God's servants to sin when they have already made progress. They fall into the worst error through thinking that they are of some importance. Next comes: *Nor let him slumber that keepeth thee.* These words are spoken as a figure deriving from the habits of men. Weary guards often suffer theft when heavy sleep steals over them; since their eyes are closed, they cannot see when they incur losses to the flock. The prophet cleverly prays on behalf of his soul that it may not be ravaged by the plundering of a hostile foe through the Lord's indifference. People speak of the Lord slumbering when we grow lukewarm in our belief in Him, for Christ keeps watch in the person in whom faith does not slumber. But if we abandon contemplation of Him, He too withdraws Himself from protecting us, as happened in the ship when the disciples grew careless, and the Lord slept. But when their faith was roused, the Lord too rose from sleep and at once shifted the perils of the deep from them.[8] So the prophet prays that he may ever keep awake before the Lord, so that he may deserve to keep his Shepherd's eyes watchful over him.

4. *Behold, he shall neither slumber nor sleep that keepeth Israel.* This

statement is similar to the preceding words. Earlier he sought that his soul should preserve what he here proclaims that the faithful people should keep. *Israel,* as we have often said, means "He that sees God." So the Lord is said not to slumber over those who see God, for the truth is that His gaze is focussed on us to the degree that our attention is riveted on Him. But God is seen most truly by those who contemplate not only His humanity but also the power of His divinity without uncertainty. On the one hand there is His incarnation as expressed in the gospel-words: *The Word was made flesh and dwelt amongst us;*[9] on the other, His divinity attested by the same evangelist: *In the beginning was the Word, and the Word was with God, and the Word was God.*[10] The person who believes these statements will be in very truth an Israel, and the Lord *shall neither slumber nor sleep* in watching over him.

5. *The Lord is thy keeper: the Lord is thy protection, over the hand of thy right arm.* He comes to the second sequence, in which he now confidently promises himself what he was seen to have sought with faith. Also notable is our statement that these words were directed at his soul in such a way as to be relevant to Christ's members by a most appropriate comparison. He says: *The Lord is thy keeper,* that is, He who made heaven and earth; and so that this guardianship could not cause any uncertainty, he added: *The Lord is thy protection.* Who could doubt that such guardianship is secure when the protection is from heaven? As for his words: *The Lord is thy keeper, the Lord is thy protection,* this is the figure of *epembasis,* which in Latin is called *iteratio.*[11] He clearly shows where the protection which he mentions can be found with the words: *Over the hand of thy right arm. Hand* is the general term applied to both right and left, but here the right is aptly mentioned, for the Lord is known to have promised every blessing with it. As Proverbs has it: *Length of days and years of life are in his right hand,* and this means eternal blessedness, whereas: *In his left hand are riches and glory,*[12] denoting the good things of this world, though there is no doubt that these can be bestowed by Him. Moreover it is His right side to which the saints are allotted when separated from the rest to obtain their rewards, whereas the left side is that mentioned when sinners are to be condemned to eternal punishment; for the saints have longed for things heavenly, whereas sinners have

sought worldly goods. We also read that sinners have given the left hand's role to their right hand; our prophet is to say of them in Psalm 143: *Their mouth has spoken vanity, and their right hand is the right hand of iniquity.*[13] But the true use of the right hand is where the bestowal of the Lord's grace is demonstrated.

6. *The sun shall not burn thee by day, nor the moon by night.* These elements in the course of their nature burn our bodies when they blaze with summer heat. But it is not the prophet's intention that we should take any thought for bodily condition, for he wishes us always to consult the interests of our souls. So we must take *day* and *night*, in other words *sun* and *moon*, as the adversity or prosperity with which the life of the human race is bounded in varying changes of fortune. As is said elsewhere: *I have cried in the day and in the night before thee,*[14] which denotes the period of our whole life, for we must always cry out to the Lord. So the Lord does not permit such persons as this to be hauled into court or to be afflicted by being confronted by some stumbling-block, for He provides them with the help of His protection. It was in this way that He guarded the people of Israel with the support of His blessings, shielding them by day with a cloud and lighting their way by night with a column of fire. This help He now manifests secretly in the case of His servants, for He defends them in times of prosperity and affliction from the most savage enemy.

7. *The Lord keepeth thee from all evil: may the Lord keep thy soul.* The divine protection is promised in various ways, for it not only delivers from adversity but also makes men blessed, and leads them to the kingdom of heaven. He added: *From all evil.* We must not understand this as the evil designated by mortal men such as the affliction of bereavements, the burden of very heavy losses, the oppression of poverty and the other tribulations which lovers of this world account as most crippling. He speaks of the evil which removes divine grace, destroys the soul, and renders void all the Lord's promises; and since he knew that in this world the saints have been tortured by great sufferings, and have attained the rewards of martyrdom at bodily cost, he added: *May the Lord keep thy soul.* He preserves the soul only in the case of the saints, who by loss of the body attain the rewards of eternal light.

8. *May the Lord keep thy beginning and thy end, from henceforth now*

and for ever. After these varied and diverse aspirations that the Lord's mercy may guard us, he comes to the end of the psalm and rounds it all off. He says: *May the Lord keep thy beginning.* It is appropriate for us to regard this as addressed to martyrs, whose beginning is to be guarded by the Lord in case they yield through the savagery of tortures, or are seduced by the enticement of flattery. So the prophet rightly prays that their beginning be protected, for without the Lord's help they cannot in any sense be wholly on their guard. As He says in the gospel: *When you come before princes and powers, take no thought how or what to speak, for it shall be given to you in that hour how or what to speak.*[15] He further adds: *And thy end,* in which lies total perfection, for until the very end of life there abides in them true and blameless confession. As He says in the gospel: *He that shall persevere to the end shall be saved.*[16] So the Lord watches over the beginning and guards the end, ensuring that martyrs both proclaim the truth and are not vanquished by any excessive punishment. But note what he added to this consummation: *From henceforth, now and for ever,* for whoever perseveres will gain eternal benefits. There can be no end where rejoicing is to continue without sense.

Conclusion Drawn From the Psalm

How well has this second step kept the prophet's feet steady and unshakeable! How well he rose above himself, for he mounted to merits of greater strength. Let us see what he achieves on the third step, after here demanding the Lord's protection with great longing.

Commentary on Psalm 121

A canticle of steps. We have listened to the previous step, and we must understand it as mounting to a higher level. But this ascent maintained with the Lord's vigilance is steady. Its advance in merit is balanced by self-prostration in mental subjection. See now how the prophet rises to the third step, rising higher than those on the second rung; he is said to inaugurate the psalm with a feeling of joy.

Division of the Psalm

In the first section, the prophet rejoices that he has been told that he will attain the heavenly Jerusalem, where the saints now reside in untroubled prosperity, and will in the Lord's company pass judgment through the bestowal of His mercy. In the second part he speaks to the citizens of Jerusalem, praying for abundance of peace for them, which he says he has proclaimed out of charity for his brethren and love of the Lord.

Explanation of the Psalm

1. *I rejoiced in the things that were said to me: we shall go into the house of the Lord.* This is a quite splendid and wholesome reason for joy, placed at the beginning to make the listeners smiling and attentive. So that you would not, as men do, regard this as a modest cause of joy, he reveals the perfect good which he says causes him to rejoice: he witnesses that he will *go into the house of the Lord.* What a worthy cause of joy, that he hastens to the place from which no-one would ever wish to depart! But we must investigate who spoke these tidings to the prophet. It was surely the holy Spirit, who spoke with silent voice to his heart. So the prophet had heard this not with the ear but with the mind, not in words but by divine inspiration; for he had inner forewarning, and burst out into these words of exultation. Next comes: *We shall go into the house of the Lord.* This is the house which takes in only the just, which contains the angels, and which attains sight of the Creator of all creatures. It is the house of longing, the house fashioned from living stones, of which another psalm remarked: *One thing I have asked of the Lord, this will I seek after, that I may dwell in the house of the Lord all the days of my life.*[1]

2. *Our feet were standing in thy courts, O Jerusalem.* Since the prophet had said that he was promised that eternal home, he now foreshadows the future, and says that he is standing in the house which he desired to attain with the utmost longing. This is to enable us to realise that holy men known to abide in the Lord's precepts are already in mind lodging in the Jerusalem to come. He is rightly said to be standing in them, because no-one falls there. Finally, observe his

words: *Our feet were standing;* they were standing in the place where they are always implanted with firm purpose. This stance does not waver, is not exhausted by any toil, but perseveres in its strength and is wearied by no fatigue. Next follows: *In thy courts, O Jerusalem.* Here he describes as *courts* the inner quarters, for the court of a house is the entrance-hall where residents cannot make their lodging. This is the figure which expresses the whole from the part.[2]

3. *Jerusalem, which is built as a city, whose sharing is in reality.* So that you should not interpret the Jerusalem which he had mentioned as the earthly abode, he denotes the heavenly city, distinguishing it with marvellous subtlety. He first says: *Jerusalem, which is built as a city.* It is indeed built, for it is constructed with spiritual workmanship from living stones every day until the end of the world. Those living stones are the confessors, martyrs, and those devoted to the Lord with pure minds. He added: *As a city,* to denote its similarity to a city. Every city is so called from its citizens, but the future Jerusalem is more deserving of the name because it is known to contain citizens of one mind. We must realise that a city in the present world contains people undifferentiated and intermingled, whereas that future city undoubtedly contains only those made perfect. The earthly city is buffeted by altercations, whereas the future city rejoices in continual serenity. This city is full of penitents, but the other knows no tears. This city sets its belief in hope, but the city to come sees God face to face. The result is that though there are two cities, there will in the future be one people of the faithful. There follows a most appropriate but opaque statement: *Whose sharing is in reality;* this means that the sharing of this city is in the Lord Saviour, who is reality in its proper sense. For reality denotes eternity, which never ceases to be what it is, but is always of one and the same kind: strength unfailing, power unchangeable, substance self-perpetuating, able effectively to perform all that it wills. It was in such terms that the Lord spoke of Himself to Moses: *I am who am,* and a little later: *He who is hath sent me to you.*[3] Another psalm addresses these words to Him: *All of them shall grow old like a garment, and as a vesture thou shalt change them, and they shall be changed. But thou art always the self-same, and thy years shall not fail.*[4] So *reality* befits the Creator alone, for the angel who thought that he had this identity then fell, for his being was not self-created, and so he could not be reality. The phrase is found also in Psalm 4: *In peace in*

the reality I will sleep, and I will rest.[5] We realise that this kind of expression is peculiar to the divine Scriptures. The sharing in this city, then, is as we have said partnership and communion with the Lord Saviour. As He Himself also attests in the gospel: *Father, I will that where I am, these also should be with me;*[6] for the Lord will be in that city, and undoubtedly the saints will share with Him in accordance with His permission. The prophet Isaiah describes this city in marvellous praise: *Thy walls shall be called salvation, and thy gates joy. Thou shalt not have the sun for the light of day, neither shall the rising of the moon shine for thee at night: but the Lord shall be for thee an everlasting light, and thy God thy glory. Thy sun shall not go down, and thy moon shall not fail: for the Lord God shall be for thee an everlasting light, and the days of thy mourning shall be ended. And thy people shall be all just, and they shall possess the land as an inheritance for ever.*[7] The apostle John in his Apocalypse also describes the astonishing mysteries of this city in his marvellous proclamation, so that you would almost believe that you were present though you know that you are elsewhere.[8] The double citation of *Jerusalem* at the end of the previous verse and in this one is the figure called *anadiplosis* or repetition of an expression. This differs from *epembasis*, mentioned in the previous psalm, for there the expression can be repeated after the interposition of several words, whereas here it is repeated with no intervening word.[9]

4. *For thither did the tribes go up, the tribes of the Lord: the testimony of Israel, to confess thy name, O Lord.* His expression *thither* denotes the city of Jerusalem, to which he earlier alluded in *whose sharing is in reality.* So that you would identify it as the heavenly Jerusalem, he added: *They did go up.* The blessed always mount to it since they make progress by continual practice. He added: *The tribes*, amongst whom the people of Israel were allotted; just as the Roman people had thirty-five *curiae*,[10] so the Jewish nation had ten tribes, corresponding with the number of Jacob's sons. By these tribes he denotes the saints who confessed the Lord Saviour as God, for to distinguish these tribes of the faithful from the ranks of the unfaithful, he added: *The tribes of the Lord.* They certainly could not have belonged to Him had they not believed in Him with unsullied mind. Clearly there were other tribes belonging to the devil, which with wicked will preferred to cut themselves off from Christ. To them he said in the gospel: *You are of your father the devil.*[11] He briefly indicated the nature of these tribes of the

Lord with the words: *The testimony of Israel,* which indicate those who provide testimony of and prove the holiness of those who see God, for testimony provides confirmation to those in ignorance, enabling them to believe that there are true servants of the Lord once they have seen blessed men prominent in worthy deeds. So that you would be in no doubt about them, he added: *To confess thy name. To confess* here means to praise, for all saints in company with the angels will celebrate the Lord's praises. This is the true testimony of Israel, when the Lord's praises are sung with most devoted love. So that future city is described with glowing blessedness and anticipated glory.

5. *Because the seats have sat there in judgment, seats upon the house of David.* He says that the people mentioned earlier as having gone up there *have sat there,* in case you perhaps regarded them as less worthy of honour. They took their seats in the place to which they went up, and in which they will judge in company with the Lord. Such great honour is promised to the saints that they are even found worthy to pass judgment in company with the heavenly Judge. As Christ Himself attests in the gospel: *You shall sit on twelve seats, judging the twelve tribes of Israel.*[12] What a position of honour and distinction worthy of admiration, that men through God's grace should become judges, whereas they had been the accused through the effects of sins! But since the Lord pronounces the twin verdicts of which we read: *Go into eternal fire,* and: *Come, blessed of my Father, possess ye the kingdom,*[13] and the rest, how will the saints be judges in company with Him? They will indeed be judges with Him, for once they are cleansed in mind and fixed in the most perfect contemplation, they will decree that the Lord's decision as apprehended by them must be carried out without hesitation. The equivalent consent of those who sit and listen makes the judgment unanimous, even though we know that the rest were silent. The expression, *they have sat,* is the use of the past tense for the future, because all God's words abide in this way, so that though they are believed to come to pass in the future, you can reckon them to have already taken place because of their imperviousness to change.

But let us examine the sense of: *The seats have sat.* The expression is justified because holy men are seats of God. By sitting in them He enlightens them with the grace of His majesty. As we read in Scripture: *The soul of the just man is the seat of wisdom,*[14] and elsewhere:

Upon whom doth my spirit rest, save on him that is humble and peaceable, and who trembles at my words?[15] Next comes: *In judgment,* which must refer to nothing other than that future judgment of which we read: *The Father does not judge any man, but has given all judgment to the Son.*[16] Though he has not stated what sort of judgment he wishes us to identify, in the light of total reason we realise that it is the judgment at which the saints will sit in company with the Lord. In the divine Scriptures you often find a message not fully expressed, but none the less allowing men understanding of what is meant in the light of reason. For example, another psalm says: *Who is the man that desireth life?,*[17] and in the gospel the Lord says: *If you will enter into life, keep the commandments.*[18] The word eternal is not added here, but we must certainly understand it; this figure is called *ellipsis,* and because necessary words are lacking, it is called a defect.[19] He next explains by his praise what these seats are with the words: *Seats upon the house of David. Upon the house* means "over Christ's household," because some of the saints there will shine more brightly than the rest of the faithful. As Paul says: *Star differs from star in glory; so also is the resurrection of the dead.*[20] If it is a mark of distinction for one of the slaves in this world to know something more of the mind of his lord than his fellow servants do, how much more wonderful can it be in Christ's house to gain some greater contemplation of the Lord, so that one is distanced from others to the degree that one is able to gaze more fully on His divinity? *David* denotes Christ, the name taken from His forbear in the flesh. Observe how the description of that city is achieved. He has stated what must be done there, how it is built, who mount to it, and what they will perform. This figure is called *characterismos,* in Latin *informatio* or *descriptio.*[21]

6. *Ask what are the things that are for the peace of Jerusalem, and abundance for them that love thee.* The prophet has reached the second narration, in which he addresses those who through the Lord's generosity will be the judges. The word *ask* is ambiguous: here it means "enquire" rather than "entreat." It is fitting for a judge to ask about and investigate everything, but at the Judgment this does not happen with words or verbal enquiry, but with silent mental reflection. As has been said, they will all judge in company with the Lord, for all will be enlightened and sanctified, and will truly recognise the truth which the Lord will declare from His own mouth. The Lord seeks peace-

makers; so does the whole troop of the saints, for they abound in charity, flourish in modesty, excel in devoted humility. The prophet desires the saints to investigate what he knows the Lord can love, but whose is the peace which he mentions? It is none other than the peace of Jerusalem, in other words, the faithful people who at the time of the Judgment are received into eternal peace. So the prophet advises them of what he knows will come: those who will judge in the company of the Lord are to take joy in such persons as both love peace here on earth and achieve the rewards of eternal peace in heaven. Because he has put *Jerusalem* at the close of the phrase, he turns to her, and embraces her with the briefest of designations: *Abundance for them that love thee.* Clearly all blessings abound in those who love Jerusalem, for those who were poor on earth will be rich in all blessings there. Those who were frail here will be indestructible there; those whose lives were transient here will be eternal there. All the blessings which can exist are seen to be included in that heavenly abundance.

7. *Let peace be in thy strength, and abundance in thy towers.* He is still addressing Jerusalem, for whom he prays for all that he knows will come, for the Lord's strength is undoubtedly the saints' peace, which is also called love, of which Scripture says: *God is love.*[22] Through love they become one, and through it they deserve to be the temple of the Creator; and whatever is promised them is granted out of consideration of love. This is the peace which no wars shatter, and no uprisings disturb; that which is bestowed through Christ's pity in the world to come will be possessed without end. Peace (*pax*) comes from the verb to spare (*parcere*) or from the verb to feast (*pascere*).[23] Next comes: *And abundance in thy towers.* This is the abundance of which he said earlier: *And abundance for them that love thee.* But here something more meaningful seems to be denoted by *towers*, so that you would realise that the abundance is not equally available to all, but is the possession of those who are better; for towers defend cities by the high obstacle which they present, and they are the first to experience the oncoming enemy. So we quite reasonably infer that the martyrs are denoted here, for they defend the Lord's city with devoted confession by making their bodies an obstacle, and like projecting structures they are seen to fight back against the enemies of the faith.

8. *For the sake of my brethren and of my neighbours, I spoke peace of thee.* He proclaims peace and denotes the signs of his peace as perfect

men do. He says that he has proclaimed the peace of the Church for the sake of his brethren and neighbours, so that once instructed by this virtue of concord, they may love and seek unity. So he carried out his own teaching; through love of his brethren he proclaimed what he knew would be of benefit to all. So his message is that a person should not teach for his own praises or benefits, but should toil with merciful heart for the sake of brethren and neighbours. As Paul puts it: *Not seeking that which is profitable to me, but to many.*[24] So he states that it was not for his own temporal advantage that he has spoken of the peace of the era to come, but for his brethren and neighbours, so that they should long for it to gain salvation, and chain themselves with the bonds of unanimity. When he says: *Of thee,* he shows that he is still addressing Jerusalem, in which the company of the saints, in other words, the most blessed unity of the people, resides.

9. *Because of the house of the Lord my God, I have sought good things for thee.* He did not wish anyone to think that his affection was devoted to anything in such a way as to appear to neglect love of the Lord, so he appended the reason why he sought blessings for Jerusalem, namely because it is the Lord's house, and whatever love is bestowed is well attributed to Him.

Conclusion Drawn From the Psalm

Let us observe the nature of the words which the prophet poured forth on the third step of love, and let us rejoice at his progress which the Lord has furthered. The higher the ascent made by any of the saints, the deeper and the sweeter are the words which he produces.

Commentary on Psalm 122

A canticle of steps. It is our pleasure to take note of how this ascent of the prophet is of benefit, and how as he seeks greater heights he gives us signs of his perfection. First he raised his eyes to the mountains, but now he has lifted up the eyes of his heart to the Lord Himself. Thus in his struggle to mount higher by spiritual steps, he has sought happily to draw near to the divine mercy. What a fine sight to see men drawing close to God and raising this sluggish mass of flesh to the rewards of heavenly grace! But this is the doing only of Him who bade Lazarus emerge from the tomb, who stretched out His right hand and saved Peter when he was drowning, who translated Elias and Enoch to heaven while they were still alive,[1] and who performed other similar miracles such as the Godhead's power performs every day. It is men who are one in charity on this earth who mount these steps; only those who have deserved to be Christ's members can hasten to their Head. So just as in our hearts we have observed this wonderful ascent, so now with attentive minds let us discuss this lofty psalm.

Division of the Psalm

The prophet was afraid to lose what he held, so he carefully maintained the position to which he had risen. Initially he piously continues to persevere in his prayers, asking that as a divine reward he may retain the gifts he has obtained. In the second section he begs the Lord to grant him mercy, because he was enduring many acts of hostility from those who insulted him at the instigation of the devil. Since they could not besmirch him by their companionship, they sought at any rate to wound him with their arrogant acts of contempt.

Explanation of the Psalm

1. *To thee have I lifted up my eyes, who dwellest in heaven.* The human race is given the wholesome advice to seek help from where they believe invincible protection will come; whereas persons puffed up in heart who preen themselves with worldly power have recourse to riches and take refuge in their transient inheritance if they are challenged by any wounding attack, so that they may exact punishment from an enemy who has had the audacity to inflict an injury. But God's servants order themselves with the most patient behaviour, and whatever the obstacle or tribulation which they endure, they raise their eyes to the Lord and look to Him in whom they have true confidence that they can be saved. Next comes: *Who dwellest in heaven.* We read that the Lord dwells in many ways; for example, in the gospel: *I dwell*

in the Father, and the Father in me.[2] He is said also to dwell in the saints, as we read in Isaiah: *I will dwell among them, and will walk among them, and they will be my people, and I will be their God.*[3] Paul too says of them: *You are the temple of God, and the spirit of God dwells in you.*[4] The gospel too attests the dwelling of both: *That all may be one, and I in them, and Thou in me.*[5] We also read that the Lord sits in heaven, as in the passage: *Heaven is my throne, and the earth my footstool.*[6] And elsewhere: *The heaven of heavens is the Lord's, but the earth he has given to the children of men.*[7]

2. *Behold, as the eyes of servants are on the hands of their masters.* Let us examine the inner meaning of these comparisons. Servants watch the hands of their masters either when they wish to be fed by them to escape the pressures of total need, or when they are ordered a beating for their faults, until they hear the word, "Enough." Both the hope of moderate treatment and the eventual end to the punishment lie in the power of masters. It is appropriate for us to act in both ways, so that we may ever raise our eyes to the Lord both when we endure some hardship and when we are beaten for some transgressions. This and the next verse are uttered with use of the figure of *homoiōsis*,[8] by which the demonstration of something lesser known is clarified by comparison with a thing better known.

And as the eyes of the handmaid are on the hands of her mistress, so are our eyes unto the Lord our God, until he have mercy on us. Some commentators wish to attach this verse too to the Lord, to the point of identifying the mistress with the Lord God, because of the text: *Christ the power of God and the wisdom of God.*[9] But in case the difference of sex may alienate some people, the passage can perhaps be understood like this: earlier he made the comparison with servants and masters, and so that the female sex should not consider itself excluded, another parallel is provided for them, for the handmaid attends on the hands of her mistress as do male servants on the hands of their masters. Then follows the statement embracing both sexes, *So are our eyes unto the Lord our God, until he have mercy on us.* The preceding parallel is clarified by the use of *so.* Whether we seek some success from the Lord, or when we bear torments of mind or body, we always raise our eyes to the Lord. He also added *our* to *eyes,* so that both sexes could interpret this as spoken of themselves. He appended: *Until he have mercy on us,* to show that both men and women should patiently seek divine blessings, and continually make entreaty to Him. The word until (*donec*) is equivocal in the divine Scriptures. Sometimes it means that something is done for a time, and sometimes for ever. An example of the temporary sense is at Psalm 109: *Until I make thy enemies thy footstool.*[10] It also means for ever, as this psalm makes clear: *Until he have mercy on us,* as though our eyes should not be on His hands even after He has taken pity on us! A similar example in the gospel is: *He knew her not until she brought forth her first-born son;*[11] but it is certain that she never knew a man at any time. So here *until* is rightly interpreted as "for ever," though it seems to mean "for a time." This type of utterance is to be accounted as one of those peculiar to divine Scripture.

3. *Have mercy on us, O Lord, have mercy on us, for we are greatly filled with contempt.* He passes to the second topic, in which he begs for mercy because of the contempt and reproach directed at him. This servant who was being battered with the continual tribulation of ills, and had set his gaze on the Lord's mercy, bursts into words which he cannot repress, and laments his need for pity with a twofold entreaty, saying that his body was toiling under sufferings, and his soul under reproaches. This experience is rightly associated with martyrs, who with God's support overcome the injury of their sufferings through vigour of spirit. To this repeated request for mercy is added the reason for it, *For we are greatly filled with contempt.* They are filled with contempt when God's servants are rent with lashes, scorched with savage flames, murdered when submerged in the deepest waters; they could not endure such treatment if they were not treated with contempt. *Greatly filled* denotes the extent of their sufferings, but they witness that they have endured these eagerly and gladly.

4. *And our soul is greatly filled: a reproach to the rich, and contempt to the proud.* Earlier he said that he was filled with the contempt of those who considered themselves happy, and he claimed that his body was torn by punitive lashes; now he says that his soul was also filled with reproaches and contempt, so that no part of him should remain immune to the injury of most oppressive suffering. He spoke of being *a reproach to the rich,* because the persecutors were wealthy and self-satisfied who with wicked reproaches rebuked the holy men for their poverty and lowliness, saying: "What advantage do you get from forgoing the world's riches and seeking future things unknown, aban-

doning present joys and loving melancholy more? Look at me; I hold what I see. Go on hoping for what you groundlessly prefer to suspect will come to pass." Next comes: *And contempt to the proud.* The proud despise the humble when they hear from them proclamations such as they scorn to obey. Since they love the things of the present, they have no truck with the future, and through their debased wickedness they attack more sharply those who strive to comply with the Lord's commands. But at the judgment to come they experience the contrary conversion. The proud who have plenty become objects of reproach and contempt. Solomon says of such people: *What has pride profited us? Or what has the boasting of riches conferred on us?*,[12] and what follows. We should clearly realise that the sequence of normal eloquence demanded that he say: "Our soul is greatly filled with the reproach of the rich and the contempt of the proud;" but since he said instead: *Our soul is greatly filled: a reproach to the rich and contempt to the proud*, this seems a peculiarity of divine Scripture. It is not to be regarded as a solecism, but as an utterance not as yet grasped by human conventions.

Conclusion Drawn From the Psalm

The prophet has by now mounted four steps, and he rightly bore with the jealousy of lunatics, for success always afflicts opponents since they imagine that one known to be zealous for his soul's progress is being impeded by their empty allegations. Let us look closely at him, remarkable as he is in perseverance in prayer, never slackening through any expressions of contempt. He heals his various afflictions and wounds by the one specific: he always lifts up his eyes to the Lord.

COMMENTARY ON PSALM 123

A canticle of steps. The prophet attests that one person in many and many persons in one mount these steps, since he clearly speaks in both singular and plural voices in these psalms. There is nothing wrong with this, for God's people form the one body of Christ, and again we know that the devoted folk resolve themselves into each and every individual of the faithful. So whether one person or a group speak the words, it is the one Church's voice. These steps are set on the path where the King Himself is known to have shown us the way to the fatherland. If through His kindness we mount these steps faithfully and humbly, we attain His sacred seat of majesty.

Division of the Psalm

The holy confessors are aware of the great dangers from which, as from the onrush of a torrent, they have escaped through God's mercy, and in the first section they confess that they have been freed from so many raging hardships solely through His pity. In the second, they give thanks that they have not been deceived by their persecutors; the roles have been reversed, and the traps of the attackers shattered, while they themselves are known to have escaped.

Explanation of the Psalm

1. *If it had not been that the Lord was with us, let Israel now say.* When sudden joy comes over us at the recollection of past dangers, it often makes us fail to observe the natural order of words. These confessors express astonishment at how they escaped their pursuers, at how tortures did not prevail over human frailty, at how, when their bodies yielded, their minds were reinforced by faith and did not cave in. They put at the beginning of the sentence a tiny version of these words, a relic of their sublime thought, but then they explain them, so that astonishment at the great dangers would not be withheld and the full import of the words would be rendered a little later. It would have been the normal statement to say: "We could not have overcome the dangers imposed on us if it had not been that the Lord was with us." The wicked tendency of our human presumption is at the same time removed from consideration, for it is not our wealth or planning or virtue which is said to have helped us, but only the Lord's pity which is known to have delivered us. Next follows: *Let Israel now say.* They recognise that it is a most healthy thing to decree that it is by the Lord's authority that such important events occur, for the rest of the blessed were rightly urged to give thanks for the source of their salva-

tion. This is the power of charity and unity, that when an individual is granted some success, all should rejoice that it has befallen them, and likewise if some reverse is sustained, all should grieve that it has affected them. So he appended below what Israel should now say; and so anyone wishing to be identified with Israel should not refuse to say such things with a pure heart.

2. *If it had not been that the Lord was with us, when men rose up against us....* The devoted confessors who began to speak at the beginning of the psalm urge Israel to recite this and the following three verses, for even if a person is by some chance freed from his dangers, he is delivered by the almighty Lord. Though one and the same judgment is implicit in all these verses, we follow our practice of setting them down individually to advise you on what is added to each to explain the sense of any other. The second verse, then, as with the first, begins with the implicit sense that Israel should say that they were freed by the Lord's grace when wicked men were making savage attacks on them; for how could their frail flesh cope, or the fickleness of their human spirit remain firm, unless the Lord was with them? When He is with us, and no vice arising from our own wickedness cuts us off from Him, we remain ever safe and unharmed, because the iniquity of persecutors does not prevail against the person shielded by the grace of divine power. So in these two verses now recounted and in the next three, we should note the figure of *anaphora*,[1] for the same words are found repeated at the beginnings of the verses. This trope has the greatest impact for stirring our spirits.

3. ... *Perhaps they would have swallowed us alive. When their anger was roused against us....* The first half of the verse goes with what precedes. This is how the sense is to be combined: *If it had not been that the Lord was with us when men rose up against us, perhaps they would have swallowed us alive.* We must place a full-stop here, so that we may take the remainder of the verse with the connection between the words sundered. With regard to his phrase, *they would have swallowed us alive,* it is not a human practice for opponents to swallow people alive; but we are swallowed alive when plunged into the evils of heresy or into the steep depths of sins with sacrilegious wickedness. This could have befallen the holy men if heavenly power had not rescued them. Next follows the other half of this verse, which must clearly be joined to the statement coming next. He says: *When their*

anger was roused against us. The sense of their roused anger is that they did not have most righteous motives, for anger and envy are lacking in judgment, pursuing as they do their desires with headlong purpose. As Solomon puts it: *Anger killeth the foolish, and envy slayeth the little one.*[2] What just motive could they have against God's servants when they had the audacity to despise the Creator of all when He was with them? *Animus* (anger) is a Greek word formed from *anemos* (wind),[3] because its movement is comparable to the swiftest breezes, or from *anaima* (bloodlessness) because it is bloodless, since it is not physical, as was stated in the book which with the Lord's help we wrote on the soul.[4]

4–5. *Perhaps like waters they would have swallowed us up: our soul hath passed through a torrent.* These short verses are likewise interconnected, for if read in this way the statement is clear and unambiguous: *When their anger was roused against us, perhaps like waters they would have swallowed us up.* By *waters* he wishes us to understand the wicked races of pagans, who were seen to have earth-bound hearts possessed by worship of idols as by the deepest flood. They sought to swallow up God's servants when they strove to induce Christians to their own forms of worship. But that divine power, which offered a hand to the apostle Peter so that he should not drown, delivered them. The ancients gave *aqua* (water) its name on the grounds that from it (*a qua*) all things come; they believed that all things were created from water.[5] Next comes: *Our soul hath passed through a torrent.* As we have already said, a torrent is a river suddenly raised by winter-showers, which we see is swift-flowing and muddy, because it does not pour out from a pure source but is befouled by the contamination of the soil. The turbulent course of this world is rightly compared with it, for the world's stream does not flow down from any spring of truth, but is the storm-filled gathering of all evils. This is the torrent from which the Lord also drank; an earlier psalm said of it: *He drinks of the torrent on the way: therefore he shall lift up his head.*[6] So Israel too is rightly said to have passed through it, for it was foretold that their Head had drunk of it. But in all this there is a single true confession, that we are freed from such great dangers solely by the Lord's pity.

Perhaps our soul would have passed through waters insupportable. We must be careful to investigate why the word *perhaps* was so often repeated in the prayer, for it is not fitting for the faithful to doubt that we could not of ourselves traverse the world's dangers if the Lord were not with us. The true Catholic Church confesses this, but it is customary in time of great danger, when delivered from the greatest disaster, to express doubt and say: "Do you think that we have escaped?" though we are in no doubt whatsoever that we have done so. In fact even in a situation of certainty elsewhere there is the statement: *Unless thy law had been my meditation, I would then perhaps have perished in my abjection.*[7] The prophet Tobias too speaks in this way: *Be converted, ye sinners, and do justice before God: perhaps he will be well disposed to you, and show his mercy to you.*[8] Elsewhere Scripture says: *Raise your eyes to heaven with weeping: perhaps the Lord will have mercy on us, and will save us.*[9] You observe the qualification *perhaps* in all these passages, though there is absolutely no uncertainty. So we rightly claim as peculiar to divine Scripture the verbal wavering expressive of great and unqualified constancy of faith; secular usage regularly confines *perhaps* to doubtful and uncertain issues. So any expression of this kind is not a failure in most vigorous faith, but a great emphasis on danger. Why should they doubt their souls' success in merging from waters insupportable when they had earlier claimed *our soul hath passed through a torrent?* He added: *Waters insupportable.* He is now calling insupportable the waters which he claimed to have endured; he could not have emerged from them if he had not endured all his privations by being strengthened through God's grace. He speaks of waters insupportable when he thinks of our weakness, for the whirlpool of sins and the storm of evil deeds cannot be endured when it finds itself cut off from the Lord's protection. By contrast, all things can be borne when God dwells in His saints, for in those circumstances error does not creep in, nor creature-comforts seduce, nor windy pride prevail, nor the malicious prompting of the ancient enemy attack us.

6. *Blessed be the Lord, who hath not given us to be a prey to their teeth.* The devoted confessors pass to the second narration, in which they thank the Lord because they were far from collapsing, as their enemies wished. Instead, those who sought to destroy them were shattered. Observe how the savage will of enemies is described: they

appeared to attack men's innocence like wild beasts, with their teeth. This is said also of the devil: *Your enemy the devil goes round like a roaring lion, seeking whom he may devour.*[10]

7. *Our soul has been delivered as a sparrow out of the snare of the fowlers.* 8. *The snare is rubbed away, and we are delivered.* The saints do well to say this, for though their bodies are afflicted, their souls are safe through the Lord's protection. The sparrow, as we have often remarked, is quite the most circumspect of birds. It nests in walls; it cleverly avoids traps laid for it, and is not easily caught, because in seeking food it always as we know proceeds with caution. *The snare of the fowlers* is any enticing sweetness in this world, in which we are trapped when we consider it to be sweet. There is a saying about women: *The eye of the courtesan is the snare of the sinner.*[11] We must take the same view of greed, of pride, of all vices. But observe the addition made: *The snare is rubbed away, and they are delivered.* This is indeed so, for the person who hastens to lay burdens on another oppresses himself. As Scripture has it: *He that hastens to dig a pit for another, himself falls into it.*[12] Moreover, observe that he says that the snare was *rubbed away*, not broken. We do not say that a thing made of leather or tow is rubbed away unless it is known to have the hardness of some metal. So it is said to be rubbed away to demonstrate by the word strength of suffering and the power of the Liberator. So they rightly say that the snare has been rubbed away and that they are delivered from it, since the fowlers are reduced to impotence, being unable to trap those whom they sought to beguile.

8. *Our help is in the name of the Lord, who made heaven and earth.* They reveal the reason why the snare was rubbed away: it was because nothing hostile can prevail against one aided by divine power. You madmen, why do you try to lay snares against the servants of Him who as you know founded heaven and earth by momentary command? It is easy for Him to destroy your traps, for He is accustomed to scatter all wicked things at will.

Conclusion Drawn From the Psalm

How splendidly the blessed devotion of confessors has mounted the fifth step, enabling them to rejoice in their advance to this fifth stage after their success in overcoming their bodily feelings with the Lord's help! The humility which is the remedy for the human race ensured that they did not fall or stagger through physical frailty. That humility enabled them to put all their hope in the Lord, and they attributed nothing good to themselves with the presumption that causes downfall.

Commentary on Psalm 124

A canticle of steps. The Lord was aware of the unstable progress of human weakness, so He fashioned this path by the steps, so to say, of the virtues, so that our longing should strive more securely for the heights, since our feet were placed on level terrain. This is how we set foot on the ridges afforded by the steps, so that we do not confront a sloping ascent. But though this saving flight of steps is seen to be constructed with suitable assistance, we do not stand firmly upright unless we are kept there by the Lord's control. The ascent, however, is mental and not physical. We mount these steps more successfully by remaining seated in the one place, withdrawn in the location of our tiny cell, than if we flit before the faces of men. The prophet cries that we must trust in the Lord so that we may not toil in vain.

Division of the Psalm

The prophet mounts the sixth step, which is in the science of numbers accounted as perfection.[1] In his initial advice he strengthens the faithful people, saying that they can in no sense be perturbed, for they have placed their trust in the Lord's strength. He gives the reason why the Lord does not allow sinners to advance beyond the lot of the just. In the second section he entreats that prosperity may attend the upright, and vengeance the wicked.

Explanation of the Psalm

1. *They that trust in the Lord, as though he were mount Sion: he shall not be moved for ever, that dwelleth in Jerusalem.* The prophetic words

address all persons in general, for those who remain constant in the true religion here on earth, and set their hope in the Lord's protection as though in Sion, the mountain of Jerusalem, stand most steady and firm. Here we must investigate the meaning of the name; *Sion* means "watching,"[2] an apt activity for the Lord Jesus Christ our Shepherd. Such a comparison of an object without sense with so great a Majesty could not be possible unless it had positive significance such as you will often find in the divine Scriptures. Elsewhere is the statement: *The mountains skipped like rams, and the hills like the lambs of the flock,*[3] and there are other passages of the same kind. So he says of the man who trusts in the Lord that like mount Sion he shall not be moved for ever, though our belief is that mount Sion like everything else will be changed at the end of the world. But the Sion here is the Lord Christ who shall not be moved; it is He who is denoted here. Observe too that earlier he wrote: *They that trust,* whereas subsequently he used the singular: *He shall not be moved;* this was clearly to signify the unity of the numerous Christian people. He added: *That dwelleth in Jerusalem.* We know that Jerusalem was utterly demolished by various races, and her citizens were often taken captive, so how can he say that its dwellers are wholly immovable? The answer is that here too we are to identify Jerusalem as the native land of heaven denoting the vision of peace, from which no-one can in any sense be moved once having attained the merit of being established in its firm foundation. In this sense we find that truth and pure reason will square with each other if we apply such terms to their appropriate sense.

2. *Mountains are round about it: and the Lord is round about his people, from henceforth now and for ever.* The shape of the earthly Jerusalem is described in this verse in such a way that it is the native land in heaven which is revealed instead to us. The earthly Jerusalem is itself on a mountain, but is set in the midst of surrounding mountains like a level expanse surrounded by lofty peaks. This type of description is called in Greek *topothesia,* and in Latin *loci positio.*[4] *Mountains* are cited in the good and the bad sense, for in both instances they are seen to tower over the general landscape with their great height. As an example of the bad sense: *In the Lord I put my trust. How do you say to my soul, Get thee away from hence to the mountain like*

a sparrow?[5] In the good sense: *Let the mountains receive peace for the people, and the hills justice.*[6] Likewise here mountains denotes holy men who dwell in the heavenly Jerusalem on all sides. To emphasise the interpretation of blessed men, there follows: *And the Lord is round about his people.* He surrounds only the person who He knows is faithful to Him. He surrounds him to lend him the help of eternal protection, and to bestow on him the accumulation of all honour. Through His nature which lies beyond description, He is everywhere wholly present, reaching into all things and containing all things. He does not, like his creatures, move from one place to be in another; and though He fills all things, He is known to attend on the good but to absent Himself from the wicked. We must understand and believe this without hesitation of the whole Trinity. The additional: *From henceforth now*, denotes this world, of which the Lord says: *Behold, I am with you all days, even to the consummation of the world.*[7] *And for ever* refers to the time when He will appear to the saints in the most powerful majesty of His light. The explanation follows why this defence is afforded.

3. *For the Lord will not abandon the rod of sinners upon the lot of the just: that the just may not stretch forth their hands to iniquity.* By *rod* is denoted the power of good and evil. In the good sense we have the words spoken of the Lord Saviour Himself: *The Lord will send forth the rod of thy power out of Sion, and thou shalt rule in the midst of thy enemies.*[8] Moses too received a rod,[9] with which he performed many miracles. In the bad sense it is given also to those who ever afflict the faithful with perverted zeal. Persecutors are a rod for martyrs; so too are masters angry with their households, as was Pharaoh, Nebuchadnezzar and the others who ruled with the harshest tyranny. But the Lord does not permit this wicked power to flourish in extended freedom, so that the faithful may realise that this discretion has been allowed to the proud for only the shortest time, to make trial of their patience; for God's servants could perhaps turn their minds to deeds of wickedness if they believed that the persecution was extending over a long period. *The lot of the just* is the Lord's inheritance, in other words the Christian religion, over which He does not allow cruel tyrants to rise, to prevent their being able to wear down the Lord's

Church by protracted persecution. By saying: *He will not abandon*, he makes it clear that even if temptation is permitted for a time, it is not left to run free in the power of him for whom an evil end and tearful death are in store instead.

4. *Do good, O Lord, to those that are good, and to the upright of heart.* Now that the people are strengthened and the constancy of their faith is enhanced, he passes to the second section, in which he briefly entreats the Lord for what he knows He will perform, namely the conferment of blessings on the good and condign punishment on the wicked. Men are *good* when they are first visited by divine grace, and then begin to desire and fulfil the sacraments. We read: *None is good save God alone*,[10] but both statements are true and perfect. If we are left to our own resources, we are undoubtedly found to be evil; if through the aid of God's mercy we attract His gaze until we become obedient, we are indeed found to be good. Next comes: *And to the upright of heart*. The upright of heart are those who follow God and do not seek to precede Him. When the apostle Peter *savoured the things of men*, he was told: *Get behind me, Satan*.[11] Those who seek to precede Him do not cease to err; those who desire to follow are undoubtedly known to be upright of heart. So the prophet prays that good may befall those who cannot detach themselves from the Lord through perverted will.

5. *But such as turn aside to evil connections, the Lord shall lead out with the workers of iniquity. Peace upon Israel.* Earlier he asked that good befall those who are good and upright of heart, and now he says that those who swerve aside can be led to evil connections. This is a fine definition of a work of iniquity; it is the evil connection which entangles us in bonds of wickedness, with the result that we cannot go free since we are held fast by nooses of such strength and size. Observe that he said: *Such as turn aside*, in other words, as disobey the Lord's commands. Those who turn aside from the commands of their Emperor perish by the same decree as those who zealously seek to commit evil.

Peace upon Israel is added as an unambiguous phrase. The peace gives promise of all outstanding things which are beyond our entire understanding, and transcend all our prayers. To express much in brief compass, this peace is the Lord Saviour Himself. But those who dispute with unity and are seen to be hostile to the Catholic people will not have this peace in any sense.

Conclusion Drawn From the Psalm

Let us consider how admirably firm this step is, enabling the prophet to recall his past ills, and to say that the Lord has lent aid during all of them. He prepares his ascent to better things, for he knows that the Lord's help has been at hand in the past. He would not have been able to mount higher if he had sought to presume on his own powers. So let us embrace this saving canon with all the feeling of our hearts, so that He who has caused us to hear of His great deeds may allow us to mount these steps.

COMMENTARY ON PSALM 125

A canticle of steps. After their enslavement to all sins, how sweetly do the voices of the blessed project themselves as they mount to the heavenly Jerusalem, so that poised on that lofty route they may comfort themselves with sacred song! Their journey is most happy, and their toil fruitful, provided that He who is the goal of their journey is always kept in their hearts. So let us lend our soul's ear and concentrate most unsullied minds, for if we drink in the holy hymn within our hearts' depths, we capture something of that blessedness.

Division of the Psalm

These most holy men who have been freed by divine pity give thanks in the first section of the psalm because they have been offered the refuge of such outstanding favour from the most savage subjection of sins, and so are found worthy of praise among the nations. In the second part they pray that their captivity may be transformed into joy, and they append the marvellous and true apophthegm: *They that sow in tears shall reap in joy.*

Explanation of the Psalm

1. *When the Lord transformed the captivity of Sion, we became like men comforted.* Here a spiritual explanation is seen to be necessary, for since in the days of David Sion is said to have endured no desolation, it remains to investigate what sort of captivity this verse appears to denote. It is clearly the captivity of the devil, under which the world was kept subject. *The captivity of Sion* describes when the wickedness of idols oppressed God's Church when its numbers were small. But it gained the transformation of freedom when at the Lord's coming the bars of hell were burst asunder. Next comes: *We became like men comforted*, doubtless because, though that earlier captivity had been lifted from us by the aid of the Godhead, it made us not wholly secure but like people comforted. Unqualified comfort comes when a promise is now to be fulfilled, whereas amidst these uncertainties of the world we get the greatest consolation when we believe that He who we know has spared us without payment is preserving his gifts for us.

2. *Then was our mouth filled with gladness, and our tongue with joy. Then* means when the coming of the Lord Saviour, as has now been said, transformed our captivity into joy, our vices into virtues, our ignorance into knowledge of things divine, our death into eternal life, so that *our mouth was* rightly *filled with gladness, and our tongue with joy*, for such blessings were bestowed on us by the Lord's gift. Here *mouth* describes the hidden depth of the heart, where joys are first sown and sprout, and through the office of the tongue burst out into a harvest of words. It is the mouth which is referred to in: *Taste, and see that the Lord is good!*[1] Even though his lips are closed, he cries out to the Lord, and the utterance of his remorseful heart is effectively heard, though his mouth is inactive.

Then shall they say among the Gentiles: the Lord hath done great things with them. The praise proclaimed by enemies is unambiguous; there is great weight of truth when a person known to have opposing sentiments gives favourable testimony. Note quite carefully that he does not say: "The Gentiles," but *among the Gentiles.* At the coming of the Lord not all Gentiles believed, but among them were some who could have uttered such words when pricked at heart. So when they saw religion flourishing among the Christian people, they attained good understanding, and they proclaimed that the Lord was truly with such people, for they showed zeal for an upright conscience, and did not desire to besmirch themselves with any superstition. Since they saw that the Christians were also exercising virtues, they said: "The Lord has decided to do great things with them," for they saw that the Christians through their prayers were having their requests fulfilled.

3. *The Lord hath done great things with us: we are become joyful.* They did not wish to leave the previous words of the Gentiles undetermined, so now they appropriate their statement and confirm it in their own persons. The Lord did great things with them when He deigned to listen to them with favour. Take note of the type of utterance which he uses: *The Lord hath done great things with us*, in other words, "He has decided to demonstrate to the Gentiles our greatness through the gift of virtues." It is appropriate for us to regard this type of utterance as another of those peculiar to divine Scripture. Next comes: *We are become joyful*, precisely as a result of such favour. Their joy was indeed abundant, since they saw that they were especially loved after having been freed from the most degrading captivity. This figure is called *diatyposis*, in other words, "description of deportment."[2] Such deportment is the label which we attach to undeviating and total perfection of mind or body in any matter.

4. *Transform our captivity, Lord, as a torrent in the south wind.* Now that they have proclaimed redemption brought by the Lord's coming, the faithful people reach the second section, entreating that their sins be again pardoned, for as Scripture says: *The just man is his own accuser at the beginning of his speech*,[3] and again: *First tell of your iniquities that you may justify yourself.*[4] So rightly they both rejoiced at the general pardon and prayed that they too be granted indulgence. There follows a beautiful comparison: *As a torrent in the south wind.* The south is a warm wind which by the force of its exhalation looses waters which are fast bound with cold, and unleashes a rushing torrent through the heat of its breath. In the same way, sins held fast by the cold of death (for they have no life in them) are loosed by the warmth of heavenly mercy, and swiftly depart like a raging torrent. To grasp the fullness of the sense we must say: "*Transform our captivity, Lord, as a torrent in the south wind* is transformed into running water."

5. *They that sow in tears shall reap in joy.* Paul teaches us that there are two kinds of sowing in this world. As he says: *He that soweth in the flesh shall reap corruption of the flesh; and he that soweth in the spirit, of the spirit shall reap life everlasting.*[5] Spiritual sowing is always *in tears,* for though the faithful through the Lord's bounty practise the virtues, they either lament their past sins or they fear to become enmeshed in future faults. Scripture well says of them: *Blessed are they that mourn, for they shall be comforted.*[6] So persons of this stamp who sow in tears attain the joys of the promised future. The prophet Osee likewise says to them: *Sow for yourselves for justice, and reap for mercy.*[7] Their sowing is their search for peace, their endurance of all things in the zeal of charity, the subjugation of their bodies by fasting, their renewal of themselves by almsgiving and devotion, and all that can contribute to the ordered way of life of the faithful. By contrast, those eager for temporal things who long for the vanities of the world sow with joy when they commit adulteries, love greed, seek exotic banquets, embrace idolatry, and commit the other sins which are done at the devil's prompting. But on the day of judgment they will reap the harvest of their deeds with grief and tears. Of them Scripture says: *There will be weeping and gnashing of teeth.*[8] Thus in one short verse the reward for good deeds, and retribution for evil ones, are made clear. This figure is called *antistathmesis* or recompense,[9] when the person who has lived an upright or a debased life receives a just reward for his deeds.

6. *Going, they went and wept, casting their seeds: but coming, they shall come with joyfulness, carrying their sheaves.* Though this verse too seems to point to good works in general, it is recognised—and others have thought the same—to be prescribing in particular almsgiving. Hence the words of Scripture: *As water quenches fire, so alms quenches sins.*[10] The word *Going* denotes the advance of a most holy life, in which they always reach their destination by taking the right path. They wept, then, when they saw the poor stripped naked, rigid with cold, disfigured by savage poverty, so that they evinced devotion in their hearts before their hands made any generous provision. Next follows: *Casting their seeds. Casting* means sending in advance into the world to come, which our deeds reach before we ourselves can get there. As Scripture has it: *But lay up to yourselves treasures in heaven, where neither rust nor moth doth consume, and where thieves do not dig*

through and steal.[11] The additional word; *Their*, is not idle, for we must contribute alms from our own labours, not from what we steal. True mercy is that which does not cause another's grief, which does not result in anyone's sad departure, for we must offer to the divine Majesty what can be obtained rightfully. Since the Lord says such gifts are given to Him, ponder whether anything can be offered to Him which is the fruit of wickedness. He added: *But coming, they shall come with joyfulness, carrying their sheaves.* Coming, they come in joyfulness, for divine mercy is in store for them because their actions on this earth have accorded with the commands of heaven. But those who have besmirched themselves here with the most evil deeds do not come to attain joy. All share the experience of coming, but only the blessed attain joy. These expressions (*coming* and *shall come*) are said to be conjugated, for they originate from words of the same kind. Earlier they had said that each individual reaps his own activity, so they continue to use the same metaphor in their truthful judgment: they added: *Carrying their sheaves.* When harvesters have finished their work, after assembling the ears of corn they carry in their laps to the threshing-floor the bundles which they have tied together in the fields. In the same way the blessed ones carry to the Lord's threshing-floor their most fruitful works. Happy is the bosom which is weighed down by the loads of wheat, so that light straw does not cheat the prayers of the harvester; otherwise he would then reap empty rewards for his toil, for he can now work no longer.

Conclusion Drawn From the Psalm

How splendidly has this seventh consecutive step prophesied to us the Lord's first coming as a prefiguration in the Old Testament! It has foretold the joy of salvation to be bestowed on the people, so that the group of eight would be left which we have earlier said relates to the Lord's resurrection. The next heading reveals this dichotomy, for its formulation is "Canticle of the steps of Solomon." Solomon means "man of peace,"[12] a term especially relevant to the Lord Christ, who reconciled the world to God, and who said: *My peace I give to you, my peace I leave to you.*[13] In short, the psalm is shown to reveal not a future prophecy but the very fruit of the womb; so it may be clear beyond doubt to all that indications of the New and Old Testaments, designated by the decades of the whole work, are contained in Psalm 71, and that here the same indications are revealed by the individual psalm-numbers.[14]

Commentary on Psalm 126

A canticle of the steps of Solomon. We have said that it is not otiose that the name of Solomon, which means in Latin *pacificus* (peacemaker),[1] is added to this heading. Whom could this epithet more appropriately fit than Him who drew together the circumcised and the uncircumcised in the cause of unity, and as the Corner-stone steadied with solid strength the walls attached to Him from different angles? Of Him Paul says: *For he is our peace, who hath made both one.*[2] There is also the fact that this is the eighth step counting from the back, and the number eight has reference to the Lord Christ's resurrection, the subject on which it is to concentrate. It denotes the New Testament to which these prophetic mysteries are addressed. Note that here and in Psalm 71 the name of Solomon is clearly inscribed to make the separation between the Testaments, so that you may realise that both Old and New are in harmony with each other.

Division of the Psalm

The prophet was exultant because he was filled with the holy Spirit, and had forseen the grace of the New Testament. To ensure that destructive presumption should not creep up on himself or on others because of this great gift, at the outset he teaches the most holy people that no-one should strive to attribute anything good to his own strength, since all things lie within the divine power. Nor should anyone seek to anticipate the time which he knows has been ordained by the Lord's decree. In the second sequence he speaks of the Lord Jesus Christ and His apostles, or of any persons who perform His commands.

Explanation of the Psalm

1. *Unless the Lord build the house, they labour in vain that build it.* Clearly the psalmist addresses builders of some sort, but it is not fitting for us to regard this as referring to those who erect squared stones with cement. Rather we must interpret them as the builders who strive to fashion each and every Christian in the truth of faith. They are the house to whom Paul says: *You are the temple of God, and the Spirit of God dwells in you.*[3] But if these men seek to build by their own powers, they are seen to labour to no effect unless the Lord's grace bestows an attitude of most genuine belief. Paul also says: *Neither he that planteth is anything, nor he that watereth, but God that giveth the increase.*[4] We must commit our energy to perform these tasks, but with the belief that it is God that can carry them through. Otherwise we may be beguiled by empty presumptions, and be seen to ignore the Author and Perfector of things, to our own destruction. Let us remember that this and the next verse exemplify the thesis called *the necessary;*[5] for the Lord's building is necessary, since without it nothing good is raised to the peak of perfection.

Unless the Lord keep the city, they shall watch in vain that keep it. He passes from the house to the city, so that accursed pride may not creep up on us individually, and so that destructive arrogance may not become dominant in holy Church. We interpret the Lord's city as the heavenly Jerusalem, a part of which still lodges on earth. In it the bishops strive to keep watch, to protect with unsleeping care the flock entrusted to them. The same injunction is given them not to be fired by harmful thoughts, and imagine that human precautions have any dominant effect, for only the Godhead can ward off dangers of attack. We become aware of the extent of Pelagian shamelessness and its wicked presumption, since the holy Spirit has decided so often to utter criticism of it which it has not endured to hear.

2. *It is in vain for you to rise before light: rise after you have been seated.* He is still addressing the teachers, so that the people may be corrected more effectively when they see that their mentors have been forewarned, for they are told: *It is in vain for you to rise before light.* It is the person who longs to be granted blessedness in this world who rises before light, whereas the true Light, the Lord Christ, endured many sufferings here, deigning to undergo the gibbet of the cross for

our salvation. All this is demonstrated by a most splendid comparison. The person who rises before light still walks in darkness, and cannot advance his journey because of the blackness of the night; similar to him are the persons who strive to dwell untroubled in this world before obtaining the joys of resurrection. They are told: *Rise after you have been seated,* in other words, endure being humbled first, and after your ascension seek the rewards of joys; for the seating mentioned denotes humility and not distinction. The following verse reveals that this is the exact sense intended; for to instruct us by His own clear example, our Head sat when He said: *My soul is sorrowful even unto death,*[6] and He rose when He said: *All power is given to me in heaven and in earth.*[7] We find the phrase, *before light,* used also in the good sense; as Jeremiah says: *I have spoken to you before dawn, and you have not heard me, and I have sent to you all my servants the prophets before dawn, saying: Return each of you from his evil path.*[8] If you concentrate your mind on them, you see that though these passages seem contradictory, they both speak of Christ. This psalm says that no joys are to be taken before light, that is, before the Lord's second coming; while Jeremiah warns the people to abandon wickedness before dawn, that is, before Christ's first coming, so that they cannot be found on crooked paths. So the two prophets have touched upon the Lord's two comings.

You that eat the bread of sorrow: when he shall give sleep to his beloved. He has made clear the persons to whom he said: *It is in vain for you to rise before light;* by his own witness it is perfect Christians who *eat the bread of sorrow,* for another psalm says of them: *Tears were my bread day and night,*[9] and: *Thou wilt feed us with the bread of tears, and give us for our drink tears in measure.*[10] Their sorrow is indeed their bread, since they refresh themselves with affliction, and console themselves with this world's sadness. Bread nourishes us, and this is the effect of the purity with which the faithful consider that punishment is inflicted on them not for death but for salvation. The next words explain when those people earlier ordered to sit are to rise, namely at the time when the faithful are welcomed into rest; for them death is sleep and untroubled intermission. God's *beloved* are those who seek Him with zealous love. One can infer from this passage the great gifts bestowed on them, since they have received such a title, for one addressed as God's beloved is undoubtedly adorned with eternal blessedness.

3. *Behold, the inheritance of the Lord, the children: the reward, the fruit of the womb.* The prophet wished to show that he had spoken the previous words with reference to Christ's faithful, so he passes to the second topic in which he now points to the Lord Christ. He says: *Behold, the inheritance of the Lord, the children;* understand "of the Church." They have been born of water and the holy Spirit, and are known to be the Lord's inheritance. The identity of these children is next explained: *The reward, the fruit of the womb.* The fruit of this womb, the offspring born of the Virgin, the reward is the Lord's entire inheritance, which on rising again is sent to possess heaven, and will rejoice with the Lord in eternal blessedness. The reward is said to have been rendered to humankind; of it Psalm 2 says: *Ask of me, and I will give thee Gentiles for thy inheritance.*[11] Paul after other comments says: *For which cause God has exalted him, and has given him the name which is above all names.*[12] His divinity received nothing to give it increase, but bestowed on the world the means of escaping the dangers of death. In this sense we speak of the people as acquired, and we proclaim the souls of the converted as a gain. In the same sense He is said to obtain the reward which we attest He at some time acquired. These and similar statements are aptly interpreted as referring to the nature in which He suffered.

4. *As arrows in the hand of the mighty, so also the children of the researchers.* An arrow is a weapon which quickly reaches its target, and flies on the straightest course. When it leaves *the hand of the mighty,* it is fired with great speed, and strikes the target. The one who takes aim is not *mighty* if the arrow goes astray; so the addition: *From the hand of the mighty,* is made to ensure that you have no doubt of the outcome, or scepticism about the arrow's speed. The apostles are well compared to these arrows, for they were directed from *the hand of the mighty,* the Lord Saviour, were quickly guided to their target, and fulfilled His commands faithfully. So that you could understand this clearly, the words that follow are: *So also the children of the researchers.* We rightly call the prophets *researchers,* for they investigated the inner depths of the Lord, and prophesied astonishing miracles to the people. Researching means investigating something hidden and making it known. Undoubtedly this was what the prophets did, for by their praiseworthy lives they deserved to be filled with the truth of holy light. The apostles are rightly called the prophets' sons; by their

preaching they came to believe, and so in a certain sense they were their offspring in faith. The blessed Paul attests without reservation that there is a kind of progeny in teaching when he says: *My little children, of whom I am in labour again, till Christ be formed in you,*[13] and in another place: *For in Christ Jesus by the gospel I have begotten you.*[14]

5. *Blessed is the man that has filled his desire with them.* The apostles, children of the researchers, desired that the believing Christian people should serve the Lord, so he calls them *blessed,* since their toil has attained their glorious aspirations. Alternatively and better, they themselves desired to enter with haste into the Lord's halls, as already stated in Psalm 41: *As the hart panteth after fountains of water, so my soul panteth after thee, O God.*[15] Paul was similarly fired by this desire when he said: *I desire to be dissolved, and to be with Christ.*[16] So they are three and four times blessed[17] who have managed to realise such longings. But this desire is not fulfilled by man's making haste; He who grants the outcome arouses such longing.

They shall not be confounded when they shall speak to their enemies at the gate. This too refers to the researchers' sons, who filled the boundaries of the world with their holy preachings. *The gate* of the city of Jerusalem is Christ the Lord; as He Himself says: *I am the gate.*[18] That person speaks at the gate who makes true proclamation of the Lord Saviour, so that men may enter through the baptism and repentance which He grants, and possess the kingdom of heaven. But we must also investigate why such a place is chosen for preachers; the answer is that the unbeliever should depart and the one who gives assent should enter. So at that place the devoted preacher both compels the unfaithful to retire and permits the committed to enter. Alternatively, words spoken at the gate are public announcements, for they are always heard by travellers.

Conclusion Drawn From the Psalm

How splendidly he mounts as far as the true Sun like a second Elias, though not borne on a fiery chariot, but raised on the steps of the virtues; not traversing the air with physical movement, but mounting the holy height in spirit. Glory to the Lord Saviour, who has revealed diverse wonders in the persons of His servants! The mortal body of

Elias journeyed through the air, but the prophet mounted to the realms above without leaving the earth. Let us ask that we who are weighed down by the frailty of the flesh may be raised up by the Lord on the wings of His mercy. For Him nothing is difficult, except when we do not believe that He can fulfil some action that is good. So let us diligently study the divine Scriptures, let us turn over the books of the New and Old Testaments if we wish to be children of the researchers. It is there that we find the Lord, if we succeed in truly studying them.

Commentary on Psalm 127

A canticle of steps. The number itself announces the splendour of this step, for it reveals to us the sacred summit of the holy Trinity by its triple trebling.[1] But since we read: *The fear of the Lord is the beginning of wisdom,*[2] we must investigate why the prophet has decided that we must keep it in mind at this stage. There are two fears which prick our hearts. The first is human fear, by which we are apprehensive of suffering physical hazards or losing worldly goods; this is clearly a temporary state, since we fear such things only as long as we dwell in the life of this world. But divine fear always mounts with us through all the advances which we make in this life. Whereas we abandon worldly fear together with the world on the first step, divine fear remains ever with us, and is adapted as a most faithful companion throughout our ascent. As has already been said in Psalm 118: *Pierce thou my flesh with thy fear, for I am afraid of thy judgments.*[3] So it is fitting that both on this step and everywhere we be instructed that fear of the Lord should be within us, for it is approved as our essential guardian.

Division of the Psalm

In the first limb the prophet recounts by certain allusions the blessings of those who fear God, so as to fire the spirits of the committed with the warmth of heaven's reward. In the second, he blesses them that they may gain eternal joys, so that none may be apprehensive of this sweetest of fears.

Explanation of the Psalm

1. *Blessed are all they that fear the Lord, that walk in his ways.* In his first words he has distinguished fear of the Lord from the terror of this world. His words: *Blessed are all they that fear the Lord,* reveal that those who with troubled mind are apprehensive of the world's dangers in loss of temporal possessions are not blessed. These dangers make men wretched, torturing them with empty fear, so that they experience no growth but a diminution, no ascent but a headlong fall. By contrast, fear of the Lord is the offspring of love, is born of charity, is sprung from sweetness. What devoted fear, consoling the timorous, refreshing the afflicted, experiencing no absence of joy unless the benefit of such fear is laid aside! Scripture says of this fear: *Come, children, hearken to me: I will teach you fear of the Lord.*[4] How advantageous the fear is by which children are instructed, how splendid the training bestowed with sweet affection! In another place we are given instruction about it: *And now, Israel, what doth the Lord thy God require of thee, but that thou fear the Lord thy God with all thy heart, and walk in all his ways, and love him, and keep his commandments with all thy heart and with all thy soul, that it may be well with thee?*[5] There is the further statement on the same point: *The fear of the Lord is holy, enduring for ever and ever.*[6] But to prevent your believing that the Lord is perhaps only to be feared when He thunders, or sends lightning, or makes lands quake, or threatens death to lawbreakers, he added: *That walk in his ways.* Fear of the Lord not only causes us to desist from wicked deeds, but also establishes us as walking in the most upright faith; those persons *fear the Lord that walk in his ways* and perform His commandments with devoted minds. But let us examine why he speaks in one place of "way" in the singular, and in another of *ways* in the plural as here. When the Lord Christ speaks of Himself, He calls Himself the Way, as in: *I am the way, the truth and the life,* and again: *No-one can come to the Father except by me.*[7] When He speaks of several ways, He denotes apostles and prophets, through whom we come to the one Way who is none other than the Lord Saviour. Jeremiah attests both usages when he says: *Stand ye on the ways of the Lord, and ask for the eternal paths of God, and see which is the good way, and walk in it.*[8] We have pointed out that this is the necessary interpretation elsewhere as well.

2. *Thou shalt eat the labours of thy fruits: blessed art thou, and it shall be well with thee.* In this and the following two verses, he recounts the blessings of those that fear God. But we must first examine why in the previous verse he spoke of the blessed in the plural, but now uses the singular: *Thou shalt eat.* It is a usage peculiar to divine Scripture to reduce to the singular something seemingly expressed in the plural. This is doubtless because mother Church, as has often been said, contains numerous blessed persons but rejoices in sacred oneness. Now let us consider why He prefers to speak of *the labours of thy fruits* though undoubtedly labours are not born of fruits, but fruits of labours. But by labours he wished to denote good works carried out in this world to yield a sweet banquet as the reward to come; for eating means being refreshed by some food, and rejoicing in its abundance. So these labours which consist of good works are apprehended at the resurrection when these words are heard: *Come ye, blessed of my Father, possess you the kingdom prepared for you from the foundation of the world.*[9] A blessed banquet this, which is not digested by the stomach, but is maintained in eternity unconsumed. There is another psalm which reveals that souls have their own food when it says: *Take, and see that the Lord is sweet.*[10] To ensure that you did not regard this as food for the flesh, he added: *Blessed art thou,* for no-one is made blessed by bodily feasting; he must be filled with spiritual gifts. Again, he did not wish you to believe that the blessed man got only modest fruits, so he appended: *And it shall be well with thee.* When things are *well,* all blessings merge with each other, and draw us to sweet joy. He is denoting those rewards *which eye has not seen, nor ear heard, neither has it entered the heart of man what things God has prepared for them that love him.*[11]

3. *Thy wife as a fruitful vine on the sides of thy house. Thy sons as olive-plants round about thy table.* We must likewise avoid the literal interpretation here too, for you observe that numerous holy men do not have wives and children, and again that wicked men possess all these things. So how can you associate things often withdrawn from good men and assigned instead to the wicked with this aspect of blessedness which has been described? *Wife* is used in the sense of sister; so we must interpret *wife* here as the wisdom of the blessed man. As Solomon says: *He who has desired to take wisdom as his spouse,*[12] and elsewhere: *Love her, and she will embrace thee.*[13] So she is the wife

of the just who grasps her husband in chaste embrace. The *vine* is the begetter of grapes, pouring forth sweet wine and reviving our hearts; in the same way this wife, which is wisdom, contributes glad fruits and brings joy to us with sweet delight. Our individual reflections are rightly called our *house*, for when we are rooted in them, we linger there as in some dwelling. The walls of this house are the two Testaments, affording the pious mind the strength and solidity of outside walls. Next comes: *Thy sons as olive-plants round about thy table.* Wisdom as wife is rightly said to have sons and not daughters. The male sex usually denotes mental strength; alternatively, when the male sex is specified, it embraces both male and female. When the psalmist says elsewhere: *Blessed is the man that feareth the Lord,*[14] it is not just the man that fears the Lord that is blessed; the woman too who fears the Lord is blessed. So they surround the spiritual table which is the Lord's altar, for they are filled with the bread of heaven. The table is called *thy table* to make clearer the glory of the bishop. We speak of bishops in these terms: "He presides over his church," "Return to your church," expressions which we know are on the lips of all. We must also investigate the fact that he preferred to compare the sons of the blessed to young olive-plants; it is because they are greener, more vigorous, and extremely strong in every way, and they bear fruit more abundantly. This fruit provides stores of food, and kindles light, and relieves tired bodies. Do not imagine that the combination of olive and vine in these comparisons is accidental. We read that the man wounded by robbers in the gospel was healed by the application of wine and oil, for these two provide sacramental protection of our life. Wine contains the severity of justice, oil the gentleness of mercy; the first can match the Old Testament, the second the New. We recognise the figure of *parabole*[15] in the comparison between vine and wife, and olives and sons, for the psalmist has compared things dissimilar in kind.

4. *Behold, thus shall every man be blessed that feareth the Lord.* Next followed the perfect end of the blessed man who fears the Lord. The words: *Thus shall every man be blessed,* as was clearly explained earlier, means "Thus shall every man deserve to be blessed who fears his Maker, who ceases to tremble at empty threats, who is filled with chaste fear of the Lord." Observe the order of words. He begins with:

Behold, thus shall every man be blessed, and so that wanton fools should not appropriate this blessing, he added: *That feareth the Lord.*

5. *May the Lord bless thee out of Sion, and mayst thou see the good things in Jerusalem all the days of thy life.* He passes to the second section, in which with the most holy devotion he asks for a benediction on those fired to every good exertion by fear of the Lord. This is to make us realise how profitable is this fear over which the holy blessing is redoubled. He says: *May the Lord bless thee out of Sion;* he means the Lord Christ who deigned to appear to men on this mountain, which in accordance with the nature of its name is always allotted to Him as the best of shepherds; for Sion, as has often been explained, means "observation." Next follows: *And mayst thou see the good things in Jerusalem.* We must explain these words repeatedly, because the intended meanings clearly depend on them. By Jerusalem is meant "vision of peace," peace here being the invisible quality which will be visible when its Author the Lord Christ is beheld with blessed mind. So he prays that he may see in Jerusalem all the things that are good; for there the Lord Himself is beheld, and He makes those who gaze on Him eternal, revealing Himself in unbroken continuity. So in the spirit of prophecy he prays on the saints' behalf for what he knows can accrue to them. But to ensure that you would not believe that these are temporal blessings, the words: *All the days of thy life*, were appended, so that the climax of eternity was enhanced by a gift beyond telling.

6. *And mayst thou see thy children's children: peace upon Israel.* He superimposed this verse on his blessings, so that the person who fears the Lord in this world may see his children's children in that era of blessedness. Undoubtedly this can befall eunuchs as well. As we have already said, *children* are those begotten from spiritual teaching. But it would have been less joyous to have obtained spiritual sons if those instructed had not begotten in turn other children. *Children's children* denotes grandchildren; they can accrue to blessed individuals accustomed to instruct people by sacred preaching. Observe that he states that this is to be regarded as one of the greatest joys, for it is inevitable that winning over a faithful person brings great joy to the one who wins him, for we know that as a result he will be invested with a great reward. It is to such people that reference is made in the story of the talent which the father of the household found to his joy had been

doubled.[16] There follows the statement which declares the summit and sweetness of that blessedness, that peace, in other words, the Lord Saviour, should rest upon that blessed Jerusalem, and make all things blessed which He embraces with the power of His majesty. This echoes the earlier words: *Mayst thou see the good things in Jerusalem;* for this is the peace which every committed person desires, groans for, sighs for; the peace for which he gladly sheds life itself.

Conclusion Drawn From the Psalm

We identify in this psalm the promises made to those who fear God, the rewards obtained by the person who with pure mind feels awe for the Lord. So let us pray most eagerly that we may deserve to obtain this fear which we seek not as punishment, but for salvation; from it sprout blessings such as never spring from worldly delights. It is right that we seek this highest gift with vehement entreaty. So as we have said, let us continually beg the Lord that by His generosity we may deserve to attain such gifts. He who bids sinners make entreaty in season and out of season has promised that He can hearken even to the undeserving among us.

Commentary on Psalm 128

A canticle of steps. The tenth step now rises to the tenth level, quitting the things of earth and uniting itself with things heavenly in glorious proximity. Let us now listen to him singing more sweetly as he is perched aloft, for the height of the steps grants us an ascent for understanding the psalms. The person who draws near to the vision of the Lord rightly makes his way upwards. But it is humility which ensures all this, for it fittingly exalts God's servants. Let us observe the content of this number, which brings a reward, for it is the denarius[1] which the rich Lord with devoted generosity grants to those who toil in His vineyard. The prophet teaches us to endure the troubles of the world patiently, for he demonstrates that the Church's sufferings are numerous.

Division of the Psalm

The prophet is filled with the holy Spirit, and in the first section he urges Israel to tell of the great struggles and the nature of the guile which they have endured from their enemies, so that none of the faithful may seem to despair because of their afflictions. In the second section he inveighs with the spirit of prophecy against obstinate foes of the Church by means of certain comparisons, calling down on them what he knew would befall them at the future judgment.

Explanation of the Psalm

1. *Often have they fought against me from my youth, let Israel now say.* Israel, in other words, God's Church, is urged to say that she has often been warred on even from her early youth. *Often* denotes the frequency of her sufferings; *from her youth* the first period of her life when from the very beginning at the devil's prompting she endured the most savage opposition. (In the same sense another psalm says: *I have been young and now am old, and I have not seen the just forsaken, nor his seed needing bread.*[2] He attached a masculine here to the neuter gender; clearly this is to be numbered among the idioms of divine Scripture.[3] *Needing bread* means that neither as a boy nor as a young man had he seen this sight which he describes.) So *from my youth* denotes from the time when the just Abel was killed by his wicked brother. Lot too in his time suffered, when that faithful man endured the many evil deeds of the Sodomites. Job bore those most notorious and numerous disasters, when the contrivances of the devil retired, overcome by the endurance of his glorious suffering. Then too God's people bore the bitter tyranny of Pharaoh. Many most holy persons were attacked by afflictions and hazards, endured the most savage contest, and when their hardship was complete won the crown of martyrdom. The Church was warred upon also in the passion of Christ the Lord Himself, when the foolish thought that she had lost the Lord whom she proclaimed as the Begetter of her life; but what the unfaithful considered to be the cause of her fall was in fact the beginning of her growth. The following phrase, *let Israel now say,* is not otiose. It refers to the present age, the time for repentance, and bids

that the rest of the faithful be instructed; whereas after the general resurrection, the Church will continually sing the Lord's praises alone. The phrase, *let Israel now say*, is to be understood throughout the three verses that follow.

2. *Often have they fought against me from my youth, but they could not prevail over me.* There was a similar exordium in the fifth of these psalms of the steps;[4] this figure is called *anaphora*,[5] the recital of the same expression at the start of several verses. We must interpret this period as the Church's old age. As the apostle says: *Little children, it is the last hour;*[6] for whatever occurs at the end of the world is most suitably called her old age. So the Church says that she has been fiercely warred on from her youth, so that you may realise that she is never brought to an end, since she is under constant attack. So she grows under the persecution of the wicked, and expands through her grief. Even though she seems to lose holy ones in this life, she is seen to gain them for the fatherland to come; so she cannot be brought to an end, since she is clearly increased by the losses which she sustains. This is what the following words make clear: *But they could not prevail over me.* She says that those who she earlier states had warred on her could not prevail over her; for the warring which develops into further conflict is not rounded off, and victory must not be pronounced when it is certain that the conflict can be renewed. The next verse explains this sentence.

3. *The wicked have wrought upon my back: they have lengthened their iniquity.* It is the most pernicious habit of evil men, when they cannot force a general imposition on a whole people, to strive secretly to exercise persuasion on individuals and thus to deceive at any rate a few people, since they have not been able to undermine God's Church by any wickedness. He bears witness here that the wicked *have wrought on his back;* they make haste to devise guile from that quarter, for they are visible from the front but cannot be seen at all from behind. The arrival of enemies from that quarter is greatly feared when they strive to confound the rear by a sudden onset. To reveal the strength of his patience, he explains the nature of the struggle, which is sometimes more greatly feared even by the stronger party. So that you would not think that these hidden attacks were momentary, he speaks of extended ambushes which the enemies of the faith continually launched with offensive intent.

4. *The just Lord will cut the necks of sinners.* Since the Lord is patient and great-souled and bears with sinners, he wishes this to be understood of those transgressors who by His mercy long to return to the satisfaction which brings salvation. Scripture attests that *necks* signifies pride with the words: *I see that this people is stiff-necked.*[7] And blessed Stephen at his passion says in condemnation of the Jews: *You stiff-necked and uncircumcised in hearts and ears, you always resist the holy Ghost, as your fathers also did.*[8] So these sinners undergo a contrary experience: their necks which they fatally raised against the Lord are subjected to His sweet yoke with the humility which brings salvation. We recall that this often befell persecutors, so that having earlier maintained their idols by the most sacrilegious compulsion, they became proclaimers of our most holy religion.

5. *Let them all be confounded and fear that hate Sion.* He comes to the second section; in this, up to the end of the psalm, he prophesies by certain comparisons to his stubborn opponents that what can undoubtedly befall them by the Lord's judgment will come to pass. They will be *confounded* when they see their perfidy condemned at that time of truth. They will *fear* the Judge who they thought was to be despised here on earth. Those who with mad hearts spurned the Lord's incarnation are the persons who *hate Sion*, that is, the Church.

6. *Let them be as grass on the tops of buildings, which withers before it is plucked up.* Abandoned buildings often sprout momentarily with grass on their tops. Before it can be gathered it withers and dies because it has insufficient roots to give it strength. Truculent sinners are linked with such grass in a most apt association, for they also often die off here before they are taken from this world's light, for they sprout on the heights of pride where they are not firmly based, whereas if they sprouted in the vale of tears, they would with the Lord's help bring their harvest to fullness.

7. *Wherewith the mower filleth not his hand, nor he that gathereth sheaves his bosom.* He continues with the image of the grass. Just as earlier in another psalm he says of the harvest of the blessed: *Coming, they shall come with joyfulness carrying their sheaves,*[9] so here he proclaims that the reapers, in other words, the angels who will assemble the people for judgment by the Lord, will not bear anything from them in hand or in bosom. In that earlier psalm, the harvesting that bore fruit was spiritual, but here it is the harvest of the flesh which rejoices

in no fertile crop of wheat, so that it fails to fill one hand and does not result in weighing down the bosom. Such is the harvest which is not sown in the Lord's field, but sprouts in the breasts of the proud, as though on tumbling gable-ends. What harvest could it bear when it *withered before it was plucked up?* His reference to *hand* and *bosom* is not idle; the hand signifies action, the bosom inner awareness, and in the activities of wicked persons neither could be found to be of any worth.

8. *And they that passed by have not said: The blessing of the Lord be upon you; we have blessed you in the name of the Lord.* It was a custom among the Jews that if passers-by came upon individuals working at some agricultural task, they bestowed grace and a blessing on them. So we read in the book of Ruth: *And Booz said to the young man that was set over the reapers, The Lord be with you: and they answered him, The Lord bless thee.*[10] Here an implication contrary to this custom is assumed, for no blessing is bestowed on wicked men who work to no effect. *They that passed by* denotes holy persons who spurn the troubled and disturbed problems of this world, and hasten to the peace and tranquillity of the next. They truly are seen to pass by what they despise out of love of the Lord. If you seek to have these passers-by justified by divine authority, listen to Moses: *I shall pass by, and see this sight.*[11] Then too in another, earlier psalm occur the words: *I have seen the wicked highly exalted, and lifted up like the cedars of Libanus. And I passed by, and lo, he was not.*[12] You observe that this word is often attached to holy men. But to ensure that the blessing should not be regarded as within the gift of human powers, there follows: *We have blessed you in the name of the Lord.* That blessing is steady and true which is imparted with mention of the Lord, from whom comes all that is profitable.

Conclusion Drawn From the Psalm

Let us observe that this psalm has mounted the tenth level, borne aloft, so to say, on twin wings; for its right wing is the proclaimed conversion of the proud after their manifold persecution of the Church, and the left is the desired confusion of those who hate Sion. The prophet utters this not because he is eager to curse, but out of feeling for the truth to come; for though we are bidden to pray even for our enemies, he revealed the nature of the truth concerning the obdurate who are doomed to perish. These words were not, however, uttered without fruit as the outcome of his great devotion, for many people save themselves by correction from the punishment which was foretold, once they realise the fate that overhangs the obstinate.

Commentary on Psalm 129

A canticle of steps. Unless we recall with concern the practice of the Church, some uncertainty can arise about why the prophet prostrates himself to offer satisfaction, when he has gained a foothold on the eleventh step. Though he was implanted on that height, and had made his way up towards enduring glory, he could still experience agitation if not destruction. A similar account was given at Psalm 127, when we said that fear of the Lord befits holy persons at every stage in this world. The Church says at Psalm 128: *Often have they fought against me from my youth,* and a little later: *The wicked have wrought upon my back,*[1] and in their ascent this people recounts the many disasters which they were still enduring in this world. So here too the closer the prophet's spirit mounted to the heights, the more he prostrated himself in devoted humility, so that bent low he could still ascend in mind, as long as he did not presume on his own merits. In his awareness of the human condition, though he had long subdued it, he bent low with greater humility, for no-one known to be implanted in our frail body can escape sin; for at what moment do we not sin in thought, or err through excess of words, or slip through thoughtless action? So there is this one safe course for the person living in this world: continually to bend low with devoted prayers, so that despite our inability to be free from guilt, we may deserve to be pardoned through the kind offices of devotion.

Division of the Psalm

The prophet's vision is mental rather than physical. To avoid being overwhelmed by massive billows of faults, in his exordium he cries out to the Lord, asking to be freed from the depth of sins and imploring the kindly deliverance of the goodly Judge from the disasters which he has recounted; for no person can be saved unless he is forgiven by God's clemency. There follows an abridged conclusion, with omission of a narration and the other constituent parts; for if they are aptly added they adorn a speech, but if inserted inappositely they are disfiguring. So our good master sought a useful and pious abridgment. He quickly reached the joys of thanksgiving so that penitents could acknowledge the abundance of grace with which they are accepted when so swift a healing is accorded them.

Explanation of the Psalm

1. *Out of the depths I have cried to thee, O Lord: Lord, hear my prayer.* The word for depth (*profundum*) stands for *porro fundum*,[2] the far bottom, whose lowest levels are wholly submerged. From here the prophet cried to the Lord so that he could be more easily heard. It was from this depth that Peter poured forth his glorious tears, and from here that the tax-collector, who had fallen so deeply into sin that he could not even raise his eyes to heaven, beat his blameworthy breast.[3] Finally from these depths Jonah, who was set in the whale's belly and had entered hell alive, spoke to the Lord with silent vehemence.[4] The whale was a house of prayer for the prophet, a harbour for him when shipwrecked, a home amidst the waves, a happy resource at a desperate time. He was not swallowed for sustenance, but to gain rest; and by a wondrous and novel precedent the beast's belly yielded up its food unharmed, rather than consumed by the normally damaging process of digestion. Jonah bears witness to this in his book when he says: *And the Lord commanded a great fish to swallow Jonas: and Jonas was in the belly of the fish three days and three nights*,[5] and the rest. In that same passage he recounted his prayers as well with prophetic truth. What an outstandingly and wholly glorious repentance, a humility which experiences no fall, grief which rejoices men's hearts, tears which water the soul! Indeed this depth, which conveys us to heaven, has no inkling of hell. So observe the power of holy prayer, believing as it does that it must be heard the more quickly, the deeper the depths from which it cried to the Lord. So finally there follows: *Lord, hear my prayer*, for those who have buried themselves in the bowels of holy

humility are all the closer to the Highest. Thus when he prayed from the depths he quickly gained the gifts of the highest Redeemer.

2. *Let thy ears be directed to the prayer of thy servant.* With this most beautiful entreaty he makes the Judge amenable to him so that a most merciful hearing may be accorded to his requests. It is the function of the eyes to be *directed*, but here the task is allotted to the ears. This is because His power, the unique force of His nature, does not hear with ears, nor walk with feet, nor see with eyes, nor taste with the mouth, nor smell with the nostrils; rather, it performs the works mentioned by a power beyond understanding. God is spirit; we read in Scripture: *God is a spirit.*[6] He is eternal, almighty, penetrating and containing all things which were created by Him, everywhere full and in totality, the Source and Medium of gleaming light. But our habitual practice is to call the power by which He sees His eyes, the power by which He hears His ears, the power by which He performs His hands, and similar expressions applied by allegory to divine activities. The prophet's phrase, *of thy servant*, rouses the mercy of the good Judge; he begs the Lord not to allow the loss of the man who He knows faithfully invokes Him.

3. *If thou, O Lord, wilt mark iniquities, Lord, who shall stand it?* Observe how the depth from which he cried to the Lord is now uncovered. By iniquity he wishes us to understand all the sin which can be committed by any wickedness. The iniquitous is the unjust; who can be exempted from association with it except Him alone who could continually embody justice? Though saintly men are seen to comport themselves in a life of commitment, they cannot wholly avoid acts of blame; idle speech incurs guilt, giving thought for the morrow is a fault, as is the deceit of dreams, preoccupation on the moment with inapposite thoughts, and other things of a like nature. The prophet, then, observed that there is no person who does not transgress with idle thoughts, or sin with empty talk, or busy himself with futile activities, and so in terror he cries to the Lord that the human race cannot attain His justice unless He bestows the aid of His mercy. *Who shall stand it?* implies a boundless burden, an unbearable weight, a devouring flame. He rightly said that the Lord's justice could not be endured, for he feared His judgments as he pondered his own deeds. This figure is called in Greek *diaporesis*, in Latin *dubitatio*,[7] when we are uncertain whether what is sought can be obtained.

4. *For with thee there is merciful forgiveness, and by reason of thy law I have waited for thee, O Lord.* In terror at the Lord's justice, by reason of which no man can morally escape punishment, he had recourse to His protective mercy. We do not merit forgiveness by our own actions, but it lies within His clemency to deign to free the self-confessed sinner. If you examine the word *propitiatio* (merciful forgiveness) with some care, you find it was effected when God lent aid to a dying world through the incarnation of His Son, so that He could release the human race when it was bound by the entanglements of sins. Next follows: *And by reason of thy law I have waited for thee, O Lord.* The law seems to be the antonym of merciful forgiveness, for the law uncovers sin, indicates the guilty, and makes the whole man subject to it. As Paul says: *I do not know sin but by the law. For I had not known concupiscence if the law did not say, Thou shalt not covet.*[8] But here we must interpret *law* as the gospel-command which says: *Bear ye one another's burdens, and so you shall fulfil the law of Christ.*[9] So this is the law which the prophet says he maintains, and by which he rightly believed that he would be saved. The word which he uses, *sustinui* (I have awaited), denotes charity, which awaits all, suffers all, and longingly anticipates its hope. It wholesomely fires the hearts of the faithful, and achieves nothing less than the perfection of Christians.

5. *My soul hath relied on thy word: my soul hath hoped in the Lord.* The repetition explains the earlier sense, enabling you to realise that in the previous verse it was the law of the New Testament which was mentioned, since you clearly recognise that the Word Itself, in other words, God's Son, is set down here. So he relied on the Word, because he believed that the Lord's incarnation would come. Only the person eager to receive a promise relies on it. To prevent your thinking that *word* here denotes some transient expression, he added: *My soul hath hoped in the Lord.* God's Word is the almighty Son of whom it is written: *In the beginning was the Word, and the Word was with God, and the Word was God. The same was in the beginning with God.*[10] This Word, when the final hour came, took flesh of the virgin Mary, and deigned to be born to banish death from the human race.

6. *From the morning watch even until night let Israel hope in the Lord.* 7. *For with the Lord there is mercy, and with him plentiful redemption.* Having now most beautifully unfolded his exordium, he passes most joyfully to the conclusion of the psalm. He is now untroubled as

regards his sins, and proclaims to the people that they must hope in the Lord Christ throughout their lives, for He can transform the most troublesome sufferings of His Church into eternal joys. *The morning watch* refers to that appearance of the Lord Saviour, when before the Jews who guarded the tomb He rose in the true nature of the body which He had resumed. *Night* denotes the close of this world; so the universal Church must continue to hope in the Lord until the world's end. Though this injunction is addressed to Israel in general, each and every person of the greatest fidelity is being advised of his own end. Ponder his words: *From the morning watch*, suggesting that once the Lord's name became more widely manifest at His coming, He is to be obeyed. Next follows: *For with the Lord there is mercy, and with him plentiful redemption.* The wonderful reason is advanced why Israel ought to have hoped in the Lord: it was because mercy lies in His hand, which can transform the wicked into the just, the weak into the immortal, the lover of the flesh into the angelic. He is accustomed to reveal this knowledge which concerns us, because human nature cannot of itself attain it. He appended the phrase: *plentiful redemption*, to indicate that the Lord's precious blood was so very rich in its fecundity that it redeemed the sins of the entire world. Like some wholesome flood it cleansed the earth of its foulness. We have put these two verses together because they are so closely interlinked as to be explained by their interrelationship.

8. *And he himself shall redeem Israel from all its iniquities.* Earlier he had called the Lord merciful and plentiful; here he reveals what He is to achieve. He will redeem Israel, then, with His precious blood, the blood which purifies rather than dyes, cleanses rather than stains. As the apostle John says: *The blood of Jesus Christ cleanses us from all sin.*[11] When he says: *He himself shall redeem*, he reveals that man had no power within him to escape. The *iniquities* are those which earlier he did not wish to have scrutinised,[12] for had they been observed he could certainly not have been redeemed. Alternatively, as some maintain, the redemption of Israel denotes the time when at the end of the world the crowd of Jews will look on Elias, and believe. This is what the prophet Malachy states with the words: *I will send you Elias, before the coming of the great and notable day of the Lord.*[13] But what benefit will accrue to the Jews now, when those others escape? How much more oppressive will be the torture of those found guilty in isolation, whilst

their posterity gains correction! It would be much preferable if those who came first in time also led the way in faith.

Conclusion Drawn From the Psalm

This psalm begins from the depths, but like the advancing sun mounts to a great height, enabling us to realise how beneficial is the repentance which we see residing at such a lofty eminence. So let us ponder how harmful is that pride which is unceasingly confronted by an abundant remedy. We do not apply a single cure to a severe illness, but confront it with manifold treatment. The tree which grows luxuriantly with great freedom through the thin air is the one most often cut down with axes. This evil of pride is struck with the sixth axe of repentance, and the nodding arms which are its branches are agitated; but at the ensuing seventh axe's blow it is cut down and at once dashed to earth and shattered. I come back to the individuals who disdain to repent at the close of their lives. Nowhere in the law is there an embargo against what wicked men are said to hold cheap; on the contrary, we are always warned never to depart from the law through the effects of idleness. So let us regard with loathing the pride which expelled the angel from the grace of celestial sweetness. Let us love the humility which has raised the faithful to heaven. Let us swiftly confess our evil deeds so that we may not meet our deserts.

Commentary on Psalm 130

A canticle of steps. When the diligent farmer has broken up the heavy soil of his rich plains with the curved plough, and has consigned fertile seeds to the cultivated fields, he climbs a treetop with joyful songs of relief, and feeds his oxen with the leaves of branches which he lops off, thus refreshing with abundant food the beasts which he had assigned to the task of continual sowing. In the same way the prophet, now that he has completed the toils of repentance, mounts the spiritual steps, and bestows on us the sweet food of songs. The whole of this psalm is concerned with gentleness and humility, with the result that the sweetness of splendid devotion renews those whom the toil of the previous confession had afflicted. So let us take the food handed to us, and taste such kindly gifts. May we be oxen fit to plough our Lord's land by the furrows prescribed! But remember that the whole of this psalm, as we have said, is aimed at bringing down pride and building up humility in every way. As the Lord says in the gospel: *Everyone that exalts himself will be humbled, and he that humbles himself will be exalted.*[1] This statement embraces the sum of both matters, for it denotes the devil in pride and the Lord Christ in humility. Thus in the compass of a few words it clearly indicates what men ought to long for and what they should fittingly avoid.

Division of the Psalm

In the first section, the prophet by his example teaches humility and gentleness to the Christian people in particular, and lays down for them most stern punishment if they do not receive the Lord's commands with the greatest humility. In the second, he changes direction, and urges Israel continually to hope in the Lord, so that strengthened by such hope they can endure all the opposition of the world.

Explanation of the Psalm

1. *Lord, my heart is not exalted, nor are my eyes lofty. Neither have I walked in great matters, nor in wonderful things above me.* A hypothetical syllogism[2] is produced here on these lines: If my heart is not exalted, and my eyes are not lofty, I become a stranger to pride. But my heart is not exalted and my eyes are not lofty. So I do become a stranger to pride. Now let us analyse the rest. This psalm proclaims humility, teaches temperance, counsels patience. When the prophet rejects what is wicked, he proclaims what is wholly praiseworthy. This figure is called *anastrophe*, when by rejection of the opposite course[3] he wishes us to understand what the divine counsels have laid down. He says that his heart is not exalted, as Pharaoh's was, when relying on the multitude of his nation he cruelly afflicted the most devoted Jews after being so often prevented from doing so by Moses. Next follows: *Nor are my eyes lofty.* The eyes were lofty of the rich

man who as we read in the gospel planned to pull down his small barns and intended to build large ones to contain an abundant harvest.[4] The psalmist added: *Neither have I walked in great matters*, Pilate *walked in great matters* when he said to the Lord Saviour: *Knowest thou not that I have power to release thee and power to crucify thee?*[5] The psalmist added finally as climax: *Nor in wonderful things above me.* Simon Magus walked in wonderful things above him when he believed that the holy Spirit could be purchased from Christ's apostles for money, so that he might obtain by payment what his merits did not possess.[6] By denying that he himself did such things, the psalmist allows us to grasp what he did perform with the Lord's help. The following verse in fact shows that this is how we must interpret it.

2. *If I was not humbly minded, but exalted my soul. As a child that is weaned towards his mother, so thou wilt reward my soul. If I was not humbly minded* is a most apt declaration, for the highest kind of wisdom lies not in arrogant self-persuasion, but in profitable attitudes induced by a devoted spirit. So he informs us that he has pondered the divine Scriptures with a simple and pure heart, unlike Arians, Manicheans, Donatists and the rest who are cut off from the true religion. If they had been willing to be humbly minded, they would not have elected to defend their depraved views. They would have turned to the truest and holiest teachers, and deserved to obtain understanding of the true faith. So the psalmist says that he was humbly minded, in the spirit of Paul's reminder: *Be not high-minded, but fear,*[7] and of a psalm elsewhere: *He that worketh pride shall not dwell in the midst of my house;*[8] and on another occasion he asks for the Lord's help in making his prayer against this vice, in the words: *Let not the foot of pride come to me.*[9] Next comes: *But exalted my soul.* He says here that his soul is not provoking danger by being raised to the height of pride to which it is ruinous to ascend. After all, saintly men exalt their souls when they strive to rouse them to embrace the divine proclamations. How can we understand anything about the holy Trinity, or soundly reflect on the blessed incarnation, if we do not raise our souls with great humility to the Lord? There is the evidence of another psalm that the soul is permitted to mount to the heights, in the words: *To thee have I lifted up my soul.*[10] It is lawful to raise the soul in the things which are the source of life, of vigour, of nourishment by the heavenly bread. But it is not fitting that the soul be exalted in debased investiga-

tions puffed up by unprofitable teaching, for these are the cause of death, of entry into hell, of condemnation to eternal misery.

He added a quite splendid and fine comparison. He says that he has desired the Lord: *As a child that is weaned toward his mother.* When a small child gets older and is prepared for taking other foods, it is usual to refuse him the milk on which he was regularly fed by his devoted mother. This is to enable him to pass to more solid food so that his body does not grow soft through being left in its tender state. But how single-mindedly and with what longing and appeal does he seek his mother! Her heart is stirred by his crying, and she almost grieves at being deprived of him. The prophet compares his feelings with that sense of longing and desire; he shows what great hope, simplicity and yearning we should feel for the Lord. *Weaned* is the expression used of those withdrawn from milk. The comparison is aptly made, for just as children suck at their mothers' breasts, so the infant faithful are nurtured by the simplicity of divine Scripture until they can be prepared for solid food. As Paul says: *I could not speak to you as unto spiritual, but as unto carnal. As unto little ones in Christ, I gave you milk to drink, not meat.*[11] The additional phrase, *toward his mother,* is not otiose, for they are still at the tender stage, and are raised towards their mother's breasts. This custom of withdrawing their sustenance is the more oppressive, for they cannot console themselves with other foods.

He appended: *So thou wilt reward my soul.* These are characteristically human words. When we are reasonably confident about some issue, we propose our own punishment. The words of Psalm 7 exemplify this: *O Lord my God, if I have done this thing, if there be iniquity in my hands, if I have rendered to them that repaid me evils, let me deservedly fall empty before my enemies.*[12] In the present passage we must rearrange the word order so that a prose-version of the verse may appear more self-explanatory: "If I was not humbly minded, as a child that is weaned toward his mother, but exalted my soul"—then follows the balancing condition—"so wilt thou reward my soul." *So* here means "If I have been rash enough to despise You, You would seem to be justified in casting me off." Or alternatively we must perhaps interpret this psalm as a declaration against people who when confronted with hardships and difficulties become impatient, and refuse to accept divine remedies. So this humble and faithful man by contrast says that his heart has certainly not hastened to show contempt merely because he was not immediately heard. He adds that his eyes did not show arrogance, for this is a tendency especially common in the young, who presume to despise their parents with fierce self-will. The comparison can indeed be interpreted in the bad sense, for a child that is weaned exalts his soul over his mother when he dares to tear at her breasts with his hands, and squalls and weeps so that his tantrums can be acknowledged. Then follows the conditional clause containing the punishment, that if he acted as earlier described, he would be renounced by the Lord, just as we know that a weaned child is refused his mother's breasts. Then, so that we may realise that this psalm is promulgated to instil the virtue of patience and humility, as has been said, he added: *Let Israel hope in the Lord, from henceforth, now and for all time.* This is so that it may not rightly appear that what is being compared with weaned children is headlong desperation on our part.

3. *Let Israel hope in the Lord, from henceforth, now and for all time.* After fittingly instructing us to espouse humility and meekness, in the second section like a good teacher he changes tack, and urges each member of the faithful to put his trust always in the Lord, and to continue in that trust for all ages. In this world we can hope, but in the next we can gaze upon the rewards for which we longed. *All time* (*saeculum*) sometimes denotes this world, and sometimes the Lord's kingdom which we believe will come. His words are: *From henceforth, now and for all time,* that is, from the present time to the eternity to come, when there will be a single age, and the changes of the seasons are happily transformed into an abiding unity. In this way the text of the psalm has ended summarily, so that the very brevity of the diction may be appropriate to the psalmist's saintly humility.

Conclusion Drawn From the Psalm

The humility which is commended at this lofty height is exceedingly wonderful. If some eremite at leisure in his cell uttered such sentiments, he would glow with the great glory of his patience, but it was a prince in the purple, one outstanding among prophets, who uttered them, to ensure that he shunned pride as eagerly as he glowed with the distinction of honours. What then is demanded of us, seeing that such were his meditations? Grant us, O Lord, the humility of the king, the patience of the prophet, for these are truly your gifts in whatever person they reside. Such virtue is not assumed at large by human will, but is granted by the generosity of Your mercy. This humility rises to a special rank of honour among outstanding virtues, for Your majesty deigned to embrace it. In short, let us ponder how greatly honoured is the humility opposed to pride, the humility set, as we see, on the twelfth step. Pride plunges people into hell, but humility leads them to heaven.

Commentary on Psalm 131

A canticle of steps. All these canticles of steps have borne the prophet upward to attain a higher hope, but this one exalted him totally, for it describes the mysteries of the Lord's incarnation. It was right that after the twelvefold aggregate of the apostles, the Lord himself should come as thirteenth,[1] since He is the Head of all. I do not think that this position befits the person of the prophet, as the glory of this great psalm can reasonably be attributed to none other than the Lord Christ; for the humble man who had previously cried from the depths could not suddenly have raised himself to such a height of glory as to seem to transcend human limits. So we must understand here the David who is greatly desired and is strong of hand,[2] whom the humility of the flesh which He assumed befits, yet the omnipotence of whose divinity is outstanding.

Division of the Psalm

Though the prophet has frequently spoken in the psalms of the Lord's incarnation, he clearly announces this great mystery above all in this step, so that he was fittingly able to mount to the glory of perfection, since he unceasingly reveals the salvation of the human race. So in the first narration he recounts the Lord Christ's words, in which we observe that He promised the Father to take no rest whatsoever unless He had injected into human breasts a love of true religion.

In the second narration he says that what had been truthfully promised by the Lord Saviour has become known, and he adds his entreaties that He may speedily manifest His saving coming, which was still suspended and delayed to a future time. In the third section he recounts that the promise made to him by the Father must be fulfilled, so that the fruit of the Virgin's womb may sit on the eternal throne of dominion, so that He may bless His Church, feed the poor, give glory to priests, prolong His power, clothe His enemies in confusion, and be overhung with the flowering and the eternal sanctification of justice. So let us listen to this psalm with eager minds, for it is deep in its meanings and abundantly significant in its words.

Explanation of the Psalm

1. *O Lord, remember David, and all his meekness.* It is the prophet's custom often to ask the Lord for help in human terms; He is asked to remember, though He could never forget anything at any time. The Godhead is not being urged to recall anything, for all that is past and future is for Him in the present. *David* means the Lord Christ, who was descended physically from David, whom He created. In a similar way we attach to a person of a later generation the names of his grandfathers and great-grandfathers, to show that he is the descendant of his ancestors. Jeremiah attests that Jesus Christ is called David when he says *And David their king I will raise up for them,* and again: *I will raise David for them as a just branch;*[3] and also Isaiah says: *I will set up one shepherd high over them, and he shall feed them, my servant David; he shall be their shepherd, and I will be their God, and David will be prince in the midst of them.*[4] It is clear that these words do not refer to David son of Jesse, for these prophets are said to have lived long after him, and their prophecy is known to refer to the future. Again, he could have said "Remember me," but to denote some other he said: *O Lord, remember David.* So we must confidently accept the interpretation seen to be approved by these great testimonies. The following words, *and all his meekness,* reveal the strength of His boundless patience. Of Him the same Isaiah says: *He was led as a sheep to the slaughter, and as a lamb before his shearer did not open his mouth.*[5] However, could the prophet have said this of himself when he recalled that he had cruelly

killed Uriah the Hethite, to obtain his wife? So this also stands out as a splendid example of His patience.[6]

2. *As he swore to the Lord, he vowed a vow to the God of Jacob.* He who swore is the Lord Christ; His clear promise is a sign of the future. The etymology of *iuravit* (he swore), as has already been said, denotes *iure oravit* (he pleaded on oath), that is, He truly and firmly promised, namely on the occasion when the Lord said to Peter who showed worldly wisdom: *Put up thy sword in its scabbard. The chalice which my Father hath given me, shall I not drink it?*[7] Again, He said to Peter in another place, so that He should not appear to depart from His purpose: *Get thee behind me, Satan: thou art a scandal unto me.*[8] Then, so that you may not regard His oath as of lesser account, hear what is said of the Father Himself: *The Lord hath sworn, and he will not repent,*[9] and again: *The Lord swore to Abraham.*[10] And later in this psalm the prophet says of the Father: *The Lord hath sworn truth to David.*[11] The phrase here, *he swore to the Lord,* shows that we must interpret *he* not as the prophet but as another; so the vow was the Son's, praying that He might by the advent of His incarnation reconcile to the Father the human race which had become hostile to Him through the effect of sins. But this vow was not made separately from the Father. All that the Father desires the Son and holy Spirit also desire, for they are known to have one nature, one power, one will. The nature of this vow is later expounded.

3. *If I shall enter into the tabernacle of my house, if I shall go up into the bed wherein I lie.* In this and the next two verses, we must interpret the words recorded by the prophet as those of the Lord Christ speaking in His human capacity. He says that He will not enter the tabernacle and mount the bed wherein He lies until He is seen to fulfil the promises which He made to the Father. *The tabernacle,* if I am not mistaken, signifies the heavenly dwelling to which after His resurrection He mounted in the flesh before the eyes of the apostles. He says that He will not enter there before He finds a place for the Lord Father in the hearts of religious persons. This was why he added: *Of my house,* to denote the heavenly dwelling; as He says elsewhere: *Heaven is my throne, and the earth my footstool.*[12] Next comes: *If I shall go up into the bed wherein I lie.* We observe that after His fashion He denotes things heavenly by means of human practices. The bed on which we lie accords us rest and an end to our toils; so His bed,

denoting His rest, must be interpreted as the completion of His most blessed passion. His words, *if I shall go up*, denote His ascension, when He mounted to heaven and took His seat at the right hand of the Father. Then the vows which He swore, which He promised, were fulfilled. As He Himself said at His passion when He had drunk of the vinegar: *It is consummated: and bowing his head, he gave up the ghost.*[13]

4. *If I shall give sleep to my eyes, or slumber to my eyelids, or rest to my temples.* Clearly the previous description cannot apply to the nature of His Godhead; we realise that it is utterly foreign to the power of His divinity that He should appear to have accorded sleep to His eyes or slumber to His eyelids. All these statements we infer reasonably relate to His humanity, for He says: *If I shall give sleep to my eyes . . . .* Sleep here is to be understood as the peace of death, of which another psalm has already stated: *I have slept, and taken my rest, and I have risen up, since the Lord hath protected me,*[14] and the rest. Next comes: *Or slumber to my eyelids.* There is a forceful explanation here of the tendency of sleep. *Palpebrae* (eyelids) get their name from *palpitare*, to flutter;[15] sleep cannot enter our eyes unless the eyelids find rest in what we may call trembling relaxation. There follows in turn: *Or rest to my temples,* for the temples of our heads certainly cannot obtain rest when our eyes are found to be wakeful and dart about with frequent movement. He first made mention of sleep, and then explained how it is attained. This was truly sleep, since it was entertained only for a period of three days, and did not impose corruption on His body, but merely rest.

5. *Until I find out a place for the Lord, a tabernacle for the God of Jacob.* We have reached the promise which was sought in the previous words but remained unspoken. He says that His vow was always concentrated on the time of the firm foundation of the Church on the disposition of His holy preaching. The Lord's place is the tabernacle of the Christian's heart, and the basilicas of the Catholic Church, in which He ever dwells as if in heaven. These were found when they were strongly built at the Lord's coming; they were surely found when He sought and found us and built us up by His devotion; and He made a tabernacle for Himself from us and in us, when He restored us to eternal life through His pity. Remember too that just as earlier the psalmist said that Christ made a promise to the God of Jacob, so here too he asserts that He solemnly vowed that the truth of His oath would be clearly fulfilled. But so that the faithless Jews may not rant that this

verse is a mere addition and not an explanation—for they have the effrontery to divert for their own destruction the divine Scriptures from the path of truth by means of certain falsehoods—they must listen to what follows, and in their confusion must now at last come to their senses.

6. *Behold, we have heard of it in Ephrata, we have found it in the fields of the wood.* After recounting the Lord's oath and His desire which He fulfilled with utter truth, the prophet passes to the second narration, in which in his own person he maintains that he has found the Lord's promise, which he had heard *in Ephrata, in the fields of the wood.* It is said that Ephrata means in Latin *speculum*, a mirror.[16] *The fields of the wood* denotes the hearts of Gentiles, which the Lord has cleansed of the thickets and entangling bushes of sins, and which lie exposed in the purity of the fields, for *campi* (fields) get their name from their extent (*capacitas*)[17] and open space; they become spruce from being bushy, cultivated from being wild, fruitful from being barren, and the temples of the Lord from being the bed-chambers of demons. So he states that what had been promised to the Jews in the image of prophecy was found in the fields of the wood, that is, among the Gentiles; for the Bethlehem where the Lord was born was also called Ephrata. In the prophet Amos's words: *And thou Bethlehem, the house of Ephrata, art surely the smallest of the tribes of Juda: for out of thee shall come forth the prince that is to rule my people Israel.*[18] And in Genesis it is written: *Rachel was buried close to Ephrata, which is Bethlehem.*[19] So clearly it was heard that the Lord would be born in Bethlehem, but that because of the faith of the Gentiles He was found *in the fields of the wood.*

7. *We have gone into his tabernacles, we have adored in the place where his feet stood.* Whereas he earlier said that he had heard in Ephrata of what he had found in the fields of the wood, he now seeks to strengthen the impact of his wholehearted devotion, and says that he has gone into the Lord's tabernacles; this was to proclaim by all the means in his power that he had entered what he entertained with the firmest hope. We must clearly investigate the fact that earlier he says that the Lord promised a single tabernacle, whereas here the prophet maintains that he enters tabernacles in the plural, in the company of faithful Christians. The prophet spoke in the plural of the Catholic Church promised by the Lord Christ, because he attached himself in

faith to the Christian people at a time when countless Churches were promised throughout the whole world. But it was not enough for him to have claimed merely to enter the Churches; he wished also to say that he had adored in the place where the most holy feet of the Lord Christ stood. *Feet* denotes the gospel-commands; as Scripture has it: *How beautiful are the feet of them that proclaim the gospel-message of peace.*[20] His feet in fact stood where the truth of faith is known to have been established; we must stand for ever where the Lord Christ, the fullness of the law and the prophets, treads. The verb stand regularly denotes constancy; as Scripture says: *He that hath the bride is the bridegroom: but the friend of the bridegroom stands and hears him.*[21] The verb stand denoted the most unshifting mind; and so we read in Scripture: *He who perseveres to the end will be saved.*[22] There is another psalm, the words of which show that sinners cannot abide in the faith: *There the workers of iniquity are fallen: they are cast out, and could not stand.*[23] Should you wish, however, devotedly to connect this verse also to historical events, it perhaps denotes the holy cross where He stood in the flesh when He was visibly nailed to it. He is rightly said to have stood where His body is shown to have been implanted. So the prophet rightly says that this place is to be adored, for it afforded us both a sign of faith and salvation.

8. *Arise, O Lord, into thy resting-place: thou and the ark which thou hast sanctified.* Once the prophet realised that the Lord Christ's promises previously mentioned had been fulfilled, he cried out to the Lord: *Arise into thy resting-place*, for he did not wish any debt to remain unpaid. He sought to make clear the outcome of events in the dispensation of the attained truth: in other words, that Christ should rise again from the world below into the enduring blessedness of His divinity. Observe that he added *thy* resting-place; for Your own majesty bestowed it on You, since You reign with the Father in equal power and everlasting glory. He did not wish you to think that the Head could abandon the members, so he added: *Thou and the ark which thou hast sanctified*, in other words, "the Church which You have deigned to sanctify by making it Your members." He did not specify the ark of Noah, or the ark of the covenant, though both of these appeared to represent a type of the Church; instead he designated her in a special way when he added: *Which thou hast sanctified.* Now observe what follows.

9. *Let thy priests be clothed with justice, and let thy saints rejoice.* He is still speaking of the members, who he prays may be taken into eternal rest by the Lord. But let us examine the meaning of: *Let thy priests be clothed with justice*, that is, arrayed in heavenly arms. As Paul says: *Having on the breastplate of justice and charity, that you may be able to extinguish the fiery darts of the enemy,*[24] in other words, be able to confront fearlessly the darts of heretics. Alternatively, *justice* denotes the Lord Christ Himself; in Paul's words: *As many of you as have been baptised in Christ have put on Christ.*[25] Next comes: *And let thy saints rejoice.* Since the saints had clothed themselves with the Lord Christ, the outcome was that they should rejoice. If putting on costly garments is a worldly pleasure, what measure of rejoicing can spring from the Majesty which makes one honoured, and clothes us in every way for salvation?

10. *For thy servant David's sake, turn not away the face of thy anointed.* The prophet recalls the evils committed by the Jewish people in the desert, or the wickedness with which they subsequently sinned before the Lord; he also foresees the suffering which they were to inflict which would bring salvation to the world but grief on themselves. So he prostrates himself in entreaty to God the Father, begging Him not to turn away from the Jewish race the face, that is, the presence, of His Anointed, which He had formerly promised through the prophets; so that He who was to reconcile the world might also efface the displeasure incurred by the Jews.

11. *The Lord hath sworn truth to David, and he will not frustrate him: of the fruit of thy womb I will set upon thy throne.* After the entreaty which succinctly but with great longing begged for the Lord's coming, the prophet's words embark upon the third narration, in which he joyfully recounts the promises of the Father to the Son. What firmer or more steadfast declaration can there be, when He by whom men swear himself swears, when He who cannot be deceived makes a promise? *David* here is not the son of Jesse, for he could have said here: "The Lord has sworn to me"; the same is true of his words at the beginning of the psalm.[26] His words: *The Lord hath sworn to David,* denote that other, the One of whom another psalm has already remarked: *I have laid help upon one who is mighty, and have exalted one chosen from my people. I have found David my servant: with my holy oil I have anointed him.*[27] And a little later: *He shall cry out to me, Thou art*

my father, my God, and the support of my salvation. And I will make him my firstborn, high above the kings of the earth.[28] This is the meaning expressed in: *He will not frustrate him.* To frustrate means to negate promises; here the psalmist says that this cannot be the outcome, because there could be no place for deception in the declaration of a promise by the most truthful Creator. Next comes: *Of the fruit of thy womb I will set him upon thy throne.* The fruit of the womb is the heavenly teaching of the Lord Saviour, from which we know that the Christian people was sprung. We have often stated that believers can be born of faithful instruction, which is a kind of womb. So the Father promises that this people is to be set on the throne of the Lord Christ, for they have been converted, and are known to utter teaching in harmony with the instructions of their Maker. When a person clearly imparts a teacher's message, he is rightly said to sit on his throne.

12. *If thy children will keep my covenant, and these my testimonies which I shall teach them: their children also for ever more shall sit upon thy throne.* He has explained his earlier words, for here too he is speaking of the apostles and of the rest of the faithful who have deserved the title of Christ's sons through purity of faith. They will be told: *You shall sit on twelve seats, judging the twelve tribes of Israel.*[29] So the Lord's throne will be accorded to them that have deserved to share his kingdom. As Christ Himself says in the gospel: *Father, I will that where I am, they also may be with me.*[30] So that you would be left in no doubt of the identity of the recipients, he expressly mentions those who with unsullied devotion keep the Lord's covenant, His testimonies, and all His teaching. He does not wish you to regard this reward as possibly transient, so he says: *For ever more they shall sit upon thy throne.* There will be no end to that age, for every reward abides there in eternity unchangeable.

13. *For the Lord hath chosen Sion: he hath preferred it for his dwelling.*
14. *This is my rest for ever and ever: here will I dwell, for I have preferred it.* The literal sense cannot be claimed for this, for we know that the Jerusalem of old endured most frequently repeated destruction and desolation; as Scripture says of it: *Sion shall be ploughed like a field.*[31] It is the heavenly Jerusalem that the name Sion connotes, harmonious in its people, united by the virtue of charity, purified by the grace of absolution; it takes joy in the perennial sight of the Lord's divinity and power. That Majesty, which is good and blessed and powerful to the

highest degree, is wholly present everywhere, but takes possession of the hearts of the blessed, and makes for Himself the dwellings which He has chosen beforehand by virtue of His mercy. The Lord's *rest* and special tabernacle is His lodging in the most devoted hearts of men. True, He is present everywhere, but we are to say that He dwells in them to a degree beyond measure and beyond understanding.

15. *Blessing, I will bless his widow: I will satisfy his poor with bread.* The Church is called Christ's widow, because she is stripped of all worldly help, and places her hope solely in the Lord. Like a widow, she suffers the shameful actions of evil men, the most cruel plunderings of the wicked. Like a woman deprived of a husband's aid, she always grieves and is always worn out, yet she enjoys the unchanging steadfastness of a most chaste mind. Paul draws this comparison when he praises the widow with the words: *But she that is a widow and desolate will hope in the Lord.*[32] Though the Church is seen to embrace both married women and virgins, she is called a widow because she is bereft of worldly protection, and has placed her hope in her heavenly Bridegroom, who has transformed her swarthiness into beauty, her error into uprightness, her cruelty into devotion, and her frailty into total constancy. An alternative view which some prefer is that *widow* denotes the synagogue which is now the Church; for the law under which she was kept subject as under a husband is now at an end, and with the accession of grace she is undoubtedly joined to Christ. She has been freed, one might say, from her former state, and has merited a heavenly marriage without loss of virginity. Paul makes this comparison as well when he says: *Know you not, brethren (for I speak to them that know the law), that the law hath dominion over man as long as it liveth? For the woman subject to a husband, while her husband liveth is bound by the law of her husband. But if her husband be dead, she is loosed from the law of her husband. Therefore, while her husband liveth, she shall be called an adulteress if she be joined with another man,*[33] and the rest. Let us also examine the expression: *Blessing I will bless.* The person who blesses once attests that he ceases to bless with that benediction; but the person who blessing, blesses, sanctifies with continual benediction, bestowing the grace of his blessing now on this side and now on that. This type of statement is called word-relation,[34] for we note that there is a close connection between the words; the same thing is seen to occur also in the next verse. Next comes: *I will satisfy his poor*

with bread. Christ's poor are truly satisfied with heavenly bread, since they are always hungry in worldly supplies. As a previous psalm had it: *The rich have wanted, and have suffered hunger; but they that seek the Lord shall not be deprived of any good.*[35] So Christ's poor are they who are short of worldly goods, but enjoy heavenly abundance.

16. *I will clothe her priests with salvation, and her saints shall rejoice with exceeding great joy.* Priests are clothed with salvation when they accept the Lord Saviour with the utmost purity of faith, and clothe themselves with His laudable mercy. As Paul says of the baptized: *As many of you as have been baptized in Christ have put on Christ.*[36] So though we have just said this, it is no shame to repeat what can reveal to us the divine mysteries: the character of teachers should be such that first they are beyond reproach themselves, and second that they instruct the hearts of the rest of the faithful. As the Lord says in the gospel: *He that shall teach and act thus, shall be called great in the kingdom of heaven.*[37] His words: *They shall rejoice with exceeding great joy,* seek to describe the enduring happiness of the saints, for he says that they not only rejoice but do so with perennial joy. Any individual can experience great mental elation and eventually subside again, but those who are never dislodged from the rewards bestowed *rejoice with joy.*

17. *There will I bring forth the horn of David: I have prepared a lamp for my anointed.* The word *there* denotes the blessed rest of which the Father earlier said: *This is my rest for ever and ever.*[38] The rest of the Father is that of the Son, and the rest of the Son is that of the holy Spirit, for the holy Trinity, one God, is not divided in blessedness or separate in power and nature. Next comes: *There will I bring forth the horn of David.* As we said earlier, here *David* is to be taken as the Lord Saviour, whose *horn,* that is, might of power, is to be demonstrated at the judgment, when eternal rewards are granted by Him to the saints. David could not have said this of himself; he was not to bestow a gift among the rest of the blessed, but was to receive his reward from the Lord. So that you would interpret *David* here as the Lord Christ, there follows: *I have prepared a lamp for my anointed,* in other words, the light of the proclamation of John the Baptist, who was truly the lamp of Christ, manifesting heavenly light in the darkness of the

world. The Lord Himself says of him: *He was a burning and shining lamp.*[39] Yes, truly a shining lamp, visible to the eyes of the spirit rather than to those of the body, and which was to direct through the whole world most abundant brightness, for it was nourished by the oil of the Lord.

18. *His enemies I will clothe with confusion, but upon him shall my sanctification flourish.* By *his enemies* are denoted heretics and pagans, or those whose lives are spent in hostility to His ordinances; the accompanying *his* signifies those of the Lord Christ. Just as the Lord's priests were vested with wholesome glory, so His enemies are clothed in the veil of confusion, for they will hear the words: *Come, blessed of my Father,*[40] but they will be told: *Go into eternal fire.*[41] So that you could recognise that the Father also does what the Son performs, here the psalmist says that the Father confounds His enemies, whereas we know that the Son will do this, for Christ Himself says in the gospel: *The Father does not judge any man, but has given all judgment to the Son.*[42] But the Son's glory is fittingly expounded by the Lord's testimony; elsewhere too the unity of their cooperation is cited in: *My Father works until now, and I work.*[43] Undoubtedly we are to understand this of the holy Spirit as well, for a statement is often made of one Person which we are to understand of the power of the whole Trinity. Next follows: *But upon him shall my sanctification flourish. Shall flourish* is cited to express the sanctity of the holy incarnation; as Paul says, it has flourished in such a way that: *Every knee should bow to him of those that are in heaven, on earth, and under the earth; and every tongue should confess that the Lord Jesus Christ is in the glory of God the Father.*[44] Clearly the phrase is an image of the countryside, for great beauty is unfolded before the eyes of the beholder when the picturesque countryside is clad in blooming colours. But how can such great praise of perennial blossoming be appropriate to the prophet David, when we read that he was made to flee the kingdom by his son, and that he is known to have committed as men do the most serious crimes against certain individuals? Whereas in all that the Lord Christ did and endured, the Father's sanctification always flourished in Him; so the present psalm is rightly applied to Him, for He is known to have been without sin.

Conclusion Drawn From the Psalm

You have heard of the prophet's progress in his ascent, and the joy with which he has filled us. Though the canticles of the steps as a whole grow in significance, we can say that these which shine forth with the brightest light in the Lord's coming are still loftier. Since the prophecy concerned the Creator, it was inevitable that this step by which all things gain increase should rise higher. In the remaining psalms of the steps there is left regard for our neighbour and love of God. If we mount these steps with pure minds, we shall attain the most glorious vision of Him.

Commentary on Psalm 132

A canticle of steps. After the most holy preaching of the previous psalm, the prophet is now perched on the fourteenth step, and proclaims to the people blessed unity, urging those who bind themselves to the Christian religion to persevere in the one accord of charity. Though some have opined that this message is to be addressed to monks, my view is that it is relevant to the harmony of Christians at large, for it is proclaimed not only to monasteries but to the whole Church, gathering into unity by a spiritual trumpet-blast all Christ's soldiers throughout the world. I do not dispute that it is addressed to saintly monasteries, but I believe that it should not be withdrawn from the general body. So the place which embraced the gathering of the faithful people was worthy of honour; clearly that assembly was established before the Lord's incarnation gained it from the Gentiles by His precious blood. That incarnation is rightly mentioned following the assembly, by means of which it is known to have been bestowed upon the world.

The Content of the Psalm

Observe that this is a second psalm without a division,[1] for it was appropriate that since it discusses unity it should contain no separation, but should remain unbroken without any difference of themes. Such indivisible units we call atoms. It has no change of spokesman, nor does it alter its theme or presentation; these are the three elements seen to engender division in psalms. These unbroken psalms perhaps correspond with the two mites which the woman dropped into the treasure-chest,[2] as a result of which we know that she obtained gifts of mercy to the full. In the same way, if we drink in the power of these psalms with devoted minds, we too will obtain remission of all our sins, for the first of them invites us to praise the Lord, and the second encourages us to love of our neighbour.

Explanation of the Psalm

1. *Behold, how good and how pleasant it is for brethren to dwell together in unity! Behold* is the utterance of a demonstrator rather than a speaker; it usually accompanies keen mental concentration and the extended finger, rather than continuous speech. *Good* is an epithet related to affection, for individuals when perfected encourage each other with shared example, and by imitating each other's virtues they ignite each other with the fire of mutual love, for doing good often lies in distancing ourselves from hostility of mind. Perfect virtue resides in satisfaction with the good which you perform. *To dwell* means continuing in the good which you purpose. This is the dwelling which the Lord seeks, not that of an enclosing wall uniting our bodies, but that which joins together our souls in an alliance of piety. (With words like this the psalmist rejects the Circumcellions,[3] who wander around different monasteries with vacillating purposes. His expression, *brethren in unity*, denotes those established under the one Father in the comradeship of faith, possessing as the Acts of the Apostles has it: *One heart and one soul.*[4] Yet those too who wander through desert wastes dwell in unity, for though they seem to be separated physically, they are known to be undivided in the harmony of faith.)[5] If you interpret the verse literally, the companionship which assembles in gatherings of brothers is also good.[6] As we read in the Acts of the Apostles: *And distribution was made to everyone according as he had need; neither did anyone say that aught of the things which he possessed was his own, but all things were common unto them.*[7] This section of

Christians will gain its praise if the harmony of spirit which we mentioned earlier is not withheld. To help you realise that this unity is no slight good, but a wonderful thing, appropriate praise attends it to the end of the psalm in mystical comparisons, so that this most precious commodity could be united with the charm of its proclamation.

2. *Like the precious ointment on the head that ran down upon the beard, the beard of Aaron, which ran down to the edge of his garment.* Clarification of the previous verse now begins, and is established by most clever comparisons. In early times some were anointed kings, others prophets, others in the highly venerated office of the pontiff; they were proclaiming by this their likeness to the Lord Christ, as in many other symbolic rituals conducted at that time; but when the Lord Christ came, He was anointed invisibly and spiritually, for we do not read that He was anointed physically as almighty King, wonderful Prophet, eternal Pontiff, when He offered Himself as a spotless Victim for sacrifice on behalf of sinners. Psalm 44 says of this ointment: *Therefore God, thy God, hath anointed thee with the oil of gladness above thy fellows.*[8] If you ask for still clearer evidence of the nature of this oil of gladness, or spiritual ointment, it is relevant to point to the time when the holy Spirit, as the gospel-reading attests, came down in the form of a dove, and hovered over the Lord Christ, the Head of the body of the Church, who was crucified, raised up on the third day, ascended to heaven, and sits at the right hand of the Father. Next comes: *That ran down upon the beard;* this refers to the holy Spirit who came down on the apostles with the strength of His power beyond reckoning, when they spoke in the various tongues of different nations. We do well to interpret *beard* as the apostles, for a beard is the mark of the most forceful manliness, remaining immovable below its head. In overcoming many sufferings by divine kindness, the apostles proved themselves to be most steadfast men through God's grace; moreover, by preserving the rules which they received from the Lord, they showed that they had remained subject to their Head. To ensure that you should not perhaps interpret *beard* as that of any man whatsoever, he added: *Of Aaron.* Aaron foreshadowed Christ's appearance, and by his priesthood already symbolically played Christ's role; we often speak of names employed symbolically for Christ, such as Solo-

mon, David, and Samson, and Aaron is likewise used here. He added: *Which ran down to the edge of his garment.* By the edge of the Lord Saviour's garment is signified the Church, for the holy Spirit descends as far as its most distant regions when sanctifying the baptised with the glory of His mercy until the world's end. The Church is likewise denoted by the tunic which could not be split during the passion. Our fathers have accordingly spoken at length in the spiritual sense about this garment. (Josephus, in the third book of his *Antiquities*, has revealed under the eighth heading the mysteries of mighty matters emanating from this passage, showing that the four colours of such garments, flaxen, purple, hyacinth and crimson, have logically denoted the world's elements. Jerome too in writing to Fabiola continues to be serviceable in this matter as well.)[9]

3. *As the dew of Hermon, which descendeth upon mount Sion.* He passes in praise to another comparison, which once again in the usual fashion reveals great secrets to us by the meaning of the names. *Dew* is thin and light rain which does not fall as drops, but soaks the hard, dry earth with the tiniest particles. It is the means by which all seeds strike root, and thanks to the temperature grow into various plants. *Hermon* is the Hebrew name for the mountain which lies beyond the river Jordan; the meaning of the name, as the Fathers recount it, is anathema.[10] So the dew of this mountain, which nurtures the sinners who lay under a solemn curse, descended on mount Sion when those sinners through the Lord's generosity attained the remedy of conversion; for *Sion* denotes the Catholic Church, which welcomes the Gentiles exposed to the danger of anathema. Perhaps you are asking why he said *which descended,* when he might better have said "ascended," since it was translated to better things. But it is common usage to say of those who attain some awareness late, "They are descending to the truth, they are descending to justice," just as if they are attaining the bright and level ground after standing on the peak of pride. This is the meaning of the dew descending from Hermon to mount Sion, that the Gentiles pass from the abode of wickedness to the pleasure of blessedness. This is what the first verse likewise proclaimed: *Behold, how good and how pleasant it is for brethren to dwell together in unity!*

For there the Lord hath commanded blessing, and life for evermore.

There (that is, on mount Sion, which is the Church and which comprises the unity of the brethren) *he hath commanded blessing,* in other words, has sent the Lord Saviour, who is the life and enduring blessedness of all believers. We have repeatedly said that the name Sion denotes the heavenly Jerusalem, the image of which is embodied in the Jerusalem on earth. The heavenly Jerusalem contains life without end, joy without interruption; it is governed and possessed by its beneficent Creator, a fact transcending every species of happiness. The use of the word *there* to denote the abode of harmony shows that no blessing is bestowed on those at variance. You observe the comparisons and the degree of admiration with which that gathering is praised, so that no-one doubts that the gift is a great one, since it is praised by Him who is to impart the reward. We must also ponder how this psalm has proceeded with a single and homogeneous thought. This figure is called *hyrmos,*[11] when the chain of an utterance preserves its tenor to the end, with spokesman and theme remaining unchanged. Already at Psalm 116 we were seen to state this, because the text cannot be divided into sections.

Conclusion Drawn From the Psalm

The benefit of unity has been demonstrated to us. It has been made clear what brotherly affection can afford us. Let us have affection for our brother as for ourselves, and let us love the Lord more than ourselves, so that this regard for our neighbours leads us to the most perfect love of the Lord. What can be more pleasant than to imitate in this life what we know is granted us as the highest gift in the blessed land to come? Let us bear here with those whom we are to love exceedingly there. This has been proclaimed to monasteries, churches, city and village communities, and hermits. No person known to possess the love of our holy religion is excluded from this brotherhood. We must not, however, leave without discussion the fact that love for brothers is here set before love of God, whereas in the commandment, *Thou shalt love the Lord thy God with thy whole heart and thy whole soul,* holds first place, *and thy neighbour as thyself*[12] comes second. It is the habit of teachers to change the order of statements to explain most aptly the usefulness of the themes. Since there is continual ascent in these psalms, it was fitting that what is said to be more outstanding than all else should be set down as the climax after everything else.

Commentary on Psalm 133

A canticle of steps. Let us observe closely with the heart's eye how the prophet has topped the steps, and mounted to the highest traces of the virtues; for he addresses the rest of his wholesome persuasion to the blessed brotherhood which he had bidden to gather in unity, urging that their blessed harmony be roused to praises of the Lord with the most burning eagerness of love, so that they may attain the crown of their activity, and may in this life imitate the sweetness which we believe will abide in holy minds in that native land of the future. It is right that a blessing be bestowed on Him to whom they have undoubtedly ascended with the greatest zeal. Now we must discuss the power of His commandment, so that its message when understood and analysed can reveal its usefulness to us. The command is: *Thou shalt love the Lord thy God with thy whole heart, and with thy whole soul, and with thy whole strength, and thy neighbour as thyself. For on these two commandments dependeth the whole law and the prophets.*[1] What a marvellous text, expressing under one head all that you can find in the holy Scriptures! For the person who loves God with his whole heart, his whole soul, his whole strength, leaves no place for vices. Where is sin to enter, when one's whole spirit is taken up with God? The devil longs for empty spaces, seeks out unoccupied areas, but when he finds God's presence he retires in great confusion. So if we love God with our whole heart, and entrust ourselves to His power with passionate devotion, we cannot leave room for faults, and we perpetually walk on the most upright ways. When vessels are brimming with some liquid, they cannot take in additional increase; in the same way, if divine love fills us totally, there will be no place of entry for sin. Next comes: *And thy neighbour as thyself.* We love our neighbour as ourselves when we do harm to no-one, but treat all with the same indulgence as we do ourselves. No person mentally agrees willingly to incur disastrous dangers, or to be hemmed in by guileful traps; all seek for themselves the foresight to avoid attack by any opposition. If we maintain with equal resolve this same attitude towards others, if we bestow on our brothers what we wish to have imposed on ourselves, undoubtedly every fault and wickedness and sin give place. This rule makes us what our heavenly Master commanded us to be. The command perhaps involves also the good angels, for since they desire that we obtain a lot commensurate with their own, they accept us as participants with them in the alliance that lasts for ever. Remember too that this is the third psalm expressive of love of the Lord, so that from this number the power of the holy Trinity can be acknowledged.

Division of the Psalm

In the first section, the prophet issues an invitation to bless the Lord; here we observe that his advice is addressed in the plural to the folk whom we mentioned earlier. Then he changes number, and blesses the people in the singular, for sacred unity is the glory and power of the Church.

Explanation of the Psalm

1. *Behold, now bless ye the Lord, all ye servants of the Lord, who stand in the house of the Lord, in the courts of the house of our God.* 2. *In the nights lift up your hands in the holy house, and bless ye the Lord.* We have set the two verses together because they are interconnected, to allow the full sense to become clearer to us. Let us first investigate why the psalmist wrote *behold* both here and in the previous psalm; the purpose is that not only the language, but also the connecting particles might demonstrate the certainty and the perfection of the content. *Now* is added because after the ascent of all these steps, only He who permitted such great progress deserved to be praised. There was first the fact that he had successfully made the ascent, and secondly that after this upward step he had no other to mount; the Lord is to be proclaimed with greater zeal when by His generosity He makes us untroubled. Alternatively there is the view of others that *now* describes time in this world, when we must exercise our spirit so that it may occupy itself in the next with eternal and undying praises. *Bless ye the Lord* means

praise, for we praise Him by blessing Him, whereas He sanctifies us by blessing us. You heard the word *servant*, and to prevent your picturing some abject creature, he added: *Of the Lord*, with the intention that the distinction of the servant should gain increase from the power of the highest Prince. Paul made himself honoured among the Gentiles by this title, for his letter is prefaced: *Paul, servant of Christ;*[2] and again he writes: *If I sought to please men, I should not be the servant of Christ.*[3] Moses is referred to in another psalm with the words: *He sent Moses his servant.*[4] So the term is already properly used of those who have attained perfection, who undoubtedly have also the title of friends. Next comes: *Who stand in the house of the Lord, in the courts of the house of our God.* He had earlier used the title *servant* as a distinction, but so that the vacillating hearts of men would not apply it to others known to be impious (though all creatures by their status are subject to the Lord), he added: *Who stand in the house of the Lord*, in other words, those whose spirit continues to dwell in the Lord by following the firm path of religion. Standing is used of those persons who do not slip from their goodly purpose through ready sinning, as for example the devil did, for he was an archangel, yet he *did not stand in the truth.*[5] The house which has been mentioned encloses the courts, for a court is the entrance-hall to a house. The courts denote either those already in the inner chambers of the Church, or those who have deserved to stand at its entrance; for undoubtedly the Church contains different areas within the grace of unity. After these words he added further evidence of firm fidelity with the words: *Our God*, meaning not any god worshipped by the Gentiles, but the God whom the true Catholic religion confesses. He added: *In the nights lift up your hands in the holy house, and bless ye the Lord. In the nights* denotes the most grisly era of this world, which is always darkened with the most crowded afflictions. So in this world we must lift up our hands when our good deeds deserve the aid of the Lord. So whenever Moses stretched forth his hands (thus presaging the cross of the most blessed passion), the arrogant boldness of Amalek was repressed;[6] and the spreading of his fingers perhaps denoted the ten commandments. Whenever he dropped his arms, the arrogance of the enemy who had lost heart revived. So our hands are to be lifted up to the Lord by means of good works, so that the devil our foe may be overcome by the majesty of heaven. Notice the significance of *Lift up;* it means "give alms more abundantly," for the Lord demands of us not only words of devotion but also deeds. He added: *In the holy house*, so that the hand which plants the alms should belong to the Christian. If heretics or pagans do this, their hands are not lifted up in the holy house; Christ accepts only the alms which the faithful Christian offers to His name. But he says that in performing this action the Lord must be blessed, so that no-one may claim any credit for himself, since it is the Lord who bestows both a merciful spirit and more generous wealth. In this way he teaches that love of the Lord is to be fulfilled both by sacred praises and by devoted works. When these have been performed, observe how worthy a recompense follows.

3. *May the Lord out of Sion bless thee, he that made heaven and earth.* Now that he has unfolded this advice in which he said that we must continue with the zeal of affection in the Lord's praises and in good works, he passes to the second section, in which in a single verse he blesses the people who persevere in steadfast unity and love of the Lord. Earlier he used the plural throughout, but he now ended the psalm in the singular, so that once he had gathered his faithful brethren in unity, the gifts of blessing could be bestowed on the people who now loved the Lord. So if we wish to be blessed, the love of the holy Trinity and the unity of the blessed Church must enfold us. Observe too how aptly a perfect conclusion has enclosed this psalm; the person who has mounted up to the heavenly Jerusalem has received as reward a heavenly blessing.

Conclusion Drawn From the Psalm

It is pleasant to recount how these steps have led all the way to the heavenly Jerusalem. On the first step he denotes loathing of the world, after which there is haste to attain zeal for all the virtues. Secondly, the strength of divine protection is explained, and it is demonstrated that nothing can withstand it. Thirdly, the great joy of dwelling with pure mind in the Lord's Church is stated. Fourth, he teaches us that we must continually presume on the Lord's help whatever the constraints surrounding us, until He takes pity and hears us. Fifth, he warns us that when we are freed from dangers, we must not attach any credit to ourselves, but attribute it all to the power of the Lord. In the sixth, the trust of the most faithful Christian is compared to immovable mountains. In the seventh, we are told how abundant is the harvest reaped by those who sow in tears. In the eighth, it is said that nothing remains of what any individual has performed by his own will; only the things built by the sponsorship of the Lord are most firmly established. In the ninth, it is proclaimed that we become blessed through fear of the Lord, and that all profitable things are granted us. In the tenth, he inculcates in committed persons the patience which he commands through the words of the Church. In the eleventh, as penitent he cries from the depths to the Lord, asking that the great power of the Godhead be experienced by the deliverance of mankind. In the twelfth, the strength of meekness and humility is revealed; in the thirteenth, the promise of the holy incarnation and the truth of the words spoken are demonstrated. In the fourteenth, spiritual unity is proclaimed to the brethren, and to them the Lord's benediction and eternal life are shown to accrue. In the fifteenth, there is awakened in the course of the Lord's praises that perfect charity than which nothing greater can be expressed, and nothing more splendid discovered. As the apostle attests: *God is love.*[7] So let us continually meditate on the hidden nature of this great miracle, so that by ever setting our gaze on such things, we may avoid the deadly errors of the world. The number of these psalms contains this further mystery: when the five bodily senses, by which human frailty incurs all sin, are overcome by the power of the Trinity, this leads us to the fifteenth height[8] of the psalms of the steps; thus the body's weakness is eliminated, and eternal rewards are bestowed on those who conquer it.

Commentary on Psalm 134

Alleluia. After this most beautiful edifice of the psalms of the steps, rising to the peak which makes men secure and blessed for ever, there comes the most apt citation of *Alleluia.* Thus holy Church can enjoy the Lord's praises, since that gift is seen to be in store for her. So let us eagerly hasten to say Alleluia with pure minds, so that by God's grace we may mingle with the saints.

Division of the Psalm

The prophet speaks throughout the psalm. Initially he says that praises are to be bestowed on the Lord because of the power of His name, for He has made what pleased Him in heaven and on earth. The prophet recounts His mighty works of different kinds. Secondly, since perfect praise of the Truth lies in the destruction of falsehood, he condemns witheringly those who worship idols. Thirdly, he exhorts the various ranks not to cease praising the Lord. In this way the demonstrative genre is attained with remarkable success in the spheres of both praise and blame.[1]

Explanation of the Psalm

1–2. *Praise ye the name of the Lord, O you servants: praise the Lord, you that stand in the house of the Lord, in the courts of the house of our God.* Following upon the previous psalms, as has been said, in which the prophet through God's pity has mounted to the peak of all the virtues, he addresses those who stand in the Lord's house, urging that after the bestowal of such great benefits they should praise unceasingly the Creator of heaven and earth. Observe too in these two verses how these instructions mount to a climax by the distinctions which are made. First he said: *Praise ye the name of the Lord.* So that you would not think that this command was imposed on each and every one, he added: *You servants, praise the Lord,* in other words, "You who are His servants, you who are committed to Him with steadfast will and believe that you have a Lord whom you do not despise through any superstition." Thirdly he says: *You that stand in the house of the Lord,* that is, "You who stand fast in your holy belief in Him with constant and unshakeable will"; doubtless this is said to contrast with those who suffered sudden eclipse and fell from the distinction bestowed on them. Next comes: *In the courts of the house of our God.* The court is the front entrance to a house of grand dimensions, in which dwellers, as we know, used to fashion a fireplace for themselves to drive out the cold; tradition relates that such places were called *atria* or courts because they were black (*atra*) from the most dense masses of black smoke.[2] Because there is no expression which does not apparently contain some arcane meaning, he says that they too must praise the Lord who are seen to have entered the first chamber of the Lord's house.

3. *Praise ye the Lord, for he is kind: sing ye to his name, for he is sweet.* Ponder the fact that he has written *praise* a third time, so as to reveal to us, through the similar nature of this praise, the indivisible unity of the holy Trinity. Manifold reasons for praise of the Lord are recounted up to the point of the division; for since all that He has done is very good, mention is made of the goodness of which He consists, for we realise that such things have welled forth from Him. The psalmist also added the description *sweet*, so that you would realise that He is not merely kind but also pleasant; elsewhere he similarly says: *Taste and see that the Lord is sweet.*[3] The expression, *sing ye*, has reference to noble actions of the body, so that we may be seen to praise the Lord by our worthy conduct in our manner of life in the world.

4. *For the Lord hath chosen Jacob unto himself: Israel for his own possession.* This verse too is still relevant to the theme of why the Lord should be proclaimed. We know that some are slightly troubled that Abraham is not mentioned here, since such possession is declared to have been promised him first by the Lord. However, the name Abraham was seen not to denote the sense which could be interpreted from the name appearing here. We have already often said that Jacob means supplanter, for in his exceeding desire for glory, he wrested the blessing due to his brother, and this is fittingly associated with the summons delivered to the mass of the Gentiles. By their belief they arrogated to themselves the Lord Saviour's coming, obtained the gifts promised to the synagogue, and outdid in their religious urgency the people which preceded them. Now after the patriarch's mystical wrestling which Jacob continuously practised with the angel, he deserved to obtain also the name Israel, because he endured with unflinching mind the pressures of so mighty a contest. Israel means "the person who sees God,"[4] alluding to the recognition gained by the Lord among His blessed ones. So He chose Jacob when He united the peoples of different nations in the assembly of the Church. He possesses Israel, for we know that at the resurrection of the blessed He dwells among all of them.

5. *For I have known that the Lord is great: and our God is above all gods.* The whole account is rendered certain, for the person who re-

counts it attests that he has had proof of what he claims. So the prophet states that he knows the truth of what he proclaims not through any vision of the flesh but through his eminence on the height of knowledge where he has beheld the mighty Lord. That most holy man saw the wondrous Majesty commanding all the powers and the virtues of the heavens; it was inevitable that he would say: *For I have known that the Lord is great, and our God is above all gods.* Not that any god exists other than God Himself; as we read in another psalm: *For who is God but the Lord? Or who is God but our God?*[5] However, this title, as we know, has been improperly applied to different powers. As we read in Exodus: *I have appointed thee the god of Pharaoh,*[6] and as Paul says: *For though there be that are called gods, either in heaven or on earth (for there be gods many and lords many); yet to us there is but one God, the Father, of whom are all things; and one Lord Jesus Christ, by whom are all things, and we by him.*[7] So He is rightly called the great God above all gods, for all things are created by Him.

6. *Whatsoever the Lord pleased he hath done, in heaven, in earth, in the sea, and in the deep.* After the earlier verses, this most true and lofty proclamation rose to the heights. This figure is called *epiphonema,*[8] a statement rising to a higher note after the recounting of events. Though the works of the Lord are beyond description, and the whole world could not succeed in recounting what He performs in the world, here the whole situation is enclosed in amazing brevity, the statement that God has done all that He pleased in heaven, on earth, in the sea, and in the deep. He says this to enable you to realise that the created things which you see were made at His pleasure, and so that you may be aware that the things invisible to human eyes could be embraced by His power. *Heaven* stands for all heavenly things, *earth* for all that is begotten on the ground; let us assume that *sea* stands for those estuaries visited by travellers in their journeys to and fro, while the *deep* denotes the ocean, which extends beyond our sight and is as some state boundless in depth. Beyond all doubt the Lord's will is fulfilled in these spheres. The psalmist next recounts the Lord's activities.

7. *Bringing up clouds from the end of the earth: he hath made lightnings into rain. He bringeth forth winds out of his stores.* If you interpret this literally, he is attesting that the secret processes of nature are fulfilled by the Lord's execution. But since later he speaks of the

Jewish people, it is appropriate to apply this verse as well to human persons. He brought up *clouds from the end of the earth* when he caused the prophets to rise from humble purposes to the heights of proclamation. They are justly compared with clouds, for by the rain of their utterances they defend us from the heat of the future judgment, since they draw down teachings which will benefit our souls. As has often been said, Scripture attests that *clouds* are to be interpreted as the prophets, with the words: *I will command my clouds to rain no rain upon it.*[9] Next comes: *He hath made lightnings into rain.* The preachings of the prophets, then, are *lightnings* when they shatter enemies, and *rain* when they cleanse committed persons from their sins and pour showers of salvation upon them by which a spiritual harvest may bud, and with God's support swell into full-grown produce. He added: *He bringeth forth winds out of his stores.* We quite justifiably interpret *winds* as the apostles, for their proclamation raced through the whole world as the swiftest of winds. Scripture says of them elsewhere: *He hath made his arrows for them that burn.*[10] Wings are allotted to the winds as well, to express the speed of their rushing to and fro, for the psalmist says: *And he ascended upon the cherubim, and he flew; he flew upon the wings of the winds.*[11] He appended the words: *Out of his stores,* from where spiritual riches could in truth emerge. Observe that throughout these eight verses he recounts with the most pleasant variation the mighty deeds of the Lord in sundry ways and with welling praise. This figure is called *auxesis,* in Latin *augmentum,*[12] since it continually rises step by step. So we do not weary of frequently repeating explanations of meanings, since as we demonstrate authority itself assumes the same tasks without tiring of them.

8. *He slew the first-born of Egypt from man even unto beast.* The prophet's words often recount these miracles so that we may grasp the Lord's power. This is to enable us to realise that they were not chance happenings, but forewarnings to offer abundant understanding of the ensuing age. If we ponder the matter more deeply, we realise that such things are happening even today. *Egypt* stands for this world, which afflicts the Christian people with various calamities, but is inspired with fear by the Lord's strength and power. Egypt denotes the affliction which does not release faithful souls without their being oppressed by grim toils in that dominion. He slays *the first-born* of the world symbolised by Egypt when through the breath of His might He

corrects persons born in original sin. *From man even unto beast* connotes "from the wiser men of this world to those who are gentle and simple." If they are not freed by the Lord's grace, they are repressed by the devil as if by the wicked tyranny of the Pharaoh.

9. *He sent forth signs and prodigies in the midst of thee, O Egypt, upon Pharaoh and upon all his servants.* He sent forth signs and wonders when at His passion the earth shook, rocks were cleft asunder, and many of the saints conquered the law of death and reached the Lord's city; this clearly happened in the midst of the world, in other words, openly and clearly. A sign is something which goes beyond the appearance which it implants on our senses, and which causes something else rising from it to enter our thoughts;[13] for example, when we see tracks, we think of the animal which has made them. A sign gets its name from the fact that it signifies.[14] *Prodigia* (prodigies) is *porro-digia*,[15] meaning "long-foretelling." Even today He achieves the same thing when He converts faithful souls by certain signs sent beforehand. *Pharaoh* means "scattering";[16] to whom will the name be more fittingly ascribed than the devil, who with his cruel aim persecutes the human race? *Upon all his servants* denotes men who obey his wishes; we speak as servants of the person whom we serve with harmonious mind. So the devil is drowned with his agents when the Christian people is freed from sacrilegious error at the font of salvation.

10. *He smote many nations, and slew mighty kings.* He labels as *nations* the harmful mobs of vices which like barbarian nations ever afflict us, but within. He says they are smitten when wounded by penitents making satisfaction; for our salvation is their wounding. He also slays *mighty kings* in us when by cleansing our faults He expels from us the impure spirits which control us through ruinous sins. They are rightly said to have been slain in their purposes because they have wholly failed to destroy us.

11. *Sehon, king of the Amorrhites, and Og, king of Basan, and he has slain all the kingdoms of Chanaan.* Though the sons of Israel through the Lord's favour brought low many kings, here only two are mentioned, doubtless so that interpretation of these names may guide us to the significance relevant to us even today. *Sehon* means "temptation of members," *Amorrhites* "those who make bitter,"[17] for those vices are bitter which seduce us from that most delightful blessedness. They have as their king the devil, who is the temptation of the members

when he changes his appearance to angel of light, to subvert the souls of the devoted by unremitting temptation in assuming the complexion and appearance of goodness. The Godhead will slay these elements in us when He frees the minds of the faithful from such slavery. Next comes: *And Og, king of Basan.* Og means "closing," Basan "confusion."[18] The king of confusion is rightly labelled a closing, for when the devil closes the path of salvation before us, he leaves us in the sacrilegious confusion in which he reigns most foully. This is why his city is called Babylon, which again means "confusion."[19] But God's power destroys all this when He leads us to the gift of His mercy. He added: *And he has slain all the kingdoms of Chanaan. Chanaan* means "humiliation,"[20] but not the humility which leads to the Lord. Those persons who fall from sacred prominence, and are sunk in a most foul manner of life, are also said to be humbled; as another psalm has it: *And he shall humble the calumniator.*[21] If such humiliation did not imply punishment, we would not read: *He that exalteth himself shall be humbled.*[22] So this humiliation is to be understood in the bad sense, and only he who took up the cross for the salvation of all has slain it.

12. *And gave their land for an inheritance: for an inheritance to his people Israel.* This verse makes clear that the previous passage is not to be interpreted literally, but taken in the spiritual sense. The land of promise was not given as an inheritance to the people of Israel, for they lost it through their transgressions. Undoubtedly behind this prefiguration of the Jews, the land of promise is being awarded to Christians for them to possess in eternal peace. So that you should grasp this prefiguration, he repeated: *For an inheritance to his people Israel;* for Israel, as we have often said, means "one who beholds God." *To his people,* precisely the Christian people, who will deserve to be called His since they have preserved His commands with salutary devotion.

13. *Thy name, O Lord, be for ever: thy memorial, O Lord, to the end of time.* After the Lord's kindnesses, worthy praise of Him ensues. He says: *Thy name, O Lord, be for ever,* as though we sought for Him something nonexistent, or as though we were seeking some profit for Him through our prayers. But this is the practice of men, to desire for God what would be considered sacrilegious if it turned out otherwise. We say: *Hallowed be thy name,* though it is clearly hallowed; *thy kingdom come,*[23] though His kingdom will undoubtedly come. But when we

say such things, we declare our wish. So he prays that the Lord's name may abide for ever among the human race, so that beginning with Christ's coming they may be called perpetually and simply Christians. Next comes: *Thy memorial, Lord, to the end of time.* The Lord's memorial is all that is contained in the holy Scriptures by way of most healthy admonition. This remains always within us when preserved with most faithful devotion. As Scripture has it: *Heaven and earth will pass away, but my words will not pass away.*[24] *To the end of time*, as has often been said, denotes everlasting day.

14. *For the Lord will judge his people: and he will comfort among his servants.* The reason for the previous praise is stated: *For the Lord will judge his people*, that is, the Jewish people, to whom he revealed great miracles and assigned His prophets so that the people would not sin. He also sent to them His own Son, so that their accursed hardness could finally be melted. But because they persisted with accursed obstinacy, He will certainly judge them, because they were unwilling to be His though He had chosen them from all nations as His possession. To them He says: *Hear, O my people, and I will speak,*[25] and elsewhere: *My people, what have I done to you?*[26] So He will judge them. But hear what follows as it concerns the faithful: *And he will comfort among his servants.* He means when He will render their promised rewards to those on earth afflicted with harsh contempt on account of His name. Scripture says of them: *Blessed are they that mourn, for they shall be comforted,*[27] and in another place are the words: *He that believeth in me is not judged, but will pass from death to life: but he that doth not believe is already judged.*[28] You observe the benefit accruing from the progress which we have described, so that having recounted the Lord's great deeds he has come all the way to His holy and awesome judgment. Now let us investigate the words of the other section.

15. *The idols of the Gentiles are silver and gold, the works of men's hands.* Now that he has sated himself sufficiently with the Lord's praises, the prophet at this second stage directs his words to bringing down the error of the Gentiles. This figure is known among grammarians as *sarcasmos,*[29] in other words, hostile derision, which wins the palm when it refutes with clear truth. So he jeers at the idols and rites of the Gentiles so that people may not worship golden statues

and gods of silver, and imagine that what has originated from man may be of service to him. How much better do they consult their interests, if they dash them to the ground and shatter them! Indeed, they are of some value if they come down in the world, and are converted into cash. So their god does not listen to them when he is undamaged, but is of more service when broken up. Observe too that the most splendid order of words descends in its manifestations of different definitions. Here the statues are described by their constituent elements, gold and silver, that is, the nature of the metals from which they are fashioned.

16. *They have a mouth, but they will speak not. They have eyes, but they will see not.* 17. *They have ears, but they will hear not. They have nostrils, but they will smell not. They have hands, but they will feel not. They have feet, but they will walk not. They will not cry with their throats,*[30] *for there is no breath in their mouths.* He moves on to different kinds of definitions, indicating and defining statues by actions which they cannot fulfil. He says: *They have a mouth, but they will speak not.* What use is a mouth that does not speak, or an eye which does not see? Or an ear that does not hear, or nostrils that do not smell, or hands that do not feel, or feet which are not moved? They are empty words without serviceable roles, unsubstantial titles; they represent transient presumption, not stable truth. Why, you men, do you aspire to harmful and mad fantasies? Why do you fashion things to cause your destruction? How much worthier it would be to subject yourselves to your Creator, and cease to cultivate the error which you have made! So the prophet Jeremiah when giving advice to the Jews in his letter says: *For their tongues are polished by a craftsman, while they themselves, laid over with gold and silver, are false things, and they cannot speak.*[31] And again: *Beasts are better than they, which can fly under a covert, or help themselves.*[32] Note that in these verses, as in Psalm 113, the statues of the Gentiles are scathingly derided, so that those who are not corrected by the first warning may be affected afresh by a repeated sense of shame.

18. *Let them that make them be like to them: and everyone that trusteth in them.* After the scorn poured upon the falsity of the Gentile deities, an apt judgment was pronounced, that those who fashioned for themselves gods without senses should themselves be deprived of the senses bestowed on them. This fate is truly appropriate for such

people, for a man abandons all reason and is void of all wisdom if he goes so far as to encompass his destruction instead of seeking his own profit. Observe too that the one condemnation embraces both craftsmen and worshippers.

19. *Bless the Lord, O house of Israel: bless the Lord, O house of Aaron.*
20. *Bless the Lord, O house of Levi: you that fear the Lord, bless the Lord.* After expressing contempt for the statues of the Gentiles, he begins the third section by saying that the Lord's praises should be hymned by the mouths of the saints. In these two verses, in enumerating the duties of different groups, he warns us that praise by the faithful must be resoundingly addressed to the true God. By *Israel* every just man in general is signified; as they look on God they offer thanks. Then he recounts them in separate groups, denoting priests by Aaron, the other ministers by Levi, and lastly all those who serve the Lord by any praiseworthy mode of life. In this way the whole devoted people according to their different sections are bidden to praise the Lord.

21. *Blessed be the Lord out of Sion, who dwelleth in Jerusalem.* Earlier he has bidden others to hymn the Lord's praises. Now, following the pattern of the good teacher, he has carried out his own injunction himself. He says: *Blessed be the Lord,* clearly denoting the Lord whom he has cited: He is Christ the King, who visited Sion, that is, His Church, at the holy incarnation. It is He *who dwelleth in Jerusalem,* the city composed of the gathering of diverse saints, the city which rejoices in eternal blessedness in the presence of its King.

Conclusion Drawn From the Psalm

This is a splendid psalm for the instruction of the most devoted people. Following such great blessings, we can do nothing other than proclaim our Lord with triple confession, as was said at the outset. Let us praise Father, Son and holy Spirit, the one and almighty God, so that the absence of differentiation in the divine nature may be mirrored in our praise. This is the true praise which renews us, this is the food by which the devoted mind is filled. Our reward lies in this work of praise by which we are so renewed that no pleasure is seen to match it. So let us proclaim Him now, that we may deserve to praise Him for ever in company with the angels. May He who is to bestow the reward in the next life grant our prayer here on earth.

Commentary on Psalm 135

Alleluia. We must again utter Alleluia, a cry whose charm is always new, though it is quite familiar from our earlier commentaries. Subjoined to it is a psalm sung with the echoing of similar words. The topics embarked upon are different, but it rejoices in the identity of its exclamation. We say not without justification that its verses are to be called "identical ending," as we have already remarked of Psalm 117, whose four verses end with a similar expression.[1] All that is said is made relevant to the Lord's mercy, without which we cannot exist at all. So it is right that the word *mercy* should be repeated quite often, since it achieves all things in us through His most generous gifts; if you investigate the root of this great mystery, our entire life depends on the Lord's clemency, and our welfare on His mercy. So the word must not be absent from our lips or our hearts, so that the divine mercy may deign to preserve us by its continual protection. Poets in imitation of this repetition have composed flowery poems with echoing effects, so transferring the sounds of the heavenly virtues to worldly pursuits. But since each and every psalm is seen to contain strengths of many kinds, we can not unreasonably adjudge that this one depicts the perfect life of the just, who undertake the Lord's commands in wholesome fashion, and continually persevere in His mercy. So let us mentally recall that these repeated motifs in verses have subtly revealed the different powers to us in Psalms 8, 23, 41, 45, 48, 56, 66, 102, 103, and 106, as has clearly been explained in those contexts. We shall explain more fully in the conclusion to this psalm the power which it is seen to have.

Division of the Psalm

The prophet speaks throughout the psalm. The whole composition is seen to be like some heavenly basket, interwoven with beautiful repetitions like strands of gold, from which spiritual blessings can be offered like luscious fruits to guests within the Church. But in the initial verses with their varied content the Lord's magnificence is first recounted, and the status of the whole world made clear. In the second section are narrated the miracles which the Lord had performed in

Egypt and among the Jewish race. The third section moves on to the Christians with a subsequent account of the Lord's blessings, so that you may realise by this repetition that there is a single Creator of all things.

Explanation of the Psalm

1. *Confess to the Lord, for he is good: for his mercy endureth for ever.* We have stated that there is most beautiful variety in the beginnings of verses, but identical repetition at the ends, so that only the first words of them need to be expounded, whereas a single explanation of the repeated sense of the ends must suffice. We must however keep in mind that the Lord's mercy is aptly appended to all the activities later recounted. We have often remarked that confession denotes both praises of the Lord and lamentation for sins. Here we must interpret it as both rather than as one or other; he teaches us that blessed persons both utter praises to the Lord continually and lament past sins. We identify the just in those who have turned from wickedness and who condemn the actions which they performed at some earlier time. As the apostle Paul says of his past deeds: *I am not worthy to be called an apostle, because I persecuted the church of God.*[2] Next comes: *For he is good*, for He indulgently listens to His praises, and is mercifully kind to those who entreat Him. He added: *For his mercy endures for ever. For ever* means eternally, since His mercy embraces enduring time. In this world He provides to create, He spares to correct; in the next, He bestows mercy on the good to award them a crown.

2. *Confess to the God of gods, for his mercy endureth for ever.* In the previous psalm, he made the hearts of Gentiles quake by deriding their statues; now he reveals the greatness and the nature of the almighty Lord by proclaiming His most glorious majesty, so that He may be regarded as God not in the sense that an angel is so called, or as a man of virtues is often so described, but as the God of gods to whom no-one like is found. A creature can be given the title of god for his outstanding distinction, as we read in Psalm 81: *I have said you are gods, and all of you sons of the most High.*[3] And again, in Exodus: *I have appointed thee god for Pharaoh.*[4] But only the holy Trinity can be called God of gods.

3. *Confess to the Lord of lords, for his mercy endureth for ever.* This statement is similar to the previous one. He is called *Lord of lords* as He was called *God of gods.* We call the holy angels lords, but only He whom all things serve is Lord of lords. He is also the Holy of holies, King of kings, the inexpressibly lofty Peak of all powers. Who could doubt that He is above all things, when His controlling power both creates all things and contains the universe?

4. *Who alone hath done great wonders, for his mercy endureth for ever.* We must understand the verb *confess,* as in the first three verses, throughout the variations of all the verses till the end of the psalm. This figure is called *apo koinou,*[5] in other words in common, so that the statement can be presented to us in full, especially as the psalm closes with this identical statement. He says, then, that the Lord alone has done great wonders, just as if He has not made manifest signs of His diverse powers through angels, apostles and His other servants. But here He is said to have performed these wonders alone, when He is proved to have fashioned the nature of the world by His word, for there is no doubt that He created His agents too. This is what the following verses make clear that we should believe.

5. *Who made the heavens in understanding: for his mercy endureth for ever.* To the very end of the psalm praise is proclaimed in honorific narration, which consists of the collected explanation of His achievements, for recounting the Lord's achievements is His praise. So this is what is meant by the earlier words: *Who alone hath done great wonders,* for He performed these things not through creatures but solely by the power of His divinity. His words: *He made the heavens in understanding,* have delineated the very power of His dispensation. He does not perform any actions by His sight or by emulating the constructions of others, but all that He has designated by the understanding of His majesty He brings to effect by the work of a moment. His will embodies the consummation of events, His decree does not permit delay; as the previous psalm put it: *Whatever the Lord pleased, he hath done in heaven and in earth.*[6] So *He made the heavens in understanding,* for they were not fashioned in any confusion or disorder or misshapenness, but brought to completion well-fashioned and adorned by their Creator's will. It should not trouble you that the psalmist spoke of *heavens* in the plural, for elsewhere too we read: *Praise him, ye heavens of heavens.*[7] Paul too says: *I was caught up to the third heaven.*[8] So it is not

given to us to define the extent of what is not explained in our reading of the holy Scriptures.

6. *Who established the earth above the waters: for his mercy endureth for ever.* After his words about the heavens, it was logical for him to speak also about the earth, for this too He made *in understanding.* This is the understanding which embraced all things, and brought them to pass by the power of His dispensation. But let us investigate why he spoke of the earth set above the waters, whereas Job says: *Who hangeth the earth upon nothing,*[9] and elsewhere we read: *He who hath poised with three fingers the bulk of the earth, what name hath he?*[10] But these statements are not found to contradict each other, for he could speak of the earth being above the waters even if it was seen to be at a great distance from them. In the same way we speak of the sky's being above us though we know that a great extent of air lies between. Alternatively, there is the suggestion of others that *above the waters* must be interpreted as adjoining the waters, for even today we speak of a town set on the sea when it is built not on the sea but adjoining it. Or at any rate we are to take it in the spiritual sense: our earth, that is, our body, is renewed over the water of sacred baptism when it is formed by the stability of religion.

7. *Who alone made the great lights: for his mercy endureth for ever.* Though the literal sense of the lights of heaven as the stars seems to be understood, it is fitting that we investigate this a little more thoroughly. *The great lights* perhaps denotes angels, powers, thrones, and dominations, who through their most holy devotion are illuminated by heavenly light; for the epithet *great* seems to set them above all things which shine in the physical world.

8. *The sun to have power over the day: for his mercy endureth for ever.* What has power over the day is the advent of the sun, for every creature accessible to the sight is made visible by it. The use of language of this kind is characteristic of the divine Scriptures; as the bible says elsewhere: *He gave them power to become sons of God.*[11] This can, however, be interpreted spiritually, for the Lord in His pity makes the sun of wisdom shine on His saints, so that they may descry what is relevant to His commands.

9. *The moon and the stars in the power of the night: for his mercy endureth for ever.* You astrologers who allot the supreme power to the dispositions of the stars, hear that moon and stars have been subjected

to the power of the night; surely they have been created not for command but rather for obedience? For what would the Creator have to do if He entrusted men's lives to the stars to arrange? Even the philosophers rightly reject you for saying that such great power lies in visible objects that you deprive the Creator of control. For us however a spiritual sense is revealed from these words. We must perhaps interpret *moon* as the Church,[12] and *stars* as the various orders abounding in sanctity: bishops, priests, deacons, subdeacons, and the rest, who like stars are seen to shine in their heavenly mode of life. All these were set in the power of the night, that is, in the darkness of the world, so that by means of them the darkened hearts of mortals may reflect the brightness.

10. *Who smote Egypt with their first-born: for his mercy endureth for ever.* So far the things which the holy Godhead created by His own hand have been mentioned; now in the second section are recounted works such as He achieved in the world through angels and servants devoted to Him. This is the twelfth kind of definition, which the Greeks call *kat'epainon* and the Latins *per laudem*.[13] This praise is maintained throughout these twelve verses, continuing to the psalm-division. Since the history in this verse is well-known, let us see what can be garnered from the spiritual sense instead. He smote the first-born of Egypt when He condemned the glory of this world which was considered preeminent, for luxury, pride, greed are so to say the world's first-born. Initially the belly gives them birth and embraces them as cherished children, taking joy in its eagerness for these things. The Lord smote them when He exiled them from the rules prescribed by His divinity; for things which are removed from the Author of life lie dead.

11. *Who brought out Israel through the middle of them: for his mercy endureth for ever.* He leads Israel out through the middle of the Egyptians when He frees His saints from association with the most wicked, and leads them into the light of His truth from their utterly foul dwelling in this world.

12. *With a mighty hand and with a stretched-out arm: for his mercy endureth for ever.* The *mighty hand* refers to action unconquerable, the *stretched-out arm* to the Lord's unique omnipotence. Mighty action is the outcome of a stretched-out arm, for the sequence of events ever reveals their Author.

13. *Who divided the Red Sea into parts: for his mercy endureth for ever.* Men of long-standing authority have stated that the Red Sea is divided into twelve parts, the same number as the tribes of the Jews are known to be. The plural *parts* is used of it here so that we should not imagine that the Red Sea was crossed by a single route. But the passage can be aptly interpreted also in the spiritual sense. The Red Sea is the churned-up depths of this world, which we cross at many points when we are converted and by the Lord's kindness hasten to the land of the living. One person attains it through almsgiving, another through continual entreaty, another through virginity, another through outstanding reputation. In this way people cross over the sea of this world to the Lord in many sectors.

14. *And brought over Israel through the midst thereof: for his mercy endureth for ever.* The earlier exposition must suffice for this verse, since it is repeated.[14]

15. *Who shook off Pharaoh and his army into the Red Sea: for his mercy endureth for ever.* He shakes off the devil and his agents into the fount of salvation when He removes them from us by the strength of His power. He spoke of shaking off as though dispelling dust, so that his speed of action would both reveal the power of divinity, and show that those people were the dregs of the earth.

16. *Who led his people through the desert: for his mercy endureth for ever.* He leads us through the desert when He makes us traverse this world unharmed. Only those who pass through the evils of this world escape them, whereas the one who cleaves to them does not attain eternal rewards. The world is called the desert because it is excluded from election by God. It is rightly so called, because it did not welcome its Maker when He came to it.

Who brought forth water from the crag:[15] *for his mercy endureth for ever.* He brings forth water from the rock when He makes the barren hearts of men spurt forth wholesome streams of tears, so that those barren through their personal aridity become suffused through God's generosity. From the crag is by way of exaggeration, for rocks are not small but huge and infrangible when extended to the size of a crag.

17. *Who smote great kings: for his mercy endureth for ever.* He smites great kings when in divine pity He quashes unholy desires in our hearts. When they die, we live; contrariwise if they chance to prevail, we must perish.

18. *And slew strong kings: for his mercy endureth for ever.* He slays strong kings when He drives demons from us as they assault us with diverse attacks. Their wicked purpose is quelled if the souls of the faithful are removed from their control. Slay, O Lord, strong kings, that you may free humble servants; deliver those devoted to You so that the most wicked one may not make us subject to him.

19. *Sehon, king of the Amorrhites: for his mercy endureth for ever.* As we have seen, an explanation of these names is already given in the previous psalm,[16] but we shall not be reluctant to repeat it, since sacred authority is shown to have repeated them for our salvation. *Sehon* means "temptation of the members," or alternatively "barren tree";[17] *Amorrhites* means "aggravation." All this appears to have reference to the devil, for he is a barren tree, and also aggravation. But the Lord kills these things in us when He guides us to His teachings through our holiness of behaviour.

20. *And Og, king of Basan: for his mercy endureth for ever. Og* means "heaping up,"[18] *Basan* "confusion." The one who heaps up our sins is none other than the devil. He is rightly called confusion, because he confounds his hangers-on, and himself retires in confusion from the judgment of the Lord. These and other such things lie slain by the Lord's power when He deigns to deliver us from such foul subjection.

21. *And he gave their land for an inheritance: for his mercy endureth for ever.* He embarks on the topic of the third narration. Though the historical sense is seen to refer to the Jews, the verse is none the less most suitably applied to the Christian people, because the blessedness promised to the Jews, now that those who fell through their own wickedness have been banished, is bestowed as a reward of inheritance on the holy and faithful Christians. Let us remember, however, that throughout the five verses in this section too that twelfth type of definition continues which we have already mentioned in the second part.

22. *For an inheritance to his servant Israel: for his mercy endureth for ever.* When he says *To his servant,* he is debarring those who resisted the Lord's commands by their wicked designs. Included in this designation are the devoted crowd among the Jews and the Christian people.

23. *For the Lord was mindful of us in our humility: for his mercy endureth for ever. Humility* properly pertains to the Christian era. It

began to be aspired to more widely when the Lord Saviour manifested it in His own person, for He demonstrated both the path of humility and the discipline of patience. So He is mindful of the humility of His servants since He is known to enjoin it upon us. The phrase, *he was mindful*, points to the secret of the holy incarnation, when at His coming He deigned to free those who believed.

24. *And he redeemed us from the hand of our enemies: for his mercy endureth for ever.* If you concentrate on the history, you see that He offered no reward to the Egyptians when He deigned to free the Jews from their hands. But because we were kept subject to the power of the devil or His agents, He accordingly paid a great price to deliver us from them by sacrificing himself. He redeemed us by various injuries and sufferings; He endured confinement, beatings and whippings. He redeemed us with nothing less than His precious blood; finally He redeemed us by revealing the miracle of resurrection. As Paul says, drawing all this together: *You have been redeemed at a great price.*[19] This was the price which was priceless.

25. *Who giveth food to all flesh: for his mercy endureth for ever.* By *all flesh* he wished us to understand not only human beings, but all that swims, flies, creeps and walks, for all things are filled by His bounty. Just as He is the Creator of all, so He is known to be the Feeder of all living things. He also feeds all spiritual creatures with the incorporeal food of His mercy. In general, all things are indigent, and it is by His gift that the whole body of creatures continues and remains in being. Alternatively, we must interpret: *He giveth food to all flesh* as perhaps referring only to the faithful whom He deigns to fill with His body and blood.

26. *Confess to the God of heaven: for his mercy endureth for ever. Confess to the Lord of lords, for his mercy endureth for ever.* Earlier he uttered these verses in identical words, except only that his earlier words, *the God of gods*[20] are here shown to have changed to *the God of heaven.* Thus we see that it has been possible to end the whole psalm with its heavenly meaning. At the close he again states that we must make confession, so as to be seen to recall everything to praise of the Lord, and so that we may believe that nothing can be achieved which lies outside the scope of His praise and mercy.

Conclusion Drawn From the Psalm

This is a marvellous psalm, deep and endowed with abundant power. We see that it gleams everywhere with the Lord's mercy as though with glowing stars. The nature of its strength and power is shown in Chronicles with the words: *When they began to praise the Lord and to say: Confess to the Lord, for he is good, for his mercy endureth for ever. The house of God was filled with a cloud, so that the priests could not stand and minister by reason of the cloud. For the glory of the Lord had filled the house of God.*[21] What words of this kind can we utter, except what divine authority is seen to witness in its own case? Though it is certain that God is present with us if we chastely sing any psalm whatsoever, we believe it more clearly when we see it strengthened by the authority of the law.

Commentary on Psalm 136

1. *A psalm of David.* The scheme of headings has now returned to the earlier convention, showing that we must ascribe merciful and most holy deeds to the Lord Saviour. We must note, however, that this hymn is not spoken by persons who rejoice, but is sung solely under the compunction of grief. The history of this event was fulfilled, as the prophet Jeremiah records,[1] when the capture of Jerusalem took place after the arrival of king Nebuchadnezzar. The most remorseful book, expressive of his devotion, survives, designated by the letters of the alphabet repeated four times.[2] But we must interpret these events spiritually, for as Paul says: *All these things happened to them in figure.*[3]

Division of the Psalm

The people of the Hebrews, who through the fault of their obduracy were many generations later to suffer in captivity under king

Nebuchadnezzar, are ushered in to speak, so that they may lament their future ills as if they were witnessed as having already passed. In the first section they recount their disasters, adding that whatever the hardships in this world they can never be in any sense forgetful of Jerusalem, though it was certain that it would be destroyed. In the second section, they direct their words to the Lord, begging Him to be mindful of the assaults made with most wicked purpose against the Church, maintaining the blessedness of those who at the outset thrust evil thoughts from their hearts.

Explanation of the Psalm

Over the rivers of Babylon there we sat and wept, when we remembered you, Sion. The remembrance of one's native soil, as known to be felt in a hostile land, is exceedingly sweet. The more bitter the present experience, the sweeter the recollection. Love of one's own abode intensifies when viewed from the place of pilgrimage. Though the prophet appears to be expounding the captivity of the Israelite people, which befell them under the Assyrians, it is appropriate that we interpret it in the spiritual sense. We realise through sustained reading that in this world there are two cities. The first is the Lord's city, called Jerusalem, the vision of peace;[4] it suffers oppression in this world, being wounded by the onset of many evils. It is humble and afflicted, resting its hope in the eternity which can never succumb to weariness. Against it stands the devil's city called Babylon, the meaning of which denotes confusion; on earth it is proud, flourishing, most joyful, watered by the vices of this world as by mighty rivers. These are the rivers, then, over which the faithful sit, enduring their captivity in this world, sighing with longing for their native land, and shedding bitter tears because they cannot attain that promised peace on earth. We must ponder the fact that he does not say "on the rivers" but *over the rivers,* for those still on the rivers are borne away by the flood of sins, whereas those sitting on the banks above the riverbed have now been rescued from those waves by the kindness of heaven. Observe that their posture is midway; he says not that they are upright (this escapes the charge of arrogance), nor prostrate (this avoids the notion of a fall), but that they are sitting humbly, shedding devoted tears over the wicked waters of sins.

2. *On the willows in the midst thereof we hung up our instruments.* Here the bitterness of grief is intensified, for the people hung up on the trees the objects of their delight with which they might have consoled themselves, as though they were superfluous; for what could their instruments achieve in that situation, when their life's hours were beset with bitter lamentations? But this record of the events is to be converted into its spiritual meaning. *Willows* are the trees on river-banks which abound in the most luxuriant greenness. Often their roots strike deep, becoming enmeshed with stakes which are cut and buried in the damp earth; they cannot be destroyed by floods though they are saturated with masses of flowing water. With them are compared saintly and faithful persons; as Isaiah puts it: *There shall spring up, as it were, grass in the midst of water, and the willow over flowing water.*[5] So it is on men like these that we hang our instruments, when we bestow them by sharing the grace from reading the divine Scriptures; for our instruments are the means of bestowing the grace of psalmody, and the cause of our joy when it is bestowed on us in turn. *In the midst thereof* means in the midst of the city of Babylon, not in the middle of the river, for the most saintly Christian must reside in the midst of the world, though he is seen to be translated in spirit to the realms of heaven.

3. *For there they that led us into captivity required of us the words of songs. And they that carried us away said: Sing ye a hymn to us of the songs of Sion.* 4. *How shall we sing the song of the Lord in a strange land?* They add to their grief the additional burden of sorrow at being reduced to such mockery: they are to pour out indiscriminately for men's pleasure their venerable hymns addressed to the Lord, and the necessity is imposed on them to recite for pagans what the Lord's people and no others are wont to hear; for the proud and arrogant victor wishes to have mounted before him relaxations and refinements derived from songs to the Lord. To them the response must be: *How shall we sing the song of the Lord in a strange land?* But to follow through the section with which we began, Paul attests that worldly concupiscence holds us subject when he says: *I see another law in my members fighting against the law of my mind, and leading me captive in the law of sin, that is, in my members.*[6] So these desires which ensnare us in conditions of captivity often press us to sing the words of the psalms in profane places and at shows, with most sacrilegious ges-

tures. But the teaching here makes clear that we must not fall in with them, for it warns us that the Lord's hymn is not to be sung in a strange land, that is, in the course of sinful activities hostile to God. The holy words of the Lord are to be confined to the holy; as Scripture has it: *Do not cast your pearls before swine.*[7] So the prophet is warning us to have no truck with such behaviour.

5. *If I forget thee, Jerusalem, let my right hand forget me.* The prophet promises never utterly to forget God's Church, laying upon himself this most stern proviso, that if it should happen that he abandoned love of Jerusalem, this will inevitably follow. The right hand of good people is the Lord Christ; in the words of Psalm 15: *I set the Lord always in my sight, for he is at my right hand, that I be not moved.*[8] So the prophet binds himself with harsh but by no means novel conditions, that if Jerusalem ever departs from his mind, he himself should pass from the Lord Saviour's recollection; for Jerusalem is the mother of the faithful, the native land of happy souls, the region of the blessed; the person who forgets her in this life is certainly not set in the Lord's kingdom in the next.

6. *Let my tongue cleave to my jaws if I do not remember thee, if I make not Jerusalem the beginning of my joy.* A second punitive condition is proposed if he forgets Jerusalem: that he be struck dumb in praising the Lord, the activity which Christians account a great reward. What is found worse than to be unable to utter words which are the means by which regular healing is granted? Psalm-singing is consolation for those who weep, a remedy for those who grieve, health for those who are sick. It is known to be a cure for the soul, the means of escape for all miseries. He who is deprived of such a gift is shut out from any benefit of consolation. Next comes: *If I make not Jerusalem the beginning of my joy.* There are beginnings of worldly joy, like the discovery of gold for the greedy, a beautiful woman for the libertine, or boasting for the arrogant. God forbid, however, that these wellsprings of joy should befit the holiness of the prophet. Let us by all means proclaim honourable occasions for joy, but they must not in any sense be preferred to holy Church. Persons who conduct themselves seriously and honourably find cause for joy in the birth of a son, as happened to Zachary in the case of John, promised to him by an angel's voice.[9] There is likewise cause for joy in the case of a son who has returned after a long time; we find this stated by way of a parable in the gospel,

when the father was overjoyed, and slaughtered a fattened steer to provide a feast for him.[10] Another cause is restoration of health after sickness, as happened to king Ezechias, who we read was granted an additional span of fifteen years after a most severe illness.[11] We must also ponder the words themselves, for the beginning of joy is always strong and always most exultant, for the will is fired at the very outset of joys, when through glowing spirits we are impelled to a joy which we scarcely believed could come to pass. Indeed, all sudden emotions are violent, and whatever endures in this world loses its heat. So to intensify the warmth of his faith, he says that Jerusalem is to be preferred as the beginning of joy, for it is right to love it more than all things. However, this and the preceding verse can also be apt for those who we earlier said were captives.

7. *Remember, O Lord, the children of Edom, in the day of Jerusalem, who say Empty it, empty it, even to the foundation thereof.* The Hebrew people pass to the second section, in which they turn to the Lord and beg Him not to allow those who are ravaging God's Church with the most savage rebukes to depart unavenged. Some have sought to interpret *Edom* as bloody, others as earthly;[12] undoubtedly both senses can signify vices of the flesh. The children of Edom are those who have most harshly persecuted the Christian people, and have failed to be converted by making any satisfaction. They pray that when the good are separated from the rest, these persecutors may be brought to mind, so that their due punishment may overtake them. As has often been remarked, this sentiment is uttered not with a solemn curse but with the intention of prophecy; our devoted love is not required in the case of those to be condemned by the Lord's judgment. Next is appended: *Who say Empty it, empty it, to the foundation thereof.* We must add to these last words "Until we reach," so that the whole statement can make sense to us. This figure is called *ellipsis*[13] or omission among the masters of secular literature, when we purposely leave words hanging, so that what has been left unsaid may be sought more longingly. So these are the words of the children of Edom who persecute the Christian people. The parallel being made is with a cistern, for if water is continuously drawn from it we undoubtedly reach the bottom. But how did it profit them to deprive Christians of the light of life in this world, when those who were slain were seen to possess eternal life instead, based on that very foundation? For the foundation of the

faithful is the Lord Christ, who cannot be torn from the just even though all the things of this world are known to be taken from them. By this action the persecutors in seeking to drain away the Catholic religion have bestowed the most blessed and abundant crowns on the martyrs.

8. *Wretched daughter of Babylon, blessed is he who repays thee with the retribution which thou hast paid us.* Our flesh is aptly called the *daughter of Babylon*, for it is known to heap confusion of sins upon us. The appropriate epithet is bestowed upon her; she is called *wretched.* What more wretched outcome could there be than that our frail possession should wax haughty after deeds so monstrous, and by means of unlawful lusts should pierce our souls with the wounds of sins? As Paul says: *The flesh lusteth against the spirit.*[14] But having mentioned the daughter of Babylon, they maintain that a most just repayment is to be rendered to her, so that just as unbridled living rouses us to vices, so when the flesh is subdued by fasting and afflictions, we can make it subject to the virtues. We render a worthy repayment to the flesh so that it may perform under compulsion what it neglects to fulfil in its pleasures. It is the blessed who render such retribution to the flesh, so that after it has impelled them to sin it may by God's help be guided to glory.

9. *Blessed be he that shall take and dash thy little ones against the rock.* They are still addressing the flesh, stating that the person who takes hold of his little ones, meaning his harmful vices, is blessed, because he has already made progress towards controlling them; for when we hold something we take it in our power, and it ceases to be free since it has begun to be enslaved by us. He added: *And shall dash them against the rock*, so that he does not linger in holding them, in case their enticing pleasure creeps over him. He shall dash them against the rock means against none other than the Lord Saviour, of whom it was written: *The rock was Christ;*[15] thus the impulses which fired us with the foulest emotions are at once shattered and dispersed. We do well to analyse their phrase: *Thy little ones*, meaning sins of the flesh born of a wretched mother. While small they are easily grasped and effectively dashed against the heavenly Rock; but once they begin to mature and reach a most vigorous manhood, a sterner struggle is commenced with them, and they are not easily overcome by our weakness. Psalm 100 likewise is seen to have warned us of this with the words: *In the mornings I put to death all the wicked of the land.*[16] But though the

present psalm has softened our spirits in devoted lamentation, and in the first section has also recounted our captivity as well with its mystical explanation, in this verse it has divulged the secrets of most savage and most secret sin, with the double aim of revealing the bane and of not concealing the remedies. At the instigation of the devil an unwelcome notion is launched into our minds; we admit there what by our own assessment we condemn, and we undoubtedly become captives to the tyranny of sin, for which we curse ourselves. But these thoughts while still little ones must be dashed against the Rock; as has been said, they must be shattered against the Cornerstone, where all evil quickly dissolves if the force of the impact is strong.

Conclusion Drawn From the Psalm

The most holy and praiseworthy devotion of the psalms of lamentation is now completed. Earlier in Psalms 73 and 78 the forthcoming captivity of Jerusalem is bewailed; here we have a third psalm on the same theme, so that the holiness of most devoted remorse can be offered through the most sacred number of the Trinity. It is indeed an exalted form of charity that the Lord bids us to show to neighbours, provided that our grief maintains due limit and measure, so that hope in the resurrection cannot be removed, and we do not suspect that the Lord has acted in any way unjustly; for even if we are fired by loving grief, we must not exceed the bounds of moderation. What we offer in the zeal of devotion should be humble and mild. The Lord Christ provides evidence of the proper measure of just tears, for He wept when He pondered the frailty of humankind, even though He was to raise Lazarus from the dead.[17] In this way the good Master sought to teach us devotion, and also to demonstrate the veracity of the humanity which He had assumed.

Commentary on Psalm 137

1. *For David himself.* Though we have said that in earlier headings David denotes "strong in hand" and "longed for,"[1] expressions clearly

befitting the Lord Saviour peculiarly, here the psalmist indicated Christ still more directly, since he subjoined the pronoun. We must utter *for Himself* with greater reverence, as though it were "for the most High" or "for the Almighty" or "for the heavenly King." Then we are to attach *David* to it, a title adopted not from His divinity, but clearly originating from the flesh which He assumed. He *Himself*, however, the Word incarnate, is the one Lord Christ, to whom the entire confession of this psalm is addressed.

Division of the Psalm

Throughout the psalm the Catholic people speaks, gathered from the entire earth. In the first narration they praise the Lord's kindnesses which have been bestowed on them, praying for patience in the future so that they can by His gift endure the opposition of the world. In the second, they pray that the kings of earth may confess the Lord on high because He deigns to reveal the miracles of His majesty in all things, and they entreat Him not to despise the converted sinners whom He deigned to create.

Explanation of the Psalm

I will praise thee, O Lord, with my whole heart, for thou hast hearkened to all the words of my mouth. And I will hymn thee in the sight of the angels. The strength and totality of this confession are denoted by the unanimity of the whole heart. When the people speaks of *my whole heart,* no part of it is left preoccupied by the ambition of this world, but is directed whole and entire to nothing but praises of the Creator, as is right. *Heart* denotes the secret recess of the mind from which we cry silently to the Lord, and our prayers are much more effectively heard than if we made them sound forth with loud shouts. If our voices strike the air, our song must proceed from the heart; and if our tongue is silent, our cry must come from that heart. The Lord is glad to hear what He is known to have created in us to His own image and likeness. Next comes: *For thou hast hearkened to all the words of my mouth.* It is the habit of the psalmist, in his aim of demonstrating the Lord's devotion, first to say that holy men have been heard, and later that they make the praises of heaven resound. He judges that this is to be applied to the faithful people now as well; as was said in Psalm 117: *I will confess to thee, Lord, because thou hast heard me.*[2] But observe the meritorious nature of the prayer in the proclamation that all their words have been heard; for the longing of just men was that the Lord Christ would come, through whom they certainly gained great increase. So all the words of His people are shown to have been justifiably heard, for we know that the world's redemption was gained through Him. They added: *And I will hymn thee in the sight of the angels.* Here the power of psalmody is revealed; he who with a pure heart sings psalms among men seems also to sing with the angels above. The addition: *In the sight of the angels,* presents proof that angels not only hear but attend to the song; we say that attention is paid to something when it can be observed with untroubled minds. Alternatively, it denotes the time when the blessed people after the resurrection will sing praises to the Lord in communion with the creatures of heaven.

2. *I will worship toward thy holy temple, and I will confess to thy name over thy mercy and thy truth, for thou hast magnified thy holy name above us.* The Lord's holy temple is the coming of the blessed incarnation, which even now the Church worships every day, when it reveres His body and blood in the sacraments of the supreme mystery. But that adoration is perfect which is accompanied by blessed confession; for the people say that they will confess to the Lord over His mercy and truth; mercy, because He deigned to come to deliver us without anyone's deserving it, and truth because He fulfilled the promises of His prophets. The person who proclaims these things with pure heart is truly acknowledged to have worshipped His temple. They added: *For thou hast magnified thy holy name above us;* they wished to show that this people had also been gathered from all the regions of the world. Whereas earlier the psalmist used the singular *I,* he now wrote the plural *above us,* for just as the saints have one voice, so the words of the faithful people belong to many. In fact, subsequently they again allot to the singular what we should notice is expressed in the plural in the description of the sacrament; for the name of the Lord was magnified above us when the power of His worship became known to us. When His name was magnified among our holy forbears, this has been extended to all ages, especially in the Christian era, when our foreheads

were signed with the anointing of the sacred chrism. Notice that we have combined two verses because the words are interrelated; thus the interlinking of the two could hold together the verses which are embraced by the one meaning.[3]

3. *In what day soever I shall call upon thee, hear me: thou shalt multiply abundant strength in my soul. Day* here denotes a bright and pure request clouded by no greed and confounded by no avarice; it shines forth from the Sun which dispels all the mists of mortality. By such prayers, then, the devoted people begs to be heard, so that filled with the Lord's strength they may deserve to escape the ambush of persecutors. If you sought to interpret *day* literally, would we then not have to pray at night, at the time when we are especially the object of the devil's deceits? So far as the faithful Christian is concerned, it is always day when he strives to be heard by means of glowing and bright entreaties. But the people's words: *Thou shalt multiply abundant strength in my soul,* showed that they would endure countless sufferings, against which they begged for such abundant help.

4. *May all the kings of the earth confess to thee, O Lord, for they have heard all the words of thy mouth.* The psalmist passes to the second section, in which the blessed people pray that the kings of the earth may confess to the Lord with humility, because all arrogance is known to be hateful to Him. *The kings of the earth* are those who wield physical sway through the gift of the Godhead, for the one known to be a slave to vices does not truly have the title of king. The addition of *all* points in particular to men of scruple and moderation, for we see that many pagan kings are either subject to animal vices or marred by debased religious practice. The people added: *For they have heard all the words of thy mouth.* They explain which kings must confess to the Lord, namely those who have merited to hear his words. Such listening befits those known to be obedient, for we say that persons who openly sneer at the sacred commands have not heard them. Observe too that one capable of hearing the glory of that proclamation does not seemingly withhold devotion without doing himself great harm. So the Jews must realise the extent of the guilt under which they are held subject through their decision merely to take in His words with their ears rather than to embrace them in their hearts.

5. *And let them sing to the Lord in canticles, for great is the glory of the Lord.* The Lord's canticles are the qualities mentioned earlier, mercy

and truth. As the psalmist says elsewhere: *All the ways of the Lord are mercy and truth.*[4] So these are the canticles which the people command those who govern their own bodies to sing, for they have spurned the displays of the world and had recourse with the utmost longing to the Lord's mercy. They append the words: *For great is the glory of the Lord;* it is indeed the Lord's glory that they should reject the world and unceasingly sing His praises, for they have abandoned the trackless wastes of the first man, and moved over to the straight ways of salvation.

6. *For the Lord is high, and looketh on the low: and the high he knoweth afar off.* The previous statement is followed by its concern. The people say that since *the Lord is high, He looketh on the low,* so that none of His subjects should imagine that He was not the object of the Lord's lofty gaze, whereas the Lord was aware that he was prostrating himself with great devotion. The divine power has no similarity to the human condition. In this world we look down on a man bent low in humility, but he becomes closer to the Lord by great exertions of self-prostration. To enable you to realise that this lowliness is precious in the Lord's eyes, there follows: *And the high he knoweth afar off. The high* denotes the arrogance which He recognises from afar because it does not draw remotely near to His grace; and to inspire the proud with fear, the psalmist wrote: *He knoweth,* so that those crazed people should not imagine that what they perform with malicious intent remains unknown to God. This mode of argument, called the *ex contrario,*[5] is assembled with the most picturesque contrast, for the humble are brought near and the proud kept wholly at a distance.

7. *If I should walk in the midst of tribulation, thou wilt quicken me: and thou hast stretched forth thy hand against the wrath of my enemies: and thy right hand hath saved me.* When the blessed people say that their tribulations will be overcome by the Lord's power, they reveal that His faithful are oppressed by many disasters in this world. They know that gold must be cleansed by fire, that a soldier gains his reward only after the greatest toils, and that faith itself wins the crown through the conflict that precedes it. Even if wicked acts of persecutors are remitted for a time, they are continually subjected to the devil's temptations, and the result is that the Christian in his longing for the native land to come aspires to joys which are delayed. So the people are *quickened* by being placed in such hardships. *Thou wilt*

quicken must be understood as "You will delight," an experience contrary to tribulation, for the living person is truly blessed if he is to be filled with the pleasure of eternal joy. Next comes: *And thou hast stretched forth thy hand against the wrath of my enemies, and thy right hand hath saved me.* The people are referring to persecutors; though in their wrath they inflict many hardships on the faithful people, they incur much greater ones through the retribution of divine justice. When converted they too endure affliction, a grief heavier than that which they imposed. They begin justly to persecute themselves, whereas earlier they refused to spare the innocent. But the people proclaim that they will be saved, for when punished by persecutors they could not be overcome by any opposition. By *right hand* is denoted the power which is the Lord Christ Himself, for *He is the power of God and the wisdom of God.*[6]

8. *O Lord, thou wilt repay for me: thy mercy, O Lord, endureth for ever. Despise not the works of thy hands.* It is a wholly perfect prayer, one such as we are advised to make, to entrust our cause to the Lord, for He can render to each and all what we merit. But to help you realise that what seems to be the opposite of an intercession has not been uttered in anger, there follows: *Thy mercy for ever,* "which You show even to those who persecute us savagely." So just as our foes are seen to afflict us because of Your name, so they too must be racked by their duty to make confession in order to achieve salvation; for they undergo a punishment which profits them, when they too suffer torment to attain eternal life. Those granted this healing of making confession have all this mercifully bestowed on them while on earth. Next follows: *Despise not the works of thy hands.* This expresses a wish which appeared to be withheld earlier. The devoted people make entreaty for their enemies who they know are to be assembled before them. Though seen to have become debased through their own fault, they are none the less undoubtedly God's work. When the people entreat that He look kindly on His work which they represent, they beg that He may show pity kindly. His work in us is good, but our own deeds are utterly perverted. So He takes pity when He gazes on His creation, whereas He condemns when He looks on our actions. So the prayer has been briefly and carefully phrased, such that it revealed the devotion of the suppliant and indicated that those enemies would be converted.

Conclusion Drawn From the Psalm

Let us pay heed to the nature of this proclamation by which the holy people has instructed us, and also to the depth of feeling of their devotion. They sought to cut out all their hearts' resentment towards their enemies, so they asked that those seen to be hostile towards them should become their comrades. Let us imitate their devoted purpose and opt to love those who afflict us. We should not regard as enemies those who are of service to us, for if we bear with them with equanimity they often bestow on us benefits which the sweetest friends cannot impart. Friends often by their flattery divert us from virtue, whereas enemies by afflicting us set us on the virtuous path. So show a desire for patience, and then you discover in an enemy more features to love.

Commentary on Psalm 138

1. *Unto the end. A psalm of David.* This repetition of *unto the end* comes after the interruption of several psalms, so it seems appropriate to explain it again, for this protracted interval virtually spells forgetfulness. We have stated that *unto the end* has two meanings. The first denotes the disappearance and end of things, when they complete their span and reach their close in a manner similar to the human condition. The second is the perfect and eternal End which is the Lord Christ. This End observes no setting, but attains the summit of total wholeness. Once we reach this there is nothing further for us to seek; He suffices for all things, since in Him lies all perfection of majesty and the fullness of all virtues. So this entire psalm—and this is also the view of the most learned father Hilary—is to be recited by the mouth of the Lord Christ. His lowliness must not however trouble or disturb anyone; to avoid this, each must have recourse to the canon of Catholic teaching, to remember that there are two natures united and perfected in the Lord Christ. The first is that by which He is God, coeternal with the Father; the second that by which He was born of the virgin Mary, and as one and the same Person deigned in time to become Man for our salvation. So the fact that He speaks in humble tones must not be a reflection on His divinity, but is to be understood

in accordance with the mystery of the holy incarnation. Once we have considered this reasoning, we can acknowledge the divine mysteries without stumbling.

Division of the Psalm

The Lord Christ speaks throughout the psalm. In the first section He recounts to the Father His death and resurrection, observing that all His thoughts are well known to the Father. In the second, He expounds the power of the Father's divinity, for in so far as He Himself is a man He cannot conceal Himself from the Father's observation in any place or at any distance. He adds that by His glorious sanctity He has overcome the world's vices, and has been preserved in the sheltering womb of His mother. In the third section He proclaims that in His role as servant He will praise the Lord Father, whose treatment of Himself has been seen to be powerful and wonderful. He adds that His own preaching and the desires of all the saints are well known to the Father. In the fourth, He maintains that the preeminence of all the faithful has been established. He bids the wicked and the obdurate to depart from Him, for they were not to be saved by any humble repentance. I believe that this psalm is to be heeded with considerable punctiliousness, for it is brimming with profound mysteries.

Explanation of the Psalm

1–2. *Lord, thou hast proved me, and known me: thou hast known my sitting down, and my rising up.* With the invocation *Lord,* Christ Jesus cries to the Father in His role as servant. The Father proved Him in the sense that He made manifest His humility, when He consented to be baptized by John though He was without sin. He was not a sinner; rather He undertook the healing of sinners. As the prophet says: *He has borne our sins and carried our infirmities.*[2] The Father has known Him, in other words, made Him plain when He said: *This is my beloved Son, in whom I am well pleased: hear ye him.*[3] He means "Hear Him saying *I and the Father are one.*"[4] There is another fitting interpretation of these words. He was proved when the devil tempted Him in the desert, and acknowledged when the temptation was dispelled, and

He was tended by angels. A third explanation is that which He Himself attests in the gospel. He was proved at the time of the passion in the devotion with which He was endowed, so that when hanging on the cross He prayed for His enemies; He was known when He made manifest the glory of His wondrous resurrection, for then His divinity became clear even to those who earlier hesitated to credit it. As the evangelist puts it: *This was the third time that Jesus manifested himself to His disciples at the sea of Tiberias after he was risen from the dead: and his disciples believed in him.*[5] The Lord Saviour's death was happily called His sitting down, for it consisted of rest, not punishment; or, as others have it, His sitting down relates to the teaching which the Lord proclaimed with heavenly holiness. He Himself in the gospel states when pointing to their teachers: *The scribes and pharisees are seated on the chair of Moses.*[6] *Thou hast known* demonstrates the figure of *hypallage*[7] which in Latin is called *permutatio;* it means "You have made me known," for all things are known to be clear to the Godhead not only when they come to pass, but also by predestination.

3. *Thou hast understood my thoughts afar off: my path and my line thou hast searched out.* 4. *And thou hast foreseen all my ways: for there is no guile in my tongue.* In these two verses the foreknowledge of the holy Godhead is revealed. *Afar off* is seen to denote not extent of place but of time, for not only does He foresee our deeds, but He also identifies our thoughts before we form them. The statement is wholly apt if fittingly applied to the Lord's incarnation; in His divinity He is the Creator, whereas in His bodily substance He was created. So no person should originate foolish lies, but should with zealous devotion understand this most certain truth; otherwise the source of our hope of salvation may be the cause of our most wretched fall. Next comes: *My path and my line thou hast searched out. And thou hast foreseen all my ways. Paths* refer to silent thoughts, *line* to just judgments, *ways* to human acts. All these were fulfilled in spotless purity by Him whom the Catholic faith proclaims as truly existing in both natures as one and the same. His expression, *thou hast searched out,* reveals the justice of His action, for though most detailed scrutiny was made, we know that no guilt was found in Him. *Thou hast foreseen my ways:* they were foreseen to the degree that we see that they were prophesied. His meekness was described with the words: *He was led as a sheep to the slaughter, and as a lamb before his shearer did not open his mouth.*[8] He

added: *For there is no guile in my tongue.* Precisely so, for truth embraces no guile. As He Himself claimed: *I am the way, the truth, and the life.*[9] He spoke nothing under the cloak of falsehood, but proclaimed to the nations for their salvation what He received from the Father; for in His human role He says: *He who sent me is greater than I,*[10] but He also said: *I and the Father are one.*[11] Both statements are true, both were uttered without guile; His double wish was to manifest the majesty of His divinity and truthfully to reveal the humility of the holy incarnation.

5. *Behold, O Lord, thou hast known all things, the most recent and those of old. Thou hast formed me, and thou hast laid they hand upon me.* Notice how true were those earlier words: *There is no guile in my tongue,* for here He clearly denoted His two natures. He says to the Father: *Behold, thou hast known all the most recent things;* this is with reference to His incarnation, which occurred in the final days. As we read in Scripture: *The lamb was slain in the evening,*[12] and as the apostle says: *Little children, it is the last hour.*[13] He added: *And those of old.* Without any doubt this has reference to His divinity; Scripture says: *In the beginning was the Word, and the Word was with God, and the Word was God,*[14] and the rest. By *things of old* He means things eternal, confined by neither beginning nor end; as we read in Daniel: *Thrones were placed, and the Old of days sat,*[15] and what follows. To make this clearer once more to our human perceptions, He repeated the same message by a change in the nature of the wording. *Thou hast formed me* means "Thou hast begotten me"; the word *form* is often used with reference also to the Godhead, as in Paul's words: *Who, being in the form of God, thought it not robbery to be equal with God.*[16] Next comes: *And thou hast laid thy hand on me.* The Father laid His hand on Him when He revealed the power of His majesty in Him; as was said in another psalm: *I have found David my servant: with my holy oil I have anointed him. For my hand shall help him, and my arm shall strengthen him. The enemy shall have no advantage over him, nor the son of iniquity have power to hurt him.*[17] Observe, then, how the Father laid His hand on Him.

6. *Thy knowledge is become wonderful through me: it has been strengthened, and I shall not be able to attain it.* He speaks of the Father's knowledge which has been proclaimed through Him all over the world. It was *strengthened* in human hearts whereas previously

men doubted it in the uncertainty of their belief. This meaning He declares also in the gospel: *Father, I have manifested thy name to men.*[18] For it was by His revelation that the venerable unity of the holy Trinity could be made plain, and knowledge of the Father became wonderful through Jesus Christ when the mysteries of the sacred law were recounted to those born of earth. Then, so that the truth of the human condition should be made plain, He added: *And I shall not be able to attain it*, for the human nature which He deigned to assume could not attain equality with the divine substance. This is what the gospel makes clear with the words: *The Father is greater than I,*[19] and again: *The Son cannot do anything but what he sees the Father doing.*[20] This is what the most deranged Arian should understand: the flesh should not have spoken otherwise, for it also awaited its destruction.

7. *Whither shall I go from my spirit? And whither shall I flee from thy face?* He comes to the second mode of narration, in which He reveals in mystical sequence that no creature can escape God's presence. Since He is most fully and entirely present everywhere, where can a person hide himself if he thinks he can evade Him? A person can lie hidden only in a place where the pursuer is not present. By saying: *Whither shall I go?* human nature makes it clear that it has nowhere to flee to, because the holy Spirit is wholly everywhere. As Solomon says: *The spirit of the Lord has filled the world.*[21] This is expressed by use of the figure called *diaporesis*,[22] when we seek what best to say. But since we realise through such preaching that the holy Spirit is everywhere, there is no doubt that the holy Spirit is seen to be coeternal and coequal with the Father and the Son; only the Trinity can be everywhere in its entirety. So irreligious suppositions must give place. We must not mentally fashion anything greater or lesser in this world. Let us return to that saving remedy; Father, Son and holy Spirit are the almighty Creator, the one God beyond understanding. We speak of His *face* by metaphor for His presence, for just as our human face possesses mere vision, so the whole of the Lord's substance knows all things with an acuteness of vision beyond description, embracing, penetrating, observing everything.

8. *If I ascend into heaven, thou art there: if I descend into hell, thou art present.* 9. *If I take my wings before daylight, and dwell in the furthest part of the sea:* 10. *Even there also shall thy hand lead me, and thy right hand shall hold me.* This seems to me the argument called the *di-*

lemma,[23] which consists of two or more propositions; whichever of them is chosen is undoubtedly prejudicial. For example, in the gospel Christ questions the Jews who misrepresented Him: *The baptism of John, whence was it? From heaven, or from men?*[24] Whichever they chose would be equally to their despite. Similarly Paul uses it of goodly matters: *Having a desire to be dissolved and to be with Christ, a thing by far the better: but to abide in the flesh is needful for you.*[25] He then added: *Which I shall choose, I know not.*[26] Similarly in this passage, speaking in His humanity, He was uncertain which of three opposing courses to choose. Now let us turn to explanation of the words, for their depth is considerable. In His capacity as Man He says: *If I ascend into heaven, thou art there*, that is, in the place where He was to be set at the Father's right hand. To grasp that the Lord is present everywhere, listen to the prophet Jeremiah: *I am a God at hand, says the Lord, and not a God afar off. If a man hide in a secret place, shall I not see him, says the Lord?*[27] Next comes: *If I descend into hell, thou art present.* This was what happened by the law of His humanity, that when His body was crucified He descended to break the bonds of those in hell, and as the most devoted Redeemer to aid the human race in its toils. He added: *Thou art present*, for He rose speedily on the third day. He then subjoined the third sentence: *If I take my wings before daylight, and dwell in the furthest part of the sea, even there also thy hand shall hold me.* This figure is called *aetiologia*,[28] or the explanation of the reason; He is explaining how He had been unable to escape God's presence. His *wings* represent the most effective speed of the divine Majesty, which raised His holy body to the realms above by the power of His divinity. When you hear the word *my*, you must comprehend the glory of His own power. So the sense is: when He has taken these wings of His before daylight, that is, at the time of the resurrection, and has dwelt in the furthest part of the sea, that is, beyond the furthest limits of this world, there His Father's hand will guide Him. Then, to reveal their joint action, there follows: *And thy right hand shall hold me;* for the Father's right hand is the almighty Word, which will embrace for ages without end the humanity which was taken up and united with it. If it seems wholly inappropriate that He should say that He is held by the Father's right hand when He himself is that right Hand, the statement is to be taken as made on behalf of His members. This form of utterance is often adopted. What must be grasped as canonical is that when He doubts, He is seen in His humanity; but when He is assured, in His divinity.

11. *And I said, Perhaps darkness will oppress me, and night shall be my light in my pleasures.* The first part of this verse is to be spoken ironically. We often make certain statements ambivalently, though we can be in no doubt about them. Take, for example, the words of another psalm: *Perhaps they had swallowed us alive,*[29] and the rest. How could darkness oppress Him, when it had no dominion over such great glory? As He Himself says: *I am the light of the world.*[30] Rather, He oppressed the darkness when by the light of His mercy He overcame the first man's blindness which was passed on to his descendants. So in this sentence in which He says: *Perhaps darkness will oppress me,* those who had the temerity to suspect dark clouds of fear around Him are being mocked; an explanation of this meaning follows when He says: *And night shall be light in my pleasures.* How could He be oppressed by darkness when night was His light in His pleasures? Night denotes the prison of hell, which He indeed illuminated when He shattered the devil's power and freed by His pity mankind whom He deigned to form to His image and likeness. *In my pleasures* refers to Paradise, from which sins expelled the first man; but by the Lord's gift the souls of saints through the resource of confession have returned to its pleasant haunts. The thief who believed was told: *Amen, I say to you, this day thou wilt be with me in Paradise.*[31] Paradise means a most lovely place, and the eternal tranquility of the most blessed sweetness.

12. *But darkness shall not be darkened by thee, and night shall be light as day: as the darkness thereof, so is the light.* The reason is given for the earlier statement, why night is a light in His pleasures. It is because *darkness shall not be darkened by thee,* but rather illuminated. *Darkness* denotes the mystical and deep content of the divine Scriptures; as we read in Proverbs: *He understands also a parable and a dark saying,*[32] and in another psalm: *Dark waters in the clouds of the air.*[33] So this darkness shall not be darkened, but rather illuminated by the Lord, for the prophets' proclamation was fulfilled at His coming. It is His custom to ascribe His own action to the Father, so that the joint work of the holy Trinity can be grasped. Next comes: *And night shall be light as the day.* The statements which had been like a dark night in their mystical complexity became bright as day when the words of the prophets were made clear. What a splendid combination of the two in: *As the dark-*

ness thereof, so is the light, for the truth is in both, whether in apparent obscurities or in bright clarity.

13. *For thou hast possessed my reins, O Lord: thou hast taken me up from my mother's womb. Reins* denotes physical strength, for when the reins are in good order, our body is enlivened by the service they offer, but when they are impaired, the body fails through excessive frailty and weakness. So He rightly says that His reins are possessed by the Father, who resides in the strength of heavenly justice and knows nothing of the sin lying in a frail body. *From my mother's womb* means from the bounds of the synagogue, because through the flesh which He assumed He was begotten of the synagogue, for we know that He was circumcised on the eighth day according to the Jewish rite. He relates that He was taken up by the Father's divinity or by His own, for the two are one. If you were to interpret the phrase as meaning merely from the virgin's womb, He is known to have been taken up by the Lord not only when He came forth, but also when He was conceived by the holy Spirit, so that this passage exstirpates the Nestorian wickedness.[34] *From the womb* means in the womb; as the Lord says to Jeremiah: *Before I formed thee in the womb, I knew thee, and in the womb I sanctified thee.*[35] All this is understood as emanating from His human nature, and is recounted in honour of His holy Father. As the words of the gospel show, it was His planned purpose to proclaim the Father, to fulfill His will, to drink the cup which He received from Him, and in no sense to distance himself from the Father's dispensation.

14. *I will praise thee, for thou hast become fearfully wonderful: wonderful are thy works, and my soul knoweth right well.* He passes to the third section, in which He praises the Father who has revealed such great wonders to Him. The Father became *fearfully wonderful* when following the Lord Christ's passion, darkness ensued, the earth shook, rocks were split, tombs gaped open, the dead rejoiced in resurrection; and Christ Himself was again seen at the holy resurrection in the same body, when He passed into His disciples through closed doors, and mounted to the heavens before men's eyes. Though he achieved these things by His own divinity, He attributed them after His fashion to the powers of the Father, so as to make clear the unity of their sacred cooperation, a point which I have often made. Next comes: *Wonderful are thy works, and my soul knoweth right well.* He

knew the wondrous work of the Father because, as He said earlier: *Night was a light in his pleasures,* because the Father had *possessed his reins,* and had *taken him up from his mother's womb.* It was inevitable that He should recognise His Father as wonderful, for His human nature, filled with the brightness of divine light, beheld Him as the most devoted distributor of such great blessings. As He says in the gospel: *No-one knows the Father except the Son, and he to whom it shall please the Son to reveal him;*[36] He knew the work of the Father right well because, as He says elsewhere: *I am in the Father, and the Father is in me.*[37] One who is externally distinct cannot have such knowledge. This knowledge is beyond reckoning, unique, beyond understanding, for they are known to abide in each other.

15. *My bone is not hidden from thee, which thou hast made in secret: and my substance in the lower parts of the earth. Os* denotes here not "mouth," but is the word for *bone,* a part actually hidden, because as we know it lies within our bodies. Who can see a man's bones when the flesh clothes them, and the skin is drawn over them and hides them? But if we seek to interpret this in the spiritual sense instead, the words more readily yield their meaning to us. When at the world's creation Eve was fashioned from Adam's rib, her husband said: *This is bone of my bones, and flesh of my flesh.*[38] When Paul speaks to married people, he explains the point of this mystery with the words: *This is a great sacrament, but I speak in Christ and in the Church.*[39] So it is clear that here *bone* must be understood as the Lord's Church. So that we can associate these words more fully with the illustration quoted, before the Lord's coming some of the sacraments of the Church were not visible, such as baptism, Christ's body and blood, and the others which became clear in the fullness of time. He added: *And my substance in the lower parts of the earth.* The lower parts of the earth were the foul religious practices of the Gentiles, which at that time differed greatly from the Jewish religion. But the substance of the Lord Saviour became known to them when they grasped the presence of the divine Word in Him, and with devoted minds accepted this through the apostles' teaching. Though the different nations were *the lower parts of the earth* because of their superstitions, they were set higher than the Jews when they took to heart the salvific rules of the Christian religion.

16. *Thy eyes did see my imperfect being, and in thy book all shall be*

enrolled: they shall be strengthened by the daylight, and none among them. The human nature which in the gospel stated that He did not know this world's end, and which said: *My soul is sorrowful even unto death*[40] and such things, attests that the Father has gazed on His imperfect being. His being is indeed imperfect, because the Church continues to gather till the end of the world; not until that resurrection will He give the promised rewards to the blessed, and then He will be *all in all.*[41] But the Godhead has already seen these events which are still reserved for the distant future; the next words make it clear that this is said with reference to the blessed, for He added: *And in thy book all will be enrolled,* precisely those who will rejoice in eternal blessedness. Just as what is written in a book is preserved because contained in writing, so what is kept in the Lord's memory remains fixed much more firmly. Next follows: *They shall be strengthened by daylight, and none amongst them,* that is, the blessed ones mentioned earlier will be strengthened by daylight, filled with perfect radiance of light from the true Sun, so that the words of Scripture are fulfilled: *As star differs from star in glory, so also will be the resurrection of the dead.*[42] Note that He did not say: "They shall be brightened by daylight," but: *they shall be strengthened by daylight;* if He had said "brightened," this could perhaps have been interpreted as merely for a short time, whereas by saying: *They shall be strengthened,* He attests that the blessing will abide for ever. He further added: *And none among them*—we must supply "shall be weakened," for at that stage all our flesh's frailty will be expelled and will depart, and all our mortality will be consumed and disappear.

17. *But to me thy friends, O God, are made extremely honourable: their principalities are exceedingly strengthened.* The fourth and remaining section of the psalm is introduced, maintaining that the honour of the saints is the glory of the Father and of himself. When He says: *To me,* He denotes himself; when He speaks of: *Thy friends,* He means the Father's. As He Himself says in the gospel: *All that is mine is the Father's, and all that is the Father's is mine.*[43] We read that the patriarchs Abraham and Moses were the first to be called the Lord's friends,[44] and subsequently the Lord Saviour said to His apostles: *I will not now call you servants, but friends.*[45] So these are the friends of the Father mentioned, whose honour redounds to the Lord Saviour, for no-one reveres His saints who does not show the devotion of a pure mind to Christ the Lord. He added: *Their principalities are exceed-*

ingly strengthened. Exceedingly means "considerably." *Strengthened principalities* denotes the episcopal sees of the apostles, which in their work of holy proclamation they founded when they established the Churches in sees apportioned throughout the world. Through God's dispensation they were chosen as the Churches' leaders, rams of the flocks, princes of the communities of the faithful, and rightly, for through their labours the devotion of the whole world was unified and solidified by the gift of the holy Spirit.

18. *I will number them, and they shall be multiplied above the sand: I rose up, and am still with thee.* Among the promises made by the Lord to Abraham in Genesis, we read that his seed would be multiplied like the sand of the sea and the stars of heaven,[46] but here He says: *Above the sand* of the sea, so that whereas in Genesis the comparison equates Abraham's seed with the sand, here the grains of sand are exceeded. The sand of the sea denotes the Jews, indicating their earthly understanding and the barrenness of their faith—*arena* (sand) derives from *ariditas* (barrenness)[47]—whereas the stars of heaven refer to the Christian people, because of the brightness of their religion and the splendour of their faith. So the Lord Christ promises that He will number the faithful people, who are found greatly to exceed the tally of the Jews, for it was inevitable that the combined numbers of the nations should exceed those of one race. He added: *I rose up, and am still with thee.* Here in quite cryptic and brief words He points to His second coming, when He will judge the world. *I rose up* denotes the time of His resurrection; *I am still with thee* the time when He sits at the right of the Father, in hiding, so to say, "for a period during which men cannot see Me, until the time when My kingdom becomes most abundantly clear to men." For *still* points to future time; not that He is at any time to be separated from the Father, but whereas He is now out of our sight, He will subsequently be visible to all nations.

19. *If thou shouldst kill sinners, O God: ye men of blood, depart from me.* 20. *Because you say in your thoughts, They shall receive their cities in vain.* In these two verses let us first mention the use of *hyperbaton*,[48] so that with the Lord's help we may be able more easily to explain them section by section. The order of words is: *If thou shouldst kill sinners, O God.* We must above all be careful not to believe that the Lord Christ is praying for the destruction of sinners, for He had undoubtedly come to save them. As He himself says in the gospel: *I have not*

come to call the just, but sinners.[49] If we analyse this verse in the spiritual sense, all our difficulties are removed. What Christ says is: *If thou shouldst kill sinners, O Lord;* God kills the sinner when he dies to sin so that he may live for the Lord. As Paul puts it: *I am dead to the law that I may live for Christ.*[50] So sinners are killed when they are translated from evil designs to a virtuous attitude. When this befalls them by the blessing of conversion, they then *receive their* previous *cities in vain,* in other words, the most evil superstitions which belong to Babylon, for now through God's kindness they have attained the fold of the Catholic Church. Since all do not deserve to attain the Catholic faith, the intermediate words are addressed to the unfaithful and obdurate who have refused to believe: *Ye men of blood, depart from me, because you say in your thoughts.* They are men of blood, then, because they live according to the flesh, and perform bloody actions. They are rightly told to depart because they have not longed to find a place in the Church. Next comes: *Because you say in your thoughts,* in other words, "You murmur against the things which were proclaimed to you by the power of the holy Spirit." So if you stick to the order of words as outlined, you will dispel from yourself all the cloud of confusion.

21. *Have I not hated them that hate thee, and did I not pine away because of thy enemies?* 22. *I have hated them with a perfect hatred, and they are become enemies to me.* The question why we are bidden to love our enemies seems to be no idle one, whereas to hate God is an accursed act, for there is a great difference between the two. On occasion our enemies rise against us with justified anger; they are annoyed because we do not render them the appropriate service, because we slander them, because we begrudge them their virtuous efforts. So we are rightly bidden to love our enemies when we happen to offend them through our fault. But when God's enemies are obdurate, they are condemned with an appropriate and solemn curse, for though created by Him and owing their entire life to Him, they become arrogant towards their Maker. So such men are rightly to be regarded with disgust, for they were unmindful of such great kindnesses. We must also take into account the verbal distinctions which are made. First He said: *I have hated them that hate thee.* Hidden hatreds can

earlier dwell in the malevolent heart, but it is a mark of the most intense wickedness to declare oneself an enemy; this denotes open and inveterate persecutors who with accursed shamelessness ravage God's holy ones. In His holy devotion He rightly says that He is pining away because of them, for while in this life He bears with them longer so that they may accept correction, they attack God's Church with rash onslaughts. As Scripture says elsewhere: *The zeal for thy house has made me pine away;*[51] the expression signifies considerable grief. We say that people pine away when they are afflicted with unending cares, and come close to death's door as their bodies fail. Next comes the ensuing verse: *I have hated them with a perfect hatred, and they are become enemies to me. Perfect hatred* consists of loving men and always loathing their vices; for in so far as they are God's creation they must undoubtedly be loved, because considered as God's works they are good. But they are to be loathed for the wickedness with which they have befouled themselves in grisly crimes, for such persons can be pleasing only to those enmeshed in similar deeds. To demonstrate to you the unity of their divinity, the Son says that they who stood opposed to the Father's commands have become His enemies. Observe too that by the fifth type of definition, called in Greek *kata tēn lexin* and in Latin *ad verbum*,[52] He defines the hatred with which He hates the Father's enemies; it is the perfect hatred begotten not by human rancour or by physical envy, but by the Lord's charity. *Odium* (hatred) gets its name from *oris repudium*[53] (rejection by mouth).

23. *Prove me, O God, and know my heart: examine me, and know my paths.* 24. *And see if there be in me the way of iniquity: and lead me into the eternal way.* No-one can say this but He who also says: *Behold, the prince of this world cometh, and in me he will not find anything.*[54] He alone is known to be free from sin who is seen also to have borne the sins of men. *Prove* denotes His patience, *know* reveals "I knew not sin, despite the agitation of my condition"; *examine* suggests a most detailed scrutiny, for no-one can deny what has happened when questioned by one with knowledge. *Paths* also refers to the activities which He continually performed with heavenly holiness. Next comes: *And see if there be in me the way of iniquity, and lead me into the eternal*

way. Observe how the good Master teaches us the perfect order of things: first He said that He was proved and known, and then examined, so that when no wickedness was uncovered He could be led to that way in which He reigns with wonderful power and everlasting glory in company with the holy Spirit. *The way of iniquity* is the work of the devil, which he never ceases to practise by means of his evil promptings in the progress of this world. The Lord rightly said that this way is not in Him who is the Rock, for no trace of the ancient serpent could be established in His unshifting presence. So His human substance did well to beg to be led into the eternal way, in which the devil's path could not be found; the Lord Christ often begs the Father for what is actually His own, so that the unity of love, power or nature between them can be recognised.

Conclusion Drawn From the Psalm

Observe here shining before us the eighth psalm which presents the two natures; these eight beat off the arrogant infidelity of those in error.[55] They should at any rate be healed by the precedent of circumcision. Just as the Jews surrendered their foreskins on the eighth day, so those in error should be schooled by this eighth psalm and abandon their idle obduracy. As has been mentioned earlier, Psalms 2, 8, 20, 71, 81, 107, 109, and here 138 discuss this matter. Even if deafness of the deepest kind attends these men, so that they are not prevailed upon by so many spokesmen, and even if they still remain obstinate in their sacrilegious belief, let us offer them syllogistic proofs since they wish to be regarded above all as dialecticians. The first proof, then, that the Lord Christ comprises two natures is on these grounds: If Christ is at one and the same time perfect God and perfect Man, as the unanimity of all the holy Fathers maintains, He consists of divinity and humanity united and perfect. Now whatever consists of divinity and humanity united and perfect must consist of two united and perfect natures, namely those of divinity and humanity. So Christ remains one and the same, and consists of two united and perfect natures, namely those of divinity and humanity. The second proof that the Lord Christ resides in two natures is this: If Christ remains one and the same, He consists of two united and perfect natures, as has has been shown, which are those of divinity and humanity. Now whatever consists of the two united and perfect natures of divinity and humanity also has its essence in two united and perfect natures. So Christ by abiding as one and the same has His essence in two united and perfect natures. The third proof that the Lord Christ always possesses two natures in Himself is this: If Christ endures as one and the same, He has His essence in the two united and perfect natures of divinity and humanity, as has been shown. Now whatever has its essence in the two united and perfect natures of divinity and humanity has two natures united and perfect in it. So Christ by continuing one and the same has in Him the two perfect and united natures of divinity and humanity. The fourth proof shows that if a person proclaims Christ as perfect God and perfect Man but denies His two natures, he subverts true teaching and his own admission that Christ is perfect God and perfect man. The grounds are these: if the one and the same Christ is perfect God and perfect Man, He has within Him the two perfect and united natures of divinity and humanity. But if He does not have within Him the two perfect and united natures of divinity and humanity, as some deranged persons claim, He is not perfect God and perfect Man, but either God alone, or Man alone, or neither God not Man. But since this is illogical and impious, and the one and the same Christ is perfect God and perfect Man, as men generally proclaim, He has within Him the two perfect and united natures of divinity and humanity. So the revered bishop Facundus,[56] whose cleverness strikes deep and demolishes heretics, recently in a communication to the emperor Justinian discussed the two natures of the Lord Christ in two exceedingly careful and clear pamphlets which I have had transcribed for you so that you have no need of commentators ancient or modern.[57] So let us now at last abandon the illicit arguments of opponents. No-one will presume to declare us as perhaps blameworthy, if following the eighth correction we announce to them the prescription which Paul proclaimed to Titus: *A man that is a heretic, after the first and second admonition, avoid, knowing that he that is such a one is subverted and sinneth, being condemned by his own judgment.*[58] One of the Fathers has well defined the nature of the heretic: "A heretic is one who is borne off track by ignorance or contempt for the divine law, and is either an obstinate deviser of new error or a supporter of another's, preferring to oppose Catholic unity rather than subject himself to it."[59]

Commentary on Psalm 139

1. *Unto the end. A psalm of David.* Though this heading is seen to be explained in the previous psalm, we are not reluctant to repeat briefly what we know is always salutary for us to hear. *Unto the end* denotes the Lord Christ; as Paul says: *For the end of the law is Christ, unto justice to everyone that believeth.*[1] Let us lift up our hearts to Him with all our strength, for in this psalm as by the voice of a herald we are forewarned that He comes as a Judge, fearful and almighty but also devoted and the object of great longing.

Division of the Psalm

Holy Church speaks throughout the psalm. In the first section she entreats the Lord that He may deign to free her from the wicked devil who seeks to undermine the devotion of the faithful people with many deceits and traps. In the second, she begs not to be consigned to that most evil tempter, now that she is certainly delivered from bitter dangers by His protection. In the third, she says that vengeance at the future judgment will visit those who afflict His poor with senseless disturbances.

Explanation of the Psalm

2. *Deliver me, O Lord, from the evil man: from the unjust man rescue me.* In her awareness of the extent of the sufferings of her members through the devil's hostility, mother Church anxiously cries to the Lord who alone can overcome Satan's wickedness, and begs for deliverance from his manifold temptation so that she may no longer be wearied and yield to him. We have learnt from the gospel-evidence that *the evil man* stands for the devil, for it says: *Now the evil man is the devil.*[2] The devil is deservedly so styled, for he is stained with the contagion of sins, so that he is no longer described as an angel of heaven but as a man of earth; the two expressions replace and interchange with each other, and even today we both call a wicked man a devil, and contrariwise as we have just demonstrated we call the devil

the evil man. There follows mention of the *unjust man* to make a distinction; here she wishes to denote in particular earth-born man, serving as the devil's trooper. So she prays with fully rounded entreaty to be delivered from both the author of sins and his followers. The characteristics identify the different individuals: the devil is called malignant, his follower unjust. The two epithets could not simultaneously befit the one person, for that is forbidden by the law of eloquence.

3. *Who have devised iniquities in their hearts: all day long they designed battles.* Dangers are always more serious when kept hidden, for they suddenly make their onset when like rivers in torrent they rush unexpectedly down. She refers to those who abandon the womb of the Church and engage in sacrilegious disputes based on perverted beliefs. She rightly begs to be delivered from these to avoid being wounded by their foul deeds. To demonstrate that their wickedness was unending, she spoke of *all day long*, so that no weariness, no length of time softened them.

4. *They have sharpened their tongues like serpents: the venom of asps is under their lips.* The malice and guile of heretics is splendidly described here. *Tongues* denotes their words which are polished on the whetstones of wickedness and seek to wound the hearts of simple people. They are aptly matched with serpents, for they vomit forth poison in their words and so are compared with deaf asps. The purpose of their striving is the desire in their obstinacy of mind never to be overcome by the truth. This figure is known as *parabole*,[3] for objects unlike each other in kind are compared in their debased natures.

5. *Keep me, O Lord, from the hand of the sinner, and from unjust men rescue me. Sinner* specifies the devil again here, for he was the first of all creatures to leave the straight path, and is known in his wickedness to have wounded Adam. Holy Church begs to be protected from his most evil power, for he is so utterly strong that he is even labelled: *The prince of this world.*[4] This is because he deceives us with many tricks and many traps, so that one cannot guard against him as he always hides himself when stealing upon us with slippery steps. His agents are mentioned next, for he strives to achieve openly through his followers what he cannot seize of his own accord by infiltrating into our minds.

They have proposed to supplant my steps: the proud have hidden nets for me. We use the word *supplant* correctly when the ground is withdrawn from our feet so that we fall heavily into dark holes. This is how the enemy attacks us. As we walk in the Lord's way, he digs pits of sins alongside, so that once he has diverted us from our most straight purposes he may trick, deceive and submerge us; for these enemies do not dare to tread the Lord's way, which belongs only to the just. *The proud* are arrogant heretics who abandon the Lord's way, and hasten to deceive the people with evil teachings rather then to instruct them. These persons set traps for holy people when they seek to entangle them with empty riddles.

6. *And they have stretched out cords for a snare for my feet: they have laid for me a stumbling-block by the wayside.* She continues to expound the evil ways of heretics. They stretch out cords, in other words, crafty and twisted objections so as to trip our human thoughts; thus they are seen to set up a stumbling-block for our minds like a snare for our feet. The snare of a cord is so placed as always to draw its bonds tighter; its hold does not soften or slip, for it encloses trapped objects in knotted coils. *By the wayside* is precisely expressed, for they trap only those who depart from the straight path of virtues. The first diapsalm now follows; a pleasant interval grants us a division here.

7. *I said to the Lord, Thou art my God: hear, O Lord, the voice of my supplication.* After these cruel snares which have been laid, after these twisted cords which have been stretched, after these evil stumbling-blocks devised by the devil's deceit, she passes to the second section. She directs her words to the Lord, pleading that she may not be consigned to these most evil traps. The Church says, as one shining with the purest faith and steady in unshakeable virtue; *I said to the Lord, Thou art my God.* This can certainly not be said by one known to be entangled in transient errors; no gathering of Arians, Sabellians, Manichees, Pelagians, Apollinarians, Eutychians, Nestorians or the other sects[5]—monstrosities would be a better definition than beliefs—can truthfully say to the Lord: *Thou art my God.* So the Catholic Church must speak these words, the bride summoned from the Gentiles, who confesses the holy Trinity in most truthful faith. Next comes: *Hear, O Lord, the voice of my supplication.* It would have sufficed to say "Hear my prayer," had she not wished some deeper meaning to be understood; for the voice of supplication is purity of

prayer and the silent cry which mounts to the Lord. Moses was silent when he was asked: *Why do you cry to me?*[6] Cain was told: *The voice of your brother's blood cries to me from the earth.*[7] So the voice of sacred action forms the most expressive cry of actual deeds, known not to men but appreciated by God alone. So she begs that the voice of her supplication be heard, because she knew that she was offering the gifts of a most just entreaty.

8. *O Lord, Lord, the strength of my salvation: thou hast overshadowed my head in the day of battle.* The repetition, *Lord, Lord,* reveals the love of His devoted prayer. This figure is called *epizeuxis*,[8] the redoubling of the same word in the same verse with no interval, a figure which we have often said is of the greatest force in rousing men's minds. When she speaks of *the strength of my salvation,* she indicates her patience and perseverance; there can be no salvation in the struggle with afflictions unless the virtue of endurance is granted through the Lord's mercy. *Virtue* is derived from *viriditas*[9] (greenness), which cannot wither away under any hardship. Next comes: *Thou hast overshadowed my head in the day of battle.* When the Church says that her head is overshadowed in the day of battle, she refers to the Lord's blessed passion. On that day of His crucifixion He was so overshadowed and protected that His mind suffered no confusion, and His flesh bore no onset of corruption; indeed, He Himself begs in Psalm 21 for help to be accorded: *But thou, O Lord, remove not my help to a distance from me: look towards my defence,*[10] and the rest. The Lord's passion is well described as the day of battle; on that day the devil was overcome, the bars of hell were burst asunder, captives were freed, and He alone triumphed by dying, for unprecedentedly He destroyed death by death.

9. *Surrender me not, O Lord, from my desire to the sinner. They have plotted against me: do not thou forsake me, lest they be ever exalted.* Anyone abandoned to possession by the devil through desires of the flesh is *surrendered from his desire to the sinner.* Paul says of such people: *Wherefore God gave them up to the desires of their heart, unto uncleanness.*[11] But to ensure that this does not happen, there ensues a wholly praiseworthy request: that just as the enemy plot to do her harm, so may the divine power deign to lend help. Finally a most just plea is entered, that those who glory in undermining the faithful peo-

ple should not be actually exalted by the destruction of the just. Next comes a second diapsalm, where we shall mark a division according to our custom.

10. *Their head goes around: the labour of their lips shall bury them.* After praying not to be consigned to her enemies, holy mother Church passes to the third section, in which she denotes the errors of the wicked, from which they cannot escape. Just as she said earlier that her hand was overshadowed by the Lord in the day of battle, so she recounts that the head of her enemies, the devil, embarks on a rotating detour, for he never attains the direct way, but is ever enfolding himself by doubling back on his tracks. The order of words is like this: *Their head goes round.* Peter likewise says of him: *Your adversary as a roaring lion goes round, seeking whom he may devour.*[12] It is a most splendid type of definition to state in one word the identity of the object sought; this is called in Greek *kata tēn lexin*, and in Latin *ad verbum.*[13] *The labour of lips* is a lie published by word of mouth; it is invented laboriously because it is fashioned by refined contrivance, whereas the truth is spoken without labour because it is uttered simply and without difficulty. So the lie from their mouths buries them when these faithless men are defeated in their claims. Malice is never so circumspect as not to contradict itself.

11. *Coals of fire shall fall upon them: thou wilt cast them out into the fire: in miseries they shall not remain.* First she spoke of their errors which they could not escape; now she tells of their punishment which is wholly salutary. *Coals of fire* are the tortures of repentance. Such fire springs from a shower of tears; as was said in Psalm 119: *The sharp arrows of the mighty, with coals that lay waste.*[14] Initially grievous remorse falls upon them, and subsequently they are cast into the fire when through the Lord's pity they are ignited by the flame of charity; and though they have long lived in quite idle tepidity, they begin to glow with holy works. The outcome for them is that they do not remain in their miseries, since through God's kindness they are transported to the side of the good.

12. *A man full of tongue shall not be guided upon the earth: evils shall draw the unjust man into destruction.* Though *full of tongue* can be used also of those eloquent in abundance of language, here it is clear that the word has particular application to those guilty of thoughtless garru-

lity. Such men are antonyms of the wise, and behave in a contrary way. The apostle James warns us: *Let every man be swift to hear but slow to speak.*[15] Men such as these are certainly not *guided* upon the earth, for they often leave the path through their fickleness. It is difficult for unrehearsed speech to be sound; as Scripture says: *In a multitude of words thou shalt not escape sin.*[16] *The unjust man* is he who despises God's rules and is betrayed by the ardour of his own desire. He is trapped by his own wickedness and submerged in the most deep and ravenous depths, for he who swerves from the Lord's commands ever ponders things harmful to himself.

13. *I know, for the Lord will do justice to the needy, and will revenge the poor.* Holy Church briefly and truthfully speaks of those tongue-wagging persons whom she must indeed blame. She says that she knows by faith through God's gift what she most certainly believes will be done. He will do justice to the needy when at the judgment He will redeem His promise, and revenge the poor of whom the Apocalypse writes: *I saw under the altar the souls of them that were slain,* and a little later: *How long, O Lord holy and true, dost thou not judge and revenge our blood on them that dwell on the earth?*[17]

14. *But as for the just, they shall give glory to thy name: and the upright shall dwell with thy countenance.* This is appointed to happen during certain serious and bitter afflictions of this time, for it is a mark of great virtue to praise the Lord when the world's attractions are removed. Job was good when he worshipped the Lord in his wealth, but how much better was he in praising Him when suffering manifold hardships! So let us be eager to offer Him greater thanks when the tempter seeks to belabour us. The enemy departs more readily when he realises that those whom he afflicts cannot do wrong; for notice the words that follow, that those who are upright do not cease to dwell with His countenance. It is an enduring vision of which we cannot tire, ever to behold Him who is the regular source of renewal for every rational creature. As has already been said in Psalm 15: *Thou shalt fill me with joy with thy countenance.*[18] That countenance represents the gift of all rewards; the person who has deserved to behold it cannot lack any blessing. But since we read: *No-one has seen God at any time,*[19] this phrase of the psalm must be referred to the time when the blessed behold the Lord not *through a glass,* but as Paul puts it, *face to face.*[20]

Conclusion Drawn From the Psalm

How salutary and sweet are the words of the most holy mother which we have heard! She has prayed for us that we may be divested of the Satanic trials which she knew were fiercely laid upon us. Once we are freed, she promises us the Lord's countenance, so that once so splendid and so great a gift is pledged to us, we may fear nothing toilsome or sad. Grant, O Lord, that just as Your servants long for You, You may reveal Yourself in the radiance of Your mercy. Let not those sins hinder us which we condemn with our own curses; we confess our faults so that we can appease You. You alone are the Judge who bestow pardon on the person who confesses. Though nothing lies hidden from You, You ask that human persons proclaim what men acknowledge that You know more truly.

COMMENTARY ON PSALM 140

1. *A psalm of David.* As the words of the heading are by now well-known through frequent repetition, we must direct our attention to the Lord Saviour. Sometimes what is said once is subject to doubt, but what is proclaimed by frequent repetition is quite definite and beyond doubt. Warnings are given us in advance by heralds, so to say, so that we may prepare our minds' concentration with suitable devotion for what is to follow. Otherwise, because the words fail to be understood, they may perhaps be heeded too negligently. In the view of more careful commentators, the prophet begs to be delivered from different errors in the course of these activities in the world; he asks that he may not fall into the net of sinners, with whom he longs to have no portion.

Division of the Psalm

The prophet is aware of human frailty entangled in the various bonds of sinners, and in the first part he asks the Lord to hear his prayer, additionally mentioning the errors from which he prays chiefly to be delivered. In the second section, he chooses rather to be convicted by the just man than to be praised by the sinner; he entreats to be protected from the snares of sinners, for he attests that he shares nothing in common with them.

Explanation of the Psalm

I have cried to thee, O Lord, hear me: hearken to the voice of my prayer, as I shall cry to thee. We must observe here an *enthymema.*[1] His proposition is: *I have cried to thee, O Lord,* and the conclusion follows, Therefore *hear me.* In this way the force of the enthymematic syllogism is achieved. The prophet in his desire to inject into the human race a mood of uninterrupted prayer, seems to have combined two different times. He says of the past: *I have cried,* denoting a prayer completed. Then he says again: *As I shall cry to thee,* clearly denoting the future. So just as no time is free of faults, so there is no time unoccupied by pious prayers, for the saving remedy against unceasing sins is continual entreaty to the devoted Lord. What point will there be in forgiveness of past sins, if future ones are seen to bind us? So a goodly end is being sought for the Christian, so that when in his final hours the pardon granted him is past, the last stage of his life may not be one of guilt. Observe that here and in the following verse he renewed his prayers fourfold, for the holy man could not be sated with so great a request; for the prayer which frees us from faults wins the heart of the Judge and wipes away sins, and mercy cannot be withheld from one who makes entreaty, for humility fires us to pray unceasingly for forgiveness. All this is achieved by the devoted Lord, for He does not wish to condemn those whom He forewarns. The Creator of the world cries out: *I desire not the death of the sinner, but that he be converted, and live.*[2]

2. *Let my prayer be directed as incense in thy sight: the lifting up of my hands as evening sacrifice. Incense* is the delightful burning of a fragrant coloured substance which when ignited on charcoal gives off a most attractive smoke to the region above, and gives pleasure to those who perfume themselves with its seductive charm. In the same way the prayer of the blessed when ignited by the fire of love obtrudes on God's sight, raised higher by the weight of humility and remorse, for the Lord takes delight in our virtues as in fragrant odours. We read in

the Apocalypse that the Lord welcomes sacred prayer as the most sweet odour, where it says: *An angel stood before the altar of the Lord, having a golden censer: and the smoke of the supplications ascended from the hand of the angel in the sight of the Lord, that he should offer of the prayers of the saints, which is before God.*[3] Next comes: *The lifting up of my hands as evening sacrifice. The lifting up of hands* denotes works of devotion performed either in almsgiving or achieved in some praiseworthy relationship. *Evening sacrifice* perhaps denotes that offering which scrupulous devotion is wont to offer up at life's end, when we show repentance and cleanse ourselves with humble entreaty; in the words of Psalm 50: *A sacrifice to God is an afflicted spirit.*[4] Our evening is when we leave the light of day at the onset of death. Notice the point which we have often emphasised, that no-one should despair provided that he cleanses his final deeds with the fount of his tears.

3. *Set a watch, O Lord, before my mouth: and a door round about my lips.* The most holy prophet begs that he may say nothing which must lead to condemnation. But he entreats correction by this double defence, that his thoughts may know no wickedness, and that a debased will may not hasten to utter foolish words. He knew that sin lies in both of these, which is why he prays to be a stranger to them; in Solomon's words: *Hedge round thy possession with thorns: set there thy silver and gold, and make a door and a bar for thy mouth, and make a yoke and a balance for thy words.*[5] *Ostium* (door) derives from *obstare* (to block),[6] for when a door is closed it blocks those coming in. The holy man realised that he must fortify with great prayers the source of such ready entrance of sin; as he had just remarked in the previous psalm: *A man full of tongue shall not be guided upon the earth.*[7]

4. *Incline not my heart to evil words, to make excuses in sins.* The second entreaty follows, that even if he chanced to utter words requiring repentance, he should not seek to excuse himself with most wicked falsehoods. This is the greatest fault under which mankind labours, that after sinning they take refuge in excuses rather than prostrate themselves with repentant confession. Clearly such wickedness is to be reckoned amongst the worst sins, for its true source also seems to occasion slower progress by the sinner towards repentance. As the First Book of Kings has it: *It is like the sin of witchcraft to rebel, and like the crime of idolatry to refuse to obey.*[8] The phrase, *to make excuses in sins,* denotes the tendency of shameless people when appre-

hended first to be found excusing themselves by some falsehood, and when thereupon found guilty to go on harnessing other excuses. This is so that their unblushing impudence may avoid coming to terms with the truth; at one time they attribute their sin to the occasion, at another to necessity, at another to other people. This figure is called *metastasis*[9] or transference, when we seek to shrug our guilt off on to another.

With men that work iniquity: and I will not be yoked with the choicest of them. The third entreaty is to be freed from the brotherhood of those who work iniquity, to avoid becoming yoked in association with them. Guilty persons are said to be yoked when two are bound together by a single chain, so that they impede each other and cannot indulge in free flight. So the prophet begs not to be bound with such men, since they are found to hinder each other through the entanglement which they share. *I will not be yoked* refers to both *men that work iniquity* and *the choicest of them.* Observe the addition: *of them,* to prevent your thinking that those called by such a name are actually the Lord's elect. Those seen to be prominent among evil men as ringleaders in crimes, robber-chiefs, and controllers of all desperadoes, are by far the most wicked.

5. *The just man shall correct me in mercy, and shall reprove me: but the oil of the sinner shall not fatten my head.* Having asked for a watch over his tongue and condemned excuses for sins, the holy man passes to the second section, in which he prefers rebukes from the just to flattery from sinners. He briefly explained the nature of the just man's correction with the words: *In mercy,* for the holy man does not rebuke in anger, but reproaches in love. Even if he gives the appearance of anger, he always adopts an inner attitude of reconciliation; in Paul's advice: *Brethren, if a man be overtaken in any fault, you who are spiritual instruct such a one in the spirit of meekness, considering yourself, lest you also be tempted.*[10] So good men regularly prefer to be reproached by the good, rather than be lauded by the flattery of the wicked; in the words of Scripture: *Better are the wounds of a friend than the ready kisses of an enemy.*[11] Next comes: *But the oil of the sinner shall not fatten my head.* Oil is often cited in both the good and the bad sense; in the good sense, as in the gospel-words: *But when you fast, anoint your head with oil, and wash your face,*[12] and in Psalm 44: *Therefore God, your God, has anointed you with the oil of gladness above your fellows.*[13] When used in this good sense, oil is the source of splendour, the nurture of light,

dispensing brightness and salvation alike. It is used in the bad sense as in this passage. *The oil of the sinner* is simulated love, extending to words alone; by flattery and soft utterances it gently sinks into our minds like the richness of oil, softening the hard edge of truth, and instead leading us in mere display to harmful thoughts of feigned love. As another psalm had it: *His words are smoother than oil, and the same are darts.*[14] Solomon too says: *The words of flatterers are soft, and finally they reach even to the inner parts of the belly.*[15] So we must always choose the injunctions which do not draw us to love of the world, but beckon us to the commands of the Godhead. The gospel-passage about the ten virgins[16] can also be aptly cited here: the five virgins who devoted their most worthy actions to the Lord, keeping their hearts glowing with the oil of teeming charity, offered themselves as the brightest of lamps to the Lord's sight. We must justly believe that they were taken to task by the just, as the prophet says here, yet none the less reproached with the zealous spirit of mercy. But the other five virgins unhappily listened to the voices of flatterers, and their heads were wholly fattened by self-deception; so their lamps went out, and they were not admitted, as it was unfitting that their foul lives be offered to the Lord of true light. Blessed Augustine in Book 59 of his *Questions*[17] has expounded this parable aptly at greater length. So let us ponder how dangerous flattery is; we know that it shuts us out from the Lord.

For my prayer is still in the things which please them. This short verse is dependent on the earlier sense. He says: *The oil of the sinner shall not fatten my head,* and follows this by adding: *For my prayer is still in the things that please them.* When he says that his prayer is still in the things that please them, he suggests that his conversion is not yet perfect, for in his prayer he was longing to attain the things to which they aspired. His entreaty was that he should become a stranger to all such things, so that he should not anoint his head with the oil of the sinner, that is, with the flattery of evil persuasion.

6. *Their judges have been swallowed up close to the rock: they shall hear my words, for they have prevailed. The rock* here as in many places denotes the Lord Christ, close to whom heretical teachers stand as judges of their people, and are submerged by a sudden devouring.

They fall into the depths because they choose not to stand on the rock. What point is there in standing close to its firm foundation when they are seen not to establish themselves on its solidity? Jerome has translated *close to,* and father Augustine has followed this in his commentary;[18] so none must dare to impugn the reading approved by the authority of such men. This rendering is seen to denote the extreme infidelity of heretics, for though they baptize, communicate, and read the sacred books as we do, they are said to stand close to the rock, but not upon it. Only those who refuse to erect frail foundations on sand establish themselves on the firm base. Next comes: *They shall hear my words, for they have prevailed.* He says that his words expressed by the text of this book have been heard by heretics. By how many passages are they refuted, by how many warnings are they rebuked to gain correction, and not to linger in their foul deeds! This statement teaches us most explicitly of the total guilt of those who hear the Lord's words, yet scorn with evil frowardness to carry them out. After so many warnings they could have acknowledged them if only they had not decided to cleave to their own opinions.

7. *As when the thickness of the earth is vomited on the ground, our bones are scattered by the side of hell.* Earlier he spoke of heretics and tyrants who refused to listen to the Lord's words; now he turns to the martyrs whom they ravaged in savage persecution. When the earth's thickness vomits forth,[19] it spreads diseases, poisons the air, and spreads far and wide a contagion dangerous to men. Similarly the sacrilegious arrogance of tyrants afflicted the bodies of the martyrs with the putrescence of their malice. These martyrs the prophet aptly terms his *bones,* for clearly they are the strongest foundations of the Christian faith. Through the Lord's help their praiseworthy constancy was neither overcome by punishment nor softened by lengthy persecution. Observe too how the refinements of the words run on like the sweetest honey; he did not say "into hell," for though they appear to die by the general lot of mankind, eternal life is accorded them.

8. *But to thee, O Lord, Lord, are my eyes: in thee have I put my trust: take not away my soul.* After speaking of the frailty of the human race, he now takes refuge in divine remedies. He reverses the order, and

asks that his soul be freed because he has put his hope in the Lord. As we have often said, you will often find this in the holy Scriptures, the reason sometimes preceding the plea and sometimes following immediately after. It is the practice of the blessed to seek to be delivered from this world; as another psalm puts it: *Bring my soul out of prison,*[20] and elsewhere we read: *Having a desire to be dissolved and to be with Christ, a thing by far the better.*[21] So here the prophet asks: *Take not away my soul;* supply "from your blessings; let my hope rest constantly on You, and my eyes ever regard You."

9. *Keep me from the snare which they have laid for me, and from the stumbling-blocks that work iniquity.* With the expressions, *snares* and *stumbling-blocks,* the prophet embraced in brief compass the ills of the whole world. He begs to be protected from them, so that he cannot be cut off by the ambush which they embody. *Snares* are the various desires of the flesh by which human minds are imprisoned in alluring bonds; *stumbling-blocks* originate with troublesome brethren who shun sacred love through contentiousness and pride. Once they chance to forfeit that preeminent gift of love, how can they gain a similar reward? Observe that he mentions stumbling-blocks after snares, for that most wicked one of old, once he has failed to deceive by snares, starts to remove from us the grace of the Godhead by means of stumbling-blocks.

10. *The wicked shall fall in his net: I am alone until I pass.* Observe the fate from which he earlier sought to be rescued so that he should not be yoked with such men, and note how the words harmonise aptly with the comparison which is drawn. Those who are encircled and enclosed by sinners will fall into the devil's net. We read however of nets in the good sense, when they trapped one hundred and fifty-three fish at the Lord's command;[22] these are known to have been a foreshadowing of the holy Church. Blessed are they who are numbered among those fish, and unhappy those who fall among this number of the wicked. *Retia* (nets) are so called because they retain (*retinentia*).[23] He added: *I am alone until I pass.* The man who is alone is he who does not (in his earlier words) walk in harness with the wicked, who confesses the holy Trinity as one God and Lord, who sets his hope in no other but the Lord alone. *Until I pass,* in other words, as long as I shall

linger in this world. The blessed are said to pass through the world like travellers, for they have no interest in its delights.

Conclusion Drawn From the Psalm

Dearest brothers, we are aware of the nature of the danger if we speak without circumspection. We know how much we ought to fear what the most holy prophet fears. When does our tongue not stealthily entice us into empty speech, or inspire us with longing for falsehood? It is the tongue which often induces us towards vices, which we can overcome with complete safety only by the single means of devoting it at all times to the Lord's praises. Let it ever speak the words in which it cannot err, let it perform the work which will benefit the soul, let it minister reverently to the Creator. We set a guard upon our mouth if we ponder diligently the Lord's commands. The person who refuses to leave the good unspoken says nothing which is evil; no error can steal in where heavenly truth overflows. If evil thoughts are withdrawn from us, if most foul deeds are set aside, if we isolate ourselves from intercourse with the wicked, then in the prophet's words we shall become *alone* for the Lord, since we are wholly uninvolved in most wicked designs.

Commentary on Psalm 141

1. *The understanding of David: a prayer when he was in the cave.* The theme of the psalm is contained in this heading, but an apposite indication of a spiritual meaning is revealed to us through physical parallels. David, the son of Jesse, fled from the prince Saul, and when he lay hidden in a cave he uttered a prayer[1] which he revealed that the Lord Christ would make in the flesh before His passion. When *understanding* prefaces this prayer, the comparison is shown to refer to Him who avoided His persecutors as He prayed and hid himself by moving to various places. This was so that the Son of God could fulfil the prom-

ise which He had made about Himself through the prophets, and reveal the truth of the incarnation which He had assumed; for this psalm includes the words of the Lord Saviour when He sought to avoid the most wicked madness of the Jews. So the flight of David was rightly placed in the heading to point to the persecution by the Jews, for David, as we have often said, denotes both that earthly king and the King of heaven. Thus in the one name is contained the meaning of the two themes. We must also remember that this is the fifth psalm labelled: *A prayer.*

Division of the Psalm

In the first section, the Lord Christ cries to the Father, recounting the wicked tricks of the persecution by the Jews. In the second, He prays to be delivered from the prison of hell, for the trust of all the faithful hung on His resurrection.

Explanation of the Psalm

2. *I cried to the Lord with my voice: with my voice I made supplication to God.* In the holy person of His venerable incarnation, He says in His customary manner that He has cried to the Lord with His voice. This figure is called *pleonasm,*[2] or excess of words, as in our usual phrases, "I made with my hands," "I heard with my ears," and the like. So that we should not regard the cry as fleeting, He added: *I made supplication,* which is performed with repeated entreaty.

3. *In his sight I shall pour out my prayer: and before him I declare my trouble.* How pure and sweet was the prayer poured out in the Father's sight, like a stream of clear water! Clearly it was issued not to sink to the depths but to reach the height of heavenly devotion. The phrase, *in his sight,* was used because the Godhead regards goodly prayers as a kind of facial gesture, and though our will cannot be observed by men it is clearly closely watched by the Godhead. The nature of this prayer is next explained: it is the *trouble* which awakes genuine and unbroken entreaties. Observe too that these words: *Before him I declare my trouble,* are spoken with the assurance of innocence, for those afflictions known to be imposed unjustly could be declared in His pres-

ence. So the devoted Advocate declares His troubles before the Father, so as to be able to obtain pardon for our sins. Note also the four modes of prayer in these two verses, as Paul states them: *Urge first of all that supplications, prayers, intercessions and thanksgivings be made.*[3]

4. *When my spirit fails me, then too thou knowest my paths.* This part of the verse follows on from the previous words. His phrase: *When my spirit fails me,* we are to understand as if He were saying: *Before him I declare my trouble, when my spirit fails me.* He wants us to realise that the troubles which He claims to be proclaiming before the Lord are many and most oppressive. But since we read that on no occasion did His spirit fail, for He fulfilled everything by voluntary suffering, we must interpret the phrase as spoken on behalf of His members. This type of explanation we know was devised with foresight by our forbears, when a person says something which cannot be in keeping with his character, as in the phrase: *And my offences are not hidden from thee.*[4] Then too the faithful spoke in this way in Psalm 83: *My soul longeth and fainteth for the courts of the Lord,*[5] and elsewhere: *My eyes have failed for thy word, saying, When wilt thou comfort me?*[6] And in the next psalm the prophet is to say: *Hear me speedily, O Lord: my spirit hath fainted away.*[7]

On this way wherein I walked, they have hidden snares for me. As we have often said, the devil hides a snare close to the way to deceive those who have dared to quit straight paths. But because the Lord Christ never strayed from His holiness, it was inevitable that the temptations which He suffered on the path of His righteousness were feeble ones, for we know that He never quitted it. He encountered them when the kingdoms of the world were shown to Him by the devil, when His hunger was tried,[8] and on the other occasions when the devil's deceit and the wickedness of evil men dared to attack Him. It was inevitable that the Lord Christ should speak in this fashion, so that even in those early times the truth of His incarnation should be made clear.

5. *I looked on my right hand and beheld, and there was no-one that would know me. Flight hath failed me, and there is no-one that hath regard to my soul.* When He says: *I looked on my right hand,* He means at the time of the way of the cross, because He could descry none of the faithful there. They were not seen standing at His right, because they had scattered through bodily fear. In the words of Scripture:

Strike the shepherd, and the sheep of the flock will be scattered.[9] Next comes: *And there was no-one that would know me,* that is, that would recognise in Him the divinity which voluntarily endured all these sufferings in the flesh which He assumed. In that flesh He said: *I have power to lay down my life, and I have power to take it up again.*[10] If they had recognised the Lord Christ in that confusion, they could certainly have been seen also on His right hand. He added: *Flight hath failed me, and there is no-one that hath regard to my soul.* He says that flight failed Him when He allowed Himself to be killed at the hands of wicked men; when flight fails, danger of death can in no sense be avoided. No-one had regard for His soul when no consolation was accorded Him, but He was left alone to His passion, though He was to die for the salvation of all. Thus the order of the betrayal has been recounted in this brief and most subtle interpretation of the words.

6. *I cried to thee, O Lord: I said, Thou art my hope, my portion in the land of the living.* He comes to the second section, in which He begs to escape the ambush of His enemies, so that the hearts of the faithful may rejoice at the gift of His resurrection. He cried, setting His hope in the Lord, when He said: *Father, into thy hands I commend my spirit.*[11] Next comes: *My portion in the land of the living.* The particular proof of this is the passage in which He said to the thief as He hung on the cross: *Amen I say to you, this day thou wilt be with me in Paradise;*[12] for Paradise is that land of the living which only the blessed will happily enter to live there for untroubled eternity. He speaks humbly and for all of us when He says that His portion is in the land of the living, for we know that it wholly belongs to Him. The remark made about the apostles is similar: *Father, I will that where I am, they also may be with me.*[13]

7. *Attend to my prayer, for I am brought very low.* He did well to say: *I am brought very low,* for as Paul puts it: *He emptied himself, taking the form of a servant, being made in the likeness of men, and in habit found as a man.*[14] In addition He was certainly humbled further when He became *obedient unto death, even to the death of the cross.*[15] If the wondrous height of His divinity had not bent low in the true body which He assumed, how could He have been crucified for the salvation of all, when He orders heaven and earth with astounding powers?

Deliver me from my persecutors, for they are stronger than I. When

He says: *Deliver me*, He is not demonstrating the weakness of His own divinity, but revealing the love of the Father; for though He had the power, as He says, to lay down His life and to take it up again,[16] He fittingly showed honour to His Father's majesty in order to represent us, maintaining the reverence of a beloved Son, *in whom the Father was well pleased*.[17] In the gospel He says: *Father, glorify me*.[18] He also cries out from the cross: *O God, my God, look upon me, why hast thou forsaken me?*[19] This was to reveal clearly the lowliness of the flesh, so as to refute the impious teachings of the Manichean. So He prays that He may be delivered by divine power from the persecuting Jews, who had become so stronger physically that they laid hands on Him and rejoiced in His death. But those most wretched of men tried to achieve all this because they saw in Him not the power of divinity but merely the bodily appearance. Paul says of them: *If they had known, they would never have crucified the Lord of glory*.[20]

8. *Bring my soul out of prison to confess thy name.* Our forbears wished us to understand *prison* here in two senses: either as the painful hardships of this world which we suffer through being set in the body, or instead as the prison of the lower world, which it is impossible to escape through the law of the human condition. The better interpretation is that of the world below, because of the hope of resurrection which with repeated entreaty He prays may come, as He begs in another psalm: *Let not the pit shut her mouth upon me*.[21] The word for prison, *carcer*, is the equivalent of *arcer*, because it prevents (*arceat*)[22] the emergence from it of those who are confined. The reason follows why He longs to free himself from this prison: *To confess thy name.* It was when it became clear that He had been brought out from the prison of the world below by the miracle of the resurrection that a confession of praise to the Father was made by all the faithful. The expression, *bring out*, denotes that He was translated from the region of death, the lowest depths, to the realms of heaven.

The just wait for me, until thou reward me. This is the confession foretold concerning the Lord's resurrection. When all the apostles were thrown into turmoil by Christ's death, they waited for just the moment when they could acknowledge the glory of the promised resurrection, and strengthen the hearts of all who were fearful. Observe the words: *Until thou reward me*, for the glory of the resurrection was nothing other than the reward for the most blessed passion. Paul says of this reward: *For which cause God has exalted him, and has given him a name which is above all names: that in the name of Jesus every knee should bow, of those that are in heaven, on earth, and under the earth; and that every tongue should confess that the Lord Jesus is in the glory of God the Father.*[23] The word *until* denotes the period of three days, after which the devotion of the just rejoiced at His resurrection. This was certainly bestowed on the Lord Christ uniquely in the humanity which He assumed; His resurrection strengthened the hearts of the just. Now let us ponder, if we can harness some insight, the clemency of our Lord, which both redeemed us from the enemy and unceasingly teaches us not to be taken captive again. He makes His rule our teaching for each day, for the purpose of His deigning to humble himself was so that we should not in the slightest degree aspire to the devil's spirit of pride. In that pride lies the fall, in humility there is always the way upwards; pride is the seed-bed of death, humility the preliminary to eternal life. So let us entreat the almighty Son that as He has accorded us a wholesome example of prayer, He may mercifully bestow on us the outcome of this most holy imitation.

Conclusion Drawn From the Psalm

This marks the conclusion of the line of psalms prefaced with the heading: *A prayer*, so now at the end of them we must make some summary observations so that through the Lord's help we may obtain a salutary stimulus to hasten to the remedy appointed to us. We must especially follow the commandments, and signing our lips with the seal of the cross we must pray to the Lord that He may cleanse our mouths which are disfigured with human foulness; in Isaiah's words: *I have unclean lips, and I dwell in the midst of people that have unclean lips.*[24] Next we must pray in words not such as human longings prompt, but those which the Godhead Himself has granted as a remedy for our wickedness. Prayer itself must come from a humble, meek, pure heart; it must confess its sins without making excuses, and in the course of bitter tears show trust in the most sweet pity of the Lord. It must not seek earthly aims, but desire heavenly ones. It must be sequestered from desires of the body, and attach itself solely to the divine. In short, it must be wholly spiritual, bestowing nothing but tears on the flesh. In so far as it is lawful, seek to behold in mental contemplation Him whom you entreat, and then you realise what sort of person you should be in offering yourself prostrate before Him. He is, as Paul says: *the Blessed and only Mighty, King of kings and Lord of lords, who alone has immortality and inhabits light inaccessible, whom no man has seen nor can see.*[25]

So such is the mighty Lord whom we should approach with all fear or love, directing our mental sight on Him in such a way as to realise that such splendour, brightness, brilliance and majesty as is conceivable to the human mind is all inferior to God, who with goodness beyond compare controls all His creatures. We must not with false presumption within ourselves form some mental picture of Him, for the hidden substance of God who made all things cannot be grasped in its essence by the knowledge which creatures possess. God has no shape, no outline; His nature cannot be assessed, nor His power grasped, and His devotion is unique. As has been most aptly remarked of Him, we can say what God is not, but we cannot grasp what He is. So we are to pray to Him who is almighty and without beginning or end, who traverses and fills all parts of the universe and every creature, but in such a way that He is wholly within Himself everywhere. He forsakes evil men not by His presence but by the power of His grace. Father Augustine when writing to Dardanus explained this at greater length.[26] The words of the prophet warn us in salutary fashion to make haste: *Come, let us adore and fall down before the Lord: let us lament before God* (then he added, so that we should not be left wholly floundering and trembling) *who made us;*[27] so that once we recognise that we have been created by Him, we may pray with confidence to our Maker. Then the humble plea which we are to utter in divine praise we virtually realise as we pray, for we gain a merciful hearing from the Lord, provided that what we ask for is in our interest. No-one is rebuffed coldly from heaven's generosity if grace is lent him to entreat with a simple and a committed heart, for a person feels that he has gained pardon to the degree that he knows that he has shed devoted tears. There is this further mark of our progress: the more a person realises that he loves and fears God, the more necessary he finds it to draw near to divine help. Thus by the Lord's kindness all the devil's guile is defeated, and by His pity our sins are overcome.

We have said as much about prayer as our mean intelligence and the nature of the occasion have demanded. If anyone desires to gain the fullest abundance of satisfaction on this subject, he must read the most eloquent Cassian, who in his ninth and tenth *Conferences*[28] has discussed the types of prayer with such power and quality that the holy Spirit seems clearly to have spoken through his mouth.

Commentary on Psalm 142

1. *A psalm of David when his son pursued him.* The history of this is very well known from reading *the Book of Kings;* for David's son Absalom is known to have driven his father from the kingdom, and irreligiously pursued him.[1] A parallel is being offered here, as some commentators claim, to the situation of every Christian afflicted in the bitterness of this world by the savage sins which are so to say his sons. But opposed to them is the healing repentance which this psalm is shown to contain. Remember however that the history of this has already been recounted in Psalm 3; but there Absalom was named because the psalmist wished the example he offers to be applied only to Judas, whereas here he goes unnamed so that each of the faithful, as we have already said, may apply the words to his own faults.

Division of the Psalm

True, the prophet has been exercised by pondering the large numbers of penitents; but the closer he draws to the praises to come, the more he turns in remorse of heart to the font of repentance, so that once he has been suitably cleansed in that solitary refuge, he may appear wholly clean before the Lord's sight. And rightly so, to avoid hearing that verdict which spells disgrace: *But to the sinner God has said, Why dost thou declare my justices?*[2] So in his initial prayer he asks the Lord Christ not to enter into judgment against His servant, but prays that the Lord's mercy may aid his troubled heart. In the second prayer he asks that he may swiftly attain pardon, so that once he has been guided on to the path of truth, he may be freed from the snares of his enemies.

Explanation of the Psalm

Hear, O Lord, my prayer: give ear to my entreaty in thy truth: hear me in thy justice. If we do not probe deeper, the sections of this verse seem at odds with each other, for whereas the prophet initially begs humbly that his prayer be heeded, he subsequently asks that he be heard according to the Lord's justice. Undoubtedly, however, the purport of the whole is tearful confession, especially as this psalm is known to be directed to the humility of penitents. Truth and justice are attributes of the Lord, militating against disputation with the suppliant, and against haling to court one who condemns himself first. It is the proud whom the Lord hales to judgment, for they believe that they have a good case. Only the one who has recourse to entreaties is known to escape judgment. The divine Majesty is not so harsh or severe in exercising power as to seek to afflict those who in the world torture themselves with recollection of their sins; for note what follows.

2. *And enter not into judgment with thy servant, for in thy sight no man living will be justified.* The intent with which he sought the Lord's justice is clear, for he now says: *Enter not into judgment with thy servant;* if justice had entailed judgment, he could not have sought what he feared. The fact that the Judge is told: *Enter not into judgment with thy servant,* should not trouble you, for the Lord Himself employs this manner of speech when He says: *Judge between me and my vineyard.*[3] Next comes: *For in thy sight no man living will be justified.* The reason is given for his unwillingness to enter into judgment with the Lord; not merely respect for His power but even the very canon of justice seems to be feared. As Scripture has it: *God hath concluded all in unbelief, that he may have mercy on all.*[4] When he speaks of no man living, he denotes mankind in general including children, who are subject to original sin unless cleansed by the water of regeneration. So Job says with total truth: *No-one is pure before thee, not even the child whose life is lived for one day upon the earth.*[5] Psalm 50 has already stated: *For behold, I was conceived in iniquities, and in sins did my mother conceive me.*[6] Whose justice will be so great that he has not sinned at some stage or period of life, when we are held in subjection through the transmission of sin, and add to it by daily failures, so that we can never be free by our own efforts, but only by divine grace? So the

Pelagian heresy must cease to proclaim nonsense, for it was condemned by so many utterances of divine Scripture before it broke out.

3. *For the enemy hath persecuted my soul: he hath humbled my life on earth.* Though the heading seemed to refer to Absalom, the enemy is described impersonally, so that we must understand this passage also of the devil. He is humbled on earth because his life is vitiated in works of the flesh, not in praiseworthy humility but in sinful decline. The penitent rightly spoke these words to indicate his affliction emphatically; in another psalm he says: *For I did eat ashes like bread, and mingled my drink with weeping.*[7]

4. *He has set me in darkness as those that have died in the world: and my spirit is in anguish within me: my heart within me is troubled. I remembered the days of old. He has set me* means "He has reckoned me" like those raging enemies who despise a person they hate, as though they consider him as already dead and buried. David was indeed set in darkness, for after the high dignity of kingship he suffered the injustice of persecution. He was regarded *as one dead in the world,* for no respect was accorded him as prophet or king, nor even the love owed to a father; the dead in the world are those known to have failed through their sins. So this man, endowed as he is with so many blessings, rightly laments that he is despised to the point of being thought wholly beyond vindication. Next comes: *And my spirit is in anguish within me, my heart within me is troubled.* An anguished spirit suggests proximity of danger, a troubled heart attests that his human wisdom is disordered, so that he set his hope more firmly in the Lord through having no confidence in his own powers. He added: *I remembered the days of old.* His heart was rightly troubled, for he was aware of his monstrous sins. *The days of old* are those stained with the ancient complexion of the old man. Just as newness of life[8] here and now begets innocence, so *the days of old* witness to sins committed.

5. *And I meditated on all thy works, and I shall meditate on the works of thy hands.* This saving recognition returned to heal him, so that when he recalled God's works he forgot his hardships. He means by the Lord's works those by which He created heaven and earth in a wondrous dispensation, those by which He bestowed blessings on the patriarchs, those by which He transported the Israelites across the sea. He says that he has often repeated mention of these so that the sweet-

ness in reading them may efface the world's bitterness. We must welcome this example appointed as the greatest remedy, so that a like healing may similarly be our salvation.

6. *I stretched forth my hands to thee: my soul is as earth without water unto thee.* Though he has prophesied the Lord Saviour's coming in countless passages, here too by stretching out his hands he formed the shape of the holy cross. The person who prays with hands extended imitates the cross of the Redeemer which was inflicted as punishment by the faithless Jews, but was none the less bestowed on believers as salvation. When Moses was warring with the Amalekites, this was how he fared: he conquered when he stretched forth his hands, he was defeated if he let his arms fall.[9] The comparison follows in which he says that his soul longs for God as the parched earth often absorbs abundant rain. The beginning of Psalm 41 is similar: *As the hart pants after fountains of water, so my soul pants for thee, O God.*[10] Notice that he said: *Unto thee*, not to anyone else, so that you would not attach this longing to evil desires.

7. *Hear me speedily, O Lord: my spirit hath fainted away. Turn not away thy face from me, lest I be like unto them that go down into the pit.* After completing the exordium, he passes to the most sorrowful narration,[11] asking for the speediest aid of a shower of mercy so that he should not be reduced to dust by being spurned by the Lord and be scattered by the wind of pride, becoming a stranger to the land of promise. So that he could be heard more speedily, he says that the spirit within him has fainted away; this often happens through excessive afflictions to those weighed down by the burden of various sufferings. As this same penitent says in Psalm 37: *My heart is troubled, my strength hath left me.*[12] Next comes: *Turn not away thy face from me, lest I be like unto them that go down into the pit.* Earlier God had turned away His face because of the arrogance of sinning, but the prophet now begs that He look upon him because he prostrated himself in remorseful entreaties; for it befits the Lord's mercy to look kindly on the humble since He despises the hearts of the proud. By *pit* we must understand the lower region of hell, where the wicked are to be plunged into eternal punishment. So such men are matched with those who spurned God's power, and who befouling the images in which they were created assumed the shape of the devil's condemnation. *Go*

down is a good description, for those who deserve to enter that pit are plunged to the lowest depths. So he entreats that he should not become like the proud, by lamenting his sins with humble satisfaction.

8. *Cause me to hear thy mercy in the morning, for in thee have I hoped. To hear thy mercy* refers to the Lord's clemency widely known through the whole world, by which He lends help to suppliants, and kindness to the afflicted. The prophet seeks to hear the gospel words: *Son, thy sins are forgiven thee.*[13] *The morning* denotes the time of pardon, for it brings light to the mind when it descends on it with blessed outcome. It is rightly called the morning, for it comes after the darkness of sins, when guilt is forgiven. Alternatively it refers to the news of the resurrection, when the angel said to Mary: *Go, tell his disciples and Peter that he has risen from the dead, as he said.*[14] The reason also follows, which must hold good: there was hope in Him who cannot deceive those who show praiseworthy trust in Him. Observe too that by such reasoning he strengthens his other requests that follow. This figure is called *aetiologia* or explanation of the cause.[15]

Make the way known to me wherein I should walk, for I have lifted up my soul to thee, O Lord. When he asks God to make the way of life known to him, he shows that the way is regarded as unknown to men. It is His lamp which reveals this road, His light which opens up these paths, for *He enlightens everyone who comes into this world.*[16] As has already been said to the penitent in Psalm 31: *I will give thee understanding, and I will instruct thee in this way in which thou shalt go.*[17] So the prophet rightly asks that the Lord should reveal to him the way of salvation, and that he should always retain knowledge of it so that it never quits his heart at any time. Attached to this is a solemn confession; what makes us deserve to obtain our requests is if we do not let our souls sink under the weight of the flesh towards the world, and we ever raise them to the Lord with the aid of the spirit.

9. *Deliver me from my enemies, O Lord: to thee have I fled.* Though the psalm-heading suggests that the prophet apparently speaks of physical foes, we must interpret this as a reference to demonic enemies who continually encompass the faithful so as to deprive them of hope in the Godhead; in Paul's words: *Your wrestling is not against flesh and blood, but against principalities and powers, the rulers of this darkness.*[18] He says: *To thee have I fled,* words uttered only by those who obey His commands. When Adam disobeyed, he fled from the Lord; so here in

contrast is revealed the attitude of a committed mind, for after the guilt of sin he says that he has not fled from the Lord, but taken refuge with Him.

10. *Teach me to do thy will, for thou art my God.* Since he longed to be the pupil of so great a Master, he did not wish to err in any way. He says: *Teach me,* as one who is ignorant, a novice, making no claims to virtue, an attitude expressed by Paul's words: *If any man thinks that he knows anything, he has not yet known as he ought to know.*[19] He added: *For thou art my God.* It is a trusting entreaty, a fitting approach, to request a blessing from the kindly Lord on the grounds that He is the Lord of the petitioner.

Thy good spirit shall lead me into the right path. Let us examine the meaning of *Thy good spirit.* It is being pointed out by this term that the holy Spirit is God, for Scripture says: *None is good but God.*[20] We read the same thing of the Son, as in: *I am the good shepherd.*[21] In this way by the sharing of epithets the equality of the holy Trinity and its power are always made clear. The good Spirit shall lead us into the right path when He subjects our bodies to His rules, so that whereas they had become misshapen through the distortion of sins, they cease to be wayward by reason of those instructions. This cannot however be achieved by human power; it is He who deigned also to create us who straightens us by recreating us. Alternatively, the right path denotes the land of the age to come, on which the upright will walk, and will ever rejoice with the Lord in great exultation.

11. *For thy name's sake, O Lord, thou wilt quicken me in thy justice: thou wilt bring my soul out of trouble.* Here is revealed the grace of the most merciful Godhead, which yields nothing to our merits, but grants everything through His kind generosity. The prophet does not claim that he will be quickened as the result of his own actions, but because of the name of the Lord Christ, for that name truly achieves the salvation of those who faithfully request it. But this quickening will come when he is recommended by grace, and the weight of justice is marvellously intermingled there; for though the Lord bestows all things without charge, it is the role of Justice itself to quicken those who make entreaty, when He sees unclean spirits cruelly attacking them. Next comes: *Thou wilt bring my soul out of trouble.* Holy souls are released from trouble as from prison, when pardon is granted them and they are commanded to quit this world. In this life pious persons

are afflicted and the just are tortured, but once holy people withdraw from this light, it marks the end of their toils. This is why Paul cries: *I desire to be dissolved and to be with Christ.*[22]

12. *And in thy mercy thou wilt destroy my enemies, and thou wilt cut off all them that afflict my soul, for I am thy servant.* The marvellous fullness of his joy is now complete. His enemies are destroyed by mercy when they are withdrawn from wicked purposes by the zeal of remorse. Undoubtedly this indicates people who escape the punishment which is their due by the remedy of supplication. He added: *And thou wilt cut off all them that afflict my soul, for I am thy servant.* Here he now states that at the time of the Judgment the devil and all wicked persons who die maintaining their obduracy will be destroyed in the course of justice. He says that they afflicted his soul because he remained in God's service. It is inevitable that they perish at the Judgment, for they are found to adopt such attitudes in order to persecute the innocent, because they identify them as God's servants. Observe that the prescribed behaviour of the penitent is fulfilled, for after hardships and painful afflictions it ends in exultation.

Conclusion Drawn From the Psalm

The affliction of the suppliants and the course of their blessed tears are brought to a close. But we must examine more carefully the meaning of this seventh prayer of penitents. Beginning with Psalm 6, he proceeded to Psalm 31, then to 37, to 50, to 101, to 129, and finally here to 142. It is perhaps the case that just as we sin in the seven days which represent the extent of a week in the world, so we may be saved by the gift of healing repentance through this same number. But as we have often reminded ourselves, we must pay great attention to the fact that these psalms begin with hardships and end with joys, to ensure that no-one despairs of the forgiveness which he realised lay in the prayers themselves. They are most sacred advocates, heavenly patrons, for they reveal the path of salvation to those enmeshed in the toils of sins. Though these psalms individually warn us to lament our sins, and through the Lord's promise lead us to the hope of joys, there lies before us that most efficacious model of the entreaty of the Ninevites,[23] when the whole population grieved, and the whole flock fasted, and the communal affliction had such power as to be able to overcome the truth of the prophet's words. From being fearful they became untroubled, from being downcast they were joyful; it was established that they were condemned to death, but they were restored to life. So let us aspire to the repentance which is the saving remedy of the human race, the consolation of those who weep, the seed of blessed joys, for it bestows the most sure hope on one and all, and imparts to suppliants *en masse* the gift of heavenly grace.

COMMENTARY ON PSALM 143

1. *David to Goliath.* The historical event represented by this heading took place in the early life of the prophet, before he became king, but the importance of its typology summons it from that outworn context to our attention to enable you to realise that everything uttered and written in the psalms bears an allegorical meaning, as we shall state more explicitly in the conclusion. It is fitting for us to be aware that this war of David was a prophecy of the Lord Christ's struggle. Just as David laid low Goliath by using a rock as the weapon of war, so the power of the devil was overcome by the Rock which is the Lord Christ.[1] These parallels are accordingly observed in this psalm as well. Not only is the victory described here which is contained in the Book of Kings,[2] nor are thanks offered for that victory alone; there are many comments apposite to the Lord Christ's struggle which we shall duly expound in their proper place. So let us be aware that this is the fourth of the psalms[3] which denote allegorically the future deeds of the Lord through the actions of David. They must accordingly be regarded with reverence and wonder throughout the whole world, since they are hallowed by sharing the glory of the number of the gospels.

Division of the Psalm

After the slaying of Goliath, which we have said was fulfilled as a deed of typological significance, the prophet in the first section thanks the Lord, saying that he has been delivered from danger in the fight now over. He prays that the Lord's coming may be swiftly announced, for through it the devil was overcome, and the consummation of the spiritual conflict waged in figure by Goliath was achieved, for at that moment the faithful were freed from great danger. In the second section, the prophet promises to hymn the Lord in the New and the Old Testaments, since he has been freed from most wicked enemies who reposed their happiness in success in this world; he states that only those whose Lord is their God are truly happy.

Explanation of the Psalm

Blessed is the Lord my God, who teacheth my hands to fight, and my fingers to war. Though victorious over a most savage enemy, and though prevailing over monstrous vices, after winning his triumph, a time when men wax especially proud and sinful, he did not preen himself with any boastful claim of self-assurance, but attributed it all to the Lord's powers, and hymned His praises with pious joy. He added the reason for this blessing: *He teacheth my hands to fight.* The Lord taught his hands to fight when he fittingly did everything to ensure the outcome of the victory so greatly desired. Clearly David was not practised in the use of arms, or well rehearsed; he had long been despised, it seemed, even in his father's house, but he suddenly appeared before his enemy as an outstanding figure. Next follows: *And my fingers to war.* Just as earlier we interpreted *hands* as activity, so here we can perhaps interpret *fingers* as saving thoughts which leap forth from our hearts like rays of the sun, as they strive cleverly to lay hold of necessary causes of things. *Fingers* is a word with many meanings, but we realise that we must interpret it according to varying contexts. So in the passage of Solomon: *Who hath poised with three fingers the bulk of the earth,*[4] several authorities think that the phrase is to be applied to the holy Trinity. The Fathers have sought to interpret *this is the finger of God*[5] in Exodus as a reference to the holy Spirit. Similarly in that book the words: *Moses received two tablets written with the finger of God.*[6] So too with the other passages which you will find varying in this way. Alternatively, *my fingers to war* bears the same sense as *my hands to fight.* This figure is called *epimone* in Greek, and *repetitio crebra sententiae* in Latin.[7] We use it well when we say that the ancient enemy is destroyed by the sign of the cross, and crushed by the firm pressure of the Rock.

2. *My mercy, and my refuge: my support and my deliverer: my protector, and I will hope in him, subduing peoples beneath me.* These titles are undoubtedly the outcome of kindnesses bestowed. Because it would have been a lengthy business to unravel the numerous examples in a single psalm, they are recounted in brief compass. This figure is called *hypozeuxis*,[8] when different words are aptly used for individual purposes. Certainly the Lord showed David *mercy* when He chose him through the prophet Samuel for the distinction of kingship, though he was the last of the brothers; *refuge*, when He gave him a stratagem against his most monstrous enemy, with the result that he felled with a stone the giant whom he could not have fought with weight of arms. He was David's *support* when He caused Saul to accept him as son-in-law; thus after earlier being subordinate in the rank of servant, David was joined in status to his lord. He was his *deliverer* when He rescued him from the hazard of the king's anger. He was his *protector* when as David lay hidden in the cave, he obtained the right to exact vengeance on king Saul. So all that had been granted him by the Lord's generosity is fittingly recounted by these individual titles. Observe too what follows: *And I will hope in him.* After receiving such great blessings, the holy man was aware that he must not abandon such hope, but the more he had received from the Lord, the more he sought. He added: *Subduing peoples beneath me.* Either David speaks here of the future, because he was to rule the people, or preferably he relates that peoples are to be made subject to him, because he saw in the spirit that they were to become subject to his seed the Lord Christ. As Psalm 2 puts it: *Ask of me, and I will give thee the nations for thy inheritance.*[9]

3. *Lord, what is man that thou art made known to him, or the son of man that thou makest account of him?* Let us listen to the king governing his devoted[10] feelings: though protected by the Lord's mighty grace after so many signal signs of virtues, he not merely confesses his own insignificance, but also makes clear through his own case that the human race is unworthy of divine blessings. When he asks: *What is man?* he reduces him to nothing, like dust shifted by a breath of wind, like mud melted into liquid earth which cannot achieve solidity. So *what is man?* is to be intoned as scornful enquiry. To it is addressed a

laudatory response: *That thou art made known to him.* How remarkable it was that the Creator of heaven and earth deigned to come to men's notice through the true body which He assumed, so that the hidden nature of the Godhead beyond our reckoning became known to the upright in faith! This figure is called *erōtēsis*, a question framed in contrast to the contrary.[11] We must similarly ask: *Or the son of man?* and a similar reply is to be made: *That thou makest account of him*—referring to none other than Your sheep, the number of the predestined, the blessed Jerusalem in which the just will ever rejoice in contemplation of the Lord.

4. *Man was made like to vanity: his days pass away like a shadow.* He explains by definition his earlier brief question, *What is man?* He is *made*, not fashioned, *like to vanity.* When Adam was created, he was truthful, simple, pure, immortal; but once he sinned at the prompting of the woman, he was *made like to vanity*, for he became subject to change, and mortal. We call a thing vain which abandons its substance and vanishes into thin air like smoke or a shadow. He himself offered a comparison to this with the words: *His days pass away like a shadow;* this is a justifiable comparison, for a shadow is visible but has no solid permanence, for when the body which forms it departs, the shadow too fades and is lost. Such would be the life of men after Adam's sin if it had not been restored by the Lord's kindness.

5. *Lord, bend down thy heavens, and descend: touch the mountains, and they shall smoke.* He has burst into open prophecy concerning the Lord Christ, broadening a little the statement which earlier he made briefly: *That thou art made known to him.* He became known to man's gaze precisely when he appeared in the lowliness of the holy incarnation, for though He remained *in the form of God*, and was coeternal with and equal to God the Father, *He emptied himself, taking the form of a servant.*[12] So the words, *bend down thy heavens, and descend*, are justified, for these events could not have happened if the divine power had not bent down. The heavens are bent down when the glory and power of the realms above descend to deliver mankind. We must interpret *mountains* here as persons who are arrogant and swollen with Satanic wickedness; the Lord touches them when He affects them with the remorse of devoted conversion. They smoked when they lamented their sins with frequent sighs and perpetual groans.

Thick smoke is exhaled from the mouth when the frame of our mortal body is stirred to the lamentation that brings life.

6. *Light forth thy lightning, and thou shalt scatter them: shoot out thy arrows, and thou shalt trouble them.* Notice that Christ's warfare is now mentioned, and the way in which the devil's horde was overcome is recounted. But though he says that the fighting was with lightning and arrows, it was the Rock which is the Lord Christ which performed this. He confronted the devil's face, since the devil always opposes His commands; that face so hard, shameless and churlish, which before the Lord's coming resisted the truth invincibly, was shattered. This is truly to be called Christ's warfare, for that engagement of David was a foreshadowing, bearing the image of this truth fulfilled. The psalmist says: *Light forth thy lightning, and thou shalt scatter them.* This is the argument called *a coniugatis*,[13] from related words. He lit forth his lightning when He poured the light of His truth into darkened sinners by the preachings of the prophets. *Scattered* means dispersed; those who had been previously devoted to the worship of idols immediately sought refuge in the folds of the Catholic Church. Next comes: *Shoot out thy arrows, and thou shalt trouble them. Arrows* denotes the apostles, who pierced men's hearts with the truth of their proclamations as if they were feathered darts, and thus healed their minds through sacred wounds. *Them* must be taken as the mountains mentioned in the previous verse.

7. *Put forth thy hand from on high: take me out and deliver me from many waters, from the hand of strange children.* At this point he directs his words to the Father. *Hand* denotes the Lord Saviour, for He is the Father's Hand by which all creation exists. He prays that Christ may come to deliver the human race. *From on high* means from the height of power, where He reigns with the Father in equality of strength and unity of substance. So the prophet asks to be freed from the multitude of waters, in other words from the people whose anger swells high, and who are roused, so to say, with the most savage storm. It is widely known that *waters* denotes peoples; as Isaiah says: *Therefore, behold, the Lord will bring upon them the waters of the river, strong and many, the king of the Assyrians.*[14] But the prophet added the identity of the people from whom he sought to be freed with the words: *From the hand of strange children*, that is, from those unable to spare the faithful because

they are born of a hostile father. Though he appears to refer to foreigners here, the passage is better understood of those whose father is the devil, of whom the gospel says: *You are of your father the devil;*[15] for those regarded by the Church, the mother of Catholics, as outsiders are *strange children.*

8. *Whose mouth hath spoken vanity, and their right hand is the right hand of iniquity.* He is still speaking of the people from whom he sought to be freed, so that he may be listened to more speedily because they are cruel and most wicked. Their mouth speaks *vanity,* for they have the audacity to be at odds with God's commands; vanity is all that is opposed to truth. Though the right hand is most often used in the good sense, he uses it here of the wicked, so that it seems to be the left instead; for in their belief that worldly things are outstanding and desirable, they account as successful all that is opposed to virtue.

9. *To thee, O God, I will sing a new canticle: on the psaltery of ten strings I will hymn thee.* He passes to the second range of topics, in which the prophet promises to give thanks to the Lord in a new canticle, after his deliverance from spiritual wickedness and savage men; in this canticle lies instruction for the new man, and the fullness of the Old Law. The new canticle is that of which another psalm says: *Sing ye to the Lord a new canticle;* and to demonstrate this newness he added: *Sing to the Lord, all the earth.*[16] It is rightly called new, for since He was not accepted by the Jews to whom the coming had been promised, He passed over to the Gentiles. It is also new because He absolves us through the water of rebirth, and because of similar features which became clear in the new teaching through the Lord's coming. Next follows: *On the psaltery of ten strings I will hymn thee.* The psaltery of ten strings is the decalogue bestowed on the tribes of the Jews. To show that both Testaments have the one Author, he promised to hymn the Lord Christ in both.

10. *Who givest salvation to kings, who deliverest thy servant David from the malicious sword. Kings* denotes just and truthful persons who as we have said rule their bodies with the Lord's help. So to these kings the Lord grants salvation when he frees them from the vices of the flesh. The Book of Wisdom says of them: *He gives kingship to kings.*[17] *Who deliverest David* has reference to the conflict with Goliath, so that the person who had been delivered physically might be spiritually the victor over monstrous vices as well. We also read of the

Lord's sword, but that is undoubtedly a sword of good intent; as Christ says in the gospel: *I came not to send peace to the earth, but a sword.*[18] So the malicious sword is the devil's, for it cuts us off from blessings, whereas the Lord's sword is kindly, for it separates us from evils.

11. *Deliver me and free me from many waters, and from the hand of strange children, whose mouth hath spoken vanity: and their right hand is the right hand of iniquity.* He has already uttered this verse in the first section;[19] he has repeated it here so that the very repetition may make wicked men more detestable.

12. *Whose sons are as new plants, steadfast in their youth.* In the earlier verses when pronouncing on the wicked deeds of the unholy, he made them loathsome; here he additionally inveighs against the blessings which they appear to possess, so that all that they manifest everywhere is disgraceful, since their very glory is accursed and rejected. The *sons* he mentions are those begotten through the proclamation of debased beliefs. They are compared with new plants, for their sturdiness derives from no proclamation transmitted by the Fathers. Rather, they have sprouted from refined and novel errors; they are steadfast in evil, implanted with wicked roots. Their strength does not derive from prophets, apostles, or any divine authority; but through a deliberately chosen perversity of novelty they have separated themselves from the unity of holy Church. We should observe that the psalmist has transmitted to the faithful this same parallel in Psalm 127, but there he speaks of saints' sons set around the Lord's table, whereas here that most sacred altar is removed from them, because they are not orthodox communicants.

Their daughters are decked out, adorned round about after the similitude of the temple. Let us ponder how subtly and how frequently he has separated heretics from Catholics. In the first comparison he removed the altar from them; now in the second he introduces daughters, which he did not ascribe to the Church in the psalm just mentioned. The first reason for this is that the female sex often indulges in random and vacillating thoughts, not possessing strength of constancy but frequently shifting to different aspirations. Secondly, he says that they do not possess natural beauty, but are decked out according to men's desires. Thirdly, he says that heretics' thoughts or preachings, which he had compared with women, do not embrace the true Church but *the similitude of the temple.* A similitude does not embrace what is true, but bears the appearance of some object which exists.

13. *Their storehouses full, bursting out of this into that. Storehouses,* what are commonly called pantries, denotes the hearts of heretics in which is stored an imposing feast of varied teachings. The more abundantly those hearts are stuffed, the more they emit diverse belchings of most wicked arrogance. If you refute them with authority, they take refuge in perverse interpretations. When with the Lord's help they are overcome also in these, they turn to the stratagems and lies of the sophists; they are vacillating and unstable because they cannot be rooted in the truth. So they are rightly compared with oppressive odours, for they deceive the hearts of simple folk with their stinking words.

Their sheep fruitful in young, abounding in their goings forth. It is more fitting for us to interpret this literally, for it is the prophet's purpose to show that such persons possess only what is fleeting and transient. They are seen to possess prolific flocks while being themselves barren in faith; the word *abounding* means overflowing with water (*unda*). As for the cattle which they are seen to have, he said that they possess them not in their comings in, but in *their goings forth,* for everything forsakes them since they themselves are doomed to perish.

14. *Their oxen fat. There is no collapse of enclosure, nor passage, nor crying out in their streets.* Here their flowing abundance is revealed, for their oxen are not lean with continual toil, but grossly fat in refined leisure, whereas they themselves are found to be thin and unfed with the truth. Next comes: *There is no collapse of enclosure.* The blessedness of the wicked is still being described, but is shown to lie in transient things. An enclosure is a wall built solely of stones, enclosing vines or protecting cultivated gardens. So the prosperity of these men is described in terms which suggest what has been erected for some useful purpose does not collapse. Next is added: *Nor passage, nor crying out in their streets.* This too he wishes to have referred to the blessings of this world; so when fathers of households wish to restore themselves by rest, there is to be no tramping through their houses nor cries of disturbance arising in the streets, so that their sleep may not be broken by untimely babbling. Thus there can be silence when they wish to rest, and encounters when they bid their friends to greet them. This figure is called *climax,*[21] when words gradually mount higher.

15. *They have called the people blessed that have these things: but blessed is that people whose lord is their God.* This verse is seen to contain two pronouncements of different kinds. One refers to those who account themselves happy, the other to the truly blessed. The prophet says: *They have called the people blessed that have these things,* that is, the things mentioned earlier. This is the judgment of those who were not students of the truth, who opt for the world's wealth and despise the kingdom of heaven; they think it blessedness to gaze on prolific flocks or to possess the fattest cattle. Listen, you men of debased opinions, listen, you madmen who believe that things sublime lie in the left hand (for we read of Wisdom: *Years of life lie in her right hand; in her left, riches and glory*).[22] Let us hear now what is said of the crowd of the faithful: *Blessed is that people whose lord is their God.* After the contempt passed on the wicked, he turns to the inner realm of Wisdom, to the voice itself of most sacred Truth. He truly defines who the blessed people are: they are those whose God is the Lord. The phrase, *whose lord,* denotes holy persons who engage in laudable behaviour. He is not said to be Lord of those who assent to wicked teachings. Those people accept Christ as Lord who are given the special title of His servants. He further added: *Their God,* with reference to those to whom He deigns to be merciful. We often read that the faithful say: *my lord and my God.*[23] If we are genuinely said to be His servants, He is truly called our Lord; thus in a few words the definition of the blessed people is established in the fullest truth.

Conclusion Drawn From the Psalm

A psalm of triumph has indeed been heard. But let us examine the significance of this song of victory, which has clearly been composed to have a bearing on the Church. Though the Lord through the agency of this holy man has revealed many mysteries of His religion, this one is seen to have been devised to announce the Church's battles which she endures spiritually; thus the proud one could be brought low by the shepherd's rock when he boasted in the presumption of his strength. So we must interpret this as an exemplar of the whole faith, pregnant with a sense of this kind: Goliath must represent the devil and his agents, and David must typify the entire Christian people, which is known to have overcome its fearful enemy through the solidity of the Rock. We must also pay great attention to the fact that after this extended chain of numerous psalms, this appears to have been set as the close, so to say, of worldly matters; for after this psalm nothing is recounted about persecutions of the Church, the bitterness of the world, the sufferings of martyrs, the afflictions of penitents, the laments of the faithful, or the execrable arrogance of Antichrist. The remaining seven are harnessed to divine praises, to express a great mystery, and they are seen to be suffused with heavenly joy. Now that we have driven off the clouds of sins, let us proceed to praises of the Lord with sunny minds.

Commentary on Psalm 144

1. *Praise for David himself.* We have shown that *David* signifies the Lord Christ by interpretation of the name itself;[1] moreover it has been demonstrated that He was so called through physical descent from His forbear. But though we seem to have this firmly established, I think that we should examine more carefully why this heading uniquely contains the words: *Praise for David himself,* since His glory is proclaimed in all the psalms. But here the praise is delineated more sharply and clearly because all the areas in which human ignorance needed instruction have been remedied, and the psalmist is bidden to devote himself to praise of the Lord alone. These praises are wonderfully unfolded distinctively and with their own strengths in the seven psalms that follow. Their peculiar nature is revealed in their conclusions as was the case also in previous psalms. It is not otiose that the Lord's praises are enclosed in this number seven, for the confession of penitents is designated by this number,[2] and the holy Spirit himself has been proclaimed with His sevenfold powers;[3] perhaps it points to that sacred mystery when the Lord ordered Moses to set seven lamps shining with enduring light in His tabernacle. Though it is certain that there is nothing without point in the divine Scriptures, I believe that the order of the Hebrew alphabet set here before the verses is especially significant. We said at Psalm 24 that this is to be interpreted with reference to two kinds of person.[4] When a psalm unfolds with all

the Hebrew letters, it denotes the just who through the Lord's grace are shown to lack no virtue; but when it does not bear the signs of all the characters, it seems to point to those in the Lord's Church not revealed as perfect in all good works. Of the intermingling of the two we read: *All sheep and oxen, moreover the beasts also of the field.*[5] In the case of this psalm, a single letter is missing from the alphabet,[6] so it seems not to indicate the higher category. In the gospel likewise the Lord said to the man who lived a praiseworthy life: *One thing is wanting to thee: but if thou wilt be perfect, sell all thy possessions, and follow me.*[7] Since all do not do this, they are seen to fall some way short of perfection. So as we give thanks to the Lord let us continually entreat Him, now that He has shown us the mystery of His love, that we who have been healed in the greater part of our merits may similarly presume to demand that by the gift of His kindness we deserve to attain the role of praising Him for ever. Alternatively, and this explanation I chanced upon later, the incomplete alphabet points to the Church, which is still developing here on earth, and is not yet cleansed by separation from the wicked, whereas the full alphabet denotes the Jerusalem to come when the assembly of the perfect will be filled by election of the saints. If you examine carefully the psalms bearing prior marks of the Hebrew letters, you will find that they reveal this.

Division of the Psalm

Christ's praises proclaimed by the blessed prophet run on through the order of the Hebrew alphabet, and unfold in three sections of narrative. The first is an unbounded promise of this praise, containing three letters of the alphabet. The second says that the Lord's praise is to be consummated in nine ways; this takes four letters. In the third part the psalmist unfolds more lengthily and clearly what he briefly proclaimed in the second part about Christ's praises, finally reminding us that the Lord must be lauded by all flesh; this part has fourteen letters. But we must note above all that the psalm has stated the quarter from which the Lord's praise can come, yet the various aspects of that praise appear incapable of being explained; for example, it says that He is to be praised in His works, but who can recount His activities worthily? It speaks of His power, but who can succeed in describing

His power? So the simple truth is that praise is bestowed on the Lord from various aspects, but in such a way that one does not believe that it can be sufficiently elaborated.

Explanation of the Psalm

ALEPH. *I will extol thee, God my king, and I will bless thy name for ever: yea, for ever and ever.* The blessed prophet is filled with the divine Spirit and has burst into speech, not presuming on human wisdom but enlightened by heavenly contemplation. He does not speak of any local or particular theme, but of the source from which all the world's weaknesses can be healed. *I will extol thee* means "I will make You known by proclaiming what You are." How could anyone believe that God can be exalted by any praise, seeing that the divine perfection cannot be bettered? *My king* is a profession of faith, for he said that he was ruled by Him whom he knew he served with a pure heart. To bless His name for ever means here to entreat Him with the charm of psalmody; he who is worthy to do this will deserve also to praise Him in the eternity to come, for what comes next is: *For ever and ever,* when there is now no end. What is happily begun is preserved with enduring gladness.

2. BETH. *Every day will I bless thee: and I will praise thy name for ever, yea, for ever and ever.* Earlier he said *I will extol thee, God,* and so that men's indifference should not imagine that it was to be done once only, the needful warning was given: *Every day,* as the days succeed each other. He who blesses the Lord here each and every day will utter praises in the next world in the company of the blessed with continual exultation on that one eternal day which is to come. The other words of this verse are identical with those of the last, so let my earlier explanation suffice.

3. GIMEL. *Great indeed is the Lord, and greatly to be praised, and of his greatness there is no end.* This is a marvellous combination, a true proclamation, to praise the Lord in such a way that you consider His greatness beyond description. Our vision of the whole of creation is insufficient; our reconsideration continues to mount all the time. Just as He is bounded by no place, so His praises cannot be limited by any eloquence, even the most outstanding. His power is indescribable, His

dutiful love beyond our grasping, His wisdom beyond explanation. It is a true definition of Him that there is no end to His sacred praises. Observe that in the words: *Of his greatness there is no end*, the psalmist never instructs you to cease proclaiming Him; even when we are silent, we are thanking Him when our way of life is praiseworthy. Though He cannot be embraced by any praises, individual phrases are a pointer, as in the words: *Great indeed*, and: *Of his greatness there is no end.* This is the fifth type of definition called in Greek *kata tēn lexin* and in Latin *ad verbum*,[8] when we intimate by individual words the thing which we seek to know.

4. DALETH. *Generation and generation shall praise thy works, and they shall declare thy power.* 5. HE. *They shall tell of the magnificence of thy majesty and of thy holiness, and shall tell thy wondrous works.* 6. VAV. *They shall speak of the might of thy more terrible acts, and shall declare thy greatness.* 7. ZAIN. *They shall publish the memory of the abundance of thy sweetness, and shall rejoice in thy justice.* He comes to the second section, in which he has marked the types of the Lord's praise with the sacred numeration.[9] Though the repetition seems to denote a generation as a boundless time (for it is clear that the Lord's works are always to be praised), nonetheless *generation and generation* must rather be applied to the two peoples: to the Jews first, chosen by the sign of circumcision, and secondly to those sprung from the Gentiles. These are the generations which have received the Lord's kindnesses. They are rightly said to sing His praises, for they are known to have obtained gifts of His devotion. But since these nine aspects—works, power, magnificence, holiness, miracles, the might of more fearful acts, greatness, memory, justice—have been presented here as a proposition, so that the Lord's praises should accordingly be sung in this same order, it is fitting that we should discuss them at the place where authority has decreed that they be more widely explained. We can perhaps under these headings label them cataracts of divine eloquence, founts of heavenly words, blessed breasts of praise from which the human race is refreshed through its devoted confession, and by which angels are afforded unceasing happiness. These statements can I think be summarily defined as the means which make summary and brief mention of what is incomprehensible and most exalted, not to its fullest extent but to the greatest degree possible. Nothing external, nothing merely probable, nothing ambiguous seems to emerge

here. Everything comes forth as the truth states it; everything is said in accord with truth. I think that these nine topics from which the Lord's praises are begotten are gathered into a great mystery, so that honour to the Trinity can be acknowledged by the number of thrice three which they embody. This number is reflected also in the sacred books which God's holy Church reads and reveres: Octoteuch, Kings, Prophets, Psalter, Solomon, Holy Books, Gospels, Epistles of the Apostles, and Acts of the Apostles together with the Apocalypse. So this number is fertile with the recollection of things heavenly.

8. HETH. *The Lord is merciful at heart and pitying.* The third and remaining narration is begun here, in which the psalmist treats at greater length the topics briefly listed in the second section. Let us now study them individually with committed minds. He began with the Lord's works, so that He is called *merciful.* The description of His merciful heart expresses the virtue of His nature, whereas His pity is the source of salvation for our frailty. He is merciful at heart in His creation, for He is given no benefits which rouse Him to make such provision; it is through the ordering of His clemency that He makes all things come to exist. He is also *pitying* when by His devotedness He restores our fallen condition, so that those who fall through sin may be raised by grace; for what person deserves by his deeds the Lord Saviour's kindnesses, when we read the general judgment that *all have sinned and need the glory of God?*[10] The words *merciful at heart and pitying* form the figure of *paronomasia,* also known as *denominatio,*[11] verbal parallelism.

Patient and plenteous in mercy. He passes to the second point of the proposition, hailed because of the Lord's power; he did not praise His power because he has held the lands in being, or controlled the seas, or tricked the sky with stars. Instead he said that He tolerates human excesses, so that those who might be punished by the law of justice are seen not to perish through the Lord's patience. As Scripture says: *I desire not the death of the sinner but his conversion, that he may live.*[12]

9. TETH. *The Lord is sweet to all, and his tender mercies are over all his works.* The third topic of the proposition is His magnificence. What is more magnificent than to be sweet to all, who by His kindness have tasted Him with devoted thoughts? As the apostle Peter says: *If so be you have tasted that the Lord is sweet,*[13] for He can be called sweet only by those who have imbibed His blessings in the spiritual

sense. Again, what is more magnificent than to bestow His tender mercies over all His works, which glory in Him as their Maker? Someone may say: "Why then are sinners to be condemned, when they are undoubtedly His creation?." But observe that the psalmist says that tender mercies are to be bestowed on the Lord's works. He crowns what He bestows on us by secret judgment through the prior gift of grace; He condemns what is built up by the devices of the devil. The force attached to the words wholly removes the difficulty. The Lord's works are always chosen, but our own works or those of the devil are undoubtedly condemned.

10. IOD. *Let all thy works, O Lord, praise thee, and let thy saints bless thee.* The fourth topic discussed is His holiness. It is the holiness mentioned earlier; all His holy ones must praise Him: the good angels, dominations, powers, principalities, or the just, and all else recognised as blessed. But since all created things are not lofty in dignity of understanding, for example, mules, rocks, logs, earth and the like, how will every created thing be able to proclaim Him? Clearly each thing praises Him by being what it is, for it causes glorification of the Creator who has made all things by a wonderful dispensation. So either the creatures themselves praise of their own accord, or the Lord's works are proclaimed as exceedingly good through their rational essences.

11. CAPH. *They shall speak of the glory of thy kingdom: and shall tell of thy power.* The fifth topic to be emphasised is His wonderful works. How marvellous God is, for He made heaven and earth, and with astonishing variety filled them with varied blessings! In the small things there is appropriate measure, in the middle-sized things just moderation, and in the great things a copious abundance of gifts. The whole is inevitably wonderful, for it is clear that the Creator of the whole universe is all-powerful.

12. LAMED. *To make thy might known to the sons of men: and the glory of the magnificence of thy kingdom.* The sixth section gives entry to the virtues. This is the narration mentioned by the psalmist in the second part, in the words: *The might of thy more terrible acts.*[14] It is through the saints' preaching that His might and the glory of His kingdom are made known, in case they might be perhaps less sought if men did not know of them. His might was also made known when Peter and John made the man lame from birth walk, and they said: *Ye*

men of Israel, why wonder you at this, as if by our strength or devotion we had made this man to walk?[15] And a little later they say that he was made whole in the name of Christ Jesus.[16] The might of the Lord was also made known when the apostles invoked His name and made manifest diverse powers.

13. MEM. *Thy kingdom, Lord, is a kingdom of all ages and thy dominion endureth through all generations.* He passes to the seventh topic, which derives from His greatness. If it is great to govern for a time, how much more splendid to have no limit to one's dominion! He first praised the Lord's kingdom for its everlasting nature, and then for the effect of His dominion. Human kingdoms exist, but are not eternal; they are strong by comparison with those of others, but they do not wield power for any longer. So the enduring nature of this kingdom is related so that you would not think that it was the kind of kingdom as you perhaps identify in this world.

14. SAMECH. *The Lord is faithful in all his words, and holy in all his works.*[17] *The Lord lifteth up all that are falling, and setteth up all that are cast down.* The eighth topic is revealed, dealing with His abundance: *They shall publish the memory of the abundance of thy sweetness,* as he related earlier in the second section already quoted.[18] He is called *faithful,* then, because He has fulfilled the promises of His coming, and not in a few of His words but in all of them. This statement is indeed appropriate only to Him who said: *Heaven and earth will pass away, but my words will not pass away.*[19] His truthfulness in promises is matched by His holiness recognisable in all His activity. This too undoubtedly refers to the Lord's abundance, when those who fall are raised, the guilty pardoned, and the battered are restored. It is then that recollection of His sweetness is noted when the power of such deeds is beheld, and there is an outburst in praise of Him who deigned to snatch the sinner from the devil's control. Note that here too two things are ascribed to the Lord: He raises up those who fall but as yet have not crashed down, and he restores those who are cast down, who are already seen to have sustained a fall. This is well observed, for we are protected from falling by His protection, and equally raised by His power so that when prostrate we can rise. Undoubtedly these and similar events can come to pass through the abundance of His sweetness.

15. AIN. *The eyes of all hope in thee, O Lord, and thou givest them*

meat in due season. 16. PHE. *Thou openest thy hand, and fillest with blessing every living creature.* Observe the entry into the ninth topic, discussion of His justice. In the two verses here and the later one, a broader explanation is given: those who listen to the Lord of mercy must also tremble at the just Judge. It is of the nature of His justice that those who do not cease to hope in Him attain the gifts of fullness from Him. The *meat* mentioned here must be understood as embracing each and every thing; some things demand physical control, and others spiritual, but to all is dispensed as one food the generosity of the Creator. So that you should not think that what is asked for will always be given, the psalmist added: *In due season.* Many make petitions, but they are happily rejected. So let us pray diligently for this one thing, that the Lord in His kindness may grant only what He knows is helpful. As Paul says: *We know not what we should pray for as we ought.*[20] We also know that all things are established in His power when He opens His hand and every living creature is filled with blessings. But it is better that we interpret *living creature* as "creature endowed with reason," for it is clear that he can be truly blessed.

17. SADE. *The Lord is just in all his ways, and holy in all his works.* The role of justice is made clear when we realise that the word itself is mentioned. The *ways* of the Lord are His dispensations and wishes; if our understanding is true, we become aware that they are always just. When He lashes us, He acts justly because He is imposing an apt penalty for our sins. So when we beg pardon, let us first confess His justice, and in this way await from Him the gifts of fatherly love. *Holy* signifies His devoted love, patience, and bestowal of all blessings, for whatever He performs is replete with praise of His powers. *Ways* refers to His dispensations, *works* to what He brings to pass. But this division is made because of our frail understanding; with Him, will is identical with action, dispensation with command.

18. COPH. *The Lord is near to all that call upon him in truth.* 19. RES. *He will do the will of them that fear him, and he will hear their prayers and save them.* These words too clearly bear upon the Lord's justice. Nearest spells kindly, distant spells angry. He is present always and everywhere; as a previous psalm had it: *If I ascend into heaven, thou art there: if I descend into hell, thou art present,*[21] and the rest. But because those who desire to have their empty longings fulfilled also call upon Him, the words, *in truth,* were added, a phrase

intended to debar all unnecessary requests; for the only person who calls upon Him *in truth* is he who asks for what the Lord himself decides is the desirable request. God truly hears the person who is seen to be given what will benefit him. What point is there in demanding excessive requests which the churlish pleader is sorry to have obtained? This was the experience of the children of Israel, when they asked for a king to be granted them, as the Gentiles had.

20. SIN. *The Lord keepeth all them that love him: but all the wicked he will destroy.* The section on justice is now briefly concluded, for both these statements have reference to the Lord's equity, that He both keeps them that love Him, and destroys sinners because of their wickedness. His statement that all sinners are to be destroyed denotes those who persist in their obduracy; for those who turn to the Lord with pure hearts thereupon cease to be sinners. As was said in another psalm: *Blessed are they whose iniquities are forgiven.*

21. TAV. *My mouth shall speak the praise of the Lord: and let all flesh bless his holy name for ever, yea, for ever and ever.* He has now expounded all the subjects which are wont to beget and bring forth the Lord's praise, and now he repeats the briefest summary of that praise to establish that what cannot be unfolded in any books or by any human powers can be enclosed in this remarkable epitome. He promises that his *mouth*, in other words the hidden region of his heart, from where he knew that he was gladly heard, will utter the Lord's praise. He also exhorts the whole of human flesh to bless the Lord Saviour; clearly this is stated by the figure of *synecdoche*, the part for the whole, for by flesh he means mankind, just as mention of souls alone does, as in the passage of Exodus: *All the souls which entered Egypt were seventy-five souls.*[22] It is the flesh which can bless the Lord with worthy praise.

If a careful student finds any themes additional to those mentioned, whether in the remaining psalms or in previous ones, which are to be applied to the Lord's praises, he should not doubt (this at least is my opinion) that they have a bearing on one or other of the modes which we have listed. He should not indict us with total failure to embrace clearly what we proclaim to be immeasurable. In my view the astute Aristotle sought to match this when he assembled topics for secular arguments with remarkable subtlety; in this way just as all discourse could be enclosed by letters, so by that combination all cultivated learning could be embraced by published judgment. From this source the dialecticians compressed their discussions in abbreviated syllogisms; from it the orators rushed along like rivers; from it the poets surround themselves with beautiful blossoms; from it satirists, historians, comic and tragic poets, were enriched, so that anything set apart from this combination seems virtually to lie beyond the tongue of man. Aristotle bestowed the title *Topics* on this collection.[23] Topics are the bases of arguments, by which the purpose of the disputant to elicit belief is achieved as though by first principles. No religious scruple condemns our reading and discussing this work, for whatever is not found to be hostile to sacred literature is investigated without harm.

Conclusion Drawn From the Psalm

In this one psalm we have heard a brief synthesis of what is widely diffused in the sacred Scriptures. Where do we not read of His works or power or magnificence or holiness or miracles or strength to perform more fearful deeds or greatness or abundance or justice? So the psalm can justifiably be called a divine storehouse, in which such a hoard of things heavenly is known to lie. It is not usual for all of them to be cited simultaneously, but praise of the Lord cannot be found without any one of them. But though he has carefully fashioned here the shape of the Lord's praise, he has emphasised that the following psalms as well are undoubtedly relevant to proclaiming Him, for this psalm is a preliminary guide to and a summary of them. You should not consider it accidental that the Lord's praises are contained in seven psalms; perhaps the words in Psalm 118 offer an indication: *Seven times a day I have given praise to thee.*[24] They are perhaps the seven candlesticks shining before the Lord which are mentioned in the Apocalypse,[25] the seven Churches to which the Lord's book was bidden to be sent. Finally, the Spirit is seven-formed, and He has bestowed those praises with divine generosity. So let us rejoice that the Lord has granted us the gift which we are to offer to His ears, but only let it be proffered with an unblemished conscience. Who can doubt that what He himself bids us offer in sacrifice is received with gratitude? What boundless devotion does the Creator show! He commands us to praise Him, and also reveals how He is to be proclaimed so that we may not fall short in our utterances; not that He has felt the need of such praises, but because He foresaw that the practice was useful for us. All His words, all His advice was given so that we should be unwilling to go astray. Finally He took on the very nature of humanity, so that in its frailty it should not perish. But let us take thought whether having received such bountiful gifts we should sin against so great a grace.

Commentary on Psalm 145

1. *Alleluia.* Once again divine authority resounds in our ears, and *Alleluia* knocks at the doors of our hearts, bidding us not to absorb ourselves vainly in empty thoughts, since it does not befit a soldier of Christ to be on furlough. The tongue too has its fruits, for a most abundant harvest is gathered if it is roused to the Lord's praise by an unsullied mind. The tongue is a spiritual member when it serves the Creator; it also commends the soul when it speaks the truth. So let us fill the air with the sweetest sounds, for this music of salvation not only charms mens' ears but also delights the understanding of angels.

Division of the Psalm

The prophet is eager that the Lord's praises be sung wholeheartedly. Initially he says that we must put no trust whatever in men, to prevent our making lukewarm entreaty of the Lord through belief that some other can grant our request. Secondly, he proclaims that all our hope must be placed in the almighty Lord. Since He is our Lord, a most beautiful definition of Him is presented from His deeds, so that the Gentiles may be convinced by such reiterated reasoning, and may abandon their errors with faithful devotion.

Explanation of the Psalm

2. *Praise the Lord, O my soul.* To ensure that his will does not idly devote itself to earthly desires, and that the impetus of his mind should

not busy itself with foolish preoccupations, the prophet offers himself wholesome counsel which he knew must be a source of profit to mankind as a whole: namely that his soul, and not din from noisy lips, should praise the Lord. Very often we recite studied words as though we are translating some foreign concept, and we feel that we have not ourselves uttered the words that we speak. The power of the soul is inflamed by spiritual vigour, and rushes here and there through different regions; with investigative reason it seeks out the sources of heavenly or earthly creatures, mingling now with those above, now with those below. But the status of these matters has been explained by me at greater length, according as the Lord has deigned to permit me, in that book on the soul which is included as Book XIII in the *Variae*.[1] So the psalmist urges his soul to praise the Lord, so that it may expel idle thoughts and busy itself with all its strength on this matter alone.

In my life I will praise the Lord: I will sing to my God as long as shall be. Let us examine the purpose of this repetition. First he bids his soul praise the Lord, and now in lending assent he promises to offer praise twice over. Praise in life means confessing to the Lord in the eternity which is more truly life, since it is afflicted by no oppression of anxieties. So he said: *I will praise,* to express the future time when angels and just men share a common lot. The phrase, *I will sing* (*psallam*), is used of this present life, for as we have often said, this word clearly suggests good works. We must interpret the verse, then, as saying that the singing goes on for ever in the next life, and is unremitting in this; the phrase, *As long as I shall be,* denotes this life, for there was to come a time when he could not continue here.

3. *Put not your trust in princes, nor in the children of men, in whom there is no salvation.* This heavenly physician first cleanses human hearts of baneful preoccupations so that he may fittingly apply saving remedies. He says that we are not to entertain hopes from demons or from men, for they cannot grant the salvation which they clearly do not possess of their own right. We must interpret *princes* as the spiritual villainies of which Paul speaks: *For our wrestling is not with flesh and blood, but against principalities and powers of this world of darkness.*[2] By *the children of men* he undoubtedly means mortals, who cannot offer salvation because they succumb to the death that is their lot. The Son of man, that is, the Son of the holy virgin, alone bestows salvation, for it is certain that He is the Saviour of the human race.

4. *His spirit shall go forth, and he shall return to his earth: in that day all their thoughts shall perish.* He gives the reason why we must not pin expectations on men. We must interpret *spirit* here as the soul; as Christ says in the gospel: *Father, into thy hands I commend my spirit.*[3] Once the soul, then, has quitted the prison of its body, the flesh disappears and returns to the earth from which it took its origin. He added *his* to *earth* to show that the flesh was sprung from it; as we read in Genesis: *God formed man of the slime of the earth.*[4] So the time of death brings an end to human thoughts, which always advance to various ambitions, now displaying eagerness for possessions, now gathering riches, now making great efforts to seek distinctions. But all these things waste away, because aspirations for them are rendered vain. As we read in the gospel of the rebuke to the rich man: *Thou fool, this night thy soul will be taken from thee, and whose shall those things be which thou hast provided?*[5]

5. *Blessed is he who hath the God of Jacob for his helper, whose hope is in the Lord his God.* Having expelled the harmful thoughts with which the human race is infected as if by most severe diseases, the prophet proceeds to the start of the second section, in which he provides what we may regard as a health-giving potion for human minds to drink. Not merely has he forbidden futile aspirations, but he has also given forewarning of what we must seek. He says that the person who hopes in the Lord becomes blessed from that very prospect. We have repeatedly said that the patriarch Jacob is cited because after the famous struggle with the angel he was the first to be called Israel, which means the one who sees God.[6] This title is aptly applied to all the chosen. *Helper* is included so that our understanding of the word may fire us to goodly efforts, for He is the Helper of those who strive to mount the steps of the virtues by their good intentions through His gift. Next follows: *Whose hope is in the Lord his God.* This continuation follows from the previous statement, for the person is blessed whose hope is known to be in the Lord His God. His mention of hope denotes endurance of present things, and longing for those to come, for no matter what the Christian suffers in this world, he is refreshed by the thought of future blessedness. But since those who worship demons could also have hope in their god, he denotes the Lord Christ in individual and varied phrases by the one technique of definition,

continuing to the end of the psalm; for in Him the hope of the faithful must rest.

6–7. *Who made heaven and earth, the sea and all things that are in them. Who keepeth truth for ever, who executeth judgment for them that suffer wrong: who giveth food to the hungry. The Lord lifteth up them that are cast down.*[7] We said at Psalm 144 that topics are introduced from which the Lord's praise is formulated; here we consider that they are again to be mentioned by most fitting references. He says: *Who made heaven and earth, the sea and all things that are in them;* undoubtedly here His praise proceeds from His works, for what can be more splendid or magnificent than to have made heaven and earth and all that are in them? His further statement: *Who executeth judgment for them that suffer wrong, who giveth food to the hungry,* clearly relates to His justice, for He will assign His equity to all by the gift of His judgment as He wills. This is the second type of definition, called in Greek *ennoematike,* in Latin *notio.*[8] He does not state what God essentially is, but what He does or has done. Our awareness can understand to a degree His actions, in so far as He allows, but it cannot investigate His essence. He says first: *Who made heaven and earth.* He is the One in whom Christians must pin their hope. Though he has included all things in this expression, *heaven and earth,* he added: *And all things that are in them,* to ensure that you would not think that some other creator exists of things however minute. Next follows: *Who keepeth truth for ever;* that is, He is the Lord Christ who says: *I am the way, the truth and the life,*[9] for it is inevitable that He speaks the truth in the world since He is known to be the heavenly Truth, whereas Scripture says of men who are under sin: *Every man is a liar.*[10]

He added: *Who executeth judgment for them that suffer wrong.* Christ is the true Judge and the eternal Helmsman who avenges the afflicted for His name's sake, and takes pity on the innocent, for they are the ones who suffer wrong, that is, injustice, when they are afflicted with harsh punishments for proclaiming the truth. He further said: *Who giveth food to the hungry.* The Creator of the world gives food to the hungry, but it is spiritual food that we must seek, so that we do not like the Jews take delight in receiving abundance in our bellies alone. The prophet Amos says: *Behold, I bring famine over the land; not a famine of bread nor a thirst of water, but famine of hearing the word of God.*[11] He added: *The Lord lifteth up them that are cast down.* This too is beyond doubt, that He raises up those who are cast down, for when the devil casts them down, the Lord lifts them up. So we must place our hope in Him whose practice it is not to cast down but to lift up.

8. *The Lord looseth them that are fettered, the Lord enlighteneth the blind, the Lord loveth the just, the Lord keepeth the stranger.* In this and the next verse we must apply the theme of: *The memory of the abundance of his sweetness.*[12] What is sweeter than to recount the deeds of His mercy and to say: *The Lord loosens them that are fettered, the Lord enlighteneth the blind, the Lord loveth the just, the Lord keepeth the stranger. He will support the fatherless and the widow, and the ways of sinners he will destroy?* The Lord Christ certainly looses the fettered, as the gospel states: *Ought not this daughter of Abraham, whom Satan has bound these eighteen years, be loosed from her sickness?*[13] But the statement can be understood not only of harrassment by an unclean spirit but also of all vices with which our minds are bound as though with ropes. Just as the devil binds when he entangles us with sins, so Christ looses when He forgives wrongs. Next comes: *The Lord enlighteneth the blind.* All sinful people are blind because they are enclosed in the darkness of sins, but they are enlightened only by Him who in the gospel smeared eyes with the mud which He made, and delivered the man enfolded in darkness to the joy of perfect health.[14] It is also said of Him: *He enlightens every man who comes into the world.*[15] He further added: *The Lord loveth the just;* who assumes love of the just except Him who can set them in eternal blessedness? Just as the devil seeks out the wicked, so the Lord loves the just. He further added: *The Lord keepeth the stranger,* in other words, the person who has quitted Babylon, the devil's city, and reached Jerusalem, the Lord Saviour's city. He preserves him so long as he remains in the lodging of the elect; as another psalm has it: *I am a dweller with thee on the earth, and a sojourner as all my fathers were.*[16]

9. *He will support the fatherless and the widow: and the way of sinners he will destroy. The fatherless and the widow* are those who gaze on the Lord with pure minds, and are stripped of human consolations. Christ supports them, for they will be defended by His protection. Once He has received them as His devotion dictates, *He will destroy* the devil, who is *the way of sinners;* in other words, He will exile him from the bounds of His kingdom, a fate which will befall each and every wicked

person at the judgment. So by the proclamation of these ten decrees the psalmist has abundantly shown the nature of the Lord, in whom the hope of the faithful must rest. Do not think that there may be a contradiction between our statement in the previous psalm that there is an arrangement of nine topics for the Lord's praise, and our saying here that we have covered ten points in proclaiming Him. You must realise that the bases of arguments are one thing, and rules for definitions another; for in the one case each individual argument is set down with a general distinction, whereas in the other the Lord's nature is suggested by various statements under the one species of definition; and as often happens, two or more definitions are assembled from the one species of arguments.

10. *The Lord shall reign for ever: thy God, O Sion, for ever and ever.* This can clearly be understood from the Lord's magnificence. What more splendid thing is there than that the Lord of Sion should reign for ever, and that of His kingdom there shall be no end? *He shall reign* seems to denote future time, when our hearts are now fixed with the most unmoving constancy on Him; for at present Christ is said not to reign wholly in His members, for their hearts from time to time are dominated by idle thoughts. But when this mortal body has put on immortality,[17] and has abandoned these harmful thoughts together with renunciation of the world, then Christ will reign perfectly among the saints when, as Scripture says: *God will be all in all.*[18] Whose Lord He is we find clearly expounded: *Thy God, O Sion.* We have already stated often that Sion denotes the Catholic Church, because of the watchfulness which she shows over the Christian people. He will reign both with her and in her, for He is blessed for ever.

Conclusion Drawn From the Psalm

The prophet through the benefit of contemplation takes his position, so to say, in the earth's last days, when we know that the world's wantonness is to be condemned. He has taught the whole creation to busy itself with the Lord's praises to avoid seeking the transient desires which are undoubtedly soon to be ended. When that future time is proclaimed to us, he clearly refers to our own day. We are at the world's close when we abandon it, and embrace death after no long extent of time. All passing desires should leave us; worldly enticements must depart. We must instead desire what we know is eternal.

Commentary on Psalm 146

1. *Alleluia.* The ensuing text explains the heading, so that there is no need for extraneous commentary, since the psalm's own words expound it. Read the beginning of the psalm, and you have explained the heading, for *Alleluia* means: *Praise the Lord.* Each of the two phrases harmoniously echoes the other, so that you can regard the heading as the start of the psalm, and reasonably regard the start of the psalm as the heading. So let us embark on this psalm trustingly and joyfully, for we are wholly acquainted with its saving message at the very outset.

Division of the Psalm

In the first theme the prophet urges the devoted people to praise the Lord, who raises the humble and depresses the necks of the proud. In the second, he says that we must eagerly hymn the Lord, who grants to those who entreat Him blessings that will profit them, whereas those who show confidence in their own powers cannot be pleasing to Him.

Explanation of the Psalm

Praise ye the Lord, because a psalm is good: to our God be joyful praise. All human work demands for itself a reward in return, so that we may console ourselves with hope of a gift in store for the toil which we undergo. But in praises of the Lord the very act carries its own reward, for what we now practise will form the repayment itself. Since it is good to proclaim the Lord, each individual is seen to obtain the gifts that were promised; he clearly obtains it when in association with the angels the saints gain the unique privilege of commencing the Lord's undying praise. So let us laud Him with all possible devotion, and while we are in the world ponder the blessed gifts to come, for what is happier than to perform now what you hope to be able to complete in that future blessedness? Our forbears tell us that a psalm is a musical instrument[1] like a harp, lute, or other instruments which match our voices with the sweetest melody; as we have repeatedly said, this denotes our most praiseworthy actions. So the psalmist recommends that the Lord's praises and the psalter should unite in a single harmony, so that just as we recite the Godhead's praises with our tongues, so we may glorify Him with the performance of good deeds. Next comes: *To our God be joyful praise;* we make joyful praise to the Godhead when our actions do not diverge from the character of the sacred words. What sort of attitude would it be, when a psalm proclaims chastity, for the singer not to refrain from impurity? Or if a psalm hymns humility, and the person reciting it is swollen with proud airs? So the Lord cannot look favourably on what is clearly rife with internal contradiction. Praise is pleasing to the Lord only when words and life are allied and at one.

2. *The Lord buildeth up Jerusalem, and gathereth up together the dispersed of Israel.* In this and the next two verses the Lord is rightly praised for His wonders and glorious deeds. When he says: *The Lord buildeth up Jerusalem, and gathereth up together the dispersed of Israel. Who healeth the broken of heart, and bindeth up their bruises. Who telleth the number of the stars, and calleth them all by their names,* the Lord is being praised as wonderful specifically for His deeds. But the first of these verses shows that the Lord does not love things which are at odds, for He clearly gathers together those that are dispersed. How can He brook in us an inconsistency between our song and our actions, when He gathers the peoples of the whole world into a blessed unity? The Lord builds the city of Jerusalem from living stones when He gathers the dispersed of Israel, who we know dwell throughout the world; as the gospel has it: *And he shall send his angels with a trumpet and a great voice, and they shall gather the elect from the four corners of the earth.*[2]

3. *Who healeth the contrite of heart, who bindeth up their bruises.* A wonderful mode of healing is announced, so that if we wish to be restored we musr make ourselves contrite in a most vigorous way. This contrition, however, is aimed at renewal and leads to full recovery; what transcends every blessing, it admits the Physician who

grants eternal health. Next comes: *Who bindeth up their bruises.* The metaphor is adopted from those skilled in techniques of healing, who bind broken and bruised bones with linen bandages when they wish to restore them, so that limbs can return to their original positions and fuse into their previous solidity. In the same way the heavenly Physician treats the hearts of penitents when they are battered with heavy affliction. He binds and strengthens them by wrapping them, so to say, with the bandage of His devoted love, and impels them to the strongest hope of recovery. As was said in Psalm 50: *A contrite and humble heart God does not despise.*[3] The tax-collector who smote his breast with continual beating was seen to have imposed on himself the contrition which he unceasingly inflicted on his guilty breast.[4]

4. *Who telleth the number of the stars, and calleth all by their names.* This too seems to reveal the Lord's power literally; the psalmist says that the stars which to us are beyond counting can be numbered by the Godhead, and they can be called by their own names, for they are all identifiable by Him to whom the sands of the sea, the drops of rain, and the hairs of men are as we know numbered.[5] When he says: *By their names,* he refutes the astrologers, who call them by alien names such as Venus, Mercury, Jupiter, Mars, Saturn, and the like. However, it is more appropriate for us to take these expressions in the spiritual sense. Earlier he had said that the contrite of heart were to be saved, and we are to take *stars* as representing them after they have received merciful healing, for they shine like stars in the darkness of this world, and they have deserved to be gathered in the number of the saints. Though the Church is seen to contain many on this earth, those who will rejoice in a share of His kingdom are none the less numbered by the Lord. A passage of Genesis attests that we can take *stars* as meaning holy men where it says: *I will multiply thy seed as the stars of heaven.*[6] Solomon too says: *But the just will shine like the stars of heaven.*[7] We know that the saints' names are cited by the Lord, for we read that they are enrolled in heaven. As He says in the gospel: *Do not rejoice that demons are subject to you: but rejoice and be glad that your names are written in heaven.*[8]

5. *Great is our Lord, and great is his power, and of his wisdom there is no number.* In this and the next verse fitting praise of the Lord is sung because of His greatness. By the words: *Great is the Lord, and great is his power, and of his wisdom there is no number. The Lord lifteth up the*

meek and bringeth down the wicked even to the ground, His greatness is announced in absolute terms. Initially when the prophet was coursing through the different areas of His praise, he was filled with wonder, and exclaimed: *Great is our Lord!* He said this precisely because His deeds were beyond counting, and His praise beyond understanding, as He gathers the scattered children of Israel, heals the afflicted at heart, numbers the crowd of the blessed, and calls each of them by his name. Who can understand the extent of His praise embracing all these things, when His greatness is so wonderful in each of them? When the psalmist calls Him *ours,* he is excluding the rites of utterly mad paganism; His power is great because He is unique, almighty, the Helmsman and Creator of all things. Next follows: *And of his wisdom there is no number.* Here we must interpret *number* as end, because number counts and limits all things that exist; how can God's wisdom be numbered when it is known to be the creator of number? If it could be numbered, it would seem to fall below number. But if number itself cannot be wholly known by us, how and by what means can divine wisdom be understood? The Creator is incomparably superior to His creatures, and so it is truthfully stated that *of his wisdom there is no number,* for in connection with the things which He created, the Sage says that God has made *all things in measure and number and weight.*[9]

6. *Lifting up the meek, the Lord bringeth the wicked down even to the ground. The meek* are those who he earlier said were contrite through tribulation and patient through regular affliction. Observe how very beautifully the contrast is achieved. The meek are lifted into heaven, the proud are thrust down to earth; by this interchange the proud man falls to the place from which the humble man is raised, and the faithful person is raised and mounts to the place from where proud Satan fell.

7. *Begin to the Lord with confession: sing to our God on the harp.* He passes to the second theme, in which he encourages the hesitant, urges the doubtful, rebukes the indifferent. *Begin* is addressed to those known to be still silent. With *to the Lord with confession,* we must supply "sing." This confession, however, urges praise and encourages worthy action, for the harp denotes the moral virtues which play an accompaniment of harmonious action; they form a true harp when they are joined in federal alliance. Just as a lyre cannot be called complete when a string is missing, so a holy man cannot be accounted perfect when deficient in any virtue.

8. *Who covereth the heaven with clouds, and prepareth rain for the earth. Who maketh grass to grow on the mountains, and herbs for the service of man.* In this and the next verse the Lord's works are recounted afresh. He says: *Who covereth the heaven with clouds, and prepareth rain for the earth. Who maketh grass to grow on the mountains, and herbs for the service of men. Who giveth to beasts their food, and to the young of the ravens that call upon him.* What mark of greater power is there than that the Creator should aid His creatures in a fitting manner? Divine Scripture often embraces this type of definition, revealing the Lord's power and might by what He performs, which is what is achieved in this and the next verse. Earlier he wrote: *Begin to the Lord with confession;* now he clearly reveals the kind of Lord to whom we are to confess. Though this section can clearly be taken literally, it is better if we regard it as expressed allegorically. We can aptly regard *heaven* here as sacred prophecy, which by divine dispensation is covered by obscurity as though by clouds, so that it fires our thoughts to seek an end which is welcomed with greater gratitude but attained with wearied longing. Next is mentioned what these clouds bring forth: they are seen to afford abundant rain, in other words irrigating streams of divine preaching. The earth for which this rain is provided is thirsty earth, for the person who fruitfully accepts the Lord's word is he who through the gift of heaven applies himself with longing to hear it. The word *prepareth* is not otiose, for unless He prepares it, no-one can attain it by his own merits. Next comes: *Who maketh grass to grow on the mountains, and herbs for the service of men.* This too must be interpreted in the spiritual sense. *Mountains* denotes holy men in whom the Lord makes grass and herbs to grow, on which simpler souls in the Catholic Church are fed like ingenuous cattle. *Grass* represents strong preaching, *herbs* gentler counsels. It was *grass* when Paul said: *I would that all men were even as myself,*[10] and *herbs* in his statement: *Let him who does not contain himself marry,*[11] and again: *I will that younger widows marry,*[12] and further: *I gave you milk to drink, not meat.*[13] These lesser precepts are rightly compared to herbs, for the phrase, *for the service of men,* denotes herbs assigned for human use. From this we clearly realise that the previous words are to be applied to men.

9. *Who giveth to beasts their food: and to the young of the ravens that call upon him. Beasts* denotes the flocks in the Church who are fed

with suitable refreshments, some with milk, others with solid food according to the judgment of the Steward, who alone can dispense what will benefit them. *Ravens* are the irreligious who clothe themselves in an irremovable black covering of sins, and do not gleam with any brightness of conversion. The young of the ravens, as the natural philosophers suggest, feed on the dew of heaven,[14] and through the blessing of their youth are as yet unaware of their parents' fare of stinking corpses. So He gives food to the sons of pagans and apostates, because they transcend the lives of their fathers by the gift of innocence. Note his additional words: *That call upon him;* only those who do not undermine the canons of Scripture with any heretical wickedness call upon Him. One must interpret this act of calling on the Lord as referring to men, for how can it apply to ravens' young?

10. *He shall not delight in the strength of a horse, nor take pleasure in the tents of a man.* After recounting the Lord's deeds, he now states the things which can be wholly displeasing to Him. *Horse* is often cited to denote pride, for the animal sticks out its neck, always presses on the reins, and speeds into swift gallops in foaming competition. The proud and swollen person is compared with it; the Godhead cannot be reconciled to him, for God chooses the meek and devoted. As another psalm has it: *Vain is the horse for safety,*[15] and elsewhere: *Some trust in chariots and some in horses, but we will be glorified in the name of the Lord our God.*[16] The tents of men are assemblies of the faithless and of mad pagans, which always develop into most wicked rites. Observe the force of the words, for he spoke of men's tents not God's, meaning those unlawful attitudes which reckless men set before themselves by their own will. *Man* too is used in the bad sense, as in: *The bloody and deceitful man the Lord will abhor.*[17]

11. *The Lord taketh pleasure in them that fear him, and in them that hope in his mercy.* Earlier he spoke of those who could displease Him; now he mentions the type of people who please Him. The Lord, then, loves those who fear Him, but not with an ignoble fear. There are many who fear, but because they despair of His mercy, they obtain no love; Judas is an example, for following his fear at the revelation of his sin, he thought that he should not make entreaty, but rather despair. The fear known to be acceptable to God is that linked with the greatest love and devoted confidence. The person who does not intend to supplicate is identical with the one who does not fear.

Conclusion Drawn From the Psalm

Undoubtedly this psalm too refers to the end of the world, when the scattered people of Israel are gathered into a single race, so that there may be one flock and one shepherd.[18] What a happy era it will be, when the living stones, more precious than any pearls, are assembled into the building of heaven and into eternal blessedness! Then the toil of each individual saint will be most sweet; grief will win them consolation, persecution will gain them eternal rest, devoted poverty will bestow on them the kingdom of heaven, and in the world to come they will rejoice that they endured all their oppressive sufferings here. Grant, O Lord, endurance of ills here, so that You can make our joy enduring in heaven.

Commentary on Psalm 147[1]

12. *Alleluia.* We return to the familiar Alleluia, but we are by no means weary of repeating it. It bears a taste which we always seek, a hearing which does not bore us, an understanding obtained without toil. Such honour is paid to this word that though it is buried in the Hebrew language it has clearly been left untranslated into any other. Greeks, Latins, Chaldaeans, Syrians, Persians, Arabs, all nations of the world retain it; all devotion to the Godhead reveres the dignity of the word with sacred piety. No-one considers it inappropriate or absurd; all hymn their joys proclaimed by the sweetness of this expression. So let us sing it with pure hearts, and concentrate on it with all our strength, so that the sweetest sound registered by our bodily ears may be matched by the heart's sincerity with which it is uttered.

Division of the Psalm

In the first section the prophet briefly addresses Jerusalem the heavenly city, urging that now that it is safely established among its citizens, it should praise the Lord with continuing joy. In the second, he recounts at greater breadth with mystical references the great kindnesses which the Lord's devoted pity has bestowed on His people.

Explanation of the Psalm

Praise the Lord, O Jerusalem: praise thy God, O Sion. This psalm, from the first verse to the end, relates that the Lord's power must be proclaimed, as you are aware when reciting the psalm itself. As has often been stated, Jerusalem means "vision of peace," which is peculiarly apt for the city which will have no association with vices and scandals. This vision of peace will be contemplation[2] of the Lord Saviour, which will be merited only by the person freed from all mental disturbance. So these two names are deservedly appropriate for that city to come, the bestowal of the reward gained and the lofty title of shepherd.[3]

13. *Because he hath strengthened the bolts of thy gates: he hath blessed thy children within thee.* The source of future blessedness is clearly shown. Though this was promised by the mouths of many prophets, it is most clearly declared in this statement. When he says that the bolts of the gates have been strengthened, he reveals that the doors of the blessed city are closed. *Sera* (bolt) is derived from *sero* (late),[4] the time at which the message is sent to the gate that freedom of entry be refused. This will happen at the time when the Bridegroom enters, as the gospel-passage about the virgins says: *They that were ready went in with him to the marriage, and the door was shut.*[5] It is closed not for the punishment of confinement, but for eternal blessedness, for no holy person will any longer emerge from there, and no new arrival will enter subsequently. What a safe and blessed haven for the just which is seen to be attained on terms which will never allow it to be lost! And rightly so, for that city has the vision of God within it, so that no-one wishes to leave because one can behold nothing similar to Him. Next comes: *He has blessed thy children within thee.* Great indeed is the blessing of children, but a much more welcome one when bestowed within the mother's womb. What a boon it is for a mother continually to behold her children flourishing, and for children to gaze uninterruptedly on their approving mother! Hence the words, *within thee,* for those consecrated by this eternal gift will never be able to depart from the Jerusalem to come.

14. *Who hath placed peace in thy borders, filling thee with the fat of corn.* With what succinct praise is that city great beyond reckoning described! What can be said to be more outstanding than she whose

territories are bounded by the gift of peace? So it can be inferred with total certainty that what we know dwells within it enjoys perennial tranquillity; and on the other hand whatever happens to lie outside her is hell. Just as blessed Jerusalem possesses peace, so unhappy Babylon will undoubtedly endure a grievous struggle; for by defining the one side he clearly revealed the nature of the other case. This figure is called *emphasis;*[6] it suggests also what it does not state. Next comes the explanation of how this peace emerges, when the faithful are filled with contemplation of the Lord Christ, for *the fat of corn* denotes the vision of the Godhead, by which the thoughts of the just are refreshed in such a way as clearly to transcend all possible satiety, since He is the true Bread which came down from heaven.[7] If He refreshes us here by sharing out His body, how totally will He satisfy in heaven those whom He fills with the full light of His divinity! That will indeed be untroubled peace and a calm inviolate, when no need hounds us, when no weariness exhausts anyone, when cold does not demoralise nor hunger oppress nor the other trials which ever war on our weakness. In heaven the alliance between body and soul is such that there is no hostile disagreement between them, but both harmonise with each other in splendid accord.

15. *Who sendeth forth his speech to the earth: his word runneth swiftly.* Now that he has described the city of the future age, the prophet passes to the second theme, in which he foretells the gifts to be bestowed on us, so that we can acknowledge the truth of what is to come by measuring present blessings. *Speech* is the Word of the Lord Father, who came down to earth when He took on the lowliness of the devoted incarnation. *Sendeth forth:* with the spirit of prophecy he unfolded the present era, though he seemed to be addressing this to the future. But his expression, *sendeth forth,* does not indicate that one lesser is sent, but reveals the harmony of holy unity. The speech of this almighty Word has run so swiftly that the speediest acknowledgment of the holy Trinity has filled the world with wondrous haste, transforming cults of idols through the manifestation of Truth itself.

16. *Who giveth snow like wool, scattereth mist like ashes.* 17. *He sendeth his crystal like pieces of bread: who stands before the face of his cold?* After prophesying the Lord's coming, he next explains by metaphorical allusions what His blessings provide. This figure is called *parabole,*[8]

for things dissimilar to each other in kind are compared. All the things mentioned, snow, mist, crystal, cold are ills of this world which grip tight mortal hearts with the frost of sins, and cause them to remain in a rock-like stupor unless they are melted by the Lord's warmth. But let us observe how apt healing is afforded in each case. He says: *Who giveth snow like wool. Giveth* means "makes," just as in common speech we say "He gave us an indication" when we state that we have been shown and taught something. So He makes snow like wool, so that what previously was frozen with bitter cold is transformed into woolly softness. This happens precisely when He has guided men's hearts when at their coldest through sins to the warmth of satisfaction. *Snow* describes man when he removes himself from the Lord; *wool,* when he has deserved to attain His healing. *Mist* denotes all sin, for it is always performed in cloudy darkness, but through the Lord's agency it is dispersed like ashes when its mass is dissolved by the grace of confession. *Crystal* is ice which has hardened for many winters, becoming like glass; the liquid hardens like rock, but wholly retains its essence. Obdurate sinners are rightly compared with it, for they are gripped tight with the coldness of infidelity, and they freeze over every day. The Lord also casts them out like pieces of bread when they are converted, and He makes them perform His mighty deeds, through which the hungry people can feast on heavenly bread. *Frusta* (pieces) is the word we use for parts of anything; it also denotes different gifts of teaching which the Lord has quite often taken from sinners and deigned to demonstrate through His saints. Next comes: *Who stands before the face of his cold?* Mention of the presence of His cold does not imply that it originates from Him, but perhaps that He allows it to exist. Examples of such usage are: *God hardened Pharaoh's heart,*[9] and elsewhere; *I the Lord make good and create evil.*[10] So no-one can withstand the cold which He does not remove, for it can condemn men through their sluggish foolishness. The danger is overemphasised so that greater gratitude may be owed to that most splendid liberation.

18. *He sends out his word, and it shall melt them, and his spirit shall blow, and the waters shall run.* At the coming of the Word no darkness, no cold, and not even the hardness itself should abandon hope, for those summoned are freed from their ills and melt into a most whole-

some liquid. In this way what had been bound fast by the frost of sins, through the Lord's devotion flows freely to achieve healing. As is said elsewhere: *There is no-one that can hide himself from his heat;*[11] for the hardness of the hazardous cold vanishes through the action of His spirit as though by the breath of the south wind, when the heap of sins is dissipated. They submit their diseased necks to the grace of humility, and once they have been melted into most healthy liquids they pour forth streams of spiritual blessings. This happened in the case of the persecutor Saul, and even today it happens with numerous individuals; those who lately were dried up in their obstinate purpose become subsequently well-watered by the current of preaching.

19. *Declaring his word to Jacob, his justices and his judgments to Israel.* Jacob and Israel denote the Church, for these two survived as the names of one person, just as from two peoples one has been formed, which on the one hand is well called Israel, and on the other is correctly termed Jacob. For now any faithful individual is an Israelite, and earlier anyone who pleased the Lord by pure devotion was a Jacob; we know that the Lord declared His word and His justices to him.

20. *He hath not done in like manner to every nation, and his judgments he hath not made manifest to them.* It appears that this verse is to be understood as saying that though the Christian religion has embraced all the Gentiles, He has not spoken to any of them face to face, nor divided the sea, nor rained with manna, nor covered their dwellings with a cloud, nor burned their holocausts with divine fire, nor performed any of the other acts visibly dispensed to the Jewish people by the gift of heaven. The visions granted physically to the Jews' eyes are granted to us spiritually.

Alleluia. Often we are struck by the fact that we find *Alleluia* placed at the close of certain psalms. It perhaps denotes those wholly concerned with the Lord's praises, not interposed with reference to any other matter, but continuing as they begin to the very end with praise of the Lord. But we cannot be dogmatic about this, for it is always dangerous to speak definitively on such questions. It is better for a person to confess that there are matters too deep for him than to be blamed for some facile assumption. So we must leave it to the reader's discretion to follow what he chooses in what we have thought worth suggesting in this or in other novel matters.

Conclusion Drawn From the Psalm

So far in the conclusions to the four preceding psalms which have sung the Lord's praises, we have stated the purpose with which they have been framed: all of them seem set up to prepare us for those that follow. The very order of the psalms is seen to denote a marvellous arrangement of topics. It was fitting to begin with the commands of the divine proclamation, to turn next to the world's recalcitrance which we must avoid, and thirdly to speak of the assembly of the Church; fourthly, the psalm now ended has bidden the gathered Jerusalem to hymn the Lord's praises, for it has been delivered from the various dangers of this world, and as we know is established in eternal rest. So he appends the message that the most holy band, gathered from the regions of the world, should rejoice in threefold exultation, so that in this most holy activity the grace of the Trinity may shine forth everywhere.

Commentary on Psalm 148

1. *Alleluia.* This part of our prayer is confined to a few syllables, but when we meditate on it, it grows ever wider. When the mind's eye gazes on it, it ejaculates the sweetest ideas of a novel kind. When uttered by the reader, it is a proclamation of praise, but when the people respond with it, it is a hymn. Thus the single word, though appearing unchanged in itself, encapsulates so diverse a mystery. This psalm is to be handled carefully, for the prophet by mention of a few creatures impresses on all of them that they must sing the Lord's praises. Those with reason and understanding must do this with their own faculties, whereas those lacking understanding or thought must do it through those which praise the Lord's works with the wisest reflection.

Division of the Psalm

The prophet reflects that all the Lord's works are contained in the things of heaven and earth. In the first part, he urges the things of heaven to utter praises; in the second, he uses allegorical allusions in counselling the things of earth to hymn the Lord with devotion of mind. To both sections he appends one worthy justification, that it is right for a creature to praise its Creator.

Explanation of the Psalm

Praise ye the Lord from the heavens, praise ye him in the high places. Since all heavenly things continually pour out hymns to the Lord, we must examine why the prophet first urges that to be done which is unceasingly fulfilled. It is a human tendency to tell men, when we see them working in the fields: "Work on"; or when they are reading: "Read on"; or when they are building: "Build on." So this exhortation can be uttered, it seems, to intensify the will to work rather than to inaugurate it. But what are these heavenly things which are encouraged to utter praise? Surely the things capable of contemplation of the Lord with the most refined understanding, through His gift. Fired with perennial love, they together hymn their Creator with sweet rejoicing. Since they are immortal, so their praises are not bounded by any close. *In the high places* denotes the more worthy essences which human beings in their weakness rightly proclaim to be lofty in their eyes, since they themselves are forced down by weakness of the flesh. It is right that each and every thing praise its Maker, in accordance with the limitations of the gift which it has received.

2. *Praise ye him, all his angels: praise ye him, all his virtues. Angel* in Greek means messenger, Latin *nuntius.* When one of the heavenly Virtues is dispatched to perform some work, he obtains this title from his office, for he is called an angel because of the name of his function, not of his nature. Next comes: *Praise ye him, all his virtues.* This is their generic title, in which are contained all the creatures which wax proud through the dignity of the heavenly army. Perhaps in this verse angels are cited before Virtues because the agent through whom the Lord's commands are fulfilled is accounted more honourable. It was a

most splendid thing to make the angels begin the Lord's praises, for they are accounted outstanding among creatures.

3. *Praise ye him, O sun and moon: praise him, all ye stars and light.* Sun, moon and stars according to some are governed by their own spirits, but because they are exposed to physical eyes, they are regarded on a reasonable estimate to be lower than the invisible Virtues, even though we see that they adorn heaven's beauty with their handsome light. Those which our sight attains are indeed bright and fine, but they are clearly material; inevitably they give place to those which exist with power unseen. So the prophet has bidden sun, moon and stars to praise the Lord either on their own account or through other substances which have feeling and expression, because the Creator's kindness has given them the right to exist. When we reflect on all these sources of light, they can provoke great wonder in us, for they give mortal eyes the faculty of sight, and they themselves exist with such gleaming brightness. To these was added *light* in general, so that by such association it would rouse the other things that contain light, and were not mentioned specifically, to the Lord's praises.

4. *Praise him, ye heaven of heavens, and the waters that are above the heavens.* Though we read in Genesis that a single sky was created, the apostle Paul too has cited heavens in the plural, for he says that he was transported to the third heaven, and discovered there things such as could not be revealed to man.[1] Here too they are cited in the plural, which perhaps squares with that account. We speak of a single palace when it is bounded by many wings and open spaces, so we can perhaps speak of parts of heaven as heavens, since its constituent parts and its folds are demonstrably one. Genesis recounts that there are waters above the heavens with the words: *He divided the waters that were under the firmament from those that were above the firmament.*[2] Both these hidden areas he denotes as offering great praise, seeing that the fine substance of the heavens remains stable; and though the waters set above it are heavier, they flow down only when bidden. Though heaven's substance is to be accounted clear, bright and outstanding, being worthy of such notable and great inhabitants as it possesses, I have not established that it is alive, and it is rash to argue on the basis of human beliefs a thesis which the authority of divine literature does not record. There is no doubt, I think, that *waters that are above the heavens* are those that descend as rain; as Genesis attests: *The flood*

gates of heaven were opened, and rain fell upon the earth forty days and forty nights,[3] and the rest. It is hardly necessary to investigate this, since all things are bidden to praise the Lord either through themselves or through rational substances.

5. *Praise the name of the Lord. For he spoke, and they were made; he commanded, and they were created.* In this verse he instructs us that the Lord is to be praised for His works; for what is more worthy than that the creature should praise the Creator, in other words that the nature of the universe should praise its Maker? Then, to refute the opinions of philosophers with the voice of Truth Itself, he said: *For he spoke, and they were made. He* denotes the Lord Saviour, for He is the Word made flesh, by whose command all things were created, as the gospel-truth declares: *All things were made by him, and without him nothing was made.*[4] Paul too says: *Who is the image of the invisible God, the firstborn of every creature, for in him were created all things in heaven and earth, visible and invisible, whether thrones or dominations or principalities or powers. All things were created through him and in him.*[5] So that most bogus view of the philosophers must be laid to rest, who think that the world could exist of itself coeternal with the Godhead.[6] He spoke, then, when He said: *Let there be light, and there was light.*[7] *He commanded* means "He decided and established," as another psalm shows: *He hath commanded his covenant for ever.*[8] *Made* and *created* convey a certain differentiation, if we ponder them more carefully. We too can make, but we cannot create. Since he had used the general term *made,* he added what was peculiar to the Godhead, so that you could understand *made* in the sense of *created.*

6. *He hath established them for ever, and for ages of ages: he hath made a decree, and it shall not pass away.* This passage too announces the power and strength of the Lord with the words: *He hath established them for ever, and for ages of ages: he hath made a decree, and it shall not pass away.* This is to remove all doubt that God is almighty, for what He has established continues in being without change, since this conclusion is applied to the things of heaven. But we read of the world to come: *There will be a new heaven and a new earth,*[9] so how can one say of the present heaven: *He hath established them for ever?* There is however no doubt that all things have been established by God. Though man himself dies, he is *established* in God's eyes when he rises again; similarly heaven and earth remain in God's sight when they are

made new. Once they have laid aside their roughness or corruptible character, nature itself is made better and abides, since it has been bidden to exist in eternity. As Paul says about the transformation of our bodies: *When the corruptible has put on incorruption, and the mortal puts on immortality.*[10] A *decree* means a law or condition, so that we may realise that all things are in His power. It cannot pass away because the Almighty established it, and Truth has promised it in return.

7. *Praise the Lord from the earth, ye dragons and all ye abysses.* Now that he has run through the heavenly substances, the prophet passes to the second section where he warns earthly objects, animate or inanimate, to unfold the Lord's praises through the wisest natures. A dragon has a body furrowed with scales, which is exceedingly long like a snake's; it is fired by natural heat, and to abate its body-temperature it dwells in watery caves. It does not creep along the ground, but when it decides to move it is said to fly along. It feeds on elephant-flesh; with remarkable strength it squeezes with its coils the limbs of those huge animals, so that it extracts their life-breath as though they were flies.[11] With *abysses* he ponders the depths of sea-waters, which must summon forth all the reasons for praise of the Lord. Observe the order of the expressions. The first substance mentioned is that of creatures with feeling, the second is that of objects bereft of it, so that the Lord is to be praised in virtue of all created things. However, as we have said on the authority of the Fathers that this psalm is a hymn of the blessed to be sung when this world is transformed, we must interpret *dragons* and *abysses* here as abrasive and strong-minded characters who are converted in this world, and honoured by offering praises to the Lord in the native land to come.

8. *Fire, hail, snow, ice, stormy winds which fulfil his word.* Fire, hail, snow and ice denote by the allegory previously mentioned men who in this world have passed from the wild conduct of extreme wickedness to the most tranquil enthusiasm of devotion. Note what finally follows: *Stormy winds which fulfil his word.* Who are they who fulfil his word but those who have ceased to be storm-tossed and evil, and have deserved to attain the grace of confessing Him?

9. *Mountains and all hills, fruitful trees and all cedars.* 10. *Beasts and all cattle, serpents and feathered fowls. Mountains* denotes men raised high with swollen power, *hills*, moderate men who handle affairs

evenly, *fruitful trees*, those converted from the hardness of sins who have brought forth most sweet fruits of good manners. *Cedars* denotes totally arrogant and proud people; *beasts*, the cruel and unrestrained; *all cattle*, the common, boundless crowd; *serpents*, the poisonous and crafty; *feathered fowls*, the philosophers whose custom it is to speed with the swiftness of their thought through the natures of objects in the world. From all these kinds of men Christ prepares His chosen, so that they can be gathered at the resurrection by troops of angels.

11. *Kings of the earth and all people, princes and all judges of the earth.*
12. *Young men and maidens, the older with the younger. . . .* We have often said that *kings of the earth* are holy men who govern their bodies, control their flesh and do not permit it to fulfil the enticements of its will. *All people* refers to the crowds which assemble together before the Lord with the eagerness shared by many. *Princes* we aptly regard as high-ranking powers in the world, and so that you should interpret them as noblemen and men of power, observe what follows: *And all judges of the earth.* We often see it happen that they suddenly abandon worldly power, and love to enter the service of the Lord. *Young men* means those on fire with the heat of youth who are converted to cool moderation. *The older with the younger* denotes a mixed-age group, for the Lord is able to summon from both sexes and every age those whom He chooses. To justify your relating all this to human persons, observe what follows.

13. *Let them praise the name of the Lord, for his name alone is exalted: the confession of him is above heaven and earth.* This passage too is proclaimed in virtue of His magnificence and uniqueness. In the words: *For his name alone is exalted: the confession of him is above heaven and earth,* His magnificence is undoubtedly being made known in the whole world. Up to this final statement higher creatures are kept in abeyance, so that the faithful people may praise the Lord when established, as they shall be, in that native land of the future, when we know that they are released from the bonds of sins. Next follows the most just reason why the Lord must be proclaimed: it is because *his name alone is exalted.* It is exalted because in Paul's words before Him: *Every knee bows, of things in heaven, on earth, and under the earth.*[12] The psalmist added: *The confession of him is above heaven and earth.* Here *confession* denotes the praise paid to Him by all rational creatures after

the renewal of this world. He spoke of *above heaven and earth*, for neither heavenly nor earthly things can be found equal to those praises.

14. *And he shall exalt the horn of his people. A hymn to all his saints: to the children of Israel, a people approaching to him.* Here the hymn wells forth wholly in virtue of the Lord's sanctity. When he says: *He shall exalt the horn of his people. A hymn to all his saints: to the children of Israel, a people approaching him,* undoubtedly the Lord's holiness and His gifts are being praised, for He will deign to glorify His saints by granting them a share in His gift. *Horn* is used for power, as we have often said; for in this world it is brought low because of the hardships and griefs which the faithful people endure, but in the next it will be exalted, for there all their glory is made manifest. The reasons are first, that they deserve to be at His right hand; second, they will judge in company with the Lord; and third, they will pass into eternal peace and joy, so that they are rightly said to be exalted, for through His wondrous devotion they attain contemplation of the Lord himself. This happens, in Paul's words: *When he shall have delivered up the kingdom to God the Father, when he shall have brought to nought all principality and all power and virtue,*[13] for he must reign until He puts all enemies beneath His feet. Next comes: *A hymn to all his saints.* These words are a promise; they represent the highest perfection of total blessedness. What the saints will deserve is to praise the Lord, the song which they sing when they are crowned by His eternal gift. Once they have obtained this, they will lack nothing more; they will have there all that cannot be grasped here: the manna of heaven, satiety which knows no surfeit, a gift beyond understanding, the continual performance of this task, and a constant and burning zeal for it. The *hymn,* then, is the saints' song directed to the Lord's praise, in which soul and body harmonise with perfect purity. We may appear to utter such praise eagerly here and now, but we can complete it only defectively. He added: *To the children of Israel, a people approaching to him.* He reveals to which saints that hymn is entrusted, namely the children of Israel, who are declared to have that title not only by race but also by faith. The name *Israelites* we properly give to those who by right belief have deserved to behold the Lord with the eyes of the heart; Israelites are those known to approach the Lord Christ by obedience

to His commands, whereas those who do not execute His commands are far from Him. So only the person who is His member is closest to Him, for the member cannot be separated from the Head.

So far as the final *Alleluia* is concerned, we must understand here too what we said in the case of the previous psalm; for repetition at such a slight interval causes boredom rather than understanding in the listener.

Conclusion Drawn From the Psalm

Let us observe the beauty and the power with which this psalm gleams forth. The voices of heaven are mentioned, which as yet cannot be heard because of the frailty of our bodily state. Heavenly creatures and earthly substances utter praise to the Lord; melodious songs are sung so that the Lord may be lauded with the harmonious delight of His creatures. Indeed, at the very outset he mentioned the speculative science of astronomy, which secular teachers have investigated in great detail, and which they have considered should be defined like this: "Astronomy is a discipline which contemplates the courses and all the shapes of the heavenly constellations, and with investigative reason surveys the dispositions of the stars in relation to each other and to the earth."[14] They say that by the annual course of the stars the year is composed of the fourfold division of the seasons; and they state that this is the source from which the rain-clouds come, the earth's produce is created, the cold weather develops, the warmth in the air takes its existence, and all that is necessary throughout the world can at God's command be supplied through the agency of the stars. Our Christian forbears have stated that we must not shun this knowledge, so long as we recognise it as a discipline which investigates the motions of the stars in their natural yearly course. But when the slippery slope of error enters, and directs astronomy towards the role of astrology, expressing the belief that the future lives of mortals are to be inferred from the course of the stars, the astronomers must then be accursed and blinded instead, when they reckon that they foresee what the Creator has decided to conceal from us for our profit. They further say that the planets speed on fixed courses opposite to the movement of heaven, and that the fabric of heaven, which keeps itself in being by rotary motion, possesses a pleasurable harmony which is sweet and unceasing.[15] But let us ascribe the obedience of natural objects to the dominion of the Creator, who bids His creatures obey Him by that very power with which He brought them into existence.

Commentary on Psalm 149

1. *Alleluia.* We are reminded to keep this term in constant use, for we are aware that it is fittingly appended to both New and Old Testaments. It is set before the Old at Psalm 104, in which the miracles in Egypt and the blessings at the Red Sea are described; here we are taught that it prefaces a new canticle, in which lies the total consummation of the whole of religion. It is accordingly placed everywhere, for we realise that it must be uttered on every occasion. It is a term to be revered with great devotion; the angels sing it, and on earth the prayers of the faithful often incorporate it.

Division of the Psalm

In earlier psalms the prophet recommends praises to the Lord in countless admonitions. Here too he says first that a new song must be sung in various ways to the Lord Christ, for by His devotion He has built the universal Jerusalem from the whole population of the world. Secondly, he describes the joys and powers of the saints, and says that the punishment of sinners is the glory of the just.

Explanation of the Psalm

Sing ye to the Lord a new canticle: let his praise be in the church of the saints. In this and the three ensuing verses the Lord's greatness is praised with reference to His works, for in the words: *Sing ye to the Lord a new canticle: let his praise be in the church of the saints,* he is saying that the Lord is to be proclaimed because of His works. The prophet was set in this world in body only, and in thought and faith he mingled with the host of angels in that native land in which he prompts the blessed people to sing a new canticle. The new canticle is the secret of the holy incarnation, the wondrous nativity, the saving teaching, the suffering which is the mistress of endurance, the resurrection which is the most certain proof of our hope, the seat at the right hand of the Father which denotes strength and unique power. But so that you should not believe that this praise can be hymned everywhere and by each and all, there follows: *Let his praise be in the church of the saints.* You can say that this denotes the Catholic Church, which is indeed the Church of saints, or the heavenly Jerusalem which is also undoubtedly the abode of the saints; for *church* (*ecclesia*) means assembly, and there is no doubt that this can refer to one or the other.

2. *Let Israel rejoice in him that made him, and let the children of Sion be joyful in their king.* Israel and Sion are different names, but the power of the saints is one and the same, for Israel means the one who sees God, and Sion means observation; both clearly refer to the blessed people who are urged to rejoice and glory in their King the Lord Christ, for they have seen that He who they believed in this world would come in His majesty, is almighty, the Donor of the eternal reward. Will there be any limit to their joy in beholding the Lord of the world who they believed died here for the salvation of all? We cannot rightly measure this joy, but we are sure that what this great truth promises surpasses all blessings.

3. *Let them praise his name in chorus: let them sing to him with the timbrel and the psaltery.* In the previous verse he said that we must rejoice in the Lord Christ, and now he says that the Lord's name is to be praised in chorus. This is the chorus which by then suffers no dispersal or weariness or scandal, but is gathered on the worth of its merits, and ever abides in the most loving unity. Another psalm explains the nature and scope of this chorus in the words: *From the rising of the sun unto the going down, praise the name of the Lord.*[1] The chorus is that gathered from the world's beginning from the aggregate of nations; it can be fully mustered only in the homeland to come. Next comes: *Let them sing to him with the timbrel and the psaltery.* We have stated that the timbrel and psaltery are praiseworthy acts performed in this world as services to God, which are no longer observed in that homeland, but they will be in evidence there when there is rejoicing as we glory in them. What saddens us here delights us there; what afflicts

us here cheers us there. As we read in Scripture, *Blessed are they who suffer persecution for justice's sake, for theirs is the kingdom of heaven.*[2] So all these, whether timbrel or psaltery, hymn the Lord in the world to come, for they are known to be practised or endured in this life for His name.

4. *For the Lord is well pleased with his people, and he will exalt the meek unto salvation.* We read that the Creator found all his works pleasing in the nature of the world, but we also read that God repents or is glad, according to their changed nature. So we read: *It repents me to have made man,*[3] but elsewhere: *I shall rejoice upon one doing penance more than upon ninety-nine just who need not penance.*[4] We attribute these changes of attitude to the Godhead as metaphorical allusions deriving from our feeble nature. When the prophet says: *For the Lord is well pleased with his people,* He means "When He has made the people rejoice in perfect bliss, when He has made equal with the angels and made truly His own those who He has decreed are to be crowned by His gift." He will be *well pleased* when as Paul puts it: *He will be all in all.*[5] *The meek* denotes the patient who have endured various evil sufferings in this world, but have remained untroubled in most holy commitment to God's kingdom. *Unto salvation* means in eternal life, with which the just Lord will repay them at the judgment.

5. *The saints shall rejoice in glory: they shall be joyful in their beds.* From this point to the end of the psalm the strength and power of the Lord is proclaimed. What greater strength is there than to bestow such great power on His saints that by His gift they gain victories over their enemies? But when he says: *The saints shall rejoice in glory: they shall be joyful in their beds,* they now attain the happy status which embraces the joys of the saints and the power of those who believe in Christ. But let us now observe how the saints' rejoicing is described. *Glory* denotes repeated praise consisting of good deeds; the just rejoice in it *in their beds,* that is, in the depths of their hearts. As Paul puts it: *For our glory is this: the testimony of our conscience;*[6] for they rejoice in the region accessible only to the knowledge of Him who deigned to bestow it. They rejoice particularly since they weigh the fact that they have a Lord whose goodness finds expression in bestowing pardon on the guilty, grace on sinners, enduring glory on the undeserving. By contrast the foolish person in this world departs from himself, rejoices in people's gossip, and imagines that he deserves the

praise with which lying words exalt him. So the saints have a doctrine of glorying, and put limits to their joy, ascribing to Him all the blessings which He bestows. If there is no limit put on happiness, there is no joy, but destruction.

6. *The rejoicings of the Lord are in their throats, and two-edged swords in their hands.* 7. *To execute vengeance upon the nations, chastisements among the people.* We must observe how beautiful, how useful these differing expressions are. Earlier he said that the saints rejoice in their beds; now he says that the Lord's rejoicings are set in their throats, the sense being that they never cease to praise whether in thought or in tongue Him from whom they obtain eternal gifts. He also moves on to explain the power that they wield, with the words: *And two-edged swords in their hands.* The two-edged sword is the word of the Lord Saviour, of which Christ Himself says in the gospel: *I have come not to send peace to the earth, but a sword.*[7] It is two-edged because it contains the two Testaments. First it separated Jews from Gentiles; subsequently it segregated and cut off only the Christians from the enticements of the whole world. There is one sword, but two ways of cutting which He grants to the chosen peoples at various selected moments of time. So the prophet says that these swords are in their hands, in other words, in the power of the saints; as Scripture has it: *The word of the Lord came to the hand of Aggeus the prophet.*[8] So the blessed ones will assume this power and pass judgment in company with the Lord; as Scripture says: *You shall sit on twelve seats, judging the twelve tribes of Israel.*[9] For note what follows: *To execute vengeance upon the nations, chastisements among the people.* This truly takes place when they shall judge in company with the Lord.

8. *To bind their king with fetters, and their nobles with bonds of iron.* 9. *To execute upon them the judgment that is written: This glory is to all his saints.* He explains what the two-edged sword performs: it binds the kings of the earth with fetters, from which there is no freedom to depart. It also clamps bonds of iron on the nobles of the world, so that they are oppressive when borne, and they cannot rupture their links by any show of strength. This is truly a new song, that the poor who were mocked in the world can pass judgment on the princes of the earth. Next follows: *To execute upon them the judgment that is written,* meaning that of which Paul says: *Know you not that we shall judge angels?*[10] Who can conceive of such a miracle? Who can mentally

grasp such great glory, that proud and wicked sinners should experience as judges those who they thought were to be slaughtered here on earth like cheap cattle? So that you would not perhaps imagine that the apostles alone would pass judgment, he added: *This glory is to all his saints.* All participate with Christ in judgment who do not oppose His commands, for with devoted will they too share in His decisions. But though the power and glory of the saints have been described in this varied account, none of them is found to have all the rewards of virtues in their totality. Christ Jesus is the only one of whom Paul says: *For in him dwelleth the fullness of the Godhead corporeally,*[11] that is, in substance. Since the Lord possesses all blessings perfectly and wholly, He bestows on each as He wills; as John says, He is clearly the fullness of all the saints.[12]

Conclusion Drawn From the Psalm

We must carefully observe how the preceding psalm is linked to this one in the task of praise, and how a certain differentiation divides them. In the first he encouraged all creatures to proclaim the Lord, but this one more separately and specifically showed that Israel must sing a new canticle and become joyful over their own Lord, who has made them gather from the crowd of nations. Also mentioned is the power which is to be bestowed on the saints at the judgment, so that the Lord's strength can be acknowledged in their glory. In this sense it is both associated with the previous psalm in its task of praise, and distinct from it in the peculiarity of its themes.

Commentary on Psalm 150

1. *Alleluia.* See how once again that herald of salvation is brought back before us, to speak not of bodily sustenance but of heavenly abundance. The city of God is urged to gather from the circumference of the world, and to sing with tongue and heart. So let us sing with total concentration this Alleluia, which through the Lord's ordering has brought the entire corpus of psalmody to its high point. Just as

transient earthly fire hastens to the upper regions and raises its ruddy crest to a peak, so this psalm gradually grows and flits upward to the heights of heaven by the steps of the virtues. If with the support of the Lord's right hand we too mount with it in devotion of spirit, we shall be granted access to the End which brings salvation, and which is bounded by no limits.

Content of the Psalm

It was right that this psalm which mounts to the harmonious unity of all the saints should not have a division, because it has guided the close of the whole book of psalms to the power of the indivisible Trinity; moreover, it deals with the whole content as a single thought, without any apparent change of spokesman or theme. This is the figure called *hyrmos*,[1] by which the course of a speech preserves its uniformity to the end. It is short, so that it may not induce weariness; it abounds in musical instruments, so that it could be made most suitable for spiritual marriage, and could be sung with marital joy in the assembly of the heavenly Jerusalem. Its purpose is praise by the saints' gathering to the Lord, who has restored them to His image and caused them to lay aside the frailty of flesh and blood. He has now set them in that blessedness to conform with His glory, so that they may be filled with abundance of all blessings. As Paul says of them: *He has blessed us with all spiritual blessings, so that we should be holy and unspotted in his sight.*[2]

Explanation of the Psalm

Praise ye the Lord in his saints: praise him in the firmament of his power. We must carefully observe the pleasurable sweetness with which this book of psalms ends, and how it looks back to its beginning. The prophet says that now that the saints have been received in the heavenly Jerusalem, it is right to praise the Lord, that is, it is right for those to whom He has revealed the shape of right behaviour. Earlier it was said of Him: *Blessed is the man who has not walked in the counsel of the ungodly,*[3] and the rest; for the saints are those who by His generosity have deserved to imitate Him. There is a fitting explanation of the kind of reverence owed to the saints; it is the Lord who is to be praised because they are justified, and not they themselves, for His glory should be hymned first since He permits the deeds which are to be acclaimed. Veneration is however to be accorded to the just, because they have received divine gifts. Next follows: *Praise him in the firmament of his power.* The strength of his power lies in the fact that He endured destruction for the salvation of all, and by virtue of His power overcame death itself, together with its most wicked founder; He sundered the bars of hell, and led strong believers to the kingdom of heaven.

2. *Praise him for his powers, praise him according to the multitude of his greatness.* Here he now instructs us that the Lord must be praised for His power and greatness. He says: *Praise him for his powers, praise him according to the multitude of his greatness.* From now to the end of the psalm he explains by mystical allusions how He is to be praised. His power is as was stated in Psalm 8: *Thou hast subjected all things under his feet, all sheep and oxen: moreover the beasts also of the fields.*[4] And as Paul says: *Before whom every knee bows, of things in heaven, on the earth and under the earth.*[5] Let us also ponder the nature and extent of what is enjoined on the blessed people, for there follows: *Praise him according to the multitude of his greatness.* Who, I ask, can possibly praise Him according to the multitude of His greatness, when Psalm 144 says: *Great is the Lord, and greatly to be praised, and of his greatness there is no end?*[6] But if you observe to whom the present verse is addressed, namely the spiritual powers who have greater strength to achieve this activity of praise, no doubt will remain. Since the Lord's power is without limit, He is proclaimed according to His greatness, when He shall be praised without end.

3. *Praise him with the sound of trumpet: praise him with psaltery and harp.* Here musical instruments are set in order in a meaningful way. The trumpet is to sound to the King, the psaltery to God, the harp and the rest to the Bridegroom. Obviously these instruments do not exist in heaven, but clearly all are to be ascribed in mystical allusion to the Lord Christ. The trumpet is a thin tube, formed from parts of horn joined together, or from some metal; at one end is a round hollow and at the other a narrow mouthpiece. When filled with intake of breath, it amplifies with fearful sound; it is used in times of war, or made available for royal visitations. The arrangement of the psaltery is op-

posite to that of the harp; at the top it has echoing mouths, so to say, of wood, where it catches the sounds of the strings coming from below, and directs them upwards, matching the words with most pleasant melody. The harp has its wooden belly set below; having received the sounds of the strings coming from the top, it transmits them in unified and pleasurable sweetness. All these instruments represent human actions, and are figuratively said to make the Lord's praises resound.

4. *Praise him with timbrel and chorus: praise him with strings and organ.* As we have said, these verses too up to the end of the psalm are appropriate to marriage-hymns. A timbrel consists merely of two drums joined together at their tops; hide stretched over them gives off a resounding reverberation. Musicians beat the hide in disciplined rhythm, and play a melody with repeated resonance. A chorus is a gathering of several voices ordered to achieve a pleasant harmony. Next comes: *Praise him with strings and organ.* Some persons suggest that since other instruments besides the psalm and harp could be found to play by the plucking of strings, the psalmist was speaking of strings in general so as to allot to the Lord's praises the whole of that class of musical instrument. An organ is a sort of castellation fashioned with different pipes, from which is produced a most abundant sound by creating wind from bellows. To ensure that this is ordered with seemly melody, its interior is constructed with wooden keys, which the fingers of organists press in controlled fashion, and thus achieve a loud and most pleasant tune.

5–6. *Praise him on fine-sounding cymbals, praise him on sweet-tinkling cymbals: let every spirit praise the Lord.* So that we should interpret the earlier expressions as allusions to the saints, he passes further to the human voice. But we must ponder the distinction made between these words. We must take *fine-sounding cymbals* as our lips, justifiably listed among musical instruments because there is a certain likeness to cymbals, and human voices, as we know, produce through the lips the sweetest harmony. Harmony is the fusion of different objects reduced to one accord. We know that this happens in the case of human voices, when the timing and the syllables are guided to a single agreement of sound. So the cymbals are our lips which are struck to control in a most specific way the sound of our vocal chords, and when they are roused most devotedly to serve the Lord, they sound forth in saving tones. *Sweet-tinkling cymbals* are very small vessels made of mingled metals; they have their hollows in the sides, and when shaken with artistic rhythm, they give forth a high-pitched sound with delightful harmony. But since our most holy prophet wanted all his words to be understood in the spiritual sense, he ended the book with a most fitting close: *Let every spirit praise the Lord.* What must praise the Lord is emphatically not flesh and blood, not worldly ambition, not the enticements of the secular world, but that which has the higher place in the nature of things, that which is redolent of heavenly things, that which desires eternal rewards. So he offered a brief and perfect statement for the whole work, that all things must praise the Lord spiritually. So after the completion of the psalms, the perfection of the entire discipline of music was allotted to them; the blast of the trumpet, the strumming of the harp, the tinkling of cymbals, the voices in chorus, that sweetest combination of spiritual harmony which is not heard with bodily ears, but is caught by contemplation of a most pure mind.

Just as we began in Psalm 1 with mention of syllogisms, so we must end with a similar conclusion. We fittingly began with a categorical syllogism, the purest and chief of all syllogisms, so we now also conclude our work with one, for it is appropriate that the end should match the beginning since in sacred literature everything must be found to harmonise with the rest. We must assemble a categorical syllogism here in this way: Let every spirit praise the Lord. He whom every spirit must praise is the true God. So the Lord is the true God. This is indeed a splendid form of utterance, which impels an unwilling individual to confess what he had earlier refused to concede. Indeed, we have shown that the series of psalms is crammed with points of grammar, etymologies, figures, rhetoric, topics, dialectic, definitions, music, geometry, astronomy, expressions peculiar to divine Scripture, in so far as the Lord has deigned to grant this. Thus those who have already read these features may gladly acknowledge them, and those who are as yet novices may observe them most clearly delineated without coming to grief.

Conclusion From the Psalms

The beautiful and wondrous order of the psalms has been unfolded, bounded indeed by a mystical number, but boundless in sacred powers. Their extent is known only to Him who embraces the sands of the sea, the drops of rain, the natures of all creatures in their calculable quantity. But though we cannot wholly grasp it, investigation of it is useful because when surveyed it is ever found to be more abundant. How many new features still remain to be described, and how numerous are the faithful whose brains will be exercised with careful application until the end of the world! But this truth will be recognised in its fullness only when the Lord Himself deigns to bestow His contemplation; however, so far as human intelligence could trace it, the entire series of psalms has been surveyed in its twofold mystery. First, as has been said on the authority of the Fathers, it embraces the mysteries of the Old and New Testaments, for seven decades are relevant to the sabbath, which undoubtedly is connected with the earlier form of religious worship; and then eight decades are ascribed to our own time, for with sacred devotion we revere the Lord's resurrection on the eighth day. Secondly, we have observed that through the Lord's generosity the earth was cleansed of its sins after one hundred and fifty days,[7] when the flood covered the earth. So the spiritual depth of the psalms with their perennial cleansing purifies the sin-stained hearts of men until Judgment Day; and from this we experience a saving flood which washes clean our minds befouled with sins.

What in fact is there that one cannot find in this heavenly chest of the divine scriptures? If you search for Genesis, there is an explanation here of how the world was made. If you mention a prophet, who has said so much about the Lord's incarnation? If you long for the gospel, it clearly reveals in countless places the passion and resurrection of the Lord Christ. If you want an apostle, listen to this teacher and consoler who both proclaims the future judgment to correct us, and often prays for sinners. Not to extend the discussion longer, if you read with the greatest care, you find all that is done in heaven, on earth, in the sea, in the world below aptly recounted in their due places. Bishop Athanasius attests this in a splendid sermon,[8] in which he analyses the virtues of the psalms with inquiring truth, and proves that all that is embraced by the content of sacred Scripture is to be found in them. If it is not impious to say so, the psalmist makes comprehensible the nature of God in two words, *Today I,* though from no books or codices can it be understood as it is explained in this brief statement, and as it is in some degree inferred from what it does not say; for in Psalm 2 the Father says to the Son: *Today I have begotten thee.*[9] In two words here there is subtle clarification of what seems to be possibly beyond human understanding. The book embraces both New and Old Testaments in such a unique way that you can truly realise that a spiritual library is built up in this book. If Paradise is considered desirable because four gliding rivers are known to lend it beauty, how much more blessed is the soul watered by the springs of one hundred and fifty psalms!

The divine power in its action has not confined itself within this number. Many different wonders are revealed on a wider front, whether understood in part or as yet wholly unknown. For example, in the case of the one hundred and fifty-three fish which the apostles' nets drew up from the depths of the sea,[10] the inclusive number of saints is explained. Again, we read that Noah's ark, built as a forerunner of holy Church, was three hundred cubits long, fifty wide, and thirty high; Origen as is his wont based many sacramental parallels on this.[11] So it is undoubtedly clear that the Creator and Craftsman of the world, when He ordered all the things of heaven and earth, made all that was created according to measure, number and weight; as the wisest authority says: *Thou hast ordered all things in measure, in number, and in weight.*[12]

Now to strengthen our memory let us briefly impart what we see is more broadly stated earlier. First, it is appropriate to remember what was said of the wide variation in the headings. We must also recall that the spokesmen are most appositely changed in the course of psalms, and that their conclusions are especially framed to counter heretics. Other issues are why the Hebrew alphabet is used in the psalms; why one psalm is seen to be formed from parts of others; why psalms are intercalated; why repetition of verses is found in psalms; the interpretation of Hebrew names; the psalms described as "identical-ending"; the fifteen psalms of the steps; why the seven psalms of penitents are taught; why the words and tears of those who grieve for the city of Jerusalem are poured out; why the series of psalms ends with praise of the Lord, in which is explained the number of ways in which He is foretold, though His praises cannot be unfolded in any books or by any human powers.[13] So this variety of the psalms is perhaps aptly compared to the most precious stone called the topaz, or to the most handsome peacock, which shows off the different colours of its body whenever the eye of the beholder is trained on them.

These are the points which we have covered to the best of our poor ability, in so far as the Lord has deigned to allow it. I ask you, masters rich in your abundant reading of heavenly literature: spare this novice, pardon me in my confession to you, be well-disposed to me. It is hard to find any work of man which does not permit of some query; as the apostle James attests: *If any man offend not in word, he is a perfect man.*[14] But if some persons launch calumnies against sacred literature, what will they do to the weak whom they boldly accuse? Utterances are always to be related to the disposition of the speaker. If we seek to destroy everything by argumentative disputation, by our unguarded opposition we condemn instead devoted commitment. But now it is time to turn our hearts to the Lord, towards whom all our efforts should strive, and whom the close of our toil should attain.

Prayer

Lord, You are the true Teacher and Donor, Advocate and Judge, Giver and Adviser, awe-inspiring yet merciful, Plunderer and Consoler. You give sight to minds that are blind. You make Your commands attainable by the weak. Your devotion is such that You wish to be continually importuned. Your generosity is such that You allow no-one to despair. Grant us our enlightened requests at Your hands, and especially those things of which in our weakness we remain unaware. Receive what we have acknowledged comes from You, and spare us for what in our ignorance we have claimed is from ourselves. Lead us to the contemplation in which we can no longer go astray. Grant that I may perform the things which I have presumed to mention under Your inspiration. Grant that what I have urged others to observe may be fulfilled, so that having granted me devoted words, You may also bestow on Your servants praiseworthy action. Free us, Lover of men, from the danger which Paul mentions, that while preaching to others I may myself be found false.[15] You truly know how weak we are; You recognise the nature of the foe who oppresses us. In our uneven contest and our mortal weakness we seek You, for the glory redounds to Your majesty if the roaring lion is overcome by the feeble sheep, if that most violent spirit who fell from heaven and is held subject here by Your warfare is overcome by the great weakness of our flesh. Then, even if through Your forbearance we suffer his power for a time, we shall certainly not be devoured by his insatiable jaws. Make him sad by reason of mankind's joy, for he ever rejoices when we fail. Amen.

NOTES

LIST OF ABBREVIATIONS

ACW	Ancient Christian Writers
Adriaen	M. Adriaen, ed., *Magni Aurelii Cassiodori Expositio Psalmorum* (CCL 97 and 98, Turnhout 1958)
Boylan	P. Boylan, *The Psalms* (2 vols., Dublin 1921)
CCL	Corpus christianorum, series latina
CSEL	Corpus scriptorum ecclesiasticorum latinorum
Martin	J. Martin, *Antike Rhetorik* (Munich 1974)
MG	*Patrologia graeca*, ed. J. P. Migne (Paris 1857–66)
ML	*Patrologia latina*, ed. J. P. Migne (Paris 1844–55)
ODCC	The Oxford Dictionary of the Christian Church[2] (Oxford 1974)
O'Donnell	J. J. O'Donnell, *Cassiodorus* (Berkeley and Los Angeles 1979)

PSALM 101 [PS. 102(101)]

1. Below, 6 and 10 f.
2. 2 Tim. 4.7.
3. See Psalms 17(16), 86(85), 90(89).
4. See Psalms 6, 32(31), 38(37), 51(50).
5. 2 Cor. 11.29.
6. Lam. 3.44. One wonders if the author of *The Cloud of Unknowing* chose this title with the scriptural passage in mind.
7. Hab. 1.2.
8. A reminiscence of Virgil, *Ecl.* 2.59.
9. Cf. 1 Cor. 14.15.
10. Walpole, *Early Latin Hymns* No. 82, regards the hymn of which these lines form a part, *Bis ternas horas explicans,* as probably by Nicetas of Remesiana, because of possible reminiscences of his *De psalmodiae bono.* But see now J. Svöfférfy, *Die Annalen der lat. Hymnendichtung* 1 (Berlin 1964) 52.
11. Isa. 1.11 f.
12. Ps. 51(50).19.
13. Ps. 51(50).11.
14. "Dwelling on," "repetition"; see above at Ps. 13(12).1.
15. The words are clearly connected.
16. Prov. 15.30.
17. John 6.51.
18. Lam. 4.8.
19. This psalm inspires other Fathers to compare the pelican with the desert-hermit; see Augustine, *En. Ps.* 101.7; Paulinus of Nola, *Ep.* 40, and ACW 36.344 f.
20. Similarly the night-raven is the symbol of the anchorite; see n. 19 above.
21. On the sparrow as an image of the penitent, see the references in n. 19 above.
22. "Comparison"; see at Ps. 1.3, etc.
23. See the list of *argumenta* at *Inst.* 2.3.15.
24. See at Ps. 22(21).9 above.

25. Ps. 51(50).4.
26. Ps. 75(74).9.
27. 'Attenuation'; see at Ps. 22(21).7, 38(37).6, etc.
28. 1 Cor. 1.27.
29. Jer. 5.6.
30. 1 Peter 5.8.
31. It is difficult not to think of the fate of Boethius here.
32. Ps. 119(118).71.
33. Gal. 4.4 f.
34. 2 Cor. 6.2.
35. This is the *argumentum a tempore*, one of the *argumenta extrinsecus* in Cassiodorus' discussion in the *Institutes*.
36. Ps. 98(97).1.
37. Ps. 11(10).5.
38. Eccli. 6.24 f.
39. Eccli. 6.30.
40. Cf. 1 Cor. 12.8 ff. and 30.
41. Cf. Acts 2.4 ff.
42. Ezech. 37.21 f.
43. Eph. 4.5 f.
44. 1 Cor. 15.28.
45. Doubtless he thinks especially of the Epicurean doctrine with regard to the first, and of the Aristotelian doctrine of the eternity of the heavens with regard to the second.
46. Ps. 148.5.
47. See above at Ps. 9.2.
48. Matt. 6.25.
49. Dan. 2.20 f.
50. Gal. 4.19.
51. 2 Tim. 1.2.
52. John 17.24.
53. Ps. 50(49).18.
54. See above, n. 4.

Psalm 102 [Ps. 103(102)]

1. See above at Ps. 11.2.
2. 1 Cor. 15.54.

3. Matt. 25.41.
4. Matt. 25.34.
5. 2 Tim. 4.8.
6. Cf. Matt. 14.17.
7. Matt. 5.7.
8. Rom. 12.19.
9. Exod. 32.9.
10. This is the figure which combines words of similar sound but dissimilar meaning, sometimes as here suggesting cause and effect; cf. *Ad Herennium* 4.32.
11. Rom. 2.4.
12. Ps. 50(49).21.
13. Matt. 5.45.
14. Matt. 25.41.
15. Rom. 11.25 f.
16. Rom. 11.32.
17. Luke 16.26.
18. Eccli. 30.1.
19. Cf. Heb. 12.6.
20. John 14.6. On the definitions, see *Inst.* 2.3.14.
21. He refers to the Pythagoreans, whose doctrine of the transmigration of souls is attested by Xenophanes and others.
22. See above at 84(83).11. Martianus Capella distinguishes *parison* from *isocolon* by stressing that isocolon has verbal equivalence of syllables, whereas *parison* has not.
23. See Augustine, *En. Ps.* 102.23 (= CCL 40.1471).
24. See above at Ps. 3.3.
25. See Ps. 8.2 and 11(10).

Psalm 103 [Ps. 104(103)]

1. See above at Ps. 81(80).3.
2. Augustine, *En. Ps.* 103, *serm.* 4.19 (CCL 40.1535).
3. The word should mean "prior exclamation"; it is included in the grammarian Tryphon's list of tropes. See Martin, 262.
4. "Comparison"; see above at Ps. 1.3.

5. Cant. 3.6, 5.10.
6. Cf. Eph. 5.27.
7. Eph. 5.8.
8. Cf. John 19.23 f.
9. Ps. 148.4.
10. Acts 1.9.
11. "The notional"; see above at Ps. 1.1.
12. The Latin of the psalm reverses the two nouns; the Douai translation has 'who makest thy angels spirits'.
13. Luke 12.49.
14. Ps. 24(23).1.
15. 1 Cor. 3.11.
16. *Hyperbaton* is more usually used of the transposition of words or phrases; see above at Ps. 37(36).9.
17. Ps. 36(35).7.
18. John 19.11.
19. Gen. 15.16.
20. Gen. 9.11.
21. John 7.38.
22. Matt. 16.18.
23. Luke 6.30.
24. The quotation is untraced.
25. Ps. 23(22).5.
26. Ps. 34(33).6.
27. Matt. 15.13.
28. So Augustine, *En. Ps.* 103, *serm.* 3.15 (CCL 40.1513).
29. This sentence praising such foundations as Vivarium itself is probably one of the additions made in the second recension; see the Introduction, p. 5 in ACW 51.
30. Wisd. 5.6.
31. Matt. 5.45.
32. Mark 14.41.
33. Cf. Mark 15.33.
34. Cf. Matt. 26.74 f.
35. A ludicrous etymology.
36. In §11 above.
37. The alleged connection is fanciful.
38. 1 Cor. 1.24.

42. See on Ps. 78(77).24.
43. Luke 19.10.
44. 1 Cor. 15.19.
45. Ps. 1.4.
46. Ps. 41(40).14.
47. John 1.51.
48. Mark 14.36.
49. The first is Ps. 78(77).
50. See above at Ps. 7.1.

Psalm 105 [Ps. 106(105)]

1. See Exod. 15.1, 15.20.
2. Cf. Judges 5.1 f.
3. Matt. 5.45.
4. Mark 10.18.
5. Virgil, *Georgics* 2.43 f., *Aeneid* 6.625 f.
6. Matt. 24.13.
7. "The qualitative"; see *Inst.* 2.3.14.
8. Luke 2.29 ff.
9. Ps. 105(104).3.
10. John 8.56.
11. Augustine, *Contra Iulianum* (ML 44.641 ff.).
12. Not in the rhetorical handbooks, but clearly equivalent to *congeries verborum* (Quintilian 8.4.26, etc.).
13. Ps. 105(104).38.
14. John 20.29.
15. Exod. 15.1.
16. Here, as elsewhere, Cassiodorus applies a figure of speech (*kakozēlon* usually describes affectation of style) to describe a psychological or moral condition.
17. Luke 22.15.
18. Exod. 21.17.
19. Ps. 118(117).18.
20. Num. 16.1 ff.
21. Num. 16.31 f.

22. Num. 16.35.
23. There is no basis for this etymology.
24. Cf. Exod. 32.1 ff.
25. Ps. 40(39).2.
26. Above at Ps. 69(68).5.
27. Exod. 32.31 f.
28. Baal-Peor was the god of the Midianites; see Num. 25.
29. Cf. Num. 25.7 f.
30. Num. 20.10.
31. Jos. 1.7.
32. *Scandalum* actually means a trap or snare, and then a stumbling-block.
33. See above at Ps. 3.4.
34. Eph. 2.2.
35. 2 Tim. 2.26.
36. Luke 19.10.
37. Titus 3.5.
38. In fact it is the concluding doxology to the fourth part of the Psalms.
39. Ps. 106(105).6.

Psalm 106 [Ps. 107(106)]

1. See at §16 below.
2. Servius, the Virgilian commentator, describes the refrains in Virgil, *Eclogue* 8, by use of this expression.
3. "Circumlocution"; see above at Ps. 72(71).8.
4. Gen. 13.14.
5. A false etymology.
6. 1 Cor. 7.7.
7. See at Ps. 84(83).11.
8. Cassiodorus wrongly implies an etymological connextion between *intercalaris* and *callis*.
9. John 16.7.
10. Isa. 61.1.
11. Cf. Tob. 9.3.

12. The reference is probably to Ps.-Augustine, *Contra Varimadum* III (ML 62.411 ff.): "in his testimoniis unitas Trinitatis ostenditur." See Fischer, *Biblica* 23 (1942) 154.
13. Apoc. 17.15.
14. Ps. 39(38).12.
15. The words have no etymological connection.
16. See §3 above.
17. See at Ps. 1.1.
18. The derivation is false.
19. So Varro, *L.L.* 5.34.
20. So Varro, *L.L.* 5.37.
21. Cf. Matt. 21.19; Luke 13.6 ff.
22. See Jerome, *Vita Pauli* (ML 23.23 ff.).
23. 1 John 2.19.
24. See at 3 above.
25. *En. Ps.* 107.1 ff.

Psalm 107 [Ps. 108(107)]

1. Psalms 57(56).8–12, 60(59).7–11.
2. The Nestorians, condemned by the Council of Ephesus in 431.
3. Unidentified.
4. See at Ps. 60(59).8.
5. So Jerome, *Tract. de Ps. 107* (CCL 78.204).
6. So Jerome, *loc. cit.*
7. Eph. 4.7.
8. So Jerome, *loc cit.*
9. Jerome, *loc. cit.* (CCL 78.205).
10. So Augustine, *En. Ps.* 59.9 (CCL 39.761).
11. Jerome, *loc. cit.*
12. Jerome, *loc. cit.* (CCL 78.206).
13. See Ps. 60(59).10.
14. Ps. 22(21).2.
15. John 14.28.
16. Matt. 26.39.
17. Ps. 107(106).16.

18. Ps. 24(23).7.
19. Ambrose, *De Incarnatione* 6.49 (ML 16.866B), attacking the heresy of Apollinarius.
20. I.e., the Arians.
21. See Psalms 2, 8, 21(20), 72(71), 82(81).
22. Cf. 1 Par. 16.

Psalm 108 [Ps. 109(108)]

1. Above, Ps. 20(19).8.
2. Mark 12.14.
3. Luke 23.21.
4. Ps. 69(68).5.
5. Though in Roman augury the left side was the favourable side, the opposite was true in Greek practice; hence *sinister* acquired its secondary meaning of "wrong" or "perverse."
6. Ps. 144(143).11.
7. Ps. 16(15).8.
8. Matt. 25.41.
9. Matt. 6.12.
10. Ps. 55(54).24.
11. Ezech. 3.17.
12. 1 Tim. 3.1.
13. 1 Cor. 9.27.
14. Acts 1.16.
15. Acts 1.20.
16. Quintilian 3.6.61 mentions these terms as equivalents for an exception to a legal statement, but clearly the sense intended by Cassiodorus is quite different.
17. The words are unconnected.
18. Ps. 51(50).11.
19. Matt. 16.18.
20. Matt. 5.7.
21. 2 Cor. 8.9.
22. Matt. 27.25.
23. John 9.27.

24. John 9.28.
25. Acts 13.46.
26. 2 Kings (4 Kings) 1.8; Matt. 3.4.
27. John 5.19.
28. John 5.26.
29. John 5.23.
30. "Repetition," cited as a figure by the fourth-century grammarian Charisius; see also Ps. 35(34).21 above.
31. Matt. 26.38.
32. Ps. 21.7.
33. Matt. 4.2.
34. Ps. 45(44).8.
35. Matt. 12.24.
36. Luke 4.22.
37. Matt. 27.40.
38. Comparison; see above, Ps. 20(19).8.
39. Matt. 27.39.
40. John 12.28.
41. Phil. 2.7.
42. Isa. 42.1.
43. Phil. 1.23 f.
44. Rom. 7.24 f.
45. For the wise virgins, cf. Matt. 25.2; the five books are the Pentateuch. The point being made is that there is a mystical correspondence between the five psalms foretelling the Passion, their five points of similarity, and the other incidences of the number five in holy Scripture.

Psalm 109 [Ps. 110(109)]

1. John 1.1.
2. "Appearance," "image"; above, Ps. 9.5.
3. Matt. 1.1.
4. Matt. 28.30.
5. John 17.24.
6. The suggested derivation is found in Varro, *L.L.* 5.167.

7. Actually Isa. 26.20.
8. Ps. 123(122).2.
9. Matt. 1.25.
10. Isa. 2.3.
11. John 1.1.
12. John 8.25.
13. Gen. 1.2.
14. John 14.8 f.
15. Matt. 5.8.
16. Isa. 26.10.
17. 1 Cor. 15.51.
18. Isa. 53.8.
19. Heb. 6.17–19.
20. Gen. 22.16 f.
21. Gen. 6.7.
22. John 6.54.
23. 1 Cor. 11.29.
24. Cf. Gen. 14.18 ff.
25. Heb. 7.26.
26. Ps. 2.2.
27. Ps. 28(27).5.
28. So also Varro, *L.L. fragmenta* (Goetz-Schoell, p. 197): *caput quod hinc capiant initium sensus ac nervi;* but explanation and etymology are false.
29. Phil. 2.9 f.
30. 2 Tim. 4.2.
31. John 1.14.
32. Rom. 6.9 f.

Psalm 110 [Ps. 111(110)]

1. Ps. 84(83).5.
2. See above on Ps. 25(24).
3. This quotation has not been traced, but cf. Hilary, *Tract. in Ps.* 118.1 (CSEL 22, 355).

4. The Vulgate does not offer these indications that the psalm is alphabetic.
5. Ps. 1.5.
6. Matt. 19.28.
7. Rom. 5.20.
8. Gen. 1.31.
9. *Psalt. iuxta Heb.* III.3 (ed. Ste Marie, 164).
10. Matt. 25.41.
11. Matt. 25.34.
12. Matt. 11.5 f.
13. Gen. 22.17.
14. "By praise"; see above at Ps. 18(17).2.
15. Eccli. 15.16.
16. See above at 21(20).8, 51(50).6, 81(80).3, 94(93).10.
17. Ps. 86(85).2.
18. Ps. 76(75).8.
19. 1 Cor. 3.19.
20. Cf. Matt. 20.1 ff. A denarius = ten asses; Cassiodorus suggests that the number of this psalm, 110, has a connection with this.

PSALM III [PS. 112(III)]

1. The minor prophets Aggaeus (Haggai) and Zacharias wrote after the return from the Babylonian captivity; the Jews were allowed to return after Cyrus captured Babylon in 538 BC, and before Darius I mounted the throne in 521. But the rebuilding of the temple promoted by these prophets took place in Darius' reign in 520.
2. "By praise"; above Ps. 18(17).2.
3. John 8.44.
4. Matt. 5.42.
5. I.e., without demanding extortionate interest.
6. Matt. 5.20.
7. Luke 13.25.
8. Matt. 25.41.
9. Matt. 25.34.

10. Matt. 19.21.
11. Dan. 7.17.
12. "Example"; see Ps. 1.4, 15(14).4, 34(33).16, etc.
13. Isa. 57.21.

Psalm 112 [Ps. 113(112)]

1. Isa. 9.6.
2. Matt. 9.14.
3. "Circumlocution"; see Quintilian 8.3.53, and Ps. 72(71).8, 106(105).3 above.
4. Ps. 108(107).6.
5. Ps. 108(107).2.
6. 12 rather than 112.
7. Jerome, *In Ezech.* 31 (ML 25.301).
8. 1 Cor. 15.41.
9. 1 Cor. 15.41 f.

Psalm 113 [Ps. 114(113A)]

1. The suggestion is unintentionally comic.
2. So Varro, *L.L.* 5.36, interpreting *colere* as "cultivate"; the etymology is incorrect.
3. See at Ps. 49(48).6 above for this "Question and answer."
4. In §3 above.
5. So Syrianus, *In Hermogenem Comm.* 2.89.20 (ed. Rabe, Leipzig 1893).
6. Matt. 3.9.
7. "Comparison"; see at 1.3, 5.11, etc.
8. See at Ps. 16(15).9, 56(55).13, etc.
9. Above, Ps. 29(28).1, 33(32).4, etc.
10. Jer. 10.9.
11. Sedulius, *Carmen Paschale* 1.268 f. (= CSEL 10.35).

12. Isa. 42.8 f., 43.10.
13. See Donatus, *Comm. in Terentii Adelphi 397: nares a naritate dictae.*
14. Rom. 1.25.
15. See at Ps. 94(93).7 above.
16. Ps. 110(109).4.
17. Cf. Fortunatianus 2.31: *anacephaleosis, id est recapitulatio vel enumeratio,* citing Cicero, *Inv.* 1.98.
18. So Varro, *L.L.* 5.18: *caelum dictum scribit Aelius quod celatum.*
19. Ps. 68(67).34.
20. Eccli. 17.26 f.
21. Ps. 86(85).13.
22. Matt. 22.32.
23. Ps. 115(114).9.

Psalm 114 [Ps. 115(113B)]

1. Ps. 49(48).19.
2. Rom. 8.35.
3. "Hasty accumulation"; see Ps. 23(22).6, 70(69).2 above.
4. See above at Ps. 5.2.
5. Rom. 7.24 f.
6. Cassiodorus regards this figure as the equivalent of apostrophe. For its normal meaning of "anticipatory statement," see Tryphon, *Trop.* 2.12, and Martin 262.
7. Cf. Heb. 12.6.
8. Cf. John 10.16.
9. Cf. Prudentius, *Cath.* 8.37 ff.
10. Cf. Luke 15.24.
11. Luke 9.60.
12. Gen. 5.24.
13. Cf. Job 1.8.
14. John 1.47.
15. 1 Cor. 15.52 f.
16. John 5.24.

Psalm 115 [Ps. 116(114 + 115)]

1. In the Hebrew version, and now in the *Nova Vulgata,* Psalms 114 and 115 appear as a single psalm. This *Alleluia* is accordingly absent there, and the numbering of verses follows in sequence.
2. Ps. 50(49).16.
3. I.e., that all men are liars.
4. "Proverb," not normally considered as a figure.
5. Acts 9.5.
6. 2 Par. 29.8.
7. 1 Cor. 4.7.
8. Matt. 20.22.
9. Verse 14 is omitted by Cassiodorus since it recurs at verse 18, and has probably been misplaced here.
10. It should be noted that Cassiodorus speaks of this practice in the past tense. Already by Tertullian's time there is evidence of the sacramental status of penance, and the notion of Penance as a second baptism, or in Jerome's expression, "a second plank for shipwreck," became common. Hence the expression "third confession" used here.
11. Luke 17.18.
12. Matt. 10.32.

Psalm 116 [Ps. 117(116)]

1. "Chain"; Cassiodorus seems to use both *hormos* and *hirmos* (Greek *heirmos*) in the same sense; see at Ps. 54(53).1.
2. See Intro. VI in ACW 51.
3. John 14.6.
4. John 1.3.
5. John 1.1.
6. Eph. 5.5.
7. Gal. 1.1.
8. 2 Thess. 2.15.
9. 2 Cor. 13.13.

10. 2 Thess. 3.5.
11. Exod. 20.26.

Psalm 117 [Ps. 118(117)]

1. Cf. Apoc. 19.1 ff.
2. For this expression used as refrain, see at Ps. 107(106).1.
3. Matt. 19.16 f.; Mark 10.17 f.
4. Matt. 12.35.
5. Ps. 114(113).21.
6. "Repetition"; see at Ps. 27(26).3, 44(43).15, etc.
7. James 4.13 and 15.
8. Phil. 2.13.
9. Jer. 17.5.
10. This sentence was added in the later recension, on which see Intro., p. 00. The relevant works of Augustine are at ML 44.549 ff.; the three Pelagians mentioned are documented in ODCC.
11. John 14.30.
12. Dan. 12.1.
13. *Gentes* is feminine but is followed by masculine *eos*. For the figure of *exallage* applied to genders, see Quintilian 9.3.6.
14. See Servius on Virgil, *Georg.* 4.309, for this strange suggestion.
15. Cf. 1 Cor. 15.53.
16. Heb. 6.14; cf. Gen. 16.10.
17. For the *a coniugatis*, see at Ps. 37(36).20, 40(39).2, etc.
18. The etymological connection between *porta* (gate) and *importare* (to bring in) is being suggested.
19. John 10.7.
20. Matt. 13.17.
21. *Gonu* and *genu* are related, but neither is connected with *angulus*.
22. The root of these words is *gōnia*, an angle.
23. Phil. 2.7.
24. Rom. 1.3.
25. Matt. 16.16.
26. See at Ps. 25(24).7, 27(26).3, etc.

27. John 5.43.
28. Ps. 43(42).4.
29. See §21 above.
30. Apoc. 1.8.
31. See n. 54 to the Intro. in ACW 51.
32. Cf. Matt. 14.17, etc.

PSALM 118 [PS. 119(118)]

1. Presumably a reference to the fact that circumcision was carried out on the eighth day of life.
2. For this calculation of 22 Old Testament books (5 books of Moses, 13 of prophets, 4 others), see Josephus, *Contra Apionem* 1.38–42, and P. R. Ackroyd in *Cambridge History of the Bible* I (CUP 1970), 114 f.
3. Cf. Jerome, *Ep.* 30.5 (= CSEL 54.246).
4. The passage has not been identified.
5. 1 Peter 2.9.
6. Ps. 51(50).9.
7. John 14.6.
8. Rom. 7.23.
9. This sentence has been added in the later recension; see the Introduction, p. 5. Primasius, the sixth-century bishop of Hadrumetum in North Africa (recaptured by Justinian from the Vandals) also wrote biblical commentaries; see ML 68.407 ff. This work on heresy is lost. The quotation at the end of the Commentary on Psalm 138 may be from it.
10. "Of what kind"; see above, Ps. 22(21).4.
11. 1 John 1.8.
12. 2 Tim. 4.7.
13. Rom. 7.19.
14. Rom. 7.20.
15. Rom. 6.12 f.
16. Eccli. 18.30.
17. John 14.6.
18. In this section I translate *nimis* as 'exceedingly', since the verse

demands a favourable meaning; but in the proverb *ne quid nimis* the word is pejorative.

19. Ps. 92(91).6.
20. Ps. 97(96).9.
21. Col. 2.17.
22. Gen. 31.52.
23. Jos. 4.5 f.
24. 1 Tim. 5.21.
25. Matt. 22.37.
26. James 2.10.
27. James 1.23 ff.
28. 1 Peter 5.8.
29. "Query"; see Martin, 284 f.
30. Ezech. 34.16.
31. Ps. 5.7.
32. Wisd. 1.5.
33. Acts 4.20.
34. Matt. 7.6.
35. Ps. 39(38).2 f.
36. Titus 3.10.
37. Ps. 36(35).7.
38. Rom. 11.33.
39. John 16.12.
40. Above, Ps. 9.2, for *synecdoche.*
41. 1 Cor. 1.5 f.
42. Exod. 20.14 ff.
43. Luke 9.60.
44. Phil. 3.20.
45. Deut. 6.5.
46. Exod. 20.17.
47. James 4.6.
48. Ps. 123(122).3 f.
49. Matt. 5.10.
50. 1 John 4.18.
51. Luke 17.10.
52. Prov. 18.17.
53. The year of jubilee; see Lev. 25.11 ff.
54. Ps. 132(131).4.

55. Ps. 121(120).4.
56. This is an addition in the later recension. Accidie or sloth is the seventh of the capital sins. John Cassian gives the classic description of it at *Inst.* 10.2 (= CSEL 17.172 ff.).
57. Rom. 3.20–22.
58. Rom. 3.20.
59. John 14.6.
60. John 15.16.
61. Ps. 84(83).11.
62. In §25 above.
63. Cf. Phil. 3.14.
64. Cf. §29 above.
65. Isa. 2.3.
66. Matt. 6.1.
67. 2 Tim. 4.7 f.
68. 1 Cor. 1.30.
69. 1 Cor. 2.8.
70. Matt. 10.18.
71. Cf. Luke 22.34 ff.
72. Heb. 12.6.
73. §32 above.
74. Rom. 5.5.
75. 2 Cor. 6.12.
76. Matt. 10.33.
77. The dictionaries do not confirm this statement; Cicero in particular often uses *exercitatio* in the good sense.
78. See the opening remarks in §44.
79. Gen. 9.15.
80. Exod. 2.24.
81. Matt. 5.5, 10.
82. See above, Ps. 52(51).11.
83. Luke 21.19.
84. *In saeculum saeculi;* cf. Ps. 37(36).27, etc.
85. Ps. 37(36).25.
86. Eph. 5.19.
87. 2 Cor. 5.6.
88. 1 Cor. 4.5.
89. Ps. 124(123).8.

90. 2 Cor. 10.17.

91. There is a clear etymological connection between the two words.

92. Deut. 10.9.

93. Ps. 80(79).8.

94. Matt. 5.8.

95. 1 Cor. 13.12.

96. *Proinde* (CCL) cannot be right; I render *providens.*

97. Acts 21.13.

98. Ps. 57(56).8.

99. John 14.1.

100. Isa. 5.18.

101. Prov. 5.22.

102. Rom. 7.25.

103. Cf. Exod. 11.5.

104. Cf. Acts 12.6.

105. Cf. Matt. 25.8.

106. In §57.

107. Heb. 3.14.

108. Ps. 45(44).8 f.

109. §33 above.

110. §71 below.

111. Matt. 23.12.

112. Luke 17.5.

113. Matt. 7.24.

114. James 4.6.

115. It is clear from Quintilian 9.3.66, echoed by Cassiodorus here, that the Latin equivalent is *adnominatio,* not *denominatio* as in the CC text (but cf. Ps. 103[102].8).

116. Ps. 68(67).16.

117. The etymology is mistaken, but the attempt to establish a law of vocalic mutation is noteworthy.

118. Ps. 102(101).26.

119. Ps. 95(94).5.

120. Ps. 148.5.

121. Ps. 36(35).7.

122. Rom. 11.33.

123. Matt. 19.17.

124. Rom. 2.13.
125. Matt. 5.44.
126. Matt. 25.34.
127. The same verb *confundere* is used in §78 ("Let the proud be ashamed") and in §80 ("that I may not be ashamed").
128. Ps. 9.7.
129. Ps. 84(83).3.
130. 1 Cor. 1.24.
131. John 1.14.
132. Ps. 119(118).45.
133. John 8.56.
134. Matt. 9.17.
135. Acts 1.7.
136. John 19.30.
137. Matt. 10.22.
138. Luke 21.33.
139. Isa. 60.19.
140. Ps. 24(23).1.
141. Phil. 1.21.
142. Gal. 2.20.
143. Ps. 41(40).2.
144. Rom. 5.5.
145. Ps. 34(33).2.
146. 1 Cor. 10.31.
147. Deut. 32.7.
148. Matt. 26.3 f.
149. Cf. Gen. 27.27 ff.
150. Cf. 1 Sam. (1 Kings) 3.
151. Cf. Dan. 13.45 ff.
152. Rom. 10.3.
153. 1 Cor. 10.21.
154. Ezech. 3.1, 3.
155. Prov. 1.15 f.
156. Ps. 73(72).27.
157. Ps. 97(96).10.
158. 2 Peter 1.19.
159. Luke 12.35.

160. John 1.9.
161. John 8.12.
162. John 5.35.
163. John 1.8.
164. Matt. 5.34.
165. The connection of *iurare* with *ius* is clear, but *orare* is irrelevant.
166. Matt. 11.28.
167. Matt. 5.45.
168. See §65 above.
169. §66 above.
170. Wisd. 3.1.
171. John 10.27 f.
172. Cf. Matt. 27.3.
173. Cf. 1 Sam. (1 Kings) 15.20.
174. Cf. Gen. 4.8.
175. Ps. 124(123).7.
176. Deut. 30.19.
177. Isa. 43.10.
178. 1 Tim. 5.21.
179. Matt. 11.29.
180. Matt. 25.34.
181. Matt. 5.44.
182. Luke 14.26.
183. Eccle. 3.5.
184. Eccle. 3.17.
185. Cf. Cicero, *Topica* 11; Boethius, *In Topica Ciceronis* 2 (= ML 64.1065 ff.).
186. Eccli. 2.11.
187. Ps. 32(31).10.
188. Ps. 6.9.
189. Ps. 40(39).2.
190. Cf. Luke 18.13 f.
191. 1 Cor. 15.53 f.
192. Rom. 2.12.
193. Prevaricators in the strict sense are persons who collude with opponents in a court of law, but later the word acquires the simple

sense of transgressors. Cassiodorus poses the question whether the Gentiles can be regarded as transgressors, since they are ignorant of the law of the Old Testament.

194. Rom. 2.14.
195. Phil. 1.21.
196. Luke 2.29.
197. Cant. 2.5.
198. Matt. 6.13.
199. Rom. 1.28; 1 Tim. 1.20.
200. This was the accepted etymology in antiquity (cf. Justinian, *Inst.* 1.3.3), but it is almost certainly incorrect.
201. Matt. 4.9.
202. Isa. 14.13 f.
203. Cant. 5.12, 4.1.
204. Ps. 28(27).9.
205. Luke 11.3.
206. Antiochus IV Epiphanes of Syria (175–65 BC), frustrated in his attempt to conquer Egypt by the Romans, turned his anger on the Jews and compelled them to conform to Greek religious practices. His career was prophesied by Daniel at 11.21 f.
207. Isa. 49.8.
208. 2 Cor. 6.2.
209. Cassiodorus has taken over this description of the topaz from Ambrose, *In Ps. 118 serm. 16.42*, who likewise compares it to the chrysoprase. The ultimate source is Pliny, *H.N.* 37.
210. Eccli. 3.22.
211. See above, Ps. 17(16).13.
212. Isa. 7.14.
213. Isa. 52.10.
214. Mark 10.14.
215. James 2.10.
216. For the other examples of *antiphrasis*, see Quintilian I 6.34, *lucus quia umbra opacus parum luceat;* and *Grammatici Latini*, ed. Keil, I 276.13: *antiphrasis est dictio ex contrario significans . . . ut bellum dicitur quod minime sit bellum, et lucus quod minime luceat.* Mart. Cap. 4.360 echoes the *lucus* reference.
217. Cf. 1 Sam. (1 Kings) 24 and 26.
218. 1 Sam. (1 Kings) 18.7.

219. Ps. 6.7.
220. Ps. 42(41).4.
221. Above, 6.7.
222. Leo the Great, *Ep.* 82.1 (= ML 54.1103).
223. Acts 5.17 f.
224. Ps. 69(68).10.
225. 1 Kings (3 Kings).19.10.
226. Cf. Num. 25.8.
227. Luke 24.32.
228. Jer. 20.9.
229. Luke 12.49.
230. Acts 13.22.
231. John 14.6.
232. Rom. 8.35.
233. §129 above.
234. In §141.
235. Exod. 14.15.
236. Lam. 3.27 f.
237. Luke 24.1.
238. §103 above.
239. Ps. 21.12.
240. Matt. 26.46.
241. Matt. 5.10.
242. Above, Ps. 20(19).8.
243. Ps. 139(138).8–10.
244. For these examples, cf. Gen. 4.8, 14.18, 22.10.
245. 1 Cor. 3.11.
246. Ps. 123(122).3 f.
247. 1 Cor. 13.9.
248. Ps. 22(21).7.
249. Luke 14.11.
250. Prov. 18.17.
251. "By etymological relation"; above, 36.20.
252. John 11.26.
253. Ps. 143(142).2.
254. Ps. 101(100).1.
255. Compare Festus (p. 260 Lindsay): *pacem a pactione conditionum putat dictam Sinnius Capito.*

256. Matt. 10.22.
257. Exod. 19.8.
258. 1 Cor. 13.3.
259. Gen. 1.1.
260. Matt. 24.35.
261. Eccli. 1.16.
262. Matt. 25.34.
263. Matt. 25.41.
264. Matt. 10.17 f.
265. Matt. 5.44.
266. Rom. 13.1.
267. Matt. 22.21.
268. Cf. Matt. 17.26.
269. Matt. 10.28.
270. Matt. 6.24.
271. The fifth of the *effecta argumenta* at *Inst.* 2.3.15 is that of *a differentia.*
272. The hymn *Bis ternas horas explicans* (Walpole, *Early Latin Hymns*, no. 82) has at 9 ff.: *ut septies diem vere/ orantes cum psalterio/ laudesque cantantes Deo/ laeti solvamus debitum.* Walpole in suggesting Nicetas of Remesiana as the author does not advert to this passage as evidence for composition by Ambrose. The passage is important as evidence of the monastic office at this date. See above, Ps. 102(101), n. 10.
273. Ps. 34(33).2.
274. Prov. 24.16.
275. Ps. 79(78).12.
276. Gen. 4.15.
277. John 14.27.
278. 1 Cor. 1.23.
279. Cf. Luke 2.29 ff.
280. 2 Tim. 4.7 f.
281. Ps. 141(140).2.
282. Eccli. 2.11.
283. A fanciful connection.
284. Ps. 45(44).2.
285. Matt. 13.35.
286. Ps. 19(18).3.

287. Cf. Matt. 12.36.
288. Isa. 53.1.
289. Ps. 118(117).16.
290. Ps. 130(129).2.
291. Matt. 25.34.
292. Cf. Matt. 18.12.
293. Cf. John 10.16.
294. Heb. 1.13.
295. Referring to the alphabetic division of the psalm.
296. This calculation is presumably a conflation of Gen. 5.31 and 7.6.
297. The Greek letters are the first two letters of the name Jesus. Thus the number 118 combines the symbols for Christ and his Church.

Psalm 119 [Ps. 120(119)]

1. The heading before each of the Psalms 120(119)–134(133) is *Canticum Graduum*, usually rendered in English as "Gradual Canticle." The theories of the meaning of the phrase are discussed in Boylan II. 277 f. Cassiodorus accepts Jerome's explanation in his *Commentariolus:* "The fifteen psalms of the steps lead up to the heights by a kind of progression." The fifteen steps are the stairs from the Women's Court to the Men's Court in the Temple at Jerusalem. They were mounted on the first day of the Feast of Tabernacles by the Levitical singers.
2. See the Conclusion to Ps. 119(118) above.
3. Ps. 84(83).6 f.
4. Cf. Isa. 38.5.
5. Ps. 32(31).1.
6. Isa. 58.9.
7. Gen. 3.1.
8. Gen. 3.5.
9. See above at Ps. 119(118).9.
10. Ps. 64(63).8.
11. Isa. 6.6 f.
12. Eccle. 4.2.
13. Phil. 1.23.

14. So Jerome, *Hebrew Names* (CCL 72.63); Augustine, *En. Ps.* 119.7 (CCL 40.1783).
15. Cf. Gen. 25.13.
16. Eph. 2.14.
17. Rom. 12.18.
18. Matt. 5.44.

Psalm 120 [Ps. 121(120)]

1. Cf. Luke 18.13.
2. See above at Ps. 1.2.
3. Ps. 119(118).120.
4. Ps. 84(83).3.
5. Ps. 119(118).18.
6. Ps. 19(18).9.
7. 1 Cor. 3.7.
8. Cf. Matt. 8.24.
9. John 1.14.
10. John 1.1.
11. "Repetition"; see above at Ps. 3.3.
12. Prov. 3.16.
13. Ps. 144(143).8.
14. Ps. 88(87).2.
15. Matt. 10.19.
16. Matt. 10.22.

Psalm 121 [Ps. 122(121)]

1. Ps. 27(26).4.
2. The figure of *synecdoche;* see at Ps. 9.2 above.
3. Exod. 3.14.
4. Ps. 102(101).27 f.
5. Ps. 4.9.

6. John 17.24.
7. Isa. 60.18–21.
8. Cf. Apoc. 4.1 ff.
9. For *anadiplosis*, see at Ps. 24(23).9; for *epembasis*, 3.3.
10. The *curia* was a parish or grouping of neighbours in the early Roman state. There were ten to each of the three tribes, making thirty in all, not thirty-five as Cassiodorus states.
11. John 8.44.
12. Matt. 19.28.
13. Matt. 25.41 and 34.
14. On this unidentified quotation, see Augustine, *En. Ps.* 121.37 (CCL 40.1810).
15. Isa. 66.2.
16. John 5.22.
17. Ps. 34(33).13.
18. Matt. 19.17.
19. Above, 51.11. Quintilian 8.6.21 says that it is regarded as a *vitium*, though he himself calls it a figure of speech.
20. 1 Cor. 15.41.
21. "Characterisation"; see at Ps. 9.26 above.
22. 1 John 4.16.
23. *Pax* is in fact cognate with *pango*, I agree.
24. 1 Cor. 10.33.

Psalm 122 [Ps. 123(122)]

1. Cf. John 11.43; Matt. 14.31; 2 Kings (4 Kings) 2.11; Gen. 5.24.
2. John 14.10.
3. Actually Lev. 26.12.
4. 1 Cor. 3.16.
5. John 17.21.
6. Isa. 66.1.
7. Ps. 114(113).16 (113.24 in Cassiodorus' numeration).
8. On *homoiōsis* (resemblance), Martin 262 cites Tryphon II.198 (Spengel, *Rhetores Graeci* III), a likely source elsewhere for Cassiodorus.

9. Cf. 1 Cor. 1.24; the point is that "power" and "wisdom" are feminine in Latin.
10. Ps. 110(109).1.
11. Matt. 1.24.
12. Wisd. 5.8.

Psalm 123 [Ps. 124(123)]

1. See above at Ps. 27(26).3.
2. Actually Job 5.2.
3. *Animus* is akin to *anemos* in Greek.
4. *Animus* has no connection with *anaima*. The *De anima* (text in CCL 96.504 ff.) was written c. 538–40, perhaps at Ravenna; see O'Donnell 103 ff., and Intro.
5. The etymology (cf. Festus, *De significatione verborum*, ed. Lindsay p. 2) is fanciful. Thales, the first Ionian physicist, posited water as the first principle.
6. Ps. 110(109).7.
7. Ps. 119(118).92.
8. Tob. 13.8.
9. Judith 7.18 ff.
10. 1 Peter 5.8.
11. Cf. Hilary, *Tract. in Ps. 123.9* (ML 9.678), and *Eccle.* 7.27.
12. Eccli. 27.29.

Psalm 124 [Ps. 125(124)]

1. See above, Conclusion to Ps. 6.
2. For slight variations in interpretation of Sion, see ACW 51 and 52, Index 3.
3. Ps. 114(113).4.
4. "Topography"; cf. Cicero, *Ad Atticum* 1.13.5.
5. Ps. 11(10).2.
6. Ps. 72(71).3.

7. Matt. 28.20.
8. Ps. 110(109).2.
9. Cf. Exod. 7.
10. Mark 10.18.
11. Mark 8.33.

Psalm 125 [Ps. 126(125)]

1. Ps. 34(33).9.
2. See above at Ps. 31(30).10; cf. Martianus Capella 5.524: *diatuposis est descriptio vel deformatio cum rebus personisque subiectis et formas ipsas et habitus exprimimus.*
3. Prov. 18.17.
4. Isa. 43.16.
5. Gal. 6.8.
6. Matt. 5.5.
7. Osee 10.12.
8. Matt. 8.12.
9. Not in the handbooks.
10. Eccli. 3.33.
11. Matt. 6.20.
12. Jerome, *Hebrew Names* (CCL 72.138); Augustine, *En. Ps.* 126.2.20 (CCL 41.1857).
13. John 14.27.
14. The point being made is that in this group of psalms 120(119)–134(133), the first seven relate to the O.T., and the other eight to the N.T., just as the first seventy psalms are claimed to relate to the O.T. and the other eighty to the N.T.

Psalm 126 [Ps. 127(126)]

1. See n. 12 on preceding Psalm.
2. Eph. 2.14.
3. 1 Cor. 3.16.

4. 1 Cor. 3.7.

5. The argument *a necessario* is one of the *argumenta extrinsecus* discussed by Cassiodorus at *Inst.* 2.3.16.

6. Matt. 26.38.

7. Matt. 28.18.

8. Jer. 7.13.

9. Ps. 42(41).4.

10. Ps. 80(79).6.

11. Ps. 2.8.

12. Phil. 2.9.

13. Gal. 4.19.

14. 1 Cor. 4.15.

15. Ps. 42(41).2.

16. Phil. 1.23.

17. An echo of Virgil, *Aeneid* 1.94.

18. John 10.9.

PSALM 127 [Ps. 128(127)]

1. Cassiodorus as elsewhere ignores the hundred, and visualises 27 as 3 × 3 × 3.

2. Eccli. 1.16.

3. Ps. 119(118).120.

4. Ps. 34(33).12.

5. Deut. 10.12 f.

6. Ps. 19(18).10.

7. John 14.6.

8. Jer. 6.16.

9. Matt. 25.34.

10. Ps. 33.9.

11. 1 Cor. 2.9.

12. Wisd. 8.2.

13. Prov. 4.6.

14. Ps. 112(111).1.
15. "Comparison"; see above at Ps. 1.3.
16. Cf. Matt. 25.15 ff.

Psalm 128 [Ps. 129(128)]

1. This Roman coin means "containing ten (asses)."
2. Ps. 37(36).25.
3. Cassiodorus writes *egentem* (masculine) here, but *egens ad loc.;* the Vulgate has *quaerens.*
4. Cf. Ps. 124(123).
5. See above at Ps. 27(26).3.
6. 1 John 2.18.
7. Exod. 32.9.
8. Acts 7.51.
9. Ps. 126(125).6.
10. Ruth 2.4 f.
11. Exod. 3.3.
12. Ps. 37(36).35 f.

Psalm 129 [Ps. 130(129)]

1. Ps. 129(128).1 and 3.
2. The etymology is acceptable.
3. Cf. Matt. 26.75; Luke 18.13.
4. Jonas 2.3.
5. Jonas 2.1.
6. John 4.24.
7. "Uncertainty"; cf. Martianus Capella 5.523: *diaporesis est addubitatio. . . .*
8. Rom. 7.7.

9. Gal. 6.2.
10. John 1.1 f.
11. 1 John 1.7.
12. See at §3 above.
13. Mal. 4.5.

Psalm 130 [Ps. 131(130)]

1. Luke 14.11.
2. See above at Ps. 7.6.
3. The normal sense of this figure is "reversal of normal word order"; see above at Ps. 24(23).5, 53(52).5.
4. Cf. Luke 12.18.
5. John 19.10.
6. Cf. Acts 8.18 ff.
7. Rom. 11.20.
8. Ps. 101(100).7.
9. Ps. 36(35).12.
10. Ps. 25(24).1.
11. 1 Cor. 3.1 f.
12. Ps. 7.4 f.

Psalm 131 [Ps. 132(131)]

1. The sequence of *Cantica graduum* began at Ps. 120(119), so this is the thirteenth of the series.
2. For these meanings, see above at Ps. 2.1.
3. Jer. 30.9, 23.5.
4. Actually Ezech. 34.23.
5. Isa. 53.7.
6. Reading *patientiae* for *paenitentiae* in CCL.

7. John 18.11.
8. Matt. 16.23.
9. Ps. 110(109).4.
10. Deut. 30.20.
11. Ps. 132(131).11.
12. Isa. 66.1.
13. John 19.30.
14. Ps. 6.3.
15. Cf. Lactantius, *De opificio Dei* 10.2 (CSEL 27.32); Servius, *In Aen.* 4.30.
16. Cf. Augustine, *En. Ps.* 131.11 (CCL 40.1916).
17. Varro derives *campus* equally fancifully from *capere.*
18. Actually Micheas 5.2.
19. Gen. 35.19.
20. Isa. 52.7.
21. John 3.29.
22. Matt. 10.22.
23. Ps. 36(35).13.
24. Eph. 6.14 and 16
25. Gal. 3.27.
26. See §1 above.
27. Ps. 89(88).20 f.
28. Ps. 89(88).27 f.
29. Matt. 19.28.
30. John 17.24.
31. Jer. 26.18.
32. 1 Tim. 5.5.
33. Rom. 7.1 ff.
34. See at Ps. 37(36).20 for the *coniugata.*
35. Ps. 34(33).11.
36. Gal. 3.27.
37. Matt. 5.19.
38. See at §14 above.
39. John 5.35.
40. Matt. 25.34.
41. Matt. 25.41.
42. John 5.22.

43. John 5.17.
44. Phil. 2.10 f.

Psalm 132 [Ps. 133(132)]

1. The first is Ps. 117(116).
2. Cf. Matt. 21.2.
3. The Circumcellions were originally bands of religious fanatics, groups of Numidian Donatists who in the fourth century lived round the shrines (*circum cellas*) and frequently attacked churches or landed estates. For the evidence offered by Augustine, Optatus and others on their activities, see W. H. C. Frend, *The Donatist Church* (Oxford 1952) 171 ff. Cassiodorus' description suggests that in his day the groups were of a less violent tendency.
4. Acts 4.32.
5. This is an addition in the second recension; see the Introduction, p. 5 in ACW 51.
6. That is, in monastic foundations.
7. Acts 4.35 and 32.
8. Ps. 45(44).8.
9. The words in brackets are from the second recension. The Josephus passage is at *Ant. Jud.* 3.7; the Jerome reference is *Ep.* 64 (CSEL 54.586).
10. Mount Hermon actually lies to the north in what was Coele Syria. Jerome, *Hebrew Names* (CCL 72.86) renders Erma as *anathema*, and Ermon as *anathema tristitiae.*
11. For *hyrmos* and *hormos*, see at Ps. 117(116).1 above.
12. Matt. 22.38 f.

Psalm 133 [Ps. 134(133)]

1. Matt. 22.37, 39 f.
2. Rom. 1.1.
3. Gal. 1.10.

4. Ps. 105(104).26.
5. John 8.44.
6. Cf. Exod. 17.11.
7. 1 John 4.8.
8. The forced explanation of the number fifteen is that the five senses are multiplied by the three Persons of the Trinity.

Psalm 134 [Ps. 135(134)]

1. See above at Ps. 29(28).1.
2. This, the correct explanation, is found in Servius, *Ad Aen.* 1.726; Varro, *L.L.* 5.161, suggests a connection with the town of Atria.
3. Ps. 34(33).9.
4. Above, Ps. 22(21).4.
5. Ps. 18(17).32.
6. Exod. 17.1.
7. 1 Cor. 8.5 f.
8. See at Ps. 23(22).6; Quintilian 8.5.11 describes *epiphōnēma* as *summa acclamatio*, the climactic exclamation following upon narrative or argument.
9. Isa. 5.6.
10. Ps. 7.14.
11. Ps. 18(17).11.
12. "Climax"; see at Ps. 69(68).5.
13. Cassiodorus is acquainted with Augustine's theory of signs, on which see P. Brown, *Augustine of Hippo* (London 1967) 261 ff.; J. N. D. Kelly, *Early Christian Doctrines*[4] (London 1968) ch. 16.
14. Varro, *L.L.* 7.14, notes the connection between *signum* and *significare*.
15. The word is cognate with *prodicere*.
16. So Augustine, *En. Ps.* 135.19 (CCL 40.1951).
17. On these victories, see Num. 21.25 ff. For the meaning of the names, see Augustine, *En. Ps.* 134.20 (CCL 40.1951); Jerome, *Hebrew Names* (CCL 72.84 and 61).
18. So Augustine (n. 17). Jerome, *Hebrew Names* (CCL 72.79) rejects this interpretation.

19. Above, Ps. 65(64).1.
20. So Augustine (n. 17) and Jerome, *Hebrew Names* (CCL 72.63).
21. Ps. 72(71).4.
22. Matt. 23.12.
23. Matt. 6.9 f.
24. Matt. 24.35.
25. Ps. 50(49).7.
26. Mich. 6.3.
27. Matt. 5.5.
28. John 3.18, 36.
29. See at Ps. 94(93).7. Martin 264 cites Tryphon for this usage; he is a possible source for Cassiodorus here and elsewhere.
30. *They have nostrils . . . with their throats* does not appear in the Vulgate.
31. Bar. 6.7.
32. Bar. 6.67.

Psalm 135 [Ps. 136(135)]

1. Ps. 118(117).1–4.
2. 1 Cor. 15.9.
3. Ps. 82(81).6.
4. Exod. 7.1.
5. See above at Ps. 32(31).11.
6. Ps. 135(134).6.
7. Ps. 148.4.
8. 2 Cor. 12.2.
9. Job 26.7.
10. Isa. 40.12.
11. John 1.12.
12. On this symbolism, see H. Rahner, *Greek Myths and Christian Mystery* (London 1962) ch. 4.
13. "By praise"; see at Ps. 18(17).2.
14. See §11 above.
15. This section does not appear in the Vulgate.
16. See Ps. 135(134).11.

17. For the alternative meaning, see Hilary, *Tract. in Ps.* 134.20 (ML 9.762); Jerome, *Hebrew Names* (CCL 72.84).

18. Cassiodorus here offers a different interpretation from that at Ps. 135(134).11; here his translation corresponds with that of Jerome, *Hebrew Names* (CCL 72.83).

19. 1 Cor. 6.20.

20. See §2 above.

21. 2 Par. 5.13 f.

Psalm 136 [Ps. 137(136)]

1. Jer. 25.

2. Referring to *Lamentations*.

3. 1 Cor. 10.11.

4. So Jerome, *Hebrew Names* (CCL 72.121); Augustine, *En. Ps.* 136.1 (CCL 40.1964).

5. Isa. 44.4.

6. Rom. 7.23.

7. Matt. 7.6.

8. Ps. 16(15).8.

9. Cf. Luke 1.13.

10. Cf. Luke 15.11 ff.

11. Cf. 2 Kings (4 Kings) 20.6 f.

12. So Jerome, *Hebrew Names* (CCL 72.65); Augustine, *En. Ps.* 136.18 (CCL 40.1976).

13. See Ps. 52(51).11 above.

14. Gal. 5.17.

15. 1 Cor. 10.4.

16. Ps. 101(100).8.

17. Cf. John 11.35.

Psalm 137 [Ps. 138(137)]

1. See at Ps. 2.1.

2. Ps. 118(117).21.

3. Cassiodorus regards the two sentences in §2 as separate verses.
4. Ps. 25(24).10.
5. See at Ps. 26(25).4.
6. 1 Cor. 1.24.

Psalm 138 [Ps. 139(138)]

1. Cf. Hilary, *Tract. in Ps.* 138.1 (CSEL 22.744).
2. Isa. 53.4.
3. Matt. 17.5.
4. John 10.30.
5. John 21.14.
6. Matt. 23.2.
7. "Exchange"; above, Ps. 14(13).2.
8. Isa. 53.7.
9. John 14.6.
10. John 14.28.
11. John 10.30.
12. Exod. 12.6.
13. 1 John 2.18.
14. John 1.1.
15. Dan. 7.9.
16. Phil. 2.6.
17. Ps. 89(88).21–3.
18. John 17.6.
19. John 14.28.
20. John 5.19.
21. Wisd. 1.7.
22. 'Doubt'; Cf. Ps. 130(129).3 and Martianus Capella 5.523: "We use this figure when we ask for advice from the jury about what we should attempt." Other references at Martin 287.
23. Servius, *Ad Aen.* 2.675; Martin 127 n. 28.
24. Matt. 21.25.
25. Phil. 1.23 f.
26. Phil. 1.22.

27. Jer. 23.23 f.
28. Above, Ps. 16(15).9.
29. Ps. 124(123).3.
30. John 8.12.
31. Luke 23.43.
32. Prov. 1.7.
33. Ps. 18(17).12.
34. It will be recalled that the Nestorian heresy proclaimed that there were two separate Persons in Christ, the divine and the human, a doctrine condemned at Ephesus in 431.
35. Jer. 1.5.
36. Matt. 11.27.
37. John 14.11.
38. Gen. 2.23.
39. Eph. 5.32.
40. Matt. 26.38.
41. 1 Cor. 15.28.
42. 1 Cor. 15.41 f.
43. John 17.10.
44. Cf. Exod. 33.11; 2 Par. 20.7; etc.
45. John 15.15.
46. Cf. Gen. 22.17.
47. The mistaken etymology is found at Servius, *Ad Aen. 1.172*, citing Varro (cf. Goetz-Schnell's edn. of Varro, *L.L.*, p. 211).
48. Above, Ps. 37(36).9.
49. Matt. 9.13.
50. Gal. 2.19.
51. Ps. 119(118).139.
52. Above, Ps. 17(16).13.
53. The etymology is false.
54. John 14.30.
55. He refers to the Arians.
56. Bishop Facundus of Hermione in North Africa was embroiled in the sixth-century Monophysite controversy as one of the supporters of the Three Chapters, the three subjects condemned by Justinian in his edict of 543-4 against Theodore of Mopsuestia, Theodoret of Cyrus, and Ibas of Edessa. He visited Constantinople, and published there his *Pro defensione Trium Capitulorum* in February 548,

arguing that condemnation of the Three Chapters entailed a rejection of the Christology proclaimed at Chalcedon in 451. After pressure by Justinian on Pope Vigilius, the Three Chapters were condemned at the Second Council of Constantinople in 553, and Facundus was temporarily excommunicated. For the text, see ML 67.527 ff.; discussion in O'Donnell 134, 168 ff.

57. This final clause was added later at Squillace; see Introduction, p. 5 in ACW 51.

58. Titus 3.10 f.

59. Perhaps the definition of Primasius of Hadrumetum; see at Ps. 119(118).2 above.

Psalm 139 [Ps. 140(139)]

1. Rom. 10.4.
2. Matt. 13.39.
3. "Comparison"; see at Ps. 1.3.
4. John 14.30.
5. On these sects, see Intro. VI.
6. Exod. 14.15.
7. Gen. 4.10.
8. See at Ps. 35(34).21.
9. Varro, *L.L.* 5.73, derives *virtus* from *virilitas* not *viriditas*, but all three words are cognate with *vir* (cf. Cicero, *Tusc.* 2.43).
10. Ps. 22(21).20.
11. Rom. 1.24.
12. 1 Peter 5.8.
13. See at 17(16).13.
14. Ps. 120(119).4.
15. James 1.19.
16. Prov. 10.19.
17. Apoc. 6.9 f.
18. Ps. 16(15).11.
19. John 1.18.
20. 1 Cor. 13.12.

Psalm 140 [Ps. 141(140)]

1. See at Ps. 21(20).8 above.
2. Ezech. 18.32.
3. Apoc. 8.3 f.
4. Ps. 51(50).19.
5. Eccli. 28.28 f.
6. The incorrect derivation is also proposed by Servius, *Ad Aen.* 6.43.
7. Ps. 140(139).12.
8. 1 Sam. (1 Kings) 15.23.
9. See Martin 40.
10. Gal. 6.1.
11. Prov. 27.6.
12. Matt. 6.17.
13. Ps. 45(44).8.
14. Ps. 55(54).22.
15. Prov. 18.8.
16. Cf. Matt. 25.1 ff.
17. Augustine, *Quaestiones* 83.59 (ML 40.44 ff.).
18. See Jerome, *Psalt. iuxta Hebraeos* 141.6; Augustine, *En. Ps.* 140.19.
19. Referring to the eruption of volcanoes from such mountains as Vesuvius.
20. Ps. 142(141).8.
21. Phil. 1.23.
22. Cf. John 21.11.
23. The words are not connected.

Psalm 141 [Ps. 142(141)]

1. Cf. 1 Sam. (1 Kings) 24.
2. See at Ps. 74(73).7.
3. 1 Tim. 2.1.
4. Ps. 69(68).6; Cassiodorus makes Christ the spokesman here.

5. Ps. 84(83).3.
6. Ps. 119(118).82.
7. Ps. 143(142).7.
8. Cf. Matt. 4.1 ff.
9. Zach. 13.7.
10. John 10.18.
11. Luke 23.46.
12. Luke 23.43.
13. John 17.24.
14. Phil. 2.7.
15. Phil. 2.8.
16. Cf. John 10.18.
17. Matt. 3.17.
18. John 17.5.
19. Matt. 27.46.
20. 1 Cor. 2.8.
21. Ps. 69(68).16.
22. For the fanciful etymology, see Servius, *Ad Aen.* 1.54.
23. Phil. 2.9 ff.
24. Isa. 6.5.
25. 1 Tim. 6.15 f.
26. Augustine, *Ep.* 187.4 f. (CSEL 57.92 ff.).
27. Ps. 95(94).6.
28. Cassian, *Conf.* 9 f. (CSEL 13.248 ff.).

Psalm 142 [Ps. 142(143)]

1. Cf. 2 Sam. (2 Kings) 15 ff.
2. Ps. 50(49).16.
3. Isa. 5.3.
4. Rom. 11.32.
5. Job 15.14.
6. Ps. 51(50).7.
7. Ps. 102(101).10.
8. Cf. Rom. 6.4.
9. Cf. Exod. 17.11.

10. Ps. 42(41).2.
11. On the structural presuppositions, see above, Ps. 6.1.
12. Ps. 38(37).11.
13. Mark 2.5.
14. Mark 16.7; Matt. 28.6.
15. Above, at Ps. 16(15).9.
16. John 1.9.
17. Ps. 32(31).8.
18. Eph. 6.12.
19. 1 Cor. 8.2.
20. Mark 10.18.
21. John 17.11.
22. Phil. 1.23.
23. Cf. Jonas 3.5 ff.

Psalm 143 [Ps. 144(143)]

1. The typology of David and Goliath foreshadowing Christ and the devil is pervasive in the Fathers; see Ambrose, *Exp. in Ps.* 118.11; Augustine, *En. Ps.* 33.4; Gregory, *Mor.* 18.14; etc.
2. Cf. 1 Sam. (1 Kings) 17.
3. See Ps. 7.26, 33.
4. Actually Isa. 40.12.
5. Exod. 8.19.
6. Exod. 31.18.
7. See at Ps. 13(12).1 for this 'frequent repetition'.
8. 'Subjoining'; see at Ps. 1.1.
9. Ps. 2.8.
10. Reading *piis* for *plus* of CCL.
11. See at Ps. 119(118).9.
12. Phil. 2.6 f.
13. See at Ps. 37(36).20.
14. Isa. 8.7.
15. John 8.44.
16. Ps. 98(97).1 and 4.

17. Actually 1 Sam. (1 Kings) 2.10.
18. Matt. 10.34.
19. In §§7–8 above.
20. Ps. 128(127).3.
21. See at 3.4.
22. Prov. 3.16.
23. John 20.28.

PSALM 144 [PS. 145(144)]

1. For the interpretation of the name David, see at Ps. 2.1.
2. See at Ps. 6.1.
3. The seven gifts of the Spirit go back to Isa. 11.2.
4. See on Ps. 25(24).1.
5. Ps. 8.8.
6. The letter NUN is omitted, but the verse, which is missing in the Massoretic text, appears here as part of §14, and in the Vulgate as part of §13. See the note at §14 below (n. 17).
7. Mark 10.21, Matt. 19.21.
8. See at Ps. 17(16).13.
9. I.e., the Hebrew alphabet.
10. Rom. 3.23.
11. See at Ps. 103(102).8.
12. Ezech. 18.32.
13. 1 Peter 2.3.
14. See §6 above.
15. Acts 3.12.
16. Cf. Acts 4.10.
17. In the Vulgate this is part of verse 13. It is probable that NUN has fallen out before it, and hence the suggestion that it is deliberately omitted is otiose.
18. See §5 above.
19. Matt. 24.35.
20. Rom. 8.26.
21. Ps. 139(138).8.

22. Exod. 1.5.

23. The claim that Greek writers developed various genres of literature by imitation of the Old Testament goes back to Josephus and Philo (see H. Chadwick, *Early Christian Thought and the Classical Tradition* [Oxford 1966] 13 ff.), and was taken up by the Fathers. Aristotle's *Topics* was known to Cassiodorus through Boethius' translation; see ML 64.909 ff. Cassiodorus suggests here that the catalogue of divine attributes in this psalm has inspired Aristotle's ordering of the *Topics*.

24. Ps. 119(118).164.

25. Apoc. 1.12 ff.

Psalm 145 [Ps. 146(145)]

1. As is explained in the Introduction, the *Variae* is a collection of imperial letters which Cassiodorus himself drew up in twelve books; he followed this with his treatise *De anima* in the years 538–40. See O'Donnell, chs. 3–4.

2. Eph. 6.12.
3. Luke 23.46.
4. Gen. 2.7.
5. Luke 12.20.
6. See at Ps. 22(21).4.
7. This last sentence is part of verse 8 in the Vulgate.
8. "Notion", "conception"; see at Ps. 1.1.
9. John 14.6.
10. Ps. 116(115).11.
11. Amos 8.11.
12. Ps. 145(144).7.
13. Luke 13.16.
14. Cf. John 9.1 ff.
15. John 1.9.
16. Ps. 39(38).13.
17. Cf. 1 Cor. 15.54.
18. 1 Cor. 15.28.

Psalm 146 [Ps. 147(146+)]

1. See Preface and Ps. 4.1. The word originally denotes the twanging of the bowstring, and then of the strings of a musical instrument.
2. Matt. 24.31.
3. Ps. 51(50).19.
4. Cf. Luke 18.13.
5. Cf. Matt. 10.30.
6. Gen. 22.17.
7. Wisd. 3.7; cf. Dan. 12.3.
8. Luke 10.20.
9. Wisd. 11.21.
10. 1 Cor. 7.7.
11. 1 Cor. 7.9.
12. 1 Tim. 5.14.
13. 1 Cor. 3.2.
14. Cassiodorus has taken this over from Jerome, *Tract. de Ps.* 146 (CCL 78.333): *pulli corvorum dicuntur de rore vivere. sic enim physiologi dicunt. . . .*
15. Ps. 33(32).17.
16. Ps. 20(19).8.
17. Ps. 5.7.
18. Cf. John 11.16.

Psalm 147 [Ps. 147(147+)]

1. It will be recalled that in the Greek numeration Psalms 146 and 147 are regarded as separate compositions, whereas in the Hebraic tradition, as now in the *Nova Vulgata,* they are put together as Psalm 147. Cassiodorus combines both by numbering the verses of the two as though they were a single psalm, whilst writing separate Introductions and Conclusions for each.
2. A repeated theme.
3. The sense of Sion is here extended to the supervision exercised by the shepherd over his sheep.

4. Varro, *L.L.* 7.6 more correctly connects *sera* with *serere*, to bar, rather than with *sero*, late, as Cassiodorus fancifully does.

5. Matt. 25.10.

6. See at Ps. 25(24).7.

7. Cf. John 6.41.

8. "Comparison"; see at Ps. 1.3.

9. Exod. 10.20.

10. Isa. 45.7.

11. Ps. 19(18).7.

Psalm 148

1. Cf. 2 Cor. 12.2.

2. Gen. 1.7.

3. Gen. 7.11 f.

4. John 1.3.

5. Col. 1.15 f.

6. The doctrine reached its fully developed form in Aristotle; see D. Ross, *Aristotle*[5] (London 1949) 95 ff.

7. Gen. 1.3.

8. Ps. 111(110).9.

9. Isa. 65.17; cf. 2 Peter 3.13; Apoc. 21.1.

10. 1 Cor. 15.53.

11. For the lore about the dragon reproduced here, see Pliny, *H.N.* 8.32 ff.; Augustine, *ad loc.*

12. Phil. 2.10.

13. 1 Cor. 15.24.

14. The definition is found also in Cassiodorus' *Institutiones* 2.7, where astronomy as the seventh of the liberal arts is discussed. At *Variae* 1.45.4 in the year 507 he tells Boethius: "By your translations Latin readers now have . . . Ptolemy's astronomy"; and Courcelle has suggested that Boethius' lost translation is being cited here.

15. Here Cassiodorus retails traditional ideas of stellar movement as propounded by Aristotle and reproduced by Cicero at *De natura deorum* 2.49 ff. We cannot of course be certain how much of this he found in Boethius' lost version of Ptolemy.

PSALM 149

1. Ps. 113(112).3.
2. Matt. 5.10.
3. Gen. 6.6.
4. Luke 15.7.
5. 1 Cor. 15.28.
6. 2 Cor. 1.12.
7. Matt. 10.34.
8. Ag. 1.1.
9. Matt. 19.28.
10. 1 Cor. 6.3.
11. Col. 2.9.
12. Cf. John 1.16.

PSALM 150

1. See at Ps. 54(53).3.
2. Eph. 1.3 f.
3. Ps. 1.1.
4. Ps. 8.8.
5. Phil. 2.10.
6. Ps. 145(144).3.
7. Cf. Gen. 7.24.
8. Athanasius, *Ep. ad Marcellinum* 11 (MG 27.22 ff.).
9. Ps. 2.7.
10. Cf. John 21.11.
11. Cf. Origen, *Hom. 2 in Genesim* (MG 12.170 ff.), and the cautionary note of Adriaen, *ad loc.*
12. Wisd. 11.21.
13. On the structural facets of the book, see Intro.
14. James 3.2.
15. Cf. 1 Cor. 9.27.

INDEXES

1. Old and New Testaments

2. Authors

3. General